MOON HANDBOOKS®
MINNESOTA

© TIM BEVER

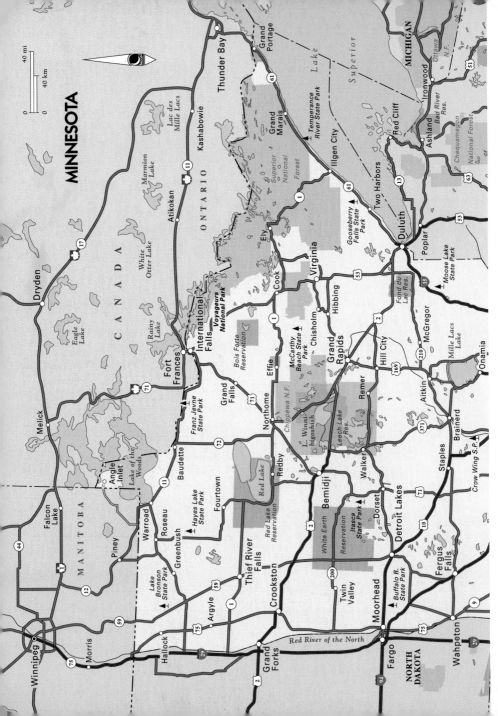

MINNESOTA

the St. Paul Winter Carnival

MOON HANDBOOKS®

MINNESOTA

FIRST EDITION

TIM BEWER

AVALON
TRAVEL

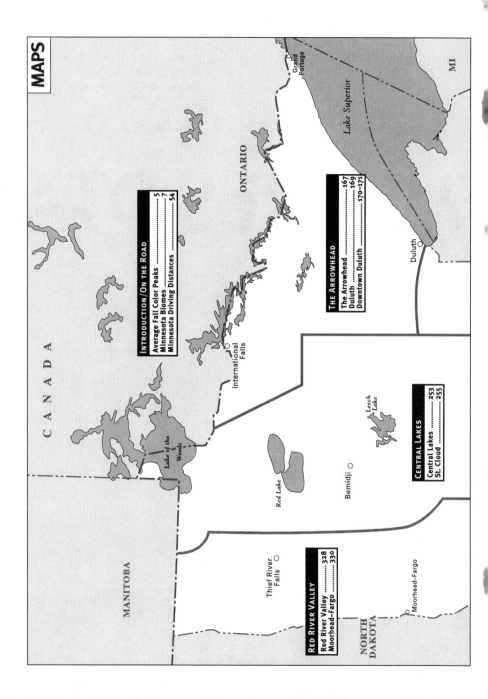

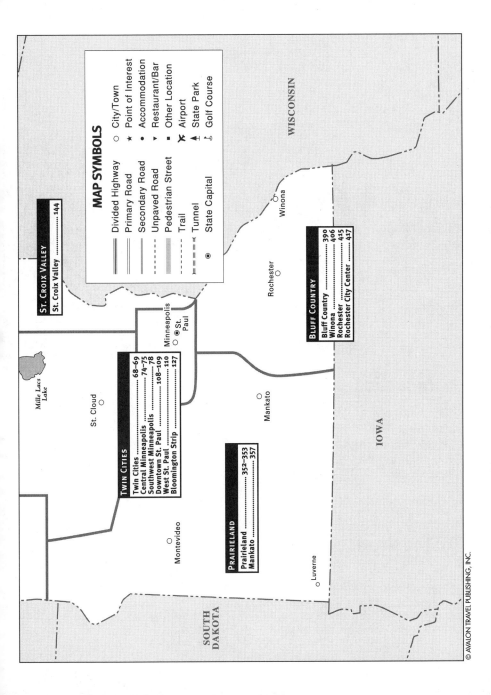

MAP SYMBOLS

Divided Highway	○ City/Town
Primary Road	★ Point of Interest
Secondary Road	● Accommodation
Unpaved Road	▼ Restaurant/Bar
Pedestrian Street	■ Other Location
Trail	✈ Airport
Tunnel	▲ State Park
◉ State Capital	⌄ Golf Course

ST. CROIX VALLEY

St. Croix Valley 144

TWIN CITIES

Twin Cities 68-69
Central Minneapolis 74-75
Southwest Minneapolis 78
Downtown St. Paul 108-109
West St. Paul 110
Bloomington Strip 127

BLUFF COUNTRY

Bluff Country 390
Winona 406
Rochester 415
Rochester City Center 417

PRAIRIELAND

Prairieland 352-353
Mankato 357

SOUTH DAKOTA

WISCONSIN

IOWA

Mille Lacs Lake

○ St. Cloud

○ Montevideo

Minneapolis ○ ◉ St. Paul

○ Mankato

○ Rochester

○ Winona

○ Luverne

Contents

Introduction 1

Known for remote wilderness adventures, the North Star State also offers a generous slice of Middle America, with acres of rich farmland, the nation's biggest mall, and genuinely nice citizens always eager to strike up a conversation. You'll also discover urbane cityscapes, vibrant immigrant populations, and world-class art.

On the Road 34

Learn about Minnesota's myriad outdoor activities, unique cuisine, and accommodations options from houseboats on the Mississippi to resorts "Up North." All of the practicalities are covered here.

Twin Cities ⟋

Despite their proximity, these twins have distinct identities. Slick and modern, Minneapolis boasts nationally known museums and sophisticated nightlife, while St. Paul charms visitors with its Victorian architecture, downtown parks, and old European feel. Together, they offer one of the richest cultural landscapes in the Midwest.

St. Croix Valley ⟋

The towns along the St. Croix River offer stunning natural scenery and a glimpse of rural Minnesota, just minutes from the Twin Cities. Time-warped small towns like Marine on St. Croix and Afton give the valley its character, while more touristed Stillwater is known for elegant bed-and-breakfasts and shopping.

The Arrowhead

Road-trippers, hikers, cyclists, and vacationing families all flock to Lake Superior year-round. Inland, the stunning Boundary Waters offer extraordinary adventure in vast untamed wilderness. And don't shortchange Duluth, Minnesota's third-largest city and a wonderful blend of small-town charm and big-city pizzazz. This is Minnesota at its best.

Central Lakes 252

*Abundant in lakes, forests, and wildlife, this is
Minnesota as it exists in the national imagination—it
was writer and comedian Garrison Keillor's inspiration
for his fictional Lake Wobegon. It's also where native
Minnesotans come to unwind.*

Red River Valley 327

*The heart and soul of Minnesota agriculture lies here,
along the Dakota border. Among the fields you'll find
lakes, hills, and the "Other Twin Cities"—Moorhead and
Fargo, North Dakota—which offer a taste of urban life.*

Prairieland 350

This remains Laura Ingalls Wilder country, even though most of the prairie has been plowed under for farming. The often overlooked southwestern corner of the state is notable for several Native American spiritual sites and offbeat attractions like the world's largest ball of twine made by one man.

Bluff Country 389

Tall limestone bluffs line the Mississippi River in the southeastern corner of the state, known for great trout fishing and fantastic bike trails. It's also significant for its large Amish settlements and the unsung city of Rochester, which is well worth a visit.

Resources 451

Tim Bewer

© MARGARET KLEMT

Though he was born next door in the land of cheese, Tim Bewer's Minnesota roots run deep. After emigrating to the United States from Wales at the start of the 20th century, his great-grandfather moved into a Minneapolis boardinghouse where he eventually married the Norwegian owner's daughter. They later ended up on a Wisconsin farm.

Bewer gave up a career as a legislative assistant to become a writer and photographer and has since covered topics ranging from autism to punk rock, but focuses on his first love—travel. He has written, updated, and edited books on Wisconsin, New York, Ecuador, and El Salvador and his work has also appeared in newspapers and magazines in the United States, Canada, and Great Britain. Someday, if he can ever find the time, he will finish his novel.

He has lived most of his life in Minnesota and Wisconsin and even after travels to over half of the states and even more countries, he still considers the Upper Midwest to be the most beautiful place on earth. He spends most of his free time hiking, canoeing, juggling, searching for the perfect burrito, or just loafing around Lake of the Isles. Though he lives in Minneapolis, his itchy feet take him Up North or overseas as often as possible. He can be reached directly at moonminnesota@yahoo.com.

Introduction

Few states can match Minnesota's diversity of habitats, making this a dream destination for those who love the outdoors. The boreal forests of the northeast fade into the tallgrass prairie of the southwest, while in between are the lakes—far more than the sloganned 10,000. While some of the state's natural beauty is as modest as its citizenry, the glaciers that once swept over the state have sculpted some phenomenal landscapes. The bluffs below the Twin Cities are a stunning backdrop to the Mississippi River, the best of the rocky Lake Superior shoreline is as lovely a coast as you'll ever see, and the Boundary Waters are unlike anywhere else on earth. While Minnesota's glorious wilderness is well known, there is so much more to explore. From skyscrapers to sod houses, from timeless steamboat towns on the Mississippi and

St. Croix rivers to Wobegonic farm country, and from Minneapolis's world-class arts scene to a record-setting ball of twine, even seasoned travelers are likely to be astounded by the variety that Minnesota offers.

If there is one thing that does tie the state's disparate corners together it's the people. Minnesota Nice is an easy butt of jokes—as *A Prairie Home Companion* and the movie *Fargo* demonstrate—but the modesty and decency are real. Most Minnesotans have also clung tightly to their cultures. The Scandinavian and German roots of the early European settlers run deep, Hmong and East African immigrants are at home in cities large and

the picture-perfect Burntside Lodge in Ely

© TINA BEYER

MINNESOTA'S TOP ATTRACTIONS

Banning State Park
Blue Mounds State Park
Boundary Waters Canoe Area Wilderness
Canal Park, Duluth
Forest History Center, Grand Rapids
Grand Portage National Monument
Great River Road south of Lake City
Harkin Store, near New Ulm
Historic Fort Snelling, Minneapolis
Hjemkomst Center, Moorhead
Itasca State Park
Jeffers Petroglyphs
Laura Ingalls Wilder Museum, Walnut Grove
Mall of America, Bloomington
Minneapolis' Art Museums
Minneapolis Sculpture Garden, Minneapolis

Otter Trail Scenic Byway
Paul Bunyan Statues, Brainerd, Bemidji, Akeley
Soudan Underground Mine State Park
Split Rock Lighthouse State Park
Summit Avenue, St. Paul
Superior Hiking Trail
Tettegouche State Park
Vince Shute Wildlife Sanctuary, Orr
Waterfalls on the North Shore

Top Five on the Wacky Side
Ed's Museum, Wykoff
House of Balls, Minneapolis
SPAM Museum, Austin
Twine Ball, Darwin
Two-Story Outhouse, Belle Plaine

small, and some of the country's most traditional Native American communities live on in the north. When you add the state's high wages and low cost of living, it's not too surprising that the quality of life here is second to none—Minnesota has topped Morgan Quitno's "Most Livable State" statistical survey every year since 1997. Don't be surprised if, after your visit, you just can't bring yourself to leave: every year thousands of people arrive as visitors and return as residents.

The Land

Minnesota covers 84,068 sq. miles, making it the 12th largest state in the nation and just a wee bit smaller than Great Britain. The Twin Cities, a little south of the state's waistline, sit right on the 45th parallel, halfway between the equator and the North Pole. Angle Inlet (49.22° North), up at the top of the Northwest Angle, a chunk of land completely cut off from the rest of the United States due to a surveyor's error, is the northernmost town in the Lower 48. Minnesota's lowest elevation is at Lake Superior, 602 feet above sea level, while its highest point, Eagle Mountain (2,301 feet), is just 13 miles from the lake near Grand Marais. The rest of the state works out to an average elevation of 1,200 feet.

Officially, the Land of 10,000 Lakes has 11,842. Red Lake, at 288,800 acres, is the largest entirely within the state's borders, with Lake Mille Lacs coming in a distant second at 132,520 acres. Due to the myriad lakes, Minnesota has more shoreline than California and Florida combined, or so they say. Including wetlands, over 6 percent of Minnesota's surface area is water. Some 92,000 miles of rivers and streams cross the state with the Mississippi River, the granddaddy of them all, accounting for 681 of them.

GEOLOGY

Beginning some 2.7 billion years ago and lasting for over a billion and a half years, the shifting of tectonic plates and volcanic activity created immense mountain ranges in Minnesota. During this time, the Canadian Shield, a layer of bedrock underlying most of Greenland, half of Canada, and extending into the northeast United States, was formed. In Minnesota this massive slab extends down to the upper reaches of the Minnesota River Valley where some of the planet's oldest rock, Morton Gneiss (estimated at 3.6

billion years), is exposed in several places. The Canadian Shield is also often revealed along Lake Superior and the Boundary Waters Canoe Area Wilderness (BWCAW), lending a special beauty to the northeast. Also during this time iron particles settled at the bottom of the great sea that covered the state forming the Vermilion, Mesabi, and Cuyuna iron ranges. Over the rest of the Precambrian era, seas continued to sweep in and out and, along with the wind and ice of early glaciers, wore away the once mighty mountains. During the Paleozoic era (540–245 million years ago), when animals evolved, and the Mesozoic era (245–66 million years ago), the age of dinosaurs, Minnesota was floating down around the equator and had a tropical climate. As the North American continent broke away from the supercontinent Pangaea, it drifted north to cooler climes.

Two million years ago the Quaternary period, commonly referred to as the Ice Age, began. During this time the Laurentide Ice Sheet, centered near Hudson Bay, advanced and retreated four times. The first three glaciations, separated by long ice-free periods, reached well into the middle of the United States covering all of Minnesota. Despite such a long, active, and violent past, Minnesota as we now know it didn't begin to really take shape until about 75,000 years ago when the last advance of ice, the Wisconsin Glaciation, swept south. The ice sheet wiped away just about everything in its path, though it spared the southeast and southwest corners. The glaciers began their latest retreat about 12,000 years ago. As they melted away, the various glacial lobes deposited the countless tons of rock and other earthly debris they had picked up on the trip south. This moraine formed most of Minnesota's hills and, when massive chunks of ice got buried in it, the lakes and wetlands. The meltwater cut most of its riverbeds, including those of Minnesota's four largest rivers: the Mississippi, its first major tributary, the Minnesota, the St. Croix, and the Red River of the North.

While gently rolling hills cover most of the state, its four corners are each a unique exception. The northeast has many steep, rugged hills, the final remnants of Minnesota's former mountains, while the Red River Valley in the northwest is unbelievably flat (see Red River Geology in the Red River Valley chapter). The southeast corner has many deep, highly eroded valleys with much exposed bedrock and many caves. The southwest corner is more or less flat except for some deep river valleys and the long tall Buffalo Ridge, a plateau that stretches well into South Dakota. Perhaps Minnesota's most unusual geological quirk is that its waters empty in three different directions: south to the Gulf of Mexico via the Mississippi River, east to the Atlantic Ocean via Lake Superior, and north to Hudson Bay via the Red River of the North.

JUST HOW MANY LAKES ARE THERE IN THE LAND OF 10,000 LAKES?

The simple answer is . . . a lot. It seems that the only thing people can agree on is that there are far more than the titular 10,000. I've seen official publications from various state and municipal agencies and other respectable sources claim 10,000-plus, 11,842, more than 12,000, 12,034, over 15,000, and 15,291. Before you decide that Minnesotans can't count, let's back up a minute. In order to determine how many lakes there are, we have to define exactly what a lake is. According to the *Merriam-Webster's Collegiate Dictionary,* a lake is "a considerable inland body of standing water." So what's considerable? Proud Minnesotans, who are most likely to cite the "over 15,000" total, aren't lying, just exaggerating a bit by counting even the smallest ponds. For their own purposes the Department of Natural Resources classifies a lake as a body of water 10 acres or larger and it has officially tallied 11,842 of these. While this is as close to a final word as there is, even this answer is not set in stone because many factors like rainfall, shoreline erosion, and sedimentation can alter a lake's surface area. So, when the DNR resurveys Minnesota's bodies of water, ponds that missed the cut last time might be added to the tally while some lakes might drop off the list.

CLIMATE

Minnesotans love to talk about, and in the company of outsiders boast about, their weather, and they have plenty of fodder for the discourse. Minnesota lies at the same latitude as France, but lacks an ocean to moderate the climate, leading to a true theater of seasons and occasional extremes like tornadic thunderstorms and blizzards, as well as extreme temperatures. Meteorologists here really earn their pay—there are no "weather girls" or comedic Willard Scott–like "weather reporters" on the local TV news. Despite the occasional flare up, Minnesota's weather is usually very pleasant.

> *In Minnesota the 10 o'clock news is just the window dressing for the 10 o'clock weather.*
>
> **Howard Mohr, How To Talk Minnesotan**

Temperatures and Precipitation

Statewide summer (June–Aug.) and winter (Dec.–Feb.) mean temperatures are 67 and 11 degrees respectively, though the northern and southern tiers differ by as much as 15 degrees. There are occasionally July frosts in the north, and January has brought temperatures in the 60s to the south. You never know exactly what you will get during the autumn. Duluth, for instance, has seen 37 inches of snow during a Halloween storm, but also a Thanksgiving high of 66 degrees. Minnesota's record high temperature is 115°F (July 29, 1917, Beardsley) beating out such notorious hot spots as Atlanta (105°), Los Angeles (112°), and El Paso (114°). The all-time low is 60 below zero (Feb. 2, 1996, near Tower), still 10 degrees warmer than the record for the Lower 48 (Jan. 20, 1954, Rogers Pass, MT).

While temperatures are warmest in the southwest corner and coolest in the northeast, precipitation runs contrary, increasing from about 18 inches in the northwest to 32 inches in the southeast. Most falls during the May to September growing season. Total annual snowfall is around 40 inches in the south and over 60 inches in the north. There is at least one inch of snow on the ground an average of 110 days each year—160 in the northeast and 85 in the southwest. Minnesota sees about 16 snowstorms with an inch or more of accumulation in an average year, though usually only one of those is a full on blizzard. While an inch or two of snow will slow down travel a bit, a winter storm doesn't become a real nuisance to Minnesotans until about six inches have fallen.

Lake Effect

Lake Superior is so big that it creates its own weather. With an average annual temperature of just 39 degrees, Superior cools the surrounding air in the summer and warms it in the winter, moderating the climate by as much as 15 degrees over inland temperatures. The effect does not extend very far because it is blocked by the Sawtooth Range and pushed back

AVERAGE TEMPERATURES

All temperatures are listed in degrees Fahrenheit.

	July high/low	January high/low
Worthington	83/59	21/1
Montevideo	86/60	22/1
Mankato	86/61	24/3
Rochester	81/60	20/2
Winona	85/61	24/4
Minneapolis/St. Paul	84/63	21/3
St. Cloud	82/57	18/-2
Brainerd	81/56	18/-5
Moorhead	83/58	15/-3
Thief River Falls	82/56	14/-6
Bemidji	79/56	13/-9
Grand Rapids	79/55	15/-7
Duluth	77/55	16/-2
Grand Marais	70/52	22/3
Ely	78/56	15/-6
International Falls	78/54	11/-10
Angle Inlet	78/53	10/-12

AVERAGE FALL COLOR PEAKS

MANITOBA

ONTARIO

Mid to late September

Mid September to early October

Lake Superior

ND

MI

WISCONSIN

Late September to early October

SD

Late September to mid October

Early to mid October

IOWA

© AVALON TRAVEL PUBLISHING, INC.

Minnesotans will tell you that the state is at its most beautiful immediately after a wet snow when everything is painted white and sparkling in the sun.

Spring usually comes in like a lion and races through like a cheetah, lasting as little as a couple of weeks. Often, because the weather can change so dramatically, you can't even be sure when it begins. You might be wearing a T-shirt one afternoon and shoveling snow the next morning.

Overall, Minnesota summers are truly glorious with daytime temperatures mingling around the 80 degree mark most of the time and only short stretches of rain. Also, there is plenty of time to enjoy the wonderful days since the sun hangs in the sky well into the evening.

Autumn is indisputably the best time of the year in Minnesota weather-wise. Unlike the state's notoriously short springs, the mild temperatures and stable atmosphere (resulting in lots of sunshine and very little precipitation) of autumn often lasts well into November, sometimes even December. Late September through early October is my pick for the best time to travel across the state; not only is the weather ideal, but you'll find fall colors, fewer visitors, off-season discounts, and no mosquitoes.

by the winds that normally blow out of the west. Some of Minnesota's larger inland lakes have a similar effect in the summer, but to a much smaller degree. Lake Superior also creates its own snowstorms. When moist air blows inland from the east and up the hills lining the North Shore, it condenses and falls as snow, making the North Shore the snowiest part of the state by far.

When to Go

More than just about any place on the planet, Minnesota experiences all four seasons. Understandably, winter gets most of the press. It usually comes on around Thanksgiving and white Easters are the norm, though there are usually mild stretches at the beginning and end—golfers often get in a few early December rounds. With so much to do when the white stuff is on the ground, most Minnesotans see winter not as a challenge but an opportunity. Come November, many are champing at the bit awaiting the first snow. Most

AVERAGE FALL COLOR PEAKS

Fall colors follow the weather, not the calendar, so there is no way to predict peaks, but this chart is a pretty good guide. The Minnesota Office of Tourism's **Leaf Line,** 651/296-5029 or 800/657-3700, www.exploreminnesota.com, is your best source of up to date fall color information.

INTRODUCTION

© TIM BEWER

Corn mazes are fast becoming an autumn tradition.

Flora and Fauna

FLORA

Three of North America's eight major biomes converge in Minnesota: Coniferous Forest, Deciduous Forest, and Prairie Grassland. Minnesota is the only place where these three communities come together, and one of the few non-mountainous regions on earth to contain any three biomes in such a small space. This convergence results in a tremendous statewide biodiversity. On a macro scale the change from one to the next is quite sudden, though on the ground the zones co-mingle, creating biologically rich areas many miles wide containing species from both.

The largest biome in Minnesota, the **Coniferous Forest,** covers 40 percent of the state. While it only dips into a few northern reaches of the eastern United States, this region extends north across most of Canada and Alaska before petering out into arctic tundra. It is also common in the high elevations of the Cascade, Sierra Nevada, and Rocky mountain ranges. Vegetation must contend with shallow soils and a short growing season, so most species have evolved to economize energy use. The dominant trees are pines, (red, white, and jack), spruce, fir, aspen, and birch. The tallest tree is the **eastern white pine,** which often tops out above 100 feet, though Minnesota's state tree, the **red (Norway) pine,** is not far behind. Vast open peatlands, some of the largest in the world, are spread throughout the central and western parts of the region and contain the unique **tamarack,** a conifer which sheds its needles in the winter, turning a beautiful orange in the process.

The **Prairie Grasslands** of the Great Plains follow the entire western border of Minnesota and sweep across most of the south. This is the state's most fractured landscape, but the prairie that hasn't been lost to the plow is some of North America's most diverse. Nearly 1,000 species of grass and forb thrive in the nutrient-rich soils of the Minnesota prairie, and small individual plots can contain over 200 species. Despite this incredible richness, five grasses, **Big and little bluestem, Indian grass, prairie dropseed,** and

MINNESOTA BIOMES

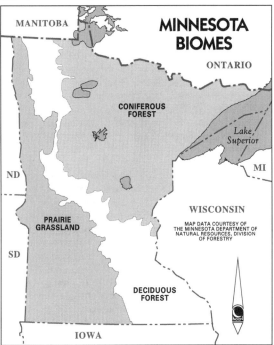

MANITOBA

ONTARIO

CONIFEROUS FOREST

Lake Superior

ND

MI

WISCONSIN

MAP DATA COURTESY OF THE MINNESOTA DEPARTMENT OF NATURAL RESOURCES, DIVISION OF FORESTRY

PRAIRIE GRASSLAND

SD

DECIDUOUS FOREST

IOWA

© AVALON TRAVEL PUBLISHING, INC.

paticas, **anemones, bellworts,** and **Dutchman's britches** that bloom before the canopy of leaves returns. Other shade-tolerant species, like **asters, elm-leaved goldenrod,** and **woodland sunflower,** wait until the summer to flower. North of Polk County onwards into Canada, the forest consists mostly of scattered stands of aspen interspersed with the prairie—known as **brush prairie** or aspen parkland; it is sometimes considered a separate biome.

FAUNA

Because of its high diversity and density, Minnesota's wildlife is a top attraction. While hitting a hiking trail increases your odds of a close encounter, it's possible to see some of the most fantastic examples, like moose and bald eagle, from your car, so always keep your eyes peeled. Also

porcupine grass, account for as much as three-quarters of the vegetative cover in dry prairies. It's the flowers that really capture the imagination though: favorites include **wood lily, purple coneflower, gray-headed coneflower, pasqueflower, purple and white prairie clovers, goldenrods,** and **asters.** Prairie wetlands, home to **small white lady's-slippers** and **golden alexander,** are scattered through the region and make up a large percentage of the northern reaches. **Bur oaks,** their thick bark resistant to fire, sometimes manage to invade a prairie, creating an **oak savanna.**

Though it covers most of the eastern United States, in Minnesota there is just a narrow band of **Deciduous Forest** separating the prairie and the coniferous forest. The most common trees are oak, maple, elm, basswood, hickory, butternut, birch, and aspen. The **sugar maple,** turning bright yellow to deep reddish-orange, is the most spectacular fall color tree. Spring sees a profusion of ephemeral wildflowers like **trillium, he-**

© TIM BEWER

Hole-in-the-Mountain Prairie near Lake Benton

see the sidebar "Minnesota's Signature Species" in this chapter.

Mammals

Eighty species of mammal inhabit Minnesota. Those you are most likely to encounter are **raccoon, eastern cottontail,** various **squirrels** and **chipmunks,** and **white-tailed deer,** all of which are common throughout the state—even in Minneapolis and St. Paul.

Eight thousand **moose** lumber across the northern tier of the state, the majority of them in the northeast corner. While spotting a moose is a distinct possibility, you have little chance of seeing any of the few dozen **elk** that call Minnesota home. Once common in the state, the only remaining herd—about 25 strong—lives near Agassiz National Wildlife Refuge (NWR), though others wander down from Canada into the far northeast counties and some have begun to spend much of the year south of the border. The occasional **caribou,** also once common in northern Minnesota, still slips across the border from Canada, but there are no more breeding populations.

Black bears are common in the northern half of the state, with the population having risen to 27,000 in recent years. Some of Minnesota's

white-tailed deer, the most common large mammal in Minnesota

black bears are actually colored a light brown, but this is just a minor variation; they are still the same species. Visit the Vince Shute Wildlife Sanctuary near Orr for a guaranteed close encounter with a wild *Ursus americanus.*

Three big cats, **lynx, bobcat,** and **mountain lion** roam the state's northern forests, but are very rarely seen. Also count yourself lucky if you spy a **badger, river otter, pine marten, fisher** or **timber wolf.**

Birds

As a result of habitat diversity, well over 400 species of bird have been recorded in Minnesota, with 313 of them residents or regular visitors. No species typifies Minnesota more than its official state bird, the **common loon,** which is prevalent in the northern two-thirds of the state with a few even nesting in the Twin Cities metro area. Other common Minnesota waterbirds include **mallards, Canada geese, great blue heron, great egret, Black-crowned Night-Herons,** and **Double-crested Cormorant.**

Red-tailed hawks and 30 species of **warbler** (24 in the northeast) are some of the defining forest species, and the state's northern forests are home to many **Great Gray Owl** and **Boreal Owl.** The Lake Superior shore attracts **herring gulls** and many species of migrating **hawks.** Arctic species like **gyrfalcon** and **snowy owl** migrate to northern Minnesota each winter. The most common birds on the prairie are **Savannah Sparrow, Western Meadowlark,** and **bobolink.**

Sandhill crane, bald eagle, osprey, and **Greater Prairie-Chicken** all came very close to disappearing from Minnesota, but thanks to ongoing habitat restoration, reintroduction, and other environmental projects, they have been saved. The first three are thriving again (20 pair of bald eagle even nest in the Twin Cities metro) and sightings are actually quite common in much of the state these days. The Prairie-Chicken is still very rare, only hanging on naturally in the northwest and along the Minnesota River at the Lac qui Parle Wildlife Management Area (WMA) where they were recently reintroduced. **Sharptailed grouse** is another species whose numbers have been dramatically reduced, but they still

© TIM BEWER

wild turkey

converge on over 200 dancing grounds in the north of the state each spring to mate.

Reptiles and Amphibians

Most of Minnesota's reptiles and amphibians are found in the southeast corner, which has the warmest climate, but many species, such as the northern leopard frog, snapping turtle, and common garter snake, range across the entire state. Most survive the winter freeze by burrowing below the frost line or hibernating at the bottom of lakes and streams.

Seventeen of the state's 29 species of reptiles are snakes. Largest amongst them is the brown and yellow **gopher snake,** which can grow in excess of six feet and is most common in grasslands along the St. Croix, Mississippi, and Minnesota Rivers. Gopher snakes, as well as the slightly smaller **fox snake,** which has a similar range, are non-venomous, but resemble timber rattlers and, because they sometimes vibrate their tails along the ground when frightened, are often confused with them. Actual rattlesnakes elevate their tails to rattle. The **western painted turtle** is by far the state's most visible reptile. They inhabit just about every body of water with a log or rock to bask on.

Frogs account for half of Minnesota's 22 amphibian species. One of the most interesting is the **bullfrog,** the United State's largest frog species, reaching eight inches in body length. Adult bullfrogs eat almost anything they can swallow, including fish, snakes, turtles, other frogs, rodents, and birds. Though they naturally inhabit just the far southeast corner of Minnesota along the Mississippi River, there are now many healthy, introduced populations elsewhere in the state. Just as exceptional are the **eastern** and **Cope's gray treefrog,** nearly identical looking species distinguished primarily by their calls. They can change their skin color to match their surroundings and are excellent climbers. Their range extends throughout most of the state, and on summer evenings they are commonly found clinging to cabins and other rural buildings waiting to snare insects that fly by.

The most common and widespread of Minnesota's seven salamander species is the **tiger salamander,** which thrives in all kinds of habitats in all parts of the state. Black with yellow spots, they can reach lengths of over 13 inches, though eight to ten is more common. It is not the state's largest salamander though; that honor falls to

RARE TURTLE CROSSING

the wholly aquatic **mudpuppy,** which measures 13 to 16 inches.

Fish

While the state abounds in the usual game fish like **walleye, muskellunge, northern pike, bass, perch, bluegill, crappies, salmon,** and **trout**—more about these in the fishing section of the On The Road chapter—Minnesota's waters have several other unique piscatorial residents.

The largest of Minnesota's 157 fish species is the **lake sturgeon,** a relic from the age of dinosaurs with no teeth or scales and, like sharks, cartilage instead of bone. Back in the 19th century, before they were nearly fished to extinction for the caviar market, anglers caught eight-foot, 300-pound sturgeons in Minnesota. They are making a slow comeback today, thanks to the Clean Water Act and strict fishing regulations, though few top out over 100 pounds. They are found in many lakes and rivers (to the surprise of everyone a six-foot, 105-pounder washed up on the shore of Lake Harriet in Minneapolis in 1998), though the

healthiest population is in Lake of the Woods. Not too far behind in the monstrous category are **flathead catfish,** which also sometimes exceed 100 pounds, though the Minnesota record catch is 70. They only live in Minnesota's largest rivers.

Some other fish that haven't changed in millions of years are **paddlefish** and the **longnose** and **shortnose gar,** all with massive snouts. The nose of the appropriately named paddlefish resembles a canoe paddle and has sensors that detect the electrical impulses emitted by the microscopic plankton it eats. Though they can grow up to 140 pounds, in Minnesota, where they are rare, the largest are just over 50 pounds. The much smaller gar have long cylindrical snouts filled with razor-sharp teeth and skin so tough that it can't be cut with a fillet knife.

THREATENED AND ENDANGERED SPECIES

Like most other places in North America, the first European settlers to arrive on the scene either plowed, drained, or logged much of the state's original habitat, creating permanent changes—the effects of which most plants and animals are still feeling today. The loss of habitat is the primary reason for the disappearance or decline of most species. Pollution, hunting, and dam construction are a few other causes. Minnesota currently lists 28 animal species as endangered and 31 as threatened. Nearly 100 others are species of special concern, meaning they aren't in imminent danger but require careful monitoring. The plant kingdom has 68 threatened and 69 endangered species with 145 on the special concern list.

The only mammal on Minnesota's list of threatened species is the **eastern spotted skunk** (noted for spraying its opponents while doing a "handstand" on its front feet).

The two most notable birds at risk are the **trumpeter swan** and **peregrine falcon,** both state-threatened species once completely extirpated from Minnesota. The Department of Natural Resources (DNR), Minnesota Zoo, University of Minnesota's Raptor Center, and private organizations have worked together to successfully reintroduce them to the state and both continue to increase in number: biologists recently counted 700 trumpeter swans and 24 breeding pairs of the high-diving falcons. Thankfully the long-term outlook for both is excellent. On the other hand, the state-endangered **piping plover,** hanging on by a feather on Lake of the Woods, and the prairie-dwelling **burrowing owl,** which is gone as a nesting species and only arrives every few years as a vagrant, are in a very precarious position.

The animal group in the gravest danger in Minnesota, and around the country, are **mussels.** Over half of the 49 species of mussel found in Minnesota are threatened, endangered, or of special concern, and at least two species have recently disappeared. Like frogs, mussels are valuable biological indicators so the current trend doesn't speak well for the state's waterways. Many disparate factors—all of human origin—including reduced water quality, dam construction, stream channelization, and, in the past, overharvesting for use as buttons and the cultured pearl industry, affect their declining numbers. The invasion of the zebra mussel has also severely harmed many species of native mussels. Thousands of zebra mussels can attach themselves to a larger native mussel, eventually killing it. This rapidly reproducing species with few predators arrived in the United States on a freighter from the Black Sea in the mid-1980s and has spread rapidly through the Great Lakes and up the Mississippi River. It appears that these exotics may also be a threat to fish populations.

MINNESOTA'S SIGNATURE SPECIES

Minnesota's state bird, the **common loon,** is easily its most beloved wild resident. Over 12,000 of these ancient birds, one of the earth's oldest living bird species, reside on lakes in the northern two-thirds of the state—only Alaska has more. With speckled black and white bodies and dark iridescent heads loons are beautiful creatures, but it's their haunting calls—a long, sad wail and a maniacal tremolo—that so enchant people. Helped by the extra weight of their dense bones these large birds can dive down 250 feet and remain underwater for up to 10 minutes in search of a meal. Their distinct red eyes help them see underwater. They're not bad in the air either and have been clocked at 75 mph. While they are masters of seas and sky they are horribly clumsy on land. The only time they go to shore is to nest, and this they will only do on the cleanest and quietest of lakes with long stretches of sheltered and undeveloped shore. Come early June, when the eggs hatch, you'll catch the solid-black fledglings sailing on their parents' backs to stay warm and out of the mouths of hungry fish and turtles.

Over 5,000 **moose** reside in the northern corners of Minnesota. The giants of the north have long spindly legs, shoulder humps, and thick flaps of skin (called a bell) hanging from their throats, and the male's flat antlers spread six feet wide. A full grown adult can stand six and a half feet high at the shoulder and weigh 1,300 pounds. Despite their size moose can sprint at 35 mph and outswim two people paddling a canoe. The name, coming from the Algonquin language, means twig eater and these do get them through the winter, but the rest of the year they prefer leaves and aquatic vegetation—they can close their nostrils when foraging below the surface. Moose have a keen sense of hearing and smell, but their eyesight is so poor that they have been known to mistake cars for potential mates.

While the **timber wolf** was wiped out from all the rest of the lower 48 by the early 1960s, a small population held on in Minnesota. Since bounties were eliminated at that time and the Endangered Species Act was passed in 1973 they have staged a remarkable comeback. Today over 2,600 wolves roam the northern third of the state and they are expanding their territory south. A typical pack averages around seven wolves and defends an 80-mile territory. Adults stand three feet tall, often exceed 100 pounds, and are seemingly all muscle. With their "steel-strong jaws," they are efficient killing machines, but, despite the widespread belief to the contrary, they are no threat to humans. Wolf advocates are quick to point out that there has never been a documented case of a healthy, wild wolf killing a human in North America. They don't howl at the moon either.

INTRODUCTION

Both of Minnesota's venomous snakes, the **timber rattlesnake** and **massasauga,** threatened and endangered respectively, are discussed under the Health and Safety heading, though if you leave them alone there is little reason for concern. The **paddlefish,** mentioned above, is Minnesota's only threatened fish.

The endemic **dwarf trout lily** (aka Minnesota trout lily) is the state's only federally endangered plant species. It survives in about a dozen locations just south of the Twin Cities in the forests of Rice, Goodhue and Steele counties, and, because each of the few remaining colonies are genetic clones, they are especially vulnerable to disturbances. It usually blooms in late April. Once wildly abundant in the state's deciduous forests, **American ginseng** was almost brought to extinction in the mid-19th century when the root became a valuable export to China (the Chinese believe that, as a folk medicine, our ginseng is more powerful than theirs) and it has never fully recovered. It is now listed as a species of special concern. Of Minnesota's three biomes, the prairie, which is the most fractured landscape, has the most plant species at risk. While once abundant and widespread, both the **western prairie fringed orchid** and the **prairie bush clover** are now federally threatened species and the latter is one of the rarest plants in the Midwest. Farming caused most of the destruction of the prairie, and while new technologies have allowed expansion into areas once unworkable, a new and growing threat to this vanishing ecosystem is the alternative medicine fad. People sneak into nature preserves under cover of darkness and dig up whatever plant is the hot new trend, as well as everything else around it, completely destroying large swatches of prairie.

History

FIRST ARRIVALS

The Beringia land-bridge theory that the first humans in the Americas migrated from Asia to North America over the Bering Strait 12,000 years ago has been seriously challenged. The discovery of important new archaeological sites, such as Serra Da Capivara in northeast Brazil, Monte Verde in southern Chile, and Meadowcroft in Pennsylvania, appear to show that humans had arrived in the Americas in several waves as much as 20,000–30,000 years ago, though these later figures are somewhat speculative and remain in dispute amongst experts. It appears the first peoples of the Americas came by boat from the South Pacific and only later by foot from Siberia. The evidence found so far shows that the first peoples in North America probably arrived about 14,000–16,000 years ago. Despite these exciting new finds, there is still no reason to think that humans came to what would become Minnesota any time before about 9,000–10,000 B.C. since most of the land was covered by ice before this.

Little is known about the first Minnesotans,

the nomadic **Paleo-Indians,** who followed the melting glaciers north, hunting large game such as mastodon, musk ox, giant bison, giant beaver, and giant sloth along the way—which is why they are sometimes referred to as the Big Game Hunters. It is assumed that they did not make pottery or fabrics since none from this time have been found. What has been uncovered in large numbers are their weapons. The finely made projectile points were attached to spears and thrown by atlatls, a powerful and accurate weapon. After these megafauna became extinct (debate continues about whether overhunting or climate change was the primary factor for their disappearance) around 6,000 years ago, so did the Paleo-Indian way of life.

With less game to sustain them, the hunter-gatherers of the **Archaic** period began to settle down into longer-term campsites near bodies of water and rely more on what they could find locally. They still hunted (now bison, white-tailed deer, beaver, muskrat, and rabbit became the main game), but also learned to fish and relied more on harvesting edible plants like acorns, cherries, blueberries, and plums. Technology advanced and people made knives, scrapers, axes, and drills. Toward the end of this period people began to construct burial mounds, and those living along the northwestern Great Lakes, including Minnesota, pounded tools out of copper nuggets. Trading was common during this time so these early metal implements spread widely.

After 1000 B.C. the **Woodland** culture began to rise in the Ohio River Valley, climaxing in the area's Hopewell societies. There were many large societal advances during this time, but most came slowly to Minnesota. Most notable was the manufacture and use of pottery. Tools became more specialized and eventually these people learned to use bows and arrows making hunting easier. People soon settled in permanent villages, and their sedentary lifestyle led to the cultivation of plants such as sunflowers, ragweed, and wild rice. People made simple jewelry, decorated their pottery, and became increasingly ceremonial. Burial mounds became larger, more complex, and more common as the importance of individual leaders grew. Few of the estimated 10,000 burial mounds in Minnesota remain today, though good examples can be found in Indian Mounds Park in St. Paul and at the Grand Mound State Historic Site near International Falls. For unknown reasons the Woodland culture began to decline around 500–600 A.D., but it lingered on in Minnesota until about 1700 A.D. in the northern part of the state.

Beginning about 1,000 years ago, a new series of cultures known as **Mississippian** either moved in and replaced some of the Woodland peoples or the Woodland peoples evolved into them. Mississippian culture was heavily influenced by ideas from Mexico and it flourished across the eastern half of the United States. Cahokia, its spiritual and cultural heart, was a city of over 30,000 people across the Mississippi River from present-day St. Louis. In Minnesota, which was again far from the center of power, the influence was tempered somewhat. Villages grew large, possibly upwards of 800 people, and were often fortified. Agriculture became important, with corn (a Mexican import) the most important crop, followed by beans, squash, sunflowers, and tobacco. Wild rice became the staple crop in the north where

corn did not grow well. Pipes carved from stone quarried at what is now the Pipestone National Monument in southwest Minnesota spread across North America due to their deep spiritual import. Though several cultures related to the Cahokians, such as the **Great Oasis** and **Cambria,** lived amongst each other in Minnesota, the **Oneota** were the most advanced and widespread.

By the time Europeans first arrived in the state the Mississippian cultures had largely faded away, though their modern descendents the **Dakota** (aka Sioux) were spread across the center of Minnesota and occupied the majority of the state. Other Mississippian progeny, the **Iowa** and **Oto** tribes, remained in the far south. The **Cree** controlled the far north and the **Assiniboine,** descendents of but enemies with the Dakota, inhabited the northwest corner. Some **Omaha** and **Cheyenne** might have been in the southwest corner and far west-central regions respectively, though we may never know for sure.

The **Ojibwe** (aka Chippewa or Anishinaabe), Minnesota's other major historic Indian culture, were centered around Sault Ste. Marie in Upper Michigan when the French came up the Great Lakes. Beginning in the 1640s the League of the Iroquois, in an effort to monopolize the fur trade, began to attack other tribes in the area and most Ojibwe fled west, eventually settling in northern Wisconsin and forcing some Dakota villages to pick up and move west in the process. As they became more enamored with the goods they received from the French in return for the furs they trapped, the Ojibwe moved into Northern Minnesota to occupy the most fertile lands. The resulting animosity between the two tribes would eventually lead to over a century of on-again, off-again war between them; the Ojibwe usually came out on top.

EUROPEAN CONTACT

The Spanish (and Portuguese), in the latter part of the 15th century, blazed the trail west looking for the East. Their goal was to circumvent the Arabs, reach the courts of the Great Khan, and establish methods to appropriate the riches of the new lands. Along the way, the natives, if any, were to be "pacified" under papal hegemony. After England came to naval power under the Tudor monarchies and began taking swipes at the French, the New World became the proving ground for European powers.

New France: Black Robes and the Fur Trade

The French were relative latecomers to maritime, and thus expansionist, endeavors, and thanks to the Reformation, conveniently freed of papal dicta for divvying up the new continent and its inherent wealth. Nevertheless, Spanish strength closed them out of much of the Caribbean and Gulf Coast. The up-and-coming English established a foothold in what would become the mid-Atlantic colonies. France was effectively forced to attempt to penetrate the new land via the northern frontier.

Jacques Cartier first opened the door to the Great Lakes region with his exploration of the St. Lawrence River in 1535 during his second expedition to find the Northwest Passage to the Orient. He sailed as far as what would become Montreal and spent that winter at the future site of Quebec City with the Iroquois. They told him stories of vast seas and wealthy kingdoms to the west. Cartier, figuring these waters must be the coveted maritime route to Asia he had been seeking, claimed the entire river valley for France. His tales, however, lacking mention of lustrous gold and silver, failed to woo Frances's insular King Francis I, who was busy fighting Spain and invading Italy. As a result, the French, content to fish the shoals of Newfoundland, left the scattered outposts to simmer for another 40 years—except for several fur traders, who, it turns out, were on to something.

When, with an eye to creating a permanent "New France," the French did establish sparse settlements in the early 16th century, they were dismayed by the lack of ready riches, the roughness of the land, and the bitter weather. However, the original traders possessed one superlative talent: forging relationships with the natives, who became enamored of French metal implements—firearms in particular. Eventually, the French found their coveted mother lode: beavers. Paris hatmakers discovered that beaver pelts made a superior grade of felt for hats, and these soon became the rage in Paris and other parts of Europe. As beaver was readily available and easily transportable to France from the wilds, it became the lifeblood of the colonies, sustaining the region through the mismanagement and general vagaries of both British and French rule.

Facilitating both the fur trade and French control over the colonies were the missionaries of the Society of Jesus—the Jesuits. These "Black Robes" (so-called by the Huron and Ottawa because of their long dark frocks) first arrived during a time of atavistic religious fervor in France. The Franciscans had originally set down here but found the task of conversion too daunting for their small order. The Jesuits became the foundation upon which New France operated, serving crucial secular and religious needs. The traders needed them to foster harmony with Native Americans. More important, the often complicated French system of operation required that all day-to-day affairs be carried out at the local level. By 1632, all missionary work in French Canada was under the auspices of the Jesuits. The Jesuits also accompanied *voyageurs* (literally "travelers," but specifically it refers to the men who paddled the canoes for the New World fur traders) as New France attempted to widen its sphere of influence westward. Eventually, the Black Robes themselves, along with renegade fur traders, were responsible for the initial exploration and settlement of present-day Minnesota.

Samuel de Champlain, who first arrived in Quebec in 1603 as part of a fur trading party and later was given charge of New France, was obsessed with finding the Northwest Passage. Convinced that the Great Lakes were the way to the riches of the East, he personally explored Lakes Ontario and Huron, where, in 1615, he made first contact with the Ojibwe who would become the French's most important partners in Minnesota. Men such as Ètienne Brulè and Jean Nicolet were dispatched west to trade and foster good relations with the natives and explore sea routes along the way.

THE VOYAGEURS REACH MINNESOTA

Brulè explored Lake Superior as early as 1618, two years before the Mayflower landed at Plymouth Rock, but he never reached the western shore. Following Champlain's death in 1635 the official desire to push west withered, and it wasn't until 1660 that the first Europeans set foot in what would become Minnesota. On their second illicit trading journey along the south shore of Lake Superior, Pierre Esprit Radisson and his brother-in-law Mèdard Chouart, sieur des Groseilliers, an enterprising duo of unlicensed traders, spent the winter of 1659 with the Ottawa in northern Wisconsin during which time they became the first Europeans to meet the Dakota. The following spring they reached the "Head of the Lake" at present-day Duluth and paddled up along the lake's western shore before returning to Montreal where they expected to welcomed as heroes. Instead French officials confiscated their colossal haul of illegally obtained fur. Radisson and Groseilliers soon allied with the British and headed for Hudson Bay where their explorations led to the formation of the Hudson's Bay Company which, ironically, later played a large role in the downfall of the French empire in North America.

Following Radisson and Groseilliers, a few others poked around Lake Superior's western shore, including Father Claude Allouez, who contributed greatly to a 1670 Jesuit map of the lake. No one, however, headed inland until 1679 when Daniel Greysolon, Sieur du Lhut (Duluth's namesake) paddled up the St. Louis River, crossed overland to Lake Mille Lacs, where he forged an alliance with the Dakota at the village of Izatys, and claimed all this land for King Louis XIV. A year later the Dakota, who apparently weren't too impressed by du Lhut's overtures, seized a group of explorers traveling north from Illinois to explore the upper Mississippi River and held them captive near Mille Lacs before du Lhut returned to secure their release. Upon his return to Europe, one member of that fateful party, Father Louis Hennepin, published *Description of Louisiana,* an account of their ordeal. Though full of inaccuracies, the first book written about Minnesota

became a best-seller. Hennepin and the rest of his party were the first Europeans to see the Falls of St. Anthony, the future site of Minneapolis.

Fur traders soon followed du Lhut and Hennepin and were operating along the Mississippi and Minnesota Rivers. In 1686 Nicholas Perrot built Fort St. Antoine on the Wisconsin side of the Mississippi River at Lake Pepin and in an elaborate ceremony three years later renewed the French claim on the area to avert the British who were eyeing the area as they expanded their own fur trading operations. Fort Bon Secours, the first white settlement in Minnesota, was built by Perrot soon after just below Lake Pepin. A few more small posts were later constructed in Minnesota, including the short-lived Fort l'Huillier near Mankato in 1700, but most New World positions were abandoned at the start of the 18th century as France fought a vast and expensive war against the British across the European continent.

The War of the Spanish Succession ended in 1714 and a few years later the French revived their quest for beaver pelts and the legendary Northwest Passage. The last French explorer of any significance in North American was the Canadian-born Pierre Gaultier de Varennes, sieur de La Vèrendrye, who built Fort St. Charles on Lake of the Woods in 1732. This Jesuit mission and fur trading post thrived despite its remote location. La Vèrendrye passed on the opportunity to enrich himself in the fur trade and spent most of the rest of his life venturing west desperately searching for the Pacific, eventually expanding the French influence all the way to the Canadian Rockies. By the 1750s the fur trade was thriving and several other large forts had sprung up in Minnesota, including La Jonquière near Brainerd.

NEW REGIMES

The Dakota initially tolerated the French partnership with the Ojibwe because their longtime enemies served as an intermediary, bringing valuable French goods to the Dakota. When the increasingly expansionist French moved into Minnesota permanently and fostered alliances with (and supplied weapons to) the Cree and Assiniboine to the north, also both enemies of the

Dakota, the Dakota attacked Fort St. Charles in 1736. The Ojibwe decided to forge their relationship with the French, increase their territory, and settle old scores by attacking the Dakota. Allied with the Cree and Assiniboine and supplied with firearms and military advice by the French, the highly motivated Ojibwe slowly swept across Dakota territory in Minnesota, Wisconsin and Canada. At the bloody, three-day Battle of Kathio (about 1750) the Ojibwe routed the Dakota in their spiritual and political heart on the western shore of Mille Lacs. Though this was the decisive clash (that is, assuming it really happened; some historians doubt that it did), the war continued, and so did the Dakota exodus to the south and west. By 1780 the Dakota had been pushed completely south of the Minnesota River where many forest-dwelling people were forced to adapt their lifestyles to the prairies.

The French and British were at each other's throats again by 1754. The French and Indian War, the North American campaign that led to the Seven Years' War in Europe (1756–1763), began with the British, led by a 23-year-old George Washington, trying to evict the French from western Pennsylvania to cement their growing control over the fur trade. The British trounced the French on both continents in this, the last of four major conflicts between the colonial powers during the previous 75 years. The decisive British victory in North America came at Quebec in 1759; Montreal fell the next year and the overseas aspect of the war was over. King Louis XV fought on in Europe for a few more years but eventually signed the Treaty of Paris, which stripped France of almost all its overseas possessions. Great Britain took Canada and all territories east of the Mississippi. Spain had received all French land west of the Mississippi a year earlier in a scheme to keep it out of British hands. The crushing victory not only gave Britain domination of North America, but also left them unrivaled in worldwide colonial supremacy.

Under the British and Spanish Flags

Spain did nothing with its lands in Minnesota, but the British continued searching for a water route to the Pacific and trading for furs with the Ojibwe

and Dakota. To appease the Ojibwe, who had been close allies of the French, the British continued to employ French voyageurs to trade and transport furs. Jonathan Carver spent two years exploring in and around Minnesota as part of a larger expedition to find the Northwest Passage and published a wildly exaggerated and frequently inaccurate (except for those passages he plagiarized from earlier French explorers) account of his journey. *Travels Through the Interior Parts of North America, in the Years 1766, 1767, and 1768,* the first English language book about Minnesota, was an immediate and enduring success going through 32 printings. British fur traders opened dozens of trading posts in Minnesota's interior and also made Spanish Louisiana their domain since no one was there to keep them out.

THE AMERICAN REVOLUTION

Twenty years after Great Britain acquired the American land east of the Mississippi River, the 1783 Treaty of Paris, which also recognized the independence of the United States, took it away. No fighting took place in or even near Minnesota during the Revolutionary War, and fur traders continued their work paying scant regard to the battles in the East since a British defeat was unimaginable. Their defeat sent shock waves around the world, but just a quick ripple through Minnesota. Life for the British in Minnesota, a western outpost far too remote for the Americans to worry about, continued on just as before.

The year after the treaty was signed, Simon McTavish's newly organized North West Company, the primary competitor of the Hudson's Bay Company, based their inland operations at Grand Portage. All pelts coming out of northern Minnesota and western Canada, as well as the trading goods going back west, passed through this gateway, which was conveniently located as far west as the voyageurs could travel in a year and still make it back to Montreal. This isolated site had been a busy trading center for many decades, but McTavish transformed it into one of the most important fur trading posts in the New World. It was from Grand Portage that Alexander Mackenzie set out on his famous expeditions to find the Northwest Passage. In 1789 he journeyed northwest along the eponymous Mackenzie River to the Arctic Ocean and four years later headed west to the Pacific becoming the first person to travel across the continent north of Mexico. His journeys proved what most had come to assume—that the Northwest Passage was merely a legend.

In 1800 the French briefly returned to Minnesota after they reacquired the Louisiana Territory from Spain, but the land west of the Mississippi joined the United States just three years later when Thomas Jefferson and Napoleon completed the Louisiana Purchase. That same year the North West Company's Grand Portage settlement was abandoned. Inland operations were moved up the shore to Fort William in Canada under the assumption that it wouldn't be long before the Americans would try to tax them.

The Americans Take Control

Though the North West Company packed up their main base, trade at most of their other outposts continued unabated. In order to secure their hold on the new land and its inhabitants, both British and Indian, 20 soldiers led by Lieutenant Zebulon Pike set out on the first U.S. expedition through Minnesota in 1805. His orders were to find the source of the Mississippi River, choose sites for army posts, reel in the British, and foster peace between the Dakota and Ojibwe. Land along the Mississippi at the mouths of St. Croix and Minnesota Rivers was purchased from the Dakota for future military posts, but this was the only goal of the expedition that was truly met. He misidentified the mighty river's source as Leech Lake and the North West Company never kept their promise to begin paying duties on their furs.

Although many factors contributed to the War of 1812 (1812–1815), it was the quest for land that ultimately led the Americans to declare war against the British. The Dakota, Ojibwe, and most other northeastern tribes fought alongside the British, who almost immediately retook

Because the 1783 Treaty of Paris was based on errant maps, nit-picking over the exact boundary along Minnesota continued until 1931.

most of the Great Lakes region before the Americans put up a strong, and often successful, fight there. Though the British had also sacked Washington, D.C., torching the Capitol and White House in the process, two years of fighting had resulted in a near stalemate. Thus, the Treaty of Ghent, which required each side to return conquered territory and join a commission to formalize the Canadian border, was a logical move.

The Convention of 1818 set the U.S.-Canadian border between Lake Superior and Lake of the Woods as the Pigeon River and then the forty-ninth parallel west of Lake of the Woods, but because the 1783 Treaty of Paris was based on errant maps nit-picking over the exact boundary along Minnesota continued until 1931. Following the (theoretical) drawing of the border, British traders finally faced reality and left Minnesota or accepted the American offer to remain and become citizens. John Jacob Astor's American Fur Company filled the void in Minnesota and elsewhere in the western United States until the fur trade crashed in 1840s.

The United States officially staked its claim in Minnesota in 1819 with the construction of Fort St. Anthony (renamed Fort Snelling upon its completion in 1825) high atop a bluff at the confluence of the Mississippi and Minnesota Rivers. Even before the massive, limestone fortress was finished a sawmill and flourmill were established at the nearby Falls of St. Anthony and steamboats had ascended the Mississippi to the small settlement. For a decade and a half this was Minnesota's main white settlement and its founding marked the beginning of modern Minnesota history.

Even up to this point little was known of Minnesota beyond its major rivers, the Minnesota, St. Croix, and Mississippi, and the source of the latter had still not been identified, though it was an essential landmark for many treaties. A bevy of explorers, some on government business, set out for the thrill and glory of the adventure, all seeking the fame sure to befall the discoverer of the source of the continent's greatest river. In 1832

Henry Rowe Schoolcraft, who had been poking around the state for over a decade, set out on an official mission to quell disturbances between the Ojibwe and Dakota, as well as to vaccinate as many of them against smallpox as possible. Though diligent in his orders (Douglass Houghton, the party's doctor, vaccinated over 2,000 people), he also decided to solve once and for all the great mystery of the Mississippi. So confident was he this time that he derived the grand name Itasca (in Latin "true head" is *veritas caput* and Schoolcraft just trimmed the outer syllables) before even setting out. Schoolcraft's Ojibwe guide Ozawindib led him upstream to what the Ojibwe knew as Elk Lake and though he wasn't the first white man to visit it, none before had recognized its importance. Schoolcraft gained eternal fame for his explorations, but his most important work came as an ethnologist and he is regarded as the foremost pioneer of Native American studies.

Land Rush

By 1837 four states—Ohio, Indiana, Illinois, and Michigan—had been carved out of the Old Northwest and tens of thousands of immigrants had flowed into what would become Wisconsin, but most of the land in Minnesota remained with the Dakota and Ojibwe nations. That year the inevitable began and the Ojibwe and Dakota signed treaties relinquishing their lands (5,000 sq. miles worth) between the Mississippi and St. Croix Rivers. Congress ratified the treaties the next year and on July 15, the very day word of the final agreement reached Fort Snelling, settlers branched out to make claims. Pierre "Pig's Eye" Parrant, an aging voyageur with a nasty disposition, settled at the future site of St. Paul and built a shanty tavern. The eventual state capital soon became a steamboat port and trading center, replacing Fort Snelling as the most important settlement on the Upper Mississippi River.

While some settlers came here to claim land and farm, most, including a large number of New Englanders, had their sights set on the vast and valuable stands of timber. Orange Walker and L. S. Judd came to the St. Croix River from Illinois and had a sawmill, the state's first (besides the small one used for the construction of Fort Snelling), running at their new town, Marine on St. Croix, by August of 1839. Franklin Steele also had lumbering in mind when he made his claim at the Falls of St. Anthony on the Mississippi River, an obvious place to build a sawmill, but it would take him a decade to get things up and running. His settlement later evolved into Minneapolis.

MINNESOTA TERRITORY

When Wisconsin was admitted to the union in 1848, the land between the Mississippi and St. Croix Rivers, which had been part of the Wisconsin Territory, was not included in its borders, leaving thousands of people in political limbo. A group of influential, though self-appointed, civic leaders hastily schemed amongst themselves and at an August summit in Stillwater elected Henry Sibley, a director of the American Fur Company, to represent them in Washington. Though technically Sibley had no right to a seat in Congress, a point that both he and his opponents were well aware of, the country was in all out Manifest Destiny fever prompting legislators to accept him as a delegate. Despite partisan bickering and a white population below 4,000 (5,000 being legally required for territorial status) the Minnesota Territorial Act was passed in March of the next year. The new territory had the same borders as the current state on all sides except the west, where it stretched out to the Missouri and White Earth Rivers, making it twice the size of the present state. The only part of the Stillwater Convention plan that went awry was the timing. Minnesota was a thoroughly Democratic state, but the law was signed too late for Democratic president James K. Polk to appoint Sibley as territorial governor. The choice instead fell to his successor Zachary Taylor, a Whig, who chose Pennsylvanian Alexander Ramsey. Sibley, who would later be elected the state's first governor, was unanimously chosen as Minnesota's first official delegate to Congress.

Before word of the new territorial status reached this far west (the first boat of the season arrived up the Mississippi with the good news in April of 1849), Minnesota had but a handful of towns and no more than two dozen buildings stood in St. Paul, but by the time Ramsey stepped off the boat in May his new home had already doubled in size. When the legislature convened in September, 1,000 people had arrived and stores, hotels, bowling alleys, a school, and the state's first newspaper (the *Minnesota Pioneer,* now the *Pioneer Press*) had all sprung up in the capital. Growth in the rest of the state remained modest, however, and the 1850 census tallied just 6,077 residents.

The first order of business for the new government was land. Ramsey and Sibley almost immediately set to work securing funds from Washington with which to negotiate treaties. In 1851 the Dakota relinquished most of southern Minnesota, some 20 million acres, in exchange for $1,665,000—about seven cents an acre. Not only did the United States fail to honor all terms of the treaties in the coming years, but at the official ceremony the chiefs were tricked into signing another document agreeing to use $275,000 of the just-appropriated funds to repay debts owed to fur traders. While the issue of traders' debts was legitimate, the total claimed for them was grossly exaggerated. This whole underhanded affair was partly to blame for the Dakota Conflict (see The Dakota Conflict in the Prairieland chapter) a decade later.

Ramsey and his agents continued to buy land from the Ojibwe and by 1857, when all but a small stretch of land along the northern border had been ceded, the territory's population had swelled to a previously unfathomable total of 150,092. Most of these eager pioneers were American-born farmers who took horse and plow to the southern prairies to raise wheat, while others swept through the great forests of the north with ax and saw. Speculators penciled in hundreds of new villages with enough homesites for over eight times the population and railroad lines that were never built. The financial Panic of 1857 dampened many grand plans and created a fair share of ghost towns, but it didn't suppress overall enthusiasm for Minnesota's future and a constitutional convention was held that year.

STATEHOOD

Minnesota officially joined the union as the 32nd state on May 11, 1858, but like the rest of the nation it was in for a tough haul over the next seven years—the depression resulting from the Panic of 1857 struck Minnesota particularly hard because of the excessive land speculation, a severe drought in 1862 and 1863 created food shortages, and in April 1861 Confederate troops fired on Fort Sumter, sending the young nation into Civil War. Governor Ramsey, who had been elected in 1859 in part because his Republican Party echoed the anti-slavery convictions of the majority of Minnesotans, was the first governor to offer troops to the Union cause, doing so a day before President Lincoln even requested volunteers. While the battles of the Civil War raged far away, war struck home in 1862 when Chief Little Crow led the Dakota in a devastating, though ultimately unsuccessful, rebellion (see The Dakota Conflict in the Prairieland chapter).

The Civil War had the unexpected effect of reviving Minnesota's economy since wheat and timber supplied Northern armies. The state's first railroad, a 10-mile route between Minneapolis and St. Paul, opened in 1862. By 1867 rail connected the Twin Cities to Chicago, an important event since frozen rivers prevented steamboat traffic for much of the year. The Homestead Act

OFFICIAL MINNESOTA STATE SYMBOLS

Bird: Common Loon
Butterfly: Monarch
Drink: Milk
Fish: Walleye
Flower: Pink-and-White Lady Slipper
Gemstone: Lake Superior Agate
Grain: Wild Rice
Muffin: Blueberry
Mushroom: Morel
Photograph: "Grace," by Eric Enstrom
Song: "Hail! Minnesota"
Tree: Norway Pine

of 1862, which allowed Americans and immigrants who had started the naturalization process 160 acres of free land if they built a dwelling on it and lived there for five years, eventually brought hundreds of thousands of new farmers to the state. Most newcomers were New Englanders, while immigrants came primarily from Britain, Ireland, and Germany. To promote foreign settlement, the State Board of Immigration was established in 1867 and, because of similar climates, it focused its efforts on luring Scandinavians. With the ringing endorsement of earlier immigrants from Norway and Sweden, hundreds of thousands arrived by the end of the 19th century, and today Scandinavians collectively constitute, by far, the largest ethnic group in the state. German is the largest single nationality.

Progressive Politics

Three industries dominated Minnesota's economy in the second half of the 19th century: logging, agriculture, and iron mining. Logging yields doubled in each decade between 1860 and 1900, with two billion board feet felled at the turn of the 20th century. During this time Minnesota was amongst the leaders nationally in the amount of lumber supplied to the growing nation, but throughout it all agriculture was the state's lifeblood, and the vast majority of Minnesotans were farmers living in the south and west. By 1860 wheat was the primary crop and it continued to increase in importance so that by 1878 the golden grain accounted for nearly three-quarters of the state's agricultural production. The total might have risen higher, but the blizzard of 1873, followed immediately by a four-year grasshopper plague, forced a reluctant move toward crop diversification.

During the 1880s and 1890s the percentage of land cultivated with wheat dropped by more than half, but overall production still increased substantially and Minnesota led the nation in wheat production during these decades. With the boom in wheat around the state and the active development of new technologies, men like Cadwallader Washburn and John Pillsbury made Minneapolis a world-famous flour-milling center. Mill City, as it was known, thrived as the na-

tion's leading flour producer for half a century. Minneapolis's supremacy in this one industry attracted tangential businesses like banks, railroads, and food manufacturers, turning it into Minnesota's metropolis. Had it not been for wheat, St. Paul would almost surely be the state's leading city instead.

Despite growth in agriculture, farmers' discontent was almost universal. At the mercy of the railroads that charged extortionate shipping rates and habitually cheated them at the scales, they were routinely forced into debt. The 1870s was a particularly challenging decade since the natural disasters came side by side with a severe downturn in the national economy (the Panic of 1873), cutting prices for their products. Their first champion was Oliver Kelley, a farmer from Elk River, who believed cooperatives and scientific agriculture were the answers farmers needed. Kelley had founded The Grange in 1867 to promote these ideals and lobby against the monopolistic pricing of the railroads. They also opposed many of the practices of millers, farm-equipment dealers, and bankers. Surprisingly they had little trouble convincing the governor and legislature to take on the railroads; a railroad commissioner was appointed and rates were fixed in 1871. The railroads, however, simply ignored the new directives. Two years later the Grangers move directly into politics when former Congressman and Lieutenant Governor Ignatious Donnelly, a brilliant public speaker, formed the Anti-Monopoly Party. Several Anti-Monopolist legislators, including Donnelly, were sent to St. Paul the next year but had no success reeling in the railroads, and the party quickly faded away. While they affected little legislatively, they did herald the progressive era in Minnesota and the tradition of third party movements that continues to this day. The Anti-Monopoly Party was followed by the Greenback Party, Farmers' Alliance, and Populist Party, all of which continued to campaign for rural issues, largely by promoting currency expansion that would have assisted indebted farmers. Donnelly, who became famous nationally for his crackpot books on Atlantis and other bizarre topics, was involved in all of them, but never again won elected office.

The first iron was shipped out of Two Harbors from the Soudan Mine up on the newly discovered Vermilion Range in 1884. Six years later iron was found on the even richer Mesabi Range, and Minnesota soon became the nation's leading iron-producing state, an honor Minnesota has maintained ever since. The mines also helped make Duluth the Great Lake's largest port. Tax revenues endowed the Iron Range boomtowns with some of the best schools and public services in the nation, but the difficult and dangerous conditions that the miners labored in bred anger and protest. In later years the Finns, many of whom were Socialists who had fled the Russian Czar's crackdown on the political left, were well known as effective organizers and agitators.

When organized labor joined the reform cause in the 1890s they brought great success to the Populist Party in both Minnesota and the nation. Though the Populists were Minnesota's second party, by the 1894 elections they faded when the Democrats, led nationally by firebrand populist William Jennings Bryan and locally by former Republican and political moderate John Lind, co-opted many of their positions. In the 1898 elections Lind became the state's first Democratic governor since Henry Sibley won the initial election in 1857, but it didn't exactly break the Republicans' hold on the executive; Lind was defeated two years later and the GOP took 10 of the next 15 governorships.

EARLY 20TH CENTURY

Despite the death of the Populist Party, the first decade of the 20th century saw progressive ideals like trust-busting and government reform expand beyond partisan politics. In 1901 Governor Van Sant spearheaded the national effort to bring the hammer down on the Northern Securities Company railroad monopoly, a crusade President Theodore Roosevelt enthusiastically supported. However, the reform movement really came to head with the 1904 election of the humble Democrat John Johnson. Over the course of his three terms the moderate Johnson promoted tax reforms, appointed nonpartisan judges, expanded powers for the Bureau of Labor, reformed

the insurance and banking industries, and further regulated the railroads. Not unlike the state's most recent populist governor, Jesse Ventura, Johnson took repeated verbal shots from both the Right and Left but remained exceedingly popular with the public and gained national prominence. His legitimate presidential potential was dashed by his untimely death in 1909. Johnson's successor, Republican Albert Eberhart, another Swede, continued to take on corporate industrialism, signed the state's first workers' compensation laws, and pushed through a sweeping program of government reforms, though he did so out of political necessity rather than personal or party conviction.

As World War I raged across Europe and dominated the political debate in this country, renewed agrarian discontent swept the Nonpartisan League into Minnesota. This political pressure group supported some socialistic programs like state ownership of grain elevators and flourmills. Though Nonpartisans had taken control of the governorship and legislature in North Dakota, where the movement had been born, they had less success in the more industrial Minnesota. The labor movement had strengthened during this time too, and by 1914 over 400 labor organizations were operating across the state, pushing for reforms like the minimum wage and the eight-hour day. Arthur C. Townley, the league's founder and a Minnesota native who had moved the headquarters to St. Paul in 1917, realized that to succeed in the state he would need to forge an alliance with labor.

Almost overnight in 1918 the new Farmer-Labor Party, capitalizing on the post-war depression, became the state's second largest political party. By 1923 it held both of the state's U.S. Senate seats and, on the heels of the Great Depression, the flamboyant Floyd B. Olson took the governorship in 1930. The party lost support by the end of the decade, supporting increasingly radical ideas like the public ownership of banks, transportation, utilities, and other essential services. By 1938 a more moderate Republican Party was back on top in the state when Harold Stassen, the Boy Governor, took office at age 31 and Republicans won both houses of the legislature. Both Stassen and the revitalized party accepted most of the major New Deal programs like Social Security and promoted "enlightened capitalism" as an alternative to the socialistic aims of the Farmer-Laborers. The moderate stance kept the Republicans on top of the political scene in Minnesota until the mid-1950s.

The state's tradition of championing reform continued in 1933 when the first sit-down strike took place at Austin's Hormel meat packing plant. After three days Hormel agreed to submit their wage dispute to binding arbitration. The next year the Minneapolis Teamster Strike, one of the most important events in American labor history, resulted in over 200 strikers injured, four killed, and a declaration of Martial Law. Not only did the truck drivers and warehouse workers win the right to organize, but the tragedy resulted in the National Labor Relations (Wagner) Act of 1935, which guaranteed all workers the right to organize and bargain collectively. It also prohibited interference in union action by employers and established national standards for resolving labor disputes.

Though the state was rapidly industrializing, farming and mining remained vital to the economy. The lumber industry in Minnesota had peaked in 1899 and the last of the virgin forests were felled by the 1930s, but iron had taken up the slack and by then over half of the ferric ore mined on earth came from Minnesota. The increasing prevalence of automobiles brought visitors to Minnesota's many lakes, allowing tourism to replace logging as one of the state's leading three enterprises.

WORLD WAR II TO THE PRESENT

Nationally, the Democratic Party, under the guidance of President Franklin D. Roosevelt, had moved sharply to the left in response to the Great Depression, and it was only natural that when the Republicans became the party of choice in Minnesota the Farmer-Labor Party and the Democrats would merge. Though politicians had promoted the union for many years, the Democratic-Farmer-Labor (DFL) Party was officially

forged in 1944. Soon liberal DFLers like Hubert H. Humphrey, Eugene McCarthy, and Walter Mondale took to the national stage. Humphrey, one of the architects of the merger, served four terms in the U.S. Senate before resigning to become the vice president under Lyndon Johnson. While Humphrey, liberal in every other way, supported the United States' involvement in the Vietnam War, McCarthy, a five-term Congressman and two-time U.S. Senator, was a leading proponent of withdrawal from Southeast Asia. The two battled it out for the Democratic presidential nomination in 1968 with Humphrey winning the party's endorsement but narrowly losing to Richard Nixon in the only election that mattered.

Minnesota's second vice president was former state attorney general and two-term U.S. Senator Walter Mondale, who served under Jimmy Carter. While DFL politicians have spent more time in the spotlight and the party has been in control more often than not from the 1950's on, power in both St. Paul and Washington has seesawed between the Democrats and Republicans.

World War II naturally led to increased iron production in Minnesota's mines, but at the same time it became clear that the high-grade iron ore was running out. In response, the state invested heavily with research funding and tax breaks to encourage mining companies to begin extracting iron from abundant low-grade taconite. The world's first taconite plant opened at Silver Bay in 1956, and a decade later taconite production exceeded regular ore—the last direct ore shipment left the Mesabi Range in 1984. The industry has run boom and bust and the importation of cheap foreign steel remains a leading issue for Minnesota's congressional delegation.

World War II not only stimulated the iron industry, but it also spurred Minnesota's industrial sector (led by industries like 3M, Honeywell, and Medtronic), and by 1948 manufactured goods exceeded the value of farm products for the first time. Though agriculture remains vital, the resulting diversification distinguishes the state's economy today. The overall solid economy of the past half-century has made Minnesota the fastest-growing state in the Midwest and Northeast regions of the country. While the state's immigrant numbers had peaked early in the 20th century, a new wave, tens of thousands strong, came from Southeast Asia in the late 1970s and early 1980s and Minnesota now has the United States' largest per capita (and second overall) Hmong population. Thousands of East African refugees, principally Somali, have also flocked to the Twin Cities during the 1990s.

Two of the most remarkable events of Minnesota's 20th century came right at the end. The Mall of America opened in 1992 and proved doubters wrong by thriving. And, in a shocker that still has some people waking up in the morning and pinching themselves to see if it was all a dream, former professional wrestler Jesse Ventura was elected governor in 1998.

Government

Minnesota's parties are the most unusual feature of the state's political scene. In recent decades the state's leading party has been the left-leaning DFL (Democratic-Farmer-Labor) which resulted from a merger of Farmer-Labor Party and the much smaller Democratic Party after World War II. The right got into the autonomy act in the 1970s: following the Watergate scandal, Minnesota's Republicans distanced themselves from the national disgrace by changing their name to the Independent Republican Party. The Independent was dropped during the party's wave of national success in the mid-1990s. Internally the party struggles with its identity as opposing internal forces simultaneously try to keep them near the center and pull them further to the right. The latter faction has the upper hand these days and is shifting the whole state to the right.

The newest player in Minnesota politics is the Independence Party of Minnesota, which sits squarely in the middle of the road. They began as part of the Reform Party, Ross Perot's anti-deficit crusade of the late 1990s, but split in 2000 when the right wing demagogue Pat Buchanan took control of the national party. Since its founding, only three party members have won a seat at the polls: one state senator who had previously served three terms as a Republican, a county commissioner, and in 1998, in a scenario so unlikely and bizarre that the writers for the WWE wouldn't have dreamed it up, former professional wrestler Jesse "The Body" Ventura was elected governor. Ventura's tenure as the state's executive was, as the *Star Tribune* called it, "a riotous four years of controversy, publicity-seeking, outside moneymaking, tri-partisan gridlock and, yes, governance."

DFL and Republican critics were outspoken from the start (an inevitable aspect of political life that the thin-skinned Ventura did not handle very maturely) though his approval ratings polled high throughout most of his term, only dropping strongly near the end. Some Minnesotans considered the plain speaking Ventura a political messiah, while others agreed with Garrison Keillor, who called him "the greatest joke Minnesota ever played on itself"; only a handful held a middle-ground opinion. Even his critics, however, had no choice but to begrudgingly respect his candor, his independence from special interests, and his commitment to personally important, though publicly unpopular, issues such as a refusal to issue religious proclamations. Ventura, saying 12 years of public service was enough (four in the navy, four as mayor of Brooklyn Park, and four as governor), chose not to run for reelection. His fervent hatred of the media and a March 2002 *Star Tribune* poll showing only 31 percent of Minnesotans felt that he "deserves to be reelected" were no doubt significant factors in his decision. It is too early to tell if the Independence Party will have much success beyond its most visible spokesman, though it is very unlikely.

The Green Party of Minnesota earned major party status following the 2000 presidential elections. It has won a handful of local races, though as of yet it is taken no more seriously statewide than the Greens are at the national level. The party is growing fast though, and some think it could soon replace the Independence Party as the main third party in Minnesota—thus directly benefiting the Republicans. White Earth Reservation activist Winona LaDuke helped raise the party's profile when she ran as the Green's vice presidential candidate for the 1996 and 2000 elections.

As its parties demonstrate, politically Minnesota has a strong independent streak, though historically it is one of the nation's more liberal states. Both traditions extend back to the mid-19th century when farmers began agitating for reform. The independence temper peaked in 1913 when party affiliation was banned in the House and Senate, a policy that lasted 60 years. Democrats have won every presidential election in the state since 1960 with the exception of Richard Nixon's victory in 1972—most by wide margins—yet Minnesotans have consistently seesawed between the left and right in Congressional, gubernatorial, and state House of Representative elections over the same period. The DFL took control of the state Senate in 1972 (the first year legislators again began running with party labels) and hasn't let go since. Currently their lock on the Senate is tenuous, while the Republicans hold a much firmer majority in the House and won the governorship back in 2002 with the election of Tim Pawlenty.

Economy

Surprisingly the industries most closely associated with Minnesota—agriculture, forestry, and mining—amount to just a small fraction (2.2 percent in 1999) of the state's Gross State Product (GSP). Even many Minnesotans are unaware that the North Star State, with over 90 percent of the country's primary industries represented, has one of the most diverse economies in the nation. Generating $36 billion (21 percent) of the state's $173 billion GSP service industries are the state's leading—and fastest growing—sector. Following service are finance, insurance, and real estate services; manufacturing; and trade, each with approximately 18 percent of the GSP.

Also, despite perpetual bellyaching by business groups about the state's high taxes and tough environmental laws, the economy is consistently one of the strongest in nation. Throughout the 1990s and on into the 21st century, job and GSP growth in Minnesota soundly outpaced the national average; unemployment in all major industries and for all major occupations has consistently been several points lower that the national rate, exports outpace imports by over 50 percent, and per capita income has risen to 11th highest in the nation. Additionally, with 19 of them headquartered here, Minnesota ranks fourth in the nation in the number of *Fortune* 500 companies per capita. Target, U.S. Bancorp, 3M, Best Buy, Northwest Airlines, General Mills, and Hormel Foods are some of the best known.

AGRICULTURE

In the mid-19th century, pioneers plowed up the prairie and created a checkerboard of farm fields and pastures. King Wheat was the crop of choice for most of them and by 1878 it accounted for nearly three-quarters of Minnesota's agricultural output. Farmers diversified in the 1880s and 1890s and the percentage of land cultivated with the golden grain dropped by more than half, but production still increased substantially and Minnesota continued to lead the nation. Minneapolis became the state's largest milling center, and it topped the nation in flour output for half a century beginning in the 1880s. Even though farming today accounts for just a tiny fraction of the state's economy and, for the most part, only occurs in the southern and western tiers, Minnesota still ranks sixth nationally in total farm income with annual receipts topping $7.5 billion. One significant factor behind the agricultural success is that Minnesota farmers have always been national leaders in supporting cooperative business organizations.

The top five agricultural products are, in order, soybeans, hogs, corn, dairy products, and cattle; together they account for nearly 75 percent of all agricultural cash receipts. Also, Minnesota raises more oats, sugar beets, green peas, and turkeys than any other state; is second for sweet corn, wild rice, and canola; and comes in third with soybeans, flaxseed, and hogs. Other crops ranking in the top ten include corn, wheat, dairy products, sunflowers, honey, potatoes, eggs, and chickens.

NATURAL RESOURCES
Mining

The first iron mine opened in northeastern Minnesota in the 1880s and the state has been the nation's leader in ore production ever since. Virtually all of it was dug out of the Vermilion, Cuyuna, and Mesabi iron ranges in northern Minnesota. Although World War II led to record production years, it was clear that the depletion of the state's high-grade iron ore was imminent. The legislature took its first action to protect the iron industry in 1941 by reducing taxes on taconite (an abundant low-grade iron bearing rock) hoping this would encourage its production. Engineers had been trying for decades to develop a cost-effective process to extract the iron from the solid rock and, thanks to generous state funding, Dr. E. W. Davis at the University of Minnesota School of Mines perfected one by the end of the decade. Reserve Mining constructed North America's first taconite plant (now owned by Northshore Mining) at Silver Bay and shipped the first load of iron pellets to eastern steel mills in 1956. The plant's completion came none too soon as ore extraction peaked at 89.5 million tons (over 80 percent of the nation's total output) in 1953. Though Minnesota's last direct iron ore shipment from the mighty Mesabi Range didn't come until 1984, taconite production exceeded that of regular ore by 1967.

Only the Mesabi Range, by far the largest of the three, is still worked these days, but it manages to provide two-thirds of the United States' supply of iron ore. The nearly $1 billion the iron mines contribute to the economy is just half a percent of the state's GSP, but it keeps many of the communities on the Iron Range alive. The mining companies employ over 5,000 people directly and many more jobs in associated industries such as transportation are directly liked to iron. The Mesabi still has enough ore to keep the mines operating at current rates for over 200 years, but that may not matter. Due to cheap steel imports, iron production has been declining for decades and temporary shutdowns have become par for the course. After Cleveland-based LTV Steel declared bankruptcy, they shut their Hoyt Lakes mine and taconite plant in January 2001, putting 1,400 people out of work.

In 2002 President Bush, in an effort to prop up the struggling U.S. steel industry (there were 30 bankruptcies and 20,000 jobs lost between 1997 and 2001), slapped 8–30 percent tariffs on imported steel. The action infuriated foreign governments, most notably Japan, South Korea, and the European Union, who were quick to point out how the hypocritical protectionist move flies in the face of the president's rhetorical support for free trade. They have lodged formal complaints with the World Trade Organization. Even with this help many analysts expect Big Steel to die soon, a prediction that does not bode well for the future of the Iron Range.

There is relatively little mining besides iron, though Minnesota also leads the nation in granite production, most of it quarried around St. Cloud, and is near the top in sand, gravel, clay, and peat.

Forestry

Minnesota was the leading lumber producing state for most of the last half of the 19th century, but the Paul Bunyan cut-and-run era of logging died out in the early 20th century. Today about one third of the state is forested—only half what it was before the lumberjacks cleared the land. Though logging is just a shadow of its former self, government reforestation efforts allowed the industry to survive, and today around 900 loggers harvest mostly small pulpwood trees like aspen. The associated paper and wood manufacturing companies are much bigger players in the economy and employ nearly 60,000 people, but still only account for 0.8 percent of the GSP. There are large paper mills in International Falls, Duluth, Cloquet, Grand Rapids, and Sartel.

MANUFACTURING

Manufacturing surpassed agriculture as the state's top industry in 1948 and today it is a strong third with most plants centered around the Twin Cities. Food processing leads the manufacturing sector with meatpacking, dairy products, and sugar refining all major contributors. Relatively little milling takes place in Minnesota today, though many of the leading companies like Cargill and General Mills remain headquartered in the Twin Cities. On the marketing end the Pillsbury Doughboy, Jolly Green Giant, and Betty Crocker all hail from Minnesota. Other major players outside the edible realm are industrial and commercial machinery, including computers and office machines; printing and publishing; fabricated metal products; and, as mentioned above, paper and wood products.

Surprisingly, high-tech industries are leading the manufacturing sector's rise. It all began in the 1980s with computing pioneers Control Data and Cray Research. Today the Twin Cities are a well-known leader in e-commerce technology, particularly software distribution, but Minnesota has really distinguished itself in the medical field. International leaders like Medtronic, inventors of the cardiac pacemaker, and St. Jude Medical are just some of hundreds of members of Medical Alley, the influential trade association for Minnesota's health care industry. Throughout the 1990s job growth in high-tech fields—particularly scientific instruments, computer and office equipment, and software—far outpaced the national average. Minnesota's high-tech payroll in 2000 was around $7 billion, seventh in the nation—it was second for the manufacture of medical instruments and supplies. That same year it ranked fourth nationally in the number of U.S. patents issued per capita, a strong indicator of available talent and commitment to research. This has all come about without a giant like Microsoft or Dell Computer to generate a multitude of spin-off companies, or an abundant local source of venture capital. Minnesota's success comes from several factors, not the least of which is the highly educated workforce. Another unique advantage Minnesota has is that unlike other high-tech hotspots, such as the Silicon Valley, there is a very low employee turnover because people who come to Minnesota generally want to stay here. The state has recently begun a push to make Minnesota a lead in biotechnology.

TOURISM

Although much of the state remains off the beaten path, tourism is a growing industry and over 13 million out-of-state travelers came to Minnesota in the year 2000, and just as many Minnesotans took an internal vacation; together they generated over $9 billion in sales and created 130,000 jobs. Half of all visits are to the Twin Cities, and the top five activities are shopping (the Mall of America effect), scenic touring, city sightseeing, fishing, and visiting parks.

The People

Minnesota's population of 4,919,479 (according to the 2000 census) ranks 21st in the nation, though its population density of 61.8 people per square mile is 31st. Fifty-five percent of Minnesotans live in the seven-county Twin Cities metro area, which is the fastest growing part of the state. Another 20 percent live in the triangle formed by the Twin Cities, Duluth, and Moorhead, leaving a lot of open space in the rest of the state. With a growth rate of around 10 percent during the 1990s, Minnesota was the fastest growing state in the Midwest. Its five most populous cities are Minneapolis, 382,618; St. Paul, 287,151; Duluth, 86,918; Rochester, 85,806; and Bloomington, 85,172.

The state's ethnic breakdown is 89.4 percent white, 3.5 percent black, 2.9 percent Asian, 1.1 percent Native American, and 3 percent biracial or other. Hispanics (who may be of any race) totaled 2.9 percent of the population. Although per capita immigration totals are average compared to the rest of the nation, more refugees choose Minnesota than just about any other state.

Although immigration peaked at the beginning of the 20th century, few Minnesotans have completely let go of their heritage. Just about every town still celebrates at least some of the traditions of its founders in annual festivals, and local historical museums usually feature cultural displays from the motherland. Scandinavian traditions are the most widespread and still so ingrained that the Swedish and Norwegian royal families visit Minnesota occasionally. Lutefisk and lefse (see Minnesota Cuisine in the On The Road chapter) remain vital to many family celebrations; a multitude of cities have Scandinavian import stores; and most Minnesotans still love a good Ole and Lena joke. The newest immigrants, like Somali and Hmong, have brought their own food, crafts, and traditions to the state and Native American pride is as strong as ever.

Native Americans

Since the time the first Europeans came in search of furs, the Native Americans residing in Min-

nesota have been almost exclusively the **Dakota** and **Ojibwe.** Historically bitter enemies, the Ojibwe, with the help of the French, swept across the state slowly pushing the Dakota south and west. The current distribution of reservations, Ojibwe over the northern half of the state and the Dakota south of the Minnesota River, generally reflects the balance of power that was achieved between them by the time Europeans began to appropriate their lands. The Dakota have four reservations, all under three acres, while the Ojibwe, by far the larger of the two, have seven reservations, none smaller than 48,000 acres. The Dakota lands are so small because following the Dakota Conflict (see The Dakota Conflict in the Prairieland chapter) they were expelled from the state and only a few later returned, at which time the government granted them new lands.

© TIM BEWER

Pow-wows are held throughout the state and throughout the year.

Minnesota, with just under 55,000 Native American residents, has the 14th largest Native population in the United States. Only about a third actually live on the reservations, while nearly 40 percent live in the Twin Cities metro.

Europeans

While many Europeans came to the New World hoping to strike it rich, most were fleeing poverty or religious and political persecution. Minnesota's land rush began at the end of the 1830s and most people were drawn here by cheap land, though others sought logging and iron mining jobs. Initially most settlers came from the eastern United States and Canada, though some northern European immigrants arrived during the early years, too.

The first arrivals in Minnesota were the **French** who spread the fur trade across the Northwest. Most of the French who came to Minnesota did so not directly from Europe, but through Canada. The most notable of the French-Canadians were the **Meétis,** an ancestral mix of French and Native American, who ran ox-cart trains of furs and supplies between St. Paul and Winnipeg. Despite the important role the French played in Minnesota history, they are now so completely assimilated that about the only cultural remnant are place names.

Despite the widespread reputation of its Scandinavian heritage, **German** is actually the most common ancestry of today's Minnesotans, and it has been that way almost from the start. Germans settled across the whole of the state but with the densest concentrations in the southern and central counties, as towns like Cologne, Hamburg, Heidelberg, New Germany, New Munich, and New Ulm attest. Minnesota remains one of the country's most ethnically German states, and New Ulm is not only the nation's most German city, but has the greatest percentage (66 percent) of any single ethnicity amongst cities with 5,000 or more residents.

Collectively the state's **Scandinavian** descendents outnumber the Germans, and they have left the most indelible mark on Minnesota. The rush of **Norwegians** and **Swedes,** who share not only similar backgrounds in Europe but also similar experiences in early Minnesota, began in the 1850s. More Norwegians and Swedes came to Minnesota than went to anywhere else in the world; and more than the next two states, Wisconsin and North Dakota, combined. Scandinavian ethnic supremacy in the state was achieved by the end of the 19th century and immigration en masse didn't tail off until around 1930. Even today, Thief River Falls and Cambridge are respectively the nation's most Norwegian and Swedish cities of 5,000 or more residents. While the climate and advertising were factors in their choice, the primary reason so many chose Minnesota was timing: lands were opening up for settlement in Minnesota just as food shortages, overpopulation, and economic strife hit the homeland. They settled throughout the state (statistically Swedes are a little more common in the north and denser Norwegian distribution is found in the south and west) and dominated state politics even before surpassing Germans in number.

The **Danish** population, a much later arrival than other Scandinavians, is only about a fifth the size of either that of the Swedish or Norwegians, but it is still one of the largest Danish communities in the United States. Tyler, in the far southwest, is Minnesota's main hotbed of Danish culture. For the most part the **Finns** came even later than the Danes did, though in equal numbers, and Minnesota's Finish descendents also constitute one of the largest such populations in the United States. Though some farmed in south-central Minnesota, most notably around New York Mills, the vast majority dug the mines of the Iron Range. The "Red Finns," as they were known across the north, were persistent and effective union organizers and fought hard for improved working conditions—they were often severely persecuted for their efforts. Authentic Finnish saunas are still prevalent across the northeast. The number of **Icelandic** immigrants was minimal, but because the population of the island was so small, the percentage of Icelanders who left their homeland and came to Minnesota during the end of the 19th century was higher than for most other countries. Surprisingly, instead of taking up fishing along Lake Superior as would be expected, almost all took up sheep farming on the

ST. URHO'S DAY

There is no St. Urho (pronounced OOR hoe with a heavy trilling of the R), but that doesn't stop Minnesotans from celebrating his heroic deeds. Legend has it that thousands of years ago wild grapes once grew in Finland. (This fact has been proven by studying the archaeological remains of bears). When a plague of grasshoppers descended on Finland, Urho drove the locusts into the sea by loudly exclaiming *Heinäsirkka, heinäsirkka, mene täältä hiiten* (Grasshopper, Grasshopper, get the hell out of here!) and waving his pitchfork. Having conquered the locusts and saved the grapes he thus became the patron saint of the Finnish vineyard workers. To honor this great linguistic feat Finnish women and children, dressed in royal purple, line up along lakeshores at sunrise on March 16th and recite the magnificent Urho's mighty words. The men, wearing green costumes, gather atop the hills and upon hearing the chant change into purple garb. When the ritual is over the celebrants dance the polka, drink wine and grape juice, and eat the traditional *moyakka* (fish soup) that, according to the fanciful Ode to St. Urho, gave him the strength to succeed. Although it has yet to be proven by scholars some Finns contend that the Irish stole the idea of celebrating St. Patrick, the Emerald Isle's patron saint, from them. The strongest evidence of this claim comes from the fact that St. Patrick's Day lands on the day immediately following St. Urho's Day. Apparently the Irish felt a celebration of their own would be a good reason to party for two days instead of just one.

None of the above tale is true, of course, though the real story behind St. Urho is just as entertaining. Urho was born to Richard Mattson in the spring of 1953 at Ketola's Department Store in Virginia, Minnesota. Mattson's tall tales of the Finnish saint who drove the poisonous frog out of Finland, initially created as a counterpart to the Irish's beloved St. Patrick, eventually led to actual celebrations in his hometown. The frogs were changed to grasshoppers by Dr. Sulo Havumäki, a psychology professor at Bemidji State University who helped spread the legend.

St. Urho's Day is now celebrated in towns with Finnish heritage across the United States and Canada—there are even St. Urho's pubs in Finland—though it is still primarily a Minnesota thing. Menagha, home to a giant fiberglass St. Urho statue,

has the best known celebration. Some of the festivities include a costume-Changing of the Guard, Finnish music, and plenty of *moyakka*. The highlight of the celebrations in the town of Finland, Minnesota is the crowning of Miss Helmi—all contestants are male. Other Minnesota towns that celebrate this holiday include New York Mills, Silver Bay, and Finlayson. It's now a big enough deal in some towns that celebrations begin on March 15th while others, for some reason, ignore tradition and hold the festivities on the 23rd. There is more about the heroic saint and the celebrations in his honor at www.sturho.com.

Ode to St. Urho
—by Gene McCavic and Richard Mattson, Virginia, Minnesota

Original Finglish version
Ooksi kooksi coolama vee
Santia Urho is ta poy for me
He sase out ta hoppers as pig as pirds
Neffer peefor haff I hurd tose words
He reely tolt tose pugs of kreen
Braffest Finn I effer seen
Some celebrate for St. Pat unt hiss nake
Putt Urho poyka kot what it takes
He kot tall and trong from feelia sou
Unt ate kala moyakka effery hour
Tat's why tat kuy could sase toes peetle
What krew as thick as chack bine neetles
So let's give a cheer in hower pest vay
On Sixteenth of March, St. Urho's Tay

English translation
One two three five
St. Urho is the boy for me
He chase out the hoppers as big as birds
Never before have I heard those words
He really told those bugs of green
Bravest Finn I ever seen
Some celebrate for St. Pat and his snakes
But Urho boy got what it takes
He got tall and strong from sour milk
And ate fish soup every hour
That's why that guy could chase those beetles
What grew as thick as jack pine needles
So let's give a cheer in our best way
On Sixteenth of March, St. Urho's Day

prairies of Lyon, Lincoln, and Yellow Medicine counties in the far southwest.

Minnesota's fourth largest immigrant group, the **Irish,** made their new homes primarily in the southeast corner of the state and, unlike most other Irish immigrants to the United States, farming was their principal livelihood. One of the first ethnic groups to arrive in large numbers in Minnesota, the roughly 12,000 exiles from the Emerald Isle living here in 1860 constituted one fifth of the state's foreign-born population. The Irish continued to arrive in large numbers through the early 20th century and because, unlike other foreigners, they arrived with a mastery of the English language, a large number became political leaders of the state's new towns. While always outnumbered by Germans, St. Paul is still considered an Irish town.

British immigrants were also early arrivals and included enough **Welsh** that when the push for statehood began, the proposed constitution was translated into their ancient tongue. Though best known as miners, most Welsh in Minnesota came to farm. A few **Cornish** miners relocated from Michigan with the discovery of iron ore in the northeast. Though most eventually relocated elsewhere in the United States, their practical meat-and-potato-filled pasties remain an Iron Range staple to this day. **Scots** were noted fur traders and Simon McTavish's North West Company set up its inland operations at Grand Portage, but few settled here permanently when Minnesota joined the United States. Many **English** professionals relocated here in the 1870s to start new lives as gentleman farmers, and though they gained fame across the state from newspaper accounts of their crimson foxhunts and horse races, they weren't cut out for rural living and the grand settlements failed.

While **Russian** and Eastern Slavic (**Ukrainian, Belorussian,** etc.) immigration dates back to the 19th century, the main surge began in the 1990s following the collapse of the Soviet Union. Many Russians chose Minnesota because they liked the climate, and they were one of the largest immigrant groups of that decade. Today's Ruso-Minnesotans tends to be highly educated professionals, and they include many

Jewish and Pentecostal Christian refugees. Most settled in the Twin Cities.

While **Poles,** most of whom arrived in Minnesota between 1900 and 1915, settled across the state, the most distinct community has always been in Winona, where the Church of Saint Stanislaus Kostka and the Polish Cultural Institute memorialize the city's Polish past and present. **Czechs** and **Slovaks** came during the same time, but in smaller numbers. The former are pretty widespread around the state (though most notably in New Prague, where much effort has been made to keep the culture), while the latter took residence almost exclusively in Minneapolis.

Almost all of the **Serbian, Croatian, Macedonian, Slovene,** and **Montenegrin** (the peoples of the former Yugoslavia) arrivals worked the mines of the Iron Range. The Iron Range was, in fact, Minnesota's great melting pot. Three dozen ethnicities came to dig and, at the turn of the 20th century, half the population was foreign born. This accounts for the tremendous number of taverns in Iron Range towns—the multitude of ethnicities worked together during the day, but drank alone at night. In the 1990s a group of **Bosnians** fled the civil war and ended up in Pelican Rapids.

Other nationalities who migrated here in small but significant numbers include the **Italians** who came to the cities, principally St. Paul and Duluth, as well as the Iron Range to strike it rich, while **Dutch** immigrants and their descendants are predominantly rural. The small number of **Swiss,** who were at Fort Snelling as early as 1821, settled throughout the state.

Africans

African Americans are the largest minority group in Minnesota. Although black migration to Minnesota began in earnest after World War I—as Southerners came north looking for factory work—Africans have been in Minnesota from the start. They first came as fur traders back in the late 18th century, most famously the Bonga (sometimes spelled Bungo) family. Pierre had settled in north-central Minnesota after gaining his freedom and opened a series of trading posts across the region. His son George, educated in

Montreal, garnered such respect and fame as a trader, explorer, interpreter, and negotiator that his death in 1885 was reported in newspapers around the country. Bungo Township and Bungo Brook in Cass County are named for the family.

In the early 19th century many slaves accompanied their owners to Fort Snelling, none more famously than Dred Scott, who unsuccessfully sued for his freedom based upon his two years of residence in free territory. The case, which reached the Supreme Court, and its far-reaching legal ramifications fanned the already strong antislavery fires of Minnesota and the rest of the North. The census of 1850, the year after Minnesota officially became a territory, tallied 39 "free colored," and they earned the right to vote in Minnesota in 1868. Minnesota was one of the few states to grant this right prior to passage of the 15th Amendment. Following the Civil War, new arrivals came slowly but steadily up the Mississippi River. Many settled in rural areas to farm, but most eventually made their way to the Twin Cities. Today 91 percent of Minnesota's 172,000 blacks live in the Twin Cities metro, though an increasing number have relocated to other parts of the state in recent years.

East Africans, principally **Somalis,** but also **Ethiopians, Eritreans,** and **Sudanese,** are the newest group of immigrants in Minnesota, arriving as refugees in large numbers in the mid-1990s. For some of those years Somalis were the largest immigrant group coming to Minnesota, and today there are an estimated 15,000 in the state—the largest Somali population in the United States. Most live in Minneapolis, but other significant populations are found in St. Paul, St. Cloud, Rochester, Marshall, Owatonna, and Mankato. The numbers will certainly grow as families reunite across the ocean.

Hispanics

Hispanics are the most widely-distributed minority group in the state. Two-thirds of Minnesota's Hispanics are of **Mexican** descent, though over 20 countries from Central and South America and the Caribbean are represented. Hispanics have been arriving since the mid-19th century, but only in large numbers since the last

half of the 1990s. Minnesota had a grand total of two residents of Mexican descent at statehood, but a population explosion of sorts led to the tripling of that total by 1880 and a further quadrupling by the turn of the 20th century. One of those 24 was an oboe player named Luis Garzoón who, while on tour with the Mexico City Orchestra in 1886, fell ill and was left behind—he remained in Minneapolis for over 50 years.

Labor shortages north of the border during World War I drew many Mexicans to the United States looking for work and, in Minnesota, a few migrant workers found employment in the sugar beet fields. By the 1920, as the sugar industry expanded, thousands of migrants came for a few months each summer, and some, finding work with the railroads or in meat packing plants, decided to stay. By the 1930s, the state's Hispanic population exceeded 3,500 and the total reached 53,884 by 1990. The next decade, thanks in part to the state's low unemployment rate, saw the number truly explode to 143,382—a 266 percent increase—and Minneapolis surpassed St. Paul as the city with the largest Latino population. The population is primarily urban, with nearly 96,000 in the Twin Cities metro, but thriving populations exist in southern and western agricultural towns like Willmar, Worthington, Pelican Rapids, St. James, and Albert Lea, where many former migrants have "settled out" to work in these towns' food processing plants. Despite a decreased need for field workers due to new technologies the state's farm fields still see thousands of migrant workers each summer.

Asians

Like all the state's other minority groups, Minnesota's Asian residents are centered in the Twin Cities, with 85 percent of the nearly 142,000 calling the metro area home. More reside in St. Paul, most notably in Frog Town, than any other city. While significant immigrant populations have come from **India, China, the Philippines,** and **Vietnam,** it is the state's 41,800 Laotian **Hmong** that are most noteworthy. Nearly one-quarter of the nation's Hmong live in Minnesota (only California has more, but if the current trend of relocating from California continues,

INTRODUCTION

Minnesota will surpass the Golden State very soon), and during the 1990s the population increased nearly 250 percent. The first Hmong arrived in Minnesota in the late 1970s following the Vietnam War. Hoping that they could carve out an independent homeland, many Hmong joined the United States in the fight against the North Vietnamese. When the war was lost, tens of thousands of Hmong, facing reprisals by the government that they had fought against (most, in fact, had nothing to do with the war, but the often violent revenge was indiscriminate), fled to refugee camps in Thailand and, over the next two decades, slowly picked up their lives and filtered into other countries, primarily the United States. As the Hmong are traditionally an agrarian people residing in small mountain villages, the Twin Cities now has the world's largest urban Hmong population. Many continue to farm, and Hmong vendors are regulars at local farmers markets, where their beautiful traditional crafts are also sold. While some of the older generation still harbor dreams of returning to Laos and have had a tough time adapting to their new home, integration has not been a problem for the next generation. Mee Moua of St. Paul, whose family fled Laos when she was five, was elected to the State Senate in 2002, becoming the first Hmong legislator in the nation.

> *Minnesotans are different from the rest of us. . . . Minnesotans hold the door for you. Minnesota men don't leave the toilet seat up. Minnesotans do not blow their horns behind you when the light turns green; they wait for you to notice. Minnesotans are nicer than other people.*
>
> **Charles Kuralt,**
> **Charles Kuralt's**
> **America**

CONDUCT AND CUSTOMS

Minnesotans are a fiercely independent, resilient, and self-reliant people. Harrison Salisbury, the *New York Times'* Pulitzer Prize-winning journalist, once attributed much of his success to "the Minnesota spirit, skeptical, contrarian, often out-of-step, hostile to the Bigs." This deeply ingrained temperament explains why many of the small, struggling towns you pass through in western farm country haven't died

out yet, why Minnesota leads the nation in sales by business cooperatives, and why large chains have a harder time pushing out Mom-and-Pop restaurants and retail stores than most places in the country.

As pervasive as the state's independent streak is, the defining quality of the native Minnesotan (it must be in the water because it seems to rub off on transplants, too) is what has come to be called "Minnesota Nice." Minnesotans are friendly, easy-going, eager to please, humble (often to the point of self-deprecation), and do not want to stand out too much. Apologies are offered for simple acts like returning something to a store or ordering a hamburger without a pickle, and sincere pleases and thank yous are the norm. Some people joke that it should really be called Minnesota "Ice" because people can be so reserved; but don't be fooled—being quiet and restrained is considered polite here. No matter how frequently Minnesota Nice is joked about, it remains a point of pride.

Language

The language played up in movies such as *Fargo* is real but uncommon. The Minnesota tongue spoken by most natives has a more typically neutral Midwestern diction, but it does share some of those now famous characteristics and vocabulary. Space does not permit more than a cursory scan of the many delicate subtleties of formal Minnesotan, but Howard Mohr, in his definitive text *How To Talk Minnesotan,* lays them out in hilarious detail. "Minnesotan is not a musical language," Mohr explains. "Some people with an ax to grind have said it is the musical equivalent of a one-string guitar. What I say is, what's wrong with a monotone—at least you don't startle anybody." Minnesotans are not an excitable bunch and, unless discussing a Viking Super Bowl victory (which would be exciting because the purple and gold have choked in the big game all four times they've made it) or bagging a thirty-point buck, their conversations reflect this. Again, Mohr says it best. "Get that excited about something in Minnesota and you might as well paste a bumper sticker on your forehead that says I'M NOT FROM AROUND HERE."

All joking aside, there are several uniquely Minnesotan words and phrases you are sure to hear. The state's true workhorse phrase is **you bet.** It can be a positive response to just about any question—"Were the fish biting today?"—or even most statements—"It's gonna be a hot one." As Mohr explains, "You bet is meant to be pleasantly agreeable and doesn't obligate you to a strong position." You bet also replaces "You're welcome" as the most common reply to a thank you. **You betcha** serves as an enthusiastic "you bet."

Yah, which is drawn out when spoken (*yaahh*), is an equally versatile word. It usually means "yes" or "sure," but it can also mean "Really?" when pronounced with a rising tone. Yah also serves as a verbal filler like "um-hmm." A **Yah, for sure** construction offers added emphasis.

Uff da is the only Norwegian expression that has survived assimilation. It is a general exclamation similar to "Oops" or "Damn it," though uff da is never impolite. Charlie Brown's "Good grief" could be expressed as Uff da.

A uniquely Minnesotan word, one you are likely to encounter either in menus, newspapers, tourist brochures, or on Garrison Keillor's *A Prairie Home Companion,* is **hotdish**—this is just Minnesota vernacular for casserole. It should also be pointed out that during the winter Minnesotans go **sliding** rather than sledding.

Less common than the others, and used primarily by women, the **Oh, for . . .** construction ("Oh, for fun!," "Oh, for cute!," "Oh, for gross!," etc.) is an exclamation that can describe things good or bad.

On the Road

With the exception of mountain climbing, you can enjoy every conceivable outdoor activity in Minnesota and then some. The hiking, paddling, and fishing are world class, and Lake Superior even attracts a handful of surfers year-round.

HIKING

The undisputed champion of long-distance hiking trails in Minnesota is the **Superior Hiking Trail** (SHT), which runs nearly 200 miles along the length of the North Shore passing through some of the loveliest scenery in the state. Readers of *Backpacker* magazine recently ranked this the second best long-distance trail in the country. The SHT is now a segment of the **North Country** **National Scenic Trail** which, when completed, will stretch over 4,000 miles from New York to North Dakota. Both trails are covered in detail elsewhere in this book.

For a day hike or just a half-hour stroll, you can't do any better than Minnesota's state parks. The system's 1,255 miles of trails cover every possible environment and fitness level and are impeccably well marked and maintained. Most Minnesotans will tell you that the most scenic trails run though thick forests and past the raging waterfalls of the eight parks hugging the North Shore. I can't disagree; but the truth of the matter is that wherever you find yourself in the state, you are never far from a great hike. Even in western farming country, oases like Blue Mounds, Maplewood, and Lake Bronson all have fantastic trails. If you ever pull into a state park and find crowded picnic areas, beaches, or campgrounds, don't be discouraged—few trails get heavy enough traffic to be annoying, and you'll generally be out there all alone, or at least it will feel like you are.

© TIM BEWER

GET IT BEFORE YOU GO

You can order state park permits, obtain free maps and brochures about state-owned lands, and get answers to almost any question from the **DNR Information Center.** They are located in downtown St. Paul at the DNR Central Office, 500 Lafayette Rd., and are open weekdays 8 A.M.–4:15 P.M. You can make a request by phone at 651/296-6157 or 888/646-6367 (in state) or email at info@dnr.state.mn.us. Most of the information is available online at www.dnr.state.mn.us or you can order what isn't. Also at the same website is the **Recreation Compass,** an interactive map with links to information about Minnesota's parks, forests, wildlife areas, rivers, etc.—including federally owned lands. While still a work in progress it can be a handy resource.

For a $3.50 fee you can buy hunting and fishing licenses, wildlife stamps, or a ski pass by phone at 888/665-4236 or online at www.wildlifelicense.com/mn. There is no need to wait for them to arrive in the mail as they are valid instantly.

The state's two national forest's millions of acres are also full of great trails. The Chippewa has over 160 miles, while the Superior's total trail mileage tops 400. Hiking in the Boundary Waters Canoe Area Wilderness (BWCAW) isn't limited to portaging your canoe. Options run from the wild and challenging **Border Route** and **Kekekabic** long-distance trails to short, easy trips, all with great scenery along the way.

People tend to dismiss the state's other public lands, like National Wildlife Refuges (NRAs), or Scientific and Natural Areas (SNAs), as day-hiking options, but this is a mistake. Most have some wonderful hikes and the trails (if there are any) will always be peaceful.

BIKING

With rarely anything more challenging than gently rolling hills between all its amazing scenery, Minnesota can be great for traveling by bike. The only flaw is that the sparse population means country roads in most of the state are unlikely to be paved, leading you onto heavily traveled highways all too often. However, drivers tend to be courteous and paved shoulders are the norm so the added traffic shouldn't deter you. Despite, or often because of, Minnesota's southeast corner's many long climbs, most saddle jockeys consider it the top place to tour on two wheels. Besides mixing rural farm scenery, including the state's largest Amish community, with unique glacial topography, the back roads are well maintained. West-central Minnesota between St. Cloud and Fergus Falls, the center of Minnesota's dairy industry, has many paved back roads and little traffic on the trunk routes. A day or two along the Otter Trail Scenic Byway through Otter Tail County is hard to beat.

What Minnesota lacks in paved roads it more than makes up for in paved trails. Minnesota is a leader in converting abandoned railroad beds into trails and has more miles of paved rails-to-trails than any other state—250 at last count—and more are added every year. The **Root River** and **Harmony-Preston Valley** state trails in the southeast, the **Paul Bunyan State Trail,** and the **Willard Munger State Trail** outside Duluth are probably the most scenic.

Off-road riders will find a lot to like here, too, from extreme single track to quiet forest touring trails. The **Chippewa** and **Superior National Forests** have hundreds of miles of seldom-followed paths to ride, and the state forests have hundreds more of even lesser used trails. The state parks with the most extensive trail systems are **Myre-Big Island, Gooseberry Falls, Savanna Portage, McCarthy Beach, St. Croix,** and the **Minnesota Valley State Recreation Area.** Many of the state's downhill ski areas, most notably **Giants Ridge** and **Lutsen Mountains,** open up trails to mountain bikers in the summer, and these are justifiably popular.

The Minnesota Office of Tourism's handy *Explore Minnesota Biking* brochure has a comprehensive listing of paved and mountain bike trails. The DNR Information Center has free maps of most of the long-distance and state forest off-road trails.

ON THE ROAD

ON THE ROAD

LEAVE NO TRACE

Leave No Trace is a wilderness ethic designed to minimize your impact when visiting the outdoors. It has been officially adopted by federal agencies including the U.S. Forest Service, U.S. Fish and Wildlife Service, and the National Park Service, and should be followed every time you venture into the wild.

The core principles are:
Plan Ahead and Prepare
Travel and Camp on Durable Surfaces
Dispose of Waste Properly
Leave What You Find
Minimize Campfire Impacts
Respect Wildlife
Be Considerate of Other Visitors

For more specific information about these guidelines check out www.LNT.org or call 800/332-4100.

ROCK CLIMBING

It's been said that Minnesota has the best rock climbing between Seneca and Boulder. Generally speaking there are four climbing areas: the perpetually busy **Interstate State Park** just an hour from the Twin Cities; the sometimes empty **Blue Mounds State Park** in the far southwest; the extensively bolted **Barn Bluff** near downtown Red Wing; and the endlessly varied **North Shore,** which includes some spectacular sea cliffs at Tettegouche State Park (please respect the decades old no-chalk tradition). Climbers in state parks must get a free permit from the office before going up.

The only current statewide climbing guidebook out there is the invaluable *Rock Climbing Minnesota and Wisconsin* by Mike Farris. Farris provides regular updates on his website at www.hamline.edu/~mfarris/guide.

CANOEING, KAYAKING, AND RAFTING

With over 11,000 lakes, 92,000 miles of rivers and streams, and the wild Lake Superior coast,

of course the canoeing and kayaking are good here. The pinnacle of paddling in Minnesota is the world famous **Boundary Waters Canoe Area Wilderness** (BWCAW), a million acres of portage-linked lakes and streams. The remoter parts of **Voyageurs National Park,** the largest water-based park in the nation, offer a similar, though definitely less wild, experience. The **Superior National Forest** (SNF) beyond the BWCAW also has some wonderful, but often overlooked, rivers and lakes.

Most of the state's rivers offer quiet canoeing with a mix of natural scenery and rural life. Although experienced paddlers can find some challenges, beginners generally have little to worry about since most rapids, if there are any, are tame. Overall, the **Kettle, Cloquet,** and especially the **St. Croix** along Minnesota's border with Wisconsin come most highly recommended for a wilderness experience. While the number of streamside towns and farms increases as you move south,

© TIM BEWER

© TIM BEWER

that doesn't necessarily mean that heading north is always the best option. The scenic rivers cutting the deep valleys of Minnesota's southwest, like the **Cannon** and **Root**, are rightly popular and poking around the **Mississippi River** backwaters in the far south can be a lot of fun, too.

Although most of the state is pretty flat, the northeast has no shortage of white water, with many rivers along the North Shore dropping over 200 feet per mile. Kayakers experienced or foolish enough to run some of these monsters should note that for the most part there is only enough water in the spring or after very heavy rains. The **St. Louis River** below Cloquet, with rapids up to Class V and a steady flow through the entire season, is the state's premier whitewater route, while the **Kettle River** through Banning State Park is another popular choice. **Superior Whitewater Rafting** in Carlton offers the only commercial white-water rafting trips in Minnesota down the St. Louis. Construction of a world-class white-water park on the Mississippi River in downtown Minneapolis is scheduled to begin in 2004.

The **Lake Superior Water Trail** is drawing an increasing number of sea kayakers each year. New campsites and rest areas continue to be built and,

though it will likely be near the end of the decade before all work is completed, the plan is to have a campsite or rest area every three-or-so miles along the state's entire shoreline. Eventually, if all goes to plan, it will be part of a circuit around the entire lake. Because of the perpetually cold water and fickle temperament of the lake, beginning paddlers should take a guide or at least stay very close to shore. The larger lakes of Voyageurs National Park are also great sea kayaking territory.

The best single source of information is Greg Breining's *Paddling Minnesota,* published in cooperation with the Department of Natural Resources (DNR). The **Minnesota Canoe Association,** 952/985-1111, www.canoe-kayak .org, is also an excellent resource. The DNR publishes detailed, pocket-sized maps for two dozen rivers (each of those shown on the Minnesota Canoeing map) showing rapids, portages, put-ins, campsites, and the like—get them free by calling the DNR Information Center. The DNR's Trails and Waterways website (www.dnr .state.mn.us/canoeing/routes.html) has descriptions of these rivers, a list of local outfitters, and water level reports updated by 2 P.M. every Thursday. You can also get this water level information by calling 651/296-1151. The Minnesota Office of Tourism publishes the handy *Explore Minnesota Canoeing* brochure with general information on the major paddling areas and the businesses that serve them.

BIRD-WATCHING

Minnesota's remarkable variety of habitats leads, naturally, to excellent birding and many people come here with binoculars and field guides in hand. In total, over 313 regular visitors, plus another 114 casuals, accidentals, and extinct, have been recorded in Minnesota. While birding opportunities are excellent year-round, winter birding in Minnesota stands out. Arctic species like the Common and Hoary Redpoll, gyrfalcon, Ross's gull, and snowy owl head south to Minnesota. There are also exciting resident species, like the spruce grouse, three-toed woodpecker, and boreal chickadee, who reach the southernmost ends of their nesting range in Minnesota.

Where to go depends on what you want to see and when you visit, but many people consider the **Sax-Zim Bog** north of Duluth to be the single best birding site in the state because of the ease of spotting northern species that are tough to find elsewhere. On the other hand, some of these species can be seen in Duluth where there is a greater overall variety of birdlife. The endlessly varied **Agassiz NWR** north of Thief River Falls has gained a good reputation among bird-watchers nationwide.

Minnesota lies right at the heart of the Mississippi Flyway, one of North America's four main migration corridors, and this brings some tremendous congregations to the state each fall. Anywhere from 40 to 140,000 (the record count for a single day is nearly 50,000) raptors soar past Duluth's **Hawk Ridge** between August and November. Other fall migration hotspots include **Lac Qui Parle WMA** along the upper reaches of the Minnesota River, where as many as 200,000 Canada geese flock; and **Weaver Bottoms** along the Mississippi River north of Winona, which sees upwards of 12,000 tundra swans in single a day. Hundreds of bald eagles overwinter along the **Mississippi River,** with Minnesota's greatest con-

centrations around Wabasha and Red Wing. The **Minnesota Valley NWR,** just a stone's throw from the Mall of America, is one of the best urban birding sites in the nation.

Several good birding books are listed in this book's Resources section, but none are as invaluable as Kim Eckert's *A Birder's Guide To Minnesota.* The *Explore Minnesota Wildlife* brochure available from the Minnesota Office of Tourism has quite a bit of useful information, and you can also pick up species checklists at most state parks, NWRs, and national forests. There is a wealth of information on the website of the **Minnesota Ornithologists' Union,** www.cbs.umn.edu/~mou, including recommended birding spots, lists of local birding groups, guided trip announcements, and the definitive Minnesota species checklist. The MOU's **Rare Bird Alerts** are available online or by phone. For statewide sightings call 612/780-8890 or 800/657-3700. Dial 218/728-5030) for Duluth and the North Shore, and 800/433-1888 for the northwest. The MOU's $25 annual membership, which includes their bimonthly newsletter *Minnesota Birding* and the quarterly journal *The Loon,* is a real bargain. Anyone heading to the Red River Valley should get a

© TIM BEWER

In Minnesota there are nearly as many bait shops as lakes.

copy of the 32-page **Pine to Prairie Birding Trail** booklet (available free from all area tourism agencies), which details 43 top sites between Fergus Falls and Warroad. The brochure includes a checklist of 275 regular species; you can read weekly birding reports at www.mnbirdtrail.com. The Audubon Society has also developed the similar **Great River Birding Trail** along the Mississippi River and the **Minnesota River Valley Birding Trail** (www.birdingtrail.org). For maps and information call 651/290-1695.

If you want someone to lead the way while you are here, check the MOU's website for a list of birding trips, or for extended excursions consider the following tour operators: **Victor Emanuel Nature Tours**, 800/328-8368, www.ventbird.com; **Wings**, 888/293-6443, www.wingsbirds.com; or **Preferred Adventures**, 800/840-8687, www.preferredadventures.com.

FISHING

Many a professional angler will insist, with good reason, that the best fishing in the United States is in Minnesota. With all those lakes, not to mention 15,000 miles of fishable streams, how could the fishing not be great? Some 2.3 million people drop a line in Minnesota waters each year, spending $1.9 billion in the process. The state leads the nation in the sale of fishing licenses per capita and is second only to California in the total number sold. The love of fishing explains why Minnesota has more recreational boats per capita, one for every six people, than any other state. While they welcome everyone, the majority of resorts cater to anglers, and they can provide you with everything you need from the boat to the worm.

Of the two dozen game species in Minnesota waters, none excite anglers like the state fish, the **walleye.** Though found across the state, generally the action is hottest in the large cool lakes of the north-central and northeast. And though more than four million are taken each year 75–90 percent are naturally produced. People talk so much about walleye that some forget Minnesota has the most varied **bass** fishing in the nation. Largemouth are most plentiful in central Minnesota, while the largest smallmouths swim in the north-

east. Minnesota's northern and central lakes also produce copious trophy **muskie** and **northern pike.** The largest rivers are well known for their **catfish.** Flatheads topping 60 pounds swim in the Mississippi, St. Croix, and Minnesota Rivers, while the more widespread channel cats can exceed 20 pounds in and around the Red River of the North. Other popular Minnesota catches include **tiger muskie, sauger, bullhead, crappie** (black and white), and **sunfish.** The latter even out-bite walleye, making it the most caught fish in the state.

Fly fishers focus on the 2,600 miles of **trout** streams carving the valleys of the southeast and climbing the hills along the North Shore. The brown trout is the top catch, while rainbow (steelhead) and the native "brookie" round out the state's inland trout species. The DNR has been experimenting with a winter catch-and-release season in Beaver Creek and Whitewater state parks.

Lake Superior, deep and always cold, adds another dimension to the Minnesota angling experience. Lake trout are the most frequent catch, while walleye, rainbow trout, and **salmon** (Chinook, pink, and coho) are all frequently landed. Duluth is charter boat central, but you will find licensed captains in just about every sizable town along the North Shore.

Regulation, Maps, and Information

In order to ensure the future of fishing in Minnesota, the DNR has enacted an extensive and somewhat complicated set of fishing regulations, and there are a variety of new rules created every year. Always inquire locally before casting a line. All anglers should also pick up the annual *Minnesota Fishing Regulations* booklet, available free wherever licenses are sold.

Anyone age 16 and older must posses a Minnesota fishing license and penalties for fishing without one can be pretty severe, potentially including jail time and confiscation of your boat. A standard license for the season is $18 for Minnesota resident and $35 for nonresidents. Discounts for seniors, married couples, the disabled, and shorter durations apply. Lifetime licenses are also available. Trout and salmon stamps are generally required for designated lakes, streams, and Lake Superior. Licenses and stamps can be bought at bait shops, sporting goods stores, marinas, resorts, hardware stores, gas stations, and DNR offices; by phone at 888/665-4236; or online at DNR at www.wildlifelicense.com/mn.

The open season for walleye, northerns, muskie, and bass is roughly mid-May through mid-February; trout streams are open mid-April to the end of September; trout in lakes are legal mid-May through the end of October, except lake trout which close at the end of September, but reopen roughly January through May. Crappie, sunfish, bluegill, perch, bullhead, rock bass, white bass, catfish, and whitefish can be taken year-round, though bag limits vary. Lake Superior seasons are a whole other story. Anglers who plan to fish any border or reservation waters should inquire locally about different seasons, regulations, and licenses.

While local bait shops can tell you what's biting and where, the *Explore Minnesota Fishing* brochure published by the Minnesota Office of Tourism offers a good overview of the opportunities in each part of the state. The DNR Information Center can also help with general inquiries. The DNR's Lake Finder website (www.dnr.state.mn.us/lakefind) has lake surveys, depth maps, stocking reports, and other information for over 5,000 lakes statewide. The lake depth maps are also available for sale at Minnesota's Bookstore in St. Paul.

Ice Fishing

As author Thomas Huhti so perfectly explains in *Moon Handbooks Wisconsin*, "Driving the truck out on a frozen lake to a village of shanties erected over drilled holes, sitting on an overturned five-gallon pail, stamping your feet quite a bit, and drinking a lot of schnapps is a time-honored tradition in the Great White North." Despite what one would assume, the ice fishing scenes from *Grumpy Old Men* were not exaggerated for comic effect; if anything they were understated to make them believable to the rest of the country. Shantytowns connected by plowed and signed roads spring up on lakes across the state between December and March. Frostbite Flats, a temporary city of 5,500 homes on Mille Lacs, is the most fa-

mous. Many of these fish houses, ranging from simple wooden shacks to "sleepers" decked out with furnaces, electrical generators, and even satellite TV, are available for overnight rental by the day or week.

Ice fishing isn't difficult, but there are a few things first-timers need to know. If there is a big crowd out on the ice you can probably assume it is safe, but never take ice safety lightly. Every year several knuckleheads foolishly push the limits and lose their vehicles or even their lives. If there is any doubt about the ice, ask. Resort owners, bait shops, sheriff's departments, and the DNR will usually have the most current ice conditions. Of course, wear warm clothing, especially waterproof boots and warm socks, to keep your feet dry and warm. A depth finder keeps you from making Swiss cheese out of the ice while looking for the perfect spot. And bring a cooler so the beer doesn't freeze.

HUNTING

Love it or hate it, hunting is an indelible part of Minnesota life. Nearly 600,000 people take up a gun or bow each year, and the first deer hunt is an important rite of passage for many kids. The littered six-packs and Stop sign targets found all too often around wildlife areas and public forestlands show that many trigger-happy idiots still roam the woods, but most hunters are, in fact, far more conservation minded than the average citizen. The revenue raised by hunting licenses and stamps, as well as funds donated by conservation organizations like Ducks Unlimited, Pheasants Forest, and the Izaak Walton League, have paid for over half of the one million acres of wildlife management land found around the state. Thanks largely to hunters, Minnesota has more public wildlife lands than any other state east of the Mississippi. And, ethical considerations aside, in many cases hunting is an essential management tool—I know a vegetarian ecology professor who takes up a rifle during the deer season. The financial benefits to rural communities and the state as a whole can't be ignored either. Hunters spend about $530 million annually in the state on hunt-related products and services.

Minnesota has 110 legal game species. Deer, geese, duck, ruffed grouse, and pheasant are some of the most popular. Any questions you have about seasons (most are between Sept. and Dec.), locations, or licenses can be answered by the DNR Information Center. Licenses can be obtained at sporting goods stores, bait shops, resorts, hardware stores, gas stations, and DNR offices.

GOLF

Believe it or not, Minnesota ranks number one in the nation in golfers per capita, and some 480 courses have been carved into the Minnesota countryside to meet demand. Like most things Minnesotan, greens fees are a veritable bargain, and the season usually runs from April through October, though over the past several years warmer-than-average autumns have extended playing time into November and even a few Decembers. The season may run year-round in Arizona, Florida, and other hotspots, but who wants to walk nine holes under the sun of a Southern summer?

Without question, Minnesota's two best courses are **Interlachen** in Edina and **Hazeltine National** in Chaska, which both *Golf Digest* and *Golf* magazines rank in their top 100 for the United States—but you'll have to befriend a member to get a whack at them. Public courses widely considered as the state's best include **The Classic at Madden's** (Brainerd), **Giants Ridge,** (Biwabik), **Legends** (Prior Lake), **The Pines at Grand View Lodge** (Nisswa), **Rush Creek** (Maple Grove), **Superior National** (Lutsen), and **Wilds** (Prior Lake).

The Minnesota Office of Tourism publishes the *Explore Minnesota Golf* brochure with a comprehensive list of courses. The Minnesota Golf Association's **Minnesota Golfer website,** www.mngolfer.com, has a searchable database with detailed information about all of the state's courses.

> *Minnesota is very golf-wise . . . there is a misconception about the fact that the season is so short. If you don't mind a little cool weather, you can get seven months of golf in, and there aren't many places in the United States where you can do that, comfortably. So, it's no surprise to me that Minnesota is becoming a golf Mecca.*
>
> *Arnold Palmer*

WINTER PURSUITS

Downhill Skiing and Snowboarding

Though Minnesota is no French Alps or Colorado Rockies, ski bums could do a lot worse—and pay a lot more. Nineteen downhill ski areas dot the state and most are open by early November thanks to man-made snow. Minnesota's big three, **Lutsen Mountains** (the Midwest's largest and highest), **Giants Ridge, and Spirit Mountain,** sit just a few hours from each other in Minnesota's northeast corner. Most others are spread out across the southern half of the state. Snowboards are allowed at all of them, but Spirit Mountain and Giants Ridge have large terrain parks and are hands down the best bets for shredding.

The www.mnsno.com website has a nearly complete list of ski areas, plus information on slope conditions and ski schools.

Cross-Country Skiing

Skinny skiing is excellent right across the whole of Minnesota, and large parks that don't have groomed trails are the exception rather than the rule. The **Gunflint Trail** area, with over 200 km of signed and well-maintained trails along it, is arguably the top spot to stride and glide, but even Twin Cities' parks like **Murphy Hanrehan** in Savage, **Battle Creek** in St. Paul, and **Lebanon Hills** in Eagan will challenge experienced skiers. The Three Rivers Park District trail system (in and around Minneapolis) has more lighted ski trails than any other place in the nation. Skiers should also know about the cross-country skiing focused **Maplelag Resort** near Detroit Lakes and **Giants Ridge** which, though best known for downhill skiing, has 70 kilometers of cross-country ski trails that have hosted World Cup events and Olympic tryouts. Special candlelight skiing nights are held in most state parks and along other popular trails.

Skiers 16 and older must carry a **Minnesota Ski Pass** on most public trails—including all in the state parks and national forests. A daily pass costs $3; a season pass is $10. Passes can be purchased by phone (888/665-4236); on-line (www.wildlifelicense.com/mn); and at sporting goods stores, resorts, hardware stores, gas stations, and DNR offices. Daily passes are sold at most state parks, but seasonal passes are not.

A great source for trail reports is **Adelsman's Cross-Country Ski Page**, www.skinnyski.com. They also feature race information, weather forecasts, and more. Another invaluable resource, the *Explore Minnesota Skiing* brochure published annually by the Minnesota Office of Tourism, has a fairly comprehensive list of trails.

Snowshoeing

The classic wood and rawhide tennis-racket style snowshoes are more likely to be found decorating a resort wall than strapped to someone's feet. High technology has made this ancient art one of the fastest growing sports in the nation. Today's modern shoes are constructed with aircraft-quality aluminum frames and high-grade polymer decks, allowing these smaller, lighter models to carry just as much weight and be far more maneuverable than the classic styles. And, unlike

© TIM BEWER

Snowshoeing is popular in Minnesota.

cross-country skiers, shoers with an adventurous spirit and a good sense of direction can go almost anywhere. Small streams, thick woods, and steep hills can all be crossed without a hitch.

The learning curve for mastering the higher, wider step required for walking with webbed feet is about as flat as for chewing gum and, other than the shoes themselves, no special equipment is needed. Some people use poles for balance, but they really aren't necessary unless you are venturing off into very steep or rocky terrain. Minnesota's state parks are a great place to give snowshoeing a try. With the obvious exception of groomed ski trails, snowshoeing is allowed anywhere, and shoes can be rented from many park offices. Shoes can also be found at most of the same places that rent cross-country skis. The "anywhere but groomed trails" rule applies to most public lands, from county parks to the national forests.

Dogsledding and Skijoring

Dogsledding's popularity is increasing in Minnesota and so are the opportunities for rookies to give it a try. Most large resorts in the north can arrange it for you, and many mushers have their own operations. Either just go for a ride or, after about 45 minutes of instruction, drive your own team. Several sled dog races are held across the north, most notably the John Beargrease Sled Dog Marathon, running 400 miles along the North Shore from Duluth to Grand Marais and back. It is considered the toughest race in the Lower 48. Watching the dogs is a beautiful and exhilarating experience.

Skijoring is a highly pared-down version of dogsledding; just strap on your cross-country skis and harness your dog (or dogs) to your waist. There are fewer opportunities to try this simple, fast-growing Scandinavian import, but many of the outfitters and resorts that arrange dogsledding can hook you up—literally. If you want to try it on your own, check out Skijor Now, 651/486-6824 or 888/486-6824, www.skijornow.com; or the Arrowhead Trading Co., 218/387-1343 or 800/739-1239, www.skijoring.com. Both companies sell equipment and offer information about getting started in the sport.

Snowmobiling

Snowmobiling is more than just a popular pastime in Minnesota—for many it's nearly a religion. Minnesota is second in the nation with over 280,000 registered sleds, or roughly 10 percent of all snowmobiles in the United States and Canada. Minnesotans so love their hobby that they just assume the snowmobile was invented here and this "fact" is widely promoted, even though that honor truly goes to Wisconsin. Minnesota is, however, home to Arctic Cat and Polaris, two of the world's four largest snowmobile manufacturers.

Beginning with the first substantial snowfall, an impressive 20,000-mile winter highway system with road signs, billboards, and bridges is laid out across the state, making it possible to travel straight through from Luverne to Grand Marais by snowmobile. Restaurants, hotels, and other businesses advertise what trail they are located on and set up parking lots for riders. Even schools have lots for students' sleds. Most of these trails are maintained by volunteers from local snowmobile clubs, but the state and local governments recognize how important the thousands of riders who descend on the state are and also pitch in. Riders drop about $150 million into the local coffers annually and allow many resorts and hotels to stay open year-round.

Snowmobile rentals are fairly common, though not exactly cheap—expect to pay $125 a day at the very least. If you bring your own sled to Minnesota you'll need a $16 trail use permit, available from sporting goods stores, resorts, hardware stores, gas stations, and DNR offices; by phone (888/665-4236), or online (www.wildlifelicense.com/mn). Snowmobiles with studs must also have a $13 metal traction device sticker and are prohibited from paved trails. All riders under 18 must take a snowmobile safety course, and the directive is being extended to adults. To find out dates and times of classes statewide, call 800/366-8917. Since requirements differ for nonresidents, it is best to inquire before arriving.

The best source of information for riders is the Minnesota United Snowmobilers Association, 763/577-0185, www.snowmobile-mnusa.org. The Minnesota Office of Tourism publishes the handy *Explore Minnesota Snowmobiling* brochure.

Shopping

Thanks in large part to the enormous Mall of America in Bloomington, over half of all out-of-state visitors list shopping as at least one reason for coming. (Scenic driving is a distant second at 35 percent.) In general, the quality and uniqueness of Minnesota's gift shops and galleries is directly related to their proximity to the state's eastern border: the Twin Cities, Stillwater, Duluth, the North Shore, and most Mississippi River towns will all appeal to discriminating shoppers.

If you like the idea of picking up farm fresh produce while out on the road, get a free copy of the **Minnesota Grown Directory** from the Minnesota Department of Agriculture, 651/296-5029 or 800/657-3700. It lists hundreds of homegrown vendors selling everything from blueberries to bison burgers.

Crafts

Minnesota's diverse cultures afford some interesting shopping opportunities. Native American arts are found throughout the state. Beadwork and silver jewelry are most common, though the least Minnesotan. Baskets made of birch bark can be true works of art, while other birch-bark items, like toy canoes, make cheap mementos. Though sold across the nation, pipestone carvings (discussed in detail with the city of Pipestone in the Prairieland chapter) are truly unique to Minnesota. If you have any interest in purchasing some, you should go right to the source, since not only is the quality likely to be higher, but you will not find anything even resembling the selection outside of Pipestone.

Also common at craft fairs and in gift shops are Scandinavian folk arts, like rosemaling—a decorative painting characterized by flowers and flowing scrolls—and chip carving. Most large and mid-sized cities have gift shops selling Scandinavian items exclusively.

Although the Hmong population is the nation's second largest, their handiwork is less common. The principal craft is *paj ntaub* (pronounced pahn dow), which combines reverse appliqué with intricate embroidery to create colorful geometric designs containing hidden symbolism. While traditionally the "flower cloths" are part of the elaborate costumes worn at weddings, New Year's celebrations, and other important events, you can buy wall hangings, bedspreads, Christmas tree skirts, wallets, and much more with the artistic patterns. A new take on the ancient art that developed in the refugee camps of Thailand and has proven very popular in Minnesota are storycloths, which tell family histories or stories of the Hmong's exodus from their tribal homelands. Prices are high, but a quick look at the intricacy shows why; large quilts or wall hangings can take months to complete. The best place to look is the Hmong Arts, Books, & Crafts Store, 298 University Ave. W., 651/293-0019, in St. Paul. You will also find artists selling their creations at crafts fairs and farmers markets.

Many people go to Lanesboro and Harmony just to buy Amish crafts, principally basketry, quilts, and furniture. The selection and quality in the shops is excellent, but many signs in front of farms invite shoppers to stop by homes (never stop by a home without a sign and never stop on a Sunday) and purchase direct from the source. Others park their horses and buggies along busy highways to sell to passing motorists.

Antiques

Stillwater, Red Wing, and Minneapolis are the state's leading antiquing centers, but many of Minnesota's tiniest towns, if they are located near a busy highway, will have an antique store, and these are where you stand a decent chance of stumbling upon a real find. The Minnesota Antiques Dealers Association publishes an annual directory of member stores that will likely be of interest to the dedicated shopper; it is available by calling 612/874-9680.

© TIM BEWER

Taxes

Taxes are high in Minnesota, but visitors won't likely notice since prices, compared with the rest of the country, are very low to begin with, and gas prices are about the national average. The statewide sales tax is 6.5 percent and a handful of cities and counties tack on an additional half or one percent. There is no sales tax on most clothing and groceries.

Accommodations

If you will be visiting Minnesota on any weekend between Memorial Day and Labor Day, it would be wise to make lodging reservations as far in advance as possible. This is not to say reservations are always necessary. It can take some effort, but for the most part you'll be able to find a room or a campsite on short notice anytime you visit, unless a large festival happens to be going on that weekend. One major exception is the North Shore, where it is almost impossible to find a room on short notice from mid-June right on through to the end of September, plus weekends in October, February, and March.

The Minnesota Office of Tourism's website (www.exploreminnesota.com) has a handy lodging search where you can choose not only by location (either region, city, or lake) but also specific amenities and features, such as whether pets are allowed, is it a lakefront property, or do the rooms have fireplaces. They also maintain a list of special offers and a link to a site that offers online booking.

Prices

Unless otherwise stated, prices in this guide are for double occupancy rooms on weekends during the summer high season and do not include sales tax, the 3 percent statewide lodging tax, or any local hotel taxes. Some large resorts also tack on their own service charges, a shamefully deceptive practice. When applicable I do what the resorts should and calculate these into the listed price. Like airlines, most hotels price by occupancy, so the sooner you book the better your chances of getting a deal. Ignoring regional variations (what's overpriced in Hibbing might be a bargain in St. Paul), generally you get what you pay for. A hotel priced more than the competition probably has newer rooms or more/better facilities; I've tried to point out when this is not the case.

Almost all hotels, resorts, and B&Bs charge their highest rates during the busy summer season and have discounted prices in the spring and fall. Summer rates on the North Shore last until the end of October, when the last of the fall color has blown away. Winter is a mixed bag. The majority of resorts and even some hotels close up shop, while those near the state's largest downhill ski areas see their highest occupancies, and thus highest prices. Across the north, where snowmobiling, cross-country skiing, and ice fishing are big business, it is quite common for rates to be just as high in the snowy season as during the summer. Off-season prices, regardless of when they occur, can be over 50 percent less, though 20 percent is more typical. In the larger cities, you will usually find significant hotel discounts (often as much as 50 percent) on weekends when business travelers are at home, while similarly substantial discounts in the country come during the week when the tourists are at work.

AAA and AARP members get significant discounts at just about all hotels, though many will automatically give the same reduced rate to anyone who simply asks if there are any specials.

HOTELS AND MOTELS

No part of the state, even the agricultural south and west, is short on quality hotels. All the major national chains are here, of course. The amenities and quality at some chains can vary, but they are priced accordingly and are usually fine. Family-run hotels and motels are an increasingly rare breed, and while they largely occupy the budget end of the lodging spectrum there are some that compete head to head with the upper-end chains. Don't make the mistake of ruling a place out just because you've never heard of it: no matter what level of comfort you need, the locally-owned establishments usually offer the greatest value. Admittedly, some lower-end properties can be pretty grubby, but if you are unsure you can always ask to see a room first. I've only included places where the rooms were clean. Recommendations from rating agencies like AAA or Mobil carry a lot of weight and can be an invaluable guide when making a decision.

Just about every hotel serves a free continental breakfast in the morning: the more expensive the bed, the more extensive the spread. It won't be more than just coffee and rolls at the cheapest lodges, but even some mid-range hotels do well by the morning meal. Whirlpool tubs are now a very common hotel amenity, and they won't always add a lot to the price, so if you'd like a little pampering ask for one when booking a room.

RESORTS

A week "Up North" at the lake is a summer ritual for most Minnesota families, and those who don't have their own cabins usually take up residence at their favorite resort. Resort, it should be pointed out, has a different definition in Minnesota than it does in Colorado or Cancún. Sure, there are plenty of fancy lodges with four-star facilities, golf courses, organized activities for the kids, and the like, but the classic Minnesota resort is a dozen or so rustic cabins with faux wood paneling, linoleum floors, furniture the owners bought back in the 1950s, and fully-equipped kitchens for frying up the day's catch. Most people raised in the Upper Midwest, myself included, have fond memories of a week at the lake in a cabin just like this and are happy to relive them again and again. Clearly these aren't for everyone, but many get so much repeat business that they don't advertise. Not all of the small, family-run resorts are stuck in a time warp, so if you're looking for something a little fancier and more modern, but with the same olden-days character, you'll have no problem finding it in most regions.

There are some things that all resorts have in common, no matter what the era. First, all are on a lake or a river. Each cabin comes with its own boat at the better resorts, and in most other cases

resort life, Minnesota style

© TIM BEWER

boats will be available to rent. Few resorts rent cabins for less than a week during the summer; daily and weekend rentals are a bit easier to come by the rest of the year. Although the majority of resorts close up shop for the winter (those listed in this guide are open year-round unless otherwise indicated), the popularity of winter sports makes it the peak season for some. There is often animosity between cross-country skiers and snowmobilers, and if you are a fan of one sport you may not be welcome or feel comfortable at a resort specializing in the other—it's usually not an issue, but it's still a good idea to check ahead of time. You may encounter pricing terms such as Housekeeping (HSK), meaning cabins have kitchens and no meals are included; American Plan, which includes three meals a day; Modified American Plan, which signifies only breakfast and dinner are provided; and European Plan, meaning you pay for all of your meals out of pocket. Always ask whether linens, dishes, and towels are provided; often they aren't or they cost extra.

> *A week "Up North" at the lake is a summer ritual for most Minnesota families; those who don't have their own cabins usually take up residence at their favorite resort.*

While there are plenty of resorts listed in this book, I would still recommend calling the local chamber of commerce or tourism office if you're interested in this type of lodging. Tell them what sort of vacation you are looking for so they can recommend a list of resorts that best fit your needs. The *Explore Minnesota Resorts* brochure published by the Minnesota Resort Association in conjunction with the Minnesota Office of Tourism includes over 700 of them. It is also available online at www.hospitalitymn.com/guides/guide.asp.

BED-AND-BREAKFASTS

The European B&B concept, where people open a portion of their home to overnight guests, has taken off in a big way in Minnesota—the Minnesota Bed & Breakfast Guild has over 170 members—though they tend to be less informal than their continental cousins. If you had to describe the typical Minnesota B&B it would be an antique-filled, 19th-century Victorian home,

but this would belie the wonderful variety of establishments. Bed-and-breakfasts have also been born in farmhouses, log cabins, sod buildings, churches, train cars, lighthouses, jail cells—even a converted chicken coop.

The biggest misconception about B&Bs is the price. Rates at B&Bs are often comparable with hotels, and many agree that the personalized service is worth a little bit extra in any case. Admittedly, a few are drastically overpriced, but on the other hand, some of the more expensive rooms are quite spectacular. Though price usually isn't one of them, B&Bs do have a few downsides. Late afternoon check-ins are the norm and pets are almost always prohibited. Policies on children vary widely so always inquire, whether you have some of your own or want to ensure that none will disrupt your stay.

There aren't too many historic inns in Minnesota, but they are a wonderful option when available. Most of these lovely, restored buildings have the look and feel of a bygone era. Though they function like hotels, they tend to list themselves with B&Bs because it carries more prestige. Larger and generally more expensive than B&Bs, they do offer some of the same personal touches.

The *Explore Minnesota Bed & Breakfast and Historic Inns* brochure, published by the Minnesota Bed & Breakfast Guild in conjunction with the Minnesota Office of Tourism, is likely to be useful. It is also available online at www.hospitalitymn.com/guides/guide.asp.

HOSTELS

Hostels offer budget priced, dorm-style accommodation, though a few private rooms are usually available, too. Many people stay in hostels solely for the friendly, communal atmosphere. The downside is that there are usually curfews and mid-day lockout times.

Minnesota has just one Hostelling International (HI)-affiliated hostel, Mississippi Headwaters, in a historic log building in Lake Itasca State Park. Their Spirit of the Land Island Hostel on the edge of the BWCAW has shut down, but there's a good chance it will reopen in the not too distant future. HI hopes to open a 150-bed Twin Cities hostel in the historic cavalry barracks at Fort Snelling State Park, but it is a long-term project and probably won't be done any time soon, if ever. A one-year membership in HI costs $25 for adults ($15 seniors, free for those under 18) and is available at their hostels or from Hostelling International's Minnesota chapter, 125 SE Main St., Suite 135, 612/378-3773, www.himinnesota.org. Members get discounts of $3 or more at all of HI's 4,500 hostels worldwide, as well as discounts at many businesses.

The City of Lakes International House and Kaz's Home Hostel are good independent hostels in Minneapolis, while the Old Barn Resort has a hostel along the Root River Trail in Preston. Minnesota State University–Moorhead and Duluth's College of St. Scholastica operate summer-only hostels.

HOUSEBOATS

You really are the captain of your own ship when you travel by houseboat. Take in the scenery and soak up the sun by day and moor up in a secluded cove at night; or if you want to spend a night on the town, dock up at a marina. The RVs of the aquatic world have everything a hotel room would, plus fully equipped kitchens and outdoor lounge space. Many models also include an outdoor grill, hot tub, waterslide, and separate bedrooms. Some companies will even deliver groceries or other supplies right to your boat. All boats have ship to shore radios for emergencies.

Absolutely no experience (or license) is needed to pilot a houseboat. Most companies will give you a short course on piloting and navigation, enough to make you an expert before you even leave the port. If you are uneasy about the driving, most companies can arrange a captain for your first day, or even the entire trip. Costs vary as widely as the size and style of boats do, but as a *very* rough estimate expect to pay about $1,500 for a three-night rental or $2,500 for a full week in a luxury vessel holding up to 12 people, or $500/three nights and $800/week for low-end models sleep-

ing four in the off-season. Count on $25–50 per day in fuel, depending on the size of the boat and the amount of cruising you plan to do.

Rentals are primarily available along the Mississippi River below the Twin Cities and in the Voyageurs National Park area, but their popularity is spreading to some other large northern lakes. *Houseboat* magazine's website, www.houseboat.net/mn.html, has a good list of houseboat rental companies, or check the lodging section of the Minnesota Office of Tourism's website, www.exploreminnesota.com.

CAMPING AND RV PARKS

Camping just doesn't get any better than in the Boundary Waters Canoe Area Wilderness (BWCAW), a million-acre labyrinth of lakes with nearly 2,200 primitive campsites accessible only by canoe or foot. A night under the stars, serenaded by wolves and loons, is likely to be the highlight of a trip to Minnesota. Plan your visit as far in advance as possible since permits are required for overnight visits. Voyageurs National Park has another 210 breathtaking boat-in sites; unlike the BWCAW, Voyageurs isn't a wilderness area so motorboats are allowed, otherwise the camping can be nearly as good. Camping along the upper reaches of the St. Croix National Scenic Riverway can also be excellent.

Minnesota's excellent state park system contains nearly 4,400 campsites. A few of the state park campgrounds are large and packed but, as a rule, are quite good. There are several options besides the usual drive-in campsites. For tranquility and seclusion choose the cart-in, canoe-in, bike-in, or backpacking sites available at well over half of the parks. The popular cart-in option lets you easily transport your gear to relatively isolated campsites, allowing the best of both backpacking and car camping. Walk-in sites, available in many parks, are part of the main campground, but set back a short ways from the road, allowing at least the illusion of solitude. There are no drive-in sites at all at Afton, George Crosby Manitou, Glendalough, John Latsch, Lake Maria, and Split Rock Lighthouse State Parks. Upper Sioux Agency State Park has a pair of Dakota-style tepees. Those who want the experience of camping without actually having to do it can rent a rustic camper cabin. These simple 12-foot by 16-foot cabins, located in park campgrounds, sleep five or six people in bunk beds. Most are wheelchair accessible and have screened porches, but none have indoor plumbing and you must bring your own sleeping bags. About half have electricity and fireplaces and are available year-round. They are located at Banning, Bear Head Lake, Crow Wing, Glendalough, Hayes Lake, Jay Cooke, Lake Maria, Lake Shetek, Maplewood, Mille Lacs Kathio, Minneopa, Myre Big Island, Sakatah Lake, Savanna Portage, Whitewater, Wild River and William O'Brien State Parks. Because of their popularity, reserve as early as possible.

Depending on what facilities are available, state park campsite prices range $7–12 plus $3 for an electric hookup. Minnesota seniors or campers with disabilities pay half price Sunday–Thursday for regular campsites. Camper cabins cost $30 with electricity and $27.50 without. You can make reservations or check availability online at www.stayatmnparks.com or call 866/857-2757 (TDD 866/290-2267) from the United States or Canada, and 605/718-3030 from anywhere else in the world. Phone lines are open 7 A.M.–10 P.M. daily. Campsites can be reserved 3–90 days in advance when paying by credit card, and 10–90 days in advance when paying by check. The steep $8.50 reservation fee is nonrefundable.

While Minnesota's state forests have few visitor facilities, about a third do have campgrounds, though even the most modern lack electric hookups and showers. All sites are first-come first-served and those with developed facilities, such as drinking water and pit toilets, charge $9. Backpacking throughout the forests is allowed, but not encouraged.

Like the state forests, campgrounds in Minnesota's national forests are generally smaller and quieter than those in the state parks. An added bonus is that most campgrounds generally only fill up on Memorial Day and Labor Day weekends so reservations are not needed, though they're not a bad idea for peace of mind. Only two of the 23 "developed" campgrounds in the Superior National Forest have electricity: Fall Lake near Ely

and Whiteface Reservoir near Aurora. Prices range $6–12. An additional 16 rustic campgrounds with pit toilets, none with more than six sites, are free. Most of the developed campgrounds in the Chippewa National Forest are also small, quiet, and rustic. Only two, Stony Point near Walker and the Norway Beach Recreation Area near Cass Lake, have showers and electrical hookups. Rates range $12–18. Reservations for all national forest campgrounds can be made online at www.reserveusa.com or by calling 518/855-3639 or 877/444-6777 (TDD 877/833-6777). If you don't know exactly where you want to camp, it is easiest to book by phone. The lines are open 7 A.M.–11 P.M. April 1 through Labor Day and 9 A.M.–6 P.M. the rest of the year. Reservations are accepted up to eight months in advance and there is a $9 fee—it costs $10 to change or cancel a reservation. Free non-reservable backcountry sites with fire grates and latrines, accessible by canoe or boat, are located along lakes and rivers throughout both forests. Backpacking is also allowed almost anywhere in the forests' millions of acres, just pitch your tent well away from water and trails.

If possible, I highly recommend camping in the state and national parks and forests. Most private and municipally-owned campgrounds are just a place to park and plug in your RV and have nothing to do with nature. On the other hand, if that's your thing there is no shortage of options and many are listed in this book. For a detailed listing of nearly 250 of them, get a copy of the *Explore Minnesota Campgrounds & RV Parks* brochure published by the Minnesota Resort Association in conjunction with the Minnesota Office of Tourism. It is available online at www.hospitalitymn.com/guides/guide.asp.

Most campgrounds, whether public or private, are open early May through mid-October; though like many things in Minnesota, the exact open and close dates are often determined by the weather. A few, including many of those in the state and national parks and forests, keep some sites available during the winter, but you should always call ahead to check exactly what the situation is. Usually facilities such as showers and electricity will be shut off and, in many cases, you must walk or ski in since the area is not plowed.

Food

The Twin Cities have just about any type of cuisine that you could hope to find, and even some you probably wouldn't, like Sri Lankan, Peruvian, and the nation's first (and maybe only) Kurdish restaurant. Mid-sized cities like Duluth, Rochester, and St. Cloud aren't nearly as well endowed, but have enough choices to please everyone. Other than pizza and Mexican-like fast food, Chinese is the only ethnic food you can expect to find outside the larger cities. Unfortunately, with few exceptions, small town Chinese tends to be appallingly bland. (I recommend asking your meal to be made hot and spicy—if you are lucky it will be, otherwise it might at least qualify as medium.) On the other hand, almost every Chinese joint outside the Twin Cites offers a budget priced all-you-can eat buffet so you can gorge yourself for about six or seven dollars. Authentic Mexican restaurants are sprouting up across the south and west as more immigrants settle in agricultural areas.

Like everything else in Minnesota, the food tends to be a real bargain. Throughout most of the state an entrée in an average restaurant will fall in the $5–10 range. In the Twin Cities prices tend to be a few dollars higher, but still well below the national average. Portions are invariably large throughout the state.

MINNESOTA CUISINE

While any blue-blooded Minnesotan regards the hotdish (local vernacular for a casserole) as a gourmet meal, Midwestern cuisine should not be dismissed out of hand. Featured prominently are locally grown ingredients like cranberries, raspberries, morel mushrooms, pumpkin, wild rice, fresh fish, and wild game such as venison, elk, grouse, and pheasant—sounds pretty good, right? Most of the poshest Minneapolis and St. Paul restaurants specialize in imaginative uses of these ingredients, using them in various ethnic recipes and creating new takes on American classics, but even small town greasy spoons feature them.

Walleye, the most prevalent Minnesota specialty, is usually served batter-fried, and menus will often have multiple variations of it. Nearly as common these days is **wild rice,** which was historically so important to the Ojibwe (it once constituted as much as a quarter of their diet) that it remains a sacred food and its harvesting a sacred event. Wild rice, or *manomin* (good berry) to the Ojibwe, has a slightly nutty flavor and is a remarkably versatile ingredient. While most common as a side dish or soup ingredient (a good wild rice soup is a truly glorious thing!), it is also used to make tortilla chips, bread, beer, pancake flour, and much more. Wild rice is still harvested from the shallow lakes of northern and central Minnesota by the Ojibwe, though its increased popularity has led to the creation of commercial paddies where water levels can be controlled. Gourmets claim that naturally grown rice is a superior product, though there is absolutely nothing wrong with the cultivated variety. However, if your only experience with wild rice is from Uncle Ben, then you haven't really tasted it.

Pasties (PASS-tees), stuffed pastry pockets with the look of mini-calzones, are a great snack, though they can easily make a meal. The basic filling is potato, onion, carrot, and beef, though pretty much anything can, and does, go inside. Chicken, ham and cheese, pizza, veggies, and breakfast (ham and eggs) are some variations. They were brought to Minnesota by Cornish miners (who took them into the tunnels with them for lunch), and they remain an Iron Range fixture but are found in bakeries and restaurants elsewhere in the state. **Potica** (po-TET-sa), a walnut-filled sweet bread brought by south Slavic immigrants, and **Porketta,** a highly-seasoned pork roast, are other Iron Range specialties.

Maple syrup from Minnesota often beats out New England-produced in competitions so be sure to pick some up when you see it for sale. Of course I haven't tried them all, but I can't believe that anyone does it better than Wild Country Maple Syrup near Lutsen.

Though you won't find it on too many menus, the state's most distinctive cuisine is Scandinavian.

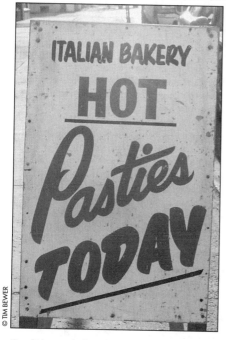

ITALIAN BAKERY HOT Pasties TODAY

© TIM BEWER

gelatinous, foul-smelling mess. When done right it is a flaky, foul-smelling mess. Traditionally Norwegians top it with butter and Swedes with a cream sauce, while a mustard sauce helps many non-fans get it down year after year. Minnesotans consume several tons of it annually, mostly during family get-togethers and church suppers between October and December. A few churches also host communal **Lapskaus** (a traditional Norwegian beef stew) dinners, which might include a side course of sing-along. If you want to sample some of this ethnic cuisine, you can always pick some up at Scandinavian gift shops and even many grocery stores. Microwaveable lutefisk dinners are a new option.

You might also stumble upon the German immigrant-bred tradition of the **Friday night fish fry** (Catholics were once prohibited from eating meat on Fridays), where filets of perch, cod, walleye, or whitefish are deep-fried, usually in a beer batter, and served as all-you-can-eat feasts along with french fries and coleslaw. If you're not from Minnesota you'll be surprised to find how popular they are—unless you're from Wisconsin, in which case you'll be shocked by their scarcity. Not surprisingly, they are most common near the Badger State border. While many restaurants do fish fries, you are just as likely to find good ones at churches, VFWs, and American Legions.

Fish boils, where chunks of fish, potatoes, and onions are cooked up outdoors in a large communal cauldron, are sometimes found along the North Shore, usually during town festivals, but some restaurants also prepare them on weekends. A boilmaster, equal parts chef and showman, finishes the preparation by dumping fuel onto the flames creating a short-lived inferno. This boil-over not only garners a collective cheer from the crowd, but also sends the fat and other undesirables up and out of the cauldron.

DRINK
Wine

Visitors are often surprised to learn that a dozen commercial wineries operate in frosty Minnesota, and even more surprised at how good some of the finished products are. Minnesota's sandy soil

Swedish meatballs are well known throughout the country, but it's the three L's, **lutefisk, lefse,** and **ligonberries,** that most intrigue visitors. These and other Scandinavian staples are largely reserved for church and lodge suppers and family get-togethers, but you'll find them on the occasional restaurant menu. Lefse comes in many varieties, but the most common combines potato (occasionally rice), flour, butter, and salt; the mix is rolled flat and baked on a griddle producing a bread that resembles a large, thick tortilla. Traditionally lefse was wrapped around meat or fish—today it is mostly eaten on the side with butter and a sprinkling of sugar, brown sugar, or cinnamon, or with a spread of jam. Ligonberries, which are similar to cranberries (and are sometimes called mountain cranberries), also make their way on to dinner plates. A much greater culinary adventure is lutefisk—dried North Atlantic cod reconstituted in water for three days, soaked in lye for another three, and then put back into water for up to a week—yes, really! If not prepared properly it becomes a is generally ideal terrain for growing grapes, and vintners who are willing to cut their vines down from the trellises and bury them each winter can grow popular varieties, such as chardonnay and pinot noir.

Minnesota's growing viticulture industry (The Minnesota Grape Growers Association is one of the largest such groups in the nation) can't compete with Tuscany, southern France, or the Napa Valley, and never will, but relatively speaking it is booming. As new wineries continue to open around the state, some envision a Napa of the North in the not-so-distant future. It's far fetched, but it could happen. The state of Minnesota considers the potential great enough to budget $200,000 annually to the University of Minnesota's Horticultural Research Center for wine research.

The first, largest, and according to many epicureans, best winery in the state is **Alexis Bailly Vineyard** in Hastings. Stillwater is home to **Northern Vineyards,** a cooperative of several small, southern Minnesotan winegrowers and **St. Croix Vineyards,** both of which also turn out superior vintages and have devotees who consider one or the other the state's top winemakers. Their products are found in larger liquor stores and many top restaurants. Other wineries, like **Carlos Creek** near Alexandria, **WineHaven** in Chisago City, **Morgan Creek** in New Ulm, and Luedke's near Princeton, tend to have a more limited regional distribution, though you can always pick up a bottle directly from the source. Instead of wine, Lake City's **Great River Vineyard** produces top-quality grape juice, grape jelly, and table grapes.

Because of the difficulty and added work of producing top-quality grapes, it is only natural that most Minnesota vintners have also chosen to use other fruits, like raspberry, strawberry, plum, and apple. Lanesboro's **Scenic Valley Winery,** the **Forestedge Winery** by Walker, and the **Minnestalgia Winery** in McGregor, do them exclusively.

All of the wineries mentioned here are open to the public for visits or tastings.

Beer

The **August Schell Brewing Company** is a real beer lover's kind of enterprise. Family-owned and operated at the same New Ulm location since 1860, they take great pride in maintaining their German brewing tradition. Just about everything they make, including six seasonals, gets high marks from beer connoisseurs, but their Pils is usually considered tops. Schells also purchased the recipe for Minnesota's venerable Grain Belt line when the Minnesota Brewing Company went bankrupt.

The fast-growing **Summit Brewing Company** is a deeply beloved craft brewer of English- and German-style beers. Summit Extra Pale Ale, their very flavorful flagship brew, is available all over the state and is on tap almost everywhere beer is served in the Twin Cities, while their India Pale Ale "dazzled" internationally renowned beer expert Michael Jackson. They also brew the unusual Great Northern Porter and four seasonals.

Several creations by **James Page,** Minneapolis's leading microbrewer, have won medals at the Great American Beer Festival, including their Burly Brown Ale and Iron Range Amber Lager, two standard but flavorful brews, plus Boundary Waters Golden Lager, which is made with wild rice. Another of their unique creations, Finnegan's Irish Ale, is crafted with potatoes.

Duluth's highly regarded **Lake Superior Brewing Company** currently brews four year-round beers, including the mildly chocolaty Sir Duluth Oatmeal Stout and their flagship Special Ale, plus four seasonal beers. You'll have no problem finding their products in Duluth and along the North Shore.

Minnesota's most adventurous brewery is the tiny, Stillwater-based **St. Croix Beer Company,** which sells St. Croix Maple Ale, fermented with maple syrup, and Serrano Pepper Ale, made with chili peppers.

Purchase

Most restaurants and bars take last call at 1 A.M. though some cities, including Minneapolis and St. Paul, have recently extended closing time to 2 A.M.. Liquor stores must close by 10 P.M., except in Minneapolis and St. Paul where they lock up at 8 P.M. Monday through Thursday— all are closed on Sundays, Thanksgiving, and

Christmas day. Like everywhere else in the United States, the legal drinking age in Minnesota is 21.

You can only purchase liquor and wine to take away in liquor stores, though 3.2 beer (beer with an alcohol content of 3.2 percent or lower) is sometimes available in convenience and/or grocery stores. The phrase "Off Sale" (or something similar like "On and Off") emblazoned on many bars signifies that an establishment has a license to sell alcohol to go. Many small towns, and even some medium-sized ones, operate their own municipal liquor stores, and these are often the only place to buy carryout alcohol in town.

Transportation

BY CAR

Though major cities, and many of the small ones in between, are connected by public transportation, to really see Minnesota you need your own vehicle. Three interstates, I-35, I-90, and I-94 (I-29, which skirts the border through the Dakotas, is also convenient), cross Minnesota, so getting here is easy.

Minnesota has designated 20 official Scenic Byways, but the system is something of a joke. The problem is that these signed routes primarily stick to the busier trunk lines, instead of leading off the beaten track. Don't get me wrong, you won't be disappointed if you follow any of these official tours, it's just that overall you'll find much more natural beauty and rural Americana (and a lot fewer McDonald's) along the back roads. A few major exceptions to this rule are the **Otter Trail Scenic Byway, Rushing Rapids Parkway, North Shore Scenic Drive, Historic Bluff Country Scenic Byway,** and **Great River Road** below Lake City, which truly deserve special designation—though even here, take time to poke around beyond the designated routes. The North Shore Scenic Drive has been designated an official All-American Road (the country's premier designation) by the Federal Highway Administration. Finally, I don't care what anyone else says, driving through the endless farm fields of the often-otherworldly Red River Valley makes for a wonderful day.

With relatively few people, Minnesota has little in the way of traffic congestion. Not surprisingly the Twin Cities do not fit this mold; though it's nothing like New York City or Los Angeles. Not only is traffic volume heavy, but Minnesota Nice does not apply to drivers who make sport out of not letting you merge.

The Minnesota Department of Transportation maintains a 24-hour, statewide road condition hotline (currently the numbers are 651/284-0511 or 800/542-0220, but these will soon be replaced by the new 511 system) that points out detour and construction information, as well as road weather information. For the Twin Cities you can also call 651/633-8383.

Rules of the Road

Drivers, front seat passengers, and all children aged four to ten must wear seat belts. Children under age four must be in a federally approved car seat. Motorcycle helmets are required for any drivers or passengers under 18 or anyone driving with a learners' permit. All drivers must have insurance. The maximum speed limit on the interstates is 70 mph, though it is reduced to as little as 45 mph in urban areas, and the top speed on state expressways is 65 mph. Radar detectors are legal.

Rentals

Rental cars are available in any town you can get to by train (except Staples, and no disrespect intended, but you probably wouldn't want to go there anyway) or airplane. Expect to pay about $45/day and $175/week for a compact car with unlimited mileage from one of the big national companies. Liability insurance is mandatory in Minnesota and will add another $10/day or so, but most personal policies cover rentals so read your policy before you shell out the extra cash. Local firms often have cheaper rates, but do most of their business with people whose cars are being repaired and so tend to have mileage restrictions.

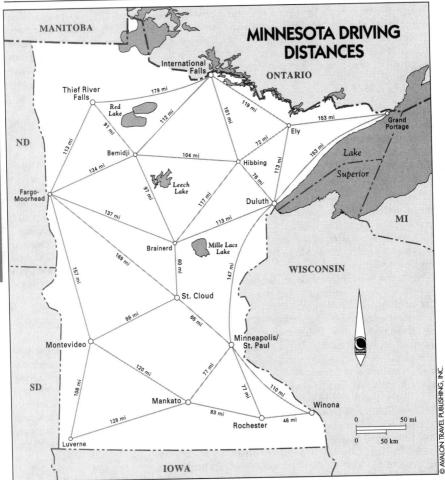

MINNESOTA DRIVING DISTANCES

MANITOBA

ONTARIO

International Falls

Thief River Falls

Red Lake

179 mi

112 mi

101 mi

118 mi

153 mi

Grand Portage

ND

91 mi

113 mi

Bemidji

104 mi

72 mi

Ely

153 mi

Lake Superior

134 mi

Leech Lake

97 mi

Hibbing

78 mi

113 mi

MI

Fargo-Moorhead

137 mi

117 mi

Duluth

113 mi

Brainerd

Mille Lacs Lake

169 mi

60 mi

147 mi

WISCONSIN

157 mi

St. Cloud

98 mi

65 mi

Montevideo

120 mi

Minneapolis/ St. Paul

77 mi

110 mi

SD

108 mi

Mankato

77 mi

Winona

128 mi

83 mi

Rochester

46 mi

Luverne

0   50 mi
0   50 km

© AVALON TRAVEL PUBLISHING, INC.

IOWA

All but a few companies require renters to be 25 years of age and those that will do business with someone as young as 21 will charge more for the privilege. In all cases you will need a major credit card and a valid drivers' license.

If you want to see the state in style, companies in both Minneapolis and St. Paul rent Harley Davidson motorcycles.

Winter Driving

The first and only rule of winter driving is, be prepared. Take a few minutes to winterize your vehicle: top off the antifreeze (it should test to at least 35 degrees below zero) and wiper fluid; keep the gas tank in an older car at least two-thirds full to prevent condensation that can freeze the fuel line; and inflate your tires to the manufacturer's suggested psi—despite the myth, underinflated tires do not provide more traction. Also, do as locals do and keep an emergency kit—warm blanket, nonperishable munchies like candy bars (which offer quick energy), a container of sand or kitty litter, and a small snow shovel—in the trunk. A flashlight, flare or reflectors, and a first aid kit are good additions. Of course you shouldn't drive without an ice scraper and jumper cables.

Winter driving is second nature for Northerners (few things are more entertaining for us than watching news footage of a Southern city crippled by a one-inch snowstorm), but if it's new to you there are a few techniques to remember. Above all, just SLOW DOWN! Posted speed limits are only meant for dry and clear conditions. Impatient drivers are always dangerous drivers, but especially when there is snow on the road. Allow at least twice as much distance between your car and the one in front of you than you would normally, and try to anticipate lane changes, turns, and stops so you can brake sooner and more gently. If you are driving a manual transmission, downshift to reduce your speed instead of using the brakes. Use extra caution on bridges and overpasses because these are the first spots to freeze. At temperatures below zero, intersections are another problem spot because car exhaust will no longer evaporate, but instead forms black ice. If you do skid, immediately remove your foot from the brake (fight that instinct!) or accelerator and steer in the direction you want the car to go; be prepared to countersteer if you overcorrected the first time. Extra weight in the trunk of a rear-wheel-drive car can aid traction. No matter how cold the temperature is outside, take the time to scrape the ice off *all* your windows, as well as your lights, before you drive.

If for some reason you are stranded in your car during a blizzard, tie something colorful to the antenna and stay with the vehicle—help will find you. Make sure the exhaust pipe is not blocked by snow and crack the window slightly when running the heater to prevent carbon monoxide poisoning.

BY AIR

Minneapolis-St. Paul International Airport (MSP), 612/726-5555, conveniently located right on the edge of the Twin Cities, is one of the Midwest's largest hubs and has flights to cities around the globe. Airlines that serve the airport are Air Canada, 800/426-7000, www.aircanada.com;

AirTran, 800/247-8726, www.airtran.com; America West, 800/235-9292, www.americawest.com; American, 800/433-7300, www.aa.com; American Trans Air, 800/435-9282, www.ata.com; Comair, 800/927-0927, www.comair.com; Continental, 800/525-0280, www.continental.com; Delta, 800/221-1212, www.delta.com; Frontier, 800/432-1359, www.frontierairlines.com; Icelandair, 800/223-5500, www.icelandair.com; KLM, 800/374-7747, www.klm.com; Northwest and Northwest Airlink, 800/225-2525, www.nwa.com; Sun Country, 800/359-6786, www.suncountry.com; United and United Express, 800/241-6522, www.ual.com; and US Airways, 800/428-4322, www.usairways.com.

Rochester International Airport, 507/282-2328, has American and Northwest Airlink, serving Chicago and Minneapolis respectively. **Duluth International Airport,** 218/727-2968, is served by Northwest, who makes frequent connections with the Twin Cities. United has service from Denver and Chicago O'Hare to **Hector International Airport,** 702/241-8168, in Fargo, North Dakota, just across the state's western border.

Small airports in Bemidji, Brainerd, Chisholm-Hibbing, Grand Rapids, International Falls, St. Cloud, and Thief River Falls are all served exclusively by Northwest Airlink. Regular round-trip tickets to the Twin Cities start at about $175–200, though the flight can cost as little as $50 when it is an add-on to a connecting Northwest flight—but they sometimes charge as much as $600 for that additional leg.

To find a good fare to Minnesota, it's important to know that Northwest Airlines accounts for over 80 percent of all flights, and thus holds a monopoly on many routes. Though Northwest brazenly denies it, they price many of these accordingly.

BY BUS

Public bus routes cover a majority of the state, though service is pretty infrequent to all but the largest towns. **Greyhound,** 800/229-9424, www.greyhound.com, has the most extensive service in the state. The discounted **Friendly Fare,** with rates ranging from $49 each way for a trip under 500 miles to $109 for a 3000-plus mile journey, requires a seven-day advance purchase, though almost every in-state route is already priced lower than this. Another good deal is the two-for-one **Companion Fare,** which is valid for all round-trip travel when purchased at least three days in advance. Students, seniors, children, and military personnel all qualify for additional discounts. Some travelers might want to bypass the discounts since the full fare "unrestricted" tickets allow unlimited stopovers along the route.

Greyhound's **Discovery Pass** program lets you choose from dozens of options for unlimited travel in the United States and Canada. The nationwide **Ameripass** varies from 7 ($199) to 60 ($549) days, while for just a little more you can get the **CanAm Pass,** which tacks on most of Canada. The nationwide **International Ameripass,** available only to foreign travelers, ranges from $135 for a four-day ticket to just $494 for sixty days. This, along with the **International CanAm Pass,** can be purchased online or at foreign travel agents, but not at Greyhound terminals in the United States. All of these passes are also valid on dozens of other carriers across the country, including Minnesota's Jefferson Lines. Call 888/454-7277 for Discovery Pass information or purchases.

Smaller carriers are **Jefferson Lines,** 800/451-5333, www.jeffersonlines.com (they are partnered with Greyhound and, from a rider's perspective, are essentially the same—you can even book Jefferson tickets on the Greyhound website), which runs from Texas up to Winnipeg, Canada, with a couple of routes across the south of the state; Lorenz Bus Service, 612/784-7196, which runs from Minneapolis through the middle of the state up to the Iron Range; and **Happy Time Tours and Travel,** 807/473-5955 or 800/473-5955, www.httours.com/transportation.htm, of Ontario, Canada, whose vans make round-trip runs between Duluth and Thunder Bay on Sunday, Monday, Wednesday, and Friday.

Nearly a dozen companies (each detailed with the respective city it serves) run van service between the Twin Cities airport and towns across the state and beyond. Some of the cities served include Hastings, Red Wing, Lake City, Wabasha, Winona, Northfield, Rochester, Mankato, Will-

mar, Morris, St. Cloud, Sauk Centre, Little Falls, Brainerd. Buses also go to the Wisconsin cities of La Crosse, Eau Claire, and Hayward, and to Decorah, Iowa. Ticket counters for all of them are in the Lindbergh Terminal, just below the baggage claim area. Reservations are highly recommended and, in some cases, required.

Getting Schedule and Fare Information: Although city listings in this book contain phone numbers for local bus terminals, they are primarily to ask directions; most do not have fare or schedule information available. Call the numbers above instead.

BY TRAIN

Depending on where you are coming from, the train can be a good way to get to Minnesota; however, because of limited service and inconvenient hours, it is nearly useless for getting around the state.

Amtrak, 800/872-7245, www.amtrak.com, provides service between Chicago and Seattle/Portland on the **Empire Builder,** which passes through Minnesota once a day in each direction with stops in Winona; Red Wing; St. Paul; St. Cloud; Staples; Detroit Lakes; and Fargo, North Dakota (for Moorhead). Though no trains go there, Amtrak provides connecting bus service to Duluth. The train is a comfortable and generally affordable way to reach Minnesota, and car rentals are available in all of the towns Amtrak serves except Staples. The primary downside to rail travel is that for points west of St. Paul, arrivals in both directions are in the wee hours of the morning.

Amtrak rail passes are some of the best travel bargains around, like the **Explore America Fare,** which allows three stops during a 45-day period in the off-peak (essentially not summer or Christmas) season. The price varies by the number of regions you visit, but is just $279 for the central United States. Amtrak also offers an **Air Rail** option, allowing you to travel in one direction by train and the opposite with United Airlines. Call 800/321-8684 for information on Air Rail travel. Students, seniors, veterans, and children are all eligible for various discounts on passes and regular tickets.

The controversial North Star Line, a state-run commuter rail project between Minneapolis and St. Cloud, strongly supported by all the communities along its route, could become a reality in the next few years, but don't count on it. Other long-term rail plans, such as connections from Hastings and Northfield to the Twin Cities, have an even less certain and certainly more distant future.

BY BOAT

The New Orleans-based **Delta Queen Steamboat Co.,** 800/862-2452, www.deltaqueen.com, has been running paddlewheel riverboats up the Mississippi since 1890. Although things have changed significantly on the river since the 19th century, it is still a timeless trip. Boats still come all the way up to St. Paul (sometimes stopping to much fanfare in Red Wing, Wabasha, and Winona) several times a year, with most runs timed to meet fall colors. A classic seven-day trip from St. Louis costs as little as $1,225 per person, though the fanciest suites run nearly $4,000. The price includes meals, entertainment, and use of all onboard amenities. Discounts apply for early bookings.

TRAVEL TO AND FROM CANADA

Minnesota has eight border crossings with Canada, one by Grand Portage, another at International Falls, and the rest along the western border from Baudette on. The four easternmost ones are open 24 hours year-round, while the others close at either 10 P.M. or midnight. U.S. and Canadian citizens do not need a passport to cross the border, though proof of citizenship must be supplied—a birth certificate and a photo ID is the best option if you do not have a passport. Though security and scrutiny have increased along the border since the terrorist attacks of September 11th, and you should expect thorough searches and questioning when coming south, overall crossings are still quick and smooth, even at the Fort Frances/International Falls port of entry, the state's busiest.

Officially U.S. Customs allows 200 cigarettes, 50 cigars, or 4.4 pounds (2 kgs) of loose tobacco and one liter of alcoholic beverage to be brought into the country duty free. Returning to Canada you can bring $50 (Canadian) worth of goods duty free, excluding alcoholic beverages and tobacco products, if your stay exceeded 24 hours. If you stay in the United States for 48 hours or more, the duty exemption is $200 (Canadian); the limit rises to $750 (Canadian) if you stay for seven or more days. For stays of two days or more, the exemption can include 200 cigarettes, 50 cigars, or 6.4 ounces (200 gms) of tobacco and 40 ounces (1.14 L) of liquor, 1.6 quarts (1.5 L) of wine, or nine quarts (8.5 L) of beer.

U.S. and Canadian citizens and permanent residents who wish to cross the border by boat along the North Shore of Lake Superior, Lake of the Woods, or through the wilderness of the BWCAW/Quetico Provincial Park area can apply for a **CANPASS-Remote Area Border Crossing Permit.** Applications and instructions are available online at www.queticopark.com/rabc. BWCAW outfitters can take care of the paperwork for you. You can also apply in person at the Pigeon River Port of Entry near Grand Portage, the Fort Frances Port of Entry at International Falls, and the Rainy River Port of Entry by Baudette, but a decision can take 48 hours.

For any general border crossing questions, call the U.S. Customs Service in Minneapolis at 612/348-1690, www.customs.ustreas.gov/travel or the Canada Customs and Revenue Agency, 800/461-9999 (within Canada) or 204/983-3500 (from the United States), www.ccra-adrc .gc.ca/customs.

ON THE ROAD

Information and Services

TOURIST INFORMATION

The **Minnesota Office of Tourism,** 651/296-3000 or 800/868-7476 (800/627-3529 TTY), explore@state.mn.us, www.exploreminnesota.com, can answer just about any Minnesota questions you have. Counselors are available from 8 A.M. to 5 P.M. weekdays, while a host of recorded information on topics such as snow depths and fishing reports is available 24 hours. The website has a lot of information, but it's not the most user-friendly site on the Web.

If you are driving to Minnesota, chances are you will pass one of the six **Travel Information Centers** that have been set up along the major highways along the border. At all of them you can pick up a plethora of brochures on all parts of the state, and the staff are very friendly and knowledgeable. You can also stop by the **Explore Minnesota USA** store in the Mall of America.

Maps

The foldout road map available free from the Minnesota Office of Tourism is more than adequate to get you around the state. The less detailed Minnesota map published by AAA (free to members, otherwise $3.50) is also fine, while their Twin Cities map (free to members, otherwise $3.95) is excellent. If you want to explore any back roads during your trip, you can't do any better than the *Minnesota Atlas and Gazetteer* published by DeLorme and available in any good book or outdoors store for $19.95. Chambers of commerce in all but the smallest communities covered in this guide publish a map of their towns.

If you'll be spending a lot of time in the outdoors, one of the DNR's 51 Public Recreation Information maps could prove handy. PRIM maps show all county, state, and federal public lands and plot campgrounds, fishing piers, boat launches, parking lots, long distance trails, and the like. They cost $4.95 and are available at DNR offices, state parks, and a few large sporting goods shops. Anyone really heading out into the wild should have 1:24,000 scale U.S. Geological Survey

(USGS) topographical maps. These $4 maps show just about every hill, stream, road, and building. To order these or other USGS maps, see http://mcmcweb.er.usgs.gov/topomaps or call 888/275-8747.

Some of these maps, and many others, are available through **Minnesota's Bookstore,** 117 University Ave., 651/297-3000 or 800/657-3757, (651/282-5077 or 800/657-3706 TTY), part of the state's Department of Administration in St. Paul. They are open Monday–Friday 8 A.M.–5 P.M. or you can order online at www.comm.media.state.mn.us/bookstore. **The Map Store,** 111 Kellogg Square, 651/227-6277, also carries most of these.

INFORMATION FOR GAY AND LESBIAN TRAVELERS

Minnesota's reputation for tolerance is justified and same-sex couples are unlikely to encounter any problems, but throughout most of the state discretion is still the best approach. In the Twin Cities, pretty much anything goes. Both Minneapolis and St. Paul have active gay scenes, and in Uptown Minneapolis gay couples are prevalent.

The best overall resource is **OutFront Minnesota,** 612/822-0127 or 800/800-0350, www.outfront.org. Their website has a wealth of information about the Twin Cities scene and a little bit about the rest of the state. You can pick up the free biweekly *Lavender* magazine (www.lavendermagazine.com), which covers the Twin Cities gay scene, at coffeehouses, theaters, bookstores, and other spots across the Twin Cities.

MEDIA

The most widely read magazine covering the North Star State is *Minnesota Monthly,* a slick publication from Minnesota Public Radio that looks at the lighter side of Minnesota from travel to art to beauty tips. It's heavy on the celebrity and has way too many ads, but there is usually something interesting between the covers.

Mpls.St.Paul is an equally ad-packed monthly

MINNESOTA EVENTS SAMPLER

Minnesotans are celebrating something or other every weekend throughout the year. While most events take place in the summer season, quite a few festivals revel in winter's wonders. This brief list highlights some of the state's most popular and peculiar events. A nearly complete roster of statewide happenings is also available at www.exploreminnesota.com/events.

Icebox Days: International Falls, late January

Brainerd Jaycees Ice Fishing Extravaganza: Brainerd, late January

St. Paul Winter Carnival: St. Paul, late January

International Eelpout Festival: Walker, mid-February

John Beargrease Sled Dog Marathon: North Shore, late February

Grumpy Old Men Festival: Wabasha, late February

Dylan Days: Hibbing, late May

Buffalo Days: Luverne, early June

SPAM Jam: Austin, mid-June

Grandma's Marathon: Duluth, mid-June

Scandinavian Hjemkomst Festival: Moorhead, late June

Rochesterfest: Rochester, late June

Judy Garland Festival: Grand Rapids, late June

Bean Hole Day: Pequot Lakes, early July

Two Harbors Folk Festival: Two Harbors, mid-July

Heritagefest: New Ulm, mid- July

Wilder Pageant: Walnut Grove, mid- to late July

Minneapolis Aquatennial: Minneapolis, late July

Blueberry Arts Festival: Ely, late July

Song of Hiawatha Pageant: Pipestone, late July and early August

Minnesota Fringe Festival: Minneapolis, early to mid-August

Bayfront Blues Festival: Duluth, mid-August

Grand Portage Rendezvous Days: Grand Portage, mid-August

Minnesota State Fair: St. Paul, mid- to late August

Potato Days: Barnesville, late August

Defeat of Jesse James Days: Northfield, early September

King Turkey Days: Worthington, mid-September

Apple Festival: La Crescent, late September

Fish House Parade: Aitkin, late November

ON THE ROAD

lifestyle magazine for the Twin Cities' wealthier set. Their forte is making recommendations, from the driest martini to the best doctors, and their opinion carries a lot of weight around town.

The Boundary Waters Journal, a thick quarterly published out of Ely, covers travel and natural history for the Boundary Waters Canoe Area Wilderness, the surrounding Superior National Forest, and the adjoining Quetico Provincial Park.

Lake Superior Magazine is a top-quality bimonthly covering the entire Lake Superior region, but as it is published in Duluth, the Minnesota portion gets a great deal of coverage. The photography is invariably excellent.

The hard to find *Big River* is an enthusiastic bimonthly focusing on the past, present, and future of the Mississippi River between St. Cloud, Minnesota, and the Quad Cities of Iowa and Illinois.

The *Lake Country Journal* is a bimonthly lifestyle magazine for north-central Minnesota, though you will find it for sale in the Twin Cities.

MONEY

If you can, either come to Minnesota with American dollars or don't leave the airport without changing most of the foreign currency you think you will need. It's not that you can't do foreign exchange elsewhere, but only a handful of banks and high-end hotels in the largest cities offer this service, and even then usually only for the most common currencies. The exception to the rule are Canadian dollars, which are not only easy to exchange at banks across the north, but, depending on the exchange rate, can get you some serious savings since many businesses in the north accept Canadian dollars at par—generally you need to be a Canadian citizen to get this discount.

The scarcity of exchange facilities doesn't matter very much anymore, since Automatic Teller Machines (ATMs) are found just about everywhere these days. Though you will usually pay $1.50 fee each time you use one, the favorable exchange rates should more than offset that. There is at least one ATM attached to most banks and convenience stores in the state, though keep in mind that many small towns have neither. Both credit cards (primarily Visa, MasterCard, and American Express)

and traveler's checks (in U.S. dollar denominations) are widely accepted, though it would be best to ask first in small town hotels and restaurants.

Tipping

Remember, restaurant servers are paid well below minimum wage and so rely on tips to make a living; unless you've done it you can't realize what a difficult job it can be. Fifteen percent is the accepted norm, with a slight boost or reduction to reflect exceptionally good or poor service. With room service, always check the bill since a tip is often already included. Taxi drivers also get about 15 percent, assuming they help you with your luggage, and $1 per bag is standard for airport skycaps and hotel bellhops. Valet parking is worth $1–5 depending on the weather and how far away they have to drive your car. Tipping isn't expected by hotel housekeepers, but if you are staying more than one night a couple of bucks is a nice gesture for an otherwise thankless job.

TELEPHONE AND INTERNET

Minnesota has seven area codes. Any 800, 866, 877, or 888 area code is toll free, while you pay (usually at exorbitant rates) for any 900 calls. **Dial 911 statewide for emergencies.**

Public pay phones are widely available on busy street corners and outside convenience stores and gas stations. Only the smallest towns will not have one. They are maintained by a variety of public companies, and most charge 50 cents for local calls; those that still charge less will not give change if you use two quarters. Dialing directions are usually posted on the face of the phone, but when in doubt simply dial "0" for an operator who will direct your call. Try to avoid this though, since you will generally pay $1–3 for this service. Most universal phone cards have a high fee for use of pay phones, so they aren't advisable for local calls, but even with the fee they will save you a lot on long distance calls.

Internet cafés are rare in Minnesota, though they are listed in the text if they exist. It is not much of a problem since most public libraries, even in very small towns, have free Internet access, and most allow visitors to use their computers. The downside is that there is often a wait, especially after school has let out for the day.

A list of helpful Minnesota-related websites is found at the end of this book.

MEASUREMENTS

Minnesota, like the entire country, shuns the metric system and, except for cross-country ski trail distances, which are usually given in kilometers, you will rarely encounter it. A U.S.-Metric conversion table is found in the back of this book if you need it.

TIME ZONE

Minnesota is in Central Standard Time (CST), one hour behind New York, six hours behind London, and two hours ahead of Los Angeles. Daylight Saving Time (clocks are turned forward one hour, moving one hour of sunshine from the morning to the evening) begins on the first Sunday of April and ends on the last Sunday of October. If you will be crossing into Canada, note that the portion of Ontario along Lake Superior is Eastern Standard Time, one hour ahead of CST. The rest of Canada that borders Minnesota is CST.

Health and Safety

A visit to Minnesota is not completely devoid of risk, but none of the potential concerns are extreme and simple common sense is pretty much all you need to stay safe and healthy.

911 is the statewide emergency number.

WEATHER
Wind Chill
The first thing a winter visitor to Minnesota has to understand is that wind chill is not just something northerners brag about. It is real and it can be very dangerous. The wind chill factor represents the temperature that it feels like when the wind is blowing. More precisely, it is an estimated measure of the rate that exposed skin will lose body heat due to the combination of wind speed and temperature. So, for example, if the temperature outside is 5° F and the winds are blowing at 30 mph, your body will lose heat just as fast as if the temperature were 19° F below zero and the winds were calm. Because the wind chill is not an actual temperature, it cannot cause water to freeze above 32° F or chill your car's engine beyond the actual air temperature, no matter how hard the wind is blowing. However, the faster the winds, the faster any object will cool down. And, though factors like the sun or evaporation rate, both of which also can affect the apparent tempera-

ture, are not part of the equation (WC = 35.74 + 0.6215T - 35.75(V0.16) + 0.4275T(V0.16) where T = air temp. and V = wind speed; in case you were wondering), it is a very useful and important guide. Children, the elderly, and those with circulatory problems should stay inside if the wind chill hits 50° F below zero and everybody, no matter how well dressed, should stay put if it drops below minus 70° F.

Frostbite
A low wind chill (or just a low temperature) can quickly lead to frostbite, the freezing of skin. The initial symptoms of redness and pain are followed by a loss of feeling and color. Fingers, toes, ears, and the tip of the nose are most susceptible. If your skin does freeze, rewarm it slowly by immersing the affected area in warm (not hot) water. If that is not possible, use body heat, an armpit for example. Do not use a heat source, such as a fire or radiator, because the affected areas can burn easily. As it thaws, the skin turns red and painful with a severe tingling or burning sensation. If damage was limited to the skin, there will probably be no long-term effects, but if blood vessels were damaged, amputation might be necessary. Severe cases need immediate medical assistance. This is also a good idea for minor cases, since there could be other complications, such as infection or hypothermia.

Hypothermia

A much more serious cold weather concern is hypothermia, a life-threatening condition where core body temperature falls below 95°F, the point at which the body can no longer produce enough heat to warm itself. Symptoms come on slowly and include uncontrolled shivering, slurred speech, confusion, drowsiness, loss of coordination, pale and cold skin, and bluish lips. Because the cold affects brain function, the victim may not even be aware of his or her own condition and must rely on companions, even when insisting he or she feels fine.

While severe cold is the quickest route to hypothermia, it is a potential danger all year long. In warmer temperatures (even up to 50°F) it can occur in people who are fatigued, malnourished, dehydrated, or chilled from wearing wet clothing. A very common cause is falling into lakes. Immersion in water below 70°F, which most of Minnesota's lakes are for the majority of the year (Lake Superior never rises above 54°F beyond the shore), will cause a lightly clothed person to lose heat faster than they can produce it. According to the DNR, most hospitalized hypothermia victims consumed excessive amounts of alcohol. Besides inducing foolish and risky behavior, alcohol has several physiological effects on the body that actually lower body temperature.

Anyone suffering from hypothermia needs immediate medical attention. If that is not an option, get the victim out of the cold as best as possible, either into a warm room or at least shelter them from the wind and insulate them from the cold ground. People with hypothermia are at high risk for cardiac arrest, so be as gentle as possible if moving them. Remove any wet or constrictive clothing and cover them with warm blankets or a sleeping bag. A metallic emergency blanket that conserves body heat should be in every backpack and canoe; they weigh just a couple of ounces and cost just a couple of dollars. Warm the body SLOWLY, starting with the chest, neck, head, and groin. In the wilderness, sharing body heat, skin-to-skin, is the best method of recovering victims. If they are conscious, give them warm (nonalcoholic) beverages and food. Even someone found out in the cold, unconscious and with no apparent pulse, should be treated. Many people who appeared dead on initial examination have been revived, especially those who have fallen into very cold water.

Winter Dress

Prevention is the best medicine for cold weather ailments. The key to staying warm in the winter is to wear loose-fitting layers. Not only is this the most effective for warmth, but you can shed layers as your exertion level rises, avoiding sweating, which leads to later chills or worse. A thin layer of wool, silk, or synthetics that can wick away sweat should be worn against the skin with a wind- and waterproof, breathable outer shell. Insulating layers of wool and lighter weight polyester fleeces will keep you warm even if wet. Cotton should be avoided as much as possible (completely if you are venturing outdoors) because it retains moisture. Over half of body heat lost escapes through the head, so a good hat, one that covers the ears, is a must. Mittens are warmer than gloves and large ones can be worn over gloves. Your feet, which are exposed to the most moisture, need warm socks, preferably a thin inner sock, a wool outer sock, and warm waterproof boots.

Tornadoes

Minnesota lies near the edge of, but outside, Tornado Alley, the region of maximum tornado frequency in the United States, and only averages 20 twisters a year (out of about 1,000 nationwide), though a record of 72 was set in 2001. Most are minor as far as tornadoes go. Minnesota has had tornadoes in every month from March through November, with the greatest numbers, about six per year on average, occurring in June. July, May, and August follow in historical frequency, and these four account for almost 90 percent of all touchdowns. Twisters can come at any time of day, but the greatest danger is between 2 P.M. and 9 P.M. They have struck all parts of the state, though the incidence rises as you go south.

Because they are rare, you don't need to worry much about tornadoes, but you do need to know what to do if you should be so unlucky. Tornado watches and warnings are announced on TV and radio, and emergency sirens will sound for the latter. A watch simply means that conditions are favorable for the development of a tornado; you should be alert for sudden changes in the weather. A warning signals that a tornado has been sighted by a person on the ground or is indicated on Doppler radar, and if a warning is announced near you seek shelter immediately. The best place to be is in a basement under something sturdy, like the stairwell or a table, and away from windows. If there is no basement, seek shelter in an interior room in the middle of the building, again away from windows. If you are in a car, drive at a right angle to the path of the tornado. If it is bearing down on you, get out of the car and seek shelter in a building or find a depression (such as a ditch) in the ground and lie flat with your hands over your head.

OUTDOORS

Lyme Disease

The biggest concern for those venturing into Minnesota's outdoors is Lyme Disease, but like most things, with just a bit of simple protection, there's no need to worry. The disease, caused by the bacterium *Borrelia burgdorferi,* is transmitted by the bite of the tiny deer tick. Deer ticks are smaller, and thankfully much less common, than wood ticks, which rarely carry the disease. It is important to note that bites rarely lead to infection, and the incidence of the disease is much lower in Minnesota than New England.

Lyme disease is almost always caught from May through July when nymphal-stage ticks are feeding. Adult ticks can also spread Lyme, but since they are much larger (an unfed nymph is no bigger than a poppy seed, while the adult grows to sesame seed size), people are much more likely to spot them and thus remove them quickly. A tick must be attached for at least 24 hours, usually 48 or more, before the bacteria can spread. If you have become infected, a distinctive "bull's-eye" rash may occur at the site of the bite in 7 to 14 days and is accompanied

Mosquitoes are jokingly referred to as Minnesota's state bird on many postcards and coffee mugs. They are most abundant in the early summer.

by fever, fatigue, headache, muscle and joint pains, and other flu-like symptoms. See a doctor if any of these symptoms occur following a bite. In almost all cases, if diagnosed in the early stages, Lyme disease can be cleared up with standard antibiotics. While not life threatening, if left untreated it can lead to arthritis or complications of the nervous system or heart.

Prevention is easy: wear light-colored clothing so you can easily spot any ticks crawling on you, tuck long pants into socks to reduce access to the skin, and use a good insect repellent. Even if you follow all of the above advice, ticks are persistent so you should do a daily tick check on yourself and your pets after spending time outdoors. If the above steps don't work, remove embedded ticks with a tweezers by grasping as close to the mouth as possible—do not grab the body as this might squeeze the infected contents into the wound—and slowly pull. Cleanse the bite with an antiseptic.

Mosquitoes and Biting Flies

Minnesota has a few bloodthirsty flying insects that can be serious annoyances. **Mosquitoes** are the most likely to put a damper on summer fun. Jokingly referred to as Minnesota's state bird on many postcards and coffee mugs, mosquitoes feed from May until the first frost but are most abundant in the early summer and are rare in the fall. They prefer to feed at dusk, but may be encountered at any time of the day. Southeast Minnesota, away from the Mississippi River, is relatively mosquito free due to the lack of lakes.

Of the four biting flies in Minnesota, the biggest nuisance are **black flies** (sometimes called buffalo gnats), which fly in swarms. Only a few species can bite through the skin with their razor-like mouths but dozens of them buzzing around your head can still be pretty damn irritating. Thankfully black flies produce just one generation a year and they only feed over a three-week period, generally from mid-May through June. They are only active during the day.

If you will be spending much time in the outdoors during the summer, you will want to use an insect repellant. Even if you aren't planning on visiting the great outdoors, bring along some bug dope just in case. Repellants containing the chemical DEET last the longest and are the most effective (though they do little to discourage black flies), but there can be side effects if too much is absorbed through the skin; this is primarily a concern for long-term use and most people use it with absolutely no problems. Still, to be on the safe side, use a brand containing no more than 35 percent DEET (those with higher percentages aren't much more effective anyway), do not put it directly on children's skin, and do not use it at all on children under two. Effective non-DEET repellants using eucalyptus and soybean oils are available, too. The downside of these alternatives is that they have to be applied more frequently, and some people attract bugs so easily that only DEET will be truly effective. Long-sleeved shirts and pants are also helpful, and a hat makes a world of difference with the black flies that like to buzz around the head. Black flies are reportedly attracted to dark colors so wearing a light-colored shirt might help.

Giardia

No matter how clean and pure the water looks in Minnesota, you should never drink it straight from the source or you might just win weeks of diarrhea, abdominal cramps, bloating, flatulence, fatigue, and nausea. The culprit is *Giardia lamblia* (aka *G. duodenalis, G. intestinalis,* and *Lamblia intestinalis*), a hardy single-celled parasite found in lakes and streams worldwide. Symptoms begin one to two weeks after ingestion and continue for one to four weeks in most people, though chronic infections can last months or years and lead to weight loss and nutritional deficiencies. Giardiasis, as the illness is called, usually resolves itself, though a doctor should be consulted if there is dehydration, blood in the stool, or symptoms that persist beyond two weeks. Children and pregnant women should see a doctor immediately. Water can be purified by boiling (one minute is enough for Giardia and most other biological hazards, but five is

often recommended to kill them all), filtering (choose one with an absolute pore size of at least one micron, 0.2 is best, or one NSF rated for "cyst removal"), or treating (iodine kills almost everything, though it doesn't taste so good).

Poison Ivy and Sumac

Coming into contact with poison ivy or poison sumac might cause a red rash, blistering, and extreme itching that can last up to two weeks. Poison ivy is found in wooded areas throughout the state and prefers moist, shaded spots; it is common along riverbanks, paths, and fencerows. It grows primarily as a woody vine; however, if it is growing in full sunlight it will become a shrub. The primary method of identification is by its leaves, which grow in groups of three—always remember "Leaves of Three, Let Them Be." The size and shape of the leaflets can vary considerably, but are usually 2–4 inches in length with pointed tips, smooth or toothed edges, and shiny faces; the middle leaflet has a longer stalk than the two on the side. Small yellowish-green, five-petaled flowers bloom in May–July, and clusters of small white berries emerge from August–November. In the fall the leaves turn red.

Poison sumac, found in just a few places north of the Twin Cities, is uncommon. It grows as a shrub or small tree with compound leaves six to fourteen inches long having seven to thirteen pointed, toothless leaflets. The leaf stems are red, and the bark is smooth with dark spots. It has small white berries similar to poison ivy, and it prefers swampy areas.

If you are unlucky enough to brush up against either, wash the area thoroughly with cold water (hot water will open your pores and make the reaction worse) as quickly as possible. You generally have at least an hour to wash away the poisonous urushiol oil before it is absorbed into the skin, but for some victims symptoms can begin in as little as ten minutes. Washing with rubbing alcohol during the first six hours can also help remove the oil and prevent or diminish symptoms. Ask a pharmacist about lotions to relieve the itching, though if it is severe you should see a doctor. A pre-exposure, over-the-counter lotion called Ivy Block reacts with the urushiol, blocking the allergic reaction. It must be applied 15 minutes before contact and lasts up to four hours. Anywhere from 10 to 35 percent of people are immune, but since sensitivity can vary over one's lifetime, or just from the amount of exposure, it is always best to avoid it.

Thin Ice

Thin ice claims several lives each year in Minnesota. Generally speaking, four inches is considered safe for walking or skating, five inches for snowmobiles, and eight–twelve inches for cars and small trucks. The main problem is that ice is never uniform. Ice formed over currents will be weaker, so be especially cautious around bridges, outside river bends, and near the lakeshore. Also, don't assume that just because you see tracks that the ice is safe. Many Minnesotans, ever impatient to begin their winter rituals, rush out too early. Local bait shops, resorts, and sheriff's departments are your best source of advice. If you plan on going out on a lake or river, carry something sharp, such as picks, screwdrivers, or even large nails, to pull yourself out with if you fall through. If you are driving on a lake, keep your windows down to facilitate a quick escape.

Snakes

Of the 17 species of snake in Minnesota, just two are venomous and both are rare and found only in limited areas in southeast Minnesota, primarily right along the Mississippi River. The **timber rattlesnake** is large, ranging three–six feet in length with a diamond-shaped head and a thin neck. They have black bands across the back, though the primary color can vary from yellow to gray or brown. It lives in deciduous forests and steep, rocky bluffs. The **massasauga,** also a rattlesnake, measures just 17–39 inches and is also stout with a triangular-shaped head. It has black or dark brown blotches against a lighter brown or gray background. The preferred habitat is low, swampy areas close to marshes, lakes, and rivers. Some herpetologists doubt this snake even resides in the state anymore. Both are timid and slow to rattle or strike. Bites are rare and rarely fatal.

It has been over a century since anyone has died from a snakebite in Minnesota, but they should still be treated as a medical emergency. First, keep the victim calm and limit physical exertion as much as possible. Squeeze and suck venom from the wound. Remove jewelry since swelling can occur rapidly. Keep the stricken limb below the heart. Attempt to identify the snake, killing it if possible, but do not waste time or put yourself at risk; observing symptoms is enough information for a doctor to choose the proper anti-venom. Get the victim to a hospital as soon as possible. Note the times that symptoms first occur. DO NOT cut the wound, use a tourniquet, or apply ice. Any of these would do more harm than good. If you use common sense—look where you sit, step, or place your hands; wear hiking boots; and don't molest snakes—you have little to worry about.

Several other species of snake, while not venomous and thus harmless, will bite when handled or cornered, so all snakes should be given a wide berth when encountered.

Bears

Despite their reputation, bears are more of a nuisance than a danger. Bears are common throughout northern Minnesota, but while attacks on humans are not unheard of, they are *extremely* rare. If you do run across a bear, stay calm and back away slowly; it will likely leave the moment it senses you. Occasionally bears will woof, snap their jaws, slap the ground, stand upright, or make a bluff charge. While frightening, these actions are not a prelude to an attack. If you are in your campsite, or for some other reason it needs to be the bear that leaves instead of you, shout, bang pots, or throw rocks and wood at the bear. Do not be gentle, though make sure it has an escape route before you begin. Capsaicin (hot pepper) sprays are another effective, and harmless, bear repellent. Food raids are the real concern with bears since they will seek out and eat anything that even smells or looks like food. Keep your campsite clean: never eat or store food in your tent, do not burn or bury food scraps at your site, store all food and anything else with a strong odor, such as toothpaste, in your car. If you are camping in the wilderness, hang your food in a tree ten feet off the ground and four feet from the trunk and any branches. There are many campsites in the BWCAW without standing trees, so it would be wise to take a bear-proof storage container—local outfitters sell and rent them. These precautions must be followed even on islands, since bears are excellent swimmers.

Deer-Vehicle Collisions

Of all the animals in Minnesota, Bambi is the one most likely to do you harm. Annually there are some 20,000 deer-vehicle collisions reported in the state, and the Minnesota Department of Transportation estimates that twice as many go unreported. These crashes, or crashes as a result of attempts to avoid deer, cause an average of $2,000 in damage per car and even result in two or three deaths annually. Deer dodging is not just a rural problem. In urban areas with abundant parks and no predators, deer populations can shoot as high as 100 per square mile, four times the highest rural population. Nearly one third of deer-vehicle collisions occur in the seven-county metro area.

Always keep an eye out for deer, especially in wooded areas and where deer warning signs are posted. Deer will cross roads throughout the year and at any time of the day, but they are most active at dawn and dusk and during October and November (while in rut and thus moving around much more than usual) and March and April (when some of the year's first greenery sprouts on roadsides). If you spot one anywhere near a road, decelerate as safely as possible because panicked deer will sprint off unexpectedly in any direction, sometimes right in front of a car, and if you see one deer there are likely to be more nearby. And, though instincts say otherwise, hitting a deer is often safer than swerving out of its way, which might result in losing control of your vehicle or hitting another one.

According to the DNR, studies have shown that whistles and other warning gadgets attached to vehicles do not frighten deer. An experimental deer alert system is currently being tested by the state. Motion detectors installed alongside roads with high collision rates activate amber lights atop the regular deer warning signs, alerting drivers to slow down. If it proves successful, the system will be expanded.

CRIME

Crime is not something visitors to Minnesota need to worry very much about, though don't be lulled into forgetting common sense. The Twin Cities have the usual big city problems, but like elsewhere these are largely limited to the poorest neighborhoods where tourists (or other city residents for that matter) are unlikely to go. Neither Minneapolis nor St. Paul are anywhere near the most dangerous cities nationally, and crime rates have been dropping for years. Morgan Quitno's most recent annual national crime survey, based on FBI-compiled crime statistics, ranked Minneapolis 30th and St. Paul 86th amongst U.S. cities. Just follow the usual simple precautions—don't flash valuables, don't carry more than you are willing to hand over, and remember that there is safety in numbers—do so and you will almost certainly have no problems. Outside the Twin Cities the chances of something serious happening to you aren't zero, but pretty close.

Whether you are leaving your car parked in downtown Minneapolis or at a remote trailhead in the Boundary Waters, always lock valuables in the trunk. In the winter don't leave your car running (either to warm it up or keep it warm) when it is unattended. Every year there are a few cases of thieves driving off with a target they found too easy to resist.

Twin Cities

. . . Minneapolis and St. Paul, an island of lifestyle in an ocean of cornfields and soybeans, where there is good espresso and Thai food and The New York Times and a couple orchestras and a dozen theaters and movie houses that show foreign and indie flicks and Ruminator Books has about three hundred shelf-feet of poetry and you can get almost anything people in New York or Los Angeles have and yet live on a quiet tree-lined street with a backyard and send your kids to public school.

Garrison Keillor, In Search of Lake Wobegon

With downtowns just eight miles apart, the Twin Cities moniker is certainly appropriate, but it is definitely a fraternal pairing. The English journalist Trevor Fishlock quipped that Minneapolis and St. Paul "are divided by the Mississippi River and united by the belief that the inhabitants of the other side of the river are inferior." This tale of two cities no longer has the acrimony of the past, when census counts were illegally padded in an effort to outrank the other, but these friendly rivals have not completely lost their competitive edge. The recent debate over where to build a new baseball stadium got personal, and the two still go head-to-head to attract new businesses.

While people who have never been here naturally lump the two together, visitors will quickly see the differences. Energetic Minneapolis with soaring skyscrapers is the more modern and cosmopolitan of the two, while conservative St. Paul with its winding

Minneapolis

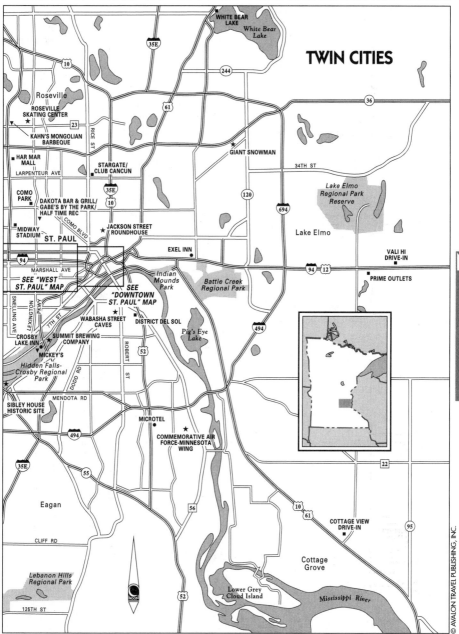

TWIN CITIES

TWIN CITIES HIGHLIGHTS

Bell Museum of Natural History, Minneapolis

First Avenue & 7th St. Entry, Minneapolis

Historic Fort Snelling, Minneapolis

Historic Murphy's Landing, Shakopee

Holidazzle Parades, Minneapolis

Mall of America, Bloomington

Minneapolis Institute of Arts, Minneapolis

Minneapolis Sculpture Garden, Minneapolis

Minnesota History Center, St. Paul

Minnesota Landscape Arboretum, Chanhassen

Nye's Polonaise, Minneapolis

Paddleford Packet Boat Company, Minneapolis and St. Paul

Science Museum of Minnesota, St. Paul

St. Anthony Falls Heritage Trail, Minneapolis

Steamboat *Minnehaha*, Excelsior

Summit Avenue, St. Paul

Walker Art Center, Minneapolis

streets and downtown parks promotes its European charm. In a nutshell, Minneapolis is slick and St. Paul is sober—though ironically two of the most notable developments in recent years are the return of nightlife to downtown St. Paul and the historic restoration along Minneapolis's Central Riverfront. Citizens tend to reflect their cities' demeanors. Some smug west bank natives consider St. Paul as nothing more than Minneapolis's most enjoyable suburb, while St. Paulites naturally judge their neighbors as arrogant. These exaggerated perceptions make easy fodder for storyteller Garrison Keillor on his radio show *A Prairie Home Companion.*

Despite all the differences, the many similarities best define the area. Twin Cities residents are full of hometown pride; prices are lower than in most similarly sized cities elsewhere in the United States; and the quality of life here is second to none. Also, you don't have to head out of town to enjoy the outdoors—the riverside parks are stunningly beautiful, especially as fall color takes hold, and around 800 of the state's nearly 12,000 lakes lie across the metro.

While many locals find little reason to go "across the river," exploring either without at least a quick visit to the other would be a mistake. The combination of the best of both makes for a wonderful trip indeed.

MEDIA

In a sense, the Twin Cities maintain competing daily newspapers, though realistically the *Star*

Tribune is the Minneapolis paper, while the smaller *Pioneer Press* focuses on St. Paul. Far and away the best source for arts and entertainment information is the free alternative weekly *City Pages.* Its primary competition is the free monthly *Rake,* which positions itself between the mildly irreverent City Pages and the fully yuppified *Mpls.St.Paul,* which is sold at newsstands and bookstores. *Pulse* is a left-leaning weekly put out on a shoestring budget every Wednesday that also has arts and entertainment listings. *Lavender* is a free biweekly covering the Twin Cities gay scene.

Twin Cities radio offers everything every other big city does, from corporate pop music to lunatic right wing political rants. **WMNN** (1330 AM) airs 24-hour news with weather and traffic updates every ten minutes. **KFAI** (90.3 and 106.7 FM) is a volunteer-run public radio station with global programming schedule so at any time you are as likely to hear punk and zydeco music as an Eritrean talk show. It's worth checking **KUOM** (770 AM), the U of M's student radio station, frequently to see what's playing since it could change from Muddy Waters to Mudhoney at any time.

GETTING THERE AND AWAY
By Air

Minneapolis-St. Paul International Airport, or MSP, 612/726-5555, is one of the Midwest's largest hubs and conveniently located between Minneapolis, St. Paul, and the Mall of America. Almost all commercial flights (except Sun Country) use the **Lindbergh Terminal.** A list of all airlines serving the Twin Cities and relevant contact information is found under Transportation in the On the Road chapter.

By Train

Though located in St. Paul, the **Amtrak** station, 730 Transfer Rd., 651/644-6012, is a bit closer to Minneapolis's downtown. The eastbound train heads out at 7:05 A.M., stopping in Red Wing and Winona, while the westbound departs at 10:25 P.M., with stops in St. Cloud, and Fargo, North Dakota—the train arrives about an hour before each of these times. A connecting bus service, booked as part of your train ticket, lets you continue on to Duluth or Eau Claire, Wisconsin.

By Bus

The modern **Greyhound** station, 612/371-3325, in Minneapolis is right downtown. There are upwards of three daily departures for Duluth ($21 one-way), six for Fargo ($32 one-way), and twelve to Chicago ($61 one-way). **Jefferson Lines** also has a few buses coming through each day with Rapid City, South Dakota ($69 one-way), and Kansas City, Missouri ($59 one-way), being notable long-distance destinations. **Lorenz** runs one bus a day to Virginia, Minnesota, taking a roundabout route past Lake Mille Lacs. There's also a little bus station, 651/222-0507, in St. Paul just west of the capitol at 166 West University Avenue.

By Boat

The magnificent **Delta Queen Steamboat Co.,** 800/862-2452, www.deltaqueen.com, is the most magnificent way to arrive in St. Paul. See the On the Road chapter for information.

GETTING AROUND

By Bus

Overall the Twin Cities' **Metro Transit** bus system is pretty good. The regular cash fare is $1.25 for local routes and $1.75 for express routes. Add $.75 during rush hour, weekdays 6–9 A.M. and 3–6:30 P.M. Seniors and youth (ages 6–12) ride for $.50 (except during rush hour when they

pay regular fares). Disabled riders (all buses are equipped with ramps) pay $.50 at all times. The fare is valid for unlimited travel on any combination of buses for 2.5 hours, though you must get a transfer when boarding. A ride anywhere within the either city's Downtown Zone costs just $.50. A **Day Pass,** good for 24 hours of unlimited travel from the time of first use, costs $6 and is valid throughout the entire metro area. They are sold at each of the three transit stores, one in each downtown and the other at the Mall of America, and some 150 retail outlets; call 612/349-7686 to find out where to buy one.

For travel to or from the airport, bus 7 (though only the C, D, E, F, and G service) runs along 4th Street in downtown Minneapolis, and bus 54 (A and M service) hits the majority of downtown St. Paul. A letter after the route number in these and all other cases signifies the final destination of that particular bus; this information will also be displayed on the sign on the front of the bus, but if you have any doubts ask the driver. If you need routing or other information, call 612/373-3333.

By Taxi

There is no shortage of cabs in either downtown, though hailing one isn't easy—your best bet is to stroll by a hotel. Expect a fare of $2 and $1.60 per mile after that. A ride between the airport and either downtown or between downtowns will cost about $25. **Suburban/Green & White Taxi** covers the entire metro area and has 24-hour radio dispatch. Call 612/522-2222 in Minneapolis, 651/522-2222 in St. Paul.

Organized Tours

Down In History Tours, 651/292-1220, www .wabashastreetcaves.com, serve up a bevy of unique two-hour Twin Cities trips like the St. Paul Victorian Tour or adults-only Twin Town Tacky Tour featuring off-beat stops. Their most popular outings are the gangster tours. Led by costumed reenactors, they revisit the homes and hideouts of the most infamous crooks of the Roaring '20s. Tours run late May through September at noon. All tours depart from the **Wabasha Street Caves,** 215 S. Wabasha St. near downtown St. Paul (though you can arrange to be picked up in Minneapolis for that city's mob tour), and cost $20. They also give 45-minute tours ($5) of the caves themselves, once a fashionable nightclub, now a hall rented out for private events.

If you just desire a more ordinary excursion, there are several other options available. **Twin Cities Tours,** 612/821-1174, www.twincities-tours.com, lead personalized tours with a focus on the Cities' neighborhoods and off-the-beaten-path places, but your chauffeur/guide will take you pretty much wherever you desire. Prices are $45/hour (plus 18 percent tip) for Lincoln Town Car transport and $55/hour for six-person vans. **Metro Connections,** 612/333-8687 or 800/747-8687, www.metroconnections.com, offers sev-

eral local tours, including half-day Twin Cities highlights and Native American (each about $25). The Native-owned **Native Tours,** 763/571-8184 or 866/489-6583, www.nativetours.com, lead half-day tours of the Twin Cities with a cultural bent for $45 between May and September. Both Metro and Native have departures from Minneapolis and St. Paul area hotels, as well as the Mall of America. From May through September **Gray Line Tours,** 952/469-5020 or 800/530-9686, offers a four-hour Twin Cities bus tour for $25 and the same tour with an added paddlewheel boat ride on the Mississippi River for $35. Buses depart from the Mall of America only, and tickets are sold at the Explore Minnesota USA store.

Minneapolis

TWIN CITIES

The larger, more polished, and—as St. Paulites would say—pompous half of the Twin Cities is truly a world-class city. Capped by a trio of internationally renowned art museums and the Guthrie Theater, arguably the best regional theatrical companies in the country, few cities this small can boast of such superb and diverse cultural opportunities. The vibrant nightlife spans punk rock karaoke to poetry slams, while the still thriving music scene has born such legends as Prince, Morris Day and The Time, Hüsker Dü, The Replacements, Soul Asylum, Babes in Toyland, and America's newest rock 'n roll heroes Dillinger Four. The city is as beautiful as it is energetic. The shimmering skyline belies the many historic structures preserved behind it and, with the mighty Mississippi rushing through the heart of town and 22 lakes dotting the rest of it, the appropriately named City of Water (*minne* is the Dakota word for water and *polis* is Greek for city) is not lacking in natural beauty either. When you get here take your time. Minneapolis may be small, but it has so much to offer visitors that you'll need at least a couple of days to do it justice and several more to experience it all.

History

Minneapolis was born at St. Anthony Falls, the

"Niagara of the West." Settlers to roll into the area immediately after an 1838 treaty with the Dakota opened up the river's east bank. Franklin Steele set out from Fort Snelling by moonlight and beat all other intended claimants to the falls, though because he lacked financing it would take 11 years before he could develop his town. When the money finally came through, he erected a dam, opened a sawmill, and plotted the town of St. Anthony. Minneapolis technically began on the opposite shore in 1849 when Colonel John H. Stevens received permission to operate a ferry and so built his home there. Though a few farmers soon joined him, this land, still a part of Fort Snelling's holdings, wasn't officially opened up for settlement until 1855. Despite the delay, west bank supremacy was such a foregone conclusion that right after the Territorial Legislature created Hennepin County in 1852, the first commissioners chose that side as the county seat, even though no town existed.

Though Scandinavian and French Canadian immigrants came to both towns in large numbers, many educated New Englanders also settled here in order to strike it rich when the United States opened up the West. Naturally hydropower made lumber the initial industry, and by 1852 four mills trimmed the pine brought down the Mississippi, though the falls were also a major tourist attraction and many wealthy Southerners—plus some East Coast luminaries like Henry David Thoreau—traveled up the Mississippi by steamboat to see them. The luxurious Winslow Hotel opened in St. Anthony in 1857 and helped the towns prosper. In 1860 St. Anthony had a population of 3,258 and 2,564 more lived in Minneapolis. The Civil War (1861–1865) ended the tourist trade and stunted the region's growth, though following General Lee's surrender settlers headed out into the prairies and money once again poured into the towns fronting St. Anthony Falls. When the state legislature officially incorporated Minneapolis in 1866, it combined the two small communities into one.

The same year the Winslow turned down its first bed, industrialists dug a canal along the river's west bank, creating the West Side Milling District. As wheat replaced big bluestem on the western prairies, new flourmills continued to open and by 1870 a dozen were grinding the golden grain, while 18 sawmills also operated in the area. Ten years later another dozen flourmills, utilizing the most modern methods available, were turning out not only more flour than anywhere else in the world, but the absolute best flour money could buy. These mills not only made Minneapolis a major city—the population swelled from 13,000 in 1870 to 165,000 by 1890—but ensured that it, rather than St. Paul, became the state's metropolis. Flour had eclipsed lumber in importance, though the latter continued to thrive and, as the 19th century spun into the 20th, Minneapolis also enjoyed a short run as the nation's largest lumber center; however, the forests were soon felled and most of the sawmills had shut down by 1910.

A variety of factors, including cheap electricity, eliminated the need for waterpower to produce flour, so Mill City's 50-year run as the "Flour Milling Capital of the World" came to an end in 1930. The last commercial mill at the falls closed in 1965; however, companies that had been born on the river—Pillsbury, General Mills, and Cargill—evolved into diversified food manufacturers and remain headquartered here. Addi-

tionally, the Minneapolis Grain Exchange, established in 1881, remains one of the world's largest commodities markets—about one million bushel are traded daily.

Suburban flight hit Minneapolis during the mid-20th century, but unlike most large Middle-American cities the downtown remains a vibrant shopping and social center. Significant civic investment began in the 1950s and, though it involved razing many gorgeous historic buildings, it also included the creation of the first all-weather pedestrian skyway and the country's second downtown pedestrian mall. The skyline was forever changed in the 1970s with the construction of the 57-story IDS tower, and the upward growth has continued largely uninterrupted ever since. Downtown's evolution continues today with expanding options in the Warehouse District and the conversion of the western riverfront into a cultural destination.

Orientation

The heart of the city is **Nicollet Mall,** a 12-block pedestrian/transit corridor lined with restaurants and shops. Busy Hennepin Avenue divides downtown and, in general, you shop on the east and play to the west; dining is good on both sides, though there is a growing preponderance of forgettable corporate chains right on Hennepin itself. The historic **Warehouse District,** the center of the city's entertainment scene, covers the northwest corner of downtown. The renovated buildings are now filled with swank restaurants and nightclubs, and this is where the beautiful people come to be seen, though there is something for all tastes here. The biggest addition to downtown in recent years is **Block E,** a glitzy entertainment project with a deliberate Times Square theme. Seventy blocks of downtown are linked by a seven-mile elevated indoor skyway system (open weekdays 6:30 A.M.–10 P.M., Sat. 9:30 A.M.–8 P.M., and Sun. noon–6 P.M.) that will keep you warm in the winter and dry when it rains. There is no shortage of parking downtown; the three municipal ramps along 2nd Avenue North are both the largest and the cheapest.

Right across the river from downtown, where the city began, historic **St. Anthony Main** has

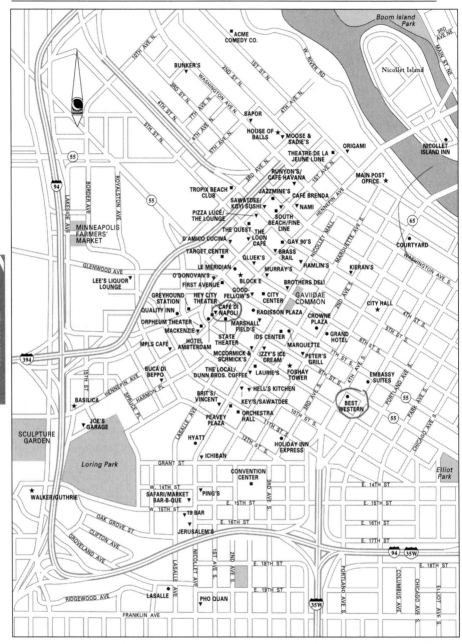

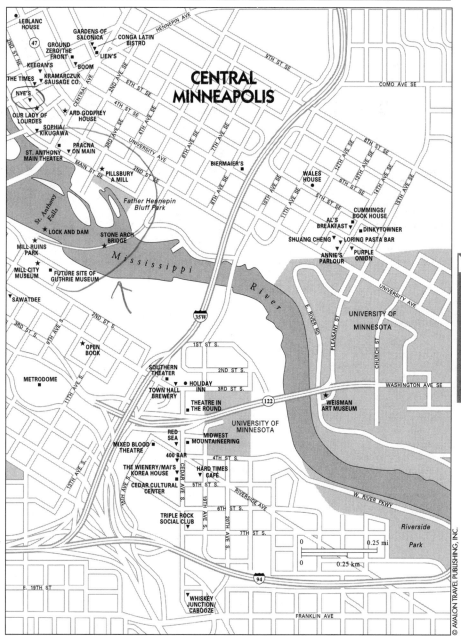

CENTRAL MINNEAPOLIS

TWIN CITIES

© AVALON TRAVEL PUBLISHING, INC.

© TIM BEWER

the skyway

many of the city's oldest buildings, and the great river and skyline views attract many for a meal and/or a stroll. **East Hennepin Avenue** behind Main Street has plenty of good restaurants, including Nye's Polonaise, a truly unique landmark. If the current pace of redevelopment continues, this may soon become *the* place to be in the city. Collectively East Hennepin and all the other neighborhoods of northeast Minneapolis are known as **Nordeast.** This working-class region, known for the figurative church and bar on every corner, maintains strong Eastern European roots though it now has a much wider international flair, especially along Central Avenue. East of the falls, on the edge of the University of Minnesota Campus, is **Dinkytown,** a fun four-block commercial district with student-focused shops, bars, and restaurants. Note that all addresses east of the river have a SE or NE suffix with Hennepin Avenue forming the north-south divide.

The University of Minnesota (U of M) campus stretches across the river to the **West Bank,** now filled with as many East African immigrants as students. The eclectic mix of restaurants and live music venues makes it one of the most enjoyable nightspots in the city and, don't worry, the

southern end isn't nearly as rough and tumble as it appears at first glance.

Nicollet Avenue, between downtown and Lake Street, has been officially designated **Eat Street,** and dozens of restaurants representing cuisines from all corners of the globe line it. **Uptown,** often fancifully described as Minneapolis's answer to Greenwich Village, is the trendiest neighborhood in town. Officially, Uptown is just a small area centered on Hennepin Avenue and Lake Street, but realistically the triangle formed by Lake Street and Hennepin and Lyndale Avenues is a continuous commercial district and, like its counterpart in New York City, has a little of everything. After the Warehouse District, this is the city's best late-night option.

The **Chain of Lakes**—Lake Calhoun, Lake Harriet, Lakes of the Isles, and Cedar Lake—which run up the city's southwest side, are the crown-jewels of Minneapolis's 22 lakes. These park-encased gems are one of the things that make the city such a wonderful place to live, and naturally they are ringed by some of the city's fanciest homes. Paved bike and pedestrian trails hug their shores and, since motorboats are prohibited, sailors, windsurfers, and paddlers have the waves to themselves.

SIGHTS

Mississippi Riverfront

The Father of Waters has only one natural waterfall, **St. Anthony Falls.** The 50-foot drop was known as Minirara (Curling Water) to the Dakota and Kakabikah (The Severed Rock) by the Ojibwe before Father Louis Hennepin honored his patron saint (Anthony of Padua) by bestowing it with the boring modern name. Hennepin was one of the first Europeans to see this spot when his Dakota captors led his exploration party past in 1680. Today a stroll through the old milling district is both a beautiful and educational experience. The two-mile **St. Anthony Falls Heritage Trail** follows the riverfront past the falls, ruined mills, and other sights comprising this National Historic District, and numerous historical markers recount the fascinating natural, engineering, and industrial history along the way. A good place to begin the tour is on the east bank at Old St. Anthony, where many of the renovated mid-19th century buildings now house shops, restaurants, and watering holes—perfect for a bit of refreshment after you complete your loop. Perched above Main Street is the small but towering **Our Lady of Lourdes Church,** 612/379-2259, the city's oldest church still in continuous use. Originally built in the Greek temple style by the First Universalist Society in 1854, the Catholic French-Canadian St. Anthony of Padua parish purchased it 20 years later and added the bell tower and other features. To fund restoration projects, the parish office sells frozen *tourtieres* (meat pies). The nearby **Ard Godfrey House** is detailed below. Heading down Main Street you'll pass the **Pillsbury A Mill,** a National Historic Landmark and the only mill building still open—though it's now used only for storage and research. When finished in 1881 it was the world's largest and could turn out 5,000 bushels a day. Across from the mill is **Father Hennepin Bluff Park.** You can either walk alongside it or follow the steps down to the trails, bridges, and overlooks at the river's edge.

Past the park the trail crosses the river over the one-of-a-kind **Stone Arch Bridge.** Beginning in 1881, 600 men worked around the clock for 22 months to finish this vital link in James J. Hill's railroad empire. Trains crossed the 23 granite and limestone arches for 101 years, but today bikers and pedestrians roll and stroll across the 2,100-foot span to take in the panoramic views. The singular structure, built of 100,000 tons of stone, is now not only an icon for the city, but a National Civil Engineering Landmark.

The west end of the bridge passes the **Upper St. Anthony Falls Lock and Dam,** 612/333-5336, the last of the 29 locks along the Upper Mississippi that connects Minneapolis with the Gulf of Mexico. The 49-foot lift accounts for over 10 percent of the river's total rise between here and St. Louis. The visitors center with informational displays (including the complicated process of shoring up the waterfall with the concrete apron) and an elevated viewing platform are open daily 8 A.M.–6 P.M. from April through November.

The ancient looking—if you ignore the steel beams and engine remnants—industrial ruins next to the lock comprise **Mill Ruins Park,** 612/313-7793. Archeological excavations will continue on the walls, canals, and tailraces for several more years. Between June and October, guides lead hour-long tours of the ruins on weekends at 1 and 3 P.M. Call in advance to have your child join a simulated archeological dig on the last weekend of the month. Both cost $5.

Rising within the ruins of the Washburn-Crosby A Mill, also a National Historic Landmark, is the **Mill City Museum,** 704 S. 2nd St., 612/341-7555. The creatively constructed glass center has exhibits about milling and associated topics, such as railroads, agriculture, and waterpower. Perched above it all is an 8th floor observation deck. The museum is also the place to pick up brochures or query the eager staff about the riverfront area and join Minneapolis Heritage Preservation Commission guides for free summer walking tours. The museum is open Tuesday–Saturday 10 A.M.–5 P.M. (open until 9 P.M. the first Thurs. of the month) and Sunday noon–5 P.M., plus Monday 10 A.M.–5 P.M. during the summer. Admission is $7.

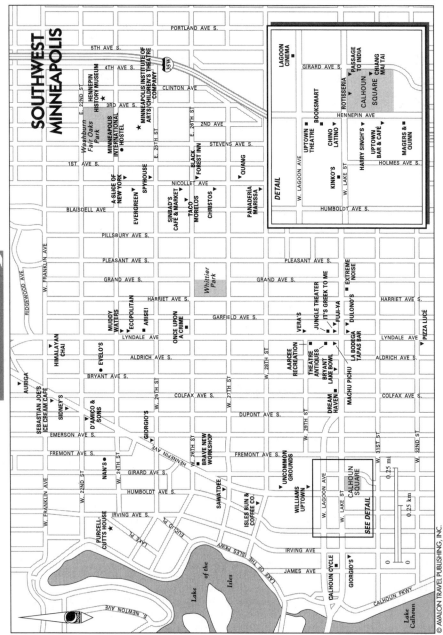

SOUTHWEST MINNEAPOLIS

DETAIL

LAGOON CINEMA
GIRARD AVE S.
PASSAGE TO INDIA
CHIANG MAI TAI
BOOKSMART
ROTISSERIA
CALHOUN SQUARE
HENNEPIN AVE.
UPTOWN THEATRE
CHINO LATINO
HARRY SINGH'S
UPTOWN BAR & CAFÉ
MAGERS & QUINN
W. LAGOON AVE
KINKO'S
W. LAKE ST.
HOLMES AVE S.
HUMBOLDT AVE S.

PORTLAND AVE S.
5TH AVE S.
E. 22ND ST
4TH AVE S.
3RD AVE S.
HENNEPIN HISTORY MUSEUM
MINNEAPOLIS INSTITUTE OF ARTS/CHILDREN'S THEATRE COMPANY
35W
CLINTON AVE
Washburn Fair Oaks Park
MINNEAPOLIS INTERNATIONAL HOSTEL
E. 25TH ST
E. 26TH ST
2ND AVE
STEVENS AVE S.
BLACK FOREST INN
1ST AVE S.
QUANG
A SLICE OF NEW YORK
SPYHOUSE
NICOLLET AVE.
EVERGREEN
SINBAD'S CAFÉ & MARKET
TACO MORELOS
CHRISTOS
PANADERÍA MARISSA
BLAISDELL AVE
PILLSBURY AVE S.
PLEASANT AVE S.
PLEASANT AVE S.
RIDGEWOOD AVE
W. FRANKLIN AVE
GRAND AVE S.
Whittier Park
GRAND AVE S.
HARRIET AVE S.
HARRIET AVE S.
MUDDY WATERS
ECOPOLITAN
ARISEI
ONCE UPON A CRIME
GARFIELD AVE S.
VERA'S
JUNGLE THEATER
IT'S GREEK TO ME
EXTREME NOISE
FUJI-YA
DULONO'S
PIZZA LUCÉ
HIMALAYAN CHAI
LYNDALE AVE
EVELO'S
ALDRICH AVE S.
W. 28TH ST
AARICE RECREATION
THEATRE ANTIQUES
BRYANT LAKE BOWL
LA BODEGA TAPAS BAR
LYNDALE AVE S.
ALDRICH AVE S.
BRYANT AVE S.
MACHU PICHU
AURIGA
COLFAX AVE S.
W. 27TH ST
DREAM HAVEN
COLFAX AVE S.
SEBASTIAN JOE'S ICE CREAM CAFÉ
SIDNEY'S
D'AMICO & SONS
GIORGIO'S
W. 25TH ST
DUPONT AVE S.
W. 29TH ST
W. 31ST ST
W. 32ND ST
EMERSON AVE S.
W. 26TH ST
BRAVE NEW WORKSHOP
FREMONT AVE S.
FREMONT AVE S.
UNCOMMON GROUNDS
NAN'S
W. 24TH ST
GIRARD AVE S.
HENNEPIN AVE
HUMBOLDT AVE S.
SAWATDEE
WILLIAMS UPTOWN
CALHOUN SQUARE
W. 22ND ST
W. FRANKLIN AVE
IRVING AVE S.
ISLES BUN & COFFEE CO.
W. LAGOON AVE
W. LAKE ST
SEE DETAIL
PURCELL-CUTTS HOUSE
LAKE PL.
EUCLID PL.
LAKE OF THE ISLES PKWY
IRVING AVE
CALHOUN CYCLE
GIORGIO'S
CALHOUN PKWY
Lake of the Isles
JAMES AVE
S. NEWTON AVE.
Lake Calhoun

0.25 mi
0.25 km

TWIN CITIES

historic St. Anthony Main

Coming back across the Mississippi along the Hennepin Avenue Bridge, you will descend onto the 50-acre enigma that is **Nicollet Island,** home to both one of the city's best known landmarks and one of its most delightful hidden gems. The Nicollet Island Inn is the city's most distinctive lodging choice, and its fancy restaurant is popular with families celebrating big events. Tucked away on the other end of the island is a colorful 19th-century neighborhood of large, gingerbread houses built between the 1860s and 1890s when this was one of the most fashionable neighborhoods in the city. After lapsing into a decrepit backwater during the 20th century, most of the architectural mélange has been fixed up and is once again a dream locale.

Art Museums

The **Walker Art Center,** 612/375-7622, began in 1879 when lumber baron Thomas Barlow Walker's art collection outgrew his house. He added a new wing to his mansion and opened the Midwest's first public art gallery, which has now grown into an internationally-renowned modern art center holding over 9,000 works. Best known for its major exhibitions of cutting-edge 20th century art, the Walker is a multifaceted center, and the performing arts do not take a back seat to visual so there are always music, dance, film, and similar events going on. A massive expansion is under way. The galleries are open Tuesday, Wednesday, Friday, and Saturday 10 A.M.–5 P.M., Thursday 10 A.M.–9 P.M., and Sunday 11 A.M.–5 P.M. Admission is $6, though all Thursdays and the first Saturday of each month are free.

Across the street from the Walker is the largest urban sculpture garden in the country. Best known for the iconic *Spoonbridge and Cherry,* the 11-acre **Minneapolis Sculpture Garden**'s landscaped grounds contain over 40 mostly massive sculptures. The small **Cowles Conservatory** has some horticultural displays, but most interesting is the palm room's 25-foot *Standing Glass Fish* by Frank Gehry, the design architect of the Weisman Art Museum. Unfortunately, picnics are not allowed at this great spot. However, you can cross the Irene Hixon Whitney Bridge to Loring Park for an outdoor meal; read what must be one of the world's "longest" poems as you amble over. The park is open daily 6 A.M.–midnight and free tours are given on weekends at

1 P.M. from May through October. The conservatory is open Tuesday–Saturday 10 A.M.–8 P.M. and Sunday 10 A.M.–5 P.M., plus extended hours after Walker and Guthrie Theater events. Admission is free.

For such a large building, the University of Minnesota's **Frederick R. Weisman Art Museum,** 612/625-9494, displays a small collection; however, the building itself is the highlight of the collection. Perched above the Mississippi River, the wonderful jumble of shapes was once described as an "exploding silver artichoke." Inside the naturally lit galleries, equal space is given to both temporary exhibitions of contemporary art and highlights from the 13,000-piece permanent collection, which is especially rich in American art from the first half of the 20th century. There is a great view of the river and downtown from the second floor terrace. The Weisman is open Tuesday, Wednesday, and Friday 10 A.M.–5 P.M., Thursday 10 A.M.–8 P.M., and weekends 11 A.M. to 5 P.M. Admission is free.

There is something for everyone at the Twin Cities' largest and most popular art museum. The encyclopedic collection of the **Minneapolis Institute of Arts,** 2400 3rd Ave. S., 612/870-3131, spans the globe and the ages with the oldest of the more than 100,000 objects dating back to 20,000 B.C. Highlights include paintings by masters such as Rembrandt, Monet, and Georgia O'Keeffe, a varied African collection, 17th and 18th century Chinese period rooms, and one of the world's premier assemblages of Prairie School objects. The MIA's 20 or so changing exhibitions offered annually are just as diverse. It is open Tuesday, Wednesday, Friday, and Saturday 10 A.M.–5 P.M., Thursday 10 A.M.–9 P.M., and Sunday 11 A.M.– 5 P.M. Admission is free.

For something completely different, explore the incomparable **House of Balls,** 212 3rd Ave. N., 612/332-3992, the "gallery, workshop, laboratory, provocation" of Allan Christian. Electrician by day and artist by night, Christian sculpts a dizzying array of works from found objects like bottle caps, frying pans, bones, plumbing, pistons, false teeth, silverware, and, most famously, bowling balls. Visitors are encouraged to handle the sculptures, some of which

© TIM BEWER

the wonderful jumble of the Frederick R. Weisman Art Museum

ARTS AND MUSEUMS PASS

The Arts and Museums Pass available from the Greater Minneapolis Convention & Visitors Association gives you free admission over five consecutive days at the following museums: the American Swedish Institute, The Bakken, Bell Museum of Natural History, Walker Art Center in Minneapolis and the James J. Hill House, Minnesota Children's Museum, and Science Museum of Minnesota in St. Paul. At $20 the pass is a good bargain if you'll be visiting several of these. It also provides various discounts on purchases at the Frederick R. Weisman Art Museum, Minneapolis Sculpture Garden, Minneapolis Institute of Arts, Minnesota History Center, and Minnesota Museum of American Art—all of which have free admission. The passes are for sale at the Minneapolis Information and Visitors Center and the Walker Art Center in Minneapolis as well as the Explore Minnesota USA store at the Mall of America.

have interactive parts, and nearly everything is for sale—you just have to be brave enough to make an offer. Though hours are by chance, it is usually open Saturday noon–4 P.M. and most evenings between about 9 P.M. and midnight, more or less. You can actually get a good look through the windows, so it is always worth stopping by. There is no charge, but you ought to leave a couple bucks.

Science Museums

From hummingbirds to moose, nearly 500 Minnesota animals are on display at the University of Minnesota's **Bell Museum of Natural History,** 612/624-7083. Equal parts art and science, the lifelike dioramas feature all of Minnesota's habitats from the prairie to the boreal forest, and famed wildlife artist Francis Lee Jaques, who lived in Minnesota for much of life, painted several of them. The kid-friendly Touch and See Room, overflowing with bones, hides, mounts, and live reptiles, lets you get up close and personal with nature—it was the first facility of its kind opened in the nation. Open Tues.–Fri. 9 A.M.–5 P.M., Sat.

10 A.M.–5 P.M., Sun. noon–5 P.M. Admission $3; free on Sundays.

While the Bell looks at the natural world, **The Bakken,** 612/926-3878, takes on technology. Founded by Earl Bakken, inventor of the first wearable pacemaker and many other medical devices, the unique museum specializes in the history of electricity and magnetism in medicine and the life sciences. Aimed principally at kids, though also of interest to adults, the galleries have hands-on displays about batteries, X-rays, magnets, and the like, plus there is an eletrarium with electric fish and Frankenstein's lab comes to life during a 12-minute multimedia presentation. Also, some of their 2,500 antique scientific instruments are always on display. Kids can participate in special programs on Wizard Wednesdays and Family Science Saturdays, while scholars can peruse some 11,000 volumes in the library. It is all housed in an expanded 1928 Tudor-style mansion overlooking Lake Calhoun. The museum is open Tuesday–Saturday 10 A.M.–5 P.M. and admission is $5.

History Museums

Here in the Scandinavian-American heartland, the castlelike **American Swedish Institute,** 2600 Park Ave., 612/871-4907, a tribute to a century and a half of the Swedish experience in America, attracts some 100,000 visitors a year. The museum's collection includes traditional outfits, folk art, the nation's largest collection of Swedish art glass, and original belongings carried from the old country by the state's early Swedish immigrants. The center also offers language and folk art classes, sponsors weekly special events, and houses terrific gift and book shops. Even if you have no interest in anything Swedish, stop by to see the mansion it is housed in. Swan Turnblad, an immigrant newspaper publisher and self-made millionaire, built his 33-room home between 1904 and 1908 with the intention of transitioning it into a Swedish cultural center one day. Turnblad spared no expense during construction: the ceilings are decorated with painted plaster sculpture, a third of the rooms have imported *kakelugnar* (porcelain tile stoves), and 18 craftsmen spent two years shaping the astounding woodwork. The museum is open Tuesday, Thursday, Friday, and

Saturday noon–4 P.M., Wednesday noon–8 P.M., and Sunday 1–5 P.M. During November and December, the Saturday hours expand to 10 A.M.–5 P.M. Admission is $5, except for the first Wednesday of each month when entry is free.

Also filling a retooled, though much less grand, mansion is the little **Hennepin History Museum,** 2303 3rd Ave. S., 612/870-1329, with rotating exhibits of random artifacts from Minneapolis and its county. The museum is open Tuesday 10 A.M.–2 P.M., Wednesday–Sunday 1–5 P.M. (closing at 8 P.M. on Thurs.). Admission is $2.

If you can visit the **Minnesota Air Guard Museum,** 612/713-2523, you'll see 19 vintage fighter, transport, and spy planes, plus jet engines, uniforms, and the world's largest display of Air National Guard unit patches. Following the September 11, 2001, terrorist attacks, access to the museum was suspended, though they do expect to reopen. It is located at the northeast corner of Minneapolis-St. Paul International Airport, off Highway 55.

Historic Buildings

The highlight of the Minneapolis Institute of Arts' world-famous Prairie School collection is the 1913 **Purcell-Cutts House,** 2328 Lake Pl., one of the country's most outstanding realizations of this uniquely American architectural style. Architects William Purcell and George Elmslie designed the house for Purcell and his family, though after a few years they moved to Philadelphia and sold the house to the Cutts family. The second owners, recognizing the significance of their purchase, made no significant alterations during their 66-year residency. The exterior contains all the classic Prairie School elements—a horizontal design, extensive eaves, earthen colors, and banks of geometrically-paneled art-glass windows—but it's the phenomenal and occasionally playful interior, which you can tour the second weekend of each month, that qualifies it as a masterpiece. The open floor plan, with versatile rooms that can serve multiple functions, showcases the Prairie School philosophy of unified design, and each sun-lit room features extensive woodwork, stencil designs, and subtle artwork. Much

of the furniture, like lamps, bookcases, and a writing nook desk, was built-in and the MIA has exactingly reproduced the rest. The hour-long tours are available Saturday 10 A.M.–1 P.M. and Sunday 12:30 P.M.–2 P.M. and cost $5. Call 612/870-3131 to reserve a spot.

No longer much of a presence on the Minneapolis's skyline, the 32-story Washington Monument-shaped **Foshay Tower,** 821 Marquette Ave. 612/359-3030, still manages to stand out in a crowd. Wilbur Foshay, who earned his wealth in shady utilities dealings during the Roaring '20s, spent $3.7 million building the first skyscraper west of the Mississippi, and "The best address in the Northwest" opened to great fanfare in August 1929. Foshay spent $116,000 on a three-day bash to mark the occasion, going as far as commissioning John Phillips Sousa to write and conduct a special one-performance-only march. Just two months after his grand opening the stock market crashed and Foshay, whose fortune existed solely on paper, lost everything, including his beloved tower—a conviction for mail fraud sent him to Leavenworth for three years. Not until the 775-foot, 57-story IDS Tower went up in 1971 did the Foshay lose its status as the city's premier icon. Today, dwarfed by its many new neighbors, the views from the 31st-floor outdoor observation deck are only waist-high, but still pretty spectacular. A small museum has a few historical displays on the man and the building. Currently both the tower and museum are closed due to security concerns, though they will likely reopen someday.

The cornerstone for the **Basilica of St. Mary,** 88 N. 17th St., 612/333-1381, the nation's first basilica and one of the finest examples of Beaux Arts architecture in the country, was laid in 1908. It took six years to complete the French and Italian Renaissance exterior with its 250-foot copper dome and monumental face. Another decade was spent on the phenomenal interior, which is filled with large stained-glass windows, carved stone, ornamental plaster, and an altar designed to be the finest in the land. The nave measures 140 long by 82 feet wide and may have been the largest of any church in the world when built. The Basilica is open daily 6:30 A.M.–5 P.M., and

the Purcell-Cutts House, a Prairie School masterpiece

free tours are available at 2 P.M. on Tuesday, Wednesday, and Thursday and after the 9:30 and 11:30 Sunday masses.

Costumed guides lead you around the quaint, yellow **Ard Godfrey House,** 612/870-8001, the oldest surviving frame house in Minneapolis. Franklin Steele, the man who laid the first claim to land at St. Anthony Falls, brought the millwright Godfrey out from Maine in 1847 to build a dam and sawmill. Godfrey, impressed by the new settlement, sent for his family the next year and built his home with the first lumber sawn at his mill. Originally erected at Main Street and 2nd Avenue, it was moved four times before ending up in this park, just a stone's throw from its original home. The Woman's Club of Minneapolis has restored and refurnished the property as it appeared in the 1840s. The house is open Friday–Sunday noon–3:30 P.M. from late May through September. Admission is $2.

At some point during your visit, be sure to stroll down to **Minneapolis City Hall,** 350 S. 5th St., 612/673-3000, a massive Romanesque building that took almost 20 years to build and nearly bankrupted the city before it was finished in 1905. *Father of Waters,* a Larkin Goldsmith Mead sculpture carved from the largest block of marble ever taken from Michelangelo's Carrara quarries, is Minneapolis's answer to Paul Bunyan. It sits surrounded by the marble and stained glass inside the Fourth Street entrance's rotunda. Atop the 345-foot tower are the 14-foot hands of the four clock faces (larger than those surrounding Big Ben) and a 15-bell carillon. The bells are played from a Schroeder-sized keyboard in the rotunda—call to find out when. The best listening spots are in the plazas on the opposite sides of the building, and you can hear them in the rotunda through speakers. A tour brochure is available at the information desk, plus free guided tours are available on the third Wednesday of each month at noon.

More famous than historic is the 1892 Victorian house at 2104 Kenwood Parkway, near Lake of the Isles—the original home of Mary Richards on **The Mary Tyler Moore Show,** set (though not actually filmed) in Minneapolis. Mary later moved to the colorful Riverside Plaza, 1525 S. 4th St., a move she never would have made in real life. A life-sized statue of Mary tosses her tam, ala the show's opening credits, at the corner of Nicollet Mall and 7th St.

Tourist Transit

The **RiverCity Trolley,** 612/204-0000, lets you tour Minneapolis in style and learn a little history along the way. Either take a quick tour of the city or hop on and off at any of the two dozen stops to sightsee. The downtown route hits all the city's highlights, including the Walker Art Center, Minneapolis Sculpture Garden, and Nicollet Mall—it even crosses the Mississippi River over the Stone Arch Bridge—while the Chain of Lakes Tour runs through the city's scenic south side stopping in Uptown and at the Minneapolis Institute of the Arts. The downtown route runs every half-hour 10 A.M.–3 P.M. (no Monday service) between May and October. The Chain of Lakes trip departs every hour starting at 10:30 and only runs weekends after Labor Day. Both tours last about an hour. A two-hour ticket costs $10, while all-day and three-day passes are $15 and $20. Tickets can be bought on the bus; bring exact change.

The **Paddleford Packet Boat Company,** 651/227-1100 or 800/543-3908, and their *Anson Northrup* mock-paddlewheeler departs from the north end of **Boom Island Park** and cruises through the Upper Saint Anthony Falls Lock. Boats depart daily at noon and 2 P.M. during the summer, plus weekends at 2 P.M. during May and October. The price is $12. They also offer much less frequent lunch, dinner, and fall color trips.

The **Como-Harriet Streetcar Line,** 651/228-0263 or 800/711-2591, part of a route between downtown Minneapolis and Lake Minnetonka that operated from 1880 to 1954, has been revived by the Minnesota Transportation Museum. Three beautifully restored classic cars, built between 1908 and 1946, run for a mile between Lake Harriet and Lake Calhoun. The 15-minute trips depart from the Linden Hills Station, a reproduction of the 1900 original, now filled with streetcar photos and artifacts; it is located on the northwest shore of Lake Harriet at West 42nd Street. Passengers may also board at the Lake Calhoun platform just south of West 36th Street. The cars run weekdays 6:30 P.M. to dusk, plus weekends and holidays 12:30 P.M.–dusk from mid-May to mid-September. Weekend service is also available during October and the first half

of May. The regular fare is $1.50, and free tours of the carbarn, where volunteers restore vintage streetcars, are available one Sunday a month (usually the second) 12:30–4:30 P.M.

Historic Fort Snelling

Perched high above the confluence of the Mississippi and Minnesota Rivers, Fort Snelling was built by the U.S. Army's Fifth Regiment of Infantry between 1819 and 1825 to administer America's new Northwest frontier. When the land was opened to settlement, people branched out in both directions to found towns that would grow into Minneapolis and St. Paul. Today, after rebuilding the crumbling stone fortress in the 1950s, the Minnesota Historical Society runs a remarkable living history museum. After brushing up on 19th-century current events in the Fort Snelling History Center, 612/726-1171, you'll walk out to 1827, where costumed reenactors lead tours and demonstrate bygone skills. You can watch them skin a beaver, forge horseshoes, mend clothing, fire muskets and cannons, bake bread, and explain how to bleed a patient with a fever. Plan on several hours to properly experience everything. During the summer this National Historic Landmark is open Wednesday–Saturday 10 A.M.–5 P.M. and Sunday noon–5 P.M. with just the Saturday and Sunday hours in May, September, and October. Admission is $6.

Fort Snelling State Park

The historic fort only takes up a sliver of the 3,400-acre state park. Most of the rest is bottomland forest extending down the Minnesota River. Though this is an urban corridor, wildlife is surprisingly abundant and, if you get out on the 18 miles of trail, you'll likely encounter some, even out on busy Pike Island separating the Mississippi and Minnesota Rivers. The easy **Pike Island Trail** skirts the island's edge, staying in sight of the rivers most of the time. Most of the rest of the trails, a mix of paved and gravel surfacing, run along the Minnesota River and connect to regional bike trails outside the park. Come winter, 12 miles of trail are groomed for cross-country skiing and a trail through the center of Pike Island is packed for winter hiking.

© TIM BEWER

new recruits at Historic Fort Snelling

Paddlers can rent canoes to run the river or look for wildlife in Gun Club Lake. Other park facilities include historical exhibits in the visitors center, a swimming beach on Snelling Lake, and accessible fishing pier. If you are driving here from Minneapolis or St. Paul, ignore the signs for Fort Snelling Historic Site and take the Post Road exit off Highway 5, though you can walk downhill from the fort. Call 612/725-2389 with any park questions.

Minnehaha Park

Centered on the 53-foot waterfall made famous by Henry Wadsworth Longfellow's epic poem *The Song of Hiawatha* ("In the land of the Dacotahs/ Where the Falls of Minnehaha/ Flash and gleam among the oak-trees/ Laugh and leap into the valley.") Minnehaha Park is one of the city's most popular playgrounds. There are multiple overlooks of the falls, and the shady path through the glen below it is quite serene. The statue *Hiawatha and Minnehaha* stands on the island immediately above the falls.

A trio of historic buildings sit just to the west of the falls. Back in the 19th century, Minneapolis residents coming to the park stopped at the petite 1875 **Minnehaha Depot,** 651/228-0263, so cute it was nicknamed The Princess by Milwaukee Road employees. The restored interior is open Sundays and holidays 12:30–4:30 P.M. during the summer. Admission is free. The **John H. Stevens House,** 612/722-2220, was the first settler's home built on the west bank of the Mississippi River in 1849. When the house was set to be razed, civic-minded citizens came to its rescue and 7,000 children and a team of horses pulled it to the park. You can visit the interior of the home to see the period furnishings and historical displays on Friday 10 A.M.–2 P.M. and Saturday–Sunday 1–5 P.M. from mid-May through mid-September. Admission is $2. The **Longfellow House,** 612/370-4969, is a two-thirds-size replica of the poet's Massachusetts home. The bright yellow building serves as an information center for the park and the Grand Rounds Scenic Byway. It is open Tuesday–Saturday 10 A.M.–5 P.M. and Sunday (plus holiday Mondays) noon–4 P.M. Admission is free.

On the west side of the park you can watch boats pass through **Lock and Dam #1** (actually the third in the series of 29 along the Upper Mississippi River) from an elevated boardwalk. The lock is open for viewing daily 8 A.M.–dusk from April through October. Guided tours are also available; call 612/724-2971 to get the schedule.

Grand Rounds National Scenic Byway

The Grand Rounds, 612/661-4800, is an urban byway like no other. The signed route runs right through downtown's St. Anthony Falls historic district and briefly passes the industrial northeast, but most of the 50-mile route follows the city's rivers and lakes—including the Mississippi River and the urban wilderness of **Theodore Wirth Park**—along forest-lined boulevards. You can make the rounds at a leisurely pace in about three hours, though it's easy to spend twice that if you make a lot of stops—and you should. Pick up a map and information about recreational opportunities along the trail at the Longfellow House in Minnehaha Park, or let the many informational kiosks guide you.

RECREATION

Bicycling

The **Grand Rounds National Scenic Byway** is best seen on two wheels and there are separate paths for bicyclists along most of the 50-mile route. The 12-mile Chain of Lakes segment circling Lake Harriet, Lake Calhoun, and Lake of the Isles, known to cyclists as the **Four Lakes Loop,** is by far the most popular ride. Another wonderful ride, especially during fall, is the seven-mile stretch along the **Mississippi River** between the Stone Arch Bridge and Minnehaha Park. Neither tour feels even remotely urban, and bike rentals are available near both; see Getting Around below.

On the Water

Naturally there is plenty of paddling in the City of Water. The **Mississippi River** downstream of downtown runs through a deep, tree-lined gorge and it's easy to forget that you are in the midst of a major metropolis, though on the downside you will be sharing the scenery with a fair number of motorboats. The recommended run is to put in on the east bank of the river at the U of M and make a four-mile trip downstream to the Ford

Dam before retracing your path. Another, rather unique, option is to begin your journey further upstream at St. Anthony Falls and travel through the locks and dams. Construction of a world-class white-water park below the falls is scheduled to begin in 2004. Many people sail and windsurf on Lake Calhoun and Lake Harriet, the largest of the **Chain of Lakes,** while the smaller Lake of the Isles, Cedar Lake, and Brownie Lake (connected by narrow channels) get plenty of canoe action. Canoe rentals for use on the lakes are available at the pavilion on the northeast shore of Lake Calhoun. Also, both **Aarcee Recreation,** 2910 Lyndale Ave. S., 612/827-5746; and **Midwest Mountaineering,** 309 Cedar Ave. S., 612/339-3433, rent canoes. Midwest also has sea-touring and white-water kayaks.

Skating

If you want to ice skate just find a park; the city freezes over 30 rinks and clears a patch on Lake of the Isles. They also offer indoor skating at the **Parade Ice Garden,** 612/370-4846, for $3 per session. Priced much higher ($7), but with added character, is the gorgeous, glass-enclosed **Depot Rink,** 218/339-2253, at 5th Ave. S. and Washington Ave., attached to the Courtyard Hotel. Both have skate rentals ($2 and $6 respectively) and lockers available. The Parade is open year-round, while the Depot takes the summer off. Times are highly variable so call for details. **Peavey Plaza,** on the Nicollet Mall next to Orchestra Hall, is the Minneapolis version of New York City's Rockefeller Plaza, though not nearly as popular and there is no skate rental or warming shelter.

Skaters who prefer concrete to ice should follow the recommended bike routes above or, between November and April, head to the **Metrodome,** which for a few hours several days a week becomes the Rollerdome, 612/825-3663. For $6 you can speed down a pair of concourses on some remarkably smooth concrete. Skate rentals are available and safety gear is free.

NIGHTLIFE

Though many locals like to complain, there aren't many cities of comparable size that can match

Minneapolis's after-hours entertainment offerings. There is no better source of what's on than the free weekly *City Pages,* available all over the city. The *Star Tribune*'s FreeTime section, published on Friday, is also very thorough.

Rock

Few clubs anywhere in the world can boast a historic set list as impressive as the **First Avenue & 7th St. Entry,** 701 1st Ave. N., 612/332-1775. Most famous as the club where Prince rose to stardom in the movie *Purple Rain,* this legendary venue—big names play the two-story mainroom while up-and-comers are relegated to the crusty confines of the 250-person Entry—has hosted just about every rock band that's ever mattered since it opened in 1970. Due to its strong support of local musicians and an impressively diverse calendar it remains, far and away, the best venue in the city.

So many national acts play Minneapolis and there is such terrific homegrown talent that, despite its success and popularity, First Avenue is far from

monopolizing the scene. Many other First Avenue-sized bands play **The Quest,** 110 N. 5th St., 612/338-3383, an elegant space formerly owned by the man formerly known as the Artist Formerly Known as Prince (who called it Glam Slam). The **Fine Line Music Café,** 318 1st Ave. N., 612/338-8100, mostly books mellower acts for a somewhat older crowd. To the chagrin of many music fans, the **400 Bar,** 400 Cedar Ave. S., 612/332-2903, with its horrible stage setup and inflated drink prices (in all fairness, the sound is really good for a bar), continues to book some of the best underground and up-and-coming bands.

Blues, Reggae, and R&B

The West Bank is Minneapolis's blues Mecca. The **Cabooze,** 917 Cedar Ave. S., 612/338-6425, is a neighborhood joint that just happens to pull in occasional big names like Kenny Wayne Shepherd, George Clinton, and Johnny Winter. **Whiskey Junction,** 901 Cedar Ave. S., 612/338-9550, just two doors down, is a biker bar with top local blues bands on weekends and

© TIM BEWER

the venerable First Avenue

PARTYING WITH THE PURPLE ONE

The artist sometimes known as Prince isn't quite as reclusive as his reputation suggests. He occasionally attends Timberwolves basketball games and is sometimes spotted in VIP rooms with his entourage at clubs like Jazzmine's, The Lounge, First Avenue, and his former venture (then called Glam Slam) The Quest; though don't expect to chum around with him. About the only opportunity to actually meet him is, surprisingly, at his Paisley Park Studios out in suburban Chanhassen. Occasionally the studio opens its doors for late night parties and every once in a while the host plays DJ for the night or takes his band up on stage and jams through the wee hours; usually though he doesn't even show up. The alcohol-free events usually start around 1 A.M., but come early because space is limited. Cover charges range from nothing to $7. Members of Prince's NPG Music Club will get notice of upcoming parties, or those who don't want to shell out $100 to join (for all you get it's actually a good deal if you're a fan), should check the unofficial but very detailed www.prince.org.

For the past few years Paisley Park has also hosted a weeklong summer Prince Celebration with music workshops and exclusive listening sessions, plus Prince and his band nightly perform rare material and acoustic sets, as do other R&B stars. A weekly pass for the most recent event cost $250. Various day-passes and single event tickets are also available. Check the above sources for details on future celebrations. If you can't get a pass you can still join in Prince-mania since many fan groups host concurrent gatherings in Lake Ann Park across the street from the studio.

a rollicking Monday night open jam. Many of the hottest local bands—mostly funk and R&B— have regular gigs across town at **Bunker's,** 761 Washington Ave. N., 612/338-8188. **Famous Dave's Barbeque & Blues,** 3001 Hennepin Ave. S., (in Calhoun Square), 612/822-9900, is a popular Uptown restaurant with live local and touring bands seven nights a week—though the weekends are reserved for blues, there's reggae, Cajun, and salsa many nights.

Folk

The nonprofit **Cedar Cultural Center,** 416 Cedar Ave. S., 612/338-2674, hosts over 150 traditional musical (and a few dance) performances a year. The calendar spans the globe, from American folk to Afro-pop, and many of the biggest names in their genre, like Greg Brown and Baaba Maal, grace the stage. The sound is excellent and there isn't a bad seat in the house; the only negative is that they close up each summer.

A trio of traditional pubs host Irish bands, but **Kieran's,** 330 2nd Ave. S., 612/339-4499, with a famous Wednesday night jam and bands through Saturday, is the best known. Live bands take the stage Thursday–Saturday at **O'Donovan's,** 700 1st Ave. N., 612/317-8896. Sunday is jam night at **Keegan's,** 16 University Ave. NE, 612/252-0880, and bands are also booked on Mondays and Thursdays.

Jazz

Jazz aficionados tend to converge on St. Paul, but it's worth seeing who is playing under the starry-night ceiling at **Jazzmine's,** 123 3rd St. N., 612/630-5299; on the massive stage in **The Times Bar & Café,** 201 Hennepin Ave. E., 612/617-8098; or overlooking the river at **Sophia,** 65 Main St. SE, 612/379-1111. All three are gorgeous locations with great food and the first two have Sunday afternoon brunches with bands.

Polka

Truly in a class by itself, **Nye's Polonaise,** 112 Hennepin Ave. E., 612/379-202, is probably the only nightspot where twenty-somethings mingle amiably with eighty-somethings. Ruth Adams and The World's Most Dangerous Polka Band hold court Thursday through Sunday, as they have since 1967, with a variety of other bands the rest of the week. Ruth isn't the only living legend employed by Nye's; Lounge singers "Sweet Lou Snider" and Ward Dunkirk tickle the ivories in the adjacent restaurant.

You can share a boot of Teutonic beer and dance to some squeezebox action every weekend at **Mario's Keller Bar,** 2300 University Ave. NE, 612/781-3860, below the Gasthof zur Gemütlichkeit German restaurant.

Dancing

Too many clubs come and go to pin down the dance floor du jour, but the following are safe bets. The city's biggest rock clubs, **First Avenue** and **The Quest,** are also some of the best places to dance, and not just because they stay open past bar time. The beautiful people hang at the mellow **The Lounge,** 411 2nd Ave. N., 612/333-8800, where you can retire to couch-filled and candle-lit wings between spins on the small dance floor; and the larger and livelier **South Beach,** 325 1st Ave. N., 612/204-0790, which also combines a cigar bar and martini lounge. These clubs mix up the styles night after night, while it's pretty much all top 40 at **Tropix Beach Club,** 400 3rd Ave. N., 612/333-1006, a large meat market crawling with an 18+ crowd.

Outside the Warehouse District is **Ground Zero,** 15 4th St. NE, 612/378-5115, an unpretentious industrial-looking club with a more colorful clientele and a penchant for techno and trance—their adjacent space, The Front, is hopping on weekends with a mix of current hits and 70s grooves. Bondage a Go-Go spices things up a bit on Thursday and Saturday nights. DJs at the U of M student-filled **Dinkytowner,** 412 1/2 14th Ave. SE, 612/362-0427, are noted for spinning world beat several nights a week. The nightly entertainment also includes live bands, independent film, and poetry open mics.

You can salsa every night of the week in Minneapolis. Best bet for Latin rhythms of all kinds is **Conga Latin Bistro,** 501 Hennepin Ave. E., 612/331-3360, where the dance floor is swinging most nights. The music is live, and the dancers some of the city's liveliest, weekends at the **MPLS. Café,** 1110 Hennepin Ave. S., 612/672-9100. **First Avenue** and **The Quest** also have salsa nights during the week.

Comedy

Currently the leading venue for stand up is the Warehouse District's **Acme Comedy Company,** 708 N. 1st St., 612/338-6393. There's a popular open mike on Monday and touring headliners every Tuesday through Saturday. Tickets are $10, or you can get dinner and a show for $22. The fast growing **ComedySportz,** 3001 Hennepin Ave. S., 612/870-1230, has an Uptown outlet in Calhoun Square. Two teams of "actletes" compete head to head for laughs and points in various improvisational, audience-directed games. The shows are appropriate for children, but not dumbed down for adults. They perform on weekend nights at 8 and 10:30. Tickets are $10 for the early show and $8 for the second act. **Brave New Workshop,** 2605 Hennepin Ave. S., 612/332-6620, the country's longest-running satirical review, started in 1958 and counts Al Franken and Louie Anderson as alumni. It's sort of a less-scripted *Saturday Night Live,* with some of the past shows entitled "2000 Years And Still No Jesus," "Minnesota! It's Not Just For Lutherans Anymore," and "Viagra! The Second Coming." For the most part, regular shows run Thursday–Saturday and cost around $20, plus they have free and cheap performances featuring improv class students other days of the week. Shows can get a little racy and are not recommended for kids under 16 or adults who are easily offended.

Eclectic

On any given night, the 100-seat theater at the ultra-trendy **Bryant Lake Bowl,** 810 W. Lake St., 612/825-8949, might be hosting film, music, dance, theater, performance art, trapeze, or shadow puppets. And, if the show is a dud go knock down some pins. If that weren't enough, the Grain Belt beer sign fronting the building delivers on its promise of "Good Food" and its lemon basil organic chicken, rather than a menu typical of tenpin alleys. The beer and wine lists are also excellent.

On the second Friday of the month, the Walker Art Center, 612/375-7622, hosts **Walker After Hours.** Combining culture, conversation, and cocktails the event—which could just as well be called Walker Singles Night—features live bands, films, free hors d'oeuvres, and cash bar with an always-popular martini of the month. It runs 7–10 P.M. and tickets cost $14.

For information about what is happening at the **University of Minnesota**—which could be just about anything—call 612/625-5000.

Taps and Taverns

Unlike the trendy nightspots the Warehouse District is best known for, **Runyon's,** 107 Washington Ave. N., 612/332-7158, comes pretty close to being a neighborhood bar and has some of the best buffalo wings you'll ever nibble on. Tapping its first keg in 1981 **The Loon Café,** 500 1st Ave. N., 612/332-8342, an attractive and oddly minimalist sports bar, helped revitalize the Warehouse District and has since grown into a local institution. The above-average meals (try one of their chilies!) means it's packed during lunch, and the proximity to the Target Center means you might not even get in before a Timberwolves game. Minneapolis's Gluek Brewing Company opened their Bavarian-style beer hall here in 1902, and though the interior woodwork and glass windows are reconstructions due to a fire, **Gluek's,** 16 N. 6th St., 612/338-6621, retains its Old World charm. Amongst the many beers on tap is Gluek's, still brewed in the nearby town of Cold Spring. The highly regarded kitchen turns out everything from bratwurst to pesto quesadillas. Naturally Block E's **Hard Rock Café,** 612/343-8081, just a block away, has plenty of Prince memorabilia. **MacKenzie,** 918 Hennepin Ave., 612/333-7268, is a casual bar with Scotch flair and a popular after-theater stop. You can continue a tippling tour of the British Isles at **The Local,** 931 Nicollet Mall, 612/904-1000; **Brit's,** 1110 Nicollet Mall, 612/332-3908; and the three Irish pubs listed under Folk above.

Minneapolis's most highly regarded brewpub is the **Town Hall Brewery,** 1430 Washington Ave. S., 612/339-8696. Not only are the food and brews consistently good, but the historic yet casual confines, trimmed with a mirrored backbar, tile floor, and tin ceilings, offers a nice counterpart to the typical West Bank bar. One of those more colorful neighbors is the **Triple Rock Social Club,** 629 Cedar Ave. S., 612/333-7399, owned in part by Erik Funk, singer/guitarist of the band Dillinger Four. They have a commendable beer roster and a vegan-friendly menu, while Bikini Kill, Al Green, and the MC5 combine to make the jukebox one of the best in town. When their expansion is finished, they plan to book live bands.

Williams Uptown, 2911 Hennepin Ave. S., 612/823-6271, is a two-for-one taproom offering twenty-somethings 370 beers. That's right, 370 beers—300 bottles and 70 on tap. Upstairs usually resembles a frat party, though a somewhat mellower bunch heads downstairs for the free peanuts and popcorn. It is uncomfortably crowded on weekends and the prices are a bit high, but great daily specials let you get around that.

With lovely views inside and out **Pracna On Main,** 117 Main St. SE, 612/379-3200, is a great place to nurse a drink. Pracna's current incarnation started the riverfront revival in 1973, though an earlier version in this same spot that opened in 1890 lets it promote itself as "Minneapolis's oldest restaurant."

Northeast Minneapolis is known for its numerous neighborhood taps, and **Mayslacks,** 1428 4th St. NE, 612/789-9862, is a classic amongst classics. Once owned by professional wrestler Stan Mayslack, the tall wooden booths, pressed tin ceiling, garlic roast beef sandwiches, and live polka on Sundays add up to some wonderful Old World charm. Up the street **Tubby's,** 2500 4th St. NE, 612/789-7301, is a simple saloon offering punk rock karaoke every Friday night.

Gay and Lesbian

Serving the community since the 1950s, the unassuming **19 Bar,** 19 W. 15th St., 612/871-5553, is just your average neighborhood tavern with darts, pool tables, and a jukebox—except that they do not serve any hard liquor. Across the river the upscale **Boom,** 401 Hennepin Ave. E., 612/378-3188, has videos playing on flat screen TVs and a very trendy crowd. **The Saloon,** 830 Hennepin Ave., 612/332-0835, below the Hotel Amsterdam, is a wild pickup bar full of boys just wanting to be seen and DJs spinning all week long. More low key is the **Brass Rail,** 422 Hennepin Ave., 612/333-3016, with karaoke, drag shows, and male dancers, all enjoyed by a very wide-ranging crowd. The **Gay 90's,** 408 Hennepin Ave., 612/333-7755, has been described as "the Mall of America of gay bars." There are three dance floors, seven bars, a restaurant (serving $11 all-you-can-eat prime rib on weekends), karaoke, male strip shows, and the La

DISCOUNTED TICKETS

TC Tix offers day-of-show discounts, usually half price or two-for-ones, for dozens of the top performing arts and sports venues in the Twin Cities. Some of the varied venues participating are Brave New Workshop; Bryant Lake Bowl; Cedar Cultural Centre; Chanhassen Dinner Theatres; First Avenue; the Historic State, Orpheum, and Pantages theatres; Orchestra Hall; Ordway Center for the Performing Arts; and Target Center. You can find out what is available by calling 651/288-2060 or checking www.tctix.com, though tickets must be purchased in person at their Target Center office. They are open Monday–Saturday 11 A.M.–6 P.M. and Sunday noon–5 P.M.

Femme drag show. The DJs are excellent, so it attracts a large number of straight dancers and has become too mainstream for many gays who no longer frequent it.

OTHER ENTERTAINMENT

Theater

Minneapolitans love their theater. Around 100 companies fill the city's stages and, outside of New York, no other American city has more live theater seats per capita than Minneapolis. Famed New York City-based director Sir Tyrone Guthrie opened the **Guthrie Theater,** 612/377-2224 or 877/447-8243, in 1963 to promote the level of creative development that Broadway theaters no longer could. It soon grew into a Tony Award-winning organization known far and wide for its innovation presentations of both classic and contemporary plays. One-hour backstage tours are available at 10 A.M. on Saturdays and some Wednesdays for $5. The Guthrie hopes to move into its exiting new space overlooking the Mississippi River by the spring of 2005. The highly physical **Theatre de la Jeune Lune,** 105 N. 1st St., 612/333-6200, founded by a combination of French and American actors, is known for new takes on old works, though it has also produced its own award-winning plays. The multicultural **Mixed Blood Theatre,** 1501 4th St. S., 612/338-

6131, has a reputation for breaking the rules. They stage their often cutting-edge work in a converted firehouse. The Twin Cities' oldest community theater, **Theatre in the Round,** 245 Cedar Ave., 612/333-3010, staged its first production in 1952. Most of TRP's ten annual productions are classics, and they have such a reputation for quality that the press regularly reviews its productions. The highly acclaimed **Jungle Theater,** 2951 Lyndale Ave. S., 612/822-7063, produces a wide variety of works in its modern home. Recognized as the pioneer of theater for children and families, **The Children's Theatre Company,** 2400 3rd Ave. S., 612/874-0400, has been adapting classic literature—like *The Adventures of Tom Sawyer, Charlie and the Chocolate Factory,* and *Dr. Seuss' Green Eggs and Ham*—since 1965. A trio of historic theaters in downtown's brightly-lit Hennepin Avenue Theater District host numerous touring shows, many making a final run for fine tuning before debuting on Broadway. The **State, Orpheum,** and **Pantages** theaters opened between 1916 and 1921 as vaudeville stages and have been gorgeously restored to their former opulence. The box office for all three is at the State Theater, 805 Hennepin Ave. Call 612/339-7007 for ticket or other information.

Dance

Like theater, Minneapolis's dance scene is strong. The premier venue for all styles is the U of M's **Northrop Memorial Auditorium,** 84 Church St., SE, 612/624-2345. The stage has the same "Balanchine Basketweave" design as the New York City Ballet's stage at Lincoln Center, and since the 1970s the Northrop Dance Season has hosted the biggest companies from around the world. On a smaller scale you can't beat the intimate **Southern Theater,** 1420 Washington Ave. S., 612/340-1725. Their calendar is comprised largely of local acts working outside the mainstream. You never know who will be on stage during their Balls Cabaret, every Saturday at midnight—call 612/340-0155 ext. 25 and it could even be you.

Classical Music

The critically acclaimed **Minnesota Orchestra,** 612/371-5656, founded in 1903 and almost

TWIN CITIES

always ranked in the nation's top ten these days, performs over 200 concerts a year; most are held in the lovely and modern Orchestra Hall at 1111 Marquette Ave. The 95-member band performs both the classics and the contemporary, and their various albums have earned four Grammy nominations. The superb, 200-voice **Minnesota Chorale,** 612/333-4866, known nationally for their innovative programming, often performs with the orchestra.

Freebies

Minneapolis's parks are busy all summer long with live performances. Something is happening almost daily over the lunch hour and early evening in **Peavey Plaza,** the fountain-filled park along the Nicollet Mall. Bands are playing outdoors at **St. Anthony Main** every weekend, and there's also a Wednesday concert across the bridge on **Nicollet Island. Loring Park** has Movies and Music on Monday nights during July and August—a band takes the stage at 7 P.M. and plays until dusk, when a classic film rolls. The nightly concerts at the **Lake Harriet Bandshell** are always popular.

Cinema

There is no problem finding a good film in this town. The U Film Society, 612/627-4430, shows some amazing international films rarely shown in this country at the **Bell Auditorium,** while its partner, the **Oak Street Cinema,** 309 Oak St. SE, 612/331-3134, is noted for retrospectives. Together these U of M campus theaters have by far the most eclectic schedule around, and just about anything might get screened at either.

Over in Uptown, Landmark, the national art-house chain, runs the aging 900-seat **Uptown Theatre,** 2906 Hennepin Ave. S., and the modern **Lagoon Cinema,** 1320 Lagoon Ave. S. The information line for both is 612/825-6006.

All the biggest bombs and blockbusters out of Hollywood are on the 15 screens downtown at Block E's **Crown Theatres,** 600 Hennepin Ave., 612/338-5900, while the five-screen **St. Anthony Main Theater,** 115 Main St. SE, 612/331-4723, just across the river, mixes things up a bit.

Spectator Sports

The **Minnesota Vikings** played in four of the first eleven Super Bowls—and lost all of them. Home games are played in the aging **Hubert H. Humphrey Metrodome** and though they almost always sell out long before game day, ticket information is available by calling 612/338-4537. Despite their devotion to the team, taxpayers have so far balked at building a new stadium. If the state doesn't step up soon owner Red McCombs, a Texan with no hometown allegiance, will probably look for greener pastures.

Taking over the Metrodome in the summer for baseball are the American League's **Minnesota Twins,** though their future is also in doubt since only the courts prevented Major League Baseball from eliminating the team after the 2001 season. Call 612/338-9467 or 800/338-9467 for ticket information—upper deck seats are just $5. The National Basketball Association's **Minnesota Timberwolves** take to the court at **Target Center,** and tickets are priced as low as $10. Call 612/673-1600 to order tickets. The **Lynx** are Minnesota's WNBA affiliate and play a 35-game schedule at the Target Center during the men's off-season. Tickets start at $8 and can be ordered in advance at 612/673-8400, though they are always available at tip off.

The NCAA Division 1 **University of Minnesota Golden Gophers** men's hockey team (nine-time WCHA conference and five-time national champs, including 2002 and 2003) is perpetually one of the best in the nation, both the men's and women's basketball teams are usually competitive in the Big Ten conference, and most Minnesotans can't even remember the last time the football team was any good. Few sports fans anywhere in the nation are more boisterous than the hockey backers at the **Mariucci Arena,** while the fanaticism is a only a little more tempered across the street at **Williams Arena** ("The Barn") for the men's basketball games—both sports usually sell out well in advance. Until a new campus stadium is built, the football team must make the short trip across the river to the Metrodome, where they very rarely attract enough fans for a sell-out. In non-revenue sports, men's baseball, wrestling, and golf, and women's

milk carton boat race during the Minneapolis Aquatennial

© TIM BEWER

volleyball and hockey are also top programs nationally. Tickets for all sports are available from the Minnesota Athletics Ticket Office, 612/624-8080 or 800/846-7437, in the Mariucci Arena.

EVENTS

The **Minneapolis Aquatennial** celebrates summer with dozens of free events across the city over 10 days at the end of July. Downtown hosts Grande Day and Torchlight parades and what is claimed to be the largest fireworks display west of the Mississippi. Out on the lakes there are sailing regattas, milk carton boat races (the concept originated here), a sand sculpture contest, and the Life Time Fitness Triathlon with the largest purse for an international-distance triathlon.

With well over 100 theater, comedy, spoken word, and dance acts taking the stage at nearly two dozen venues, the **Minnesota Fringe Festival** has grown into the largest of its kind in the nation. It is held over 10 days in early August, and all tickets are just $10.

Although activists from across the political spectrum march in it, Minneapolis's **MayDay Parade** is principally a mobile arts festival celebrating the arrival of spring. Oversized puppets, along with stilt walkers, musicians, costumed revelers, and other creative spirits, travel south along Bloomington Avenue to Powderhorn Park, delighting some 50,000 spectators.

The **Holidazzle** parades, made up of illuminated floats, storybook characters, musicians, and dancers, are so popular they run it two dozen times a year. The half-hour procession glides down the Nicollet Mall every Wednesday through Sunday at 6:30 P.M. between Thanksgiving and Christmas. If you want a spot in the heated skyway, claim it early, or stop at the City Center mall for information about heated grandstand viewing.

ACCOMMODATIONS

Hotels and Motels $50–100

Downtown: The **Hotel Amsterdam,** 828 Hennepin Ave., 612/288-0459 or 800/649-9500, is an unabashedly gay hotel, though all are welcome, and with a great downtown location and rates starting at $50 ($250/week) they do attract many straight guests traveling on a budget. The friendly staff know everything there is to know about the scene, while the lounge is a great place to meet people. All rooms are European style with shared bath and no air-conditioning.

The best values are at the **Best Western Downtown,** 405 S. 8th St., 612/370-1400 or 800/372-3131; the **Holiday Inn Express,** 225 S. 11th St., 612/341-3300 or 800/870-0114; and **Quality Inn,** 41 N. 10th St., 612/339-9311 or 800/423-4100, which, with few business customers, keep a steady price throughout the week. All are smaller, low-rise properties with pool, whirlpool, and exercise equipment—the Best Western also has a sauna—featuring sub $100 rates. None are connected to the skyway, but access is less than a block away from each if you need it.

The much fancier **Radisson Plaza,** 35 S. 7th St., 612/339-4900 or 800/333-3333, has a great location, top-notch service, a sauna, whirlpool, and fitness center. On weekends it's a great bargain at $99; rates start at $199 during the week.

A good choice for families is the **Courtyard,** 225 3rd Ave. S., 612/375-1700 or 800/321-2211, part of the beautiful Milwaukee Road Depot redevelopment, which comes with an indoor water park, game room, fitness center, and an adjoining skating rink. Rates for standard rooms can be as little as $94 ($139 weekday). They also offer two-dozen unique luxury suites in the original depot building.

South: Budget travelers might want to consider the very basic **Snelling Motel,** 5346 Minnehaha Ave., 612/721-4841, which has rooms from $50 a night, though you can do better for not much more at some of the city's B&Bs.

Hotels and Motels $100–150

Downtown: The aptly named **Grand Hotel Minneapolis,** 615 2nd Ave. S., 612/339-3655 or 866/843-4726, filling a renovated 1912 building, is the city's most elegant hotel and the place you are most likely to run into celebrities. The lobby and rooms have copious marble, granite, and decorative woodwork, plus all guests get free use of an adjoining fitness club. Rooms start at $149 on the weekends and are at least $100 more during the week.

The **Embassy Suites,** 425 S. 7th St., 612/333-3111 or 800/362-2779, has an unexpected art deco theme extending from the black tile floor in the tropical garden atrium right down to the padded headboards. Their two-room suites, all fitted with a microwave, refrigerator, and minibar, are a good deal at $109 ($169 weekday). Guest facilities include a small pool, fitness center, sauna, steam room, and a pair of whirlpools. A major renovation is planned, but hopefully none of the Miami Beach look will be lost.

The classy **Marquette Hotel,** 710 Marquette Ave., 612/333-4545 or 800/328-4782, is part of the massive IDS Center. The rooms ($109 weekends, $199 weekdays) are modern, large, and come with plenty of little extras, plus there is a sauna and exercise room. Basil's, the hotel's high-priced restaurant, is where Mary Tyler Moore lunched in the opening credits of her TV show, and her table is still frequently requested.

A wonderful eighth-floor, outdoor patio sets the **Northstar Crowne Plaza,** 618 2nd Ave. S., 612/338-2288 or 800/556-7827, apart from its peers. It also features a fitness center and excellent customer service. Rooms start at $109 ($152 weekdays).

The **Hyatt Regency,** 1300 Nicollet Ave., 612/370-1234 or 800/223-1234, is one of the city's largest and busiest hotels. All rooms, usually priced from $125 ($224 weekdays), got a makeover in 2002 and guests can use their small pool and modest exercise equipment or get discounted day passes for the on-site health club.

The **Nicollet Island Inn,** 95 Merriam St., 612/331-3035 or 800/331-6528, has the most character of any Twin Cities hotel. The solid 1893 limestone building in the center of the Mississippi River has been beautifully renovated, but maintains many original features. The 24 individually-decorated rooms start at $140 throughout the week.

University: The misleadingly named **Radisson Metrodome,** 615 Washington Ave. SE, 612/379-8888 or 800/333-3333, sits smack in the heart of campus (but not very close to the Metrodome) and is as large and fancy as most of the downtown hotels in this category. There is a small on-site fitness center, and guests can also get a free pass to the adjacent University Recreation Center. A free shuttle will take you downtown. Rooms start at $104 weekends and $149 weekdays.

Over on the West Bank the **Holiday Inn,** 1500 Washington Ave. S., 612/333-4646 or 800/448-3663, has large rooms with great views from $119 all week long. Overlooking downtown from the 14th floor is a small pool, whirlpool, sauna, and fitness center.

Hotels and Motels $150–250

The city's newest hotel towers above Block E. **Le Méridien,** 601 1st Ave. N., 612/677-1100 or 800/543 4300, a luxury chain with a high-tech/minimalist theme they've dubbed "Art + Tech." Rooms are $189 ($229 weekdays) and feature edge-lit handcrafted etched glass headboards, a wall-mounted 42-inch plasma screen television, plus all the little things you'd expect for that price. There is also a small fitness center, and the hotel has an arrangement for guest use of the large Northwest Athletic Club across the street.

B&Bs

The **Wales House,** 1115 5th St. S., 612/331-3931, is a pleasant European-style guesthouse right on the edge of the U of M campus. Mingle with the other interesting guests—90 percent are here on university business and about half are from overseas—in either the casual TV lounge, four-season porch, in front of the gas fireplace in the semiformal living room, or over the mostly organic continental breakfast. The 10 guestrooms are simple, but a good value at $55 with shared bath and $65 with private bath.

A more typical B&B is **Evelo's,** 2301 Bryant Ave. S., 612/374-9656, a simple but lovely 1897 Victorian home with a largely intact interior and many period furnishings. The three simple and homey guestrooms share 1.5 baths and cost $70. The morning meal is a small, all-vegetarian affair. Similar in style and location, but just blocks from Lake of the Isles, is **Nan's,** 2304 Fremont Ave. S., 612/377-5118. The bright 1895 Victorian isn't fancy, but still has some lovely stained glass and other original features. The three guestrooms, priced $65–70, share a bath. A full breakfast is served each morning.

Fancier is the 1896 **LeBlanc House,** 302 University Ave. NE, 612/379-2570, across the river. The two guestrooms have private baths with one

attached and the other across the hall; they cost $110 and $100 respectively. The continental breakfast has a Swedish touch.

The castlelike **1900 LaSalle Guesthouse,** 1900 LaSalle Ave., 612/874-1900, part of the Van Dusen event center, focuses mostly on business travelers, but considering that the restored 1892 mansion has three of the most luxurious rooms ($149 each) in the city, it's worth consideration by travelers, too. The rest of the neighborhood can't live up to the grandeur of the mansion, but it's convenient to downtown.

Hostels

Minneapolis has a pair of very distinct independent hostels. Most convenient is the **Minneapolis International Hostel,** 2400 Stevens Ave. S., 612/522-5000, info@minneapolishostel.com, which sits in a renovated mansion right across the street from the Minneapolis Institute of Arts. Despite having 49 beds—spaced out between nine two-, four-, six-, eight-, and 20-bed rooms—the patio, lounge with fireplace, and colorful bedding make it surprisingly homey. There's also a game room, movie room, Internet access, kitchen, laundry, secure storage, free parking, and no curfew. Rates are $20 for a bed and $40 for a private room, and you must show an out-of-town ID.

For a truly homey experience, join the Kaszynski family at **Kaz's Home Hostel,** 612/822-8286, in south Minneapolis. After retiring, they opened up one room in their home and charge just $10 per person per night. There's an 11 P.M. curfew, and the house is closed during the day. They'll give you the address when you make a reservation; two bus lines run direct to downtown.

FOOD

African

Red Sea, 320 Cedar Ave. S., 612/333-1644, is a good place for a first sampling of East African cuisine. Eating the Ethiopian dishes off communal platters with the *biddena* (a spongy flatbread made with *teff*) makes for a fun dining experience. Entrées run $5–14, but the sample platters, from $10, are the way to go. Open daily for breakfast, lunch, and dinner.

Simple **Safari,** 1424 Nicollet Ave., 612/872-4604, has a small menu of authentic Somali dishes rounded out by a few Middle Eastern standards like gyros. Most of the heaping platters, including the spaghetti with goat meat, cost about $8. Open daily for lunch and dinner.

American

Minneapolis's oldest restaurant, **Peter's Grill,** 114 S. 8th St., 612/333-1981, opened in 1914 and relocated in 1985, but the art deco setting is straight out of the 1940s. The menu is as classic as the decor and runs from $4 sandwiches to $15 steaks. Open weekdays for breakfast, lunch, and dinner and Sat. for breakfast and lunch.

Smaller and simpler, but equally timeless, is the lunch counter at **Hamlin's Coffee Shop,** 512 Nicollet Mall, 612/333-3876, which goes back to at least 1926, and they did their best to keep the original look when forced to remodel in the 1980s—the photos by the entrance show they did quite well. Their classic roster of burgers and sandwiches go for about $5, and the malts are really good. Open weekdays for breakfast and lunch.

Key's, 1007 Nicollet Mall, 612/339-6399, is a Twin Cities home-cookin' favorite with some big city touches on the menu, like grilled salmon and a jerk chicken sandwich. The portions are enormous, the food is terrific, and it's all in the $5–10 range. Their fantastic breakfasts are served all day. Open daily for breakfast and lunch, and Monday–Saturday for dinner.

The **Uptown Bar & Café,** 3018 Hennepin Ave. S., 612/823-4719, a longtime neighborhood gathering spot, has a large menu ranging from classics like a hot roast turkey sandwich and liver and onions to a veggie taco and gyro hash platter. Portions are huge and meals average just $6. Open daily for breakfast, lunch, and dinner, and they have live rock bands many nights.

Bakeries

Words can not adequately describe the glory that comes out of the oven at **Panadería Marissa,** 2750 Nicollet Ave., 612/871-4519, and everything is so cheap that you can afford to sample lots of new things. The *churros* are as good as

any south of the border. Open daily early to late. I guarantee you won't soon forget the taste of the cinnamon buns at **Isles Bun & Coffee Co.,** 1424 W. 28th St., 612/870-4466. Open daily for lunch and dinner. Several branches of **Dunn Bros. Coffee** sell the sweet **Taste of Scandinavia** bakery creations, including the one downtown at 925 Nicollet Mall, 612/332-7545. Open daily for breakfast and lunch.

Barbecue

Famous Dave's Barbeque, 3001 Hennepin Ave. S. (in Calhoun Square), 612/822-9900, is a local institution but also a national chain. The award-winning St. Louis-style ribs are the specialty of the house, but they splash the sauce on chicken, beef brisket, burgers, and catfish. Most items are in the $7–12 range, but they have some great lunch specials. Open daily for lunch and dinner. They have live blues nightly.

Market Bar-B-Que, 1414 Nicollet Ave., 612/872-1111, has been going strong since 1946. Sandwiches are about $7, while plates of beef, chicken, or pork (with the sauce served on the side) are as little as $10. Open daily for lunch and dinner.

Breakfast and Brunch

Eating at **Al's Breakfast,** 413 14th Ave. SE, 612/331-9991, a 14-seat closet in Dinkytown, is a legendary Minneapolis experience. You'll have to decide if it's worth the wait, though anyone who's ordered a short stack or one of the creative omelets will tell you that it is. Open daily for breakfast and lunch.

The menu at **Hell's Kitchen,** 89 S. 10th St., 612/332-4700, has no peers. Feast on eggs Benedict with bison instead of bacon, lemon-ricotta hotcakes, walleye hash, and wild rice porridge. They are most proud of their crab cakes, served with a poached egg. Most everything is over $10, but you get what you pay for. Open daily for breakfast and lunch.

The **Nicollet Island Inn,** 612/331-3035, may not have the biggest Sunday brunch buffet in town, but their legendary spread is considered by most to be the best. For $26 they will pamper you with made to order omelets, smoked salmon, imported cheese trays, prime rib, champagne, and much more. Also on Sundays you can brunch with live jazz and gospel respectively at **The Times Bar & Café,** 201 Hennepin Ave. E., 612/617-8098; and **Jazzmine's,** 123 3rd St. N., 612/630-5299.

Other good morning choices include **Hamlin's Coffee Shop, Key's, Red Sea, Sidney's,** and **Uptown Bar & Café**—each detailed elsewhere in this section.

British

Step into **Brit's,** 1110 Nicollet Mall, 612/332-3908, and you've entered a classic pub atmosphere, though during the summer the best seats are on the upstairs patio surrounding the bowling green ($5 per person per hour). The "Bill of Fayre" hits the best and worst of British pub grub from fish and chips and tandoori chicken to scotch eggs (most entrées average $8), and they'll pull you a pint of any of a dozen English ales and lagers. Open daily for lunch and dinner.

Burgers

If you don't mind paying $10 for a burger, stop in at **Joe's Garage,** 1610 Harmon Pl., 612/904-1163, and grab a table on the Basilica-facing rooftop patio. The bevy of burgers aren't all from cows—there's also turkey, lamb, spicy Asian pork, and yellow-fin tuna—and toppings like gorgonzola and caramelized onions are appropriate for the trendy crowd that gathers here. Other menu choices include portobello fettuccine and red Thai curry risotto, plus there is a fun drinks list. They add $6 deli sandwiches during lunch. Open daily for lunch and dinner.

Annie's Parlour, 313 14th Ave. SE, 612/379-0744, does good burgers and 15 flavors of malts for $4. The second floor Dinkytown institution has views of downtown and an outdoor deck. Open daily for lunch and dinner.

Caribbean

In business since the early 1980s, **Harry Singh's,** 3008 Hennepin Ave. S., 612/729-6181, serves up a now legendary *roti-dhalpourie*—a delectable toasted flatbread overflowing with curried vegetables or meat for $7. Do take a chance ordering

off the creative (nonalcoholic) drinks list, but don't dare try the "hot-hot" sauce unless you are a chili expert. Open Tues.–Sat. for lunch and daily for dinner.

Chinese

Seafood is the specialty at **Shuang Cheng,** 1320 4th St. SE, 612/378-0208, and regulars recommend ordering off the daily specials board, but you won't go wrong with whatever you choose from their huge Szechuan and Cantonese menu. Entrées range $5–20. Open Mon.–Sat. for lunch and dinner and just dinner on Sunday.

Evergreen, 2424 Nicollet Ave., 612/871-6801, specializes in Taiwanese cuisine and has a little of everything from Mandarin beef to herb soup, but what sets it apart are the surprisingly lifelike mock meats—beef, shrimp, and squid to name a few. Entrées average $8. Open daily for lunch and dinner.

Though the pricey menu items average $12 at **Ping's,** 1401 Nicollet Ave., 612/874-9404, they also have a popular $7 weekday lunch buffet. Open daily for lunch and dinner.

Coffee and Tea Houses

All places listed here are open late every day of the week, like a coffee house should be. **Moose & Sadie's,** 212 3rd Ave. N., 612/371-0464, is a fairly large but subdued downtown space that has maintained as much of the original warehouse architecture as possible. A glass wall keeps the smokers' haze in check.

You are never more than a few blocks away from a good cup o' joe on Hennepin and Lyndale Avenues. **Uncommon Grounds,** 2809 Hennepin Ave. S., 612/872-4811, is as classy a coffee house as you'll ever take a seat in, while a more colorful crowd gathers at **Muddy Waters,** 2401 Lyndale Ave. S., 612/872-2232. Though large, **Vera's,** 2903 Lyndale Ave. S., 612/822-3871, remains cozy and has a completely separate smoking section and also a great outdoor garden and good food.

Trendy **Spyhouse,** 2451 Nicollet Ave., 612/871-3177, is filled morning to night with students from the nearby Minneapolis College of Art and Design.

Across the river, the student-filled **Purple Onion,** 326 14th Ave. SE, 612/378-7763, in Dinkytown has little decoration, but tons of character.

Quality matters immensely at pint-sized **Himalayan Chai,** 713 W. Franklin Ave., 612/871-5152, where friendly owner Swadesh Shrestha gets all his teas from his family's farming cooperative in Nepal.

Cuban

The swank **Café Havana,** 119 Washington Ave. N., 612/338-8484, is like the Old Havana ride at a Cuban theme park. The glamorous, cigar-smoking patrons probably couldn't care whether the food was from Cuba or Cambodia and don't mind shelling out an average of nearly $20 per plate. Open Tues.–Sat. for dinner; reservations are a good idea.

Deli

The lines extending down the hall tell you how good the New York-style **Brothers Deli,** 50 S. 6th St. (skyway level), 612/341-8007, is. Corned beef and pastrami (shipped in from the Bronx) sandwiches are just $5. Open weekdays for lunch.

Eastern European

As your eyes adjust to the dim lights, **Nye's Polonaise,** 112 Hennepin Ave. E., 612/379-2021, fades into view like a dream, but the sparkly red and gold vinyl, wood paneling, and gigantic martinis are real. There have only been superficial changes since Nye's opened in 1949, and much of the clientele has regularly filled the booths all these many years. It's principally a supper club menu of steak and seafood, with added Polish specialties like pierogis and pork hocks. Platters run $7–50 with most of it under $20. A lounge singer holds court in the restaurant every night, and you can dance off the calories in the adjacent polka bar. Open daily for dinner and Mon.–Sat. for lunch.

One block over is the equally venerable **Kramarczuk Sausage Company,** 215 Hennepin Ave. E., 612/379-3018, where for about six bucks you can get a grilled Ukrainian sausage, Hungarian goulash, or pastrami sandwich. A butcher shop adjoins the cafeteria so you can take their Old World recipe sausages, bakery, and cheese home with you. Open Mon.–Sat. for breakfast, lunch, and dinner; Sat. is accordion night.

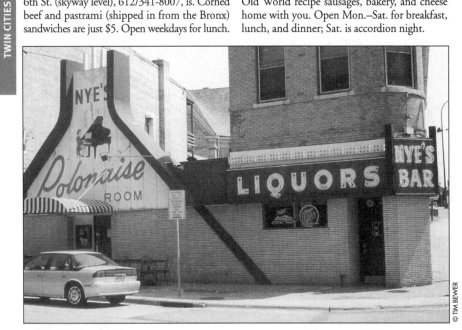

© TIM BEWER

a Minneapolis original

Eclectic

While the wall of candles and pint-sized margaritas are two reasons why **Chino Latino,** 2916 Hennepin Ave. S., 612/824-7878, is the trendiest dining spot in the Cities, it doesn't get by on attitude alone. Their open kitchen takes diners on a wonderful culinary tour of the vaguely equatorial "Hot Zone" as they have dubbed it. There's Philippine *paella,* Jamaican jerked chicken, Brazilian surf and turf, *chipotle* salmon sushi, Indonesian *satay,* and a Polynesian *pupu* platter, just to name a few—they even have *cuy* (guinea pig) if you give 48 hours notice. Most dishes are enormous and meant to be shared, and half the fun of eating here is sampling as much as your group can. Their drinks list is just as much fun as the food menu. It's possible to get out of here for around $10 per person, but most people shell out at least three times that. Open daily for lunch and dinner; weekend reservations are a near necessity.

Had Salvador Dali been an interior designer, he might have dreamt up the wonderful madness at the **Loring Pasta Bar,** 327 14th Ave. SE, 612/378-4849. The name actually belies the variety coming out of the open kitchen which, besides saffron chicken linguini and portobello mushroom ravioli, has non-pasta choices like spinach and walnut pesto pizza, Szechuan salmon, and a 20-oz. steak. Neither the food nor service is spectacular; still they are good enough to draw even their critics back again. Piano and guitar players set the mood during lunch and dinner, and after nine it evolves into a nightclub with live bands most nights. Prices are a reasonable (but very un-Dinkytown-like) $8–20. Open Mon.–Sat. for lunch and daily for dinner.

The **MPLS. Café,** 1110 Hennepin Ave. S., 612/672-9100, has a mostly Mediterranean menu, but besides the Spanish tapas and *paella,* wood-fired pizzas, and Moroccan lamb sandwich, other international choices, like nachos and jerk chicken, work their way into the seasonal menus. Prices run $8–28 and the wine list is excellent. Live French, flamenco, jazz, and salsa bands make for a fun evening. This is the perfect after (or before) theater destination. Open weekdays for lunch and daily for dinner.

Marshall Field's Marketplace, 612/375-2200, on the Nicollet Mall between 7th and 8th Sts., is a grand food court on the lower level where the choices range from sushi to strawberry smoothies to stuffed cabbage to spinach tortellini. They are open weekdays for lunch and dinner, and you can get a lot of food for under $5.

If you are looking for cheap fast food downtown, head to the skyway where small shops and food courts abound; most are only open weekdays for lunch.

Fine Dining

If you want presentation and pretension to top off your dining experience, then Minneapolis has no shortage of choices that will wow you. Reservations, of course, are strongly recommended at all of them.

The unbelievable Zig-Zag Moderne art deco decor, which makes you feel as if you are dining in a 1930s movie, would be reason enough to choose **Goodfellow's,** 40 S. 7th St., 612/332-4800, but it's the food, service, and 800-bottle wine list that has garnered it just about every national culinary honor available. As many ingredients as possible are bought right from the source, locally when possible, and the creative minds in the kitchen seem to know no bounds, as "rice paper wrapped salmon with satsuma orange, baby bok choy, and citrus aioli will attest," though it's not all so chi-chi. As for price . . . let's just say that appetizers on the dinner menu start at $13, though you can also get a lunch entrée for around this price. Open weekdays for lunch and Mon.–Sat. for dinner.

Named for owner Vincent Francoual, one of the city's most creative and respected chefs, **Vincent,** 1100 Nicollet Mall, 612/630-1189, has been wowing Minneapolis since opening its doors in 2001. Vincent is always pushing the envelope with creations like "rice flakes crusted Alaskan halibut with pineapple mango Moroccan couscous." The wine list doesn't disappoint either. At $20 a plate average it's not cheap, but for what you are getting it's remarkably affordable and the lunch menu is about half this. A chef's table is available for $67 per person. Open weekdays for lunch and Mon.–Sat. for dinner.

The chef-owners at **Auriga,** 1930 Hennepin

Ave. S., 612/871-0777, focus their efforts on using locally grown ingredients when creating their international menu. Seasonal choices might run from pumpkin ravioli to smoked salmon, and most entrées are priced in the $10–20 range. This casual yet romantic spot has rightly won its fair share of local awards and has a fantastic wine list. Open daily for dinner.

French

The view inside **Sophia**, 65 Main St. SE, 612/379-1111, is as lovely as the skyline scenery outside. The menu runs from an $8 goat cheese gratin appetizer to a $26 filet mignon, and they don't even stock a bottle of wine under $20. Open weekdays for lunch and daily for dinner. Sophia also serves up live jazz every night except Sunday.

German

The **Black Forest Inn**, 1 E. 26th St., 612/872-0812, is loved as much for its ivy-draped beer garden as for its food—probably more—but that's not to dismiss the *schnitzels, schweinebraten,* or any of the other hearty traditional offerings that range $5–17. Open daily for lunch and dinner.

With costumed waitresses and roaming accordion players, **Gasthof Zur Gemüutlichkeit**, 2300 University Ave. NE, 612/781-3860, is like a Bavarian theme park, though they haven't neglected the food and beer. Sampling the *schnitzel* and sharing a Das Boot of beer makes for a fun dining experience. Entrées average $10. Open Tues.–Sun. for dinner.

Greek

Fans of *mousaka, tigania,* and *baklava* are in for a real treat in Minneapolis, where three standbys with equally comprehensive menus race neck and neck in annual awards. Dinner platters (including soup or salad) average $11 at the Cypriot-owned **Christos** (2632 Nicollet Ave., 612/871-2111, open daily for lunch and dinner), one of Eat Street's most popular restaurants. The similarly priced **It's Greek to Me**, 626 W. Lake St., 612/825-9922, (open Tues.–Sun. for lunch and dinner) has the most varied menu and loveliest decor, plus an outdoor patio.

The trendy **Gardens of Salonica**, 19 5th St. NE, 612/378-0611, (open Mon.–Sat. for lunch and dinner) has the smallest menu, but is priced about $2 less per plate.

Ice Cream

Though they made their name in St. Paul, **Izzy's Ice Cream**, 825 Nicollet Mall, 612/338-0022, has an outlet hidden away inside the lovely Medical Arts Building. Open weekdays for breakfast and lunch. **Sebastian Joe's Ice Cream Café**, 1007 W. Franklin Ave., 612/870-0065, makes 20 flavors daily, plus serves a full range of bakery and caffeinated drinks. Open daily for breakfast, lunch, and dinner. Beware the free samples at **Caruso's Gelato**, 3001 Hennepin Ave. S. (in Calhoun Square), 612/822-2629—they may convince you their small cones are indeed worth $3.50. Open daily for lunch and dinner.

Indian

Little **Passage to India**, 1401 W. Lake St., 612/827-7518, does everything right: classy decor, attentive service, and excellent food. The menu covers the whole of the country, and there are even half a dozen Indonesian dishes. While entrées are $10 and up, everything is half price Monday–Thursday until 4:30 P.M., and the daily lunch buffet is a steal at $6. Open daily for lunch and dinner.

Irish

What sets **The Local**, 931 Nicollet Mall, 612/904-1000, apart are the trio of almost museumlike Victorian pub decors. The menu runs from pub pies to pork chops and has some great sandwiches, but in the evening they serve a lot more glasses of whiskey and pints of Guinness than meals. Entrées, averaging about $10, are a bit on the pricey side, though the weekend brunch menu is a good value. Open daily for lunch and dinner.

Other extensive and similarly priced Irish menus are available at **Keegan's**, 16 University Ave. N., 612/252-0880; **Kieran's**, 330 2nd Ave. S., 612/339-4499; and **O'Donovan's**, 700 1st Ave. N., 612/317-8896. All three are Irish-owned and have more genuine pub atmospheres—Keegan's is an official Guinness Irish Pub Concept property.

Italian

Just like the people who live around it, **Figlio,** 3001 Hennepin Ave. S. (in Calhoun Square), 612/822-1688, is both classy and hip. Though some foodies object, most agree the food here is excellent. Pastas and wood-fired pizzas are all about $10, while some of the other items on the menu, like seafood jambalaya and New York strip steak, can cost much more. Now if only they would just turn down that damn music. Open daily for lunch and very late for dinner.

Those who don't like Figlio, either for the food or the atmosphere, should head down the street to **Giorgio's,** 1601 W. Lake St., 612/822-7071. The changing, one-page menu of delectable pastas range from $10 to $15. The recipes are Tuscan-inspired, but draw from the whole of Italy with some creative touches. If the menu at the Lake St. locale doesn't appeal to you, then walk down the street and try the even more cramped original at 2451 Hennepin Ave. S., 612/374-5131. Open daily for dinner and Tues.–Sun. for lunch. Reservations are recommended.

D'Amico Cucina, 100 N. 6th St., 612/338-2401, is frequently cited by local and national reviewers as the best restaurant in Minnesota. As long as you have spare cash to throw around (the tasting menu is $75), the food, 500-plus bottle wine list, service, and ambience are going to impress you. Open Mon.–Sat. for dinner. Reservations recommended.

The same people who wow the elite at D'Amico Cucina please the masses at **D'Amico & Sons,** probably the Twin Cities' most popular Italian restaurant, if only because there are so many of them, six in Minneapolis alone. The informal deli-cafés turn out good pastas and even better wood-fired pizzas for about $8. They have locations at 555 Nicollet Mall (in Gaviidae Common), 612/342-2700 (open daily for lunch); 2210 Hennepin Ave. S., 612/374-9374 (open daily lunch and dinner); and the Minneapolis Institute of Arts. Kids eat free on Sundays after 2 P.M.

Neither the family recipes, the decor of the main dining room, or even the owner has changed since the **Café Di Napoli,** 816 Hennepin Ave., 612/333-9019, opened here in 1938. Pizzas and pastas average $9, and the trip back in time makes it definitely worth a visit. Plus, it's a kid favorite. Open Mon–Sat. for lunch and dinner.

The festive and fast growing **Buca di Beppo,** 1204 Harmon Pl., 612/288-0138, chain got its start in this kitsch-filled basement space on the edge of downtown. Their basic and tasty southern Italian "immigrant cooking" is served in heaping platters ($10–20) intended to share, so the more the merrier. Individual portions are available. Open daily for dinner and weekends for lunch.

Japanese

It often surprises visitors just how many good sushi bars there are here. The longtime leader is quiet and classy **Origami,** 30 N. 1st St., 612/333-8430. It is open weekdays for lunch and daily for dinner. Another sophisticated, almost Zenlike (except in the karaoke room) fresh fish outlet is **Kikugawa,** 43 Main St. SE, 612/378-3006, across the river at St. Anthony Main, which has the largest non-sushi menu. Open daily for lunch and dinner. For a hip, high-energy night out try **Nami,** 251 1st Ave. N., 612/333-1999 (open weekdays for lunch and daily for dinner); **Koyi Sushi,** 122 N. 4th St., 612/375-9811 (open weekdays for lunch and daily for dinner); **Fuji-Ya,** 600 W. Lake St., 612/871-4055, (open daily for dinner); and **Sushi Tango,** 3001 Hennepin Ave. S. (in Calhoun Square), 612/822-7787, (open Thurs.–Sun. for lunch and daily for dinner). All six are reasonably priced with few selections over $5.

Ichiban Japanese Steak House, 1333 Nicollet Ave., 612/339-0540, and its tree-filled dining room is the best known spot for knife-flashing *teppanyaki,* but the boat-delivery sushi bar is popular, too. It is not easy to get out for under $50. Open daily for dinner.

Korean

Minneapolis's only Korean restaurant is **Mai's Korea House,** 414 1/2 Cedar Ave. S., 612/339-9385, a simple family-run place on the West Bank with authentic Korean entrées and Vietnamese soup for about $5. Open Mon.–Sat. for lunch and dinner.

Mexican

There are a lot of really good Mexican restaurants in Minneapolis, but the most lauded is **Taco Morelos**, 14 W. 26th St., 612/870-0053, where everything is made fresh. The menu has plenty of seafood options, and their breakfast dishes, served all day, are highly recommended. Entrées range $6–13, though a taco (either stuffed with cow's brain or more traditional ingredients) is just $2. Open daily for lunch and dinner. There are many more authentic Mexican joints on this part of Eat Street, while Lake St. east of the freeway is another happy hunting ground.

El Burrito, 618 2nd Ave. S. (in the Northstar Center, behind the Crown Plaza Hotel, 612/339-8620, wraps massive $5 take-away burritos for the downtown office crowd. Open weekdays for lunch.

Middle Eastern

Jerusalem's, 1518 Nicollet Ave., 612/871-8883, is a popular little spot topped by a big cupola at the head of Eat Street. The menu isn't huge, but it has a few less common choices, such as kibby and lemon soup. Most entrées are around $10. Open daily for lunch and dinner, and belly dancers shake the stage on weekends.

Farther down the street is the much more casual, but similarly scrumptious, **Sinbad's Café & Market**, 2528 Nicollet Ave., 612/871-6505. Half grocery and half restaurant, there are deli sandwiches from $3 plus a lunch buffet and entrées off the menu for $7. There is occasionally live Arabic music. Open Tues.–Sun. for lunch and dinner.

Natural Foods

The **Café Brenda**, 300 1st Ave. N., 612/342-9230, boldly proclaims itself as a "Natural Restaurant Extraordinaire," and this beloved gem delivers. Even though fish, chicken, and turkey comprise half the menu, choices like Southwestern mock duck tacos and wild mushroom and pistachio make Brenda's many a vegetarian's favorite restaurant. Ingredients are often organic and many dishes, including some fantastic desserts, are vegan. Entrées run $8–15. Open weekdays for lunch and Mon.–Sat. for dinner. Reservations recommended.

The wonderfully creative **Sapor**, 428 Washington Ave. N., 612/375-1971, out on the edge of the warehouse district, isn't quite as virtuous as Brenda, but they also use mostly organic ingredients in their whimsical world cuisine. You'll find entrées like miso-baked salmon, fortina cheese and polenta skewers, and butternut squash croquettes with green-chile pepita sauce. The wine and beer lists are excellent, and the service impeccable. Expect to pay about $20 for an entrée at dinner or half that at lunch. Open weekdays for lunch and Mon.–Sat. for dinner.

Simpler and more affordable than the others is **Sidney's**, 2120 Hennepin Ave. S., 612/870-7000. Everything, which is primarily pizza and pasta, is prepared from scratch, and many ingredients are organic. The menu contains many creative dishes, like Mardi Gras fettuccini (with a Cajun tomato sauce) and peanut butter and jelly pizza, all for about $10. They are open daily for breakfast, lunch, and dinner.

Pizza

Dulono's, 607 W. Lake St., 612/827-1726, doesn't do anything fancy; they just serve up some of the Twin Cities' best thin-crust pizza. A 16-inch one-item pie is $14. Live bluegrass bands take the stage on weekends. Open daily for lunch and dinner (until 3 A.M.).

Pizza Lucé, 119 N. 4th St., 612/333-7359, and 3200 Lyndale Ave. S., 612/827-5978, is not your average pizzeria. Roasted eggplant, barbecue chicken, and goat cheese are some of the more unusual of their fifty-plus toppings, and they even offer a vegan cheese alternative. Open daily for lunch and dinner (closing no earlier than 1 A.M.).

You can get New York-style thin crust by the slice at countless places along the skyway downtown plus elsewhere in town at **A Slice of New York**, 2407 Nicollet Ave., 612/871-4334; and **Rotisseria**, 1409 W. Lake St., 612/822-7400.

Seafood

All other Twin Cities seafood restaurants pale in comparison to **Oceanaire Seafood Room**, 1300 Nicollet Ave., (in the Hyatt), 612/333-2277. The main ingredients are flown in from both coasts and beyond, though the downside is that you need really deep pockets to enjoy it. Almost all entrées are over $20 and wines peak at $460 a bottle. Open daily for dinner. Reservations are required for the dining room, though walk-ins can still dine at the oyster bar.

A little less expensive than The Oceanaire is **McCormick & Schmick's,** 800 Nicollet Mall, 612/338-3300. The menu, changing twice daily, also features steak, and it all ranges from $8 to $27. It has a lovely interior full of decorative wood and glasswork and some private, velvet-draped booths, as well as one of the city's best happy hours. Open weekdays for lunch and daily for dinner.

Great places for seafood with a twist include **Shuang Cheng** and **Machu Pichu** listed in the Chinese and South American sections.

South American

Machu Pichu, 2940 Lyndale Ave. S., 612/822-2125, defines itself with seafood such as a shrimp *ceviche* and steamed halibut, though the *empanadas* also come highly recommended. The Peruvian dishes start at $11 and run up to $25. Open Tues.–Sat. for dinner, with live music from across the continent on weekends.

Rotisseria, 1409 W. Lake St., 612/822-7400, does Peruvian-style rotisserie chicken plus New York-style pizzas. Open daily for lunch and dinner.

There's real Ecuadorian flavor, right down to the imported Guitig and Inca Cola, on the north side of town at the simple **Sabor Latino,** 2505 Central Ave. NE, 612/789-1754. Popular dishes like *ceviche de concha* (clam marinated in lemon juice) and *seco de chivo* (goat stew) all average $8. Open daily for lunch and dinner.

Spanish

The little **La Bodega Tapas Bar,** 3005 Lyndale Ave. S., 612/823-2661, is a bright and fun space with live flamenco music on weekends. The 51 finger foods range $4–8. Open daily for lunch and dinner.

Steak Houses

Minneapolis's steak original is **Murray's,** 26 S. 6th St., 612/339-0909, "home of the silver butter-knife steak." This landmark opened in 1946, and the dining room looks like they are still on the same calendar. The menu isn't extensive, but has much more than just beef, including a salmonburger, broiled walleye, and chicken pot pie. The lunch menu runs $8–18 and dinner starts at $20 and goes up fast. Open daily for dinner and weekdays for lunch. Reservations recommended.

You'll get the full four-star treatment at nationally-renowned **Manny's Steakhouse,** 1300 Nicollet Ave. (in the Hyatt), 612/339-9900. The steaks, as good as any in the world, are $29 and up, way up. A few items such as lemon pepper chicken and pork chops come in under $20, but why come here if it's not for beef? Open daily for lunch and dinner. Reservations are highly recommended.

Thai

Sawatdee isn't the only Thai restaurant in town, but it sometimes seems that way—and things wouldn't be so bad if it was. The food is always fresh and flavorful (the far north meets the Far East with their walleye in ginger sauce), and most entrées fall into the $9–12 range. They have four Minneapolis locations: 1005 Nicollet Ave., 612/341-2838; 2650 Hennepin Ave. S., 612/377-4418; 118 N. 4th St., 612/373-0840; and 607 Washington Ave. S., 612/338-6451, all open daily for lunch and dinner except the Nicollet Ave. location, which is closed Sundays. The Hennepin and Washington Ave. locations have lunch buffets.

The swank **Chiang Mai Thai,** 3001 Hennepin Ave. S. (hidden away behind Calhoun Square), 612/827-1606, gets quite noisy, but everything on the menu is truly sublime, and the plates are always piled high. It's only a bit more expensive than Sawatdee. Open daily for lunch and dinner, and weekend reservations are a good idea.

Vegetarian

Whether you want something truly unique or just want your dollars to support supreme environmental values, **Ecopolitan,** 2409 Lyndale Ave. S., 612/874-7336, is worth a try. As one of the nation's first raw-foods restaurants, every ingredient is organic and vegan and, despite the limited rules of engagement, the menu is very creative: pesto pizza, burritos, and marinara sauce with shredded zucchini fettuccini, plus salads and juices, of course. Prices are reasonable, too, with nothing over $10. They also have an oxygen bar and a store selling environmentally-friendly products. Open daily for lunch and dinner.

Uptight city officials consider the **Hard Times Café,** 1821 Riverside Ave., 612/341-9261, a blight on the neighborhood, while many of its Bohemian fans—students, professors, artists, and the occasional derelict—consider it a second home. Ironically the smokiest restaurant in town has one of the healthiest menus—burritos, veggie wraps, and tempeh reubens cost about $5. They are open daily for breakfast, lunch, and dinner and stay open until 3 A.M. weekdays and 4 A.M. weekends.

A quick scan of the menu board at **The Wienery,** 414 Cedar Ave. S., 612/333-5798, might send a vegetarian right out the door. This little West Bank dive serves up top-quality bratwurst, polish sausage, and the like, *but* surprisingly tasty veggie versions of most wursts are also available. Either way, all options are heaped with toppings of your choice and cost about $3.

Open daily for breakfast and lunch and Mon.–Sat. for dinner.

Evergreen, Pizza Lucé, and the **Triple Rock Social Club,** each detailed above, are a vegan's dream come true, while vegetarians should also check out all of the places listed above with Natural Foods.

Vietnamese

Everything on the menu at **Quang,** 2719 Nicollet Ave., 612/870-4739, is fresh and delectable, making it the city's Vietnamese leader. Entrées average about $6. Open daily except Tuesday for lunch and dinner. **Pho Quan,** 1815 Nicollet Ave., (no phone), is a real dive serving real, and really tasty, Vietnamese soup and stir-fry. A $4 medium bowl is more than enough for a meal. Open daily for lunch and dinner.

SHOPPING

Minneapolis's shopping central is the **Nicollet Mall** downtown, and the best place to begin browsing is at 7th Street where you'll find a **Marshall Field's** and the **City Center, IDS Crystal Court,** and **Gaviidae Common** malls—the lat-

Lake of the Isles, one of nearly two dozen lakes in Minneapolis

© TIM BEWER

ter anchored by **Sak's Fifth Avenue** and **Neiman Marcus.** For Minnesota products—food, books, T-shirts and the like—head to **Love From Minnesota,** 612/333-2371, in the Crystal Court. Art lovers should budget some time to browse the galleries in the **Wyman Building,** 400 1st Ave. N., over in the Warehouse District. There are exclusive antique and interior design galleries scattered around the district.

The **Minneapolis Farmers' Market,** 312 East Lyndale Ave. N., is open daily 6 A.M.–1 P.M. from late April through Christmas. Between May and October an adjunct market hits the Nicollet Mall between 5th and 10th Streets 6 A.M.–6 P.M. on Thursday and 8 A.M.–3 P.M. on Saturday.

The **Uptown** area has many wonderful one-of-a-kind shops, though generic chain stores like the Gap have infested the corner of Hennepin Ave. and Lake St. **Calhoun Square,** a small indoor shopping center, has a pseudo street market with some interesting vendors. Hennepin is one of the state's best antiquing spots, while Lyndale Avenue also has some good antique outlets including **Theatre Antiques,** 2934 Lyndale Ave. S., 612/822-4884, a vintage superstore. Many of the city's cutting edge art galleries also line Lyndale. **Extreme Noise,** 407 W. Lake St., 612/824-0100, an all-volunteer, not-for-profit collective, is one of the best punk rock music stores anywhere.

Bookstores

The main **Barnes & Noble,** 612/371-4443, is downtown at 801 Nicollet Mall. The downtown **Borders,** 600 Hennepin Ave., 612/339-4859, is in the Block E complex, while a smaller location is in Uptown at Calhoun Square, 3001 Hennepin Ave. S., 612/825-0336. No independent can compete with the big boys' overall selection, though for some specific interests there are many other options. **Birchbark Books,** 2115 W. 21st St., 612/374-4023, is a small neighborhood bookstore with a good Native American section: not surprising since it is owned by novelist and poet Louise Erdrich. **Uncle Edgar's,** 612/824-9984, and **Uncle Hugo's,** 612/824-6347, share a building at 2864 Chicago Ave. and stock mystery and science fiction titles respectively. They have so many titles, new and used, that there isn't enough room on the shelves.

Once Upon a Crime, 604 W. 26th St., 612/870-3785, and **Dream Haven,** 912 W. Lake St., 612/823-6161, also with a mix of new and used titles in the same subjects, are smaller, but better located. The **Amazon Bookstore Cooperative,** 4432 Chicago Ave. S., 612/821-9630, (there is no connection to the Internet giant Amazon.com who just stole their trademark, though an amicable settlement was reached before the case reached the courts) is the oldest women's bookstore in the country. **Arise!,** 2441 Lyndale Ave. S., 612/871-7110, has a large stock of leftist literature.

Excellent used bookstores include **Magers & Quinn,** 3038 Hennepin Ave. S., 612/822-4611; **BookSmart,** 2914 Hennepin Ave. S., 612/823-5612; **Laurie's,** 921 Nicollet Mall, 612/338-1114; **Biermaier's,** 809 4th St. SE, 612/378-0129; **Book House,** 429 14th Ave. SE, 612/331-1430; **Cummings,** 417 14th Ave. SE, 612/331-1424; and **Lien's,** 507 Hennepin Ave. E., 612/362-0763. There is no better place to pick up a read for the road than the **Friends of the Minneapolis Public Library Bookshop,** 250 Marquette Ave., 612/630-6177, where paperbacks are $.50 and hardcovers are no more than $3.

Bibliophiles might also want to stop by the **Open Book,** 1011 Washington Ave. S., 612/215.2650, literary arts center to see if any interesting exhibitions or workshops are going on.

INFORMATION AND SERVICES
Tourist Information

The Greater Minneapolis Convention & Visitors Association, 612/348-7000 or 888/676-6757, www.minneapolis.org, runs the **Minneapolis Information and Visitors Center** downtown at the Convention Center. It is open weekdays 10 A.M.–7 P.M., Saturday 10 A.M.–6 P.M., and Sunday noon–5 P.M.

Post Office

The monstrous main post office, located along the river at 100 S. 1st St., 612/349-0359, is an art deco gem; buy a stamp just for a chance to see the 1,000-foot lobby, lined by the longest brass light fixture in the country. Lobby hours are weekdays 5:30 A.M.–11 P.M.

Internet Access

You can surf the Web downtown at **Woodson Coffee Co.,** 430 1st Ave. N. (next to D'Amico Cucina), 612/359-0169, and **Kinko's,** 80 S. 8th St. (in the IDS Center), 612/343-8000. Kinko's also has 24-hour branches in Uptown at 1430 W. Lake St., and on the U of M campus at 612 Washington Ave. SE. The following coffee houses—**Moose & Sadie's, Purple Onion,** and **Spyhouse**—each detailed above, have wireless access for customers.

GETTING AROUND

By Bus

General city bus information is detailed in the Twin Cities introductory section. A transit store and information center at 719 Marquette Ave. is open weekdays 7:30 A.M.–5:30 P.M. An all-day or three-day pass on the **RiverCity Trolley,** described above, can be a good way to get around, since it hits most places of interest.

By Train

The city's new light rail system, the **Hiawatha Line,** will connect downtown's Warehouse District to the Mall of America, stopping at Fort Snelling and the airport along the way. Service to Fort Snelling is scheduled to begin in April 2004, and the entire line should be open by the end that year.

Car Rentals

Major car rental companies with downtown locations include **Avis,** 829 3rd Ave. S., 612/332-6321 or 800/230-4898; **Budget,** 229 10th St. S., 612/332-5218 or 800/527-7000; **Enterprise,** 110 S. 10th St., 612/677-1319 or 800/736-8222; and **Thrifty,** 1313 Nicollet Mall (at the Millennium Hotel), 612/333-2050 or 800/847-4389.

You can travel in style with a Harley, Moskito Scooter, or exotic car from **Midwest Motorcycle,** 215 Washington Ave. N., 612/338-5345 or 888/237-5853.

Bike and Skate Rentals

Calhoun Cycle, 1622 W. Lake St., 612/827-8231, is ideally located right by Lake Calhoun and Lake of the Isles and also rents in-line skates. **Campus Bike,** 213 Oak St., 612/331-3442, is on the east side of the U of M campus.

St. Paul

Those who paid attention in school will remember that St. Paul (pop. 287,151), not Minneapolis, is the capital of Minnesota. Political supremacy aside, the "Last City of the East," plays second fiddle to its larger sibling for all but its most fiercely loyal residents. Yet, when it comes to interesting attractions, St. Paul doesn't lag very far behind Minneapolis at all, and the many structures from the city's past, most notably the historic homes along Summit Avenue, are the most popular destinations for tourists. Downtown has taken a sharp turn toward the modern in recent years, but it still has pockets of the European charm city boosters boast of.

History

It has been said that the Mississippi River gave birth to the city, but Pierre "Pig's Eye" Parrant, a famously nefarious character, was its midwife. Parrant, an aging voyageur who got his nickname from his blind "marble-hued and crooked" eye, moved down the river from Fort Snelling in 1838, immediately after the land was opened to settlers, to open a ramshackle saloon. Others soon followed, some for the steady supply of whiskey and others to take advantage of the ideal steamboat landing: all took to calling the settlement Pig's Eye Landing. Sadly, in 1841 a pious French missionary named Lucien Galtier built a tiny log chapel here and pressured residents to adopt its name for the village.

St. Paul soon replaced Fort Snelling as the most important settlement on this stretch of the Mississippi, although it wasn't exactly a bustling metropolis yet; just 30 families, mostly French Canadians, called it home in 1845. In 1849 Minnesota became a territory and St. Paul its capital. Things changed virtually overnight when word reached the people of Minnesota. St. Paul nearly doubled in size in just three weeks, and by the fall of that year nearly 1,000 hopeful settlers had bought a one-way steamboat ticket. Some haughty boosters even predicted that St. Paul would become the new national capital.

Back then, as today, Germans and Irish, in that order, made up the majority of the population, though the city is usually still thought of as an Irish enclave, in part because the Irish were dominant in politics from early on.

The many structures from the city's past, most notably the historic homes along Summit Avenue, are the most popular destinations for tourists.

The first railroad came to St. Paul in 1862 connecting it with St. Anthony (now a part of Minneapolis), though it wasn't until the next decade that rail began to replace the paddlewheel. James J. Hill centered his railroad empire here and made St. Paul the gateway to and transportation center of the entire Northwest and the city prospered along with him. Mark Twain visited in 1882 during his trip up the Mississippi River (that would be chronicled in his classic book *Life on the Mississippi*) and was very impressed. "St. Paul is a wonderful town," he said. "It is put together in solid blocks of honest brick and stone, and has the air of intending to stay." Stay it did, of course; most new arrivals, though, did not. In the peak year of 1888, nearly 150 trains a day serving 13 lines brought eight million passengers through the city's Union Depot, but most stopped only briefly before moving out to claim land in the Minnesota frontier.

The 20th century saw ups and downs as prohibition brought a horrible crime spree to the city, while the opportunities provided by the World Wars brought many of the city's poorest into the economic mainstream. During the Roaring '20s infamous gangsters like John Dillinger and Baby Face Nelson found St. Paul to be a safe haven; as long as they didn't commit crimes in the city, Police Chief John O'Connor left them alone. The so-called O'Connor system worked for a while, but the city grew increasingly lawless, and kidnapping was a growth industry. By the early 1930s, law enforcement officials in Washington, D.C., had labeled St. Paul "poison spot of the nation" and a clean up began. Not long after Dillinger, now officially "Public Enemy Number One," famously shot his way past police and escaped from his apartment on the morning of March 31, 1934, the city cracked down on other no-longer-welcome criminals and closed the brothels and gambling halls.

Little of note happened in St. Paul over the rest of the century and while the city stagnated, Minneapolis gained its clear supremacy. Recent years, however, have brought billions of dollars in new development to downtown, including the RiverCentre convention complex, which includes the Xcel Energy Centre arena, plus new museums, major housing developments, and office buildings. The changes have all led to a rapid economic and attitudinal resurgence for the city.

Orientation

St. Paul stretches 29 miles along two sharp bends in the Mississippi River. **Downtown** sits on the steep north bank of the first bend and is centered on **Rice Park. Lowertown,** the eastern half of downtown, is a largely residential area with many artists occupying converted warehouses. The historic district surrounds the tree-filled and stream-divided **Mears Park,** a great place to take lunch. A five-mile elevated, indoor skyway system weaves across much of the area connecting hotels, restaurants, theaters, and the like. **West Seventh Street,** just beyond the Xcel Centre, has several good bars and restaurants and is downtown's busiest entertainment district. Parking is rarely a problem downtown, and you can even still find some free short-term street parking on the edge of Lowertown. The RiverCentre Ramp attached to the Science Museum is huge, well situated, and cheaper than most others—enter in the back off Chestnut Street.

Running west of downtown across the city are the Victorian mansions of **Summit Avenue** and the restaurants and specialty shops of **Grand Avenue.** The lovely neighborhood behind the

M

TWIN CITIES

Cathedral of St. Paul is known as **Cathedral Hill** and is home to several of St Paul's top restaurants. Asian businesses of every variety line University Avenue between the Capitol and Lexington in an area known as **Frog Town.** West of Frog Town and centered on the maddeningly busy intersection of Snelling and University Avenues is the **Midway** neighborhood with some worthy restaurants, stores, and bars. The whole of University Avenue is still somewhat gritty, but the influx of Asians in the east and commuters in the west has put the area rapidly on the upswing. The upscale **Highland Park** neighborhood in the far southwest of the city has enough good restaurants to make it worth a visit, especially if your hotel is out in the southern suburbs. Head south of the river for south of the border flavor along Concord Street in the **District del Sol,** the hub of St. Paul's Hispanic community.

SIGHTS

Minnesota State Capitol

This spectacular edifice looming over downtown, topped by the world's largest unsupported marble dome, is a true architectural masterpiece. This, the third capitol, was designed in 1895 by the famed Cass Gilbert (who also drew up the plans for the U.S. Supreme Court and New York City's Woolworth Building) and opened for business ten years later. It rises 223 feet and has an exterior of Georgian marble, an intensely controversial choice, along with Minnesota granite and sandstone. Its most unique feature is the gilded statue Quadriga (officially titled *The Progress of the State*) perched over the main entrance. The four horses, representing Earth, Fire, Water, and Air (nature), are reined in by two women symbolizing Industry and Agriculture (civilization). The charioteer riding into the future is Prosperity. The entire artladen interior, from the grand rotunda to the painted hallway ceilings, is equally spectacular. Don't miss the Governor's Reception Room (yes, you can just walk right in), the most ornate part of the building. Before visiting any of it though, pick up the self-guided tour brochure from the first floor Information Desk. If you happen to

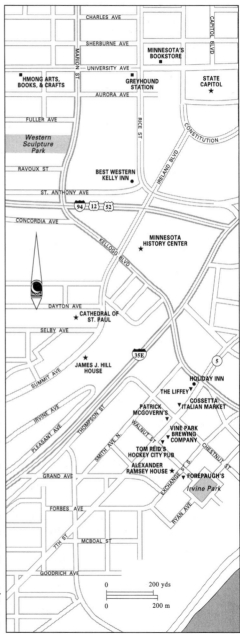

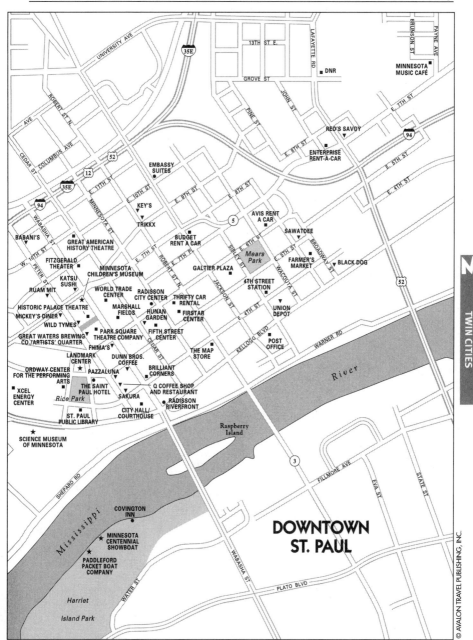

DOWNTOWN ST. PAUL

TWIN CITIES

© AVALON TRAVEL PUBLISHING, INC.

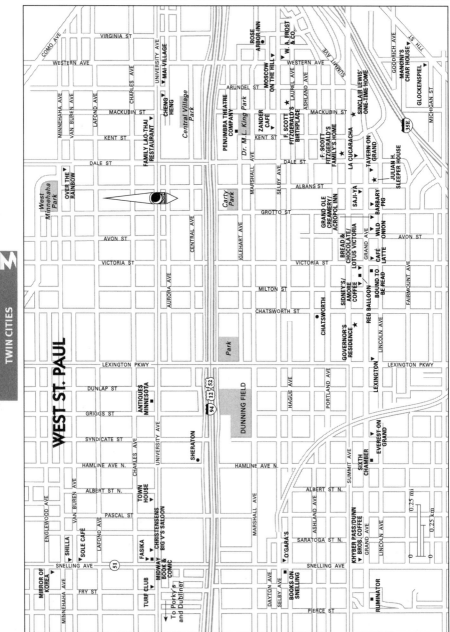

© TIM BEWER

Minnesota State Capitol

Prince. Much of the museum is hands-on, and you can climb aboard a 24-ton boxcar, touch a beaver-pelt top hat, and listen to a loon. Don't miss the Home Place Minnesota Theater, a 15-minute multimedia presentation about the state as told by Minnesotans, both famous and ordinary, that shows throughout the day. Museum hours are Tuesday 10 A.M.–8 P.M., Wednesday–Saturday (plus Mon. during the summer) 10 A.M.–5 P.M., and Sunday noon–5 P.M. Admission is free.

Landmark Center

St. Paul's castlelike Landmark Center, 651/292-3225, makes a dazzling backdrop to Rice Park. The 1902 Old Federal Courts Building, as lovely inside as it is out, has been transformed into a cultural center with ongoing performances and exhibitions. Take at least a few minutes to look around the grand atrium, and learn the in-depth history of the building's construction, occupation, and preservation on a free 45-minute tour (Thurs. 11 A.M. and Sun. 1 P.M.). The building is open Monday–Wednesday and Friday 8 A.M.–5 P.M., Thursday 8 A.M.–8 P.M., Saturday 10 A.M.–5 P.M., and Sunday noon–5 P.M.

The Landmark Center also houses a pair of museums. The underappreciated **Minnesota Museum of American Art,** 651/292-4355 (open Tues., Wed., Fri., and Sat. 11 A.M.–4 P.M., Thurs. 11 A.M.–7:30 P.M., and Sun. 1–5 P.M.), ringing the second floor, has a small but interesting collection from the 19th and 20th centuries. Down in the basement is the small **Schubert Club Museum of Musical Instruments** (open weekdays 11 A.M.–3 P.M.). Admission to both is free.

Landmark Plaza memorializes former St. Paulite Charles Schulz with bronze statues of Charlie Brown, Snoopy and other *Peanuts* characters.

City Hall and Courthouse

The 1932 Saint Paul City Hall and Ramsey County Courthouse, 15 W. Kellogg Blvd., is an art deco masterpiece. Built during the depths of the great depression, the dramatic 20-story building was designed "to symbolize 20th century pride in progress, industry, and democracy." The ornate Zig-Zag Moderne interior is

come when the house or senate is in action, you can watch from the third floor galleries. The building is open to the public weekdays 9 A.M.–5 P.M., Saturday 10 A.M.–4 P.M., and Sunday 1 to 4 P.M. Free guided tours, which, weather permitting, take you up to see Quadriga, depart on the hour. Call 651/296-2881 with any questions.

Minnesota History Center

The Minnesota History Center, 651/296-6126, is a modern monumental building constructed primarily of Minnesota materials. It houses the library and offices of the Minnesota Historical Society, gift and book shops with North Star State merchandise, the Café Minnesota, and, of interest to most visitors, the History Center Museum. The third floor displays examine the entire history of the state, from 3.6 billion-year-old geology to the present day. Exhibits focus more on telling stories than just displaying period artifacts, though there are, of course, plenty of the latter, including a Dakota birch bark canoe from 1835; the *Yankee Girl,* a ten-foot boat sailed across the Atlantic in 1979 by Gary Spiess; ancient pottery; and the Purple Rain outfit worn by

TWIN CITIES

highlighted by the otherworldly Memorial Hall, where dark blue Belgian marble, bronze trim, and a mirrored ceiling surround *Vision of Peace,* a 36-foot Native American apparition carved from Mexican onyx by Swedish sculptor Carl Milles. The three-story lobby sits just inside the Fourth Street entrance.

Science Museum of Minnesota

Minnesota's most visited museum takes visitors on a journey from the ancient world to the future of high technology. The excellent collection is chock full of interactive exhibits of interest to both kids and adults. You can make a tornado, pilot a riverboat, experiment on cells, see dinosaur fossils, play the musical staircase, and much more. One of the most interesting sections is the often-overlooked Collections Gallery where the varied assortment of items includes a shell collection, pottery, two-headed turtle, Egyptian mummy, and quack contraptions from the late Museum of Questionable Medical Devices. The museum also hosts a **3D Laser show** and **Omnitheater** showing large-format IMAX films on a 70-foot-tall domed screen. During the summer the museum is open Monday–Saturday 9:30 A.M.–9 P.M. and Sunday 10:30 A.M.–5:30 P.M.; the rest of the year the hours are the same except for closing at 5:30 P.M. Monday–Wednesday. A combo ticket costs $13 for the exhibits, Omnitheater, and Laser show; $12 for the exhibits and Omnitheater; $9 for the exhibits and laser show; and $7 for just the exhibits or the Omnitheater. Call 651/221-9444 for additional information.

Mississippi National River and Recreation Area

Interestingly, the National Park Service's Mississippi National River and Recreation Area (MNRRA) possesses almost no land. Instead, they coordinate preservation, education, and recreation with various local agencies along a 72-mile stretch of the river between Anoka and Hastings. Their **Mississippi River Visitor Center,** 651/293-0200, at the Science Museum is the place to get information about recreational activities, historic sites, and events along the Mighty Mississippi (and there are a lot of them) and

learn about the natural and cultural history of the entire river from its source at Lake Itasca to the Gulf of Mexico. Information is also available about other regional National Park Service properties. Admission is free and they are open the same hours as the museum.

Minnesota Children's Museum

Kids can have a blast and learn something in the process at this museum designed exclusively for them. Hands-on exhibits, aimed at toddlers to ten-year-olds, let kids make paper, work in a warehouse, shop in a market, and crawl through an anthill. The museum, located at 10 W. 7th St., 651/225-6000, is open Tuesday, Wednesday, and Friday–Sunday 9 A.M.–5 P.M., Thursday 9 A.M.–8 P.M., plus Monday 9 A.M.–5 P.M. in the summer. Admission is $7.

Irvine Park Historic District

Not quite as grand an address as Summit Avenue, the many stately homes from the last half of the 19th century are a very lovely sight nonetheless—

Alexander Ramsey House

SUMMIT AVENUE

The longest stretch of Victorian homes in the nation runs over four miles from the edge of downtown to the Mississippi River along this stately avenue. The most fantastic mansions stand at the far east end and though it's not an unbroken chain the drive is lovely all the way across town. Beginning in the 1850s and peaking during the 1880s, the movers and shakers of Minnesota's moneyed class attempted to outdo each other with their massive and elaborate designs leading Frank Lloyd Wright to reportedly call it "The worst collection of architecture in the world." While many are excessively pompous you'll surely disagree with his assessment and enjoy the conceited legacy of St. Paul's elite. It's an easy drive, of course, but to really appreciate the boundless grandeur you should get out and bike or walk. Guided tours of the neighborhood depart from the James J. Hill House (described below) on Saturdays at 11 A.M. and 2 P.M. between May and September. The 90-minute walks cost $6 and reservations are recommended.

Perched high above downtown, right at the beginning of Summit Avenue, is the **Cathedral of St. Paul,** 651/228-1766, an even a more domineering landmark that the capitol. The nation's fourth largest cathedral, modeled after St. Peter's in Rome, was built of St. Cloud granite between 1906 and 1915. Its domed steeple rises 306 feet and up to 5,000 people can attend services. Naturally the original Saint Paul features prominently in the interior artwork though the most unique aspect are the Shrines of the Nations surrounding the sanctuary with the patron saints of the country of origin of Minnesota's first settlers. Free tours are offered at 1 P.M. on Monday, Wednesday, and Friday. You can visit on your own daily 8 A.M.–6 P.M. except on Friday when it closes at 4.

The **James J. Hill House,** 651/297-2555, a National Historic Landmark across the street is truly something special. Hill constructed the Great Northern Railway (which earned him the nickname Empire Builder) and was one of the ten richest men in America when he spent nearly a million dollars on this home in which he only lived about four months each year. Completed in 1891 the red sandstone mansion encompassed 36,000 sq. feet on five floors, making it to this day one of the largest private residences ever built in the Upper Midwest. But it is the fine detail, not the large scale, that makes the house so remarkable. Public rooms, including the 100-foot long reception hall, are lined by stained glass, crystal chandeliers, and hand-carved oak and mahogany woodwork, the latter extraordinary for both the quality *and* quantity. There is even artwork in the back of some of the 22 fireplaces. The pinnacle of elegance is the dining room with a gold-leaf ceiling, hand-tooled leather wallpaper, and original furnishings built specifically for the home. Many clever and advanced (for the day) mechanical systems were employed in the design; one of them, Hill's personal pipe organ, is sometimes played on Saturdays. Ninety-minute tours of the home, including the servants' quarters and work areas, begin every 30 minutes from 10 A.M. to 3:30 P.M. Wednesday through Saturday. Admission is $6. Many concerts, lectures, and other special events are held here.

continued on next page

© TIM BEWER

Cathedral of St. Paul

TWIN CITIES

SUMMIT AVENUE (cont'd)

To see how a more typical upper class home looked during the Gilded Age's peak book a tour of the **Julian H. Sleeper House,** 66 Saint Albans St. S., 651/225-1505. Seth Hawkins has turned his home into a museum of decorative arts and just about everything is authentic to the era. Eastlake furniture, oriental carpets, wall pockets, and over 500 owls fill the house and during a visit you'll hear interesting stories about the how and why of 1880s interior design. A pair of rooms are set aside for Dr. Hawkins' other interests: one holds the largest collection of President James Garfield memorabilia outside the museum in Garfield's Ohio hometown, while the basement houses an exhibition of Slovenian history and culture. Admission is by donation and guided tours (you must call ahead) are available at just about any time, even evenings.

Another house open for tours is the **Governor's Residence** at 1006. Visitors can look around the suitably stately 1912 English Tudor mansion on Thursdays 1–3 P.M. between May and Sep-

tember. The free tours last about half an hour. Call 651/297-2161 with any questions.

Though author **F. Scott Fitzgerald** echoed Wright's sentiments about the street, proscribing it "a mausoleum of American architectural monstrosities," he resided in his family's apartment at 599 (which he described as "a house below the average on a street above the average.") in 1919 while writing *This Side of Paradise.* Fitzgerald was born just a few blocks off Summit in the even more modest brick apartment building at 481 Laurel Ave. Sinclair Lewis lived at 516 while writing his play *Hobohemia.*

© TIM BEWER

Summit Avenue homes

especially those fronting the village green–style park. The most prominent is the **Alexander Ramsey House,** 265 S. Exchange St., 651/296-8760, one of the nation's best preserved Victorian homes. Built by Minnesota's first territorial governor and second state governor, the 1872 Second Empire mansion remained in the family until 1964 when they turned it, and all the original furnishings, over to the Minnesota Historical Society. Not only do you get to admire the walnut woodwork, crystal chandeliers, and other opulent embellishment, but you'll learn about life for the city's elite in the 1870s. Top-of-the-hour tours, led by actors portraying the family's servants, are available Friday and Saturday from 10 A.M. to 3 P.M. The hours are expanded between Thanksgiving and Christmas when the house is decorated for the holidays. Admission is $6. Architectural and historical walking tours of the neighborhood, departing from the Ramsey

House, are offered once a month from May to September and cost $6.

Jackson Street Roundhouse

This hodgepodge collection of railroad memorabilia is really for rail fans only. Housed in and around a 1907 steam locomotive maintenance shop are old rail cars, the original turntable, and various other bits of train memorabilia. The most interesting part is the workshop where you can see engines in various states of repair and disassembly, and on Saturdays you might even see volunteers working on them. Kids can take a ride on a miniature train. It is open Saturday 10 A.M.–5 P.M. and Sunday 1–5 P.M. Admission is $3. Call 651/228-0263 for information.

Parks

Harriet Island, an expansive riverside park across from downtown hosts, among other things, a riverwalk, outdoor stage, restaurant, bed-and-breakfast, yacht club, and the Minnesota Centennial Showboat. The island is also the home base of the **Paddleford Packet Boat Company,** 651/227-1100 or 800/543-3908, whose paddleboat sightseeing cruises run the Mississippi to Fort Snelling. Boats depart daily at noon and 2 P.M. during the summer, plus weekends at 2 P.M. in May and October. The price is $12. They also offer much less frequent lunch, dinner, and fall color trips, some of which pass through the locks.

Como Park, 651/266-6400, is a 450-acre stretch of green surrounding Lake Como. The free **Como Zoo,** 651/645-1014, isn't the best of zoos, but most of the animals do have room to roam. The real gem of the park is the **Conservatory,** a bargain at just $1. The 100-foot-tall Palm Dome at the center of the massive greenhouse contains many palms, orchids and other tropical foliage. A sunken garden and bonsai room are some of the displays branching off from the dome, while the lovely Como Ordway Japanese Garden sits outside. Both the zoo and conservatory are open daily at 10 A.M. closing at 6 P.M. from April through September and 4 P.M. the rest of the year. The 1914 **Cafesjian's Carousel** is another popular attraction.

Six large burial mounds, piled up some 2,000 years ago by the Hopewell peoples, sit on the highest point of the bluffs lining the river east of downtown. To get to **Indian Mounds Park** take 7th Street East to Mounds Boulevard and follow it south for about a mile and a quarter. Everyone will likely find something they like at **Western Sculpture Park** whether it's the giant armadillo, the three-story metal tower, or one of the 20 other oversized statues residing across the freeway from the History Center.

Summit Brewing Company

Minnesota's favorite local brewery leads visitors through their small, modern bluff-top plant every Tuesday, Thursday, and Saturday at 1 P.M. After getting introduced to the ingredients, you'll see the brewing and bottling rooms up close and then at the end of the 45-minute tour you can sample what you've just watched them make. Reservations (651/265-7800) are required on Saturdays.

RECREATION

Though it is mostly industrial south of downtown, the bluff-lined **Mississippi River** is quite beautiful to the west. It's a scenic trip by kayak or canoe, but you'll be sharing it with quite a few speedboats, which is why few people paddle it. Most active Twin Citians prefer to follow the river by bike, and paved trails follow both sides of the river all the way to Minneapolis. To make a really nice loop, head out from Harriet Island down to Fort Snelling and Minnehaha Park in Minneapolis, continue up the river and return to downtown via Summit Ave. It's about a 20-mile trip.

If you'd rather hike the river, then go to **Crosby Regional Park** and the adjoining **Hidden Falls Regional Park,** which together have about seven miles of riverside trails. The 6.5 miles of hilly, wooded trails at **Battle Creek Regional Park,** half of them some pretty wild single track, offer some of the best biking and cross-country skiing in Twin Cities. The principal trailhead is off Winthrop St. by Afton Rd.

The paved **Gateway State Trail** runs from Cayuga St., alongside I-35E (not too far from the capitol) to Pine County Park about four miles north of Stillwater. The scenery is urban and urban sprawl for most of the route (punctuated by the **50-foot snowman** at along Hwy. 36 in North St. Paul), but eventually you escape to the rural countryside.

NIGHTLIFE

There is no truth to the rumor that St. Paul has no nightlife, though this is one case where the capital city does envy Minneapolis. There is no better source of what's on than the free weekly *City Pages* available all over town.

Rock

A fancy Country and Western bar that opened at the end of World War II, the **Turf Club,** 1601

University Ave. W., 651/647-0486, took a chance and made a change to a rock format letting up-and-coming bands play. The switch paid off and now even touring acts play on occasion. Cover charges are always low, if there's one at all. The owners of **Christensens Big V's Saloon,** 1567 University Ave. W., 651/645-8472, just a few doors down from the Turf Club, know a good thing when they see it and have since emulated their neighbor by also booking upstart alternative bands. The **4th Street Station,** 2001 E. 4th St., 651/298-0173, in Lowertown is best known as the place to see heavy metal bands, but they also have a variety of other acts and DJs spinning dance discs during the week.

Jazz

St. Paul has got Minneapolis beat when it comes to the jazz scene. Both **Artists' Quarter,** 408 St. Peter St., 651/292-1359, a downtown basement club with a movie-set-perfect ambience and the **Dakota Bar & Grill,** 1021 E. Bandana Blvd., 651/642-1442, about a 20 minute drive from downtown, feature the best local and national jazz acts. **Brilliant Corners,** 334 N. Wabasha St., 651/224-3688, is simple downtown space beloved for its loose, musician-friendly atmosphere. No alcohol is served, so the music bounces on into the wee hours of the morning, and sometimes the big names that headlined at the other two clubs come to sit in after their advertised gigs.

Blues

As popular as it has become, the **Minnesota Music Café,** 499 Payne Ave., 651/776-4699, still seems to be one of the Twin Cities' best kept secrets. Besides great bands seven nights a week and a large sunken dance floor ensuring good viewing by all, the walls also serve as a Minnesota music hall of fame.

Folk

The original **Dunn Bros. Coffee,** 1569 Grand Ave., 651/698-0618, a very relaxing space by Macalester College, has musicians almost every night. Have a craic with the best Irish bands and open jams at **The Liffey,** 175 W. 7th St., 651/556-1420; **Dubliner Pub,** 2162 Univer-

sity Ave. W., 651/646-5551; and **Half Time Rec,** 1013 Front Ave., 651/488-8245. The classic main bar of the latter served as Slippery's in the movie *Grumpy Old Men* and there's a bocce ball court in the basement.

Dancing

Stargate, 1700 Rice St., 651/488-9393, is St. Paul's hottest dance club, and they play mostly Top 40 and House. If hip-hop is more your style, head down the street to the tropical-themed **Club Cancun,** 1638 Rice St., 651/489-8466. The **Wild Onion,** 788 Grand Ave., 651/291-2525, is a casual bar and grill by day with a small and fun dance floor at night. On Wednesday and Thursday nights Sensación Latina plays for salsa fans at the swank **Fhima's,** 6 W. 6th St., 651/287-0784, downtown. Crowds kick up their heels to the live big bands on Thursday "Swing Night" at the **Wabasha Street Caves,** 215 Wabasha St. S., 651/292-1220. The bands play 7–10 P.M., but if you are a neophyte come at 6:15 for a lesson. The regular nights are all ages, but the 21 and older crowd gets the floor to themselves one Friday a month at 8 P.M. Entry is $7 on Thursday and $8 on Friday.

Comedy

Flanagan's Wake is a wild and inventive interactive Irish wake dinner theater. It is staged by the Minneapolis-based comedy troupe **Brave New Workshop** at the Historic Palace Theatre, 17 West 7th Place. Show times are Thursday and Friday at 7 P.M. and Saturday and Sunday at 5 P.M. Tickets are $40 or $45. Call 612/332-6620 for reservations.

Bars

Longtime favorite **Patrick McGovern's,** 225 W. 7th St., 651/224-5821, is always relaxed—unless packed before a Wild game—and they serve the world's greatest turkey sandwiches. Don't let the name fool you though, that's the only thing Irish about it. Another game day favorite is **Tom Reid's Hockey City Pub,** 258 W. 7th St., 651/292-9916, owned by the current Wild color man. **Wild Tymes,** 33 W. 7th Pl., is another busy downtown sports bar that also does live music and karaoke.

O'Gara's, 164 Snelling Ave. N., 651/644-3333, a St. Paul institution, comes pretty close to being all things to all people. It's a neighborhood bar and grill with better than average pub grub and half a dozen of their own microbrewed beers, plus they host a variety of live bands (there's a lot of tribute acts on the main stage, plus jazz bands in the smaller Shamrock Room) in the adjoining wings. A young Charles Schulz lived upstairs. Green Bay Packers fans will want to spend Sunday afternoons at **Gabe's by the Park,** 911 N. Lexington Pkwy., 651/646-3066, where the city's many faithful cheer on the Green and Gold. Get there early if you want a table. They also run a shuttle to St. Paul Saints baseball games.

Gay and Lesbian

The longest running gay bar is the **Town House,** 1415 University Ave. W., 651/646-7087, which, though it hosts live bands and a Thursday drag show, attracts a pretty mellow crowd, as does **Over the Rainbow,** 719 N. Dale St., 651/487-5070, a simple neighborhood bar with a dance floor upstairs and a mostly lesbian clientele. Tops for dancing is **Trikkx,** 490 N. Robert St., 651/224-0703, with DJs spinning six nights a week.

OTHER ENTERTAINMENT

The pageantry surrounding the **Ordway Center for the Performing Arts,** 345 Washington St., 651/282-3000, begins with the liveried footmen greeting you at the lobby entrance and continues into the spectacular 1,900-seat Main Hall. And the calendar, from big time Broadway and West End productions to children's puppet theater, lives up to the venue.

The beautifully renovated **Fitzgerald Theater,** 10 E. Exchange St., 651/290-1221, with its double balcony design was one of the nation's premier theaters when completed in 1910. Best known as the home of Garrison Keillor's *A Prairie Home Companion* radio variety show, the Fitzgerald also hosts other musical, theatrical, and special events. Advanced tickets to PHC are nearly impossible to come by (check www.prairiehome.org if you want to try) but you can always join the

hopefuls out front for day-of-show rush tickets. There are no hard and fast rules about what it takes to get one of these on-stage seats, but generally it's a good idea to be in line by noon to wait for the sale at 4:15 P.M. The number available for each performance varies week by week, but it is usually around 40–60. Rush tickets cost $10 (cash only) and you may only purchase two.

Classical Music

The **St. Paul Chamber Orchestra,** 651/291-1144, founded in 1959, is the first and only full-time professional chamber orchestra in the United States and has been hailed as one of the world's best. When they are not on stage at the Ordway, they are off touring North America, Europe, or Asia. **The Minnesota Opera,** 612/333-6669, also puts on its lavish productions, both traditional and contemporary, at the Ordway.

Theater

The stunning **Minnesota Centennial Showboat,** 651/227-1100, is a 175-foot floating theater docked at Harriet Island. Crowds are encouraged to hiss the villain and cheer the hero at the melodramas produced by the U of M's theater department. The creative **Great American History Theatre,** 30 E. 10th St., 651/292-4323, truly manages to make the history of Minnesota and the Midwest exciting and entertaining. Their original productions range from dramas about the state's pioneers to an Andrews Sisters musical revue. The award-winning **Penumbra Theatre Company,** 270 N. Kent St., 651/224-3180, is one of the nation's oldest and most respected African American theater companies and the oldest professional theater company of any kind in the city. The **Park Square Theatre Company,** 20 W. 7th Pl., 651/291-7005, produces a classics repertoire and has a good reputation.

Freebies

During June and July a variety of bands, all on the lighter side, play Rice Park on Mondays and Mears Park on Tuesdays over the lunch hour. The music moves to Harriet Island on Hump Day evenings at 7 P.M.

Cinema

The **Grandview 2,** 1830 Grand Ave., 651/698-3344, and the **Highland I & II,** 760 S. Cleveland Ave., 651/698-3085, are classic early-20th-century cinemas, with the balconies converted into second screens. Both show standard Hollywood fare, though the Highland sometimes shows independent films, too. The Science Museum's immense **Omnitheater,** 120 W. Kellogg Blvd., 651/221-9444, has large-format IMAX films. It has the nation's first convertible dome, allowing movies to be projected on a full-vision spherical screen or large flat screen when appropriate.

Spectator Sports

The **Minnesota Wild,** a year 2000 National Hockey League expansion team, skates at the Xcel Energy Center, meeting a true need in hockey-mad Minnesota. They fill the gap left by the 1993 departure of the North Stars, whose owner, Norm Green, in one of professional sports' all-time lowest moves, packed up and followed the cash to Dallas where they became the Stars. Tickets, starting at $10, can be bought in person

at the Xcel Energy Center box office or by phone through Ticketmaster, 651/989-5151. The first three seasons have been total sellouts, though walk-up tickets are sometimes available.

The **Saint Paul Saints,** part-owned by Bill Murray (yes, that Bill Murray) and Mike Veeck (son of former White Sox owner Bill Veeck "the greatest public relations man and promotional genius the game of baseball has ever seen") play baseball in the Northern League, an independent organization about the equivalent of AA minor league ball. While there are far fewer of them, Saints fans are just as dedicated as those of MLB's Twins. And all the special promotions like fireworks, theme nights (e.g. Star Trek, Disco, and Gilligan's Island), and the between-inning gimmicks mean you don't need to enjoy baseball to enjoy a night at the ballpark. Home games are played in the classic all-bleacher **Midway Stadium.** There has long been talk about building a new riverfront stadium, but if St. Paul has its way that will be the new home of the Twins. Tickets are no more than $8 and as little as $3. The ticket office can be reached at 651/644-6659.

snow-sculpting contest during the St. Paul Winter Carnival

EVENTS

When a haughty New York reporter claimed in 1885 that St. Paul was just "another Siberia, unfit for human habitation" in the winter, St. Paulites didn't protest with letters to the editor, they created the **St. Paul Winter Carnival** to prove him wrong. The 10-day festival, commencing the last Friday in January, features ice- and snow-carving competitions, dogsled rides, broomball tournaments, softball on ice, a parade, and a giant snow slide in Como Park. Indoor activities include bonspiels, art exhibits, concerts, and a grand ball. Though the carnival is famous for its ice castles, they are built only occasionally; however, one is planned for 2004. Another unique aspect is reenacting of the festival's silly legend. Boreas (the King of Snows) battles Vulcanus Rex (the King of Fire) and his minions until spring ceremoniously triumphs over winter.

The **Minnesota State Fair** has everything other state agricultural fairs have—livestock shows, a carnival midway, washed up rock stars on the grandstand, car races, and food on sticks—only a lot more of it than most; the 360-acre fairgrounds are the nation's largest. The Great Minnesota Get-Together runs for 12 days ending on Labor Day and tickets cost $8.

St. Patrick's Day, Cinco de Mayo, and the **Hmong New Year** are also large celebrations in St. Paul.

ACCOMMODATIONS

Hotels and Motels $50–100

Downtown: The **Best Western Kelly Inn,** 161 Saint Anthony Ave., 651/227-8711 or 800/528-1234, is out on the edge of downtown, but still within walking distance—or just ride their shuttle van. For $89 you get a sauna, whirlpool, and a rather large pool, along with decent rooms. St. Paul's largest hotel, the **Radisson Riverfront,** 11 Kellogg Blvd. E., 651/292-1900 or 800/333-3333, has 475 rooms, plus a fitness center and a rather public pool and whirlpool area. Its smaller sister property, the **Radisson City Center,** 411 Minnesota St., 651/291-8800 or 800/333-3333, has a better pool, fitness center and somewhat

larger rooms. Both are connected to the skyway and sometimes have rates as low as $99, but expect to pay more most of the time. The **Holiday Inn,** 175 7th St. W., 651/225-1515 or 800/448-3663, which sits right across the street from the RiverCentre and got a complete renovation in 2001, also drops its prices below the $100 mark if not too full, though expect to pay a little more here, too. Amenities include a pool, whirlpool, and fitness center.

West: The **Sheraton,** 400 Hamline Ave. N., 651/642-1234 or 800/535-2339, just off the freeway between downtown St. Paul and Minneapolis, is as fancy as many of the downtown hotels and has a pool, whirlpool, and fitness center. Rooms go for as little as $99. Other hotels on this side of town are much more down-market. The **Days Inn,** 1964 University Ave. W., 651/645-8681 or 800/329-7466, just a couple blocks from the Amtrak station, is starting to show its age, but is still decent enough at $79. Down along the river toward Fort Snelling and the Mall of America—just a short drive to downtown—the simple **Crosby Lake Inn,** 1810 7th St. W., 651/698-0821, has rooms from $60.

East: The **Exel Inn,** 1739 Old Hudson Rd., 651/771-5566 or 800/367-3935, just about five minutes from downtown, has small and simple rooms for less than $60.

Hotels and Motels $100–250

Downtown: Built in 1910 by the same people behind New York City's Grand Central Station, **The Saint Paul Hotel,** 350 Market St., 651/292-9292 or 800/292-9292, has no equal in the state for luxury. Nationally recognized for its elegance and service, rooms come with all the expected amenities and then some, plus high tea is served in the lobby under Waterford chandeliers. There is a decent-sized fitness center up on the 12th floor with motivational views. The regular weekend rate is $149, though specials are sometimes offered so always ask. Every room at the **Embassy Suites,** 175 10th St. E., 651/224-5400 or 800/362-2779, is a two-room suite and faces the impressive palm-filled atrium, home to a family of ducks and a wayward sparrow. The full range of facilities includes a pool, whirlpool, sauna, steam room, and fitness center, plus each room is equipped with a microwave, refrigerator, and wet bar. Their free shuttle takes you around downtown and even out to the Grand Avenue area. They charge as little as $119.

B&Bs

Cathedral Hill's elegant **Rose Arbor Inn,** 341 Dayton Ave., 651/222-0243, is a great house with a great host in a great location. The four pleasantly appointed guestrooms, priced from $125, have private baths and all but one has its own fireplace. You'll get a continental breakfast in the morning, but this is actually a B&D (Bed and Dinner) and your stay includes a four-course meal (vegetarian or other dietary needs accommodated) prepared by owner Pamela Hiller, who previously cooked in some of the Twin Cities' top restaurants.

St. Paul's original bed-and-breakfast is the **Chatsworth,** 984 Ashland Ave., 651/227-4288 or 877/978-4837, a homey 1902 Victorian house just blocks off Summit Avenue. The six guestrooms range from $99 for those with a shared bath to $169 for the largest and fanciest. Weekends require a two-night stay.

The most unusual lodging in the city is the **Covington Inn,** 651/292-1411, a floating B&B docked at Harriet Island. The former towboat's four plush rooms each have a private bath and, naturally, a nautical theme. Rates run $180–235.

FOOD
African
Many people get a gleam in their eye when they talk about the small and simple menu of cous cous, lentils, chicken, and other Algerian delights ($6–10) at **Barbary Fig,** 720 Grand Ave., 651/290-2085. Open daily for lunch and dinner except closed all day Tues. and Sun. for lunch.

For an authentic taste of Ethiopia, there's **Fasika,** 510 Snelling Ave. N., 651/646-4747. All dishes, including the recommended sample platters, are under $10. Open daily for lunch and dinner.

American
The **Café Minnesota,** 651/297-4097, in the Minnesota History Center, is far from the average cafeteria. Besides the basics, the changing menu might feature sweet and sour pork, shrimp gumbo, grilled swordfish, and calzones. There are always some distinctly Minnesotan dishes, too, like chicken and wild rice hotdish, ravioli stuffed with pumpkin, and wild rice soup. Best of all, few choices exceed $6. Open weekdays for breakfast and daily for lunch.

The wildly popular **Café Latte,** 850 Grand Ave., 651/224-5687, is another gourmet cafeteria and rightly the busiest restaurant on Grand Avenue. Soups, salads, and sandwiches—with lots of vegetarian options—all go for around $5. There is a separate pizza/wine bar in back and high tea, served 1–5 P.M. daily, is $10. Don't let the long lines scare you off; they move fast and there is plenty of seating upstairs. Open daily for breakfast, lunch, and dinner. You can get a small sampling of Café Latte's sandwiches and amazing bakery at their less crowded **Bread & Chocolate,** 867 Grand Ave., 651/228-1017, outlet on the opposite corner.

Tavern on Grand, 656 Grand Ave., 651/228-9030, is a friendly neighborhood bar and grill with a Northwoods theme that is rightly famous for its walleye. You can get it in several forms, including a sandwich for $8 or a two fillet platter for $18. Open daily for lunch and dinner.

Mickey's Diner, 36 W. 7th St., 651/222-5633, a 1937 art deco dining car (one of just two listed on the National Register of Historic Places) offers a chance to eat in history. Don't go just for the setting though; the classic stick-to-your-ribs meals are fantastic and you can stuff yourself for around $6. The other Mickey's, 1950 W. 7th St., 651/698-8387, housed in a regular brick and mortar building (though the interior is equally classic), is out towards Fort Snelling. Both are open all hours.

Key's, 504 N. Robert St., 651/222-4083, has standards like massive omelets, meatloaf, turkey dinners, and chocolate cake cooked from scratch. You can get a great meal here for around $7. Open daily for breakfast and lunch.

You can get soup, sandwiches, Grand Ole Creamery ice cream, and a good variety of coffees at little **Café Nikita,** 214 4th St. E. (Union

Depot Place), 651/222-4053, and then enjoy them in an oversized chair in a plant-filled room. Just about everything is under $5. Open weekdays for breakfast and Mon.–Sat. for lunch.

If the giant neon pig flying over **Porky's,** 1890 University Ave. W., 651/644-1790, isn't enough to get you to stop, then consider the burgers and ice cream cones for a buck and a three-piece chicken dinner for $4. There is no indoor seating at this classic drive-in, but they still do business year-round. Classic car owners show off their machines here during the summer and fall between trips up and down University Avenue. Open daily for lunch and dinner.

Bakeries

It's hard to beat the cakes, cookies, and bars at **Café Latte,** 850 Grand Ave., 651/224-5687. Also wonderful is the **Taste of Scandinavia** bakery served at the downtown **Dunn Bros. Coffee,** 367 Wabasha St., 651/767-0567. Grab a tray and tongs and help yourself at **Panadería Don Pancho,** 140 Concord St., 651/225-8744, down in District del Sol. It's worth the drive and many people come here from all over the Twin Cities to take home bags of breads and sweets.

Breakfast and Brunch

The classic **Q Coffee Shop,** 350 Saint Peter St., (in the Lowry Professional Building), 651/224-6440, is where people who know the value of a dollar take their morning meal. Large breakfast platters run $3–5. Open weekdays for breakfast and lunch.

Other good choices for the morning meal are **Café Latte, Café Minnesota, El Burrito Mercado, Highland Grill, Key's, Mickey's Diner,** and **Sidney's.** Two of the biggest Sunday brunch mother lodes are at **The St. Paul Grill** and **Carousel.**

Brewpubs

St. Paul has a pair of classy downtown brewpubs worth a visit as much for the food (ranging $6–17 at both) and outdoor patios as the beer. Both serve burgers and other pub food, but more typical menu items include a mahi mahi po boy, grilled portobello sandwich, penne *arrabiatta,* grilled

duck breast, and avocado-stuffed salmon—many of these choices come infused with the house brews. The **Vine Park Brewing Company,** 242 W. 7th St., 651/228-1355, is open Monday–Saturday for lunch and dinner plus Sundays if a big event is going on, and has the more creative kitchen of the two. The **Great Waters Brewing Co.,** 426 St. Peter St., 651/224-2739, open daily for lunch and dinner, makes some good mustards.

Cambodian

Cheng Heng, 448 University Ave. W., 651/222-5577, half of a funky little Cambodian minimall, is the Twin Cities' only Cambodian restaurant and worth seeking out. Cambodia lies between Thailand and Vietnam and so does the food, so there are many unique variations to discover, all around $6. A picture menu makes ordering easy. Open daily for lunch and dinner.

Chinese

Hunan Garden, 380 Cedar St., 651/224-7588, isn't spectacular, but it's the only Chinese restaurant downtown that isn't fast food. It has a popular all-you-can-eat weekday lunch buffet and serves all the standards for around $6. Open Mon.–Sat. for lunch and daily for dinner.

Coffeehouses

The coffee shop of choice for hip Lowertown artists, the **Black Dog,** 308 Prince St, 651/228-9274, has art on the wall, entertainment on stage, and good coffee and wine behind the counter. You can build your own sandwiches and pizza, too. Open daily for breakfast and lunch and Mon.–Sat. for lunch. With couches, board games, and even a piano, **Amore Coffee,** 917 Grand Ave., 651/222-6770, invites you kick back and stay a while. Open daily for breakfast, lunch, and dinner.

Deli

For an authentic New York-style Jewish delicatessen you'll have to head out to **Cecil's,** 651 S. Cleveland Ave., 651/698-0334, a Highland Park institution since 1949. Besides sandwiches to go and a small deli, there is a sit-down restaurant in back where a plate will cost you about $7. Open daily for breakfast, lunch, and dinner.

Eastern European

The friendly **Moscow on the Hill,** 371 Selby Ave., 651/291-1236, has Russian delicacies from across the empire, like *pelmini, blini,* and *vareniki,* ranging $10–24. The setting is beautiful, and the service is attentive. Open weekdays for lunch and daily for dinner. Reservations recommended.

Eclectic

The funky little **Highland Grill,** 771 Cleveland Ave. S., 651/690-1173, out in Highland Park can't be pigeonholed. Fun meals like pear rigatoni, spicy turkey burger, black bean falafel, blue corn pancakes, and beer battered fish and chips run $5–10. Open daily for breakfast, lunch, and dinner.

Downtown, the large **Fifth Street Center food court,** 55 5th St. E., (skyway level) has all the simple fast-food outlets—burgers, subs, pizza, Chinese, Mexican, etc—found in typical shopping malls. It is open weekdays for breakfast and lunch. The **Galtier Plaza food court,** 175 5th St. E. (enter on Sibley St.) in Lowertown is similar but smaller and also open for lunch on Saturdays. There are many more weekday-only fast-food outlets scattered along the skyway.

Fine Dining

W. A. Frost & Co., 374 Selby Ave., 651/224-5715, in a restored 1889 building, has been a St. Paul landmark since 1975. Dine on grilled marinated quail or portobello mushroom lasagna for around $20 a plate in the romantic dining room with three fireplaces, cozy bar, or huge outdoor patio. Open daily for lunch and dinner. Reservations are recommended.

Just down the street is the **Zander Café,** 523 Selby Ave., 651/222-5224. The menu at this unpretentious bistro changes every six to eight weeks, but butternut herb risotto and Portuguese fish stew are typical offerings. At $12–15 per entrée Zander isn't exactly cheap, but it is a good value for the wonderful creations you get. The wine selection is also fantastic. Open Tues.–Sun. for dinner. Make reservations well in advance.

The venerable **Lexington,** 1096 Grand Ave., 651/222-5878, served its first steak when prohibition was repealed and, with the white linens

and dim lights, it maintains a bit of an aura from that era. Hot turkey dinners, walleye almondine, lamb chops, and other solid American fare range from around $12 to $33. The $13 Sunday brunch is very popular. Open daily for lunch and dinner. Reservations are recommended on weekends.

You'll feel like a real mover and shaker when you sit down at **The St. Paul Grill,** 350 Market St., 651/224-7455, and many of your fellow diners probably are. The perfect companion to the posh Saint Paul Hotel in which it resides, the dinner menu offers simple but superb delights such as rosemary grilled chicken breast and pan-fried walleye for around $18 and highly recommended steaks for $30. The bar features nearly 200 wines and the absolute best in scotch, bourbon, and vodka. You can get lunch for about $10. It is a popular spot for pre-theater dinners and reservations are recommended. Open daily for lunch and dinner.

The **Carousel,** 11 E. Kellogg Blvd., 651/292-0408, perched on the 22nd floor of the Radisson Riverfront, has unbeatable views and a creative menu featuring entrées like walleye in a pecan batter, ostrich kebabs, and pistachio encrusted sea bass. The rotating inner ring lets you take in all there is to see during your meal. Lunch averages $12, while dinner is about double that. Open daily for breakfast, lunch, and dinner.

French

Forepaugh's, 276 S. Exchange St., 651/224-5606, occupying an opulent 1872 Victorian mansion, offers a memorable dining experience. The service is impeccable, and for what you get (and where you get it), it's very reasonably priced with nothing over $20. Open Sun.–Fri. for lunch and daily for dinner. Reservations recommended.

German

Glockenspiel, 605 W. 7th St., 651/292-9421, has the look, feel, and even smell of a real German restaurant. Traditional fare—including bratwurst, *schweinschnitzel,* and *käsespätzle*—runs $8–18 and the daily specials include a Friday fish fry and wild game Saturday. Open daily for lunch and dinner. Reservations recommended on weekends.

Greek

The **Acropol Inn,** 748 Grand Ave., 651/298-0151, a classy landmark, has been getting rave reviews for decades, though sampling their roast lamb, *papoutsaki, mousaka,* or breaded scallops doesn't come cheap. Most entrées are around $15, some steak and seafood choices nearly reach $30. Open Mon.–Sat. for lunch and dinner. You also can't go wrong at the more moderately priced **Christos,** 214 4th St. E., 651/224-6000, with its spectacular location in the grand lobby of Union Depot Place. Open Mon.–Sat. for lunch and dinner.

Ice Cream and Desserts

Some St. Paulites' eyes light up just with a mention of the **Grand Ole Creamery,** 750 Grand Ave., 651/293-1655. Their homemade ice cream, available in some 100 flavors (although only 32 at a time) is so good that there are sometimes even lines down the sidewalk in January. Open daily for lunch and dinner. You can also get a scoop of their creamy art downtown at **Café Nikita,** 214 4th St E., 651/222-4053, in Union Depot Place.

Irish

Attached to the Holiday Inn is **The Liffey,** 175 W. 7th St., 651/556-1420, an Irish pub straight out of Dublin—literally, in fact, since the etched glass and dark wood were crafted in Ireland and shipped overseas to be installed. Irish-born entrées include fish and chips, corned beef and cabbage, and shepherd's pie, while American favorites like a walleye sandwich, meatloaf, and a sirloin steak round out the menu. Prices run $6–16. Open daily for breakfast, lunch, and dinner.

Italian

Cossetta Italian Market, 211 W. 7th St., 651/222-3476, opened as an Italian grocery in 1911 and has expanded into the most popular Italian eatery in the city. Pizza, pasta, and hero sandwiches are served cafeteria style and you can get an oh-so-satisfying meal for around $5. It may look a little chaotic during the lunch rush, but don't be discouraged; the line moves plenty fast and it is absolutely worth it. Open daily for lunch and dinner.

With its swank dining room and sometimes whimsical ingredients **Pazzaluna,** 360 St. Peter St., 651/223-7000, is the antithesis to Cossetta. A few of their excellent pizzas and pastas start around $10, but the average entrée is double that. Open Tues.–Sat. for dinner, reservations recommended.

Winner of the You Can't Judge a Book by Its Cover award goes to Highland Park's **Ristorante Luci,** 470 S. Cleveland Ave., 651/699-8258. There aren't many restaurants where you can come in jeans and a T-shirt and order a $2,000 bottle of wine, but despite years as a nationally-known kitchen, Luci has not turned its back on its neighborhood roots. Like a real Italian trattoria, this fancy but unpretentious (they've got white linens, but never replaced the Pabst Beer sign from the building's previous incarnation) restaurant puts the emphasis on the food not the atmosphere so you'll find it crowded and noisy, but always friendly. If you want the elegant decor that usually comes with prices this high just cross the street to **Luci Ancora.** The original focuses

You can't judge a book by its cover.

more on the south of Italy, while Ancora tends to tackle the north. At both, a miniature first course pasta is about $10, while entrées run $15–30. Open daily for dinner. Reservations are essential.

Japanese

Saji-Ya, 695 Grand Ave., 651/292-0444, is a hip little joint with five dozen sushi options at the bar, a knife-whirling teppanyaki room, and bento trays—perfect for the outdoor deck. You can eat lunch for under $10, but dinner will cost much more. Reservations recommended. Open Mon.– Sat. for lunch and daily for dinner.

Two other more casual spots with sure-fire sushi are found downtown: **Sakura,** 350 St. Peter St., 651/224-0185, (open daily for lunch and dinner); and **Katsu Sushi,** 465 Wabasha St. N., 651/310-0111, (open Tues.–Sun. for lunch and dinner). Both are a bit cheaper than Saji-Ya and also have full menus.

Korean

All three of St. Paul's Korean restaurants—**Shilla,** 694 Snelling Ave. N., 651/645-0006; **Mirror of Korea,** 761 Snelling Ave. N., 651/647-9004; and **Sole Café,** 684 Snelling Ave. N., 651/644-2068—sit within two blocks of each other and all are quite similar in atmosphere, price (about $9 a plate), and quality of food. All are open six days a week (Shilla is closed on Mon., Mirror on Tues., and Sole on Wed.) for lunch and dinner.

Mexican

St. Paulites in the know head to **El Burrito Mercado,** 175 Concord St., 651/227-2192, for their Mexican fix. This grocery store cafeteria serves up great burritos, *tortas,* and *guisados* for just two or three dollars. Open daily for breakfast, lunch, and dinner.

Across the street, **El Amanecer,** 194 Concord St., 651/291-0758, has a full Mexican menu, but their specialty is seafood, and the extensive selection runs from fried red snapper with garlic to shrimp fajitas. Most piscotorial entrées cost around $15, while enchiladas and the like are about half that. Mariachi bands play on weekends. Open daily for breakfast, lunch, and dinner.

La Cucaracha, 36 Dale St. S., 651/221-9682,

is a long time neighborhood favorite serving old family recipes with some American modifications for about $9 a plate. The margarita selection is impressive. Open daily for lunch and dinner.

Middle Eastern

Friendly **Babani's,** 544 St. Peter St., 651/602-9964, claims to be the first Kurdish restaurant in the nation and, as improbable as it seems, they've made this out-of-the-way downtown location work since 1997. There is no need to be timid since all of the lovingly prepared items are explained on the menu, and vegetarians have plenty of choices. Lunch items cost about $7 and dinner averages around $12. Open weekdays for lunch and daily for dinner.

For some Afghan flavor there's **Khyber Pass,** 1571 Grand Ave., 651/690-0505. Platters like chicken in curry sauce and lamb kebabs are lovingly prepared and mighty tasty, though a bit pricey at around $8 lunch and $11 dinner. Open Mon.–Sat. for lunch and dinner.

Natural Foods

Everything at **Sidney's,** 917 Grand Ave., 651/227-5000, which is primarily pizza and pasta, is prepared from scratch, and many ingredients are organic. The menu contains many creative dishes like Mardi Gras fettuccini (with a Cajun tomato sauce) and peanut butter and jelly pizza, all for about $10. They are open daily for breakfast, lunch, and dinner.

Nepali

The Nepali and Tibetan cuisine at **Everest on Grand,** 1278 Grand Ave., 651/696-1666, is lovingly prepared to order and the drinks selection is a lot of fun. Most dishes are in the $9 range, though the best options are the $9 lunch buffet or one of the complete dinners for about $15. Open daily for lunch and dinner.

Pizza

Inquire locally about the best pizza in St. Paul and a majority of people will direct you to **Red's Savoy,** 421 E. 7th St., 651/227-1437, which, with candles and an aquarium, is as classy as a hole-in-the-wall can be. A large, thin-crust laden with cheese is just $9. Open daily for lunch and dinner.

For a true Italian experience visit **Punch Neapolitan Pizza,** 704 S. Cleveland Ave., 651/696-1066, where they follow the rules of Vera Pizza Napoletana, a group of Naples pizzeria owners "dedicated to preservation of Neapolitan pizza." The flaky wood-fired, brick oven-singed crust is topped with imported San Marzano tomatoes and fresh mozzarella. They are a little less conservative with the toppings, which include such options as arugula, cracked red pepper, and roasted eggplant. For all this pizza glory they charge just $10 per pie. The fairly cramped quarters out in Highland Park are only open Tuesday–Saturday for dinner.

Steak Houses

Mancini's Char House, 531 W. 7th St., 651/224-7345, is *the* St. Paul steakhouse and has been since 1954. The steak and seafood menu is priced $15–35 and the dim lights and red vinyl booths transport you back to the set of a mobster movie in the hey-day of Vegas. Open daily for dinner, reservations recommended.

Thai and Lao

Ruam Mit, 475 St. Peter St., 651/290-0067, skimps on the decorating budget but not in the kitchen, which turns out consistently fresh and flavorful Thai. The portions are huge, and very few of the 60-odd menu items exceed $10, while the small lunch buffet is just $6. Remember, when they say hot, they mean it. Open Mon.–Sat. for lunch and dinner. Also downtown, **Sawatdee,** 289 5th St. E., 651/222-5859 (see Minneapolis), in a unique converted warehouse setting, is always popular and rightly so. Open Mon.–Sat. for lunch and daily for dinner.

The simple **Family Lao-Thai Restaurant,** 501 University Ave. W., 651/224-5026, offers a taste of Laos and northeastern Thailand, like deep fried quail, papaya salads, and beef lob for about $8 an entrée. Open Tues.–Sun. for lunch and dinner.

Vietnamese

In my experience you can't go wrong with any of the plethora of authentic Vietnamese restaurants in Frog Town, though the popular **Mai Village,** 422 University Ave. W., 651/290-2585, does stand out. Most everything on the large menu is under $8, though if you've got a serious appetite try the Bò 7 Món, their $15 seven-course specialty meal. Open Mon.–Sat. for lunch and dinner.

Clearly with all the authentic Vietnamese on University Avenue the perpetual "Best of" awards won by the **Lotus Victoria,** 867 Grand Ave., 651/228-9156, must be due mostly to the location, though the food is quite good and few of their 150-plus menu items (consider trying anything with the spicy mustard sauce) exceed $10 so you really can't go wrong. Open daily for lunch and dinner.

SHOPPING

Grand Avenue is the city's most interesting shopping district with plenty of one-of-a-kind shops. You can also find some interesting s hops along University Avenue, like the tiny **Hmong Arts, Books, & Crafts,** 298 University Ave. W., 651/293-0019, and the massive **AntiQues Minnesota,** 1197 University Ave. W., 651/646-0037. The quality of the inventory at both is excellent.

The covered, open-air **St. Paul Farmer's Market** at the end of 5th Street in Lowertown has been operating since 1853. About a third of the vendors are Hmong, and a few sell some traditional crafts, too. The market runs Saturdays 6 A.M.–1 P.M. and Sundays 8 A.M.–1 P.M. from late April until early November, plus some occasional Saturdays during the winter. A smaller version operates on the Seventh Place Mall on Tuesdays and Thursdays during the summer and into October. Besides the farmers market, downtown has little shopping of note, though you can get some *A Prairie Home Companion* recordings and other merchandise at the **Fitzgerald Theater,** 10 E. Exchange St., 651/290-1221, and quality antiques along West 7th Street.

Bookstores

The best independent booksellers in Minnesota, **Ruminator Books,** 1648 Grand Ave.,

651/699-0587, has been around since 1970. Just down the street is the larger **Bound To Be Read,** 870 Grand Ave., 651/646-2665. The **Red Balloon Bookshop,** 891 Grand Ave., 651/224-8320, is a truly amazing children's bookstore, and the bookstore at the **Minnesota History Center,** 345 Kellogg Blvd. W., 651/296-6126, has an astonishing collection of local interest titles. You can get outdoor recreation maps and a handful of local interest books at **Minnesota's Bookstore,** 117 University Ave. W., 651/297-3000. The Map Store, 111 Kellogg Square, 651/227-6277, stocks a lot of what it says it does, including USGS topo maps.

Midway Book & Comic, 1579 University Ave. W., 651/644-7605, is the city's largest used bookstore, while others good used collections are found at **Sixth Chamber,** 1332 Grand Ave., 651/690-9463, and **Books On Snelling,** 145 Snelling Ave. N., 651/645-9900.

INFORMATION AND SERVICES

Tourist Information

St. Paul tourism brochures are available at the Landmark Center, Science Museum, Children's Museum, City Hall, Minnesota History Center, and the Capitol during their regular hours. You can have any and all questions answered by the **St. Paul Convention and Visitors Bureau,** 175 W. Kellogg Blvd., Suite 502, 651/265-4900 or 800/627-6101, www.stpaulcvb.org. Be sure to request their **Fun Pass** to get discounts at attractions, hotels, and restaurants in and around St. Paul. They are open weekdays 8:30 A.M.–5 P.M.

Post Office

The city's main post office is downtown at 180 Kellogg Blvd. E., 651/293-6034. They are open weekdays 8:30 A.M.–5:30 P.M. and Saturday 9 A.M.–noon.

Internet Access

If you show any library card you can get Internet access at the **St. Paul Public Library,** 90 W. 4th St., 651/266-7000. **Dunn Bros. Coffee,** 367 Wabasha St., 651/767-0567, downtown has wireless service and a couple of computers available free to anyone making a purchase.

GETTING AROUND

General **city bus** information is detailed in the Twin Cities introductory section. Metro Transit has an information station in the Firstar Center, 101 E. 5th St. (skyway level), where you can buy passes or get information. It is open weekdays 7:30 A.M.–5 P.M.

You can **rent a car** from **Avis,** 255 E. 6th St., 651/917-9955 or 800/230-4898; **Budget,** 166 E. 7th Pl., 612/727-2000 or 800/404-8033; **Enterprise,** 395 E. 7th St., 651/225-9766; and **Thrifty,** 64 E. 6th St., 651/227-7690 or 800/847-4389, all located downtown, or **Hertz,** 730 Transfer Rd., 651/644-6012 or 800/654-3131, at the Amtrak station.

The Suburbs

METRO SOUTH

Depending on your viewpoint, the towns below Minneapolis are the best or worst of suburbia. While you'll find street after street of similar looking houses and strip malls it also holds some of the region's most popular attractions. Bloomington (pop. 85,172) is Minnesota's fifth largest city and, as home to the Mall of America, has made the Twin Cities' rivalry into a bit of a three-way affair. Despite the prevailing wisdom, the area is not all tills and thrills. In contrast to the amusement parks, malls, and casinos are some excellent historic sites, a traditional Japanese garden, and a 10,000-acre National Wildlife Refuge. With so much to offer it's not surprising that the southern suburbs are extremely popular places with locals and tourists alike.

Sights

The **Minnesota Zoo,** 952/431-9500, way to the south in Apple Valley, is widely regarded as one of the nation's best. Over 2,300 animals from five continents live on the 500-acre compound, and a genuine effort is made to mimic their natural environment. Naturally northern creatures like wolves, caribou, Siberian tigers, and musk ox are a specialty, but the tropics area and aquatic hall are also excellent. Curiously, most marquee species like giraffe, hippo, lion, and elephant are missing, but they hope to change this soon. The regular shark feedings and dolphin shows are also crowd favorites. A monorail ride offers a unique (and climate-controlled) view of the outdoor animals. The zoo is open daily 9 A.M.–6 P.M. during the summer, as well as weekends in May and September; the rest of the year it closes at 4 P.M. Admission is $11. Also at the zoo is the jumbo-sized **Imation IMAX Theatre,** 952/431-4629, with a six-story-tall movie screen. Tickets are $9, though a combo ticket with the zoo is $18.

Just about six miles west of the Mall of America, but a whole world away, is the **Normandale Japanese Gardens,** 952/487-8145. Islands, bridges, a waterfall, and meticulously manicured trees are positioned around a pond at the center of the two-acre site. Created and overseen by a garden architect from Tokyo, it follows traditional design elements, though most plants are heartier varieties that can withstand Minnesota winters. The garden is located behind Normandale Community College and is open daily sunrise to sunset.

With over 75 rides, five roller coasters, and a

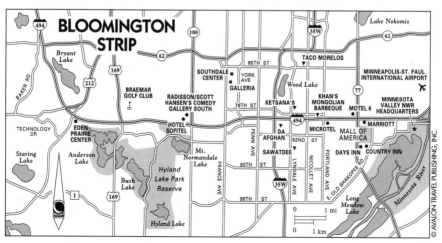

water park Shakopee's **Valleyfair!,** 952/445-7600 or 800/386-7433, is the biggest amusement park around. Also on the grounds is a jumbo IMAX theater and Challenge Park, with mini golf and bumper boats. A nightly laser and fireworks show closes the park on most summer nights. Open May through Labor Day and weekends in Sept. Admission $33 for unlimited rides, though activities in Challenge Park cost extra. Not far from Minnesota's largest amusement park is its largest "Amaizement Park." Each fall **Sever's Corn Maze,** 952/974-5000, cuts miles of paths through a cornfield. Getting lost in a corn field is fun enough, but live music, an exotic petting farm, pig races, camel rides, and a hay bale maze for the little ones lets you make an afternoon out of it. The maze is wheelchair accessible. Sever's is located next to Canterbury Park in Shakopee and is open 10 A.M.–6 P.M. beginning Labor Day weekend. Admission is $9.

Just upriver from Valleyfair! is **Historic Murphy's Landing,** 2187 E. Hwy. 101, 952/445-6901, a 19th-century living history museum spread out over 88 riverside acres. You'll ride out to the village on a horse-drawn wagon and walk amongst the nearly 40 restored and au-

thentically furnished buildings laid out in chronological order from an 1844 log fur trading post to the 1893 town hall. Other structures you'll find in between include a general store, blacksmith shop, one-room schoolhouse, train depot, and homes representing different ethnic groups—Irish, German, Norwegian, English to name a few. In many of the buildings costumed interpreters share their particular culture or demonstrate bygone skills like spinning yarn, making horseshoes, and baking bread—you can often try them yourself. Several 2,000-year-old Native American burial mounds lie at Murphy's Landing and next to it at **Veterans Memorial Park.** Special historical events, such as an old-fashioned Fourth of July and 19th-century doctoring, are held every weekend. Murphy's Landing is open weekends and holidays 10 A.M.–5 P.M. (last tickets sold at 3:30) from late May to late October. It reopens in late November (10 A.M.–4 P.M.) for the month-long Folkways of the Holidays to celebrate Christmases of various nationalities. Admission is $7.50, half price after 2:45.

In downtown Shakopee is the small **Stans Historical Museum,** 235 S. Fuller St., 952/445-

doing a little gardening at Historic Murphy's Landing

© TIM BEWER

0378, which revolves around native son Maurice Stans. He served in several high government positions, including secretary of commerce under President Nixon, before being named finance chair of Nixon's Committee to Re-elect the President (CREEP) in 1972. The displays paint a rosy, hometown proud picture of his Watergate shame. Much more interesting is Stan's African arts collection, which spans the continent and was gathered during 19 visits. The museum is open Tuesday, Wednesday, and Friday 9 A.M.– 4 P.M., Thursday 9 A.M.–8 P.M., and Saturday 11 A.M.–3 P.M. Admission is free. Next door is the house where Stans was born. No original furnishings remain, but Maurice himself restored the ground floor to the way he remembered it as a child. Someone from the museum will let you in to look around if they have some spare time.

The **Sibley House Historic Site,** 1357 Sibley Memorial Highway, 651/452-1596, in the tiny riverside village of Mendota (a Dakota name for Meeting of the Waters) sits across from Fort Snelling at the confluence of the Minnesota and Mississippi Rivers and is the oldest permanent European settlement in the state. Fur traders, long familiar with the area, had established camps by the early 1800s, and in 1824 John Jacob Astor's American Fur Company built an outpost here. A decade later future first governor Henry H. Sibley was named the post's second director and the house he erected here in 1838 is the oldest stone residence in Minnesota. It was restored and refurnished in 1910 and has been open as a historic site ever since. A few other limestone-constructed structures from that era remain standing, including the home/inn built next door by the renowned fur trader Jean-Baptiste Faribault, which now houses some museum exhibits, and a cold store used by the fur company now filled with a simulated trading post. Guided tours of the buildings depart Thursday–Monday between 10 A.M. (except noon on Sun.) to 3:30 P.M. from May through October and last about an hour. Admission is $4.

One of just four urban national wildlife refuges in the country, the **Minnesota Valley National Wildlife Refuge** is a surprisingly wild place. The 10,000-acre preserve stretches 34 miles from Fort Snelling State Park upstream along the Min-

nesota River to Jordan and, despite the adjacent development, the myriad habitats are home to abundant animals, ranging from river otter to prairie skink, though the birds are most notable—the 120 or so nesting species include bald eagle, peregrine falcon, wild turkey, and scarlet tanager. The visitors center, 3815 E. 80th St., 952/854-5900, which can give you the lowdown on hiking and wildlife watching opportunities in the many units, sits in the shadow of the Mall of America and is open Tuesday–Sunday 9 A.M.– 5 P.M. There is also an art gallery, interpretive exhibits, and snowshoe rental here.

At Fleming Field Airport in South St. Paul is the aircraft collection of **Commemorative Air Force–Minnesota Wing,** 651/455-6942. Six World War II planes are on display, including one of just four remaining P-51C Mustang prop fighters and a B-25 Mitchell medium bomber which, if you've got $1,725 to spare, you can take a ride in. Vintage military vehicles and other aircraft and crew artifacts are also on display. Their historic hanger (#3), built by the Navy in 1941 as a base to train pilots, is usually open Wednesday 10 A.M.–6 P.M. and Saturday 10 A.M.– 5 P.M., though they are often performing maintenance at other times so feel free to call and ask if you can stop by. Admission is free.

Recreation

Except for 20 miles of trail, including the most challenging mountain bike and cross-country ski paths in the Twin Cities, the 2,400-acres of rolling hills comprising **Murphy-Hanrehan Park Reserve,** 952/447-6913, have been left undeveloped (the mountain biking season only runs Aug.–Oct. to reduce erosion). To reach the trailhead, take County Road 27 south of County Road 42 and follow the signs for about a mile. Park admission is $5 Friday–Sunday (and holidays) and $3 the rest of the week (but free on Tues.). Another recommended set of trails loops through the 2,000 acres of hills and lakes at **Lebanon Hills Regional Park,** 651/438-4671. Hikers and horseback riders each have about 11 miles worth, while mountain bikers get a pair of fairly challenging loops totaling 2.5 miles. The groomed and tracked winter trails satisfy

THE HIGH TEMPLE OF CONSUMERISM

The **Mall of America** is big. Really big. It could hold seven Yankee Stadiums, 32 Boeing 747s, or 24,336 school buses. It has its own zip code. You get the idea. It is also wildly popular. Not only do the 43 million annual visitors (more than Disney World, Graceland, and the Grand Canyon combined) make it far and away the most popular destination in Minnesota: it is, by some accounts, the third most popular travel destination in America. Nearly 40 percent of all visitors come from more than 150 miles away and six percent (that's over 2.5 million a year) arrive from foreign countries. Some, particularly British, Scandinavian, and Japanese visitors, even come to Minnesota on package holidays just to shop the mall. The megamall is not just the largest shopping center in the United States; with a bank, post office, college campus, Chapel of Love (that's right, thousands of people have tied the knot here—call 800/299-5683 to be the next newlyweds), day cares, and doctor's offices, it is like a city unto itself. Sunday even sees church services in the Camp Snoopy amusement park.

Store hours are Monday–Saturday 10 A.M.–9:30 P.M. and Sunday 11 A.M.–7 P.M., though the nightclubs and many of the restaurants and attractions open earlier and close later. Mall walkers are let in daily at 7 A.M. The moment you get there pick up a map; you'll need it.

Sights and Recreation

Camp Snoopy, 952/883-8600, the mall's 7.5-acre centerpiece, is the largest indoor theme park in the nation. The 20 rides include a roller coaster, seven-story Ferris wheel, log chute, bumper cars, and several kiddie rides. Other attractions include a climbing wall, arcade, and the X-treme trampoline. You can choose to buy individual ride tickets or get a $23 wristband for unlimited thrills. The park is typically open Monday–Thursday 10 A.M.–9:30 P.M., Friday–Saturday 10 A.M.–10 P.M., and Sunday 10:30 A.M.–7:30 P.M. with slightly extended summer hours.

Over 3,000 sea creatures live beneath Camp Snoopy at **Underwater Adventures,** 952/888-3483. Walk-through tunnels in the 1.2 million-gallon aquariums let you get eye to eye with denizens of Minnesota's deep like sturgeon, muskie, and snap-

ping turtles and ocean dwellers like sandtiger sharks, moray eels, and K.G. the octopus who opens a jar to get his meals. You'll also find a touch pond with sharks and stingrays, virtual submarine ride, pirate-ship playground, and various other interesting non-aquatic creatures like scorpions. Certified SCUBA divers can swim with the sharks for $175: they provide tanks, and weights; you must provide all other gear. The aquarium is open Monday–Thursday 10 A.M.–9 P.M., Friday–Saturday 9:30 A.M.–9:30 P.M., and Sunday 10 A.M.–7 P.M. Monday–Saturday opening times are a half-hour earlier during the summer. Admission is $12; $14 during the summer.

Though there are dozens of nominees, the winner of the Only-in-the-Mall-of-America award goes to General Mills' **Cereal Adventure,** (N376), 952/814-2900, a family-friendly fun park that "celebrates the joy of eating cereal." Kids can slide down a giant spoon into an oversized bowl of plastic cheerios, learn how cereal is made, and get their mug on a box of Wheaties. Open Mon.–Sat. 10 A.M.–9:30 P.M. and Sun. 11 A.M.–7 P.M. Admission is $6.

Part store, part art gallery, and part workshop, the **Lego Imagination Center,** (S164) 952/858-8949, delights people of all ages and is one of the mall's must-sees.

© TIM BEWER

much more than just a shopping mall

Entertainment

Not surprisingly the Mall of America has a plethora of diversions, and that's besides the arcades, bowling alley, and movie theater. **Knuckleheads,** 952/854-5223, hosts comedians while dancers can choose between **Gators,** 952/854-5483, with a Florida swamp theme, and **Flashbaxx,** 952/854-5483, where you dance to the classics of the 1970s and '80s under disco balls. Dueling pianos at **Ltl Ditty's,** 952/854-5483, engage you and everyone else to belt out classic hits. All of these and more are part of the Upper East Side Entertainment District; it stays open until 1 A.M. nightly.

Accommodations

Thanks to the mall Bloomington now has more hotel rooms than either Minneapolis or St. Paul. Both the **Country Inn,** 952/854-5555 or 800/456-4000, and **Days Inn,** 952/854-8400 or 800/329-7466, claim to be the closest hotel to the Mall of America, but any difference between them is only a matter of feet. The Days Inn's recreation area has a large pool, whirlpool, sauna, and video games. The Country Inn has two small pools, a whirlpool, and exercise equipment. Rooms can go as low as $89 at each, though expect to pay a lot more. The massive **Marriott,** 952/854-7441 or 800/228-9290, with a large pool, whirlpool, and fitness center, has nearly 500 well-appointed rooms which you can also get for as little as $89. It's much fancier and only about five-minutes from the mall. All three have free airport and mall shuttles.

Food

While most of the 50-plus restaurants are exactly the generic sort you would expect to find in a mall there are a few tasty alternatives like the Southwestern-style burritos at **Baja Tortilla Grill** (S392) and the award-winning ribs at **Famous Dave's Barbeque** (S320). On the fancy end are a pair of formal restaurant chains operated by the same company; both specialize in California cuisine. The menu at the **Napa Valley Grille,** (W220), 952/858-9934, changes every other month or so, but mustard seared yellow fin tuna and spinach fettuccine are typical. The **California**

Café, (S368), 952/854-2233, has a broader menu running from wood-fired pizzas to grilled rabbit. Both charge about $20 for dinner and $12 for lunch and are open daily for both meals. If the food itself is irrelevant, there are also several theme restaurants including **Rainforest Café** (S102) and **Hooters** (E404).

Shopping

Ironically the least interesting part of the Mall of America is the shopping, which stands out more for quantity than quality—there are three Sam Goodys, four Sunglass Huts, and too many Gaps to even count. That's not to say that you won't find something interesting; with 520-plus stores to browse it's sure to happen. Choices range from the department store anchors Bloomingdale's, Macy's, Nordstrom, and Sears to specialty stores with stocks limited to nothing but magnets or farm toys. A few unique stores worth seeking out are **Lake Wobegon USA** (E350) with *A Prairie Home Companion* and other Minnesota Public Radio goods and **The Garlic Shoppe** (W326) with more garlic-infused products than you could ever imagine. **Minnesot-ah!** (E157 and N316), **Love From Minnesota** (W380), and **Explore Minnesota USA** (N129) all have North Star State souvenirs. For a more far-flung cultural flavor there's **Liten Hus** (E145), Scandinavian; **Spirit of the Red Horse** (W387), Native American; and **Irish Indeed** (N142).

Information and Services

For the lowdown on the mall stop by one of the **Guest Service Centers,** positioned at each of the main entrances on Level 1, call 952/883-8800 or 800/879-3555, or see www.mallofamerica.com. Statewide tourism information is available at the **Explore Minnesota USA** store (N129), 952/853-0182; **Highland Bank,** (W322), 952/853-0216, can change common foreign currencies; and there is also a **post office** (N254), 952/854-1849.

Metro Transit runs **express buses** from downtown Minneapolis and St. Paul to the Mall of America's Transit Station. The **Hiawatha Line** light rail project will connect the mall to downtown Minneapolis and the Airport by the end of 2004.

M

TWIN CITIES

cross-country skiers of all abilities, though most of the 14 miles of trail are graded intermediate. Short portages link seven of the lakes into a short canoe trail. The **Diamond T Ranch,** 4889 Pilot Knob Rd., 651/454-1464, adjacent to the park can take you horseback riding there.

Buck Hill, 952/435-7174, offers 13 downhill ski runs and a terrain park. Prior Lake has a pair of the state best public golf courses: **The Wilds,** 3151 Wilds Ridge, 952/445-3500; and **Legends,** 8540 Credit River Blvd., 952/226-1147.

Entertainment

It's far from the excess and glitter of Las Vegas, but Prior Lake's **Mystic Lake Casino,** 952/445-9000 or 800/262-7799, is one of the largest casinos between Sin City and Atlantic City. The **Shakopee Mdewakanton Sioux Community Pow-Wow** is held near here in mid-August.

Gamblers can also play the ponies or seven-card stud just up the road at **Canterbury Park,** 952/445-7223 or 800/340-6361, in Shakopee.

The hundreds of knights, knaves, minstrels, and jesters frolicking around the 16th-century village that is the **Minnesota Renaissance Festival,** 952/445-7361 or 800/966-8215, guarantee a good time for all. Eat lots of food and buy handcrafted wares between the real jousting matches. The merriment takes place near Shakopee every weekend from mid-August through the end of September. The **Trail of Terror,** held weekend evenings during October on the Renaissance Festival grounds, has a haunted maze, hay rides, and sideshow. Tickets are $17 for the main festival and $15 for the Halloween event.

Scott Hansen's Comedy Gallery South, 763/420-2213, at the Hotel Sofitel, gets many big name acts, while **Stevie Ray's Comedy Cabaret,** 952/835-7800, at the Radisson, 7800 Normandale Blvd., offers a night at the improv.

Hotels and Motels

Bloomington Strip: Hotels surrounding the Mall of America are listed with the mall, though both the cheapest and the poshest lodgings in the area are down the freeway a bit. The **Microtel Inn,** 952/806-0000 or 877/806-8600, has tiny rooms and a fitness center. The rooms are larger, but much, much older (a renovation is planned) at the **Motel 6,** 612/861-4491 or 800/466-8356. Both charge about $65, and the Microtel has a free airport and Mall of America shuttle. At the other end of the spectrum is the **Hotel Sofitel,** 952/835-1900 or 800/763-4835, where large rooms with all the bells and whistles go for as little as $109, but expect to pay more. It has a large fitness center, a trio of French restaurants, comedy club, and free mall shuttle.

Burnsville: The **Ramada,** 952/890-9550 or 800/666-7829, has standard hotel rooms from $71, but what sets it apart are the 28 **Fanta-Suites** with an igloo and space ship as some options. The theme rooms, each with a private whirlpool, cost $189 and special "Romance Pack-

SHAKOPEE-MDEWAKANTON RESERVATION

Total Area - 1 sq. mile
Tribally Owned - 100 percent
Total Population - 338
Native Population - 214
Tribal Enrollment - 301

In the 1880s a few of the Dakota who had been exiled from Minnesota following the 1862 Dakota Conflict began to return to their homelands near the upper reaches of the Minnesota River. In recognition of their ancestry the government began purchasing land for them at this time, but when reservations were reestablished in the 1930s the Shakopee band, with just a handful of families, was considered too small and they were lumped in with the Lower Sioux. The tribe didn't earn official recognition until 1969. Their Mystic Lake Casino, the second most successful Native American gaming enterprise in the nation by some estimates, lies just 25 miles from downtown Minneapolis and has made the Shakopee Dakota by far the wealthiest tribe in the state. While most of the 18,000 daily players go home with lighter wallets the tribe itself has hit the jackpot and reportedly most members are now millionaires.

ages" are available. There is also an indoor/outdoor pool and whirlpool.

Shakopee/Prior Lake: In town the simple but decent **Travelodge,** 952/445-5074 or 888/515-6375, charges $66 and has a whirlpool, sauna, and game room. Next to Canterbury Park the **Park Inn,** 1244 Canterbury Rd., 952/445-3644 or 800/670-7275, offers a pool, whirlpool, sauna, exercise room, and game room. At $79 it's Shakopee's best value. The **Mystic Lake Casino Hotel,** 952/445-3000 or 800/262-7799, is a ten-story, 416-room monster with pool, whirlpool, sauna, and free use a nearby health club. Regular rates start at $109.

Inver Grove Heights: Just five minutes from downtown St. Paul, the **Microtel Inn,** 651/552-0555 or 888/771-7171, charges $69.

Campgrounds

Considering that it sits squarely in the Twin Cities metro area, the 93-site **Lebanon Hills Campground** in Apple Valley is pretty good. One of the dozen basic sites is $14; add $9 for a full hook-up. If you're here to gamble the **Dakotah Meadows RV Park & Campground,** 952/445-8800 or 800/653-2267, next to the Mystic Lake Casino is the obvious place to be. Nearly 100 parking lot sites with full hook-ups and ten traditional tepees are $16 each.

Food

Bloomington Strip: Despite being hidden away in a business park **Da Afghan,** 929 W. 80th St., 952/888-5824, has garnered a loyal following thanks to impeccable food and service. Prices run $10–20. Open Tues.–Sun. for dinner, and Thurs. and Fri. for a $7 lunch buffet. Walk through the buffet line at **Khan's Mongolian Barbeque,** 500 E. 78th St., 612/861-7991, choose your ingredients, and let them fry them up for you in the open kitchen. Lunch costs $8 and dinner is $12. Open daily. For a taste of Thai, Minneapolis' popular **Sawatdee,** 8501 Lyndale Ave. S., 952/888-7177, has a Bloomington branch, and **Ketsana's,** 7545 Lyndale Ave. S., 612/869-0087, is a little diner owned by the same family as the wonderful Ruam Mit in St. Paul. Both are reasonably priced and open

daily for lunch and dinner. Minneapolis' **Taco Morelos,** 2 W. 66th St., 612/243-9699, serves their wonderful Mexican meals down in Richfield. Open daily for lunch and dinner.

Shakopee: The same people behind Minneapolis' wonderful Taco Morelos also run **Sabroso,** 1120 1st Ave. E., 952/445-0900. Open daily for lunch and dinner. The beloved **Dangerfield's,** 1583 1st Ave. E., 952/445-2245, is perched on a hill over the Minnesota River, and the screened-in deck is the place to be in the summer. The menu runs the gamut from shrimp linguini to prime rib au jus to cashew chicken wraps to pizza to . . ., you get the idea. The majority of items are under $8, and nothing is over $20. Open daily for lunch and dinner.

Shopping

There are few things you can't find in the Mall of America, but antiques are one of them; however, the 325 dealers at **AntiQues Minnesota,** 952/894-7200, take care of that. Both the **Shakopee Trading Post,** 723 1st Ave. W., 952/496-2263, in downtown Shakopee, and **First American Crafts & Gifts,** 952/496-3528, by the casinos, have high quality Native American arts and crafts from Minnesota and beyond.

METRO WEST

Other than those who live here, most people look at these communities as just the space between Minneapolis and Lake Minnetonka. Of course, there's a bit more to the area than this—but not much. The main thing the western suburbs have going for them is excellent shopping and dining.

Sights and Recreation

It won't make most people's top 40 countdown, but almost everyone will find something interesting at the **Pavek Museum of Broadcasting,** 3515 Raleigh Ave., 952/926-8198. You can watch TV on a screen the size of a doughnut or play a tune on a theramin, a musical instrument you don't actually touch. The jumbled collection contains over 1,000 radios, televisions, and phonographs from the first half of the 20th century; rows of historic vacuum tubes; a working

1912 rotary spark-gap transmitter like that used on the Titanic; and a 1950s radio studio where kids can broadcast their own show. The museum, hidden away in St. Louis Park, is open Tuesday–Friday 10 A.M.–6 P.M. and Saturday 9 A.M.–5 P.M. Admission is $5.

Golfers might want to play a round at Edina's **Braemar Golf Club,** 952/826-6793; or **Rush Creek Golf Club,** 763/494-0400, in Maple Grove, two of the state's best.

Entertainment

Although they've been doing musicals and comedies since 1974, the **Plymouth Playhouse,** 2705 Annapolis Ln. N. (in the Best Western hotel), 763/553-1600, is now best known for their renditions of Howard Mohr's classic book *How To Talk Minnesotan,* which has run in several different forms for years. Also in Plymouth, at the Radisson Hotel, is **Scott Hansen's Comedy Gallery West,** 763/420-2213, which puts many good national acts on stage, including the eponymous owner.

Accommodations

The hotels along I-394 offer easy access to downtown Minneapolis. The closest is the **Holiday Inn Express,** 763/545-8300 or 800/465-4329, where $84 rates include a small pool, whirlpool, and exercise room. The **Super 8,** 763/546-6277 or 800/800-8000, right nearby charges just $55. Rooms start at $99 at the **Sheraton,** 952/593-0000 or 888/625-5144; and $79 at the **Doubletree,** 952/542-8600 or 800/222-8733. Both offer small pools, whirlpools, fitness centers, and saunas, while the Doubletree, which is much closer to downtown Minneapolis, also has a game room.

To the south, in St. Louis Park, is the **Lakeland Motel,** 4025 Hwy. 7, 952/926-6575. The building is old, but the rooms, priced from just $60, are spotless and have some new furnishings. The nearby **Best Western American Inn,** 3924 Excelsior Blvd., 952/927-7731 or 800/528-1234, has smaller but more modern rooms for $80. Both are just a hop, skip, and a jump from Minneapolis.

Food

Edina: The dining is as trendy as the shopping at Edina's Galleria Mall. The Chicago-based **Big Bowl,** 952/928-7888, chain serves up pan-Asian fare like kung pao beef, pad thai, and a choose-your-own ingredient stir-fry for around $9. Also sustaining shoppers for under $10 is **The Good Earth Restaurant & Bakery,** 952/925-1001, which, like the name suggests, specializes in natural foods using whole grains, fresh juices, and other organic ingredients whenever possible. Galleria is also home to a **Sidney's,** 952/925-2002 (see Minneapolis).

The fashionable 50th & France neighborhood, centered on the Minneapolis-Edina border, also has a plenty of quality dining. **Tejas,** 3910 W. 50th St., 952/926-0800, is considered by some critics to be as good as any Southwestern restaurant in the Sunbelt. The menu changes with the seasons, but the grilled chicken-wild rice burrito with mango-habanero sauce and apple-endive slaw gives you a good idea of what to expect. Everything on the lunch menu is under $10, while the dinner menu is $15 and up. Open Mon.–Sat. for lunch and dinner. The funky little **Edina Grill,** 3907 W. 50th St., 952/927-7933, is the sister restaurant of St. Paul's Highland Grill; prices and hours are the same. Also, two of Minneapolis's favorite Italian eateries, **Giorgio's,** 4924 France Ave. S., 952/928-0323; and **D'Amico & Sons,** 3948 W. 50th St., 952/926-1187, have branches here. Just up the road, the burgers and malts (both $4) and white-uniformed waitresses at the **Convention Grill,** 3912 Sunnyside Rd., 952/920-6881, will take you back to the 1950s. Open daily for lunch and dinner.

I-394: Many of the expected chains are tucked in between the hotels along the freeway, but there are also some real finds. The Pan-Asian **August Moon,** 5340 Wayzata Blvd., 763/544-7017, charges $9–17 for goat cheese won tons, red curry coconut soup, and pineapple chicken. Open daily for dinner and weekdays for lunch. Across the street, **Yangtze,** 5625 Wayzata Blvd., 952/541-9469, serves traditional Chinese fare including, according to some, the best dim sum around. Entrée prices start at $4 and go up to $16 for the birds nest soup. Open daily for lunch and dinner. In the same little strip mall is the award-winning **Taste of India,** 5617 Wayzata Blvd., 952/541-4865, with an all-you-can-eat

$8 lunch buffet. Open daily for lunch and dinner. **Shelly's,** 6501 Wayzata Blvd., 952/541-9900, cooks with a patented wood-roast system to turn out a flavorful menagerie of meats from pork prime rib to trout to tenderloin steak in a North-woods-lodge environment. Prices run $10 to $30. Open daily for lunch and dinner.

Much farther down the freeway is the festive **Santorini,** 9920 Wayzata Blvd., 952/546-6722, with not only a full Greek menu, but a make-your-own-pizza and pasta bar that is very popular for lunch. Entrées average $15, and they have a good Greek-focused wine list. Nightly entertainment runs from karaoke on Wednesdays to belly dancing on Sundays with live bands in between. Open daily for lunch and dinner. Corned beef and pastrami sandwiches, potato knishes, Dr. Brown's soda, and everything else you would find at a real New York deli are available at **Zaroff's,** 11300 Wayzata Blvd., 952/545-9090. Open daily for breakfast, lunch, and dinner. There is also another **Big Bowl,** 12649 Wayzata Blvd., 952/797-9888, in the Ridgedale Mall.

Shopping

If you enjoy shopping and history, spend a few dollars at Edina's **Southdale Center,** the first totally enclosed shopping center in the United States, which opened its doors in 1956. This 150-store center was also the birthplace of mall walking. Across the street the **Galleria Mall** is packed with posh shops like Coach, L'Occitane, and Laura Ashley. A unique collection of shops and galleries is in the **50th & France** neighborhood on the Edina-Minneapolis border. Kevin Smith's big-budget breakthrough movie *Mallrats* was filmed in the **Eden Prairie Center,** but the mall has been so thoroughly remodeled that you'll barely recognize it. Over half a dozen antique stores line Mainstreet in downtown Hopkins.

LAKE MINNETONKA AND CHANHASSEN

This 14,310-acre Rorschach test has been a popular tourist destination for well over a century. Tonka, as locals and regulars call it, has a multitude of long peninsulas and deep bays that sum to 105 miles of shoreline; some early explorers even named it Peninsula Lake. The Dakota had dubbed it Minne-ho-Tonka (Water with a Big Voice, but some historians don't believe that the

Wayzata's Towne Trolley

© TIM BEWER

Dakota actually call it this) and Governor Ramsey shortened it to Minnetonka, which would translate to just Big Water. Incidentally, Minnetonka Moccasins took its name from the lake though they began, and remain, a Minneapolis-based company, while Tonka Toys got their start making trucks in a basement workshop in the lakeside community of Mound.

Settlers came in 1852, immediately after the ratification of treaties with the Dakota, and fifteen years later the first tourists rode James J. Hill's Great Northern Railroad from Minneapolis to Wayzata's (Wise etta) lakeshore. From here, people boarded paddlewheel steamers to travel to luxurious resorts across the lake. Wildlife was abundant on the shore, and men could hunt and fish at will. At Minnetonka's peak during the 1880s, 90 boats loaded passengers at the Wayzata dock—the largest, the *Belle of Minnetonka*, carried 2,500 passengers—and the wealthy and famous from across the nation came to sample the good life here. Though today, with development along nearly all of the shore, the sentiment is no longer true, it's easy to understand why back then this was widely considered one of the most beautiful lakes in the state. By the turn of the 20th century the Eastern bigwigs found other playgrounds, and the gilded run ended, though Tonka tourism didn't die. Through the early 20th century most tourists were middle-class day-trippers lured out from Minneapolis and St. Paul by modern amusement parks. Though they continued to come through the Depression, they didn't spend enough money to keep the hotels, fairs, and other businesses going. Eventually the elite returned to build grand mansions and summer homes, and the numerous posh boutiques and top-flight restaurants catering to them, along with the superb boating and sailing, has revived Tonka's status as a top weekend getaway. Fourteen communities fringe the lake, but just two small, busy cities, Wayzata (pop. 4,113) and Excelsior (pop. 2,393), see most of the action.

The city of Chanhassen, a modern sprawling suburb just below the lake, has a pair of Twin Cities favorites: the Minnesota Landscape Arboretum and the Chanhassen Dinner Theatres. It's also home to Prince's **Paisley Park Studios,**

7801 Audubon Rd., his $10 million recording, rehearsal, and film production studio. No regularly scheduled tours are available, though that doesn't mean you can't visit (see the sidebar "Partying with the Purple One").

Sights

The Twin City Rapid Transit Company's first streetcar tracks reached Lake Minnetonka in 1905. The line, which connected Minneapolis with Excelsior, served both tourists and the growing lakeside population. The rambling shoreline made expanding the lines prohibitively expensive, so the TCRT engineers built six boats to connect the rest of the lake's towns and resorts. The narrow, 70-foot boats launched in 1906 were officially called Express Boats, but the public dubbed the double-deckers Streetcar Boats, not just because of their function, but for the form as well: both the land and water people movers were painted canary yellow and had the exact same seats and benches. The service was very popular, but short-lived. By the 1920s most travel to the lakes was by car, and the service was ended in 1926; the boats were scuttled north of Big Island. The **Steamboat *Minnehaha,*** 952/474-2115 or 800/711-2591, was raised from the lake's depths with the intention of putting it on display on dry land. However, others had grander ideas and, with the assistance of the Minnesota Transportation Museum, the fully restored boat made its second maiden voyage out of Excelsior in 1996. Today a ride across the lake on this distinctive craft has become a Tonka tradition. There are a variety of trips available between late May and mid-October, with prices starting at $7—reservations are recommended. Also boarding at the Excelsior dock is the **Lady of the Lake,** 952/929-1209, a 70-foot mock paddlewheeler with narrated 90-minute public cruises around Big Island for $8.

For a look at the lake's heyday, visit the **Excelsior-Lake Minnetonka Historical Society Museum,** 305 Water St., 952/474-8956, to look at the small but interesting collection of photos and artifacts. It's worth a visit just to see the 1924 roller coaster car, which gives new meaning to the term thrill-ride. It is open Thursday 3–6 P.M.,

MINNESOTA LANDSCAPE ARBORETUM

People from across the Twin Cities make regular journeys to Chanhassen to stroll the 1,030 beautiful acres of the Minnesota Landscape Arboretum, 952/443-1400 (dial extension 5010 for the seasonal bloom report), the northernmost of its kind in the United States. Find serenity in the traditional, four-season Japanese Garden or inspiration in the home demonstration gardens. The impressive perennial and annual flower gardens are packed with 20,000 plants; both peak in July. The plant and tree collections include everything from oaks and firs to azaleas and ornamental grasses. On the more natural side there's a bog walk and a prairie restoration. Most displays are along a three-mile drive though there are also trails to hike. Picnic areas are available during the summer and seven miles of trail are groomed for cross-country skiing in the winter. Though the public education and enjoyment missions have taken center stage this remains a research facility under the direction of the Department of Horticultural Science at the University of Minnesota. Naturally the focus is on cold-hardy species and they have developed 80 species of fruit and ornamental plants since opening in 1908: apples remain a key focus.

Hour-long guided tours focus on the seasonality of the gardens. You can go on foot for free through the display gardens or by tram ($2 per person) through the rest of the arboretum. Both run daily except Monday from May through mid-October; the walking tour starts at 10:30 A.M. and the tram runs several times a day. To do it yourself pick up free audio equipment in the Snyder Building. Also in the Snyder Building is a traditional English tea service (Wed. 3:30–4 P.M., Nov. though Mar., $25), conservatory, horticultural library, and gift shop with garden books, gifts, and supplies. The arboretum hosts a plethora of horticultural classes and special events throughout the year, as well as the fun "Thursdays in the Garden" with live music and kid-focussed activities during summer evenings. The grounds are open daily at 8 A.M. closing at 9 P.M. May–September and 5:30 P.M. October–April. The Snyder Building is open Monday–Saturday 8 A.M.–5:30 P.M. (except 8 P.M. Thurs.) and Sunday 11 A.M.–5:30 P.M. between April and October and weekdays 8 A.M.–4:30 P.M. and weekends 11 A.M.–4:30 P.M. the rest of the year. Admission is $5, except free after 4:30 P.M. on Thursdays.

© TIM BEWER

the Minnesota Landscape Arboretum's Japanese garden

and Saturday 10 A.M.–3 P.M. during the summer. Admission is free. Boarding outside the museum is the other half of the Minnesota Transportation Museum's Lake Minnetonka Division, the **Excelsior Streetcar.** Old No. 78, one of the oldest operating streetcars in the country, makes 15-minute trips across town. The streetcar operates Thursday 3–6 P.M., Saturdays and holidays 10 A.M.–4 P.M., and Sunday 1–4 P.M. from the end of May through mid-October. It doesn't run in the rain. The fare is just $1.

While not an actual trolley, Wayzata's shiny red **Towne Trolley** is still fun. Monday–Saturday between mid-May and mid-October the fancy bus makes a half-hour loop through town, and you can get on and off at will. Wednesdays during the summer the trolley leaves the city for the narrated, hour-long tour around the lake. The regular rides are free, while the Gold Coast tour costs $5. The trolley rides start at the 1906 Wayzata Depot, 402 E. Lake St., which is also home to the nearly empty **Wayzata Depot Museum,** 952/473-3631. It is open weekends noon–4 P.M. during the summer and admission is free. The nearby **Minnetonka Center for the Arts,** 2240 North Shore Dr., 952/473-7361, is primarily a large art education center with classes in many media; there is often something interesting in the gallery. Open Mon.–Thurs. 9 A.M.–9:30 P.M. and Fri.–Sat. 9 A.M.–5 P.M. Admission is free. Many people enjoy a stroll through the modest formal flower and shrub gardens at **Noerenberg Memorial County Park,** 2840 North Shore Dr., just up the street from the art center, though picnics are prohibited. Boaters can stop for a picnic on **Big Island, Goose Island,** and **Wawatasso Island.**

Recreation

Excelsior's **Excel Boat Club,** 141 Minnetonka Blvd., 952/401-3880, rents pontoons, kayaks, and fish houses, and arranges fishing guides. Other boat rental options (each has pontoons and fishing boats) around the lake are **Howard's Point Marina,** 5400 Howard's Point Rd., 952/474-4464; **Minnetonka Boat Club & Rental,** 4850 Edgewater Dr., 952/474-5206; and **Rockvam Boat Yards,** 4068 Sunset Dr., 952/471-9515.

Wayzata Beach is just west of the Depot (on the other side of the Minnetonka Boat Works building), and there's another beach in **Excelsior Commons Park** just north of downtown Excelsior. Both are small but busy.

Entertainment

The theater scene out here is truly superlative—largest and oldest to be precise. Having elicited giggles and guffaws since 1940 makes Excelsior's all-comedy **Old Log Theater,** 5175 Meadville St., 952/474-5951 or 800/328-4827, the longest continually running professional theater in the country. Performances are held Wednesday–Saturday at 8 P.M. and Sunday at 7:30 P.M., with matinees most Wednesdays and Thursdays at 1 P.M. Prices are $11 for children's productions, $15 for matinees, and $20–24 for evening performances. Many people take advantage of their on-site restaurant for a pre-performance meal.

The out of the way location hasn't prevented **Chanhassen Dinner Theatres,** 501 W. 78th St., 952/934-1525 or 800/362-3515, from growing into the nation's largest dinner theater. Serving steak and seafood (for the most part, though vegetarian options are available) to as many as 1,000 guests a night also makes them the largest restaurant in the state and one of the largest in the nation. The Broadway of dinner theater has three stages, so at any one time you can choose from a musical, comedy, or drama. The price for dinner and a show runs $30–62 depending on the day, the time, and the performance. On Tuesday–Saturday nights dinner begins at 6 P.M. (an hour or so earlier on Sun.) and there's an 11 A.M. matinee on Wednesday and Saturday. Show time is usually about two hours later, depending on the performance.

There is a free **Summer Concert Series** on the lake from mid-June to mid-August. Wayzata hosts the 7 P.M. concerts on Wednesday nights at the Depot, and on Thursday the performances are in the band shell in Excelsior Commons Park.

The second weekend in September hosts the lake's biggest events. Wayzata's **James J. Hill Days** celebrates the man who first made this a tourist destination with a parade, arts and crafts fair, lumberjack shows, and dachshund races.

Excelsior holds **Apple Day** that Saturday. Over 200 artists sell their wares on the lakeshore the second weekend of June during Excelsior's **Art on the Lake** festival. In early February over 1,000 duffers whack away at tennis balls on one of three nine-hole golf courses out on Wayzata Bay during the **Chilly Open Golf Tournament.**

Accommodations

Property values are way too high for any hotels to open on the lake, so lodging choices are limited. Of course, being so close to Minneapolis the scarcity of lodging doesn't matter much. The only place right by the lake itself is the **Birdhouse Inn and Gardens B&B,** 371 Water St., 952/474-0196, a lovely and luxurious 1858 Italianate home right in downtown Excelsior. Each of the four antique-filled guestrooms (all with private bath) has unique touches like a claw-foot tub or hand-painted floors. Prices run $119–169. A popular hotel choice near the lake is the **AmericInn,** 952/475-4422 or 800/634-3444, a bit to the north in Long Lake. It has a pool, whirlpool, and exercise room and charges $100. Over by the Chanhassen Dinner Theatres the family-owned **Chanhassen Inn,** 531 W. 79th St., 952/934-7373 or 800/242-6466, has decent rooms for $68, while **Country Suites,** 591 W. 78th St., 952/937-2424 or 800/456-4000, charges $109 and has a pool, whirlpool, and exercise room.

Food

Excelsior: The place to be in Excelsior is the boat-friendly **Maynard's,** 685 Excelsior Blvd., 952/470-1800, where an expansive deck reaches out over the lake. You can still glimpse the water from the indoor tables, or sports fans can watch the game up by the bar. The menu has burgers, portabella mushroom pasta, chicken stir-fry, fish and chips, fish tacos, and much more—most of it is priced at around $8. Sunday has a stellar $15 brunch. Open daily for lunch and dinner. Two small Asian establishments in Excelsior rarely disappoint. **Ming Wok,** 205 Water St., 952/470-1010, has a mostly Cantonese menu with some Szechwan flavors running $5–15. Open Mon.–Sat. for lunch and dinner. Most of the ni-

giri sushi at **Yumi's Sushi Bar,** 28 Water St., 952/474-1720, are under $5. Open Mon.–Sat. for dinner. **Adele's Frozen Custard,** 800 Excelsior Blvd., 952/470-0035, just east of downtown Excelsior, not only serves its sinfully rich and delicious namesake delight, but also chili dogs, bratwurst, and other fun fast food all for about $3. They are open daily for lunch and dinner, though they close up shop in January and February. The **Queen of Excelsior,** 952/474-2502, docked in its namesake town, offers a Sunday brunch on the lake every Sunday from May through September. The two-hour cruises depart at 11:30 and the price is $24. Reservations are required.

Wayzata: The **Blue Point,** 739 E. Lake St., 952/475-3636, does everything right; from the setting to the service to the seafood this is one of the lake's best restaurants. Daily dinner options such as grilled Florida swordfish, smoked lobster linguini, and pheasant penne run about $21, though you can pay a lot more than this for an entrée—on the other hand, you can get a sandwich or pasta at lunch for as little as $7. They also feature live lobsters and an oyster bar. If you've got money burning a hole in your pocket this is the place to spend it. Open daily for dinner and Tues.–Sun. for lunch in the summer. The principally Italian **Portofino,** 952/475-1045, in the beautifully renovated Minnetonka Boat Works has a large outdoor deck, and the interior design allows great lake views from most tables in the dining room. Pastas average $15 and steak and seafood run $17–30, though you are mostly paying for the setting. Like most lakeside establishments it has its own dock. Open daily for lunch and dinner. For cheaper Italian there's a branch of **D'Amico & Sons,** 810 E. Lake St., 952/476-8866, (see Minneapolis) on the other side of town.

Elsewhere: Perched on the middle of the lake since 1968 **Lord Fletcher's,** 3746 Sunset Dr., 952/471-8513, is Tonka's most famous restaurant. With choices ranging from Atlantic salmon baked in rice paper with herbs served in the Old World-style dining rooms, to burgers on a lakeside deck nearly big enough to land an airplane on, Fletcher's has something for most tastes. If you don't mind the high prices (the aforementioned selections are $22 and $8 respectively) or the summer weekend mobs, you'll probably enjoy yourself here. Open daily for lunch and dinner, and you can come by boat. Nearby is the classic **Minnetonka Drive-In,** 4658 Shoreline Dr. 952/471-9383. They don't wear roller skates, but carhops still bring cheap ice cream, chilidogs, and chicken dinners right to your car. Open daily for lunch and dinner from roughly April through September.

Shopping

If shopping is your hobby you could spend a day exploring the streets of Excelsior and Wayzata; and without trying too hard you could max out a credit card or two. A couple of standout shops, both in Excelsior, are **Heritage II,** 50 Water St., 952/474-1231, with Scandinavian and British imports, amongst other things; and **Truffle Hill,** 952/470-1996, just west of downtown along County Road 19, with handmade gourmet chocolates.

The best spot for antiques is the **Wayzata Home Center,** 1250 E. Wayzata Blvd., a mall to the northeast of downtown now almost completely filled with antique shops. Everything at Gold Mine Antiques, 332 Broadway Ave. 3., 952/473-7719, in downtown Wayzata is top-shelf. In Excelsior the largest stores are **Country Look In Antiques,** 240 Water St., 952/474-0050; and **Mary O'Neal & Co,** 221 Water St., 952/470-0205. **Captain's Cargo & Gallery,** 261 Water St., 952/474-8963, primarily carries nautical items.

Both **Excelsior Bay Books,** 36 Water St., 952/401-0932, and **The Bookcase of Wayzata,** 607 E. Lake St., 952/473-8341, have good regional sections.

METRO NORTH

Though definitely part of the urban picture, the few worthy attractions in the northern suburbs have a rural personality. Because the hotels are away from the airport and Mall of America, rates tend to be lower up here.

Sights and Recreation

Jane and Heman Gibbs settled on this frontier farmstead in 1849, living in a sod house initially, and the family remained here for a century before the land was turned into the **Gibbs Museum of Pioneer and Dakotah Life,** 2097 W. Larpen-

Gibbs Museum of Pioneer and Dakotah Life

teur Ave., 651/646-8629. Costumed interpreters tell the Gibbs' pioneering story as they lead visitors through their 1867 house, farm buildings (home to sheep, chickens, pigs, and other barnyard residents), and the surrounding gardens—there's also a one-room schoolhouse. Jane had lived amongst the local Dakota as a child, and many of her native friends camped on the farm each year to visit her, so another part of the museum contains tepee and bark lodge imitations. Blacksmithing, Dakota dancing, doll making, and other special events are held most weekends. Open Tues.–Fri. 10 A.M.–4 P.M. and weekends noon–4 P.M. from May through October. Admission is $5.

Now a tony suburb, the city of White Bear Lake was Minnesota's first resort community, with a lakeside hotel opening in 1853. Upwards of 10,000 people a day made the trip from the Twin Cities at its peak around the turn of the 20th century, and in the 1930s it was a swinging getaway for artists like F. Scott and Zelda Fitzgerald and gangsters like Baby Face Nelson and Ma Barker. The resorts and amusement parks are gone, but this aspect of the past features prominently in the White Bear Lake Area Historical Society's tiny **Depot Museum,** 4735 U.S. 61, 651/407-5327. It's open Tuesday–Friday 10 A.M.–4 P.M. year-round, plus the same times on summer Sundays. Far more interesting is the historical society's **Fillebrown House,** 4735 Lake Ave. Built as a summer getaway in the 1870s and later winterized, this large, storybook cottage is a rare example of American Picturesque architecture. Hour-long tours by costumed guides discuss the house's unique architecture and explain life in those early days every Sunday from mid-June through August at 1:15, 2:15, and 3:15 P.M. Admission is $5.

The **Roseville Skating Center,** 651/415-2170, boasts an indoor ice arena, as well as the John Rose Minnesota Oval, the largest outdoor refrigerated ice surface in the country. The 400-meter track is open November to March. The rest of the year the OVAL becomes the Midwest's largest skate park. Skating, indoors or out, costs $4 and rentals (ice or in-line) are another $4. Not to be outdone, **Schwan's Super Rink** at the **National Sports Center,** 1700 105th Ave. NE,

763/785-5601, up in Blaine, has four Olympic-sized ice sheets under one roof. Open skating and rentals each cost $3. Also open to the public at the NSC is **Tournament Greens,** 763/785-5643, the mother of all miniature golf courses. The 18-hole putting course, designed and maintained by the PGA, uses real bent-grass greens for a challenging and authentic experience. A round costs $7 or $8 for two on weekdays. The **Minnesota Thunder,** a member of the United Soccer League, a Division II professional league affiliated with Major League Soccer, plays its home games at the NSC. Call 763/785-3668 for ticket and schedule information.

Entertainment

The funky little **Heights Theater,** 3951 Central Ave. NE, 763/788-9079, just over the border from Minneapolis in Columbia Heights, has been screening movies since 1926. It has been beautifully restored and today's films, spanning classics to blockbusters, are still preceded by recitals on a Mighty Wurlitzer Organ on weekend evenings.

Accommodations

Roseville is a good lodging option because it is close Minneapolis and convenient to St. Paul. Rooms at the **Radisson,** 2540 Cleveland Ave. N., 651/636-4567 or 866/444-6835, got a complete renovation in 2001 and have most of the bells and whistles of the fancier downtown hotels, but cost as little as $84. Facilities include a large pool, jumbo whirlpool, sauna, fitness center, and game room, plus they offer free shuttle service to both downtowns. The usual small and simple rooms at the **Motel 6,** 2300 Cleveland Ave. N., 651/639-3988 or 800/466-8356, are $60. It has an outdoor pool.

Over in Brooklyn Center, an easy drive to Minneapolis, the **AmericInn,** 2050 Freeway Blvd., 763/566-7500 or 800/634-4444, has a pool, whirlpool, sauna, fitness center, and game room from $89. At the **Best Western Kelly Inn,** 5201 Central Ave. NE, 763/571-9440 or 800/528-1234, in nearby Fridley, $79 gets you the same facilities and a free day pass to a nearby Bally's health club.

Food

Columbia Heights: Central Avenue has several well known Indian and Middle Eastern restaurants worth a drive. The fabulous **Udupi Café,** 4920 Central Ave. NE, 763/574-1113, serves exclusively South Indian vegetarian dishes, so you'll get to sample specialties like *vadas, dosais,* and *uthappams,* (all explained on the menu), that you don't find at the average Indian restaurant. Entrées average $7 and the small all-you-can-eat lunch buffet costs $8. Open daily for lunch and dinner. Two blocks south and four countries west, **El Bustan,** 4755 Central Ave. NE, 763/502-8888, serves dishes from Turkey, as well as other Mediterranean nations like Egypt and Lebanon, in a smart Middle Eastern decor with cozy booths. The menu is heavy on fish, and after dinner water pipes are very popular. Most entrées average $12, though kebabs and salads are under $5. Open daily for lunch and dinner. If you just want a burger you can't do much better than **Flameburger,** 4800 Central Ave. NE, 763/571-3267, a classic, 24-hour greasy spoon. A meal here isn't complete without their famous hash browns.

Roseville: Everybody seems to love **Royal Orchid,** 651/639-9999, which relocated from Minneapolis to the Roseville Marketplace mall. Most of their delectable Thai dishes cost around $9. Open Mon.–Sat. for lunch and dinner. What **India Palace,** 2570 Cleveland Ave. N., 651/631-1222, lacks in decor it makes up for with great food—many regard this as the best Indian restaurant in the Twin Cities. Prices range $8–17 and the lunch buffet is $8. Open daily. Also in Roseville are branches of **Famous Dave's Barbeque,** 2131 Snelling Ave., 651/633-4800 (see Minneapolis) across from the Har Mar Mall; **Khan's Mongolian Barbeque,** 2720 Snelling Ave. N., 651/631-3398 (see Metro South); and **Good Earth,** 1901 W. Hwy. 36, 651/636-0956 (see Metro West).

Shopping

White Bear Lake is one of the few suburban communities with any character (or even an actual downtown for that matter), and the flower-filled city center has a fair share of unique galleries, gift shops, and boutiques. The rest of the suburban wasteland pretty much just has the usual malls and big-box retailers.

METRO EAST

Quite a few farm fields remain between St. Paul and Stillwater, but urban sprawl is rapidly creeping east, and it won't be long before they are all replaced by subdivisions. It's a boring area and contains little that that can't be found elsewhere in the Twin Cities area. The one thing the eastern suburbs are not lacking in is drive-in movie theaters. The **Cottage View Drive-In,** 651/458-5965, down in Cottage Grove, and the **Vali Hi Drive-In,** 651/436-7464, in Lake Elmo, screen double and triple features respectively. Both charge $7. Besides the hotels, about the only thing that brings tourists out here is the modest **Prime Outlets** mall, 651/735-9060, with a Levi's, Eddie Bauer, and about three dozen other stores. **Lake Elmo Regional Park Reserve,** 651/430-8368, one of the largest parks in the Twin Cities metro area, also has a conveniently located campground. The 80 sites in the main camp are shadeless and widely spaced and cost $15 ($19 for a full hook-up), while pitching a tent in the grassy primitive camp area costs $10. Also scattered amongst the 2,165-acres of forest and grasslands are several lakes with a swimming beach and fishing pier, plus 24 miles of trails for hiking, biking, and horseback riding. The park entrance is a mile north of I-94 on Keats Avenue North, and a day pass costs $4.

St. Croix Valley

Some of Minnesota's most scenic towns and best state parks are tucked away along this wild border river, and all are easy day trips from the Twin Cities, though you need at least a couple of days to do the whole region justice. A drive through the valley is an engaging mix of natural scenery and country life. Stillwater, with its well-preserved downtown, elegant bed-and-breakfasts, and famous shopping, is by far the best known of the river towns, but it's really the smaller time-warped villages like Marine on St. Croix to the north and Afton to the south that give the valley its special character. They all get quite crowded on summer weekends and accommodation prices can nearly double, so plan a weekday visit if you can.

People who are particular about paddling will want to dip their oars in the upper stretches of the St. Croix or cinch up their spray skirts for some of the state's best white-water action on the St. Louis and Kettle Rivers.

History

Though modern Minnesota was born at Fort Snelling, down where the Minnesota River joins the Mississippi, it grew up along the St. Croix. The Dakota occupied the valley when French explorer Daniel Greysolon, Sieur du Lhut—the man presumed to be the first European to visit—passed through in 1680. Swarms of fur traders, first the French and

Stillwater

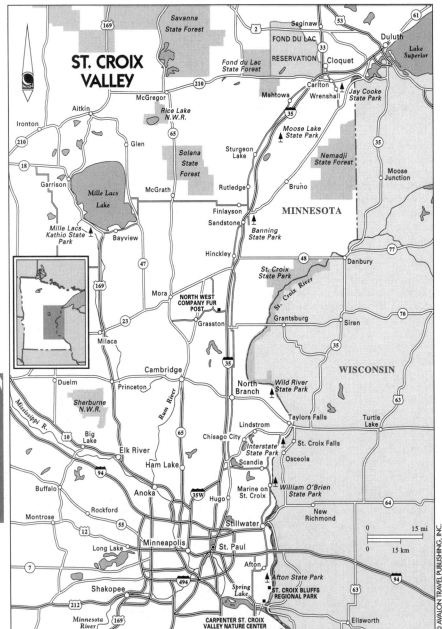

ST. CROIX VALLEY

© AVALON TRAVEL PUBLISHING, INC.

ST. CROIX VALLEY HIGHLIGHTS

Banning State Park
Franconia Sculpture Park, Taylors Falls
Interstate State Park
Jay Cooke State Park
Minnesota Zephyr, Stillwater
North West Company Fur Post
Paddlewheel Boat Tours, Taylors Falls
St. Croix National Scenic Riverway
Superior Whitewater Raft Trips, Carlton

towns they built still bear a resemblance to their original homes. Wisconsin became the 30th state in 1848 leaving the St. Croix Valley, which had been a part of the previous Wisconsin Territory, in a political vacuum. A group of influential, though self-appointed, civic leaders hastily convened an August summit in Stillwater and elected American Fur Company director Henry Sibley to represent them in Congress. Though technically he had no right to a seat in Congress, and legally there wasn't even a white population large enough to form a territory, Sibley and his allies put the Minnesota Territorial Act on President Zachary Taylor's desk the next year.

The mills were largely silent and the logging camps empty by around 1915, but immigrant farmers tried to make a living off the land. The soil was far too sandy and poor, however, and those who managed to get by struggled—others faced reality and gave up. As part of the relief effort during the Great Depression, the government bought out many of the farmers and reforested the land leaving extensive state forests and parks along the river. In 1968 the St. Croix was one of the eight original rivers added to the National Wild and Scenic Rivers System, initiating a second period of preservation by both the National Park Service and the states of Minnesota and Wisconsin.

then later the English and Americans, weren't far behind. Though some trading posts were built, there could be no settlement until the Ojibwe, who had taken over the valley by force from the Dakota, relinquished their lands in 1837. The fur trade had largely gone bust by this time, though the river would soon transport another precious cargo. Lumberjacks moved in almost immediately after the treaty was signed, sending their logs downstream to the state's first sawmill in Marine on St. Croix and later to Stillwater, which quickly grew into the river's dominant lumbering center and one of the state's ranking cities.

Many of the earliest settlers in the valley were wealthy New Englanders, and several of the

The Lower St. Croix

STILLWATER

If you want to relax and be pampered spend a night in historic Stillwater: book a table at a four-star restaurant, stroll along the riverfront promenade at sunset, take a moonlit gondola cruise, and count sheep at any of the romantic B&Bs. With Amish furniture, antique radios, and everything in between, Stillwater is also one of the best shopping locales in the state, and many people—bibliomaniacs and antique fanatics in particular—come here just for a day of retail recreation. The combination of quality, variety, and the beautiful setting truly makes this the anti-Mall of America.

History

Due to the aforementioned Territorial Convention of 1848, Stillwater boldly proclaims itself as the "Birthplace of Minnesota." The city's own birth came with the completion of the Stillwater Lumber Company's sawmill in 1844, and by 1848 Stillwater had become the river's largest community and the center of the lumbering industry. The census of 1850 listed a population of 620, second only to St. Paul with 1,083 citizens. The next year the Territorial Legislature handed out the capital to St. Paul, the university to St. Anthony (which later became Minneapolis), and the penitentiary to Stillwater. In 1854 Stillwater and St.

ST. CROIX VALLEY

Paul became the territory's first two incorporated cities. With dreams of becoming the next Chicago, Stillwater thrived through the rest of the century and had ten mills turning at its peak, but it suffered with the end of the logging era. The last log passed through the St. Croix Boom in 1914, and the city stagnated for decades though never bottomed out, largely due to the availability of jobs in the Twin Cities. The big turn around came in the early 1980s, when the historic buildings downtown were restored and empty storefronts hung signs for gift and antique shops.

The most hotly debated issue for the rapidly-growing city's future revolves around the iconic **Stillwater Lift Bridge.** The 1931 bridge, one of just two lift bridges remaining in operation in Minnesota (the other is in Duluth), can no longer handle the high volume of traffic. Plans for the construction of a nearby four-lane bridge, which could result in the destruction of the lift bridge (a compromise allowing it to stay is likely, but not assured), have been in the works since the 1970s and have been hotly debated in the courts ever since. Though clearly a worthy goal, saving the historic span is not the primary issue. Wisconsin real estate interests are naturally some of the strongest sup-porters of a new bridge, while opponents, including a majority of locals, desperately want to prevent Twin Cities urban sprawl from spreading out here any faster than it already is.

Sights

The town itself is the most interesting attraction, and you should plan to spend a good deal of time just wandering the well-preserved Main Street, though there are a few diversions at each end of the historic walk. The Washington County Historical Society's **Warden's House Museum,** 602 N. Main St., 651/439-5956, was the home of the heads of the now closed Stillwater Prison. Though the house dates from 1853, the furnished rooms appear as they would have in the 1890s, while others hold lumber era and other historical displays. The prison room includes an exhibit on the most famous inmates, the Younger Brothers, the other half of the infamous James-Younger Gang who finally met their match during a bungled bank robbery in Northfield. Jim, Bob, and Cole Younger were model prisoners and even helped found the prison newspaper. The Carriage House out back has an old high wheel bicycle and a birch bark canoe, among other things. The museum is open

ST. CROIX VALLEY

© TIM BEWER

a Stillwater moment

TAKE A RIDE

Watching the grand paddlewheelers cruise up and down the St. Croix River is one of the most enjoyable parts of a visit to Stillwater and with the **St. Croix Boat & Packet Company,** 525 S. Main St., 651/430-1234, you can join the fun. A variety of lunch and dinner cruises, priced from $18, depart more or less daily from mid-May through mid-October, though the schedules vary so you should call or stop by their office for details. Advanced reservations are highly recommended.

You can also take a much slower and more romantic cruise in authentic Venetian gondolas with **Gondola on St. Croix,** 651/439-1783. They offer rides, weather permitting, from May through October: call ahead for times or stop by their booth at the Stillwater Docks. A 20-minute ride costs $20 per person (the gondolas hold up to six people) though they also offer longer rides with cheese and cracker baskets and can even arrange violin players. Reservations are recommended though walk up rides are sometimes available.

As you cruise the beautiful valley aboard the **Minnesota Zephyr** you'll be served a five-course dinner in one of their five elegantly restored dining cars while cabaret singers perform hits from the 1940s and 50s. The leisurely three-hour trips depart from the historic Stillwater Depot, 601 N. Main St., 651/430-3000 or 800/992-6100, at 7:30 P.M. on Friday and Saturday, and noon on Sunday. Lunch and dinner trips also run other times, but on a scattered schedule so you need to call ahead. Tickets cost $65 and reservations are required, as is semi-formal attire.

The replica turn-of-the-century **Stillwater Trolley,** 400 E. Nelson St., 651/430-0352, zips up and down the city giving 45-minute narrated tours with plenty of interesting historical tidbits. The trolley, departing from in front of the Dock Café, runs daily May through October. The ride costs $10.

Hot air balloons are an increasingly popular way to take in the valley. **Aamodt's Hot Air Balloon Rides,** 651/351-0101 or 866/546-8247; **Stillwater Balloons,** 651/439-1800; and **Wiederkehr Balloons,** 651/436-8172, all soar over the St. Croix from near Stillwater.

Thursday–Sunday 1–5 P.M. from May through October. Admission is $3. The grandly named **Stillwater Depot Logging and Railroad Museum,** 601 N. Main St., 651/430-3000, is really just a small collection of memorabilia and photos in the office of the Minnesota Zephyr train rides—it is still worth a look though. The displays are free and open 10 A.M.–7 P.M. weekends year-round and weekdays when the trains are running.

Get regaled with stories of the city's history as you walk through the **Joseph Wolf Caves,** 402 S. Main St., 651/292-1220, which were used to brew beer in the late 1800s and have also served as a bomb shelter. The half-hour tours depart daily, except Tuesday, every hour on the hour between 10 A.M. and 6 P.M. and cost $5. Outside the main May through November season, tours are available Friday–Sunday 1–4 P.M. The **Main Street Steps** next to the caves lead to a wonderful and oft-photographed view of the city and river.

Recreation

P. J. Asch Otterfitters, 413 E. Nelson St., 651/430-2286, located downtown in an old grain elevator rents kayaks, cross-country skis, snowshoes, and climbing gear. They've also converted the four-story tower into an indoor climbing gym.

During the summer your kids can learn to log roll and crosscut during the two-hour **Lumberjack Sports Camps,** 651/439-5626. The cost is $10 and reservations are required.

The **Stillwater Yacht Club,** 422 E. Mulberry St., 651/439-5658, rents pontoons, fishing boats, and cabin cruisers.

Entertainment and Events

If anything interesting is on stage, it's probably at the **Washington County Historic Courthouse,** 101 W. Pine St. The popular **Valley Chamber Chorale,** 651/430-0124, performs there four times a year. The **St. Croix Boat & Packet**

Company (see the Take a Ride sidebar) has a Friday Night Music-on-the-Water cruise for $12 during the summer. Back on land the **St. Croix Crab House,** 317 S. Main St., 651/439-0024, puts blues and rock bands on stage every weekend and sometimes during week.

The city's heritage is celebrated during **Lumberjack Days** with an 1860s-style baseball game, ice cream social, grand parade, and, of course, lumberjack competitions. The festivities take place over four days in late July. Another popular gathering is the **Fine Art and Jazz Festival** the first weekend in October.

Accommodations

Stillwater has a host of historic and elegant inns, many in 19th-century lumber baron mansions, and choosing is easy because they are all excellent. Filled with the bounty from years of compulsive shopping in Southeast Asia, the exotic **Elephant Walk,** 801 W. Pine St., 651/430-0528 or 888/430-0359, info@elephantwalkbb.com, has as much character as any B&B in the state. It's like walking through a funky little museum, and you could easily spend your whole time in Stillwater examining the collection. Each of the four guestrooms has a private bath, whirlpool, and stocked refrigerator. Prices start at $169 though it's worth shelling out a $100 more for the Cadiz Garden Suite with its hidden rooftop patio overlooking the backyard garden.

No detail is overlooked at the spectacular, antique-filled **Rivertown Inn,** 306 W. Olive St., 651/430-2955, an 1882 Victorian mansion whose period decor is also of museum quality. The nine gorgeous guestrooms each have a private bath and whirlpool and run $200–250. Breakfast is served in the dining room, or you can choose to eat outside in the gazebo.

The only downtown B&B is the **Brunswick Inn,** 114 E. Chestnut St., 651/430-8111. Built in 1848 this is the oldest surviving wood-frame structure downtown and though it isn't as opulent as most other B&Bs in town, the lovely decor has a pleasant 19th century feel. The three cozy rooms have private baths with whirlpools and cost $159. Breakfast is served in the adjoining Amy's at Brunswick restaurant.

The **Laurel Street Inn,** 210 E. Laurel St., 651/351-0031 or 888/351-0031, welcome@laurelstreetinn.com, an intricate 1859 home, has a great hillside location overlooking the river and town, and the veranda is a great place for breakfast. The four antique-filled guestrooms, each with a private bath and whirlpool, run $199.

Both of Stillwater's historic hotels have large rooms and antique furnishings. The ageless **Lowell Inn,** 102 N. 2nd St., 651/439-1100, was opened in 1927. The 21 rooms, though newly renovated, ooze character. Prices start at $99 and run up to $169 for whirlpool suites. The **Lumber Baron's,** 101 S. Water St., 651/439-6000, just off the river, occupies a renovated and expanded 1890 commercial building and is equally charming. Rates run $129–189.

The historic inns and B&Bs are a big part of the Stillwater experience, but you can save a lot by spending the night "up on the hill" in a chain hotel. The **Best Western Stillwater Inn,** 1750 W. Frontage Rd., 651/430-1300 or 800/647-4039, has rooms from $87, plus a whirlpool and fitness center. At $81 the rooms at the **Super 8,** 2190 W. Frontage Rd., 651/430-3990 or 800/800-8000, aren't as good a value, but they are the cheapest in town.

Food

Many people drive in from the Twin Cities for a table at the open-kitchened **La Belle Vie,** 312 S. Main St., 651/430-3545, whose chef/owner Tim McKee has earned considerable national attention. You'll shell out at least $50 (and almost certainly a lot more) for a sublime four-course meal topped by something artsy and likely Mediterranean-inspired. Both the service and wine list meet the demands of anyone willing to indulge prices this high. Open daily for dinner and reservations are highly recommended.

About a mile south of Stillwater, **The Bayport Cookery,** 328 N. 5th Ave., 651/430-1066, is another nationally recognized kitchen. The five-course prix fixe (at least $30) menus change nightly but always follow a theme. Most have at least a touch of Minnesota, like morel mushrooms or wild game, but they might also offer something far flung, like a taste of Spain. There is

ST. CROIX VALLEY

just one nightly seating at 7 P.M. Wednesday to Sunday. Reservations are required.

Savories, 108 N. Main St., 651/430-0702, calls itself a European Bistro, though the eclectic, something-for-everyone-menu is globally inspired. For anywhere from $8–24 you can get a pizza, honey wheat vegetable pita, Szechwan noodles, or sunflower-crusted trout. Open Tues.–Sun. for lunch and Wed.–Sun. for dinner; they also do a divine weekend breakfast.

The best table with a view is at the **Dock Café,** 425 E. Nelson St., 651/430-3770, a casual Stillwater classic. The menu runs from recommended steaks to a creative sweet potato and avocado sandwich; they also serve an utterly Minnesotan wild rice-encrusted walleye. Dinner entrées average $15, while lunch comes in around $10. Open daily for lunch and dinner.

The **Gasthaus Bavarian Hunter,** 8390 N. Lofton Ave., 651/439-7128, a longtime casual favorite three miles west of town (follow Laurel St. which becomes McCusick), serves authentic Old World recipes for around $15 a plate at dinner. Vegetarians need not fear as they have a couple of meat-free options. An accordionist plays on Friday nights and Sunday afternoons, while the occasional polka band heats things up at other times. Open daily for lunch and dinner.

Darla's Grill & Malt Shop, 131 S. Main St., 651/439-9294, just does the basics like burgers and other sandwiches for around $5, but they do them well. They also have a walk-up ice cream window along Chestnut St. Open daily for lunch and dinner in the high season with reduced winter hours.

The **River Market Community Co-op,** 221 N. Main St., 651/439-0366, has sandwiches, sushi, and bakery to go. Open daily for lunch and dinner.

For dessert the top option is the legendary **Nelson's Drive Inn Dairy Store,** 920 W. Olive St., 651/439-3598. This little west side shack makes dozens of ice cream flavors, including blue moon, rum cherry, banana crème pie, plus all the standards. Open daily for lunch and dinner.

Also see the "Take A Ride" sidebar for a pair of mobile dining options.

Shopping

Two of Minnesota's largest antique stores, **The Mill Antiques,** 410 N. Main St., 651/430-1816, (in the 1870s Isaac Staples Sawmill) and the **Midtown Antique Mall,** 301 S. Main St., 651/430-0808—each with over 20,000 square feet of space and 80 dealers—sit at opposite ends of Main Street, and over a dozen more sit in between. Prices are high, but so is the quality.

Books are the city's other consumer claim to fame. King Richard Booth of Hay-on-Wye in Wales officially proclaimed Stillwater North America's first Booktown (www.booktown.com) in 1994. All silliness aside, books are serious business in Stillwater, and dedicated bibliophiles come here from across the country just to browse. The city's outstanding bookshops collectively have around 500,000 used titles on sale, about half of them at **Loome Theological Booksellers,** 320 N. 4th St., 651/430-1092, the largest secondhand theology, philosophy, and religion dealer in the world—housed, appropriately enough, in an old church. There is less volume but more variety at the **Loome Antiquarian Bookstore,** 201 S. Main St., 651/430-9805; and **St. Croix Antiquarian Booksellers,** 232 S. Main St., 651/430-0732. If you want to be a book's first owner, there's the small **Valley Bookseller,** 217 N. Main St., 651/430-3385.

The co-operatively run **Northern Vineyards,** 223 N. Main St., 651/430-1032, sells directly to the public from their downtown winery. They give tours of their on-site facility every Saturday at noon, while tastings are available any time. **St. Croix Vineyards,** 6428 Manning Ave. (next to Aamodt's Apple Farm), 651/430-3310, is just west of Stillwater. You can tour the vineyard and sample their wines weekends May through July, and daily August through December.

You probably weren't thinking about banjos, dulcimers, or guitars when you came to Stillwater, but visit **Musicmaker's Kits,** 14525 61st St. Ct. N. (behind Joseph's Restaurant along Highway 36), 651/439-9120, and you just might leave with one. This small workshop turns out acoustic instruments you assemble yourself.

ST. CROIX VALLEY

Information and Services

Someone at the **Greater Stillwater Chamber of Commerce,** 106 S. Main St., 651/439-4001, www.ilovestillwater.com, will have an answer to any questions about the area. During the June to October high season their offices are open weekdays 9 A.M.–6 P.M., Saturday 10 A.M.–6 P.M., and Sunday 11 A.M.–5 P.M. The rest of the year they're open weekdays 9 A.M.–5 P.M. and Saturday 10 A.M.–2 P.M.

Transportation

Metro Transit bus #294 runs from downtown St. Paul to downtown Stillwater, but service is very limited and inconvenient. Fares and other general information are detailed in the Twin Cities chapter.

For those arriving by boat there is public mooring at the **Stillwater Docks** and a trio of full service marinas: **Wolf Marine,** 651/439-2341; **Sunnyside Marina,** 651/439-2118; and **Stillwater Yacht Club,** 651/439-5658.

SOUTH TO THE MISSISSIPPI

Highway 95/County Road 18 heads south along the St. Croix and, except for a few quick glimpses of the river, is pretty ordinary until it hits **Afton,** a quaint village of 19th-century homes, several now housing restaurants and shops. The **Afton Historical Museum,** 3165 Saint Croix Trail S., 651/436-3500, housed in an 1868 church, has a small collection of historical artifacts with an emphasis on farming, since the first farm in Minnesota was established by Joseph Haskell just a mile west of the village in 1839. You might also catch someone weaving rugs on their antique looms. The museum is open Wednesday 1–8 P.M. year-round and Sunday 1–4 P.M. during the summer. Admission is free. The **Afton House Inn,** 3291 Saint Croix Trail S., 651/436-8883, info@ aftonhouseinn.com, was built in 1867 as a hotel, and a night here feels like a real escape. The 16 cozy rooms, most with fireplaces and/or whirlpools, range from $65 to over $150 for the most luxurious. Although there have been gaps in the lodging operation, a restaurant has operated here continuously since it opened, and currently

they have a pair of them. The pasta, meat, and seafood menu in the **Wheel Room** averages about $20 for dinner, while their more casual **Catfish Saloon** is about half that. Both are open daily for lunch and dinner. You can also dine on the river between May and October with their Sunday brunch cruises departing at noon. They cost $23 per person. Behind the Afton House the large, full-service **Windmill Marina,** 651/ 436-7744, takes care of boaters' needs.

Beyond Afton, scenic County Road 21 veers away from the river and up a steep, wooded bluff passing half a dozen orchards and farms where you can pick you own apples, strawberries, cherries, and the like. Four miles on is **Afton State Park,** 651/436-5391, established and managed for nature first and recreation second. The 1,700-acre park protects several deep wooded ravines, some lined by sandstone outcrops, that drop hundreds of feet down from the bluff tops to the St. Croix. With a mix of prairie and forest, Afton is a good park for bird-watchers. The primary reason for the park's overall peacefulness is that reaching most facilities requires a bit of a hike. The rocky beach and picnic area are a half mile downhill from the parking area. The only camping spots are the 24 widely-spaced backpacking sites reached by a long one-mile climb, or the single canoe site on the St. Croix. Most of the 20 miles of hiking trails have some long steep climbs, but the effort is usually rewarded with great views, particularly the series of loops in the north end of the park. The riverside route along the south end of the park is also scenic, and the rocky beach makes a nice stroll when not busy with swimmers. Horses are allowed on one five-mile loop, and a four-mile paved bike path runs along the entrance road and down a short stretch of the river. Most of the trails are groomed for cross-country skiing, including 2.5 miles of level, beginner trail. Surrounded by but independent of the park is **Afton Alps,** 651/436-5245 or 800/328-1328, one of Minnesota's largest ski hills with 40 trails, 18 lifts, a snowboard park, and tubing hill. The rest of the year there is an 18-hole golf course and eight miles of challenging mountain bike trails. Rentals are available.

Besides fresh food, the **Afton Apple Orchard,**

651/436-8385, just west of County Road 21 on 90th St. S., also has hay rides, a petting zoo, and a massive corn maze ($6) in September and October. A little farther down the road, **St. Croix Bluffs Regional Park** has one thing Afton State Park does not—a drive-in campground. With abundant shade, it's pretty good. The park also has 4.5 miles of hiking trails, boat access, and picnic sites. Non-electric campsites are $10 and those with electric and water hookups are $17. Park entry is another $4.

Just before hitting the Mississippi you'll pass the **Carpenter St. Croix Valley Nature Center,** 651/437-4359, a private, 720-acre facility. The small interpretive center has a few nature displays, plus animals caged and mounted. Outside are a flower and herb garden and environmentally-friendly apple orchard. Fifteen miles of scenic trail cross the forest, savanna, and restored prairie, some overlooking the St. Croix River, others leading down the bluffs to its shore. Unfortunately you can't escape the Highway 10 traffic hum. The center is open daily 8 A.M.–4:30 P.M. and until 8 P.M. the first Friday of each month from June through September.

NORTH TO THE FALLS

Highway 95 up to Taylors Falls is heavily populated, but it's still not too shabby of a drive and has some moments of true beauty.

Marine on St. Croix

Minnesota's lumber industry began here when the Marine Lumber Company cut its first pine board in 1839. Stillwater, just 11 miles to the south, didn't get its first mill for another six years, but it quickly grew into an important city while little Marine Mills, as it was then known, remains a scene right out of a New England postcard. Citizens and the post office rechristened their town Marine on St. Croix in 1917, though it took the U.S. Board on Geographic Names another 51 years to officially accept the change. Despite all the effort to get the longer name, most locals just call it Marine.

The foundation ruins of the Marine Mill can be seen in the little downtown park. Across the

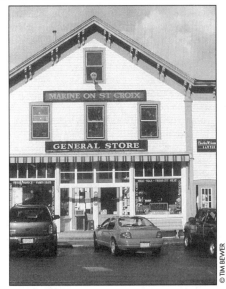

Marine on St. Croix

highway and up the hill on 5th Street, the 1872 town hall and jail now houses a small collection of historical artifacts. The **Stone House Museum,** 651/433-2061, as it is known, is open very limited hours during the summer—call ahead if you really want to visit. Admission is free. Canoe rental and shuttle service for St. Croix River trips can be arranged at **Marine Landing,** 651/433-2864, just north of town (follow the signs). The **Asa Parker House,** 17500 St. Croix Tr. N. 651/433-5248 or 888/857-9969, B&B occupies a handsome 1856 home. The four guestrooms, each with private bath, run $129–179. The small and friendly **Voyageur Café,** 651/433-2366, is a good choice for value-priced homecookin' away from home. Open Wed.–Sun. for breakfast and lunch. You can also get coffee and some organic bakery three doors down at **Tigerlilly's Coffee & Tea,** 651/433-4858. Open daily for lunch and dinner.

William O'Brien State Park

Just north of Marine on St. Croix is the popular, and often busy, William O'Brien State Park, 651/433-0500. The original 180 acres were

ST. CROIX VALLEY

donated to the state by Alice O'Brien, daughter of the eponymous lumber baron who purchased the land he had earlier cleared of trees. The park, which has had a century and a half to recover, has since expanded to its present 1,520 acres. Though it only comprises a small part of the park, the most interesting area is the beautiful and wildlife-packed floodplain forest. The highly recommended **Riverside Trail,** a paved 1.5-mile loop with interpretive signs, offers up close views of the river. Even better than walking along the water is getting right out on it. The easy paddle around Greenberg Island takes about an hour, though budget some extra time to poke around looking for wildlife and wildflowers. Canoe rental is available, and a shuttle service lets you explore more of the river. Many people are satisfied just taking it easy down by the river fishing, picnicking, or swimming in Lake Alice.

The rest of the 12-mile hiking trail system forms a series of loops across the mosaic of forest, grassland, and wetland stretching atop the bluffs. All of the trails have some rolling hills, but none are especially challenging. The most interesting and least traveled are along the west edge of the park. The two-mile **Transition Trail** is mostly wooded, but as the name suggests, offers a look at the prairie as well, while the **Rolling Hills Oak Savanna Trail,** a mile-long loop through a savanna restoration, branches off the southern end of it. In winter most of these loops are groomed for cross-country skiing, both traditional and skating.

The pair of campgrounds, one down by the river and the other up on the hill, have 125 sites (62 electric) with a mix of shady and open choices in both; there is also a camper cabin. Overall, the last two loops of the Upper Campground are the most peaceful and scenic options.

Scandia

The state's first known Swedish immigrants settled here in 1850, and it was this general area

that Swedish author Vilhelm Moberg described in his famous series of novels about famine-stricken peasants leaving the homeland to start a new life in Minnesota. The town, which chose the ancient name for Scandinavia as its own, clings tightly to its Swedish roots with cultural festivals, museums, and a few Dala horses decorating downtown. The **Gammelgården,** 651/433-5053, "Old Small Farm" in Swedish, is a museum of Swedish immigration with half-a-dozen furnished buildings from the mid-19th century. These include an 1855 immigrant house, the oldest existing Lutheran church in Minnesota (built in 1856), and an 1879 barn filled with old farming tools. The historical park also hosts the Midsommar Dag (Midsummer Day) arts and crafts festival the fourth Sunday in June, Spelmansstamma music festival the third Saturday in August, and the traditional Lucia Christmas celebration on the Sunday closest to December 13th. A smorgasbord is a part of each of these celebrations, and a lutefisk dinner is held on the third Thursday in November. The buildings, located on the south side of town along County Road 3, are open Friday–Sunday 1–4 P.M. from mid-May to mid-October. Admission is $4.

Just south of town, along Highway 3, is the **Hay Lake School Museum,** 651/433-4014. In its day the redbrick, one-room schoolhouse was quite fancy, which reflects the value the state's Scandinavian immigrants placed on education. The 1896 building is in excellent shape and is sometimes used by school groups during the week to let the students learn what life was like for children more than a century ago. The barn-shaped building in back is the Johannes Erickson Log Cabin, built in 1868 and now furnished as a Swedish immigrant might have done. The area, referred to as Historic Corner, also has a granite obelisk commemorating the state's first Swedish settlers. The buildings are open Friday–Sunday noon–4 P.M. from the start of May through the end of October. Admission is $3.

The Upper St. Croix

TAYLORS FALLS

Taylors Falls mixes spectacular natural scenery with historic architecture to create one of the best quick getaways from the Twin Cities. The first two settlers here were the well-financed Benjamin Baker and his employee Jesse Taylor who came in 1838 to open a sawmill. Baker died before the mill could be completed, and Taylor later sold his logging claims and moved on, but his name remained. The namesake falls are not the small rapids below the bridge, but a long raging tumble that now lies buried behind the hydroelectric dam just upriver from the town. Though steamboat service began immediately (iron mooring rings from this era can still be seen along the river), the city didn't really begin to grow until 1850. In 1886 one of the largest logjams ever stretched seven miles upstream from the city.

Sights

Perched on the bluff above the town is the **Angel Hill District,** populated almost exclusively by white Greek Revival homes with green trim; most were built in the 1850s and 1860s. The resemblance to a New England village is so remarkable that, I've been told, transplants from out East sometimes visit to relieve bouts of homesickness. Halfway up the hill is the simple but stately **Folsom House,** 272 W. Government St., 651/465-3125. New England lumber baron W. H. C. Folsom came to Taylors Falls in 1850 and constructed this home four years later. It stayed in the family until 1968 at which time it and most of the original furnishings were acquired by the state. Guides lead tours daily, except Tuesdays, between 1 P.M. and 4:30 P.M. from late May though mid-October, plus during the two weekends following Thanksgiving to coincide with the city's Christmas-themed **Lighting Festival.** Admission is $3.

Paddlewheel boat tours of the St. Croix River begin by chugging through the Dalles of the St. Croix and then continue down the river taking in more of the valley's beautiful scenery. Your captain will, of course, point out rock formations that vaguely resemble various objects—the Old Man of the Dalles is a remarkable looking face—and regale you with a history of the valley. There are up to four cruises a day from May through mid-October, plus Wednesday and weekend dinner cruises. The shortest (three miles/30 minutes) trip is $8, while the most expensive dinner run is $33. Call 651/465-6315 or 800/447-4958 for information and reservations. The same company operates **Wild Mountain,** seven miles north of town on Highway 16. In the summer you can get your thrills on the water slides, alpine slides, and go-kart track, and in the snowy season there are 23 downhill ski and snowboard runs, the highest dropping 300 feet. You can ride the chairlift in the fall to take in the splendid color.

You'll have to decide if there's anything clever, but there is always something interesting on display at **Franconia Sculpture Park.** Dozens of works by artists from many countries grace the 16-acre meadow along Highways 8/95, two miles southwest of town. Artists live and work communally while creating their works, which are then left on display for two years before moving to permanent homes. Plans are afoot to move to a larger and more scenic site along the St. Croix River. The park is open to visitors daily from dawn to dusk. Admission is free.

Practicalities

Two old and basic hotels offer good value. The **Springs Country Inn,** 361 W. Government St., 651/465-6565, has rooms as low as $59, plus some whirlpool suites for $95. Even cheaper is the **Pines Motel,** 543 River St., 651/465-3422, where each of the eight rooms are $52. The **Cottage Bed & Breakfast,** 950 Fox Glen Dr., 651/465-3595, info@the-cottage.com, perched on the edge of the bluff just outside of town, offers serenity and phenomenal views. The private two-room cottage costs $125. In town the **Old Jail B&B,** 349 W. Government St., 651/465-3112, has three large and distinctive suites. The namesake is in the 1884 jail, which retains the original exterior, including the iron cage door, but has been thoroughly modernized inside. In the house next to the jail are the Overlook Suite, with great views, and the ground-level Cave Suite, with its bathroom in an old beer cave extending into the bluff. Each of the latter two have kitchens and rates range $120–150.

For a meal you can't do any better than the **Chisago House Restaurant,** 361 Bench St., 651/465-5245, with its large all-American menu and outstanding food. Breakfast is served all day, and nothing on the menu is over $15. Open daily for breakfast, lunch, and dinner. Carhops at **The Drive-In,** 572 Bench St., 651/465-7831, will bring you burgers and malts for just a few bucks. Open daily for lunch and dinner, but only during the summer season. The **Rocky River Bakery,** 360 Bench St., 651/465-7655, does some scrumptious snacks and deli sandwiches. Open daily except Tuesday for breakfast and lunch.

INTERSTATE STATE PARK

One of the smallest, but most scenic and popular of Minnesota's state parks, Interstate sits right on the southern edge of Taylors Falls. The Dalles of the St. Croix, sheer pine-topped cliffs jutting up to 200 feet straight out of the river, are one of the most beautiful sights in the state. By the early 1850s they had become a major tourist destination with thousands arriving by steamboat and later railroad just to see them. That didn't stop businessmen from proposing to blast the cliffs into gravel. The citizens of Taylors Falls and St. Croix Falls, Wisconsin, pushed to preserve the Dalles as the centerpiece of a national park, but these dreams were dashed. Thankfully, the state of Minnesota set aside 298 acres as a state park in 1895, and Wisconsin opened its much larger share across the river five years later creating the nation's first interstate park. Besides being beautiful, these cliffs are now the most popular rock-climbing destination in the state with routes rated as high at 5.11. Naturally the best sites in the 37-site (22 electric) campground are those abutting the river. Park stickers from either Minnesota or Wisconsin are valid on both sides on non-holiday weekdays. Call 651/465-5711 for more information.

© TIM BEWER

the Dalles of the St. Croix at Interstate State Park

Potholes

While the cliffs get the majority of oohs and aahs, the most interesting geological formations are the potholes. In many places the torrential water from the melting glaciers that cut the Dalles formed massive whirlpools. Sand and gravel trapped in the vortices carved shafts in the solid bedrock so symmetrical it's difficult to imagine nature doing it on its own. Over 200 potholes, including the world's deepest at 60 feet, are found in the two parks, a greater concentration than anywhere else. Displays in the visitors center show how the potholes were made and also discuss other aspects of the park's history.

Recreation

A small web of trails lead past and even into the potholes and atop the Dalles. Some of these form the **Pothole Trail,** a partly wheelchair-accessible quarter-mile route with interpretive panels along it. The **River Trail** leads for nearly 1.5 miles from the pothole area to the campground.

ST. CROIX VALLEY

It's an easy hike with great views and even though it abuts the highway for part of the route, it is definitely worth your while. You could make a round-trip out of it by returning along the **Railroad Trail** on the other side of the highway. Across from the campground is the mile-long **Sandstone Bluffs Trail.** It has some great vista points, passes small Curtain Falls, and from mid-April through May the forest floor is carpeted by an amazing concentration of wildflowers. It requires a bit of a climb, but it's not too tough.

The best way to see the Dalles is from the water, and while you've got the option of the paddlewheel tour boats (see Taylors Falls), the peaceful St. Croix is prime paddling territory. The river is part of the St. Croix National Scenic Riverway, and longer trips beyond the park are popular. Good day-trip options include the seven-mile

> *The Dalles of the St. Croix, sheer pine-topped cliffs jutting up to 200 feet straight out of the river, are one of the most beautiful sights in the state.*

float to Osceola and the 17-mile trip to William O'Brien State Park. Rental and shuttle service are available at the park (651/257-3550 or 800/447-4958). You can get additional information at the National Park Service's Riverway headquarters in downtown St. Croix Falls, Wisconsin.

WILD RIVER STATE PARK

Stretching 18 miles along a remote and beautiful stretch of the St. Croix River, this aptly named 6,800-acre park was created in conjunction with the St. Croix National Scenic Riverway. A remarkable abundance of wildflowers, including trillium and wild geranium, paint the forest floor each spring. The best spots for enjoying them are the **Trillium Trail,** which conveniently skirts the campground, and the **River Terrace Loop.** You can learn about the flowers and more at the **McElroy Visitor Center** overlooking the St. Croix Valley. A wildflower garden and deck with great river valley views are outside the center.

The main park entrance is 10 miles north of Taylors Falls along Highway 95 and County Road 12, though for a more scenic drive come via County Road 16. The Sunrise River boat launch, along with its quiet picnic area, is in the west end along County Road 9. Call 651/583-2125 with any questions.

Recreation

Canoeing is obviously a top draw, and a pair of put-ins are spaced at a leisurely day-trip distance. Rentals and a shuttle service (651/465-6501 or 800/996-4448) are available for the calm and easy 10-mile trip along the park or longer journeys.

The canoeing is great, but Wild River is more than just the St. Croix. The 35-mile trail system stretches across most of the length of the park and has only the occasional steep hill. One of the most popular trails, and rightly so, is the **River Terrace Loop,** which circles the bottomland forest for 1.5 miles. Joining it at the Nevers Dam overlook (the dam was removed in 1955) is the **River Trail,** which follows the St. Croix south

© TIM BEWER

climbing the Dalles, Interstate State Park

ST. CROIX VALLEY

ST. CROIX NATIONAL SCENIC RIVERWAY

Established in 1968 as one of the original projects in the National Wild and Scenic Rivers System, the 252-mile Riverway begins in Wisconsin, where it also encompasses the entire 98-mile Namekagon River. The spring-fed St. Croix flows for 25 miles through the Badger State before becoming a border river. For the most part it's a narrow, shallow, lazy waterway winding through an often remote ribbon of wilderness—absolutely ideal canoeing territory. There are only occasional Class I rapids (a few of which can rise to Class II during high water) so it makes a leisurely trip, perfect for families. Thanks to the 60-foot tall St. Croix Falls Hydroelectric Dam the last ten miles of the Upper St. Croix are now the Indianhead Flowage and because motor boats are common here most paddlers take out at Wild River State Park.

The river hits the sheer cliffs of the Dalles of the St. Croix at Taylors Falls and after a short sprint through the narrow gorge it spreads its banks and drops its bottom. For the next fifty miles, until it joins the Mississippi, the Lower St. Croix takes its time. The first twenty miles, down to the Apple River, are officially a "slow speed zone" for motorboats and despite substantial development along the shore remain popular with canoes. Beyond the giant sandbar at the Apple's mouth the river grows some more and large motorboats are the primary users. The river is so wide below Stillwater that it is known as Lake St. Croix and sailboats join their gas-guzzling cousins on the water.

To prevent the spread of zebra mussels boaters may no longer travel upstream past the High Bridge, about 3.5 miles north of Stillwater. Personal watercraft are also prohibited above Stillwater. Boaters should also read and heed the strict no-wake regulations posted at all landings.

Camping

While the canoeing is fantastic the camping is even better. Over 100 free, first-come, first-served campsites are stretched out along the Minnesota section of the Riverway. All sites are marked by a sign and have a fire ring and a pit toilet and most also have a picnic table. The majority are individual sites which allow up to three tents and eight people, though a few designated group sites can accommodate twice as many.

Strict regulations have been enacted to protect the fragile river environment and as these are always subject to change it is a good idea to get current information before heading out. Currently campers must use designated sites about Taylors Falls. There is a one-night limit above the Nevers Dam Landing (13 miles upstream from Taylors Falls; the dam was removed long ago) and a three-night limit on the remaining stretch down to the St. Croix Falls Dam. Houseboaters may tie up for an overnight stay anywhere below Nevers Dam, but may not build fires or set up tents on the shore. There are few campsites below Taylors Falls, but camping is allowed for up to seven nights anywhere on federal land except the areas immediately south of the Dalles and around the towns of Osceola, Wisconsin and Marine On St. Croix. Another exception to this rule is that camping is restricted to islands between Stillwater and the High Bridge. Below Stillwater the Riverway is managed collectively by the states, counties, and National Park Service (NPS) and there is little public land and no designated Riverway campsites, though some state and county parks have campgrounds. The large delta at Wisconsin's Kinnickinnic State Park is a favorite with boaters.

Information

The **St. Croix Visitor Center,** 715/483-3284, is located in St. Croix Falls, Wisconsin just across the river from Taylors Falls. They can also provide you with maps and information including a complete list of area outfitters. Interpretive displays cover the St. Croix's human and natural history with a focus on Scandinavian immigration. From mid-April through mid-October the center is open daily 8:30 A.M.–5 P.M. and weekdays 8:30 A.M.–5 P.M. the rest of the year.

© TIM BEWER

the St. Croix River at Wild River State Park

for the same distance. If you head up the bluffs you can make a loop out of it by following the **Old Logging Trail,** part of a three-mile paved route connecting the campgrounds and interpretive center. It is the only trail allowing bikes. Also in the southern section of the park is the three-mile **Amador Prairie Loops,** a pair of rings circling Wild River's prairie restoration. Two seldom used trails, the five-mile **Sunrise Loop** and three-mile **Goose Creek Loop,** branch out through the bottomland forest in the north end of the park from the Sunrise River area. Both trails, particularly the latter, can be very wet but are also excellent places to encounter wildlife, as is the rolling **Sunrise Trail,** which continues five miles along the river all the way back to the southern end of the park. Twenty miles of trail are open to horses, and **Wild River Stable,** 651/257-4044, offers trail rides through the park. A three-hour trip costs $45, though many other options are available. Come winter all 35 miles of trail are groomed for cross-country skiing—the **Aspen Knob Loop,** a two-mile trail through the hilly southwest corner of the park, offers the biggest challenge—and the River Terrace Trail is packed down for winter hiking. Both skis and snow-

shoes are available for rent. A pair of easy, mile-long self-guided nature trails, **Windfall** and **Amik's Pond,** begin at the visitors center and discuss forest and wetland ecology respectively; the latter passes a beaver pond and is a good bird-watching area.

Accommodations

The campground has 96 (17 electric) mostly wooded campsites, each well screened from the others. Also in the camp area are two rustic camper cabins and a guesthouse with all the comforts of home, including air-conditioning, TV, VCR, and a fireplace. Horseback riders have their own rustic campground. The eight reservable backpacking sites are as little as a quarter mile and no more than two miles from park roads—only Buck Hill lets you camp in sight of the river. The park has another eight canoe-in campsites, and there are other National Scenic Riverway sites available. All canoe sites are first-come, first-served.

ST. CROIX STATE PARK

Minnesota's largest state park protects the scenic shore of not just its placid namesake river, but

ST. CROIX VALLEY

also the wild boulder-strewn Kettle, the first state-designated Wild and Scenic River. In 1934, at the height the Great Depression, the National Park Service bought 18,000 acres of failing farms and over the next several years, aided by the Civilian Conservation Corps (CCC) and Works Progress Administration (WPA), helped restore the land and build public facilities creating the park. Because most of the park's original design and historic buildings remain intact and in use, it has been declared a National Historic Landmark. Since then the park has nearly doubled in size, and the hardwood forests, tamarack and black spruce bogs, meadows, marshes, and streams are home to an enormous diversity and abundance of flora and fauna. Call 320/384-6591 with any questions.

Recreation

A 100-mile web of trails covers the park. Horseback riders can use well over half of them, while mountain bikers have access to 20 miles, though because they are rough and often sandy the ride isn't very popular. Biking is quite good along the park roads, and a paved five-mile trail connects the campground with the beach. The **Adventure-St. Croix Store,** 320/384-7806, by the campgrounds has mountain and road bikes for rent during the summer.

The best and most popular hiking trails are those along the rivers, particularly the three-mile **Rivers Bluff Trail** starting at the campground. The 3.5-mile **Kettle Rapids Trail** over in the west end of the park gets less use, even though it is arguably the most scenic. Not only does the nearby 2.75-mile **Two Rivers Trail** lead along both the St. Croix and the Kettle, but it is also the only riverside trail that forms a loop. The five-mile **Bear Creek Trail** crossing through the heart of the park along its namesake waterway is another worthy hike. The 12 miles of trail groomed for cross-country skiing offer several loops, most along the St. Croix, and all are level and easy. Snowshoes for exploring the rest of the park during the snowy season are available for rent at the interpretive center.

Of course the canoeing is excellent, and together the two rivers offer something for paddlers of all stripes. With seven landings between them, trips can be made of almost any length and variety, from a nearly placid paddle with just a few Class I rapids along the entire 21 miles of the St. Croix, to some moderate white water scattered along most of the Kettle. The Adventure-St. Croix Store rents canoes and provides shuttle service for anything from a one-hour outing along the park to a three-day trip.

If you are looking for a more restful getaway have a swim in Lake Clayton, climb the 100-foot fire tower, learn about geology (or just enjoy the scenery) at the **Kettle River Highbanks Overlook** perched atop the 50-foot cliffs, or cast a line into one of the trout streams emptying into the St. Croix. The **St. Croix Lodge,** an old log and stone CCC building overlooking the St. Croix River, houses human and natural history exhibits.

Camping

Canoe-in campsites on both the Kettle and St. Croix Rivers and two Adirondack-sheltered backpack sites, each about a couple of miles from the trailhead, offer the park's most secluded camping. The main campground has 211 sites in three distinct sections. All of the park's 42 electric hookups are in the mostly open Riverview Campground, which is, naturally, where most of the RVs park. The park's four walk-in sites are over here, too. The Old Logging Trail Campground loops are the most secluded of the three, and thus the preferred choice for tent campers, while the Painted Rock Springs Campground is sort of middle ground. Five camper cabins (available mid-May to mid-Sept.) and a fully equipped, six-bedroom guesthouse (open year-round) let you enjoy the park without roughing it. A separate horse camp can handle 100 horses.

North to Duluth

It's a rather monotonous 150 miles from the Twin Cities to Duluth along I-35. The towns and parks along this route aren't quaint and remote like those along the St. Croix, but they are worthy of quick visits nonetheless—especially Banning State Park—so schedule a little extra time for your drive north if you can.

NORTH WEST COMPANY FUR POST

It's always 1804 at the North West Company Fur Post, 320/629-6356, and the voyageurs wintering here will show you their lives at one of Minnesota's best living history reenactments. During your visit to this fortified outpost, authentically reconstructed on the exact Snake River site as the original, they will show you into their quarters; barter for blankets, pots, and trinkets; let you play games; and try to con you into doing some of their chores. Outside, visit the summer-style wigwam and learn how the Ojibwe benefited from the fur trade. The post is located just west of Pine City. Between mid-May and Labor Day it is open Tuesday–Saturday (plus holiday Mondays) 10 A.M.–5 P.M. and Sunday noon–5 P.M. From mid-April through mid-May, and Labor Day through the end of October, it is open Friday and Saturday 10 A.M.–5 P.M. and Sunday noon–5 P.M. Admission is free. The annual **Fall Gathering** with music and demonstrations takes place in mid-September.

HINCKLEY

Halfway between the Twin Cities and Duluth, Hinckley makes a convenient pit stop, a role it has served since the 1850s when stagecoach service began between St. Paul and Superior, Wisconsin. Lumberjacks arrived in 1869 to begin clearing the surrounding stands of white pine and the next year, when the Lake Superior and Mississippi Railroad connected St. Paul with Duluth, the town flourished. The boom went bust in a big way in 1894. That summer remains one of the

driest on record, and high winds on September 1 blew several small forest fires together creating a raging firestorm that swept across the county destroying Hinckley and five other towns in a matter of hours—over 400 people lost their lives. Though the city rebuilt, it never fully recovered. The saving grace for the town has been the Mille Lacs Ojibwe's **Grand Casino Hinckley,** 320/384-7101 or 800/472-6321. Of course there are the slots and blackjack tables, but they also brings in a host of big name musical acts that draw people up from the Twin Cities. The **Grand Celebration Pow-wow** is held here in mid-June, and the Native American gift shop in the hotel lobby is small but good. Other area shopping opportunities include **Antiques America,** 320/384-7274, a 50-dealer outlet next to the freeway; and the **Hinckley Flea Market,** 320/384-9911, on the way to the casino. The **Grand National Golf Club,** 320/384-7427 or 800/468-3517, is one of the state's top public courses.

Few visitors make it to the slowly dying downtown and really the only reasons to do so are to access the southern end of the paved **Willard Munger State Trail,** which runs 63 miles to Duluth, or visit the **Hinckley Fire Museum,** 320/384-7338. Besides telling the story of the deadly inferno, there are Native American, logging era, and railroad displays. The museum is housed in the Saint Paul & Duluth Railway Station built immediately following the fire, and the Depot Agent's residence upstairs has been furnished as it might have been at that time, though considering his salary it likely wouldn't have been so fancy. The museum is open Tuesday–Saturday 10 A.M.–5 P.M. and Sunday noon–5 P.M. (last admittance is 4:15 P.M.) from May through mid-October and admission is a rather steep $5.

Practicalities

If you are here to gamble it doesn't matter where you stay since the casino runs a shuttle service to all of Hinckley's hotels. The cheapest rooms in town ($54) are at the older but updated **Gold**

Pine Inn, 320/384-6112 or 888/384-6112, next to I-35. You can stay at the modern 281-room **Grand Casino Hinckley Hotel,** 320/384-7101 or 800/468-3517, for as little as $59, but you'll likely need to pay more. Facilities include a pool, whirlpool, sauna, and fitness center. There are also 222 RV campsites jammed together next to the casino.

The casino has half a dozen restaurants to choose from, including a coffee shop and a really good **all-you-can-eat buffet** ($7 lunch and $12 dinner) with well over 100 choices. **Tobies,** 320/384-6174, next to I-35 has been serving classic family fare to road trippers and locals since 1948. Entrées on the varied menu include burgers, salads, seafood, steak, and pasta and run $5–27. They are always open and have a take-away counter for their bakery. **Greyhound** buses stop here on the Twin Cities to Duluth run.

SANDSTONE

A sandstone quarry was cut into the Kettle River bluffs here in 1885 and this city grew up alongside it. The town was completely wiped out by the same fire that destroyed Hinckley in 1894; most of the population rode out the inferno in the river. Highway 23, aka the **Veterans Evergreen Memorial Drive Scenic Byway,** leads from here all the way to Duluth and has long been the scenic route to Lake Superior. The tiny **Sandstone History & Art Center,** 402 Main St., 320/245-2271 (the regular hours are Thurs. 9:30 A.M.–1 P.M., Fri. noon–4 P.M., and Sat. 10 A.M.–2 P.M. from mid-May through mid-Oct., though there is often someone around the rest of the week; admission is $1), built of local stone, features a diorama of the quarry and not much else. You can walk around the real thing in **Robinson Park** on the east edge of town along 3rd St., though there isn't much to see anymore. The self-guided trail map available at the museum gives a history of the site and details what remains after 50 years of cutting. If you love the twang you'll want a ticket ($10–20) for the **Midwest Country Music Theater,** 309 Commercial Ave. N., 320/245-2429 or 888/729-1033, a 300-seat venue with weekend Grand Ole Opry-style shows.

If you are going to stick around a while, or are visiting the park but not camping, consider the small and simple **61 Motel,** 1409 Hwy 23 N., 320/245-5419. It's so old that it's now a classic, but it passes the white glove test, and the owner couldn't be any friendlier. You can listen in on the local gossip while enjoying a cheap, heaping platter of home-cookin' at the no-frills **Maggie's Colonial Café,** 420 N. Main St., 320/245-2481. **Greyhound** buses stop at the Amoco gas station, 320/245-0340, just east of town along Highway 23.

BANNING STATE PARK

Banning State Park's 6,237-acres straddle the raging Kettle River, the first waterway officially designated Wild and Scenic by the state of Minnesota. White-water fanatics with sufficient skill and nerve shoot the mile-long gorge containing the spectacular rapids with names like Dragon's Tooth and Hell's Gate, several of which can hit Class IV. The same goes for Big Spring Falls, the most challenging run of them all, at the far south end of the park. The eight miles from the village of Rutledge to the take-out just before the Banning Rapids has nothing above Class I rapids and is an ideal trip for beginners, though it gets pretty shallow after June.

Banning also contains several of the most rewarding hiking trails in the state. The trails of principal interest are those along the edge of the gorge since they offer superb viewing of the river and the paddlers who brave it. The easiest is the two-mile **Quarry Loop Trail.** It follows an old railroad bed that was used in part to ship the stone from the Banning Quarry that operated here between 1892-1912. Today, most areas look quite natural and even the ruins of the two remaining building are a scenic addition. If you are curious about the quarrying operation, pick up the brochure at the trailhead. Much more interesting than the man-made cuttings are the potholes carved into the rocks alongside the Kettle River during the last Ice Age. They can be found all along the river if you look carefully. The return half of the trail is scenic in its own right, but not nearly as much as the stretch along

© TIM BEWER

rafting the Kettle River, Banning State Park

the river, so you may just want to backtrack instead of completing the loop. Continuing along the river south of the Quarry Loop are the **High Bluff Trail** and **Wolf Creek Trail,** which together lead for a little over a mile to Wolf Creek Falls. Beyond the falls the trail continues on to Robinson Park in the city of Sandstone. The **Hell's Gate Trail** and **Lower Hell's Gate Trail,** two short spurs right along the river, lead towards, but not actually to, Hell's Gate Canyon, though both are still beautiful walks.

Few people bother with the rest of the 14-mile trail system, though the riverside half of the **Skunk Cabbage Trail,** blanketed by this large and somewhat foul smelling flower in the spring (it generates enough foul heat to melt the snow and is the first plant to bloom in the spring), is very scenic; the upper half features more typical spring wildflowers. Branching off it is the three-quarter-mile **Trillium Trail,** another good spring wildflower walk. Both trails are level and easy, though the riverside half of the former can get wet in spots and there is one long climb halfway through. **Big Spring Falls** in the far south end of the park

is a lovely sight and a fun spot to explore. To get there, head to the village of Sandstone and take Third Street to Pine Street (the last turn before the bridge) and follow it to the small unmarked pull off. To get way off the beaten path, head up to the **Log Creek Arches,** large potholes worn away at the bottom, in the undeveloped northern half of the park. An official trail will probably be built up here in future; until then the curious should ask for directions at the office. None of the trails are open to bikes, though a six-mile-paved path connects the park with the Willard Munger State Trail that runs between Hinckley and Duluth. Come winter, 12 miles of trail, including the Quarry Loop and High Bluff trails along the gorge, are groomed for cross-country skiing.

The campground has 33 widely spaced drive-in sites (11 electric) and a camper cabin. Additionally there are five first-come, first-served canoe-in sites along the river, one of which can be reach by foot. Although the park boundary curves around the city of Sandstone, the entrance is four miles to the north along Highway 23. Call 320/245-2668 for further information.

ST. CROIX VALLEY

MOOSE LAKE STATE PARK

There is a Moose Lake nearby, but the focus of this park, both geographically and recreationally, is Echo Lake with its picnic area and small swimming beach. Fishing is principally for largemouth bass, northern, and panfish. Rowboats and canoes can be rented from the park office. The campground, just east of the lake, has 33 mostly shady drive-in sites (20 electric), plus a pair of secluded walk-ins. This area is known for the abundance of agates, and the **Moose Lake Geological Agate Interpretive Center** discusses and displays them. You might also find some in the park and, if you do, feel free to take them home. Five miles of seldom-used hiking trail and seven miles of groomed cross-country ski trail lead over the gently rolling hills covering the rest of the park's 1,194 acres. Tops is the westernmost of the three loops comprising the 2.5-mile **Rolling Hills Trail**. It circles a pond and is the best spot to look for wildlife, including beaver, white-tailed deer, and even bald eagle, which have nested along it in recent years. With almost no development along the shore, the two-mile **Echo Lake Trail** also has

its moments. Unfortunately you can't escape the hum of Interstate traffic on any of them. For bikers a paved spur of the Willard Munger State Trail leads 2.5 miles down to the park. Call 218/485-5420 for more information.

CLOQUET

Once the site of an Ojibwe village, the first European settlers came in 1870 when a sawmill was built at what was then known as Knife Falls. Many more people soon followed, and Cloquet had grown to 12,000 people (a bit larger than it is today) by 1918 when it and two dozen other area towns were almost completely wiped out by a forest fire. The blaze killed 453 people outright, and many more died from resulting injuries or disease. Cloquet remains a lumber town at heart, and Carlton County's top three private sector employers, all based in Cloquet, are in the forest product industries, including the massive Potlatch paper mill with over 1,200 employees.

Sights

Although Frank Lloyd Wright defined himself

ST. CROIX VALLEY

© TIM BEWER

one of Frank Lloyd Wright's lesser-known designs

FOND DU LAC RESERVATION

Total Area - 158 sq. miles
Tribally Owned - 23 percent
Total Population - 3,728
Native Population - 1,353
Tribal Enrollment - 3,847

French fur traders gave the name Fond du Lac (Head of the Lake) to the Ojibwe village they encountered at the mouth of the St. Louis River. The name stuck, and was later applied to the reservation spread across St. Louis and Carlton counties. The original boundaries cut them off from their ricing and fishing lakes to the south, but through protest and pressure the tribe successfully fought for redrawn property lines. The tribal headquarters is in the city of Cloquet.

By cooperating with outside governments the Fond du Lac band has found great success in both economic development and education. The tribe runs a pair of casinos including Fond du-Luth which is a joint venture with the city of Duluth and

the only casino in Minnesota located outside reservation boundaries. The Fond du Lac Tribal & Community College in Cloquet is just as unique since it is the only combined tribal and state community college in the United States. Opened in 1987 the college concentrates on technology and computer training. In wonderful contrast to the college's high-tech ambitions, the architecture and landscape of its property illustrates ancient aspects of the Ojibwe culture. Campus buildings are laid out in the image of a bear paw, the Ojibwe archival library is shaped like a drum, and the traditional colors of red, black, white, and yellow are incorporated throughout the campus.

One of the Fond du Lac's most famous sons is Jim Northrop, an award winning writer known in and out of the State of Minnesota. His award winning syndicated column *The Fond du Lac Follies* appears in several Native American publications and his book *Walking the Rez Road* won a Minnesota Book Award.

with such important works of art as Fallingwater and the Guggenheim Museum, he also designed the **Lindholm Service Station** at the corner of Highway 33 and Cloquet Ave. Though built in 1956, Wright initially drew up the design as part of his Broadacre utopian city project in the 1930s. Only a compulsive fan of the famous architect would make the trip here just to see the somewhat run-down and frankly rather uninteresting (though unmistakably Wright-designed) building, but if you are passing through it's worth a look. The R. W. Lindholm House, also designed by Wright, sits about half a mile south of the station, but it's not visible from the road. Just down the street from the gas station is the **Carlton County History and Heritage Center,** 406 Cloquet Ave., 218/879-1938. The usual assortment of historical artifacts includes displays on the logging industry and the fire of 1918. It is open 9 A.M.–8 P.M. on Monday and 9 A.M.–4 P.M. Tuesday–Friday. Admission is free.

While at its lower reaches the Class V rapids of the St. Louis River offer a wild ride for ex-

perienced paddlers only, the 90 miles above Cloquet is a scenic route with few rapids, all of which are easily portaged if necessary. A good number of campsites and put-ins are spread out between Highway 53 and Cloquet. The **Cloquet River,** a major tributary of the St. Louis River, which it joins just above the city, is an equally scenic and much wilder route. Above the Island Lake Reservoir it has many rapids and campsites, but this stretch is only runable after heavy rains. Below the lake, water levels depend on the amount of water released by Minnesota Power and can be pretty low from July onwards, but generally it's enough to scrape by. Call 800/582-8529 for recorded water level information.

Practicalities

The Fond du Lac band operates the **Black Bear Casino,** 218/878-7400 or 800/533-0022, just south of town. The attached hotel has a pool, kiddie pool, two whirlpools, a sauna, exercise center, and game room, and charges from $99. On the south side of town along Highway 33 is

ST. CROIX VALLEY

the **Super 8,** 218/879-1250 or 800/800-8000, with standard rooms for $77 and a couple of themed whirlpool suites for double that.

During the warmer months the obvious choice for a meal is **Gordy's Hi-Hat,** 415 Sunnyside Dr., 218/879-6125, just across the river on Highway 33. Their famous hamburgers, fishburgers, and malts are under $4. Open daily for lunch and dinner from April through September. The fun menu (wild rice Cajun shrimp, New York strip kabob, and smoked turkey club sub) at **Grandma's Café,** 1405 Hwy. 33 S., 218/878-0633, just north of the freeway, is tough to resist. Entrées average $6–22. Open daily for lunch and dinner. **Greyhound** buses stop at D's Fabricare, 12 2nd St., 218/879-1591 (right behind the Lindholm Service Station), on their way between Duluth and the Twin Cities.

CARLTON

Instead of rushing on from Cloquet to Duluth along the freeway, consider taking the scenic route through Carlton. Though it has just 7 percent the population of its neighbor Cloquet, this city of 810 is the Carlton County seat. Carlton secured its dominion back in 1889 by stealing the county records and safes from the village of Thomson across the St. Louis River. The only reason to come to town is to follow one of the scenic routes out. The 15-mile stretch of the **Willard Munger State Trail** between Carlton and Duluth is easily the most scenic part of the entire trail. Highway 210 between Carlton and Highway 23 forms the **Rushing Rapids Parkway,** a winding drive along the wild St. Louis River. At nine miles it is the state's shortest official scenic byway, but one that truly deserves special recognition. Highway 23 will lead you right in to Duluth. For a bit of an adrenaline rush let **Superior Whitewater,** 950 Chestnut Ave, 218/384-4637, take you down the **St. Louis River** on one of their rafts. The two–three hour trips cost $36 per person and no experience is necessary, but rafters must be at least 12 years old.

JAY COOKE STATE PARK

Jay Cooke State Park, 218/384-4610, sprawls over nearly 9,000 acres, but most visitors are only interested in perusing the rugged St. Louis River and the deep gorge it has cut through the mangled bedrock. One of the easiest and most popular places to take in the splendid beauty of the gorge is the swinging bridge, which spans the river right behind the River Inn Visitor Center. You don't even need to get out of your car to enjoy the spectacular scenery since Highway 210, the **Rushing Rapids Parkway,** hugs the torrential river for much of its route through the park.

The park's superb trail system extends 50 miles through all parts of the park. Naturally the trails along the river are the most popular; however, most park visitors don't get beyond the swing bridge and the campground so you won't encounter a crowd even on these. The **Carlton Trail** begins at the bridge and hugs the south bank up to the north end of the park. It's an easy three-mile in and out, or you could take the Willard Munger Bridge across the river and follow the **Thompson Trail** back through the forest and along a short stretch of the north bank. The three-mile **Silver Creek Loop** heads west from the bridge and after about a mile turns in from the river and returns through the wooded hills. For some real solitude and a good chance of an animal encounter, strike out on the rolling, seldom-used loops branching off the Silver Creek trail, like the **Bear Chase Trail, Lower Lake Trail,** and **Spruce Trail.** You can walk in history along the scenic **Grand Portage Trail,** a steep, narrow route north of the river that was used by Voyageurs during the fur trade 300 years ago to bypass the rapids—if you follow the 0.75-mile **River Trail** back along the river you'll complete a three-mile loop. Also north of the river is the paved **Ogantz Trail,** a moderately hilly mile-long loop with a pair of river overlooks along it. The paved **Willard Munger State Trail,** a 63-mile route between Hinckley and Duluth, skirts the northern edge of the park, and about eight miles of trail branching off it are open to horses and mountain bikes, including a spur to the campground. Thirty-two miles of trail are groomed for cross-country skiing, and most offer a good challenge for those who want it. You can rent snowshoes at the park office to explore the rest of the park or, if you choose, stick to the four miles of packed winter hiking trails.

Experienced kayakers can tackle the challenging rapids, while those without white-water expertise can get the same thrills with a white-water rafting trip out of Carlton. Adequate water flow is all but guaranteed all season long. The park's campground has 80 (21 electric) widely spaced and mostly shady car-camping sites, plus three walk-ins for added seclusion and a heated camper cabin. The best camping is at the four backpacking sites south of the river.

The Arrowhead

If Minnesota were to release a greatest hits album, most of the tracks would come from its northeast corner. Tucked in between Lake Superior and the Canadian border are some of the state's most interesting towns, best museums, oldest historic sites, and the deepest wilderness east of the Mississippi. The incomparable Boundary Waters Canoe Area Wilderness encompasses the best of the best of Minnesota's lakes, and if you are even remotely interested in the outdoors you simply must dip a paddle into these enchanting waters at least once in your life. In contrast to the placid borderland lakes, the waters of the North Shore rage through deep gorges and over massive waterfalls before emptying into Lake Superior. Places like Grand Marais, with its flourishing arts community, and the iconic Split Rock Lighthouse complete the North Shore mosaic. Though it is defined by the city-sized scars left behind after more than a century of strip mining, these only serve to make the surprising Iron Range, stretched out across the heart of the Arrowhead, one of the most unusual places in the state, while Duluth is simply one of the most pleasant cities you'll ever spend time in. Spread out across most of the region is the 6,600-square-mile Superior National Forest (SNF), which hosts every conceivable outdoor activity and then some. The Arrowhead is the Minnesota you've imagined, and whatever the season it just doesn't get any better than this.

Split Rock Lighthouse

© TIM BEWER

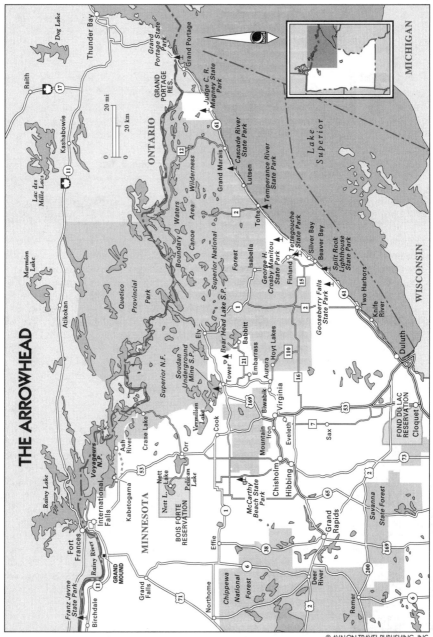

THE ARROWHEAD

THE ARROWHEAD HIGHLIGHTS

Boundary Waters Canoe Area Wilderness	**S. S. *William A. Irvin*,** Duluth
Canal Park, Duluth	**Ship watching,** Duluth
Dorothy Molter Museum, Ely	**Soudan Underground Mine State Park**
Grand Portage National Monument	**Split Rock Lighthouse**
Great Lakes Aquarium, Duluth	**State Parks on the North Shore,** all eight of them
International Wolf Center, Ely	**Superior Hiking Trail**
Ironworld Discovery Center, Chisholm	**Two Harbors Lighthouse,** Two Harbors
Mine tours, Hibbing and Mountain Iron	**Vince Shute Wildlife Sanctuary,** Orr
North House Folk School, Grand Marais	**Voyageurs National Park**

Duluth

Duluth is a city of many faces. It seamlessly blends small-town charm with a touch of big-city pizzazz, and though its 86,918 residents make it the third largest city in Minnesota it still has a wild side, as the resident bears and wandering moose will affirm. So will *Outside* magazine, which named it one of its ten American "Dream Towns." Ironically though, it is the city's gritty industrial side that is the most interesting to visitors. While it sits 2,342 miles from the Atlantic Ocean, Duluth, along with Superior, Wisconsin, its neighbor to the south, is one of the busiest ports in the world and the top on the Great Lakes. Some of the world's largest grain elevators and ore docks dominate the shoreline, and over 1,000 monstrous ships sail into the Twin Ports each year. Witnessing these leviathans up close and personal is a fascinating activity. Although Duluth has something for everyone, those with children in tow will especially appreciate the city on the lake. Many people planning a first time North Shore getaway just stop in Duluth briefly, only to regret not having budgeted more time. Don't make the same mistake; stick around for a few days and enjoy everything this wonderful city has to offer.

History

French voyageurs, who first arrived in the mid-17th century, called this area Fond du Lac (Head of the Lake) and like the Native Americans before them camped in the natural harbor for protection from Lake Superior's notoriously severe and sudden storms. Daniel Greysolon, Sieur du Lhut, a marine captain in the French army—for whom Duluth is somewhat creatively named—landed on Minnesota Point in 1679 to promote peace between the warring Ojibwe and Dakota, and fur traders soon established a small outpost in Duluth's present-day Fond du Lac neighborhood. The enterprise succeeded, though never flourished, even after 1809 when John Jacob Astor's American Fur Company built a fort here. The station was abandoned in 1849, the same year Minnesota became a territory.

Rumors of copper in the area—later proven to be nothing but rumors—and the construction of the Sault Sainte Marie Locks brought settlers back in 1853. The next year, when the Treaty of La Point turned over most of the Ojibwe's land to the Americans, a true land rush began and many predicted that a city here could rival Chicago. As a site for a city the Head of the Lake couldn't be more ideal. The natural harbor, massive and completely protected from storms, is one of the best in the world and, as the westernmost point on the Great Lakes, it is perfectly situated commercially. Wealthy land speculators from St. Paul and politicians from Washington threw money into development. Nearly a dozen small settlements, which eventually would merge into the present-day Duluth, sprang up below the steep hills on the north

THE ARROWHEAD

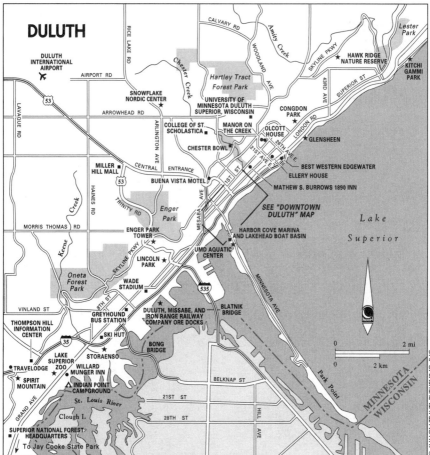

side of the bay, but most initial growth took place to the south on the broad plains of Wisconsin. Superior was the logical location for a great city, not only because the of the level terrain, but it was also closest to the natural harbor entry, linked to St. Paul by a new military road, and a future rail line wouldn't need to span the St. Louis River. By 1857 Superior had swelled to around 3,000 people, while Duluth remained a backwater. The Civil War began a few years later and put all plans for a new Metropolis on ice.

It would be over two decades before anyone again dreamt of a great city here. That person

was eastern financier Jay Cooke, who came in 1868 and decided to bring his Lake Superior and Mississippi River Railroad north from St. Paul to Duluth instead of Superior. This was the first in a series of events that gave Duluth dominance and created a rivalry between the two cities that to a small degree still exists today. Even before the first train rolled into "Jay Cooke's town" in 1870, Dr. Thomas Foster, publisher of the city's first newspaper, had declared Duluth "the Zenith City of the Unsalted Seas" and the population exploded from 14 in January of 1869 to 3,500 by the 4th of July.

THE ARROWHEAD

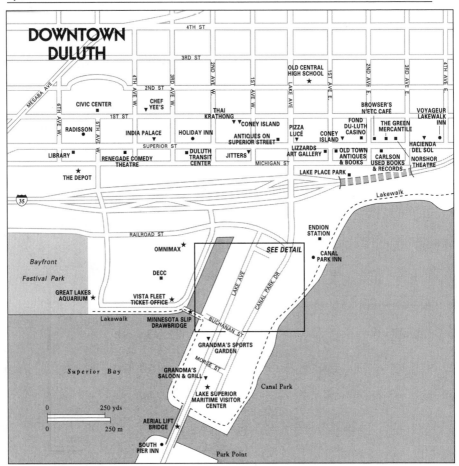

DOWNTOWN DULUTH

The bubble burst a second time in 1873 when Cooke's entire empire crumbled, inciting a stock market crash and national depression. The city officially lost its charter and most of its 5,000 citizens, but Duluth was just too strategically positioned and surrounded by too many natural resources not to fulfill its destiny. It took about a decade, but soon local logging and western wheat farming revived the Twin Ports' purpose and fueled construction of even more railroads to move these products here, plus the wharves, docks, and grain elevators needed to ship them to the East. By 1883 Duluth and its 14,000 residents were thriving and the city, through further economic ups and downs, continued to grow. Shipping eventually made Duluth-Superior the second most important urban center in all of the Northwest and home to more millionaires per capita than any other city in the world.

As the 20th century rolled in, iron mining expanded on the Mesabi Range and Duluth-Superior became the busiest port on the Great Lakes. Many of the city's heavy industries shut down or moved on over the course of the century, but tourism and shipping, along with education and health care jobs, have kept the city moving forward.

THE ARROWHEAD

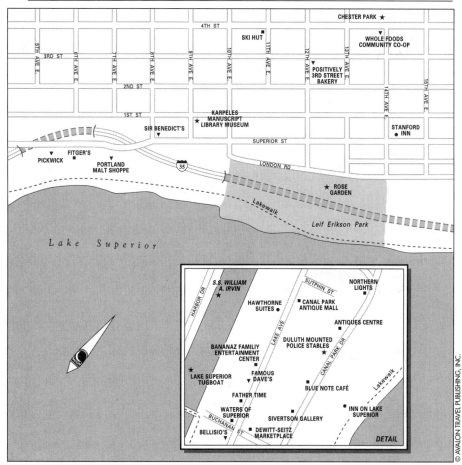

Orientation

Duluth stretches 26 miles along Lake Superior and St. Louis Bay and is less than a mile wide for much of it. Downtown is tucked right up into the steep, rocky hills that parallel the shoreline, and a few streets here are as steep as any in San Francisco, though most everything of interest sits at the bottom along historic Superior Street. Most of the action for tourists is in the adjacent Canal Park, which is not a park at all but a reclaimed warehouse district brimming with shops, restaurants, and other diversions. Many more must-see attractions are just a short stroll away along the waterfront. The seven-mile ribbon of land jutting out beyond the city is Park Point (rarely referred to by its official name, Minnesota Point), the world's largest freshwater sandbar. All but one of the city's B&Bs are to the northeast in the mansion-filled East End just beyond downtown. Today most of the town's growth is inland along Highway 53, the area known as Miller Hill, but unless you are traveling to or from the airport or are desperate for more shopping there is probably no reason to venture up this way.

Duluth has a limited **skywalk** system, which can get you out of the cold and rain, but probably the only time you'll find yourself using it is to cross from downtown hotels to the Duluth Entertainment Convention Center (DECC). Canal Park has ample **parking** for all but the busiest summer weekends. The lots are cheap, and a few on the north end are even still free. Should you find these lots full, look behind the DECC, just a short walk away.

SIGHTS
Aerial Lift Bridge
The massive bridge spanning the Duluth Ship Canal is as iconic to the Twin Ports as the Golden Gate Bridge is to San Francisco, but much more unusual. Instead of your standard seesawing drawbridge, a 1000-ton central spans rises 138 feet, like an elevator, letting ships enter the harbor. Watching one of the massive ships pass through it is a mandatory part of a Duluth visit.

Lake Superior Maritime Visitor Center
This excellent collection of Twin Ports and Great Lakes shipping past and present includes a giant steam engine (which the staff runs occasionally), a model of an ore dock, and lots of unique knick-knacks. If you want to see a child's eyes light up, let her spin the wheel in the pilothouse mock-up. Computer screens post ship arrival and departure times, and telescopes let you examine ships out on the lake waiting for their dock to free up. The center is open daily 10 A.M.–9 P.M. during the summer (it stays open through the year, but hours vary considerably so call ahead) and admission is free. Call 218/727-2497 for information.

SHIP WATCHING

There is something almost magical about watching giant ships cruise in and out of port. Things that big, it seems, just shouldn't be so maneuverable, or even be able to float for that matter. Ocean going "salties" stretch up to 730 feet long while the "lakers" can exceed 1,000 feet in length and weigh 100,000 tons when fully loaded—mostly with taconite, coal, and grain. The shipping season depends on the weather, but usually runs late March to mid-January. The **Boat Watcher's Hotline** (218/722-6489), a service of the U.S. Army Corps of Engineers, gives ship arrival and departure times for both the Twin Ports and the North Shore. The Corps also publishes the fact-filled brochure *Great Lakes Shipping: A Guide* to help you identify the various ships, fleets, and flags you'll see in harbor. It is available free of charge at the Lake Superior Maritime Visitor Center. The wonderful *Duluth Shipping News*, a free newsletter published daily during the summer, informs the curious of what cargo individual ships are carrying on that day along with their histories and statistic. Other articles offer an inside scoop on how the industry works and tell stories about the crews. You can pick it up just about anywhere in Canal Park.

The ultimate viewing spot anywhere is the **Duluth Ship Canal.** As the ships slip under the Aerial Lift Bridge they pass so close you feel like you can reach out and touch them. Display screens at the Lake Superior Maritime Visitor Center post arrival and departure times. Also in Duluth, an elevated observation platform near the Duluth, Missabe, and Iron Range Railway Company's 2,000 foot-long **ore docks** lets you see the ships being loaded with taconite pellets. From South 40th Avenue West, just south of I-35, head east on Oneota Street and follow the signs. The **Vista Fleet Harbor Tours** take you past these and other docks in the harbor.

The **Harvest States grain elevators** (the largest in the nation), across the bay in Superior, are the best place for an up close look at boats in dock. You'll see them on the right as you come across the Blatnik Bridge. You can also drive past the docks on **Connors Point,** a mile northwest of Superior's Tourist Information Center on U.S. 53. Although it sees much less traffic than Duluth's canal, ships occasionally arrive and depart through the **Superior Entry** at the end of Wisconsin Point.

Moving up the North Shore your next best bet is **Two Harbors** where you have unobstructed views of the ships pulling into Agate Bay and loading up at the ore docks. Ships can also be seen loading in **Silver Bay** and at **Taconite Harbor** much further along the coast.

so close you can almost touch it

S. S. William A. Irvin

The former flagship of U.S. Steel's Great Lakes Fleet is now a floating museum and your chance to see what takes place on board the monstrous ships you've been admiring in the port. During the hour-long tour of the former iron ore and coal vessel you'll see the 2,000 horsepower engines, elaborate guest quarters, and vast cargo hold. In the pilothouse kids can sit at the wheel and blow the whistle. For Halloween, the Irvin is transformed into a frightening "Ship of Ghouls" with a tamer family version during the day. The 610-foot Irvin, 218/722-7876, is open Sunday–Thursday 9 A.M.–6 P.M. and Friday–Saturday 9 A.M.–8 P.M., plus Sunday–Thursday 10 A.M.–4 P.M. and Friday–Saturday 10 A.M.–6 P.M. during May and from September through mid-October. Admission is $6.75. Your ticket to the William A. Irvin includes a look around the retired *Lake Superior tugboat* docked alongside it. A look around the tug alone costs $3.

Vista Fleet Harbor Cruises

Vista Fleet's 90-minute narrated cruises let you get up close and personal with the giant ships, grain elevators, and ore docks in the harbor and, weather permitting, you'll even get to cruise under the Lift Bridge. The boats depart across from the DECC. The standard tours depart daily from mid-May to mid-October and cost $10. Call 218/722-6218 for information about times and prices of their special lunch, dinner, and moonlight cruises.

Great Lakes Aquarium

The country's first and only exclusively-freshwater aquarium puts you face to face with the native residents of Lake Superior, like the five-foot lake sturgeon in the 103,000 gallon Isle Royale tank and the bizarre paddlefish, long nose gar, and slimy sculpin in one of the 19 other tanks. Divers feed the monsters of the Isle Royale tank once in the morning and again in the afternoon. Not all of the aquarium's creatures have fins. Besides 70 species of fish there are turtles, snakes, salamanders, mud puppies, frogs, ducks, and playful otters. The Great Lakes Aquarium is actually much more than just an aquatic zoo. There are also often-overlooked historical, ecological, geological, and artistic exhibits about the world's largest lake, spanning its glacial creation to current environmental threats, plus displays and wildlife

THE ARROWHEAD

from the world's other great freshwater lakes, like Baikal and Nicaragua. Plenty of interactive exhibits, like the touch tank, lock and dam exhibit, and virtual submarine, aimed at kids let them learn without even realizing it. Due to financial troubles the aquarium's future is not entirely certain and hours and prices are in flux—call 218/740-3474 for details.

The Depot

Officially it's the St. Louis County Heritage and Arts Center, but everyone calls it "The Depot," 506 W. Michigan St., 218/727-8025 or 888/733-5833, after the imposing 1892 Chateauesque-style structure's original purpose. Today it houses four museums, with the **Lake Superior Railroad Museum,** 218/733-7590, the top draw. The outstanding collection of classic rolling stock includes an 1861 wood-burning steam engine, railway post office, and rotary snowplow. Depot Square, a re-created 1910 street scene, is another must see. The hands-on **Duluth Children's Museum,** 218/733-7543, entered by descending through the a giant tree trunk, looks forward by focusing on natural history and world cultures, while the

displays of the **St. Louis County Historical Society,** 218/733-7580, look back at northeastern Minnesota. The small **Duluth Art Institute,** 218/733-7560, has rotating exhibits. During the summer the museums are open daily 9:30 A.M.–6 P.M. The rest of the year hours are Monday–Saturday 10 A.M.–5 P.M. and Sunday 1–5 P.M. Admission is $8.50.

Karpeles Manuscript Library Museum

Seemingly out of place in far off Duluth, the Karpeles collection of historical documents is one of the largest in the world, and Duluth native David Karpeles wanted one of his seven branch museums to be located here. Displays are rotated every three months so you never know what you will find, but the collection includes original copies of such landmarks as the Bill of Rights and Emancipation Proclamation, letters from Darwin and Galileo, and Wagner's *Wedding March.* It may seem dry, but it can be fascinating to see history with changes written in the margins. Located at 902 E. 1st St., 218/728-0630, it's open daily noon–4 P.M. during the summer, closing Monday the rest of the year. Admission is free.

The Depot

Leif Erikson Park

This picnic-perfect lakeside park is home to a stunning **Rose Garden** (along London Rd. at 13th Ave. E., if you're coming by car) filled by over 3,000 bushes and is also the final resting place of a half-sized replica of the **Viking ship** that Leif Erikson sailed to North America. In 1926 this very boat retraced the route from Norway before ending up here.

Glensheen

Self-made millionaire Chester Congdon spared no expense in building his opulent estate on Lake Superior, and little has changed inside the 39-room, Jacobean-style mansion since it was completed in 1908. The 75-minute guided tours take you past the wealth of custom designed furniture, hand-carved woodwork, leaded art glass windows, and the formal gardens in the surrounding 7.5-acre grounds. Glensheen, 218/726-8910 or 888/454-4536, is located at 3300 London Rd. From May through October it is open daily 9:30 A.M.–4 P.M., and Friday–Sunday 11 A.M.–2 P.M. the rest of the year. The standard visit costs $9.50 and a grounds pass is $4. Other special tour options are available.

University of Minnesota Duluth

The modern UMD campus is home to the best art museum in the northland. The **Tweed Museum of Art,** 218/726-8222, has over 4,500 objects from around the world in its permanent collection, most notably modern American works, and hosts many traveling exhibitions plus works by faculty, students, and local artists. The nine galleries are open Tuesday 9 A.M.–8 P.M., Wednesday–Friday 9 A.M.–4:30 P.M., and weekends 1–5 P.M. Admission is free. It sits right in the center of campus next to Cina Hall; follow the signs to the visitor parking lot. The **Marshall W. Alworth Planetarium,** 218/726-7129, has free public shows at 7 P.M. every Wednesday while school is in session.

Lake Superior Zoo

The zoo's residents come from around the globe, but the focus is fittingly on northern and polar species (Bubba and Berlin, the zoo's playful polar

---

Superior Street, Duluth's historic main drag, is lined with gorgeous turn of the 20th century buildings and you should take some time to admire the classic architecture of a bygone era: they don't build them like this anymore. The free ***Downtown Duluth: Architecture and Public Art*** brochure, available at the Endion Station tourism office in Canal Park, points out dozens of historic buildings on Superior Street and elsewhere. The one building not to miss, though it would be difficult to do so, is the Old Central High School which towers over the downtown. This 1892 Romanesque Revival brownstone has gargoyles and a 230-foot clock tower with chimes patterned after London's Big Ben.

Beyond downtown, the ***Walking Tour of Duluth's Historic East End*** brochure, also available free at Endion, details two dozen historic houses on Superior and 1st Sts. between 21st and 24th Aves.

---

bears, are crowd favorites), which means winter is as good a time to visit as any. It is located at 72nd Avenue West and Grand Avenue, 218/733-3777, and open daily year-round. From April through October the hours are 9 A.M.–6 P.M. dropping to 10 A.M.–4 P.M. the rest of the year. Admission is $6.

Paper Mill Tours

StoraEnso, 100 N. Central Ave., 218/722-6024, takes visitors on a fascinating one-hour tour of their high-tech papermaking facility. You'll get a video overview of the process and then see (and hear!) the giant rolls being wound. Tours start at 9 A.M., 10:30 A.M., 1 P.M., and 3 P.M. on Monday, Wednesday, and Friday during the summer. Free tickets must be reserved in advance at the Vista Harbor Dock Tourist Information Center. Open-toed or high-heeled shoes and children under 10 are not allowed.

Scenic Train Rides

Rail fans hit the jackpot in Duluth with not one, but two scenic excursions chugging out of the city. The **North Shore Scenic Railroad,** 218/722-1273 or 800/423-1273, at The Depot skirts Lake Superior on either a short 90-minute excursion or a six-hour trip all the way to Two Harbors. Other options include murder mysteries, elegant dinners, and a Pizza Train. Regardless of the trip, you'll travel in vintage passenger cars pulled by classic engines. The short excursions cost $10 and run daily at 12:30 P.M. and 3 P.M. (plus 10 A.M. Fri. and Sat.) during the summer and then weekends to October. Call for specifics of their various other options.

Heading in the opposite direction is the **Lake Superior and Mississippi Railroad,** 218/624-7549, which follows the St. Louis River for 12 miles along the original rail line connecting Duluth with the Twin Cities. They like to call their train ride a "nature walk on rails, " which pretty much sums it up. You can ride in their vintage coaches, but the best views come from the completely open "Safari Car." Trains depart across from the zoo on Saturday and Sunday at 10:30 A.M. and 1:30 P.M. from mid-June to Labor Day weekend with additional fall color trips later on. The ride costs $7.

Skyline Drive

This scenic 38-mile drive stretches right across the top of the city. The marked route roughly follows the ancient Lake Superior shoreline, often rising 600 feet above today's lake surface. Scenic overlooks are frequent and, needless to say, superb. Though the central portion of the drive passes through the city, most of the parkway leads through forest and past rushing rivers and waterfalls. You can access the east end from Superior St. at Lester Park and the west end at Becks Rd. near Gary-New Duluth. The popular eastern section is known as **Seven Bridges Road,** a narrow unpaved route, with not seven but eight stone-arch bridges, and the most scenic of the scenic overlooks.

Also along the eastern portion is the **Hawk Ridge Nature Reserve,** a 200-acre hilltop natural area owned by the city of Duluth and managed by the Duluth Audubon Society. The main overlook is located a mile east of Glenwood Ave. People flock from all over the country beginning in mid-August when tens of thousands of migrating raptors follow the air currents along the Lake Superior shoreline on their way south for the winter. As many as 48,000 hawks have been counted in just one day. The best viewing is usually from mid-September through October between about 9 A.M. and 4 P.M., and some still pass by as late as December. During the migration, Hawk Ridge naturalists conduct research and offer free educational programs for the general public. The rest of the year it's still a worthwhile destination for the 2.5 miles of hiking trails and great lake views. For more information call 218/728-5812.

Enger Park, near the middle of the parkway at 18th Avenue West, should also not be missed. A historic rock observation tower rises five stories from the city's highest point, and a Japanese garden, picnic area, and several secluded overlooks surround it.

Flightseeing

For $30 per person Orville Air, 218/733-0078, will give you a bird's-eye view of the Twin Ports during a 20-minute seaplane ride. Flights depart daily May through September from Sky Harbor Airport out at the end of Park Point.

RECREATION
On Land

While the wilderness north of Duluth beckons, don't overlook the 11,000 acres of green space right in its backyard. Twenty-three rivers and creeks rush down the hills of Duluth in a long series of waterfalls and rapids before emptying into Lake Superior. The rivers are truly wild in the spring, while later in the year they can slow to not much more than a trickle, but the settings are superb anytime. These wild waterways form the core of some of the city's best parks, and the hiking trails following them offer a near wilderness experience. The trails are often steep, of course, but generally easy to follow. From east to west some of the best hikes are **Lester Park Trail,** Superior St. and Lester River Rd.; **Congdon Park Trail** (my personal favorite), Superior St. and 32nd Ave. E.; **Chester Park Trail,** 4th St. and

WHERE'S THE THERMOSTAT?

The coldest winter I ever spent was a summer in Duluth.

While Mark Twain never uttered this frequently misattributed quote, Duluth does fashion itself as "The Air-Conditioned City." Lake Superior, with an average temperature of just 39 degrees, cools the surrounding air making the climate pleasant during all but the fiercest heat waves. If the winds blow out of the east it can keep the city's temperature down by as much as 15 degrees over the inland temperature. The lake has the opposite effect in the winter when it serves as a three-quadrillion-gallon radiator.

14th Ave. E.; **Lincoln Park Trail,** 3rd St. and 25th Ave. W.; and **Kingsbury Creek Trail,** right behind the zoo. For a scenic hike of a different nature, follow the wooded two-mile **Park Point Trail** from the Sky Harbor Airport at the end of Minnesota Ave. past sand dunes and a ruined lighthouse. Bird-watchers will have a field day out here during the spring and fall migrations.

Duluth's 4.2-mile **Lakewalk** is urban walking at its very best. Separate walking and biking lanes hug the shore from the Great Lakes Aquarium to beyond Leif Erikson Park. It not only connects many of the city's most popular attractions, but with such fantastic scenery it's a top attraction itself. After the Lakewalk the city's most popular bike routes are the **Western Waterfront Trail,** a five-mile gravel and grass path along the St. Louis River, and the 14 scenic miles of the **Willard Munger State Trail,** which lead to Jay Cooke State Park. The Munger trail continues beyond the park all the way to Hinckley and will eventually connect the Twin Ports with the Twin Cities. Both trails are best accessed at a parking area just south of Grand Avenue on 75th Avenue West. The nearby **Willard Munger Inn,** 7408 Grand Ave., 218/624-4814 or 800/982-2453, rents bikes, in-line skates, and offers a shuttle service all the way to Hinckley. **Skyline Drive,** described above, also makes for a great bike ride.

On Water

Duluth's **charter fishing** docks are located alongside the William A. Irvin, while a few captains are also docked out on Park Point. Check with the Duluth Convention and Visitors Bureau for referrals or other information.

If you'd like to give sea kayaking a try, call the **UMD Outdoor Program,** 218/726-6533, which leads beginners around the harbor. Their four-hour trips leave at 1 P.M. on Fridays and 9 A.M. on Saturdays from late June through August and cost $40. The also have a wide variety of beginner to advanced canoeing and kayaking lessons and trips to the nearby St. Louis River and Split Rock Lighthouse. Their Aquatic Center is on Park Point at South 15th Street.

Synergy Sails, based in Park Point's Harbor Cove Marina, 1003 Minnesota Ave., 218/348, 3048, will take you out on the lake in their 32-foot sailboat. You can either just sun and sightsee from the deck or take the wheel. A two-hour trip is $160 for up to four people, and an all-day sail is $500.

Because the water is shallow, and thus warm, the most popular place for a swim is the **Park Point Recreation Area,** which has lifeguards and changing rooms. There is another public beach on Park Point just five blocks south of the bridge at South 12th Street. You can also take a quick dip at the rocky beaches in **Canal Park,** behind the Endion Station Visitor Information Center, and Brighton Beach in **Kitchi Gammi Park** at the far east end of town along Highway 61.

Winter Sports

Spirit Mountain, exit 249 off I-35, 218/628/2891, 800/642-6377, has 23 runs (the biggest drops 700 feet) for skiers and snowboarders (who can also shred the half-pipes and terrain park), plus three tubing runs. A one-day lift ticket is $17. Cross-country skiers also flock to Spirit Mountain, which has 14 miles of groomed, double tracked trails with an eight-foot skating lane through a beautiful woods—a half-day trail pass is just $4.

The city grooms another 27 miles of cross-country trail (call 218/624-3062 for trail conditions) in local parks, including the intermediate level nine-mile **Magney-Snively Ski Trail** starting just off Spirit Mountain along the Skyline Parkway. One third of the nine miles of the **Lester-Amity Trail,** with beginner to advanced loops in Lester Park, are lit during early mornings and late into the evening. The **Chester Bowl Trail** is just two miles long, but it's the most challenging route in the city. The park also has a 175-foot-tall downhill run with a chairlift (a daily pass is $3.50), plus a pair of ski jumps and an ice skating oval. The private **Snowflake Nordic Center,** 4348 Rice Lake Rd., 218/726-1550, has another nine miles of trails groomed for classic and skating—a third are lit at night. Snowflake has rentals, instruction, a chalet, and even a sauna for after the trails. A day pass is $7 or $3 after 6 P.M. The **Ski Hut,** 1032 E. 4th St., 218/724-8525, and 5607 Grand Ave., 218/624-5889, rents cross-country skis as well as snowshoes.

For something out of the ordinary, let **Epic Sleddog Adventures,** 6009 Eagle Lake Rd., 218/721-3692, take you for a ride. A half-day trip costs $90, plus other options are also available.

Other Diversions

For some it will be a guilty pleasure, but there are few people who won't find something fun at **Bananaz Family Entertainment Complex,** 329 Lake Ave. S., 218/720-5868, which has video games, laser tag, mini golf, a trampoline jump, climbing wall, and much more. **Enger Park,** 1801 Skyline Blvd., 218/723-3451; and **Lester Park,** 1860 Lester River Rd., 218/525-0828, are two good 27-hole public golf courses overlooking Lake Superior.

ENTERTAINMENT

For the full scoop on what's on during the week, scan the Friday *Duluth News-Tribune*'s The Wave section or the free weekly *Ripsaw*. The biggest touring acts that make it to the Twin Ports, from musicians to circuses, play at the **DECC,** 218/727-4344, which also hosts a "Best of Broadway" series. The **NorShor Theatre,** 211 E. Superior St., 218/727-7585, mixes live music, independent films, and other special events. Both **UMD,** 218/726-8564, and the **College of St. Scholastica,** 218/723-6632, have full cultural calendars.

Nightlife

There is live music most nights at **Sir Benedict's,** 805 E. Superior St., 218/728-1192, and **Pizza Lucé,** 11 E. Superior St., 218/727-7400. The former hosts bluegrass, Celtic, and similar music, while just about any type of band might take the stage at the latter. The **Amazing Grace** bakery-coffee shop has folk artists most nights, including a Monday open mic. You might also catch some weekend jazz at the small **Blue Note Café,** 357 Canal Park Dr., 218/727-6549, around the corner. Duluth's only brewpub, **Fitger's Brewhouse,** 600 E. Superior St., 218/726-1392, is a happening bar all the time (and has pretty good food, too), but especially on weekends when jazz and rock bands take to the small stage. Down in the basement of the Fitger's Building is the large **Tap Room,** 218/728-1192, with bands every Saturday night (and sometimes others), including some touring acts, while DJs pack the place on Thursday and Friday nights. **Grandma's Sports Garden,** 425 Lake Ave. S., 218/722-4724, in Canal Park clears the floor for dancing on Wednesday through Saturday nights.

Classical Music and Dance

The **Duluth-Superior Symphony Orchestra,** 218/733-7579, performs more or less year-round at the DECC, while the **Minnesota Ballet,** 218/529-3742, puts on a couple of performances there each year. The **Lake Superior Chamber Orchestra,** 218/724-5231, holds five Wednesday evening concerts at the College of St. Scholastica each summer.

Theater

The **Duluth Playhouse,** 218/733-7555, entertaining the masses since 1914, is the state's longest continuously running theater group. They perform half a dozen shows during the year at The Depot. **Renegade Comedy Theatre,** 404 W. Superior St., 218/722-6775 or 888/722-6627, goes for laughs with every ticket. Besides the standard theatrical productions, they offer Improv Comedy Olympics on Friday and Saturday nights. The early shows are family fun, while the late performances are rated PG on Friday and R on Saturday.

The same bunch runs the **Tugboat Children's Theatre** with occasional weekend shows. **Bennett's Dinner Theatre,** 600 E. Superior St. (in Fitger's), 218/722-2829, does murder mysteries and comedies, some with audience participation, following a specially prepared Bennett's On The Lake meal. Friday and Saturday night shows are $37.50, while brunch matinees are $25. Tickets for the show minus the meal are $12.50.

Freebies

During the summer there are free concerts in various locations around the city. Chester Bowl Park hosts rock and country bands on Tuesday nights at 7 P.M., while bands of all stripes play rotating locations around town, including Glensheen and downtown's Lake Place Park, at the same time on Wednesdays.

Cinema

Cinema 8 Theatres, 218/727-5554, is just beyond the Miller Hill Mall, while for something not out of Hollywood there is the **NorShor,** 211 E. Superior St., 218/727-7585, which actually has a bar. Duluth also has a state-of-the-art **OMNIMAX Theatre,** 218/727-0022 or 888/666-4629, at The DECC.

Spectator Sports

The **UMD Bulldogs** compete in a full slate of NCAA Division II athletics, but for the fans it is pretty much all about hockey. Despite the school's small size, the men's team is a regular contender in the Division I WCHA conference and count Brett Hull among the dozens of alumni who have skated in the NHL. The women's team won the inaugural national championship in 2001 and repeated in 2002 and 2003. Men's hockey tickets cost $12, though are next to impossible to get on short notice, while women's cost half that and are always available on game day. Order tickets through the UMD Ticket Office, 218/726-8595 or 877/221-8168.

The **Duluth Huskies** play in the Northwoods League, made up of Division I college baseball players who get minor league experience while keeping their college eligibility. Home games are played at historic Wade Stadium at 34th Avenue West and Grand Avenue. General admission tickets cost $5 and are available by calling 218/786-9909.

Many of the world's best curlers compete for the **Duluth Curling Club,** 218/727-1851, whose home ice is at the DECC. The bonspiel season runs November to March, and they also have open houses if you want to throw some stones of your own.

Gambling

Downtown's **Fond du-Luth Casino,** 129 E. Superior St., 218/722-0280 or 800/873-0280, is run jointly by the city and the Fond du Lac Ojibwe.

THE GREATEST OF THE GREAT LAKES

To call Lake Superior big is to make a colossal understatement. Just take a look at the numbers. The lake's surface area covers 31,280 square miles—almost the same size as South Carolina—making it the largest lake in the world. It stretches 350 miles at its longest and 160 miles at its widest, has 2,726 miles of shoreline, and its deepest point sinks 1,279 feet below the surface. Its three quadrillion (that's 15 zeros) gallons of water constitute one-eighth of the world's fresh water supply and is enough to cover all of North and South America one foot deep. Only Lake Baikal in Russia and Lake Tanganyika in East Africa, both much smaller but deeper lakes, contain more. It isn't just the volume of water that makes this lake special; it also happens to be some of the purest and cleanest in the world.

Though the lake is usually enchanting is also has a dark side. During the worst storms waves can rage over 30 feet high. Superior has sent at least 350 ships to its bottom including the Edmund Fitzgerald which famously snapped in half near Sault Ste. Marie, Michigan on November 10, 1975. All 29 crew members aboard the 729-foot ore carrier died. It's easy to see why those who intimately familiar with her will tell you th perior deserves as much respect as admir

EVENTS

So much more than just a race to Duluthians, mid-June's **Grandma's Marathon** is one of the most anticipated dates on the city's calendar. Though the racers compete on Saturday morning, live entertainment and a health expo run all weekend, plus the post-race party is free and open to the public. Four thousand skaters follow the same route as Grandma's the second weekend in September for the **Northshore Inline Marathon,** the largest inline race in the country and an official World Cup event.

The **Bayfront Blues Festival** has the whole town swinging the second weekend in August. Dozens of acts perform on two stages in Bayfront Festival Park, and many area clubs get in on the action as well. Recent headliners have included Buddy Guy and Luther Allison. **Winterfest** begins on the first of the year and continues for six weeks with dozens of winter sports events, like ski jumping contests and snowshoe races, plus weekend activities like sleigh rides and a lutefisk-eating contest.

ACCOMMODATIONS

The Duluth area has nearly 4,300 hotel rooms, but they can fill up during summer weekends. The Duluth Convention and Visitors Bureau (CVB) can help you find rooms on short notice. If you are here to ski, check with Spirit Mountain about "Ski Free" specials they have with area hotels.

Hotels and Motels

Canal Park: The cheapest Canal Park rooms are at the **Canal Park Inn,** 250 Canal Park Dr., 218/727-8821 or 800/777-8560, with rates as low as $109, and there is a pool and whirlpool. This is the only Canal Park hotel that is not a re-cent construction, though it has certainly kept up ___ ach room at the **Inn on Lake** ___ anal Park Dr., 218/726-1111 ___ has a private balcony or patio, ___ l, whirlpool, and sauna. They ___ .

___ ites, 235 Lake Ave. N., 218/ ___ 766-2665, the only Canal Park

hotel not on the lakeshore, is a lovely warehouse conversion incorporating many of the original building features into the design. All rooms have full kitchens, and guests have use of the pool, whirlpool, sauna, and fitness center. Studio rooms start at $125, though most are much higher-price multiroom suites.

No hotel is better situated than the brand new **South Pier Inn,** 701 Lake Ave. S., 218/786-9007 or 800/430-7437, on Park Point just across from Canal Park. Most rooms look up at the Lift Bridge, and you can watch ships pass through the harbor from a private balcony. Rates start at $119, but most of the 29 rooms are whirlpool suites from $199.

Downtown: The **Voyageur Lakewalk Inn,** 333 E. Superior St., 218/722-3911 or 800/258-3911, is an older but well-kept hotel and, considering the location and $65 price, it is a great option. All rooms are more modern than the exterior would lead you to believe. Perched on a hill right above downtown is the appropriately named **Buena Vista Motel,** 1144 Mesaba Ave., 218/722-7796 or 800/569-8124, another older but spotless property. Rooms, some of them quite large, start at $60.

Both the **Radisson,** 505 W. Superior St., 218/727-8981 or 800/333-3333, and **Holiday Inn,** 200 W. 1st St., 218/722-1202 or 800/477-7089, have pools, whirlpools, saunas, great views from upper levels, and charge from $125. The Holiday Inn also has a fitness center. The fanciest hotel in town is nationally recognized **Fitger's Inn,** 600 E. Superior St., 218/722-8826 or 800/726-2982, part of a restored brewery complex right along the lake on the edge of downtown. Although suites go for $275, the regular rooms, all lavishly appointed, start at just $110.

East: Just minutes from most of the action, the large **Best Western Edgewater,** 2400 London Rd., 218/728-3601 or 800/777-7925, has a pool, whirlpool, sauna, game room, miniature golf course, free bikes, and room rates as low as $89. It's not directly on the shore, but has easy access to the Lakewalk and great views from lakeside rooms.

West: You can save a good chunk of change by sleeping on the west side of town.

The friendly, family-run **Willard Munger Inn,**

7408 Grand Ave., 218/624-4814 or 800/982-2453, sits right by the Willard Munger and Western Waterfront Trails and guests get free use of bikes. Simple rooms start at just $46, while whirlpool or fireplace suites go for $90. Right across the freeway from the entrance to Spirit Mountain is the **Travelodge,** 9315 Westgate Blvd., 218/628-3691 or 800/578-7878, with a pool, whirlpool, and sauna. The rooms, starting at $69, are fairly basic, but have some homey touches.

B&Bs

If you fancy bed-and-breakfasts, then Duluth, with a dozen in beautifully restored historic homes, is your kind of town. The Historic Bed and Breakfast Inns of Duluth website (www.duluthbandb.com) lists most of them. Each of the following, as do most others, has a two-night minimum stay requirement on weekends.

From the gingerbread house exterior to the opulent decor full of stained glass and carved woodwork, the spectacular elegance of the **Mathew S. Burrows 1890 Inn,** 1632 E. 1st St., 218/724-4991 or 800/789-1890, can't be beat. The five guestrooms, all with private bath, run $95–175.

The 18,000 sq.-foot **Manor on the Creek,** 2215 E. 2nd St., 218/728-3189 or 800/428-3189, also has a truly spectacular atmosphere. Built in 1907 by a lumber baron, it is one of the largest houses in the city, and every square inch has an elegant touch. Some of the many amenities include a fantastic sunroom, billiards room, and two wooded acres along Oregon Creek to stroll at your leisure. The seven tastefully decorated guestrooms, each with a private bath, start at $129, though it is worth paying in the $200 range for one of the rooms overlooking the creek.

A mining tycoon built the deceptively small-looking 10,000 sq.-foot Georgian Colonial **Olcott House,** 2316 E. 1st St., 218/728-1339 or 800/715-1339, in 1904 and today it is decorated as it might have been in that bygone era. Each of the six guestrooms has a private bath and fireplace and is priced around $150, though the four-room Carriage House in back is $185.

Although it is in a grand 1890 Victorian home, the **Ellery House,** 28 S. 21st Ave E., 218/724-7639 or 800/355-3794, has a very homey atmo-sphere. Each of the four guestrooms, priced from $99 to $139, has a private bath and this is one of the few B&Bs in town that welcomes children.

The 1886 orange brick **Stanford Inn,** 1415 E. Superior St., 218/724-3044, is proud to be Minnesota's first gay-owned B&B. It's much less grand than the others, but still has a few nice Victorian touches, a sauna, and is located right near the Rose Garden. Three of the rooms, each priced at $85, share two baths, while the one with a private bath is $115. It is open daily May through October and weekends the rest of the year.

Hostels

The **College of St. Scholastica,** 218/723-6084, rents out its dorm rooms to the public from June through mid-August for $25 per person (if you are traveling alone you still get a room to yourself) and also has apartments with private baths for $80.

Campgrounds

The best camping in the area is at nearby Jay Cooke State Park, but as far as municipal campgrounds go, the 50 sites along the St. Louis River at the **Indian Point Campground,** 902 S. 69th Ave. W., 218/628-4977 or 800/982-2453, are really good and cost $17 with no hookup and $23 with full hookup.

FOOD

All of Duluth's restaurants are smoke-free.

American

Grandma's Saloon & Grill, 522 Lake Ave. S., 218/727-4192, covered in unique antiques and collectibles, is a Northland institution. The menu covers such options as curried wild rice chicken salads, turkey burgers, and Cajun chicken fettuccine, all averaging $10. Open daily for lunch and dinner.

The chef-owned **Lake Avenue Café,** 394 Lake Ave. S., 218/722-2355, in the DeWitt-Seitz building offers casual fine dining and is arguably the city's best restaurant. The global menu features choices such as falafel, pizza, burritos, and a unique Thai chili. Entrées, all lovingly prepared, average $15, though some are only half that. Open daily for lunch and dinner.

Another restaurant that vies for the title of Duluth's best is its most elegant and romantic, **Bennett's on the Lake,** 600 E. Superior St. (in Fitger's), 218/722-2829, where both the food and the service match the lovely setting. Dinner choices like grilled duck with shiitake mushroom and sage crusted pork loin run $12–26, while the lunch menu is mostly salads and sandwiches for around $9. The breakfast menu has just a few choices, though the Sunday buffet is tremendous. Open daily for lunch and dinner and weekdays for breakfast.

Next to Fitger's is the classic **Pickwick,** 508 E. Superior St., 218/727-8901, family owned since 1918 though the business, in different forms, has been going since 1888. The menu is mostly steak and seafood, and it all averages out to $15. If you're lucky you'll get a lakeside seat, though the intricate woodwork makes the interior views just as beautiful. Open daily for lunch and dinner.

Not that there is anything wrong with the food, but the **Top of the Harbor,** 505 W. Superior St., 218/727-8981, is all about the location. Perched on the 16th floor of the Radisson Hotel, the revolving restaurant looks right down on the city and harbor. Lunch is mostly sandwiches for about $8, while the much more substantial dinner menu has $20 steak and seafood. Open daily for breakfast, lunch, and dinner.

At the bottom end of the spectrum, **Coney Island,** 107 E. Superior St., 218/727-1077, and 112 W. 1st St., 218/722-2772, has highly recommended burgers, hot dogs, and ice cream for under $2. Open daily for breakfast, lunch, and dinner.

Asian

The excellent lunch buffet and dinner entrées at **India Palace,** 319 W. Superior St., 218/727-8767, all average $9, and understandably some rank this classy gem amongst the city's best restaurants. Open daily for lunch and dinner.

Duluth's only Thai dining is the friendly **Thai Krathong,** 114 W. 1st St., 218/733-9774, which serves all the usual, perfectly prepared for around $8. Open Mon.–Sat. for lunch and dinner.

Taste of Saigon, 394 S. Lake Ave., 218/727-1598, in the DeWitt-Seitz building serves Vietnamese fare (and a little Chinese, too) adapted for American palates, but it's still tasty and, with dozens of choices, vegetarians can't do any better. Entrées average $8. Open daily for lunch and dinner.

There are nearly a dozen Chinese restaurants in town, but ask a local for a recommendation and it will almost surely be **Chef Yee's,** 319 W. 1st St., 218/722-3993, with dinner specials as low as $6. Open Mon.–Sat. for lunch and dinner.

Bakeries

Amazing Grace, 394 S. Lake Ave., 218/723-0075, in the lower level of the DeWitt-Seitz Building is a good choice for a savory snack or a cup of soup to keep you energized while you explore Canal Park. Open daily for breakfast, lunch, and dinner.

The small, worker-owned **Positively 3rd Street Bakery,** 1202 E. 3rd St., 218/724-8619, uses mostly organic ingredients in its wonderful cookies, brownies, and breads, yet they still managed to price them ridiculously low. Open Mon.–Sat. for breakfast and lunch.

Barbecue

Minnesota's own **Famous Dave's,** 355 S. Lake Ave., 218/740-3000, has brought their award-winning, St. Louis-style ribs to Canal Park. Most items are in the $7–12 range, and they have some great lunch specials. Open daily for lunch and dinner.

Coffeehouses

Both **Jitters,** 102 W. Superior St., 218/720-6015, downtown and the **Lakeview Coffee Emporium,** 600 E. Superior St., 218/720-4464, at Fitger's serve a good cup o' joe in a small and relaxing environment.

Deli

You really get your money's worth at **Sir Benedict's,** 805 E. Superior St., 218/728-1192, where a whopping sandwich is around $5 or get a half sandwich and a cup of soup for the same price during lunch. The cozy digs with a vaguely British pub theme overlook the lake, and the patio is immensely popular in the summer. Their global beer selection is outstanding. Open daily for lunch and dinner.

The **Whole Foods Community Co-op,** 1332 E. 4th St., 218/728-0884, turns out wonderful vegetarian sandwiches, pita pockets, and soup to go for about $4. Open daily for breakfast, lunch and dinner.

Ice Cream
There are snack stands all over Canal Park, but it is worth a trip over to the cute **Portland Malt Shoppe.** The constant crowds hovering in front of it tell you how good it is. Open only during the mid-May to mid-October high season.

Italian
At classy **Bellisio's,** 405 S. Lake Ave., 218/727-4921, pastas go for $10 at lunch and $15 during dinner. The atmosphere is romantic and the wine list impressive. Open daily for lunch and dinner.

Mexican
Hacienda Del Sol, 319 E. Superior St., 218/722-7296, isn't exactly a south of the border experience, but it is still some of the best Mexican in the northland. All the usual cost around $7, and the secluded, shady deck in back is a wonderful place for a warm-weather meal. Open Mon.–Sat. for lunch and dinner.

Pizza
The excellent and eclectic **Pizza Lucé,** 11 E. Superior St., 218/727-7400, is far from your average pizzeria. Roasted eggplant, barbecue chicken, and goat cheese are some of the more unusual of their fifty-plus toppings, and they even offer a vegan cheese alternative. A large one-topping is $13 and take-away slices are available. Open daily for lunch and dinner (until at least 2 A.M.) and delivery is free.

Grandma's Sports Garden, 425 Lake Ave. S., 218/722-4724, in Canal Park redefines thin-crust with their tasty pizzas. A large cheese is $8, while sandwiches and salads round out the menu. During the busy season they are open daily for lunch and dinner, though the hours drop down to weekends for lunch and Wednesday–Sunday for dinner the rest of the year.

SHOPPING

When you combine the variety, quality, and density of unique shops and galleries, Duluth is arguably the best shopping city in the state. The funkiest shopping in Canal Park is at the **De-Witt-Seitz Marketplace,** 394 Lake Ave. S., a beautifully converted warehouse with over a dozen stores. Amongst the choices are the **Northern Waters Smokehaus,** 218/724-7307, with highly regarded fish and gourmet cheeses, and **Art Dock,** 218/722-1451, selling work in many media by nearly 200 regional artists. The **Sivertson Gallery,** 361 Canal Park Dr., 218/723-7877 or 888/815-5814, is known far and wide for their "Art of the North" by regional, Canadian, and Alaskan artists including many Native Americans, while **Waters of Superior,** 395 Lake Ave. S., 218/786-0233, is somewhat similar. Both charge top dollar. The largest selection of antiques is at **Father Time,** 395 S. Lake Ave., 218/625-2379, but both the **Antiques Centre,** 335 Canal Park Dr., 218/726-1994, and **Canal Park Antique Mall,** 310 S. Lake Ave., 218/720-3940, are just as good. The local section at the bookstore **Northern Lights,** 307 Canal Park Dr., 218/722-5267, is excellent.

The quality shopping continues downtown where **Lizzards Art Gallery,** 38 E. Superior St., 218/722-5815, features the work of dozens of regional artists. **The Green Mercantile,** 209 E. Superior St., 218/722-1771, has a full range of environmentally responsible products. The wonderfully jumbled **Carlson Used Books & Records,** 206 E. Superior St., 218/722-8447, isn't exactly "Duluth's Finest Tourist Attraction" as they claim, but the selection is impressive. While **Old Town Antiques & Books,** 102 E. Superior St., 218/722-5426, has a huge selection of the former and only a bit of the latter, it is also worth a browse for bibliophiles. **Antiques on Superior Street,** 11 W. Superior St., 218/722-7962, has a much smaller selection than Old Town, but it's all top quality.

Just on the edge of downtown is the **Fitger's Brewery Complex,** 600 E. Superior St., with unique shops in a wonderfully renovated 1885 brewery. Native American arts and crafts are the specialty of the **Spirit Bay Trading Company,** 218/722-1839, while **The Bookstore at**

Fitger's, 218/727-9077, also has a decent local selection. While there stop by the free **Fitger's Museum** (open Mon.–Fri. 10 A.M.–5 P.M., Sat. 11 A.M.–4 P.M., and Sun. noon–3 P.M.), which displays various bits of Fitger's memorabilia around one of the original copper kettles.

Most Duluthians do their day-to-day shopping along Central Entrance and Highway 53 where the 110-store **Miller Hill Mall,** home to a **Barnes & Noble,** 218/727-0191, is found.

INFORMATION AND SERVICES

Tourist Information

The friendly and helpful **Duluth Convention and Visitors Bureau,** 218/722-4011 or 800/438-5884, www.visitduluth.com, has a pair of Information Centers. Their **Endion Station** office in Canal Park is open 8:30 A.M.–5 P.M. weekdays. The **Waterfront Center,** 323 Harbor Dr., in the DECC is open daily 8:30 A.M.–7 P.M. during the summer, with reduced hours during May and from September through mid-October. A brochure rack is available year-round at The Depot. The **Thompson Hill Information Center,** west of town off I-35, has statewide travel information.

Media

The city's daily paper, the *Duluth News-Tribune,* isn't bad, though for national and world coverage pick up either the *Star Tribune* or the *Pioneer Press,* the Twin Cities' dailies, which are both widely available. For an irreverent look at the Twin Ports pick up the free weekly *Ripsaw,* available every Wednesday all over town.

It's worth checking in occasionally to see what's playing on **KUMD** (103.3 FM), the university's student radio station, since it could change from Mozart to Motörhead at the top of the hour.

Post Office

The downtown post office is in the Civic Center at 515 W. 1st St., 218/722-1681.

Internet Access

Browser's N'Etc. Café, 201 E. Superior St., 218/726-0530, has high-speed connections for $.10 a minute.

GETTING THERE AND AWAY

By Air

The **Duluth International Airport,** 218/727-2968, just off Highway 53 on the northwest edge of town, handles 10 daily **Northwest Airlines,** 800/225-2525, flights between Duluth and the Twin Cities. Round-trip fares start at around $175—much less if it is a part of a connecting flight from elsewhere.

By Bus

The **Greyhound** station, 4426 Grand Ave., 218/722-5591, is inconveniently located on the west side of town. There are three trips a day to the Twin Cities ($21 one-way), one a day to International Falls ($20 one-way) passing through Virginia, and also one a day to Ironwood, Michigan ($31), stopping in Ashland, Wisconsin. **Happy Time Tours and Travel,** 807/473-5955 or 800/473-5955, runs along the North Shore between Duluth and Thunder Bay (see North Shore Bus Service later in this chapter for more information).

By Train

There is no passenger rail service to Duluth, but **Amtrak,** 800/872-7245, www.amtrak.com, offers a bus connection to and from St. Paul.

GETTING AROUND

By Bus

The Duluth Transit Authority bus system offers a fairly extensive service for a market this small (buses even go to Park Point and Spirit Mountain). The fare is $1 on weekday mornings and afternoons and $.50 all other times. All routes pass the downtown **Duluth Transit Center,** 214 W. Superior St., 218/722-7283, where you can get schedules and information.

As convenient as it is enjoyable, the **Port Town Trolley** travels between Canal Park, downtown, and along the waterfront every half hour between 11 A.M. and 7 P.M. during the summer. The fare is $.50.

By Taxi

Allied Taxi, 218/722-3311; **Diamond Taxi,** 218/727-8868; and **Yellow Cab,** 218/727-1515, all have 24-hour service.

By Boat

Transient dockage is available at the full-service **Lakehead Boat Basin,** 218/722-1757 or 800/ 777-8436, just south of the Lift Bridge.

Car Rentals

Avis, 218/727-7233; **Budget,** 218/727-7685; **Hertz,** 218/722-7418; and **National,** 218/727-7426, all have branches out at the airport, while **Enterprise,** 218/722-5800, sits across from the Miller Hill Mall.

North Shore

Minnesota's North Shore is one of those places that truly deserves all the accolades so freely heaped on it. Officially an All-American Road, the 150 miles of Highway 61 from Duluth to the Canadian border is about as rewarding as a drive can be. Tucked in between Lake Superior and the worn down remnants of the ancient Sawtooth Mountains you'll find improbably tall shoreline cliffs, countless waterfalls, lighthouses,

There's a waterfall every couple of miles on the North Shore.

myriad moose, and much more. The drive can be made in a couple of hours, but several days are needed to do it justice. Few places in the Midwest are better suited to fall color touring than the North Shore; the beautiful surroundings are one reason, but the lake is another. While leaves inland turn between mid-September and mid-October, Superior's warm waters delay the lakeshore peak by a couple of weeks greatly extending the season. Locals all seem to have their favorite fall color drives so ask around. Storm watching is another fall pastime—when the wind whips out of the northeast, huge waves thrash the shore.

Accommodations (and visitors) are plentiful, so during the summer and fall it is wise to make weekend reservations as far in advance as possible; even weekday reservations are a near necessity during July and August and then again for fall color.

DULUTH TO TWO HARBORS

If you want to get right up to Two Harbors, stay on four-lane Highway 61, otherwise take the exit after Kitchi-Gammi Park and follow North Shore Drive as it hugs the lake for the next 20 miles. You'll soon hit the DNR's **French River Fish Hatchery,** 5357 North Shore Dr., 218/525-0867, where trout and salmon are raised. There is a small visitors center with a video explaining the operation and a glass viewing window. In the spring and fall, when fish are being raised, you can tour one of the buildings. It is open weekdays 8 A.M.–4:30 P.M. A few miles farther up the road is **Tom's Logging Camp,** 5797 North Shore Dr.,

MY WAY OR THE HIGHWAY

There are many way to travel the North Shore besides Highway 61. The **Superior Hiking Trail** is the greatest thing to happen to the North Shore since the Ice Age. Sticking primarily to the ridgeline on its 198-mile run between Two Harbors and the Canadian Border, it has frequent vistas of Lake Superior to complement the waterfalls, gorges, and other up-close scenery. It connects seven state parks (all but Grand Portage) and many of the Superior National Forest's scenic highlights, plus it joins with the Border Route Trail at the east end, letting you continue on for another hundred miles across the Boundary Waters Canoe Area Wilderness. It's no surprise that readers of *Backpacker* magazine recently ranked it as the second best long distance trail in the country. Most access points are between five and ten miles apart so the trail is ideal for day trips. No matter how long you are hiking you can travel between most trailheads with the Superior Shuttle, 218/834-5511, www.superiorhikingshuttle.com. The 12-person van runs on a set schedule Friday through Sunday (plus holiday Mondays) from mid-May to mid-October. In general the cost is $10 for the first stop and $5 for each additional with a maximum cost of $50. Transport outside these times can be arranged for about twice the normal rate. Though not necessary, reservations are a good idea, especially on holiday weekends and during fall color. Many area resorts will also drive their guests to trailheads. Seventy-five free, first-come, first-served backcountry campsites—with latrines, fire rings, and on average room for two or three tents—are spread out along the trail. Another overnight option is Lodge to Lodge Hiking, arranged by calling 800/322-8327. The Superior Hiking Trail Association, 731 7th Ave., 218/834-2700, in Two Harbors can answer any and all questions about the trail. They also publish the very detailed *Guide to the Superior Hiking Trail,* sell maps, and lead guided hikes. Information on all of these, along with maps and descriptions of all trail segments, is available at www.shta.org.

Though it won't be finished until 2012 the **Gitchi-Gami State Trail** is already earning rave reviews. The 86-mile paved path, open to bikers, in-line skaters, cross-country skiers, and other non-motorized travelers, will run from Two Harbors to Grand Marais connecting the towns and parks in between. The route generally hugs the highway, but often runs down to the lake and up through the adjacent forest. Currently about 12 miles of the trail are paved and open to the public. These trail segments can be accessed from Gooseberry Falls State Park, Split Rock Lighthouse State Park, Beaver Bay, and Tofte. By the end of 2003 the trail should also connect Beaver

---

218/525-4120, with replica buildings from the heyday of lumbering, like a blacksmith shop and bunkhouse. Kids love feeding the deer, llamas, and pygmy goats. Open daily 9 A.M.–5 P.M. May through mid-October. Admission is $3. Right across from Tom's is the **Stoney Point** wayside, a noted storm-watching site.

Though copper prospectors came a half-century earlier, **Knife River** was platted in 1899 following the construction of a logging railroad. Like most North Shore towns it made the switch from logging to fishing when the forests were cut over. Today it is one of the few that retains a commercial fishing industry, though just a handful of people along the entire North Shore (down from 450 in the 1920s) are able to make it their livelihood. Nevertheless, tiny Knife River is still famous for its aquatic bounty, and many North Shore residents and regular visitors stop here when passing by to pick up some of the famous smoked fish. Many swear by **Russ Kendall's Smokehouse,** 218/834-5995, the most renowned outlet, while others are as just as devoted to **Mel's Fish House,** 218/834-5858. You can't really go wrong with either. If you want to get your fish the hard way, the Knife River is chock full of trout in the spring (be careful though, the Ojibwe chose the river's name because of the numerous sharp stones in it) or call the full-service **Knife River Marina,** 218/834-6076 or 800/826-7010, for charter captain recommendations. **Emily's,** 218/834-5922, opened as a general store in 1929, and now offers a B&B room with private bath for $100 and a popular restaurant. The small but creative menu of soups, salads,

Bay to Gooseberry Falls State Park and Tofte and Schroeder to Temperance River State Park. Call 218/834-6626 or scan www.gitchigamitrail.com for trail updates.

Up behind the bluffs, the rugged **North Shore State Trail** runs all the way from Duluth to Grand Marais. The 146-mile path is used primarily by snowmobilers, though the rest of the year it offers a remote and seldom used mountain bike route. The 70 miles through the Finland State Forest and Superior National Forest, starting east of Finland, is the best bet since the western half often has long stretches of standing water. Camping shelters are spaced out along the entire route. Call 218/834-6626 with trail questions.

More and more sea kayakers are discovering the joys of the North Shore and the developing **Lake Superior Water Trail** is making the journey increasingly easier. By the end of the decade there will be a campsite or rest area every three-or-so miles and the system is currently complete from Two Harbors to the Cook County line. New facilities are added every year and some day the trail will circle the entire lake. For updates and maps call 218/834-6626. Remember, those who know her consider Lake Superior an inland sea because conditions can change from placid to rough in a matter of minutes and the cold water means small

mistakes can be deadly. Beginning paddlers should take a guide or at least stay very close to shore.

With safe harbors at nearly a dozen spots and full-service marinas in Knife River, Silver Bay, Grand Marais, and Grand Portage, travelling by boat is fairly easy. Anyone boating on Lake Superior should not set out without a copy of Bonnie Dahl's *Superior Way: The Cruising Guide to Lake Superior* at the helm. Its 400-plus pages are filled with harbor maps, wilderness charts, and detailed GPS information. Even if you don't have your own boat, sailing and fishing charters operate out of several North Shore towns.

Although the limited schedule doesn't make it very convenient, you can travel along the North Shore by bus. **Happy Time Tours and Travel,** 807/473-5955 or 800/473-5955, www.httours.com/transportation.htm, makes a round-trip run between Duluth and Thunder Bay, Ontario on Sunday, Monday, Wednesday, and Friday. A few towns have scheduled stops; however, if you give the driver notice you can arrange to be dropped off and picked up at any point along Highway 61. The bus runs year-round, but always inquire ahead of time since no service is scheduled on holidays, both Canadian and American. The Duluth to Grand Marais one-way fare is $50.

seafood, and steak contains some old Scandinavian recipes and new ones like wild rice and cheese soup. There is a fish boil on Friday nights from February through mid-October. The restaurant is open daily for lunch and dinner plus weekends for breakfast; you can eat well for under $10.

TWO HARBORS

With over 3,600 residents Two Harbors is the largest community on the North Shore, after Duluth, of course. The city promotes itself as the trailhead to the North Shore, and realistically the spectacular lakeside scenery and most interesting sights do begin just beyond town. Most businesses are centered along Highway 61 (7th Ave.), though most places of interest are down along

Agate Bay, the more industrial of the twin bays. Two Harbors actually began as two communities—Agate Bay and Burlington—each named for the natural harbors on which they sat. Though the first settlers arrived in 1855, the towns didn't really blossom until iron ore was found on the Vermilion Range. This was the shortest route to Lake Superior from the Soudan Mine, and the railroad hauled its first ore to a waiting boat on Agate Bay in 1884. Ore shipments peaked in 1945, but to this day more ore is shipped out of Two Harbors than any other Great Lakes Port.

Sights

The 1892 **Two Harbors Lighthouse,** 218/834-4898, is the oldest still operating on the North Shore. You can climb the tower and see the two

Spend a night in the Two Harbors Lighthouse.

you can now tour her from the captain's quarters down to the engine room. It is open the same times as the museum and costs $3.

Paul Van Hoven Park near the museum is the closest you can get to watch boats loading at the three massive (1,300 feet long and seven stories high) **ore docks;** the breakwater by the lighthouse is another good vantage point. Ten million tons of taconite pellets depart Two Harbors annually, and arrival and departure times are posted in the window of the Northshore Botanicals gift shop, 630 First Ave., in the local newspaper, and at the Depot Museum.

The tiny **3M Museum,** 201 Waterfront Dr., 218/834-4898, commemorates the founding of Minnesota, Mining & Manufacturing, which started here in 1902. Initially they tried to mine corundum, a durable mineral used to make grinding wheels, but couldn't find any where they expected to. After nearly going bankrupt they invented sandpaper, moved to St. Paul, and grew into one of the globe's largest corporations. The handful of displays recall the company's past and promote its current products. The collection of historic Scotch Tape containers is about as exciting as it gets. Open daily 12:30–5 P.M. between May and October. Admission is $3.

North Shore Aviation, 218/834-9292 or 877/672-8687, will take you for a bird's-eye view of the North Shore. You can circle above Two Harbors for $30 per person or fly on to either Split Rock Lighthouse or Duluth for twice that. Scenic boat trips with **Grampa Woo Excursions,** 218/226-4100, depart from Two Harbors on Thursday and Fridays. See Beaver Bay for more information.

The rocky beach at the **Flood Bay Wayside,** just a little over a mile northeast of town, is excellent for agate hunting.

1,000 watt bulbs spinning and tour the assistant keeper's house, now operated as a bed-and-breakfast by the Lake County Historical Society. Also located on the grounds is a restored pilothouse from the wrecked oreboat *Frontenac* and displays about Lake Superior shipwrecks and fishing. The lighthouse is open Monday–Saturday 9 A.M.–7 P.M. and Sunday 10 A.M.–3 P.M. from May through October. Admission is $3.

The historical society looks at the rest of the county's history in the **Depot Museum,** 520 South Ave., with a historical hodgepodge in the 1907 Duluth & Iron Range Railroad depot—the building used in the movie *Iron Will.* Outside is a pair of steam locomotives, including the 569-ton Mallet, the largest ever built. From May through October the museum is open Monday–Saturday 9 A.M.–5 P.M. and Sunday 10 A.M.–3 P.M., though it has just weekend hours at the start and end of this period. Admission is $3. Docked below the depot is the **Edna G. Tugboat,** the last coal-fed, steam-powered tugboat operating on the Great Lakes. Built in 1896 she served Two Harbors for nearly a century, and

Recreation

With all the great parks near Two Harbors there is no need to do your hiking in town, but the short, easy loop of the **Sonju Harbor Walking Trail** behind the Two Harbors Lighthouse is a surprisingly scenic stroll. A paved stretch of the trail heads along the shore up to Burlington Bay. The **Avalanche Cycle Company,** 602 First St.,

218/834-0555, rents bikes and cross-country skis. **Silver Creek Sled Dogs,** 218/834-6592, lets you take a ride or mush your own team, and a full-day trip with you in the driver's seat costs $175.

Entertainment and Events

The city hosts several wonderful events during the summer. Two Harbor's biggest festival is **Heritage Days,** the first full weekend after the fourth of July, with a motorcycle rally, 4x4 mud race, soapbox derby, and lutefisk toss. Beloved by both spectators and performers, the **Two Harbors Folk Festival** features three days of music and dance the weekend after Heritage Days. There are races, clinics, and demos during the **Two Harbors Kayak Festival** the first weekend of August.

The **Two Harbors City Band,** founded in 1897, performs in Thomas Owens Park, (kitty-corner from the silver-domed Lake County Courthouse) on Thursday nights at 7:30 P.M. The show is preceded by an ice cream social.

Accommodations

The family-run **Voyageur Motel,** 1227 7th Ave., 218/834-3644, has small, basic rooms, but they are clean and a good value at $48. The newer **Country Inn,** 1204 7th Ave., 218/834-5557 or 877/604-5332, charges $94 and offers a pool, whirlpool, sauna, and miniature golf course. For something unique stay in a boxcar at **Northern Rail Traincar Suites,** 1730 Hwy. 3, 218/834-6084. All rooms are in actual train cars, though you only notice this from the outside and the hallway connecting them. Rates start at $135.

About a mile northeast of town, the fancy **Superior Shores Resort,** 218/834-5671 or 800/242-1988, info@superiorshores.com, is perched on a quiet and scenic stretch of shoreline. The wide variety of rooms ranges from standard hotel units for $109, to $439 for a decked out three-bedroom unit. All guests have access to indoor and outdoor pools, hot tub, sauna, and tennis courts. Weekends require a two-night stay.

Easily the top option for spending the night, if you can get a room, is the **Lighthouse Bed & Breakfast,** 218/834-4814 or 888/832-5606, in the restored Two Harbors Lighthouse. The three guestrooms share a bath and cost $125; all proceeds are used for lighthouse maintenance. The whole house is filled with period furnishings, and a full breakfast is served in the morning.

The city's **Burlington Bay Campground,** 218/834-2001, has over 100 campsites spread out between Highway 61 and the lake. A site with full hookups costs $21.

Food

What began as a wayside fish shack has grown into the legendary **Betty's Pies,** 1633 Highway 61 E., 218/834-3367 or 877/269-7494. Even with a new owner (don't worry, the original Betty passed on her recipes), locals and regular visitors to the North Shore continually sing its praises, and it is not just hype—these pies are amazing. There is also a small menu of soups, salads, and sandwiches, and there is often a long wait for a table. Pies start at $15 ($3 for a slice) and sandwiches are about $6. Betty's is open daily for breakfast, lunch, and dinner.

The fanciest menu is at **Kamloops,** 218/834-5671, at the Superior Shores Resort. Seafood and pastas dominate the menu, and locally caught fish is the specialty. Fish boils are held on Monday nights during the summer. The dining room overlooks the lake, and there is an outdoor deck. Open daily for breakfast, lunch, and dinner.

Despite the name and a Vietnamese cook, the large menu at the **Vietnamese Lantern,** 629 7th Ave., 218/834-4373, is almost entirely Chinese. The last Oriental cuisine before the border averages $7 a plate and is quite good. Open Mon.–Sat. for lunch and dinner.

Portside Pizza, 623 1st Ave., 218/834-6362, does a good thin-crust and has some unique toppings like cashews and sauerkraut, plus a choice of cheeses. A family-sized, one-topping 'za is $14. Kids will like the video game room. Open Mon.–Sat for lunch and daily for dinner.

Judy's Café, 623 7th Ave., 218/834-4802, is a local favorite for cheap, no-nonsense meals. Their hearty breakfasts are served all day. They are open daily for breakfast and lunch and weekdays for dinner.

Shopping

Agate City, 721 7th Ave., 218/834-2304, sells

rocks and fossils from around the world, including, of course, plenty of Lake Superior agates. It's worth a look just to see their museum-quality displays. Honey-smoked salmon is the specialty at **Lou's Fish House,** 1319 Hwy. 61, 218/834-5254, but they also sell lots of other fish, beef and turkey jerky, and Wisconsin cheese. Two Harbor's downtown antique stores, **Second Chance Antiques,** 218/834-3334, and **Home Sweet Home,** 218/834-4017, sit side by side downtown at the corner of 7th St. and 2nd Ave. There are more antiques on your way into town at the **Adventure Mall,** 218/834-9330.

Information and Services

The **Two Harbors Area Chamber of Commerce,** 1026 7th Ave., 218/834-2600 or 800/777-7384, www.twoharbors.com/chamber, has brochures for Two Harbors and elsewhere on the North Shore and will help find hotel vacancies during busy event weekends. Their office is open weekdays 8 A.M.–5 P.M. Lake County staffs the **R. J. Houle Visitor Information Center,** 1330 Hwy. 61, 218/834-4005 or 800/554-2116, www.lakecnty.com, which is housed in a historic CCC log building just east of town. From May through October it is open Monday–Saturday 9 A.M.–5 P.M. and Sunday 9 A.M.–3 P.M.; hours for the rest of the year are Wednesday–Sunday 9 A.M.–1 P.M.

The **Superior Hiking Trail Association,** 731 7th Ave., 218/834-2700, offices have maps and any other information you could want to know about one of the best long-distance hiking trails in the nation, plus books, clothing, and related items are for sale. They are open weekdays 9 A.M.–4:30 P.M. At other times you can get some trail information at the Houle Visitor Center.

Transportation

You can visit Two Harbors with the **North Shore Scenic Railroad,** 218/722-1273 or 800/423-1273, which travels here from Duluth. The two-hour layover is enough time to see the main sights, and they also allow passengers an overnight stay if you depart Duluth on Friday.

TWO HARBORS TO GRAND MARAIS

Gooseberry Falls State Park

With your first glimpse of Gooseberry Falls you'll quickly understand why this is Minnesota's most popular state park. The swift Gooseberry River shoots around a narrow bend, drops over Upper Falls into a rocky gorge, blankets the 100-foot wide rock wall forming Middle Falls, and plunges over the split Lower Falls before calmly marching on to Lake Superior. Though nearly 600,000 people gaze upon these scenes each year—the whole 90-foot drop sits just a short stroll down a wheelchair-accessible trail—a relatively small number of them venture through the rest of the 1,675-acre park.

A pair of excellent trails follows the river down to Lake Superior. The **River View Trail** starts below the falls and climbs up a ridge with a superb view of Lower and Middle falls together before hitting Agate Beach. The **Gitchi Gummi Trail** follows the much higher ridge across the river looking down upon the river's mouth from above; it's rather noisy when circling back by the Highway so consider retracing your steps instead of completing the two-mile loop. Both trails have a few climbs, but steps make them pretty easy overall. Heading upstream, the two-mile **Fifth Falls Trail** (part of the North Shore-length **Superior Hiking Trail**) hugs the river as it climbs to its namesake cascade and returns on the opposite shore. Another 12 miles of trail wind through the park's hills, most of them open to mountain bikes. Come winter most of the trails are groomed for cross-country skiing, while the Gitchi Gummi and Fifth Falls trails are packed for winter hiking. The lovely campground has 70 well-spaced, non-electric sites and there is also a kayak site on Lake Superior. Call 218/834-3855 with any park questions.

Split Rock Lighthouse State Park

On November 28, 1905, a great gale whipped Lake Superior into such a rage that six ships were wrecked and 23 more damaged within 12 miles of the Split Rock River. In response, the **Split Rock Lighthouse** was built atop this magnificent 130-

Gooseberry Falls State Park

foot cliff and began operations in 1910. Its 370,000-candlepower beacon steered ships away from the treacherous shore for 59 years before onboard navigational equipment made it obsolete. The Minnesota Historical Society has restored the gorgeous facility to its pre-1924 appearance, and when you tour the lighthouse, fog-signal building, and keeper's home the costumed reenactors share tales of their isolated, pre-road lives. Exhibits in the visitors center discuss the lives of the families who lived here, how the light station was built, and other North Shore topics. You can stroll the grounds year-round 8 A.M.–sunset, while tours are available daily between mid-May through mid-October. The visitors center's hours are daily 9 A.M.–5 P.M. during the tour season and Friday–Sunday noon–4 P.M. the rest of the year. Admission is $6 during the tour season.

Though many visitors don't realize it, Split Rock is much than just a lighthouse, and the rest of the 2,075 acres shouldn't be overlooked. This is one of the best spots on the North Shore to explore by kayak, and there are put-ins near both ends of the park's 6.25-mile shoreline, the longest of any park on the North Shore. The University of Minnesota Duluth Outdoor Pro-

gram, 218/726-6533, leads kayaking trips below Split Rock once a month during the summer. The all-day trips cost $100—equipment is provided and no experience is necessary. About half of the park's 12 miles of trail stick to the shore side of the highway, and these are available for hiking and mountain biking and groomed for cross-country skiing. There are many wonderful lakeside overlooks, but none compare to the view from the peak of the 1.25-mile **Day Hill Trail.** The easier **Little Two Harbors Trail** leads from Day Hill to the lighthouse. Turning inland the stretch of the **Superior Hiking Trail** following the waterfall-rich Split Rock River is a challenging, but rewarding, walk. Split Rock's campground is one of the best and most popular on the North Shore. All 20 cart-in sites are secluded and most come with lake views; none is more than 2,000 feet from the parking area. Though the sites are primitive there is a modern shower building. Another four backpacking sites—two are bluff top and two sit lakeside— and a kayak-only site on Crazy Bay offer even more solitude. Call 218/226-6372 for lighthouse tour inquiries and 218/226-6377 with any other park questions.

THE ARROWHEAD

Beaver Bay

A group of German and Swiss families who arrived on a steamboat in 1856 were Beaver Bay's first settlers. A nationwide financial panic the very next year caused the abandonment of all the other fledgling towns between Duluth and Grand Portage, but these hardy immigrants remained. A sawmill provided the livelihood for most of the town's first residents, and soon several Ojibwe families moved here to join them in the lumbering business. About two dozen, including John Beargrease, a legendary North Shore resident who is famous for delivering the mail by dogsled before any roads or trails existed in these parts, were laid to rest in the traditional **burial ground** behind town. There's little to see there since it is left in a natural state, but if you want to visit take the first left off County Road 4.

The best views of the North Shore's scenery are from the water, and if you don't have your own boat you can still take in the splendor with **Grampa Woo Excursions,** 218/226-4100. Two-hour, narrated cruises take in Split Rock Lighthouse and Palisade Head from late June through August. The boat departs from their office just north of town at noon and cost $20. Less frequent dinner cruises cost $65 and depart at 5 P.M. returning at sunset.

Down on the lakeshore, half a mile before town, is the **Cove Point Lodge,** 218/226-3221 or 800/598-3221, a great hotel in a great setting on 150 acres. All rooms in the lodge (from $139), built and decorated in the classic Northwoods style, face the lake, as do the large two-bedroom cottages ($339). Guests can use the pool, whirlpool, and sauna, but lazily watching the lake appears to be the most popular activity. A six-mile-spur trail loop connects to the Superior Hiking Trail. Dinner in the highly regarded restaurant runs $8–22 and walleye are their specialty. In town, the **Inn At Beaver Bay,** 218/226-4351 or 800/226-4351, has standard rooms from $40 or lofts with whirlpool baths for $75—they're basic, but a good value. The above-average restaurant has a fairly standard American menu, with burgers for $3 and steak for $17. There is live music on weekends.

A couple of stores in town are worth a stop.

Just off the highway behind the Holiday gas station the **Lake Superior Sausage Company,** 218/226-3540, makes and sells over 90 varieties of sausage from lake trout to Armenian lamb to vegetarian to maple cinnamon pork. The **Beaver Bay Agate Shop,** 218/226-4847, is worth a look even if you don't want to buy.

Silver Bay

The youngest town on the North Shore, Silver Bay was built from scratch by the Reserve Mining Company in 1951 to house workers for its new taconite processing plant, the first in North America. The ore arrives by rail from their mine near Babbitt to be processed, and over four million tons of iron pellets are shipped down the Great Lakes annually. Free tours of the **Northshore Mining** taconite plant are offered at 10 A.M. on Saturdays from mid-June to the end of August and Wednesdays during July and August. Call 218/226-3143 for reservations or information. Tours depart from the **Visitor Information Center** (no phone), a half-mile up the hill on Outer Drive, which also has a small historical display. It is open daily 10 A.M.–4 P.M. from late May through early October. Just beyond the visitors center (follow the signs) is a **scenic overlook** with signs identify the various taconite buildings and explaining the process. For a scenic drive, Silver Bay is the eastern end of the 59-mile **Superior National Forest Scenic Byway,** which connects the North Shore to the Iron Range. Call the **Silver Bay Safe Harbor and Marina,** 218/226-3121, for charter fishing recommendations. The **Mariner Motel,** 46 Outer Dr., 218/226-4488, with its red neon trim and floor-to-ceiling windows, is a mighty strange looking place, but the rooms are large and clean and cost just $50. Since the town itself isn't much of a tourist destination this is a good place to look for last-minute bookings.

Palisade Head

Arguably the most spectacularly beautiful site in the state, Palisade Head's ruddy cliffs climbs 350 feet straight out of Lake Superior. A slim road at mile marker 57 snakes to the top, where you can walk along as much of the rim as your fear lets you—needless to say, be careful. Even severe acrophobiacs should make the trip just to take in the wonderful scenery in the distance. Shovel Point, another rhyolite lava headland, crawls out of the lake to the north, and Wisconsin's Apostle Islands are visible on the horizon. Palisade Head is a part of Tettegouche State Park, the main entrance of which is just 1.5 miles away, though no state park sticker is required for visits of less than an hour. Rock climbers need free permits from the park office.

Tettegouche State Park

By far the largest state park on the North Shore, Tettegouche's (TET uh gooch) 9,346 acres are just an hour from Duluth, but make a wonderful wilderness escape. **Palisade Head** and **Shovel Point,** stunning cliffs climbing straight out of Lake Superior, make the coastal scenery some of the best on the North Shore, though most of the park sits atop the Sawtooth Range, where six lakes are nested between the steep hills and the Baptism River leaps over a succession of waterfalls and

© TIM BEWER

Palisade Head

rapids. Established in 1979 Tettegouche is one of Minnesota's newest state parks, but it's also one of the North Shore's earliest protected areas. The Alger-Smith Lumber Company set up a logging camp in the park at the end of the 19th century and gave many area lakes Algonquin names since the men were mostly from New Brunswick, Canada. In 1910, after having cleared the area's red and white pine, they sold the land to a group of Duluth businessmen who created a fishing camp. Though it changed hands a few times, all subsequent owners stewarded the land allowing today's beautiful park.

Tettegouche's 23 miles of hiking trail, including a 12-mile stretch of the **Superior Hiking Trail,** are generally quite hilly, though the myriad scenic vistas make the lung-chugging climbs worthwhile. The most popular destination is **High Falls,** a 70-foot drop on the Baptism River. The tallest waterfall entirely in Minnesota is just an easy 1.5-mile round-trip from the campground, but the most scenic route follows the **Baptism River Trail** 1.5 somewhat difficult miles up from Highway 61 passing two more waterfalls along the way. A series of interconnected loops wind around the interior lakes offering many scenic overlooks— Palisade Valley is arguably the most beautiful. A mature forest covers the park's lake area and there are even scattered old-growth white and red pine stands, such as Conservancy Pines on Mic Mac's east shore. Down at Lake Superior the popular two-mile **Shovel Point Trail** is a fairly easy walk out along its namesake cliffs; interpretive displays discuss the park's geology. In the winter the Shovel Point Trail is designated for snowshoeing, and the office rents shoes. Fifteen more trail miles are groomed for cross-country skiing with most offering a bit of a challenge. Experienced rock climbers scale Palisade Head and Shovel Point (a free climbing permit is required); paddlers can rent canoes from the park office (or just call in from the Tettegouche Camp) to explore the portage-linked Mic Mac and Nipisiquit lakes, while anglers take trout from Bear and Bean lakes and the Baptism River.

Tettegouche's varied overnight options make the park one of the best places to spend the night on the North Shore. The 34 sites (no electric,

SUPERIOR NATIONAL FOREST

Stretching 150 miles across Minnesota's Arrowhead the Superior National Forest (SNF) is home to two of the nation's premier recreation destinations: the Boundary Waters Canoe Area Wilderness and the Superior Hiking Trail. Though best known for these two heavyweights there are few outdoor activities that you can't partake of here. The three and a quarter million acres (two million of which are managed by the Forest Service) surround 2,000 lakes and rivers, some almost-mountain-like hills, and an extensive boreal forest ecosystem. All mammals typical of the Northwoods inhabit the forest, but the roughly 400 timber wolves roaming Superior are the real stars and the 163 breeding bird species are more than any other national forest. Not surprisingly the American Bird Conservancy chose this as one of its Globally Important Bird Areas.

Most of the campgrounds sit lakeside and are peacefully rustic, though if you aren't in to roughing it many of the state's best resorts and most charming towns border the forest, so after taking in the scenery during the day you can retire to elegant quarters and a gourmet meal. The Superior is so vast that for the purposes of this book the five administrative districts are treated as individual places and spread throughout the chapter. The Boundary Waters Canoe Area Wilderness spans four districts and has its own section.

Recreation

The Superior National Forest contains some of the best hiking in the entire state. Over 400 miles of trail range from quarter mile strolls to week-long wilderness treks. Several short paths let you get a good look at the wilderness scenery though the most notable routes are the **Border Route, Kekekabic, Pow Wow,** and **Sioux Hustler** trails which offer some of the best backpacking east of the Rockies. Also truly superlative, the 198-mile **Superior Hiking Trail** hugs the North Shore through much of the forest. Berry picking, wildflower searching, and fall color viewing are popular activities along all the forest's routes. Call the Forest Service's **Fall Color Hotline,** 800/354-4595, during September and October to get the up to the minute scoop on autumn's annual exhibition. Mountain bikers are largely limited to forest roads and old logging roads, though the Tofte District's **Superior Mountain Bike Trail System** has something for everyone. Mountain bikes are NOT allowed anywhere in the BWCAW or on the Superior Hiking Trail.

Come winter 300 miles of trail are groomed for cross-country skiing with most of these spread across the Tofte and Gunflint districts. This includes the **North Shore Ski Trail** which combines for 122 miles along the hills between Tofte and Grand Marais. The Laurentian District has another 65 miles while most of the trails in the Kawishiwi and LaCroix districts extend into the BWCAW—a natural winter destination since snowmobiles are banned—and so are ungroomed. Elsewhere in the forest snowmobilers have 700 miles of groomed trails to ride.

Paddling is principally about the BWCAW where you can explore over 1,000 lakes and streams, but it's not the only option. Another 13

six walk-in) in the Baptism River Campground are widely spaced. Down on Lake Superior (and unfortunately right next to the highway) are 13 cart-in sites—none are more than half a mile from the parking lot and about half have lake views, which should help you overlook the highway hum. There are also five backpack sites along the Superior Hiking Trail and kayak-accessible sites for those paddling the shore. The **Tette-gouche Camp** has four classic log cabins from the early 1900s on Mic Mac Lake, a 1.7-mile walk,

bike, or ski in from the nearest road. Three cabins sleep six, while the other is wheelchair-accessible and has room for two people; the price per couple is $60–90. The cabins have electricity but no running water; however, a modern shower building means you don't really have to rough it all that much. Meals are cooked on a hotplate or campfire, and there is also a small fridge. Each cabin comes with a canoe. Farther up the Baptism River is the modern **Illgen Falls Cabin** with all the conveniences of home for $150 per night.

THE ARROWHEAD

designated lake and river portage routes lie outside the wilderness and not only do they have great scenery, but relatively few people follow them. Even though most are short enough to run in a day, campsites facilitate overnight trips. Another bonus to these lesser-known trips is that permits and fees are not required. Obviously, with 695 square miles of surface water and over 2,250 miles of streams, fishing is popular here. The Gunflint and Tofte districts are rumored to have the best angling opportunities though you can't really go wrong wherever you cast a line. Many people fish the waters of the BWCAW for the serenity it offers and, because more big fish live to maturity, some smallmouth aficionados believe that world record bass lurk in these waters.

Camping

Superior has 23 developed campgrounds. The majority lie in the eastern end of the forest with access from the North Shore and all sit on a lake or river. Only Whiteface by Hoyt Lakes and Fall Lake near Ely have electric hookups and only the latter has flush toilets and showers—individual campsites each have a picnic table, firegrate, and tent pad. In general the camps are fully operational from mid-May into September, though they never actually close and camping (with no drinking water or other services available) is allowed at any time. About half take reservations (for a $9 non-refundable fee) at 877/444-6777 or www.reserveusa.com, though all have some first-come, first-served sites available. Surprisingly, except for summer weekends the camps rarely fill

up—and even on summer weekends it is usually possible to show up and get a site somewhere. Camping rates in summer range $6–16 depending on how developed the campground is though there is no charge after the water is shut off. There are also 16 rustic campgrounds with fewer facilities that tend to be very peaceful (none have more than six sites) and more remote. All of these free camps are in the Tofte District except for one nearby in the Gunflint District.

Many remote backpacking sites with firegrates and latrines dot the forest's lakes and trails. For more information on these free sites inquire at one of the district offices. Forest Service rules also permit you to camp anywhere on National Forest land, as long as you're 100 feet from any trail or water source and observe Leave No Trace (www.lnt.org) outdoor ethics. Though registration isn't required for backcountry camping, checking in at a ranger station before heading out is always a good idea, especially to find out about any current fire restrictions.

Information

The **Forest Headquarters,** 8901 Grand Avenue Place, 218/626-4300 (218/626-4399 TTY), r9_superior_NF@fs.fed.us, is in Duluth though you are better off getting information directly from the district ranger stations. Detailed forest information is available online at www.superiornational-forest.org. The Forest Service publishes a slew of free maps and information sheets about activities and facilities. There's also a very detailed foldout map available for $6.

It's a fully accessible two-bedroom home with a back deck overlooking the 45-foot waterfall. The price is $150 per night. Call 218/226-6365 with any park questions.

George H. Crosby Manitou State Park

Crosby Manitou is one of the best and least-known wilderness escapes on the North Shore—in part because getting there requires a long detour off Highway 61. This was the first Minnesota state park designed for backpackers, and

21 wonderful campsites are scattered about the 6,682 acres, mostly along the Manitou River. The 24 miles of hiking-only trails are generally steep and rugged, but they reward the adventurous with overlooks of the gorge and excellent wildlife and fall color viewing. Arguably the most beautiful path is the **West Manitou River Trail,** which hugs the river through most of the park. A recommended loop combines the River Trail with the relatively easy **Middle Trail** and the **Yellow Birch Trail** plus the **Misquah Trail.** It's

about a 3.5-mile hike and features four fantastic overlooks and river frontage at the back end. To the north of this is Cascades, the only waterfall in the park accessible by trail. You can return via the lovely **Humpback Trail** to make a longer loop. The park's easiest walk is the mile-long loop around Benson Lake, much of which follows a boardwalk. Five miles of the North Shore-length **Superior Hiking Trail** follows parts of each of these trails through the park. Anglers appreciate the small lake because trout are abundant and motors are prohibited. Even the less energetic should consider a picnic along Benson Lake, or just come up for the lovely drive along the Baptism River. For any Crosby Manitou questions call Tettegouche State Park at 218/226-6365.

Taconite Harbor

Six miles before you hit Tofte you can pull off to a lakeside observation point and watch oreboats loading at LTV Steel's massive dock.

Temperance River State Park

If you are short on time or energy, Temperance River State Park, 218/663-7476, is a great stop because you can get a quick taste of the best of the North Shore—wild waterfalls and rugged coast. The 539-acre property is centered on the river, so named because, unlike other North Shore rivers, there was no sand "bar" at its mouth. In less than a mile you can stroll an easy riverside path down to Lake Superior's rocky beach and jagged cliffs and then head upriver along an impossibly narrow, corkscrewing gorge to Hidden Falls on the rough **Cauldron Trail.** Along the river look for deep potholes carved into the soft lava during the last Ice Age. Many more trails run beyond the park through the adjacent Superior National Forest, including the **Superior Hiking Trail,** which leads to **Carlton Peak,** the highest point on the North Shore and a popular spot for hikers and rock climbers—a free permit from the park office is needed by the latter. The 924-foot summit, where the Superior views stretch on seemingly towards infinity, is 2.8 miles in from the park, though it can be reached in a three-mile round-trip from the trailhead on County Road 2. For an unobstructed view of Carlton Peak scram-

ble up the SNF's comparatively dinky **Britton Peak** just a quarter-mile round-trip from the County Road 2 trailhead. The campground sits unfortunately close to the highway, but this can be overlooked since many of the sites come with lake views. The 55 campsites are shady and well spaced with all 18 electric and three cart-in sites in the upper camp.

Tofte

The principal reason to stop in this little town is to tour the **North Shore Commercial Fishing Museum,** 218/663-7804. Housed in a replica fish house, the displays engagingly explain the who and how of Lake Superior's fishing industry through old equipment—including a fish table that received heavy use, as the scales still embedded in it will attest—and fascinating photos. Open daily 9 A.M.–7 P.M. from June through September and 9 A.M.–5 P.M. the rest of the year. Admission is $3. Sharing space with the museum is the **Lutsen-Tofte Tourism Association,** 888/616-6784, www.61north.com.

Tofte is linked to the BWCAW via County Road 2 (aka the Sawbill Trail), and an outfitter at each end can set you up with everything you need to paddle it. In town is **Sawtooth Outfitters,** 7213 Hwy. 61, 218/663-7643, which also has mountain bikes, sea kayaks, and cross-country skis. **Sawbill Canoe Outfitters,** 4620 Sawbill Trail, 218/663-7150, is right up at the Sawbill Lake Entry. You can get Superior National Forest information at the **U.S. Forest Service Tofte Ranger Station,** 7355 Hwy. 61, 218/663-8060. From May through September it is open daily 6 A.M.–6 P.M. and weekdays 7:30 A.M.–4 P.M. the rest of the year.

Comprising nearly half the town is the oft-lauded **Bluefin Bay Resort,** 7198 Hwy. 61, 218/663-7296 or 800/258-3346. Some of their topflight amenities include a fitness center, tennis courts, ice rink, saunas, indoor pool, and a year-round outdoor pool and hot tub. They also offer movie nights, guided sea kayak and snowshoe tours, sailing trips, and a shuttle will take you to Lutsen Mountains or area trailheads. The 53 diverse lakeside units range from studios to three-bedroom condos and most have fireplaces, decks, and whirlpools. Add the lake views and it's a great romantic getaway. Rates run $89–509. Two-day rentals are required on weekends. Bluefin Bay also holds all of Tofte's restaurants. Together the **Bluefin Restaurant,** 218/663-7296, and **Breakers Bar and Grille,** 218/663-6200, share one of the most highly regarded kitchens on the North Shore. Most of the delectable entrées like cinnamon wild rice pancakes, elk steak sandwich, duck chambord, and couscous primavera run $8–18. There are great views from the dining room and a wonderful summer deck. Open daily for breakfast, lunch, and dinner, and evening reservations are a good idea. Just up the road is the **Coho Café & Bakery,** 7126 Hwy. 61, 218/663-8032, with fancy salads, deli sandwiches, pasta, and pizza from $6–17. Open daily for breakfast, lunch, and dinner, though they close up on some weekdays during the slow season.

Lutsen

Lutsen is just barely a town, but **Lutsen Mountains,** 218/663-7281, a mile to the south, makes it one of the North Shore's busiest destinations. Besides the 85 runs, 986-foot drop, and terrain park comprising the Midwest's largest downhill ski area, there are also 17 miles of challenging cross-country ski trails, 10 miles of hiking trail, horse and pony rides, 35 miles of mountain bike trail, and a gondola ride that is ideal for fall color viewing. An unlimited day pass for the last three costs $23 and bike rentals are available. **Lutsen Rec.,** 218/663-7863, halfway up the hill, rents skis in the winter and offers paintball and miniature golf the rest of the year. Also attracting people to Lutsen is **Superior National,** 218/663-7195, with 27 of the loveliest holes you'll ever golf. Two families live and make their national-award-winning **Wild Country Maple Syrup,** 218/663-8010, out in the middle of a 320-acre sugar bush just north of Lutsen. You can watch the production in August and September and buy likely the best syrup you've ever tasted. To reach them take County Road 4 seven miles north, then west on Forest Road 164 and follow the signs.

Naturally there is plenty of quality lodging in the area. The **Eagle Ridge Resort,** 218/663-7284 or 877/754-9335, is the closest resort to the ski hill, but is best known for its heated indoor/outdoor pool which stays at 85 degrees right through the winter. Studios, with either a fireplace or whirlpool, that can sleep four are $123 per night, and they also have larger rooms. Peak weekends require a two- or three-night stay. Lutsen's most affordable rooms are at the **Mountain Inn,** 360 Ski Hill Rd., 218/663-7244 or 800/686-4669, a standard but very friendly and well-run hotel. Rooms with microwaves and refrigerators run $99–119 (dropping to almost half that in the shoulder seasons) and guests can use the whirlpool and sauna. **Lutsen Resort,** 5700 Hwy. 61, 218/663-7212 or 800/258-8736, sits down on a 1,000-foot Lake Superior pebble beach. The 31 rooms in the Swedish-style main lodge start at $109 (two-night minimum on weekends), and they also have more expensive cottages and condos for rent. Some of their many amenities include a pool, whirlpool, sauna, game room, shuffleboard, bike and kayak rentals, and par-3 golf course. Their lovely dining room is the most highly regarded kitchen in the area. The steak and seafood menu (vegetarians get a pasta primavera) runs $13–25, and there are cheaper sandwiches and the like in their Poplar River Pub. Open daily for breakfast, lunch, and dinner. Also on Lake Superior, **Lindgren's,** 5552 County Road 35, 218/663-7450, info@lindgrensbb.com, has everything you could want in a bed-and-breakfast: a great location, a building full of character, and a friendly host. The 1920s log home has a warm Northwoods lodge decor with nearly enough animal mounts to start a museum, while each of the four guestrooms, priced from $105–175, has a private bath and overlooks the lake—one has a stone fireplace and another a whirlpool. Outside is a wood-burning Finnish sauna and lakeshore bonfire pit. Weekends require a two-night stay.

Cascade River State Park

The Cascade River drops 900 feet during the last three miles of its journey, tumbling over a pair of waterfalls right before running into Lake Superior. This 2,865-acre park surrounding it stretches along miles of Lake Superior shoreline, and its 18 miles of trail let you stroll or ski along the rugged coast or climb up into the Sawtooth Range for some spectacular scenery both near and far. It's less than half a mile round-trip along the **Cascade River Trail** to reach Cascade Falls and The Cascades. The **Superior Hiking Trail** continues along both banks of the river gorge into the adjacent Superior National Forest and up to County Road 45 offering a 7.7-mile loop. Down another branch of the SHT is **Lookout Mountain.** The popular overlook on the east side is a steep 1.75-mile climb, and you can continue on to complete a 3.7-mile loop around the peak. The easy **Lake Trail** skirts two miles of gorgeous shoreline, but suffers highway hum. Five backpacking campsites with Adirondack-style shelters are scattered about the park, and an otherwise good 40-site primitive campground is situated unfortunately close to the highway. For more park information call 218/387-3053.

If a night under the stars isn't your thing consider **Cascade Lodge,** 218/387-2911 or 800/322-9543, a North Shore fixture that sits right by the park entrance and is directly connected to its trail system. Many of the guestrooms in the 1930s log lodge come with lake views, while the cabins, most with fireplaces, are oozing Northwoods charm. Naturally, due to its location, the lodge caters to outdoor sports enthusiasts and mountain bikes are available for rent. The cheapest rooms start at $72 and the cabins range $90–225.

SUPERIOR NATIONAL FOREST—TOFTE DISTRICT

The Tofte District, running up from the North Shore into the Boundary Waters features many of the best day hikes in the forest and several good non-BWCAW canoe routes. Rangers run a busy summer interpretive program with morning hikes, evening campfires, and more every Tuesday through Saturday and, though most take place at area resorts, all programs are open the public. The district is also known as a blueberry mecca and the Forest Service has management areas dedicated to increasing production and a brochure with maps directing pickers to prime sites. For additional details see the Superior National Forest overview earlier in this chapter.

Recreation

The district's most popular hike is the **Oberg Mountain Trail,** a not-too-strenuous climb with views of Lake Superior and Oberg Lake waiting at the top. The 3.4-mile **Leveaux Trail** also has great ridge-top views, though it gets much less traffic. These are some of the best fall color hikes on the North Shore, and Oberg gets almost as busy as Highway 61 at this time; even then Leveaux remains a quieter alternative. Both loops are connected to the **Superior Hiking Trail** and start on Forest Road 336 between Tofte and Lutsen.

The little-known **Hogback Lake Trail,** on Forest Road 172 between Tofte and Isabella, has six miles of peaceful loops along six small and slender lakes. It is only half a mile in to the gorgeous ridge-top views between Hogback and Scarp lakes. There are some great backpacking campsites on the lakes and trout stocked in them. West of Isabella, the **Flathorn Lake Trail**'s main summer route is a two-mile loop around its namesake, but come winter people head off to ski the 15 miles of groomed intermediate-level trails—known as Flathorn-Gegoka—branching farther into the forest. There are also pleasant and easy hikes at the **Divide Lake, McDougal Lake,** and **Ninemile Lake** campgrounds. See the Boundary Waters Canoe Area Wilderness Section for other recommended hikes.

Mountain bikers will want to stop by the Lutsen-Tofte Tourism Association for maps ($2 each) of the **Superior Mountain Bike Trail System,** 200 marked miles of everything from casual road routes to wild single-track. Cross-country skiers will also want to pick up a regional map of the **North Shore Ski Trail,** whose 122 miles spread across the Tofte and Gunflint districts. Two of the most popular sections are the **Sugarbush** and **Moose Fence** trails, both of which lie north of Tofte along County Road 2 (the Sawbill Trail) with 33 miles of easy to difficult loops.

Timber Lake-Frear Lake, 15 miles northwest of Tofte, is the most traveled of the district's four non-BWCAW portage canoe routes. The nine-mile loop covers six lakes, and on weekends all 12 campsites might be occupied. Although they are primarily used as day paddles there are also a few campsites along the five-mile **Crescent Lake-Rice Lake,** three-mile **Crooked Lake Area** routes, and six-mile **Island River** routes. Canoeing into Scarp Lake around the Hogback Trail is also scenic and enjoyable.

You can learn about natural history as you drive up the **Temperance River Watershed Tour,** a roundabout route up to the Sawbill Lake Campground; the roadside interpretive signs are only kept up spring through fall. More signs are put up for a **Fall Color Tour** from mid-September to mid-October; check at the ranger station for details.

Camping

None of the district's campgrounds accept reservations. **Sawbill Lake,** the district's largest, has 50 sites right on the edge of the BWCAW and it rarely fills up. If you want to paddle into the wilderness or take a shower (for a fee), Sawbill Canoe Outfitters, 218/663-7150, is right next door. There are 33 more sites nearby at **Crescent Lake.** The nine sites, several riverside, at **Temperance River,** halfway between Tofte and Sawbill Lake along County Road 2 (the Sawbill Trail), also don't fill up very often.

The other four developed camps lie on a line west of Tofte. The closest and thus busiest is **Ninemile Lake** with 24 sites and good birdwatching in the surrounding forest. With just three sites **Divide Lake** is more peaceful, and it has a great two-mile trail around the lake. **Little Isabella**'s 11 riverside sites are noted for their serenity. Also in a beautiful setting is the nearby **McDougal Lake,** with 21 sites, a mile-long hiking trail, and a swimming beach.

Fifteen small **rustic campgrounds** are spread across the district. These more remote and less developed sites are available free of charge.

Information

The **Tofte Ranger Station,** 7355 Hwy. 61, 218/663-8060, is located on the edge of Tofte. From May through September it is open daily 6 A.M.–6 P.M. and weekdays 7:30 A.M.–4 P.M. the rest of the year. Maps and brochures can also be

picked up at the **Isabella Work Station,** 1, 218/323-7722. It is open 7:30 A.M.– during the summer and Monday–Thursday in the winter.

GRAND MARAIS

Grand Marais is not your average small town. This bustling village of 1,353 people has more cultural offerings than many much larger cities. Artists and progressive thinkers have been arriving for decades, and today their work fills galleries and keeps the stages stirring throughout the year.

The name Grand Marais, or Big Swamp, comes from the French version of the Ojibwe name for the area, though some historians claim they did a poor translation and the actual name was Place Beside the Duplicate Waters. Trading posts and fishing camps were established here previously, including one for John Jacob Astor's American Fur Company, but a permanent community didn't take hold until 1871 when explorer and prospector Henry Mayhew came looking for iron, copper, and silver. He never found great mineral wealth, but the town he founded prospered with fishing and logging. Today Grand Marais is a good base for exploring the surrounding wilderness and a great destination on its own.

Sights

The **Cook County Historical Museum,** 4 S. Broadway Ave., 218/387-2883, occupies an 1896 lighthouse keeper's home. Most of the small but interesting collection of artifacts and photos relate to past industries, such as logging and farming, but there are some Native American and geological displays as well. From June through September the museum is open Monday–Saturday 10 A.M.–4 P.M. and Sunday 1–4 P.M., the rest of the year it is open if someone is there working, which is most likely on Saturday afternoons. Admission is free. Just down the street is the **Johnson Heritage Post Art Gallery,** 115 W. Wisconsin St., 218/387-2314, where exhibitions from local and regional artists change monthly, more or less. Even if art isn't your thing, stop by just to admire the hand-hewn log building, a replica of a

working harbor in Grand Marais

19th-century trading post that once stood here. Open daily 10 A.M.–5 P.M. during the summer and Tues.–Sun. noon–3 P.M. the rest of the year. In 1907 a forest fire destroyed most of the community of Chippewa City, which overlooked Lake Superior a mile east of present-day Grand Marais. **St. Xavier Church,** built as a mission for the local Ojibwe, survived the blaze and, after extensive restoration, is now open to visitors. Both the unique interior construction and the photographs of its congregation back in 1895 when it was constructed are worth a look. The church, known locally as the Chippewa City Church, is along Highway 61 and open summer Saturdays 1–4 P.M. Admission is free. The Cook County Historical Society, which maintains the above three properties, also has a **Commercial Fishing Museum** down by the campground. You can walk through the authentic building daily 9 A.M.–5 P.M. from late May through October.

A stroll along the breakwater to the **Grand Marais Lighthouse** (the Fifth-order Fresnel lens was carved in 1885, though the current steel skeletal tower is from 1922), still in op-eration, and past the forested cliffs of **Artist Point** is an essential trip. While tiny in size, Artist Point's beauty is immense—pack a picnic and you could easily spend half a day. Unfortunately, everybody and her sister knows about it; however, you will often find solitude by walking out to **Sweetheart's Bluff** across the bay. The short, easy trail, less than a mile round-trip, starts at the far west end of the campground, behind the orange gate.

For something a bit different you can visit a sawmill. Free tours of the **Hedstrom Lumber Company,** 218/387-2995, are available several days a week from mid-June through August, and you must reserve a space in advance. It is located five miles up the Gunflint Trail. During the summer you can get around town via **horse-drawn trolley.** The "old-time city bus" runs a regular route between the coast guard station and the campground. An all-day pass is $10.

Recreation
Both **Bear Track Outfitting,** 2011 Hwy. 61 W., 218/387-1162 or 800/795-8068; and **Wilder-**

AN EDUCATIONAL VACATION

The abundance of artists in and around Grand Marais has resulted in some special opportunities for visitors so you might want to see what is on schedule at the following organizations before planning your trip.

The wonderful **North House Folk School,** 218/387-9762 or 888/387-9762, www.northhouse.org, promotes and preserves knowledge and skills from the past. You can try your hand at making snowshoes, knives, quilts, maple syrup, bronze bells, wooden spoons, and even boats. You can also learn wilderness living skills and sailing.

Classes of a different nature are on offer through the **Grand Marais Art Colony,** 218/387-1284 or 800/385-9585, www.grandmaraisartcolony.org, which for over 50 years has offered summer workshops for writers and visual artists. You can even get university credit for some of them.

Sugar Bush Fiber Arts, 218/387-2149, has weekend and week-long classes ranging from silk scarf painting to Native American bead weaving available throughout the year.

ness Waters Outfitters, 1712 Hwy. 61 W., 218/387-2525 or 800/325-5842, equip those heading off to the Boundary Waters. Bear Track also offers fly-fishing clinics. With the BWCAW so close, some people overlook the fantastic paddling available on Lake Superior, but not **Superior Coastal Sports,** 20 E. 1st St., 218/387-2360 or 800/720-2809. Half-day and full-day trips, available mid-May to mid-September, along the area's cliffs and sea caves are $39 and $75 respectively, and multi-day trips to other North Shore locations and Isle Royale National Park are available. They also do sales and rentals for those with experience and lessons for those without.

When the lakes are frozen **Arleigh Jorgenson Sled Dog Adventures,** 218/387-2498 or 800/884-5463, and **NOMADS Adventure and Education,** 218/387-1411 or 888/753-5629, offer one-hour to multi-day mushing trips. For around $200 you can drive your own team for a full day. Overnight trips through the BWCAW and Superior National Forest offer the option of camping or staying in cabins.

The **Superior North Outdoor Center,** 9 N. Broadway St., 218/387-2186, rents and repairs bikes and leads rides through the Superior National Forest. A 4–6 hour trip is $40 per person and can be designed to suit all abilities. They also offer guided and self-guided lodge-to-lodge rides, plus rock and ice climbing trips.

Those who don't want to brave chilly Lake Superior (though a few hardy souls do) can swim at the **Grand Marais Municipal Pool,** 218/387-1275, down by the harbor on 8th Ave. The indoor complex has a diving board, whirlpool, sauna, and wading pool for the little tykes.

The **Gunflint Hills Golf Course,** three miles north on the Gunflint Trail, 218/387-9988, is a nine-hole, par-34 course with sweeping views of Lake Superior. The moose are in play.

Entertainment and Events

The focus of Grand Marais cultural life is the **Arrowhead Center for the Arts,** 11 W. 5th St., 218/387-1284 or 800/385-9585. The $3.5 million complex opened in the spring of 1998 and has made locals proud and many other cities a little envious. An eclectic schedule of theater, concerts, film, dance, and special events make for a well-rounded calendar.

For nightlife your best bet is the cozy and smoke-free **Gun Flint Tavern,** 111 W. Wisconsin St., 218/387-1563, which has a rollicking round of live blues, jazz, or reggae on the weekends and an open-mike on Wednesdays. They keep a dozen microbrews on tap and serve wine by the glass. You can rack your brain over a pizza at **Sven and Ole's** Thursday nights during their weekly trivia contest.

During the **Fisherman's Picnic,** the first weekend in August, the town battles it out in log sawing, rock skipping, and loon calling, while gorging themselves on fishburgers. Of course there are also scores of more traditional pursuits during

THE ARROWHEAD

the four-day festival. Field trips and speakers during the last weekend of October's **Grand Marais Birding Festival** naturally center around the fall migration. Some of the rarer sightings include black-headed grosbeak, purple sandpiper, and Anna's hummingbird, while Pacific loon, golden eagle, and Thayer's gull are all relatively common.

Accommodations

Operated by the friendly Pederson family for over 50 years the lakeside **East Bay Hotel,** 1 E. Wisconsin St., 218/387-2800 or 800/414-2807, has a wide variety of rooms. Single European-style sleeping rooms with shared bath go for as little as $26 (some of these even have lake views), standard doubles run $45–82, and a large two-bedroom suite with fireplace, whirlpool, and kitchen in the new wing tops out at $169. A sauna is available to all guests. Just down the beach is the **Shoreline Motel,** 20 S. Broadway Ave., 218/387-2633 or 800/247-6020, with rooms from $88. The lobby is filled with games, puzzles, and books to enjoy in your room or in front of the fireplace. The same owners run the **Aspen Lodge,** 310 Hwy. 61 E., 218/387-2500 or 800/247-6020, where all rooms have a lake view. There is a sauna, whirlpool, and the only hotel swimming pool in town. Rates start at $110. Also on the beach is the **Best Western Superior Inn,** Hwy. 61 E., 218/387-2240 or 800/842-8439, with some of the best hotel rooms around. Standard rooms are $109, while adding amenities such as balconies, whirlpools, and fireplaces can nearly double that. All but a few have lake views, and there is an oversized whirlpool.

The **Grand Marais Inn,** 1800 Hwy. 61 W., 218/387-1585 or 800/456-5258, has regular motel rooms from $90, while in back are a pair of hand-hewn log cabins with stone fireplaces built by Swedish settlers in 1925, before there was even a road here. They have been modernized with electricity and plumbing since then, but still retain a rustic atmosphere. The **Harbor Inn Motel,** 207 W. Wisconsin St., 218/387-1191 or 800/595-4566, has spotless rooms from $55.

Grand Marais has several high quality B&Bs. The **Snuggle Inn,** 8 7th Ave. W., 218/387-2847 or 800/823-3174, info@snuggleinnbb.com, has four cozy, Northwoods-themed rooms, each with limited lake views and a private bath. Owners Tim and Greg are an excellent source of hiking information and serve wonderfully creative breakfasts. Larger and more modern, the **MacArthur House,** 520 W. 2nd St., 218/387-1840 or 800/792-1840, has five large rooms and a two-room whirlpool suite, plus guests can use the downstairs whirlpool. Perched above the town, right along the SNF's Pincushion Mountain Trails, is the **Pincushion Mountain B&B,** 968 Gunflint Trail, 218/387-1276 or 800/542-1226. Each of the four guestrooms has a private bath. Bikes and skis are available for rent, and afterward guests can unwind in the sauna. All three have rooms from $90.

The city-owned **Grand Marais RV Park & Campground,** 218/387-1712 or 800/998-0959, on the west side of town has nearly 300 sites (147 full hookups, 106 water and electric). Despite its location by the waterfront, it is a very uninspiring campground and primitive sites are a whopping $21. Camp at a nearby state park or in the Superior National Forest if you can.

Food

Probably the most beloved place to eat in Grand Marais is the **Angry Trout Café,** 416 W. Hwy. 61, 218/387-1265, which serves wonderful pastas, salads, sandwiches, and fish using as many locally produced and organic ingredients as possible. Entrées run $7–19. They are open daily for lunch and dinner, but much to the chagrin of locals and tourists alike, only between mid-May and mid-October.

Victoria's Bakehouse and Deli, 411 Hwy. 61 W., 218/387-1747, is also sometimes mentioned as the best restaurant in town. The menu changes frequently, but duck á l'orange or seared pork loin with cranberry-walnut sauce, both about $15, exemplify the dinner offerings. Earlier in the day they offer cheaper deli sandwiches and salads. Open Tues.–Sat. for breakfast, lunch, and dinner.

The Pie Place, 2017 W. Hwy. 61, 218/387-1513, while specializing in the obvious, also serves up mouthwatering, made-from-scratch meals for about $5 for lunch and twice that for dinner. The menu changes weekly, and they even do free delivery—menus are found at every hotel and B&B in town. Open Tues.–Sun. for breakfast, lunch, and dinner.

For location you can't beat the lakeside dining room and large outdoor deck at the East Bay Hotel's **East Bay Restaurant,** 218/387-2800. The menu, averaging $15 a plate, consists mostly of steak, seafood, and sandwiches, though Friday is Mexican night. Open daily for breakfast, lunch, and dinner.

Sven & Ole's, 9 W. Wisconsin St., 218/387-1713, is a North Shore institution and for many a mandatory stop after canoeing the BWCAW. Pizza is their main business, but subs and pasta round off the menu. A family-sized pie with the works is about $18. The Pickled Herring Pub in back has a wide selection of local microbrews and over a dozen imported beers. They are open daily for lunch and dinner and offer delivery in the evening.

Alyce's, 5 W. Wisconsin St., 218/387-2648, is a real-deal soda fountain from 1938 with malts, phosphates, and ice cream sodas. Reasonably priced burgers, BLTs, and the like are available as side dishes to your ice cream. Open Mon.–Sat. for lunch and dinner.

My Sister's Place, 410 Hwy. 61 E., 218/387-1915, specializes in creative and bountiful toppings on burgers and hot dogs. Open daily for lunch and dinner.

It doesn't take much imagination to figure out the specialty of **World's Best Donuts,** 4 E. Wisconsin St., 218/387-1345; unfortunately, the doughnut makers hibernate in the off-season.

Tiny **Cuppa Diem,** 111 W. Wisconsin St., 218/387-9850, is the city's top choice for a caffeine fix.

Shopping

Sivertson Gallery, 14 W. Wisconsin St., 218/387-2491 or 888/880-4369, sells "Art of the North" by regional, Canadian, and Alaskan artists including a high percentage of Native Americans. Prices are very high, but the quality is excellent. Betsy Bowen's woodcut prints highlight the offerings of **Waters of Superior,** 501 Hwy. 61 W., 218/387-9766 or 877/387-9766.

Work from many more local artists is on sale at the **Eight Broadway Art Gallery,** 8 N. Broadway St., 218/387-9079. The jewelry at the **Stephan Hoglund Studio,** 107 W. Wisconsin St., 218/387-1752 or 800/678-1891, is inspired by, and often made with, materials from the surrounding environment.

The largest selection of antiques is at **Lake Superior Collectibles,** 16 1st Ave. W., 218/387-2200, which has over 5,000 square feet of everything from silverware to fishing lures. **Trailside Antiques,** 110 5th Ave. W., 218/387-2665, is tiny, but everything is high quality, much of it imported from England.

Birch Bark Gallery, 11 1st Ave. W., 218/387-2315, is a massive gift shop with a fantastic selection of Minnesota and North Shore books. **Drury Lane Books,** 12 E. Wisconsin St., 218/387-3370, also has many regional titles, and there is also a paperback exchange in the lobby of the Grand Marais Public Library, 104 2nd Ave. W., 218/387-1140.

The **Dockside Fish Market,** 418 Hwy. 61 W., 218/387-2906, better known as the fish house, is a commercial fishing operation that sells smoked and fresh fish direct to the public.

If you need any camping gear you'll probably find it at the **Lake Superior Trading Post,** 218/387-2020, on the harbor at the end of 1st Avenue West.

Information and Services

The **Grand Marais Visitor Information Center** is located at 13 N. Broadway, 218/922-5000 or 888/922-5000, www.grandmarais.com, and they will help you find a vacancy, recommend a fishing charter captain, or answer any other questions about Grand Marais. They also stock information about the Gunflint Trail, other North Shore towns, and even Thunder Bay, Ontario. They are open Monday–Saturday from 9 A.M. to 5 P.M. The **U.S. Forest Service Gunflint Ranger Station,** 218/387-1750, on Highway 61 just before town can give you the lowdown on recreation in the Superior National Forest. Open daily 6 A.M.–6 P.M. from May through Sept. and weekdays 8 A.M.–4:30 P.M. the rest of the year.

If you are arriving by boat the **Grand Marais Marina,** 218/387-1712, has 22 slips. All of the city's banks and many businesses exchange Canadian dollars.

GUNFLINT TRAIL

County Road 12, better known as the Gunflint Trail, runs 63 resort-lined miles through the Superior National Forest from Grand Marais to Saganaga Lake on the Canadian border. You can paddle into the BWCAW, roam the endless trails, and maybe spot some of the myriad moose. Specific trails, along with Superior National Forest campgrounds, are discussed below.

One of the first resorts up the trail is also one of the best. Each of the ever-so-cozy cabins at **Bearskin Lodge,** 218/388-2292 or 800/338-4170, stay@bearskin.com, are widely spaced along East Bearskin Lake and come with a fireplace and private dock. Amenities include a whirlpool and a reservable sauna. Prices start at $925/week and $155/day, though there are only weekly rentals for most of the summer. Famous for its friendliness the **Gunflint Lodge,** 218/388-2294 or 800/328-3325, gunflint@gunflint.com, has been run by the Kerfoot family since 1927, and they are so popular that during peak summer weekends rates start at $325 per night; weekday prices can be considerably less. All of the two dozen cabins have fireplaces, and some have whirlpools and saunas. They have a busy schedule of activities for young and old, offer BWCAW outfitting, and have horseback riding at their own stables. Both resorts offer boat and canoe rentals, and some of the state's best cross-country skiing is right out your door. They also offer excellent meals, but you should have at least one meal at Trail Center Lodge's **Black Bear Bar and Restaurant,** 218/388-2214, which is as close to a neighborhood tap as you can have in these parts. The menu has all the usual, but also choices like bratwurst and eggs, peanut butter and mayo burgers, Italian fried chicken, Friday fish fry, portabella mushroom sandwich, and a popular peppermint schnapps malt. Not only is the food great, but so are the Northwoods atmosphere and friendly service. It is open daily for breakfast, lunch, and dinner, though they close up in April and November.

There is no shortage of outfitters ready to send you out into the BWCAW. Two well-known and highly experienced operators, **Voyageur Canoe Outfitters,** 218/388-2224 or 888/226-6348; and **Way of the Wilderness,** 218/388-2212 or 800/346-6625, sit at the far end of the road. The latter is adjacent to the SNF's Trails End Campground and runs the high-season-only **Trail's End Café** with pizza, burgers, and the like. **Boundary Country Trekking,** 218/388-4487 or 800/322-8327, specializes in Inn to Inn trips for bikers, hikers, and paddlers, plus offers yurt cross-country ski touring. All three have lodging available on-site. For more area information contact the **Gunflint Trail Association,** 800/338-6932. They run the Gunflint Trail Information Center, 218/387-3191, in Grand Marais where Hwy. 61 meets Wisconsin St. It is open daily from early June through late September and weekends the rest of the year. Their website, www.gunflint-trail.com, has a vacancy search.

SUPERIOR NATIONAL FOREST—GUNFLINT DISTRICT

The forest's easternmost reaches surround the Gunflint Trail (County Road 12), making most recreational facilities easily accessible to those who want to head out into the wilderness by day and relax with all the comforts of home at a resort by night. For additional details see the Superior National Forest overview earlier in this chapter.

Recreation

Just about all of the district's trails are on or near the Gunflint. The first trailhead you pass, just a mile up from Grand Marais, is for the **Pincushion Trail System,** a side loop of the **Superior Hiking Trail.** The 15-mile nest of loops are generally level in the front with some good climbs towards the back, and there are some great views, especially from the Pincushion Mountain Loop at the far end. Pincushion is the most popular cross-country skiing in the area (out of seven trails offering 221 groomed miles) and the only mountain biking trails in the district, though other off-road opportunities exist on old logging roads. The next two paths are the often-muddy **George Washington Memorial Pines Trail,** an easy three-mile loop through a tall stand of pines with a swamp at the back end, and the **Northern Light Lake Overlook,** a steep half-mile climb to the fantastic views atop Blueberry Hill. Even though your odds of seeing the lumbering giants from the observation deck at the end of the **Moose Viewing Trail** aren't much better than just driving along the road, if you do find some you can observe them in a much more intimate setting—it's about a half-mile round-trip.

There are more fantastic vistas at the ends of the **Lima Mountain Trail** and **Honeymoon Bluff Overlook,** not to mention beautiful scenery along the way. From the summit of Lima Mountain, a 1.5-mile walk, you'll be rewarded with 360-degree forest and lake views, while the latter hike is a half-mile loop leading to a sunset-ready overlook of Hungry Jack Lake. Both trails have steep climbs and good bird-watching. The **Central Gunflint Trail System,** impeccably maintained by Bearskin Lodge and Golden Eagle Lodge, is some of the best cross-country skiing in the state. There is terrain for all abilities, and about half of the 29 groomed miles can accommodate skate-skiers. The Central Gunflint Trails connect to the remote **Banadad Trail,** detailed with the BWCAW section, to offer a full spectrum of skiing choices.

Right near the end of the Gunflint is the remarkable Magnetic Rock, a house-sized behemoth that deflects compass needles. The fairly easy 1.5-mile hike into the rock, naturally called the **Magnetic Rock Trail,** is a great berry-picking route. Plenty more Gunflint area hikes cross into the BWCAW, and these trails are detailed with that section.

Naturally the BWCAW is the primary paddling destination in these parts; however, for a short trip that is sure to be crowd-free, dip an oar in the 3–5 mile **Pine-Kemo-Talus-West Twin** canoe route about a third of the way up the Gunflint. It has four short portages and a pair of campsites.

If you are driving up the Gunflint Trail and want to learn more about the blowdown, pick up the *A Changing Forest* brochure at the ranger sta-

tion in Grand Marais. There are also informational kiosks along the road.

Camping

All but two of the district's campgrounds lie along the Gunflint Trail. First in from Grand Marais is **Kimball Lake.** The namesake lake is stocked with trout so the camp's 10 sites are popular with anglers, and there is a swimming beach nearby. The almost adjacent **East Bearskin Lake** and **Flour Lake** campgrounds have 33 and 35 sites respectively and are the best places to look last minute. The former offers some great paddling, both in and outside of the BWCAW. Though not far off the highway, **Iron Lake** has a real middle of nowhere feeling and despite having just seven sites it also tends not to fill up. All the way at the end of the Gunflint Trail is **Trails End** with 32 gorgeous and widely spaced sites, some of which have water hookups for RVs. This is a great base for short explorations of the BWCAW, and Way of the Wilderness Outfitters, 218/388-2212 or 800/346-6625, is conveniently located right next door. Reservations are accepted for the last three.

Devil Track Lake is the forest campground closest to Grand Marais, and most of its 16 sites sit lakeside. Also in a beautiful setting nearby are **Two Island Lake** with 38 sites and the four-site **Cascade River** rustic campground.

Information

The **Gunflint Ranger Station,** 2020 W. Hwy. 61, 218/387-1750, is located in Grand Marais. From May through September the offices are open daily 6 A.M.–6 P.M. and weekdays 8 A.M.–4:30 P.M. the rest of the year.

GRAND MARAIS TO THE BORDER

Though Grand Marais is the last town of any significance in Minnesota, Highway 61 still has a lot more to offer before taking you into Canada. This is the least developed section of the highway, and the final mountainlike stretch between Grand Portage and the border is beautiful enough to warrant the drive.

Judge C. R. Magney State Park

This wild 4,514-acre park and its famous **Devil's Kettle Falls** are just 14 miles northeast of Grand Marais, though it still receives relatively few visitors. Before the Brule River empties its load into Lake Superior, it thrashes through a mass of volcanic rock in a fit of white-water rapids and waterfalls. At one point a pinnacle splits the river sending the eastern half on a 50-foot plunge, while the western section cuts its way through a seemingly bottomless pothole. It is an awesome and intriguing sight and arguably the best hike on the North Shore. The 2.5-mile round-trip to the falls is steep with a long set of steps near the end. There is more to do here besides just taking in the striking vista of the Devil's Kettle. Nine total miles of hiking trail, including a stretch of the **Superior Hiking Trail,** follow the Brule River and Gauthier Creek through the forest, and five miles of these are groomed for cross-country skiing in the winter. Anglers have no trouble reaching their limit of rainbow and brook trout. Twenty-seven well-spaced campsites are available during the summer in the quiet and shady campground. Call 218/387-3039 for additional information.

Naniboujou Lodge

The one-of-a-kind Naniboujou Lodge, 218/387-2688, info@naniboujou.com, is as much a work of art as a hotel. It was built on Superior's shore in 1928 as an exclusive private club with such luminaries as Babe Ruth and Jack Dempsey as members, but thanks to the stock market crash the following year it didn't last long. The building languished for decades, but has been lovingly restored with modern amenities added—though the lack of phones and TVs in the rooms ensures your stay is truly relaxing. The 24 guest rooms' rates range $75–95 and many have great views, but even if you aren't staying here do yourself a favor and make reservations for lunch or dinner so you can get a proper look inside. The Great Hall dining room is painted in a kaleidoscope of Cree Indian designs and centered on a massive stone fireplace. Dinner options such as cranberry pork tenderloin, walleye sautéed with toasted almonds, or vegetarian shepherd's pie run $6–17, while lunch is comprised of sandwiches and salads for around $7; take-away box lunches are available. Naniboujou is open from mid-May to mid-October, and weekends from late December through mid-March.

Grand Portage

This little village on the Grand Portage Ojibwe reservation has a surprising array of offerings. Best of them is reliving the fur trade era at the **Grand Portage National Monument,** 218/475-2202, an excellent living history museum. From 1784 to 1803 the Scottish-run North West Company, the most profitable fur trade operation on the Great Lakes, had their inland headquarters here, and Native Americans and Europeans came from across the region to buy and sell pelts. Grand Portage was one season's journey from Montreal, and goods transported between the coast and the interior—the French Voyageur Highway extended far into northwest Canada—were exchanged here with Montreal men ("pork-eaters") wintering in the city and the North men ("winterers") remaining in the wilderness. To get here from the west they carried 180 pounds of "soft gold" over the 8.5-mile Grand Portage, bypassing a long stretch of waterfalls and rapids on the lower Pigeon River. The cedar-picket palisade and many of the buildings have been reconstructed and furnished in the 1797 style. In and around the stockade you will find exhibits on the fur trade and Native American heritage, historic gardens, and massive birch-bark canoes, while guides in period costume tell stories and demonstrate traditional skills. The **Grand Portage Rendezvous Days and Pow-Wow,** held the second full weekend of August, re-creates the annual summer gathering that was held annually during the post's existence. January's **Winter Frolic,** held in conjunction with the **Grand Portage Passage Sled Dog Race,** showcases winter life at the post with activities like sleigh rides and snow snake tossing. The short but steep **Mount Rose Trail** climbs 300 feet from the parking lot with a couple of good vistas along the way. The more adventurous can retrace the steps of the voyageurs along the **Grand Portage Trail,** a long but fairly level walk through the woods to the site of Fort Charlotte. Register with the park service in advance if you want to camp there. The

GRAND PORTAGE RESERVATION

Total Area - 76 sq. miles
Tribally Owned - 95 percent
Total Population - 557
Native Population - 322
Tribal Enrollment - 1,097

The Grand Portage Reservation sits along 18 miles of Lake Superior shoreline at the tip of Minnesota's Arrowhead. It is named after the 8.5-mile portage trail developed by early Native Americans to bypass the waterfalls and rapids on the lower Pigeon River. Both the Ojibwe and the French arrived here about 1730 and made the portage a vital link in the inland fur trade. In those days many Ojibwe worked with the fur traders and later at the commercial fishing station opened by the American Fur Company.

Residents and the tribal government have cooperated with the State of Minnesota and the Environmental Protection Agency on wildlife habitat and resource protection and in 1996 the tribe became the first in the nation to be certified by the EPA as having the technical capability to monitor its own water quality. They have played an active role in restoring and protecting Lake Superior's fish populations.

John Beargrease, a northland legend (and the man for whom the Sled Dog Marathon is named) for his years of service as the mailman before a road led up the North Shore, was a Grand Portage member though the most famous tribal member goes by the name Manito Geezhigaynce, or "The Little Spirited Cedar Tree." For 300 years this gnarled, wind-blown cedar has clung to the rocky cliffs at Hat Point on Lake Superior. Though it technically lives off the reservation this tree has played such a vital role in the spiritual lives of tribal members that they have bought the land and guides must accompany visitors.

buildings are open daily 9 A.M.–5 P.M. between late May and early October, and entry is $3. The trails are grounds are free and accessible all year.

For a look at modern Native American enterprise there is the **Grand Portage Lodge and Casino,** 218/475-2401 or 800/543-1384, just off the highway. Guests of the hotel, where the 100 rooms go from $67, can relax in the sauna and pool when they aren't testing their luck. A small collection of Ojibwe cultural artifacts is on display near the bingo hall. Another excellent hike leads to the **Mt. Josephine Lookout** with panoramic views in all directions, including Lake Superior's **Susie Islands,** important for the typically arctic plants they harbor. The fairly challenging 1.5-mile climb starts a mile east of the National Monument on County Road 17.

Grand Portage Isle Royale Transportation, 715/392-2100 or 888/746-2305, takes passengers to Michigan's remarkable Isle Royale National Park. The MV *Wenohah* heads to Windigo on the southwest end of the island daily at 9:30 A.M. and returns by 6 P.M. The trip costs $40, and day-trippers get 2.5 hours to explore—plus fantastic scenery along the way—including the sacred Witch Tree at the tip of Hat Point—

seen on countless postcards. The MV *Voyageur II* circumnavigates the island three times a week, and they will drop you off and pick you up at any point along the way. The service runs between mid-May and late October out of **Voyageurs Marina,** 218/475-2476. If you've got your own boat, the tiny marina has everything you'll need from gas to nautical charts, and they can also arrange charter-fishing trips. Each September **Grampa Woo Excursions,** 218/226-4100, offers all-inclusive, three-day boat trips to Thunder Bay, Ontario, for $445. The tours, timed to take in the fall color, pass the Susie Islands and stop at the old Canadian mining town of Silver Islet. If you are arriving from Canada between May and October, all your Minnesota-related questions can be answered at the **Grand Portage Travel Information Center** on Highway 61.

Grand Portage State Park

Tucked up against the Canadian border is one of the smallest but most beautiful state parks in Minnesota. The state's highest waterfall, creatively named High Falls (aka Pigeon Falls), drops 120 feet at a narrowing of the Pigeon River. It's no Niagara, but to call the scene awe-inspiring is not an

THE ARROWHEAD

overstatement. A half-mile paved trail and board-walk lead to a pair of overlooks of the falls, one of which is wheelchair-accessible. To get there in the winter, consider renting a pair of snowshoes from the park office. A 3.5-mile hiking/cross-country ski trail follows the Pigeon River to smaller Middle Falls. Call 218/475-2360 for information.

To see High Falls from the Canadian side park at the Ontario Travel Information Center, drop $2 in the courtesy box and follow the mile-long trail under the bridge. The loop is a bit rough and wet in a few places, but worth it since you can island hop in the rocky river right above the falls.

Boundary Waters Canoe Area Wilderness

With 1.1 million acres and over 1,000 lakes, the Superior National Forest's Boundary Waters Canoe Area Wilderness is an unrivalled dream-scape for outdoor lovers. Stretching 150 miles along the Canadian border, it is the largest wilderness east of the Rockies and one of the most beautiful spots in North America. *National Geographic Traveler* included the Boundary Waters, along with the Taj Mahal, Grand Canyon, and Venice, in its "50 Places of a Lifetime" issue.

Streams and portages connect the myriad lakes, allowing unlimited canoe travel, and not surprisingly 99 percent of visitors journey on the water; however, the wilderness surrounds some of Minnesota's best hiking trails, too. Motorboats are allowed on 19 periphery lakes, but that was a necessary part of the compromise to get the wilderness protection in the first place, and they are unlikely to impede on your experience if you are here to paddle. For the ultimate in isolation plan part of your trip through one of the dozen Primitive Management Areas (PMAs). Previously established portages and campsites are no longer maintained on these 124,000 acres, so reaching the lakes they surround requires a bit of bushwhacking. There is no limit on day use, but only one group can camp in each zone each night.

With over 200,000 visitors each year this paddlers' paradise is also the most heavily used wilderness area in the country; however, a strict permit system protects the beauty, solitude, and wildlife and ensures a quality wilderness experience. Canada's adjoining Quetico Provincial Park added another million-plus protected acres to the ecosystem, and other than the various regulations there is very little difference between the two.

NATURAL HISTORY
Geology
Sitting on a low plateau at the southern end of the Canadian Shield, a ancient slab of rock stretching from the Great Lakes up to the Arctic Ocean, the Boundary Waters are a unique Ice Age relic. The glaciers that have swept south over the last two million years bulldozed right down to the bedrock, and since they last retreated some 10,000 years ago only a very thin skin of soil—six inches on average—has formed. Along lakeshores and many other places the eroded bedrock is still exposed, lending a unique beauty to the area. This Precambrian crust is estimated to be 2.6 billion years old, making it some of the oldest exposed rock in North America. The gouging glaciers left a noticeable (if you look on a map) northeast "grain" across most of the area. Glacial meltwater filled these long, narrow basins, forming the myriad lakes that cover nearly a quarter of the BWCAW's land area.

Flora and Fauna
The BWCAW lies in a transition between the temperate deciduous forest and the coniferous northern boreal forest with the latter predominating. This mixed "North Woods forest" features white and red pine surrounded by spruce, balsam, jack pine, aspen, and birch and, because of the early limits on logging, there are still many old-growth stands along the lakes. Summer is berry time and blueberries, a favorite of both humans and black bears, ripen throughout most of July with the peak coming as the month turns into August. Wild raspberries peak about the same time, while wild strawberries are ready

the Boundary Waters Canoe Area Wilderness

weeks earlier. The odd, dead-looking plants cling-ing to nearly every large rock in the forest are lichens, a symbiotic union of fungus and algae. Of course, the storm of 1999 (see The Blow-down) has changed the forest considerably and it will be years, maybe decades, before anyone knows exactly how.

Naturally this wild corner is one of Minnesota's best wildlife-watching destinations, but the most enduring animal memories are usually not the ones seen, but those heard. The common loon is surprisingly common on these lakes—nearly all have a nesting pair—and their echoing wails on a still summer night are reason enough to pitch a tent. The territories of several wolf packs extend into the BWCAW and, if you're lucky, their plain-tive howls will float past your campsite, too. White-tailed deer and moose are a wolf's primary prey, and spotting the latter grazing in streams and shallow bays is not a rare event. Beaver and otter are common in the water, while bald eagles frequently soar above it, and you will probably see several large-eared woodland deer mice scaveng-ing around your campsite at night. Other com-mon critters include great blue heron, herring gull, spotted sandpiper, broad-winged hawk,

ruffed grouse, gray jay, white-throated sparrow, a variety of ducks, snowshoe hare, and the chat-tery red squirrel. You'd be very lucky to see a mountain lion, bobcat, lynx, fisher, pine marten, mink, northern flying squirrel, star-nosed mole, spruce grouse, black-backed woodpeckers, bo-real chickadee, or red-backed salamander, but they are all out there. In total there are around nearly 200 species of birds, 45 mammals, 12 am-phibians, and seven reptiles in the BWCAW.

Bears deserve special mention. Hundreds of the lumbering giants roam the BWCAW and, un-fortunately, the place you are most likely to see them is in camp. Keep a clean campsite, however, and you probably don't have to worry about them crashing your party—if you don't know what specific precautions to take, be sure to ask someone before you head out. If one does wander into camp you can usually frighten it off by mak-ing loud noises, though do not charge it.

HUMAN HISTORY

The Boundary Waters' early history mirrors that of the state. The first inhabitants were nomadic Paleo-Indians who followed the melting glaciers

THE ARROWHEAD

THE BLOWDOWN

On July 4, 1999 a fierce storm with straight-line winds in excess of 90 miles per hour whipped across northern Minnesota and though it lasted only 20 minutes its effect will be felt for a lifetime. The hurricane-strength maelstrom toppled 600,000 acres of forest across Minnesota and Ontario, more than half of it in the Boundary Waters Canoe Area Wilderness. The storm's ground zero was a four- to 12-mile wide and 30-mile long swath right along the Canadian border between Ely and the end of the Gunflint Trail—80 percent of the trees in this area were knocked over or snapped in half. It was one of the largest blowdowns ever recorded in North America. Though the scale of the devastation brought tears to the eyes of many, it must be remembered that these events, however extraordinary, are part of a forest's natural ecological cycle. The sunlight, once blocked by the mature trees, will allow new trees to grow and this emerging forest is actually beneficial to much wildlife including moose, lynx, and wolf.

The biggest problem is fire. There is now up to ten times the fuel available to burn, increasing not only the likelihood of wildfires, but also the severity. Millions of dollars have already been spent on storm recovery and fire mitigation and prescribed burns will continue until at least 2005. Besides the obvious visual impacts, visitors to the Superior National Forest face other changes. There will be area closures and campfire restrictions for the next many years—always check on these before beginning a trip. Also, don't pitch a tent under damaged or leaning trees. In some BWCAW campsites there are no longer trees and so bear-proof food storage containers are highly recommended. While many paddlers, understandably, now try to avoid blowdown areas this is not entirely necessary since even in the hardest spots hit some stands were not toppled, especially on shorelines—scientists suspect that growing up with more winds strengthened these trees—and so out on the lakes you might not even notice the damage. The Forest Service or your outfitter will be able to tell you what to expect in specific locales.

north hunting large game such as mastodon, musk ox, and giant beaver. The first French-Canadian fur traders—the very first may have been Jacques de Noyon in 1688—shared these waterways with the Dakota, but by the time the fur trade began in earnest in the mid-18th century the Ojibwe had taken control. The fur traders continued to paddle and portage these waters until the dwindling beaver populations and changing European fashions crashed the industry in the 1840s.

Following World War I a national interest in outdoor recreation emerged, and the profusion of automobiles brought a great influx of vacationers to the Superior National Forest, prompting the conflicts between recreationists and commercializers that continues today. Before 1919 scant regard was given to public use of national forests, though in that year the U.S. Forest Service hired Arthur C. Carhart as a landscape architect to develop new policies for multiple use. He initiated the first serious discussions within the Forest Service of protected wilderness, and one of his earliest acts was a management plan for what would

become the BWCAW. Acting on Carhart's recommendations, Secretary of Agriculture William Jardine signed a plan for the unnamed wilderness in 1926 that prohibited roads and other development across 1,000 square miles and required loggers to leave "tree screens" around lakes. Thanks to noted conservationists like Sigurd Olson and Ernest Oberholtzer, a series of state and federal laws during the 1930s, '40s, and '50s solidified and expanded these protections, and the debate helped shape the landmark Wilderness Act of 1964. Beginning in 1948 the federal government began buying out private resort and homeowners in what was then called the Superior Roadless Primitive Area. One person who stayed was Dorothy Molter, known to most as the Root Beer Lady. She lived deep in the wilderness of Knife Lake between 1934 and her death in 1986. Her nursing skills and immense popularity prompted the Forest Service to grant her a lifetime exemption, allowing her to remain at her home. By all means, visit her museum in Ely.

Restrictions on incompatible uses such as fly-ins,

mining, and snowmobiles came piecemeal and not without opponents fighting every step in court; a few even resorted to violence against preservationists. The most contentious period in its history surrounds the 1978 passage of the BWCA Wilderness Act, which established the present boundaries and codified the regulations. To the chagrin of the wilderness backers, motorboats remained permissible on about one quarter of the periphery lakes. This was, however, far from the final word, and there are still serious efforts to roll back most of the wilderness protection.

PLANNING AND PRACTICALITIES

Though you could just show up and head right out into the wilderness, there are numerous factors—not the least of which is the quota system—that make advanced planning for an overnight journey a good idea. A night under the stars is the ultimate Boundary Waters experience, though day trips can still be pretty amazing, too, and require must less advanced thought.

When to Visit

There is no best time to experience the Boundary Waters, but three-quarters of visitors set out during June, July, and August, leaving the beautiful-weather months of May and September crowd free. September also gets you fall colors. The peak of the peak runs mid-July though mid-August, though even then you can find solitude. Ice-out usually comes at the end of April, while the first snow falls and the lakes refreeze around the end of October, and there are always some who paddle right up against these limits. Blackflies are at their worst the first two weeks of June, while mosquito swarms are gone by the end of July. Late May to early June, as well as September, tend to offer the best fishing. The summer permit situation might also be a factor in when you begin your trip. Winter visitors are a hardier bunch, but skis, snowshoes, and dogsleds are an excellent way to experience the Boundary Waters' unique beauty.

Permits

Between May 1 and September 30 the BWCAW operates under a quota system, and all overnight visitors, plus daytime motorboaters, must get a permit before entering. The cost is $10 per adult per trip (children are $5), plus a nonrefundable $12 reservation fee. A $20 deposit will be collected regardless of the party size, and the rest must be paid (or the difference will be refunded if you are traveling solo) when picking up the permit. A seasonal fee ($40 for adults and $20 for youth) covers permit costs for the whole year, but does not eliminate the reservation fee or deposit.

While not required, reservations are a very good idea since you cannot count on just showing up and finding a route that suits your desires. They are handled by the BWCAW Reservation Center, P.O. Box 462, Ballston Spa, NY 12020, 518/885-9964 or 877/550-6777 (877/833-6777 TDD), www.bwcaw.org. Reservations for the coming year may be submitted beginning November 1, and those received before mid-January will join a lottery, regardless of the order they were received. Following the lottery, reservations are accepted on a first-come, first-served basis. Permits can be picked up at all Superior National Forest ranger stations; the forest headquarters in Duluth; and 75 resorts, outfitters, and other businesses. These cooperating permit stations only accept credit cards for payment, and most charge a small service fee. If an outfitter is arranging your trip they will secure your permit for you.

Overnight visitors between October 1 and April 30, plus non-motorized day-trippers throughout the year, must fill out a self-issuing permit form, which is available at the ranger stations and most entry points. No reservations are required, and there are no limits on the number of visitors. An overnight in a PMA requires first-come, first-served authorization in person from a Forest Service office.

Outfitters

An outfitter, a good one anyway, is not just a company that rents canoes and camping gear. They are, as the Ely Chamber of Commerce puts it, "biologists, historians and woods-wise guides whose knowledge and love of this area will add immensely to the pleasure you'll have on your canoe trip." They can plan a route that ideally fits your abilities and desires, and their intimate knowledge of the area (your map will be marked with scenic and historic highlights, good wildlife-viewing territory, prime fishing spots, the best campsites, or anything else that interests you) is often worth the price of your gear rental. And, speaking of gear rental, with all the portaging you will probably be doing, it pays to use their specially designed lightweight equipment. Complete outfitting includes just about everything you need for your trip from toilet paper to the tent—all you need to bring are your clothes and personal items. Most companies can also arrange transportation to the entry point and pre- and post-trip accommodation. Many will even guide your trip if you are unsure of your outdoor skills.

There are literally dozens of outfitters to choose from in the surrounding communities, and all of those listed in this guide are highly regarded, though they are far from the only good ones out there. Before choosing an outfitter be sure to talk with them. They should begin by asking you questions about the type of trip that you want to do and be willing to give you references. Also, remember that a higher price usually means better and lighter equipment so ask specifically what you are getting for your money.

Rules and Etiquette

The BWCAW's strict regulations, which will be detailed when you get your permit, are meant to maximize people's wilderness experience while minimizing their impact. First and foremost everybody should observe Leave No Trace (www.lnt.org) principals. Maximum group size is nine people and four watercraft. One rule that catches some people off guard is the ban on cans and glass bottles, though fuel, insect repellant, medicine, and personal hygiene products in their original containers are allowed. Food and drink may be stored in plastic containers, but they must be packed out.

For those traveling by water, camping is restricted to designated sites, except for people with Primitive Management Area-endorsed permits. Those following hiking trails are strongly encouraged to use the designated sites, but it is not a requirement. Winter visitors should set up camp out on the ice and make only one trail connecting camp with the shoreline. If you build a fire, burn only dead and down wood collected well away from your campsite—it is, of course, illegal to cut live vegetation. Tree vandalism is a serious problem in the BWCAW and even minor damage adds up over time. Canoes must be licensed in Minnesota or your home state. Minnesota law also requires all watercraft, including canoes, to have wearable life jackets on board, though it doesn't say you need to wear them. Motorboats are allowed only on 19 lakes, and your wilderness permit must specifically designate motorized use. Portage wheels are permitted only over a handful of portages.

One final thing to remember is to be quiet. Voices carry surprisingly far across the lakes, especially on still evenings, and loud noises not only disturb other visitors but scare off wildlife. Barking dogs do the same thing, so they are best left at home. If you must bring Fido, keep him on leash at landings and portages.

Information

Your best sources of information are the Superior National Forest ranger stations or an experienced outfitter. On the Web, check out www.superiornationalforest.org/bwcaw and www.canoe-country.com. For Quetico Provincial Park information call 807/597-2735 or see www.ontarioparks.com.

Naturally, with the labyrinth of lakes you'll be traveling, a good map is essential. USGS topographic maps are excellent for detailing the lay of the land, though they do not show portages and campsites so it is best to buy BWCAW-specific maps. However, if you plan to use GPS you'll need the USGS topos, too. The most popular maps are the W. A. Fisher Company's F-Series, which use a scale of 1.5 inches per mile, while others prefer MacKenzie Maps with their larger 2 inches to 1-mile scale. Both are excellent, waterproof, and available all over town, so you may want to make your map decision based on the number of maps needed since a single map by one company may cover your entire route as opposed to two or three from the other. Also, keep in mind that no maps are perfect and will show portages and campsites that no longer exist, which is one more reason to discuss your trip with the Forest Service or an outfitter.

An invaluable resource for neophyte campers is *Boundary Waters Canoe Camping* by Cliff Jacobson. This comprehensive book covers every fathomable situation, from paddling, camping, and orienteering basics to how to follow a moose trail. The best resource for route planning is Robert Beymer's two-volume *Boundary Waters Canoe Area.*

PADDLING

With 62 entry points and over 1,500 miles of canoe routes, recommending where to paddle is simply not possible in this book; for that you will need to rely on a Boundary Waters-specific guidebook or, much better, get local advice. However, before deciding where you want to go, you must determine what sort of trip you want to take, and there are as many possibilities as there are lakes. Some people will want to pick a single base camp and spend a weekend there. Others may want to head out for ten days of exploration, packing up and heading to a new camp every day. Many come with a single purpose, such as seeing the northern lights, spotting a moose, or casting for trout. Whatever kind of trip you want, it can't be stressed strongly enough that when poring over maps or discussing routing with an outfitter you need to be realistic about your strength and skills. It is wise to plan a couple of layover days. Regardless of whether you use these to relax or cover more territory (there is less gear to haul over portages), they will keep you on schedule if rough weather slows you down.

You don't have to head deep into the wilderness to enjoy the BWCAW's beauty, but during the summer this is a near necessity for finding solitude. The best advice for getting away from other paddlers is to portage often, and the longer the better. Most portages are a quarter mile or less, though some are over a mile. Don't forget that, unlike most other paddling trips, because of the portages weight matters here. Also, remember that elevation change rather than distance is usu-

ally a better indication of a portage's difficulty. Portage lengths are usually given in rods, and one rod equals 16.5 feet. The number of permits available for each entry point (the quota corresponds to the number of campsites available) is also a good general rule for determining the number of other canoes you will encounter, but there is not a direct correlation since few people will portage, and there is no limit on day-trippers. Generally there are more bugs and portages on the smaller lakes, so the more willing you are to "sweat and swat" the more privacy you will get. The other bonus to the smaller lakes is that most people consider them more beautiful. On lakes where motors are still allowed, you can use a towboat service to get you out to the edge of the real wilderness faster. Naturally, the Primitive Management Areas offer a more secluded experience, too.

HIKING

The Boundary Waters isn't known for hiking, but it should be. The long-distance trails through the heart of the wilderness offer world-class treks, while short easy trails probe lakes on its edge. Remember that hikers and backpackers are subject to the same permit and quota system as paddlers.

Long-Distance Trails

These rugged and remote routes have downed trees, beaver dam crossings, streams to wade, and other challenges, so they are not for inexperienced hikers. Though the trails are marked, a topographic map and compass are essential. Campsites are spread out along each of them.

The **Kekekabic Trail** runs 38 gently-rolling miles across the heart of the Boundary Waters from the end of County Road 18 east of Ely to the end of County Road 12 (the Gunflint Trail) west of Grand Marais. This trail was constructed in the 1930s for firefighting access and left abandoned until the Kekekabic Trail Club (www.kek.org) was founded in 1989 to reclaim the route for recreation. The **Snowbank Trail** is an easier 24-mile loop that starts out along the east end of the Kek and then heads north around its namesake lake passing many more along the way. It is an exceptionally scenic route with mature pine stands, shoreline bluffs, and some hilltop overlooks at the north end. The **Old Pines Trail** is a similarly beautiful S-curve off the east end that, with a return along the Kekekabic, can be added on to Snowbank to double the mileage.

As the name suggests, the **Border Route Trail** sticks close to Canada for most of its 75 miles. The fairly difficult route runs along the north side of County Road 12 (the Gunflint Trail) with over half of that passing through the BWCAW. Besides the river and lake scenery—some of the Boundary Waters' best—there are many rock ledges and stands of old-growth pine along the way. The BRT connects to the Superior Hiking Trail at the east end, and the Magnetic Rock Trail can be used as a connector with the Kek, leaving just about a quarter-mile road walk. Soon this will become the route of the **North Country National Scenic Trail.**

Two other abandoned trails revived by the Kekekabic Trail Club are the 28-mile **Pow-Wow Trail** and the 32-mile **Sioux-Hustler Trail,** both very rugged and seldom followed loops. Pow-Wow passes though prime moose and wolf habitat and features many old-growth pines. The trailhead is 17 miles north of Isabella on Forest Road 377. Sioux-Hustler originates 29 miles east of Orr on County Road 116 near the Forest Service's Lake Jeanette Campground and is noted for the many granite outcrops along it. It is the only long-distance trail not affected by the blowdown.

Ely Area

Generally a backpacking trip, the rugged and sometimes challenging **Angleworm Trail** can be hiked in a day, if you get an early start. The 14-mile loop around Angleworm and other lakes passes ridge-top overlooks and mature red and white pine stands, plus moose are often spotted in the Home Lake area. There are nine lakeside campsites, and this is a relatively popular winter camping destination. The trailhead is 17 miles northwest of Ely on County Road 116 (the Echo Trail).

All the way up by Crane Lake is the 15-mile **Herriman Lake Trail** with various loops linking four lakes. Less than half a mile down the trail, before entering the BWCAW, is a picnic site on the

Echo River. Farther in on various hilly branches you will find three lakeside campsites, a sandy beach, and many scenic overlooks. Herriman and Knute lakes are excellent fall color destinations.

Gunflint Trail Area

It's a seven-mile round-trip to the state's highest point along the **Eagle Mountain Trail.** Most of the hike is pretty easy, though it's fairly rugged and strenuous over the last half mile to the endless views atop the 2,301-foot granite summit. The trailhead is on Forest Road 170, 17 miles northwest of Grand Marais. The six-mile **Brule Lake Trail** is a little-used route to the summit starting to the west on Forest Road 326. There are two campsites on Whale Lake right below the hill.

All other area trails lie along County Road 12 (the Gunflint Trail). The **Daniels Lake Trail** is an easy 1.5-mile round-trip stroll from near the end of County Road 66 to the shore of its namesake lake. Much more challenging is the 3.5-mile **Caribou Rock Trail** starting two miles up County Road 65. Within the first 0.75 mile, you'll get beautiful overlooks of West Bearskin and Moss lakes before entering the BWCAW and passing more lakes and a handful of campsites. Both of these trails link up with the Border Route Trail.

WINTER

At 18 miles, the easy to intermediate **Banadad Trail** near the end of the Gunflint Trail is the Boundary Waters' longest ski trail and its only groomed route (use of snowmobiles to groom the trail was grandfathered into the wilderness legislation), though because it is so remote even with grooming it can be a rugged trip. It also has the distinction of offering yurt-to-yurt skiing through Boundary Country Trekking (see Gunflint Trail). Though not groomed, cross-country skiers appreciate the wilderness scenery of the **South Farm Trail,** a generally easy five-mile route eight miles east of Ely on County Road 16 that crosses its namesake lake and loops through a spruce swamp at the back end. Skiers are also the primary users of the **North Arm Trail** 13 miles north of Ely; take County Road

116 (the Echo Trail) to County Road 644. Most of the 16 ungroomed loops are intermediate level, though beginners and experts will find appropriate routes along the 26 total miles. Other popular winter ski routes are the Herriman Lake, Angleworm, and Sioux Hustler trails, each detailed above under hiking, plus the **Hegman Lake Pictographs** north of Ely, which is one of the finest examples of this style of Native American rock art in North America.

If you've never experienced dog sledding before, there is no better place to give it a try. Outfitters in the Ely and Grand Marais areas run mushing trips across the frozen lakes ranging from a few hours to weeklong adventures, and you will get to take the reins on any of them.

Ely and Vicinity

ELY

On the map, Ely appears to be at the end of the road. For people who love wilderness and beauty and solitude, on the contrary, it's at the center of the world.

Charles Kuralt

Charles Kuralt named Ely his "number one vacation destination" in the country and made several trips here annually in his later years, though the gentleman journalist certainly isn't the only one to laud Ely. Travel and sports magazines like *Midwest Living* and *Canoe Journal* regularly honor this little town set conveniently near the middle of nowhere. Five hundred lakes lie within 20 miles of Ely and this is the most popular gateway to the Boundary Waters Canoe Area Wilderness. Though most people are here to explore the outdoors, if the surrounding two million acres of public forest were to suddenly disappear the unique museums and fantastic amenities would still make this town of 3,724 a wonderful destination.

History

While modern day boosters have dubbed Ely the "Canoe Capital of the World," it was once the "Capital of the Vermilion Range." Like most other range cities, Ely began as a rough and tumble mining town—filled with tavern, casinos, and brothels—in the 1880s and was especially festive in the spring when thousands of lumberjacks poured in to blow the money they had earned over the winter. When the flamboyant, fundamentalist preacher Billy Sunday passed through during the summer of 1900 he quipped,

"the only difference between Ely and Hell is that Ely has a railroad into it."

Between 1888 and 1967, miners hauled over 80 million tons of ore out of the city's five iron mines. By 1897 the average miner took home $2 a day and, though unions eventually brought safety and justice to the miners, working the pits was never an easy life. Ely sent more men per capita to World War II than any other community in the United States, because for many joining the infantry was preferable to going underground. Tourism, the principal industry today, began back in the 1910s, and the remote fly-in resorts attracted many gangsters and bootleggers back in the 1930s. Today, besides the short-term visitors, Ely's remoteness attracts many artists and explorers who have added to the city's already singular character.

Sights

Considering that Ely lies in the heart of the largest population of wolves in the lower 48 states and that both Dr. David Mech (one of the world's foremost wolf experts) did much of his pioneering wolf research here, it is only natural that the **International Wolf Center,** 1396 Hwy. 169, 218/365-4695 or 800/359-9653, opened their education center here. For most people the highlight is the resident wolf pack living in the 1.25-acre enclosure behind the center. Though the five gray wolves can and sometimes do hide out in the forest, they tend to roam and rest up front, allowing close-up views through the massive windows. Naturalists discuss the pack and their behavior several times a day. Some visitors only take time to see the wolves, but the other exhibits are excellent and should not be missed. You'll

AURORA BOREALIS

You have to go another 800 miles or so north to reach prime viewing territory, but northern Minnesota is still close enough to regularly see the Northern Lights. This unparalleled evening show, caused by the interaction of oxygen and nitrogen atoms in the upper atmosphere with charged particles emitted by the sun, leaves a deep impression on all who see it. Auroral displays can be seen almost any time but around here your best bet is during the summer months. They tend to be more intense around the equinoxes. The colorful lights dance anywhere from just a few minutes to several hours.

learn their vocalizations and behaviors, understand the social structure of the pack, see inside a den, and hear about legend and lore back to the Middle Ages, while children can follow a wolf pup through its first year in the Little Wolf room. Besides the various talks held daily throughout the year, they also offer short off-site tracking and howling trips, plus extended adventure programs where you can accompany researchers into the field. The center, located just east of Ely on Hwy. 169, is open daily 9 A.M.–7 P.M. during July and August, daily 9 A.M.–5 P.M. from early May through June and September through mid-October, plus weekends 10 A.M.–5 P.M. the rest of the year. Admission is $7.

Hoping to emulate the Wolf Center's success is the **North American Bear Center,** 21 E. Sheridan St., 218/365-7879. Currently they run a small information center, photo gallery, and gift shop, though in coming years they plan to open a large and modern education center near town. The current exhibits are open weekdays 11 A.M.–6 P.M. and weekends noon–5 P.M. and admission is free.

The city's other must-see attraction, the **Dorothy Molter Museum,** 2002 E. Sheridan St., 218/365-4451, celebrates a most remarkable woman. In 1934, at the age of 27, this local legend dropped her life as a nurse in Chicago and moved to the deep wilderness of Knife Lake up near the U.S.-Canadian border to help run the

Isle of Pines Resort. She soon became a self-sufficient wilderness expert living in a large canvas tent for most of the year and moving to more solid quarters for the winter. Known to many as the Root Beer Lady, as many as 7,000 canoeists would stop each summer to chat and get some of her famous home-brewed root beer—chilled with ice she had cut during the winter and packed in sawdust and moss. The U.S. Forest Service had added her property to the Wilderness Area, but due to her popularity and vital nursing skills (she was also known as the "Nightingale of the Wilderness"), Molter was allowed to stay. Though she could no longer conduct business out there, nobody was prevented from making a free-will donation in exchange for a cold root beer. When the last resident of the BWCAW died in 1986, two of her cabins were hauled out piece by piece by dogsled and reassembled in Ely, and the pair form the majority of the museum. The interior of her winter cabin remains just as she left it, while the Point Cabin, formerly used by guests, holds various photos and other personal effects. Though small, give yourself plenty of time to tour the museum since most of the guides knew Dorothy and have decades worth of stories to share. The museum, located near the International Wolf Center, is open Monday–Saturday 10 A.M.–5:30 P.M. and Sunday noon–5:30 P.M. during the summer and also noon–4 P.M. on weekend in May and September. Admission is $4.

Over at Vermilion Community College the **Ely-Winton History Museum,** 1900 E. Camp St., 218/365-3226, has a small but well-presented local history collection. Exhibits cover mining, logging, Native American history, and there's even equipment from Will Steeger and Paul Schurke's 1986 dogsled expedition to the North Pole. It is open daily 10 A.M.–5 P.M. during the summer. Admission is $2.

A few other historic sites will be of interest to some. The **Pioneer Mine headframe** sits right across from Grand Ely Lodge on the north edge of what was then an open pit iron mine, but is now Miner's Lake. It may be opened for tours in the near future. On the northeast side of town, near the junction of 13th Ave. E. and Main St., is

© TIM BEWER

International Wolf Center

a hunk of exposed volcanic rock known as Ely Greenstone. Known as **Pillow Rock,** the undulating lava solidified underwater and really does look soft. There is history of a different sort at the **Ely Steam Bath,** 127 S. 1st Ave. E., 218/365-2984. Miners, loggers, and, more recently, paddlers have been coming for a good sweat at the Finnish-style sauna since 1915. Not only will you come out squeaky clean, but you'll likely have absorbed some interesting stories about the town. And remember, the top bench is for experts only; you've been warned. It costs $5 for a seat in the public rooms, or you can get a private room for $7 per person. Hours are limited so call ahead.

To see some historic sites beyond town, reserve a seat with **Burntside Heritage Tours,** 218/365-5445, or **Hegman Lake Pictograph Tours,** 218/365-5838. The former's two-hour pontoon tours of Burntside Lake cover geological and historical sites including Sigurd Olson's Listening Point; they depart from Burntside Lodge and cost $20 per person. Besides the ancient Native American rock paintings hidden away on the edge of the BWCAW, the Hegman Lake canoe trips' naturalist will discuss the area's human and natural history. The per-person price is $30

and no paddling skill is required. Both trips last two hours and reservations are required.

Recreation

The primary reason for Ely's popularity is that recreational opportunities in the surrounding wilderness are nearly limitless. The BWCAW and the rest of the Superior National Forest are covered in their own sections, though there are other options in and around town. The five-mile **Trezona Trail** is a paved route around Miner's Lake—formerly mining pits—on the north side of town. The south side follows an old rail line and is generally level, while the north side rolls over some hills; a spur at the east end connects the trail to the International Wolf Center. Trezona's south side is part of the new **Mesabi Trail** stretching 132 miles across the Iron Range from Ely to Grand Rapids, though completion of this end of the trail is still several years away. Although it's principally a snowmobile trail, some mountain bikers ride the rough-surfaced **Taconite Trail,** which stretches 165 miles to Grand Rapids. **Spirit of Wilderness,** 2030 E. Sheridan St., 218/365-3149, rents mountain bikes for $20/day. Follow the bridges for a scenic scramble around

THE ARROWHEAD

the rocky islets at **Semers Park.** Though the swimming season is short, the park also has a sandy beach for those summer days when you need to cool off. Semers is on the shore of Shagawa Lake just west of town; from Sheridan St. take Central Ave north to Shagawa Rd. and follow the signs. The **Hidden Valley Recreation Area** has 12 miles of hilly loops through a mix of birch stands and pine plantations just a mile east of town off Hwy. 169; turn by the ski jump. Though designed for cross-country skiing, the trails are open to mountain bikers in the summer. Maps are sometimes available at the trailhead, but it would be best to pick one up at the chamber of commerce. In fact, the chamber distributes maps for most area ski and bike trails.

At last count there were nearly 30 outfitters in town, all waiting to set you up with everything you need for a Boundary Waters canoe trip. About half, including most of those listed below, are member of the Ely Outfitters Association, whose helpful website (www.canoecapital.com) lets you choose an outfitter from a map or an available services comparison chart. A complete list of outfitters is kept on the chamber's website. The local wisdom is that you really can't go wrong with whichever company you choose, though the following three, each conveniently located right in town, are some of the most highly recommended. Ely's very first canoe company, **Wilderness Outfitters,** 1 E. Camp St., 218/365-3211 or 800/777-8572, started leading travelers into the wild in 1921. The **Piragis Northwoods Company,** 105 N. Central Ave., 218/365-6220 or 800/223-6565, also operates a large outdoors store—you can test a canoe on your trip before purchasing it. Also on the scene for a long time is **Voyageur North Outfitters,** 1829 E. Sheridan, 218/365-3251 or 800/848-5530. **Timber Trail Lodge and Kawishiwi Lodge,** both detailed under Accommodations, also offer complete outfitting and do an excellent job.

Although canoeing dominates the Ely outdoors scene, **dogsledding** is the area's fastest growing sport and over half a dozen companies—more than any other town in the world, according to Ely's Chamber of Commerce—can take you out for a canine adventure. Trips run anywhere from a few hours to a week and, even if you've never seen a sled dog before, you'll get to mush your own team of huskies through the BWCAW, though you can always take it easy and just ride in the basket. For overnight options you can choose to experience true winter solitude and beauty with a camping trip, or pick a deluxe lodge-to-lodge option and refresh yourself each night with four-star meals. Remote yurt camps offer another option. The first name mentioned with Ely area dogsledding trips is almost always Paul Schurke, who runs the **Wintergreen Dogsled Lodge,** 218/365-6022. The noted arctic explorer—part of the first confirmed team to reach the North Pole overland without resupply—has a reputation for not only offering topnotch fun and adventure, but also leading the most highly educational trips around. Other highly recommended companies include **Run Silent Dog Sled Trips,** 218/365-4288; **White Wilderness Sled Dog Adventure,** 218/365-6363 or 800/701-6238; and **White Wolf Dog Sled Trips,** 218/365-4288—a full list is available on the chamber's website. No matter who you choose, expect to pay between $150–$200 for a day-long trip (day trips are not available through Winter Green Lodge) and a whole lot more for lodge-to-lodge or camping trips. In most cases, appropriate winter clothing can be rented through the trip provider.

It seems a shame to spend any time golfing when you are so close to such wonderful wilderness, but if you must, the nine-hole course at the **Ely Golf Club,** 218/365-5932, is there for you. There is a popular **sledding** hill here in the winter.

Entertainment and Events

Thanks to a bit of good fortune, Ely has an active arts scene for such a small town. In 1988 a painting that hung inconspicuously in the Ely Public Library for over 50 years was discovered to be *Breakfast in the Garden,* a long-lost masterpiece by the American impressionist Frederick Frieseke. A New York collector bought the painting for over $500,000 and the city used the proceeds to create the Donald G. Gardner Trust. Besides funding the library, much of the money goes to the **Northern Lakes Arts Association,** 218/365-

5070, which sponsors a wide variety of theater, music, dance, literary, and visual arts events throughout the year, including summer band concerts in Whiteside Park.

The city's biggest celebration is the **Blueberry Arts Festival** held the last weekend in July. Besides the 250 arts and crafts exhibitors, there are copious children's activities and food vendors. The Blueberry Arts Festival is so successful that Ely repeats it the weekend after Labor Day as the **Harvest Moon Festival.** This smaller version also includes logrolling shows, and the **Boundary Waters Blues Festival** takes place the same weekend. During the 10-day **Voyageur Winter Festival,** starting the last Thursday in January, you can make a snow sculpture, watch the Spirit of the Wolf Sled Dog Race, or take a sled-dog ride of your own.

Accommodations

One of the loveliest resorts in all of Minnesota—and certainly the most photographed—**Burntside Lodge,** 218/365-3894, info@burntside.com, got its start as a hunting camp in the early 1900s. Many of the 21 ultra-cozy cabins overlooking island-studded Burntside Lake were built in the 1920s and each is unique. The National Park Service, noting both its age and architecture ("a remarkable architectural achievement in an outstanding state of preservation"), has added it to the National Register of Historic Places. Rates range from $125/875 for a night/week in a one-bedroom cabin to $295/2065 for a three-bedroom waterfront cottage—most have kitchens. Resort amenities include a large marina renting everything from kayaks to pontoons (personal watercraft are prohibited), a pair of sandy beaches, a Finnish sauna, a cappuccino bar, and one of the area's best restaurants. Burntside, located just six miles northwest of Ely, is only open from early May through the end of September.

Twenty miles east of Ely on the north shore of Lake One, right on the edge of the BWCAW, is Minnesota's lone paddle-only resort. Most of the 16 housekeeping cabins at **Kawishiwi Lodge,** 218/365-5487, have screen porches and their own dock; three can only be reached by water. Each rental includes a canoe, and they offer full outfitting for overnight trips. There are also hiking trails nearby, and guests can unwind in the sauna after a busy day. Rates range $540–$960 a week for the one- to four-bedroom cabins. They are open from May through September.

Seven miles east of Ely on Farm Lake, one of the area's best fishing waters outside the BWCAW, is the friendly **Timber Trail Lodge,** 218/365-4879, bill@timbertrail.com, an excellent choice for families. Guests have use of the sauna, and there is a game room and TV lounge in the small log lodge, plus kids activities are scheduled during the summer. They also offer complete outfitting and have fishing guides who work right out of the resort. Two- and three-bedroom lakeshore cabins run about $1000/week (discounts in the slow season are quite large), and there are some cheaper and pricier options, too. Besides the 11 modern cabins, they have four comfy motel-room kitchenettes for $65 a night and 18 campsites, many right on the lake, with full hookups for $24. Timber Trail is one of the minority of Ely resorts to remain open year-round, and cabins are available for daily rental outside the summer.

Log Cabin Hideaways, 218/365-6045, offer seven scattered and secluded cabins, most right on the edge of the BWCAW, for those who want a wilderness feel without having to rough it. Though they are rather plush in most other regards, none of the log cabins have electricity or indoor plumbing, and all but one is reached by paddling, hiking, or skiing. Only the cheapest lacks a wood-fired sauna. They can sleep anywhere from two to ten people, and summer rentals are by the week ($375–1195), while there is just a three-night minimum ($75–$185) in the winter.

Back on the quieter end of Farm Lake is the funky and artsy **Blue Heron Bed & Breakfast,** 218/365-4720, info@blueheronbnb.com, where the north-facing lake views are phenomenal. Blue Heron is located right on the edge of the BWCAW, so day-tripping right out the door, either by land or water, is wonderful. Guests have free use of canoes and snowshoes and can unwind in the wood-fired sauna. The six inviting guestrooms, all with private bath, run $110–$155 and there is a two-night minimum stay most of the year.

Houseboats are available from a pair of companies on contorted Birch Lake down by Babbitt, 15 miles south of Ely. Both **Kinsey Houseboats,** 2718 Birch River Rd., 218/827-3763 or 888/827-3763; and **Timber Bay Houseboats,** 8347 Timber Bay Rd., 218/827-3682 or 800/846-6821, charge around $550 for a three-day weekend and $1000 for a full week during the summer—overall Kinsey's prices are lower.

The newly remodeled **Adventure Inn,** 1145 E. Sheridan St., 218/365-3140, has both the city's cheapest rooms and some of its nicest—either way they are a good value. The large "deluxe rooms" have four beds for $125, while the older rooms are just $43. There's both a sauna and hot tub for guest use.

The city's only large hotel is the **Grand Ely Lodge,** 400 N. Pioneer Rd., 218/365-6565 or 877/472-6335, overlooking Shagawa Lake a mile north of town. It has a pool, kiddie pool, whirlpool, sauna, fitness center, game room, and marina with boat rental, plus guests have free use of bikes, canoes, kayaks, and paddleboats. Rooms run $140.

The **Budget Host,** 1047 E. Sheridan St., 218/365-3237 or 800/283-4678; and **Paddle Inn,** 1314 E. Sheridan St., 218/365-6036 or 888/270-2245, are two older motels with saunas and clean rooms for about $70.

If you've looking to save money but don't want to camp, check with the chamber of commerce about **bunkhouse** availability. Many outfitters keep these simple hostel-like rooms available for groups heading out to and returning from the BWCAW and will rent them to individuals when not in use. Expect to pay about $15 per bed.

Food

Many, if not most, diners choose the **Burntside Lodge,** 218/365-3894, for dinner because of the fantastic setting—the dining room in the historic main lodge surrounds a fireplace and has excellent lake views—but no one goes home disappointed in the meal. The mostly steak and seafood menu also includes pastas and some vegetarian dishes (ranging about $14–34), and Burntside is the only seasonal restaurant in the state to earn *Wine Spectator* magazine's Award of Excellence. They are open for dinner daily (reservations are highly rec-

ommended) and weekends for breakfast during their May through September season.

The **Blue Heron B&B,** 827 Kawishiwi Tr., 218/365-4720, also serves up a beautiful setting for a meal, though the global menu is like no other. Besides some set items such as salmon mousse and Spanish paella, you can also mix a meat—chicken, pork, scallops, walleye, lamb, etc.—with your choice of preparation style, everything from Thai to Honduran, for a truly unique meal. Most entrées fall on the low side of the $15–30 price range. They serve dinner Wednesday–Sunday (and a Sunday brunch), and reservations and menu selection must be made 24 hours in advance, though you usually need to do so much earlier to get a table.

The **Ely Steak House,** 216 E. Sheridan St., 218/365-7412, a casual local favorite that's as well known for their walleye as the steaks, sits downtown at the top of the hill. The menu also includes gyros, club sandwiches, shrimp alfredo, and broasted chicken, all in the $6–27 range. Open daily for lunch and dinner.

The eclectic menu makes the log cabin-ensconced **Chocolate Moose,** 101 N. Central Ave., 218/365-6343, a tourist magnet, and even if the food weren't so good the front deck would still ensnare a steady stream of diners. Blueberry pancakes, black bean egg rolls, grilled portabella sandwich, spanakopit, pizza du jour, and buffalo steak are typical choices, and the beer and wine list is vast. For the ultimate Minnesota meal try the wild rice crusted walleye. Most menu items range $5–10, while the gourmet dinner entrées are priced up to $22. So many people come just for dessert that they've installed a take-out ice cream counter. This high-season only café is open daily for breakfast, lunch, and dinner.

Tops for java is the **Northern Grounds Café,** 117 N. Central Ave., 218/365-2460, but they've also got deli, panini, and bagel sandwiches in the $6 range for lunch and a small selection of dinners, like eggplant Florentine and sautéed salmon, on summer evenings for two to three times that price. They are open daily for breakfast, lunch, and dinner in the summer, daily for breakfast and lunch in the winter, and something in between during spring and fall.

The frozen pasties from **Erica's Bakery,** 402 E. Sheridan St., 218/365-2105, make a unique BWCAW meal, and during the summer few things refresh better after an outdoors trip than a scoop of homemade ice cream from **Sherry's Northwoods,** 1114 E. Sheridan St., 218/365-8404.

The definitive Ely bar isn't actually in Ely but 18 miles to the north at the BWCAW's Mudro Lake entry point. The legendary **Chainsaw Sisters Saloon,** 218/343-6840, lacks running water and electricity, but don't worry, the beer is always cold. They are open daily during the paddling season (naturally, they've got canoe rentals) and weekends in October, December, January, February, and March. To reach it, head up the Echo Trail and turn east just past the Fenske Lake Campground.

Shopping

Naturally with all the tourists descending on town there is no shortage of Northwoods-themed shops selling loon coffee mugs and chainsaw-carved bears, though thankfully not all the shops are so generic. Internationally renowned nature photographer Jim Brandenburg lives in Ely when not traveling the globe for *National Geographic,* and much of his Boundary Waters work is sold at the **Brandenburg Gallery,** 11 E. Sheridan St., 218/365-6563 or 877/493-8017, while the **Bob Cary Art Gallery,** 117 N. Central Ave., (above the Northern Grounds Café), 218/365-6658, sells prints and paintings from this local legend. Dozens of local and regional artists not lucky enough to have their own galleries sell their creations at the **Kess Gallery,** 130 E. Sheridan St., 218/365-5066.

Crafted from moose hide using a Cree design, Steger Mukluks are not only half the weight and twice as warmth as regular winter boots, but they are fashionable enough for *Elle* and *Mademoiselle* magazines. Made right here in Ely, you can pick up a perfectly sized pair at the **Steger Mukluk Company,** 33 E. Sheridan St., 218/365-3322 or 800/685-5857. For the rest of your body take a look at **Wintergreen Designs,** 205 E. Sheridan St., 218/365-6602, Minnesota's only full-line outdoor apparel maker.

Lisa's Second-Floor Bookstore, 105 N. Central Ave., 218/365-6745, at the Piragis Northwoods Company has an immense selection of outdoor-related titles, while **Chapman Street Books,** 139 E. Chapman St., 218/365-2212, is a decent used store and also sells imported tobacco.

Information and Services

The very helpful and friendly **Ely Chamber of Commerce,** 1600 E. Sheridan St., 218/365-6123 or 800/777-7281, www.ely.org, on the west side of town is open weekdays 9 A.M.–5 P.M., plus they add Saturday hours from June through September. They offer vacancy searches, and there's an RV dump station in the parking lot.

Direct all Superior National Forest questions to the **Kawishiwi Wilderness Station,** 218/365-7561, in the lobby of the International Wolf Center. It is open daily 6 A.M.–6 P.M. from May through September. The rest of the year stop by the **Kawishiwi Ranger Station,** 118 S. 4th Ave. E., 218/365-7600, right in Ely. It is open weekdays 8 A.M.–4:30 P.M.

There is no better way to catch the pulse of Ely than to tune in to **WELY** (94.5 FM and 1450 AM) radio—once owned by Charles Kuralt. Music ranges from bluegrass to new age while other programs include the End-Of-The-Road Trading Post and Birding with Bill. The true gems of the broadcast day are the Personal and Emergency messages, broadcast several times a day. Anyone looking for lost glasses; a ride to Minneapolis; a fourth member for a bowling league; or to invite their friends, who happen to live beyond the range of telephone service, to a birthday party can spread the word to the entire listening audience.

Transportation

There is currently no air service to Ely, though **Northwest Airlink,** 800/225-2525, has offered summer service in the past and may do so again down the road. If you arrived without a car and need to get around, call **Ely Cab,** 218/365-7500.

TOWNS AND PARKS AROUND ELY

Bear Head Lake State Park

With the spectacular scenery of the BWCAW beckoning it's understandable that some people don't stop at Bear Head Lake State Park,

218/365-7229, but its 4,523 wild and rugged acres are definitely worth a visit. The park touches the shores of nine pine-rimmed lakes, and naturally most visitors head for the water. Anglers seek walleye, bass, crappies, and trout. The easiest paddling is in the sheltered North Bay of the 674-acre namesake lake, while the more adventurous can make the mile-long portage out to Blueberry Lake. Boats are allowed on Bear Head, but a 10 mph speed limit is enforced. Bear Head Lake also has a swimming beach. The 10 miles of hiking trails, each named for the lakes they circle, get you into the wild quickly. The mile-long **Norberg Lake Trail** is the easiest and most popular hike, while most of the remote campsites lie along the challenging **Becky Lake** and **Blueberry Lake** trails, both of which are rather hilly. Most miles are groomed for cross-country skiing in the winter, and the Taconite State Trail, a popular snowmobile route, links the park with Ely and Grand Rapids—though seldom used the portion through the park makes for a decent warm-weather hike, too. At least one pair of bald eagles nest on Bear Head Lake each summer, so if you spend some time here sightings are almost guaranteed. If nothing else, the camping is excellent, too. The 73 (26 electric) sites in the family campground are shady and fairly secluded, while you can truly get away from it all at the six backpack and canoe-in campsites scattered along the shores of several lakes. There is also one camper cabin and a fully-appointed three-bedroom guesthouse, both open year-round, for those who don't want to rough it.

Soudan Underground Mine State Park

The opening of the Soudan Mine in 1884 heralded the beginning of Minnesota's iron mining industry, and over the next 79 years nearly 16 million tons of ore were shipped down to Two Harbors and on to eastern steel mills. Known as "The Cadillac of Mines" for its modern safety features, this National Historic Landmark has been left almost exactly as it was when operations shut down in 1963. You begin your journey toward the center of the earth by donning a hardhat and climbing into the cage for the half-mile descent. At level 27 you'll board a railcar and journey nearly a mile into the last and deepest area mined at Soudan. There are two sets of steps and uneven footing along the rest of the tour, and though it is not very physically demanding,

Soudan Underground Mine State Park

it is definitely not for claustrophobics. Although ore is no longer extracted, the mine has buzzed with activity of a futuristic kind since 1980 when the University of Minnesota opened a **High Energy Physics Lab.** Currently, physicists are searching for dark matter and trying to measure the mass of neutrinos. The mine tours run daily 10 A.M.–4 P.M. from Memorial Day weekend through the end of September; call 218/753-2245 for availability of tours later in the fall. Tours of the physics lab are available at 11:30 A.M. weekdays and noon on weekends. The adult price is $7 for one tour or $12 for both, and they accept same-day reservations. For either be sure to bring some warm clothes since the mine temperature stays at about 50° F at all times. There is plenty more to see and do above ground while waiting for your tour to begin. The visitors center contains exhibits on Soudan's geological and mining history, and several surrounding mine buildings are open to explore. Elsewhere on the park's 1,300 acres is a five-mile hiking trail that passes more historical mining sites and some decent Northwoods scenery.

Just outside the park, along Highway 169, you'll see a sign for **Rocks and Bottles,** and if you have even a minor interest in either you'll want to stop to chat with the instantly-likable Stafford Korpi, a lifelong excavator of old dumpsites. It's more of a museum than a shop since he's not interested in the money and will only part with something if he has a duplicate of it. The conversation will quickly turn beyond his collection to other topics like politics or physics, and if you have any unanswered questions about the Soudan mine he can fill you in since he worked underground for 15 years.

Tower

The Minnesota Gold Rush of 1865 brought the first settlers to the Lake Vermilion area, though the prospectors packed up and left the next year after the only nuggets they uncovered were fool's gold. The village of Tower began in 1882 as a shantytown supply center for the Soudan Mine and was named after Charlemagne Tower, one of the men who fronted money to open the mine. Initially founded at the end of the Vermilion

Trail, a rugged path three days from Duluth by horse and wagon, the railroad soon arrived and facilitated not only mining but logging as well, and by the end of the decade Tower was a thriving city. Today it sees large numbers of tourists passing through on their way to Ely and serves as a supply center for those visiting the Soudan Mine State Park or Lake Vermilion. Vermilion, Minnesota's fifth largest lake and one of the most popular in the state for anglers and boaters, sprawls over 49,110 acres but because of its many twists and turns, there are still some places where it feels intimate. Wildlife remains abundant— at last count 14 pair of bald eagle nested around the lake and one of the 250 resident loons will sing you to sleep at night. Many of the lake's 365 islands have picnic sites and campgrounds.

If you don't have your own boat, and don't want to rent one, you still have several options to get out and see the lake. Mail is delivered on the water, and Aronson Boat Works, 218/753-4190, takes passengers on their **mailboat** during the summer. The 80-mile, 3.5-hour trip costs $12 and departs at 9 A.M. Monday through Saturday. Reservations are recommended. Aronson's is located on Pike Bay, three miles west of town on Hwy. 169. To see some of the lake's wilder residents schedule a trip out on the water with **Vermilion Wildlife Tours,** 218/753-2673. Binoculars, guidebooks, and even a camera with telephoto lens are provided, and the 20-foot boat is designed for stability to assist shutterbugs. Tours are two or more hours and rates depend on the length of trip and number of people, but start at $60/hour. To see Vermilion—or any of the thousands of other Boundary Waters area lakes—from a different angle call **Van Air,** 218/753-2331, for an aerial tour in their five-seat Cessna floatplane. A basic 20-minute fly-over costs $30 per person, though other options, such as sunset moose viewing and dinner trips, are also available. While based in Tower, you can start your tour at most Ely-area resorts.

From mid-April to mid-May you can visit the **Pike River Fish Hatchery,** 218/365-7280, where 15 million walleye are raised before being stocked into Vermilion and other lakes. Morning is the best time to visit. Located west of town by the

BOIS FORTE RESERVATION

Total Area - 212 sq. miles
Tribally Owned - 32 percent
Total Population - 657
Native Population - 464
Tribal Enrollment - 2,767

The French called this band of Ojibwe the "Strong Men of the Forest" and the name Bois Forte stuck. Today most reservation lands lie around Nett Lake and the tribal headquarters is in the small village of the same name, though the tribe also controls a special reserve on Lake Vermilion and this is where they constructed the successful Fortune Bay Casino. Wetlands cover half of the reservation though it is also marked with great timber stands and four Indian-owned logging firms operate in the area. Nett Lake, covering 7,300 acres, is the largest wild rice producing lake in the United States and most of the harvest is consumed locally rather than being sold since this is considered a superior product to what can be bought in most stores. Sitting in the middle of the lake is Spirit Island, sometimes called Picture Island, a beautiful spot covered with hundreds of human, animal, and geometric petroglyphs. Though carved thousands of years before the Ojibwe moved into this region many people still believe it is a sacred site and so they leave offerings of tobacco, clothing, and food.

Pike River Dam; take Hwy. 169 to County Road 77 and head north about half a mile to Angus Road, 200 yards past the dam. In town, at the junction of Hwys. 135 and 169, is the **Tower Train Museum,** 218/753-3041, a wee collection of historical photos and artifacts housed in a rail coach car. There is a gift shop and area tourism information in the adjacent depot. It is open daily 10 A.M.–4 P.M. from early May to early September, and they charge a buck.

There are dozens of resorts on the lake (also see Cook below). The busiest is the Bois Forte Band of Ojibwe's **Fortune Bay Resort-Casino,** 218/753-2611 or 800/555-1714, on the south shore, which has 118 rooms, 24 RV sites, and a steady stream of people hoping to beat the odds.

Among the many amenities are a pool area, 18-hole golf course, and marina. Standard rooms are $79, but there are several fancier options, too. While this resort is the future of the tribe, you can get a look at their past in the **Bois Forte Heritage Center,** 218/753-6017, (aka Atisokanigamig or Legend House). The collection is small but well presented and includes a wigwam, fur trading post, and historical and cultural artifacts. Outside is a tepee and short nature trail that passes one of the old gold mines. Open Tues.–Sat. 10 A.M.–5 P.M., with expanded summer hours. Admission is a rather steep $5. West of Tower, at the end of Pike Bay is the much more relaxing **Pike Bay Lodge,** 218/753-2430 or 800/474-5322. Once the summer estate of mining tycoon A. B. Coates, the original home, boathouse, and two other buildings have been converted into cozy cottages. Rates begin at $695/week and one-night stays are permitted in some units. To completely immerse yourself in lake life, call **Vermilion Houseboats,** 218/753-3548 or 800/262-8706. They offer weekday, weekend, and weeklong packages, and prices vary considerably with what you rent, but a 40-foot Explorer, which sleeps five people, is $645 for a weekend, while a week in the 60-foot Executive sleeps 14 and will set you back $4,500. If you want to stay in town there is the **Marjo Motel,** 712 Highway 169, 218/753-4851, which has changed little since 1956 when it was built by the same family that runs it today, though the price of the large clean rooms has risen from $2.50 to $40.

For nourishment try the home-cooked meals at the **Tower Café,** 411 Main St., 218/753-2710. Sandwiches cost just a couple of bucks, while a full chicken or walleye dinner platter will set you back about $9. They are open daily for breakfast and lunch and also have a couple of rooms for rent upstairs. The pasties made by **Erica's Bakery,** 509 Main St., 218/753-4705, are known far and wide.

Cook

Cook, a busy Highway 53 pit stop, has a few restaurants, gift shops, and even one of the oldest continuously operating movie theaters in the state (since 1939) to keep you busy for a short while, but the real action is north of town on the small end of Lake Vermilion (see Tower), which is home to a dozen resorts. Of these **Ludlow's Island Lodge,** 218/666-5407 or 877/583-5697, eight mile west of Cook on County Road 540, is the fanciest. Over half of their 18 deluxe cabins are on a private island, while the others are spread out on both the north and south shores. Besides the usual facilities there are racquetball, tennis, and sailing lessons. If you want a vacation during your vacation, they offer fully outfitted canoe trips on the Vermilion River and have a separate camping island nearby. Ludlow's isn't for those with thin wallets; weekly rates begin at $1,950. A little more traditional, but no less relaxing, is **Pehrson Lodge Resort,** 218/666-5478 or 800/543-9937, with 21 cabins spread along 2,000 feet of shore, out on Pamahan Island, or tucked up on the hillside. Children's programs are offered on summer weekdays, and there is free use of canoes, windsurfers, and sailboats. They are just six miles north of town on County Road 24, and weekly rates start at $800. While these resorts are closed in the winter, the **Moosebirds B&B,** 218/666-2627, nine miles from town on County Road 24, stays open all year. The three guestrooms in back of the General Store share a deck overlooking the lake, and a pontoon boat is available for rent. The rooms with shared bath are $79 and $89, while a private bath costs $109. In town the **Vermilion Motel & RV Park,** 320 U.S. 53 S., 218/666-2272, has large, new rooms for $53 and RV sites with full hookups for $15; guests have use of the sauna and **Greyhound** buses stop here on their way between Duluth and International Falls. According to some, the **Country Supper Club,** 218/666-5351, serves best food in the area outside of Ludlow's Island Lodge. They feature steak and seafood and also have some good pastas with prices ranging from $8–20. It is conveniently located between most of the resorts, three miles north of town on County Road 24 and half a mile west on Beatty Rd. Open daily for lunch and dinner. Surprising **Comet Coffee,** 102 S. River St., 218/666-5814, part of the aforementioned movie theater, is a good choice for a snack or a simple meal. Folk and similar artists sometimes perform here, too.

Although it's on a peninsula, not an island, the only direct access to the **Black Bay Trail** is via water, so the eight-mile route on the north end of the lake is an excellent place for wildlife viewing. Three docks on Black Bay Peninsula, maintained by the DNR, give easy access, if you've got a boat. Cross-country skiers can also travel the groomed 25-mile **Ashawa Trail.** The main trailhead is a mile north of Moosebirds on County Road 24. A ski pass is required. If you don't mind getting up long before the crack of dawn you can witness the fascinating mating dance of the male **sharp-tailed grouse.** The DNR maintains observation blinds on private land in the area. The spectacle takes place during April at about 4:15 A.M., and you need to arrive at the site well before the birds. To reserve a blind, call the DNR at 218/744-7448. Besides dispensing information about the forest, the **Superior National Forest LaCroix District Office,** 320 U.S. 53 N., 218/666-0020, has a display of Northwoods wildlife, sells nature-related items, and is stocked with area tourism brochures. Outside, a short nature trail circles a pond. The office is open daily 6 A.M.–6 P.M. from May through September, and weekdays 8 A.M.–4:30 P.M. the rest of the year.

Embarrass

Tiny Embarrass was settled in the 1890s by Finns who wanted to farm instead of mine. It took its name from the Embarrass River, which had been christened by French voyageurs (*embaras* means difficult) who had trouble navigating it due to the many downed trees along it. It wasn't until the 1950s that non-Finns began arriving in significant numbers. (According to the *WPA Guide to the Minnesota Arrowhead Country,* published in 1941, the entire township's "population of 652 includes only two persons who are not Finns.") The Finnish heritage remains strong today, and to preserve their roots and attract tourists, the community has opened a **visitors center,** 218/984-2084, along Hwy 135 west of town and started the caravan-style **Heritage Homestead Tours,** which visit several early 20th century farmsteads and other historic sites around the town. The knowledgeable guides share stories of the pioneers' lives and explain some of the clever construction methods they used to make their log structures. Tours depart twice daily, at 10 A.M. and 2 P.M., during the summer and cost $5. While some of the sites are on private property, you can visit a pair of them on your own. The **Hanka Homestead** is 1.5 miles north of the village on County Road 21, one-quarter mile west on County Road 26, one-quarter mile north Pylka Rd., and then east at the first driveway. The **Pyhala Homestead** is on Salo Rd., just east of the campground. The visitors center, with a sauna display and a good deal of information about the area posted on the walls, is open daily 9:30 A.M. until 6 P.M. (or whenever someone comes by to close it up) throughout the summer, though it is usually only staffed for the half-hour before tour departure times. If you want to take some of Finland home with you, stop in the village at **Sisu Tori,** 218/984-2155, a gift shop filled with crafts and baked goods. Outside the gift shop are several more Finnish structures, including the well-preserved **Nelimark Sauna.** Just up County Road 21 is **Timber Hall,** which locals believe is the largest freestanding log building in the United States. Regardless of its rank, at 60 feet by 144 feet it is worth a look. The **Finnish-American Summer Festival,** held the second Sunday in June, is a daylong celebration all things from the motherland including food, crafts, music, dance, and pesäpallo, a Finnish game that resembles baseball as dreamed up by the writers of *Mad Magazine.* Sticking with the Finnish theme the only lodging around is the **Finnish Heritage Homestead B&B,** 218/984-3318 or 800/863-6545, on a quiet 1901 farmstead where many of the original structures, including a wood-fired sauna, remain. Breakfast includes some Finnish selections. Rates for the five antique-filled guestrooms, one of which has a private bathroom, start at $79. The **Heritage Park Campground,** half a mile east of Sisu Tori on Salo Rd., has 10 shady campsites for $8 or $10 with electric hookups. Hiking trails here lead through the forest along the Embarrass River. The town's only restaurant is the simple and cheap **Four Corners Café,** 218/741-4200, inside the Conoco gas station across from the visitors center. It is open Tuesday–Sunday for lunch and dinner.

SUPERIOR NATIONAL FOREST— KAWISHIWI DISTRICT

Centered on Ely, the most popular entry into the Boundary Waters, surely makes Kawishiwi the forest's busiest district, though there is no shortage of solitude, especially for hikers and canoeists who travel outside the BWCAW. For additional details see the Superior National Forest overview earlier in this chapter.

Recreation

The district's most popular hike is along the beautiful **Bass Lake Trail,** six miles north of Ely on County Road 116 (the Echo Trail). The gorge holding Bass and Low lakes was once filled by much larger lakes, but in 1925 the glacial ridge separating the pair gave way, dropping the water level 55 feet in just hours. It's six miles around Bass and Dry lakes, but most hikers just head to the waterfall, about a mile in on Bass's north shore. There are campsites on Bass and several surrounding lakes. Also highly recommended is the **Secret/Blackstone Trail** out near the end of County Road 18. The five-mile path has a pair of loops around its namesake lakes. The longer and steeper back loop has numerous ridge-top vistas of lakes and bogs and a cliff well known by area rock climbers. There is a campsite just a short walk in on Blackstone Lake. The seldom-followed 0.8-mile portage into **Agassa Lake** passes through thick-forested hills and crosses a bog, making it a beautiful hike and a good wildlife-watching destination. There are also short, easy hikes at the **Fenske Lake** and **South Kawishiwi River** campgrounds, and some more excellent trails are detailed with the Boundary Waters Canoe Area Wilderness. Mountain bikers should get maps of the Forest Service's four recommended routes on little-traveled forest roads. Naturally most paddlers are here to hit the BWCAW, but canoe routes on lakes and rivers outside the wilderness do not require permits or fees and are equally beautiful. One of the most scenic and peaceful options is the 20-mile, seven-portage route running between Fenske and Bass lakes that begins 11 miles north of town along County Road 116. The dozens of backcountry campsites on this and other waterways are free of charge. Part of the forest's **Discovery Tour** auto tour runs along County Road 116. A guide booklet pointing out natural and historic sites along the way is available at the ranger station.

Camping

Fall Lake, the campground nearest to Ely (it's about 4.5 miles east on County Road 18), is the forest's largest and most developed. Many of the 66 sites have electric hookups, and this is the forest's only campground with showers and flush toilets, plus there is a swimming beach and direct access to the BWCAW. **Fenske Lake,** 10 miles up

the Echo Trail, has 15 well-spaced sites, plus a swimming beach and access to the BWCAW is nearby. South of town are the 32-site **South Kawishiwi River** and 28-site **Birch Lake** (very popular with anglers) camps, which rarely fill up. Reservations are accepted for all four.

Information

The **Kawishiwi Ranger Station,** 118 S. 4th Ave. E., 218/365-7600, in Ely is open weekdays 8 A.M.–4:30 P.M. From May through September you can also get forest-wide information at the **Kawishiwi Wilderness Station,** 218/365-7561, in the lobby of Ely's International Wolf Center, 1396 Hwy. 169. It is open daily 6 A.M.–6 P.M.

Voyageur Country

Minnesota's only national park brings hundreds of thousands of visitors to these remote forests and waters, but communing with wild bears at the Vince Shute Wildlife Sanctuary is reason alone to make the drive. Anyone with an interest in ancient Native American history will want to stop at Grand Mound, while the gateway community of International Falls has some worthy diversions.

INTERNATIONAL FALLS

Famous for its frequent mention on TV weather reports as the Lower 48's cold spot, temperatures in the Icebox of the Nation often dip in to the minus 30s Fahrenheit during the long winters; the all-time low is minus 46°. The 6,703 hardy souls who live here are rather proud of their frigid lifestyles, though you are very unlikely to encounter any of these extremes. The local Convention and Visitors Bureau (CVB), hoping to attract more visitors outside the summer months, doesn't discuss the cold very much, though they will quickly point out that the mean high temperature from June through August is an idyllic 77°. They may stay mum on the winter weather to tourists, though they actively promote the frozen north to companies who need to do cold-weather product testing. City officials, however, must also remain publicly tight-lipped about this

industry since espionage is a real concern for the companies based here.

Rainier, a quaint village of 199 with a historic Rainy Lake waterfront and Lift Bridge, sits three miles to the east on Highway 11 (turn at the giant Voyageur statue) and should be a part of any visit here.

History

As the name suggests, International Falls is tucked up along the border with Canada—its sister city of Fort Frances, Ontario, lies right over the International Bridge—though the long series of rapids that provided the second half of the name lies buried behind the hydroelectric dam. Founded in 1895 as Koochiching (it was named for the falls) the town was nearly wiped out by a fire in 1902, and the rebuilt community renamed itself the next year. Its original Algonquin moniker means Mist Over the Water referring to the thick, rainbow-filled

HOKEY SMOKE!

International Falls was the real life inspiration for Frostbite Falls, home of TV stars Rocky the Flying Squirrel and Bullwinkle J. Moose. In one episode Rocky is taken to Koochiching County Hospital.

the great Bronko Nagurski

cloud the waterfall threw up as the lake emptied into the river. Though the cold put the town on the map nationally, it is paper and tourism that keeps it going. The dam went up in 1908 and powered a paper mill on each side of the border. Today Boise Paper Solutions employs 1,150 in town and you won't just see how immense their operations are, you'll smell it too—don't worry, you get used to it quickly. Also important to the local economy are the tens of thousands of people stopping by on their way to Voyageurs National Park, which begins about ten miles to the east.

Sights

Tours of **Boise Paper Solutions,** 218/285-5011, let you see one of the world's largest and fastest papermaking machines turning out about 1,500 tons of paper per day. The free 75-minute tours are available weekdays at 8:30 A.M., 11 A.M., and 1:30 P.M. during the summer—meet at the visitors center at the corner of 2nd St. and 4th Ave. No open-toed shoes or children under age 10 are allowed, and reservations are recommended.

The Koochiching County Historical Society, 214 6th Ave., 218/283-4316, runs a pair of side-by-side museums. The excellent **Koochiching** County Historical Museum begins with the first Paleo-Indians and continues through the modern day with interesting discussions of past industries such as gold mining, fishing, and the fur trade. Highlights of the collection include a birch bark canoe, beaver felt hat, Native American crafts, and Jesuit rings. A visit here is a great way to round out your Voyageurs National Park experience. International Falls' most famous resident is commemorated in the **Bronko Nagurski Museum.** Often considered the greatest football player ever, the inaugural Pro Football Hall of Famer played both fullback and defensive tackle during nine years with the Chicago Bears in the 1930s and 1940s and was the only player to ever win All-American honors at two positions in the same year. After retirement from football and wrestling, he farmed and ran a gas station in town. Exhibits include his size-22 Hall of Fame induction ring and a copy of his first contract (for $5,000), and you can watch his exploits in a 14-minute video. The museums are open weekdays 9 A.M.–5 P.M. Admission is $2. Out in front of the museums a 26-foot **Smokey Bear** with two cubs at his feet greets visitors—locals dress them up for the winter with earmuffs, gloves, and scarves. What was once the world's largest thermometer (that honor now belongs to Baker, California, a Mojave Desert hotspot) previously told the temperature to passersby, but it has been taken down for repairs and the cost makes its future uncertain.

The private **Sportsmen's Service Wildlife Museum,** 424 3rd Ave., 218/283-2411, has about 150 Minnesota mammal and bird mounts on display including moose, wolves, lynx, lots of owls and ducks, and an albino skunk. There are also a few Native American and other historical displays. It is certainly worth a dollar. Open Mon.–Sat. 9 A.M.–4 P.M.

Most people find the free firefighting displays at the **Spot Firehouse** supper club (see Food below) interesting. The 3,000 items span toys and T-shirts to helmets and hydrants—there are even half a dozen real fire trucks.

Hawk Sightseeing, 218/286-3272, will take you on morning or evening flightseeing trips over Voyageurs National Park for $85/hour. Spotting wildlife is all but guaranteed. The floatplane can pick you up at just about any area dock and carries just one passenger.

Recreation

You can pedal, skate, walk, or ski from International Falls to Rainier and Voyageur National Park's Rainy Lake Visitor Center, a 12-mile trip, along the paved **Rainy Lake Bike Trail.** The trailhead is just east of the CVB. **Tara's Wharf,** 218/286-5699, on the waterfront in Rainier, rents bikes and paddleboats.

If you are here on a hot summer day and want to cool off, **City Beach** is located on the east side of Rainier, and there is another small, unsupervised swimming beach right in Rainier itself.

The 18-hole course overlooking the Rainy River at the **Falls Country Club,** 218/283-4491, is one of northern Minnesota's best golf courses.

Entertainment and Events

What could be more appropriate in International Falls than **Icebox Days** held the third weekend in January? Wintry events include turkey bowling, snow sculpting, cross-country ski races, a polar bear dip, and the Freeze Yer Gizzard Blizzard 10k and 5k race.

Music in the Park concerts, featuring a wide variety of local groups, take place Wednesday evenings at 7 P.M. during June and July in Smokey Bear Park.

The city's only movie theater is the **Cine 5,** 1319 3rd St., 218/283-2342.

Accommodations

Most of International Falls' hotels line Highway 53, though the fanciest is the **Holiday Inn,** 1500 Hwy. 71, 218/283-8000 or 800/331-4443, over on the shores of the Rainy River. Standard rooms start at $109, while whirlpool and river-view suites cost just a little more. Guest amenities include a pool, kiddie pool, hot tub, sauna, games, and exercise room. Also above average is the **Days Inn,** 2331 U.S. 53 S., 218/283-9441 or 800/329-7466, on the south end of town. With a whirlpool, sauna, exercise room, and prices from $75, it's a good value. The **Falls Motel,** 2101 U.S. 53 S., 218/283-8434 or 800/328-8435, is one of the city's better family-run motels, and at $55 a night it is priced cheaper than some others. There is a microwave and refrigerator in every room and a sauna for winter use.

The wonderful **Sandbay Bed & Breakfast,** 218/286-5699 or 877/724-6955, in Rainier sticks right out over Rainy Lake. All three guestrooms—priced $110–165—have private baths, kitchens, and either balconies or decks overlooking the lake. Breakfast is served just down the street at Grandma's Pantry. If you want to add a night of camping in Voyageurs National Park, Tara can arrange it.

Food

Asking local advice on where to eat usually elicits a recommendation to drive east and dine with a view at any Rainy Lake resort. In town there are some decent views at the Holiday Inn's **Riverfront Grill,** 218/283-4451, which overlooks the Rainy River and a flower garden. The dinner menu spans a raspberry chicken salad ($8) to manicotti ($10) to prime rib ($18), with a simpler sandwich menu at lunch averaging $6. Open daily for breakfast, lunch, and dinner. The Northwoods-themed **Chocolate Moose,** 2501 U.S. 53 S., 218/283-8888, has a similar menu with lower prices. Open daily for breakfast, lunch, and dinner. The **Spot Firehouse,** 1801 U.S. 53 S., 218/283-2440, was founded in 1936 by a firefighting family and is best known for the museum-sized collection of fire memorabilia, but the dining room is also highly regarded. Steak and seafood average $20, though burgers and other cheaper options are available. Open Mon.–Sat. for dinner. **Sandy's Place,** 1510 3rd Ave., 218/285-9108, is most noted for their served-anytime breakfasts. Heaping plates of omelets, pancakes, or walleye and eggs run $3–8. Open Mon.–Sat. for breakfast and lunch. With house-roasted coffees and the work of local artists on the walls, **Coffee Landing Metro,** 444 3rd St., 218/283-8316, brings a little big city to The Falls. Besides caffeine they serve some bakery and sandwiches. Open daily for breakfast, lunch, and an early dinner. There is nothing special about **Dragon China Buffet,** 218/283-2064, west of town on Hwy. 71 (in front of the International Mall), but it's there if you need some variety. The small all-you-can eat buffet is $5 at lunch and $7 for dinner. Open daily for lunch and dinner. **Tara's Wharf** on Rainier's waterfront is a popular stop for ice cream cones.

Shopping

Spruce Street Landing, a handful of small stores linked by a boardwalk in Rainier, is a fun place to stroll and shop. The **Koochiching Museums' gift shop** has authentic Native American arts and crafts and an excellent regional book selection. If you are heading into Voyageurs National Park and forgot any equipment, you can probably find it at **The Outdoorsman's Headquarters,** 1100 3rd Ave., 218/283-9337.

Information and Services

The enthusiastic **Rainy Lake/International Falls Convention and Visitors Bureau,** 301 2nd Ave., 218/283-9400 or 800/325-5766, www.rainylake.org, can find last-minute vacancies, recommend fishing guides, or answer just about any question you might have. The office is open weekdays 8 A.M.–5 P.M.

The **post office** is downtown at 400 4th St. **Coffee Landing Metro,** 444 3rd St., 218/283-

8316, has free Internet access for their customers. Canadian currency can be exchanged all over town.

Transportation

The **Falls International Airport,** 218/283-4461, just south of town, is served by **Northwest Airlink,** 218/283-4630 or 800/225-2525, which makes the 2.5-hour flight to the Minneapolis-St. Paul airport several times a day. Round-trip fares start around $200, but are much less as a segment of a longer Northwest flight. **Greyhound** buses come up from Duluth once a day and stop at the Budget Host Inn, 218/283-2577, west of downtown on Hwy. 71. If you are coming from or heading on to Canada, there is scheduled air and bus service from Fort Frances across the river. For car rental you can choose between **Avis,** 218/285-7799; **Hertz,** 218/283-4461; and **National,** 218/283-4626, all with offices out at the airport.

WEST ON HIGHWAY 11

Highway 11 hugs the sandy-banked Rainy River for most of its run through the sparsely populated and occasionally scenic border region between International Falls and Baudette. Although maps show a number of towns along the road, all but a few of them exist in name and memory only.

Grand Mound

Seventeen miles out of International Falls, at the junction of the Rainy and Big Fork rivers, is the largest Native American burial mound in the Upper Midwest. After learning about the people who built the 28-foot-tall gravesite in the Grand Mound History Center, 218/285-3332, you'll follow the trail through the old-growth forest past four smaller mounds before reaching the tree-covered behemoth. The trail continues down to the rivers, where you might see bald eagle gliding above the treetops or a fox strolling the shore. The site is open daily during the summer, plus weekends in September, 11 A.M.–5 P.M. Admission is $4.

Franz Jevne State Park

Peace and quiet are the main features of the diminutive park. Tucked into a small bend of the

Rainy River it encompasses just 118 acres, but this is one of the more scenic stretches of the Rainy and bear, wolf, and moose have all been known to wander through on occasion. A small picnic area overlooks the Sault Rapids, and anglers have foot and boat access in their search for walleye and northern. An easy three-mile hiking trail follows the Rainy before it loops back through the forest. The return half of the loop isn't nearly as scenic, so if you really liked the walk along river you might just want to retrace your steps back. The trail is groomed for cross-country skiing in the winter. The 18 sites (one electric, three walk-in) in the rustic campground are shaded and well spaced; several have covered picnic tables. There is no office so for any inquiries contact Zippel Bay State Park at 218/783-6252.

Basshenge

As you approach the turnoff to Franz Jevne State Park from the east, keep your eyes open for Basshenge, though you can't really miss it. With a name like this in the Land of 10,000 Lakes you would, of course, expect a monument to fish, but instead this work of art was the dream of Joseph Guastafeste, onetime principal double bassist with the Chicago Symphony, who has a cabin near here, and he laid 21 steel sculptures of string basses in the shape of bass clef.

VOYAGEURS NATIONAL PARK

Befitting of the Land of 10,000 Lakes, Voyageurs National Park is dominated and defined by water. Centered on four large lakes—Rainy, Kabetogama (cab a toga ma), Namakan, and Sand Point—water covers nearly 40 percent of the park's 218,055 acres. Water isn't just part of the scenery, it's the primary means of transportation, too. Except for the paths leading up to the four entry points, there are no roads in the park. To witness the hundreds of lopsided islands and slender bays or explore the rugged 75,000-acre Kabetogama Peninsula at the heart of the park, you'll have to travel by boat.

Visually Voyageurs is similar to the BWCAW, which sits just to the east, but it comes without the serenity of official wilderness designation. It

is often called America's Motorboat Park. Most people enjoy the scenery from a fishing boat, houseboat, or pontoon and the many motors—either the rumbling boats in the summer or whining snowmobiles in the winter—might affect the tranquility of your adventure. On the other hand, Voyageurs is one of the least visited national parks—more people visit Alaska's Denali National Park during the month of June than come to Voyageurs during the entire year—so it is still easy to commune with nature in peace, especially if you head out to the Kabetogama Peninsula or spend the night under the stars. Nevertheless, if you want deep wilderness head to the BWCAW; if you are looking for stunning scenery without the need for physical effort or arranging permits, Voyageurs is for you.

Human History

The French-Canadians for whom Voyageurs National Park is named first paddled through these waters in the late 17th century following routes shown them by the area's Dakota inhabitants. The first European arrival is presumed to be Jacques de Noyon, an independent fur trader who may have paddled up from Lake Superior in 1688 and built a winter outpost on Rainy Lake—though there is some doubt that he ever really came. Others followed, though the fur trade didn't truly flourish in these remote parts until the Canadian-born Pierre Gaultier de Varennes, sieur de La Vèrendrye and his party arrived on the scene in 1731. La Vèrendrye opened Fort St. Pierre and over the next three decades established a string of forts and trading posts from Rainy Lake to Winnipeg. Shortly after his arrival the Ojibwe, close allies of the French, drove the Dakota out in order to monopolize the most productive trapping lands.

While Native Americans procured the beaver and other pelts, the voyageurs transported them back to Montreal in birch bark canoes—strong and maneuverable, but light enough to be portaged around the many waterfalls and rapids. Whole fleets would paddle in from Montreal each spring bringing trade goods like guns, pots, fabric, and beads and return with their 35-foot vessels stacked high with up to two tons of bundled furs.

The roughly 1,000 miles from Montreal to Grand Portage, on the western shore of Lake Superior, was as far as they could travel in a season and still make it back before winter, so other groups of men (known as *hivernauts*) overwintered in the northwest and journeyed in from the western outposts meeting up at Grand Portage to exchange cargoes. This far more demanding western route, which passed through what is now the park, eventually expanded so deep into Canada that it also needed to be broken up, so the North West Company built Fort Lac la Pluie, across the river from International Falls. All the other major fur trading companies, including Hudson's Bay, XYZ, and American Fur Company, also based operations here at one time or another. In fact, the voyageurs' influence was so strong in these parts that the 1783 treaty ending the American Revolution specified that the American-Canadian border would follow their "customary waterway" between Lake of the Woods and Lake Superior.

The fur trade died out by 1850 due mostly to a combination of changing European fashions and the near extirpation of beaver from this part of North America. Gold fever hit Rainy Lake in 1893 and, though the finds were real, the costs of extracting the ore made it a short-lived enterprise. The mine on Little American Island, the only profitable one of the seven in the area, lasted until 1897. It was only a few years later that lumberjacks moved in to fell the valuable white pine stands. Commercial fishing, most notably for sturgeon eggs to be sold as caviar, and commercial blueberry picking also started around the turn of the 20th century, and both were very profitable. None of these industries, however, were practiced in a sustainable manner, and they all died out around the time of the Great Depression. Another short-lived but very profitable enterprise at this time was smuggling alcohol in from Canada during Prohibition. Resorts catering to anglers sprung up early in the century and, as the land healed, more and more tourists arrived. Congress made Voyageurs Minnesota's first and the nation's 36th national park in 1971.

Natural History

Voyageurs lies at the southern end of the Canadian Shield and across Minnesota's border lakes region much of this 2.7 billion-year-old bedrock—some of North America's oldest exposed rock—lies bare along the park's shorelines. The last glacier to sweep south across North America scraped away large quantities of this Precambrian layer, gouging out the area's many lakebeds. The glaciers also picked up some unbelievably large boulders in the north and deposited them in the park—some of these erratics are as big as houses and weigh 200 tons. The thin layer of soil that has accumulated over the 10,000 years since the last glaciation naturally supports a transitional boreal forest, though as a legacy of logging aspen remains the dominant tree in the park's relatively young forest. Scattered marshes, swamps, and bogs (home to insectivorous pitcher plant and sundew) sit between the many hills and outcrop ridges. Summer sees a profusion of wild berries with strawberries ripening in early July and blueberries filling out around the end of the month—most years you can pick some of both on the same trip.

Voyageurs is home to just about every animal species typical of the Northwoods. Spotting one of the park's nearly 3,000 beaver is almost guaranteed, while black bear and moose are most likely to be seen deep in the heart of the Kabetogama Peninsula. You'd have to be pretty lucky to happen upon a timber wolf, though around 50 roam these woods so you might hear one howling at night. Few of Voyageurs' 230-plus reported bird species are as beloved as the bald eagle, and the nation's symbol is frequently spied perched in trees alongside or soaring over the park's largest lakes. Other raptors you might see soaring overhead include osprey, broad-winged hawk, and turkey vulture. Out on the lakes you'll likely see common loon, great blue heron, hooded merganser, common tern, belted kingfisher, a variety of ducks, and large flocks of ring-billed and herring gulls, while spruce grouse, pileated woodpecker, boreal chickadee, scarlet tanager, ruby-throated hummingbird, and around 25 species of warbler reside across the inland forests. This is one of the best places in Minnesota to look for boreal forest birds.

Orientation and Information

Voyageurs National Park follows the Minnesota-Ontario border for 55 meandering miles. Access for most visitors is through one of the four resort areas dotting the park's periphery. Crane Lake is over at the far southeast end, while Kabetogama and Ash River sit in the middle. Rainy Lake on the northwest corner, not far from International Falls, has the only NPS Visitor Center open year-round. Each of these gateways offers lodging, food, fishing guides, water taxis, and just about anything else you could need during your trip. The northern three each have a visitors center, while Crane Lake has a sporadically open ranger station. The **Ash River Visitor Center,** 218/374-3221, and **Kabetogama Lake Visitor Center,** 218/875-2111, are both open daily 9 A.M.–5 P.M. from mid-May through the end of September. The former is housed in the historic Meadwood Lodge, a 1935 log building, while the latter has some wildlife exhibits. The **Rainy Lake Visitor Center,** 218/286-5258, with various historical exhibits, is open the same hours as the others during the summer, but stays open Wednesday–Sunday 9 A.M.–4:30 P.M. the rest of the year. There are no fees for visiting Voyageurs, though all overnight visitors require free permits. Get them at park visitors centers or self-register if the office is closed. Water-taxi service is available from resorts, outfitters, and fishing guides at each of the four gateways. Prices depend on the length of trip and number of people, but expect to pay about $50 for a short trip.

Historic and Natural Attractions

Though the red and white **Kettle Falls Hotel** sits 16 miles from the nearest road, people come from all corners of the park to stroll the grounds, have a meal or a drink in the Lumberjack Saloon, or just relax on the endless veranda. The simple, antique-filled lodge facing south toward Canada was erected on this remote border site around 1910. It is rumored to have started as a brothel and did a thriving business during Prohibition, but soon became a fashionable getaway attracting the rich and famous like Charles Lindbergh and John D. Rockefeller. Just a short walk from the hotel is the **Damtender's Cabin,** a restored 1910 log home that will be opened for tours in coming years.

Gold fever struck Rainy Lake in July of 1893 when prospector George Davis hit pay dirt on **Little American Island.** You'll learn the whole story of the Rainy Lake Gold Rush along the short, wheelchair-accessible trail, which takes you past a mineshaft, tailings piles, and other mining remnants from the only area mine that produced significant ore. Another mine can be seen on the south shore of nearby **Bushyhead Island,** and the Park Service intends to open the Kabetogama Peninsula site of Rainy Lake City, a short-lived mining boomtown, to the public in the next few years. For a glimpse of another Rainy Lake industry stop by **Oveson's Fish Camp** where an ice house, fish processing house, and camp home in use between 1958 and 1985 stand at the water's edge.

The **Ellsworth Rock Gardens** on the north shore of Kabetogama Lake features 52 terraced flower beds and over 150 geometric and animal-themed sculptures assembled out of the local granite. Built by Chicago contractor and regular summer visitor Jack Ellsworth between 1944 and 1965, this singular spot makes an ideal picnic ground.

The cliffs on the Canadian side of **Namakan Narrows,** a channel at the southeast end of Namakan Lake, feature moose, people, canoes, and other ancient pictographs. Another popular natural attraction near Crane Lake are pinkish granite **Grassy Bay Cliffs.**

You don't need your own boat to see the park. The **Sight-Sea-Er II** and **Rainy Lake** tour boats, departing from the Kabetogama Lake and Rainy Lake Visitor Centers respectively, offer a variety of tours throughout the summer season, including wildlife-watching and sunset cruises and visits to the Kettle Falls Hotel and Ellsworth Rock Gardens. Prices range $12–33 and reservations, which are highly recommended, can be made for either boat at 888/381-2873. Most resorts also do tours for their guests, and there is no shortage of companies offering boat rentals and water-taxi service. The park also offers regular ranger talks and canoeing programs. You can get information on these free (except for some of the canoe rides) interpretive programs at park visitors centers.

Well outside the park, but certainly worth a stop if you are driving by, is the 16-foot-long **Lake Kabetogama Walleye.** Climb up into the saddle for a one-of-a-kind photo-op. It sits at the junction of Highway 53 and County Road 122.

Boating

As stated above, most park visitors get around in a motorboat of some kind (personal watercraft are forbidden), though some boaters choose to sail. All of the attractions listed above are only accessible from the water, but of course part of the appeal of Voyageurs is that everywhere you go is beautiful. The most important advice for boaters is to be sure you understand the U.S. Coast Guard buoy system and can read navigation maps, which are sold at the visitors centers. Use great care if motoring beyond the buoys since many rocks and reefs are unmarked, plus water levels change considerably over the summer. For weather forecasts you can tune to local radio stations 640 AM, 1230 AM, 93.1 FM, 99.5 FM, or 104.1 FM. Park rangers monitor marine band 16 for emergencies. Minnesota law only requires a life jacket be in your boat, but these are big lakes, which means big waves, so wearing them is always advisable.

There are marinas, rentals, and free public boat ramps in each of the four gateways. The average cost of a small fishing boat is around $65 per day, while a pontoon goes for about $140. Several Crane Lake resorts have rentals docked on Mukooda Lake, an inland lake only accessible by a short portage.

Paddling

If you want to paddle through deep wilderness without another soul around, you are probably better off dipping your oar in the nearby Boundary Waters Canoe Area Wilderness than at Voyageurs. That said, you do not have to be a horsepower addict to enjoy the park, and there really is some excellent paddling here—*Canoe and Kayak* magazine has named it one of the top-ten sea kayaking destinations in the country. Plus, some of the BWCAW's drawbacks don't

come into play here: there are few portages and with no permits or quotas you can just show up and go. Most paddlers start at Ash River because it has the easiest access to quiet back bays, though the north end of Kabetogama Lake, directly accessible from the Woodenfrog Campground, has lots of small islands and relatively few boaters. A 75-mile circumnavigation of the Kabetogama Peninsula—possible with two short portages— takes about a week.

Canoe rentals are available at each of the four gateways, plus a pair of outfitters can set you up with everything you need for an extended trip: **Voyageurs Adventures,** 218/875-2037 or 877/465-2925, at Kabetogama; and **Anderson's Canoe Outfitters,** 218/993-2287 or 800/777-7186, at Crane Lake. Voyageurs specializes in sea kayaks and offers various guided trips throughout the park, from a three-hour sunset paddle ($35) to an overnight camping trip in Lost Bay ($135), while Anderson's location lets you easily fold the BWCAW into your trip.

One of the best ways to experience the park with a paddle is by taking advantage of the **Boats on Interior Lakes** program. The Park Service has placed canoes and rowboats on eight Kabetogama Peninsula lakes (Locator, Quill, Ek, Cruiser, Little Shoepack, Shoepack, Brown, and Peary), and the first-come, first-served boats can be used for day trips or overnight journeys. The cost is $10 per party per day and reservations (by phone or in person) can be made up to a week in advance. You must bring your own life jacket—if you aren't traveling with one you can rent one for a couple of bucks from area resorts.

Hiking

Voyageurs is all about the water, but if you prefer to travel by foot you will not be disappointed here. The **Cruiser Lake Trail,** Voyageurs' most adventurous hike, cuts 9.5 miles across the east end of the Kabetogama Peninsula and, together with its adjoining trails, passes a dozen lakes and nearly as many campsites—this is the best backpacking destination in the park. Though hilly, the route is only moderately challenging; still, because of the peninsula's remoteness you should have some basic outdoors skills before venturing out here. The primary path connects Kabetogama Lake's Lost Bay (about a three-mile paddle with one short portage from the Ash River Visitor Center) to Rainy Lake's Anderson Bay climbing ridges for truly remarkable panoramas—you'll be looking into Canada from the northern end of the trail—and dropping down to cross beaver dams, crystal clear trout streams, and patches of wild blueberries and strawberries. Wildlife abounds on this remote peninsula, and you might spot any of the park's most exciting species. Peary, Brown, Cruiser, and Ek lakes are all represented in the Boats on Interior Lakes program (see Paddling). Cruiser Lake, (perched 300 feet above Rainy Lake it is the park's highest), near the trail's midpoint makes a good day-trip destination, or, if you want to do the whole trail in a day, you could arrange for a water taxi to pick you up at the far end. Several other moderately difficult paths with similarly stunning scenery branch off the Cruiser Lake Trail, including the highly recommended **Anderson Bay Trail** at the northeast end. The two-mile loop leads atop the Anderson Bay Cliffs, some rising 70 feet above the water, for some magnificent long-distance views. The 2.5-mile **Beast Lake Trail** enters the Cruiser Lake system from Namakan Lake's narrow Mica Bay, and the mile-long **Jorgens Lake Trail** at the south end passes a pair of peaceful lakes.

Over on the west end of the peninsula are the **Locator Lake Trail** and the **Black Bay Beaver Pond Trail.** The former starts on Kabetogama Lake and crosses two miles of beautiful country inhabited by countless beaver. The moderately difficult (very difficult if you are shouldering a canoe) path climbs a ridge and drops through a ravine before reaching its namesake, part of a long, narrow chain of lakes through the heart of the peninsula. There's a day-use picnic area and rental boats (see Boats on Interior Lakes program above) at the end. You can probably figure out what's at the end of the Black Bay Beaver Pond Trail, a 1.25-mile-long round-trip starting just across Black Bay Narrows from the Rainy Lake Visitor Center. Many of the peninsula's portage trails, particularly **Gold, Cranberry Creek,** and **Ryan Lake,** cross through some beautiful scenery.

Over on the mainland the 24-mile **Kabetogama-Ash River Trail** (Kab-Ash for short), which links these two resort areas, accounts for over half of all the park's trail miles, and a variety of forest types and wetland boardwalks make for great wildlife viewing. There is talk of expanding the trail all the way down to Crane Lake—if this ever happens it will be a truly fantastic trek. There are also some short trails at each of Voyageurs' four gateways. Rainy Lake's option is the **Oberholtzer Interpretive Trail,** an easy 1.5-mile route that covers a cattail marsh, pine forest, and scenic views of Black Bay; the first half is wheelchair-accessible. The slightly hilly 2.3-mile **Echo Bay Trail,** a few miles northwest of the Kabetogama Lake Visitor Center, loops through a mix of aspen and conifer stands. You'll pass many areas flooded by beavers and might spot wolf tracks. The Ash River area's **Blind Ash Bay Trail** is arguably Voyageurs' most beautiful short mainland path. The hilly 2.5-mile round-trip follows a rocky ridge—there are some great views of Kabetogama Lake from atop it—and ends up looking out over the narrow namesake bay. You'll see plenty of fire-scarred trees along the route. Two scenic overlooks around the Ash River Visitor Center also have short, easy trails. Though not actually part of the park, Vermilion Gorge and Vermilion Falls, a pair of natural attractions near Crane Lake, are also worthy destinations; see Superior National Forest-LaCroix District for details.

Winter Recreation

Very few of the park's 250,000 annual visitors come when there is snow on the ground, and most of those are here to snowmobile since this is one of the few national parks where snowmobiles are allowed. Over 110 miles of well-marked trail wind over the park's frozen lakes and connect to the extensive trail system extending beyond the park; trail maps are available from the Rainy Lake Visitor Center or any area resort. Sleds are not allowed anywhere on land except for marked safety portages and the popular, though ungroomed, Chain of Lakes Scenic Trail cutting across the Kabetogama Peninsula. Pressure ridges and slush are two potential hazards, and riders should pay attention to trail signs to avoid these hazards. The speed limit on the lakes is 45 mph—it is enforced!

Despite the predilection for horsepower, silent sport lovers are not completely overlooked. The principal cross-country ski route is the **Black Bay Trail,** a nine-mile series of groomed loops for all abilities on the northwest corner of Kabetogama Peninsula, just across from the Rainy Lake Visitor Center—follow the **Rainy Lake Ice Road** to reach the trailhead. Also starting near the Rainy Lake Visitor Center is the Koochiching State Forest's **Tilson Creek Trail,** a challenging 10-mile set of loops with a spur leading right to the visitor center's upper parking lot. Also groomed for skiing are the park's Echo Bay Trail and possibly in the future the Kab-Ash Trail. Although, the beauty of snowshoes is that you can go just about anywhere, the Park Service packs three snowshoe trails to make the going that much easier. Besides the Blind Ash Bay and Oberholtzer trails described under Hiking, there is also the winter-only **Sullivan Bay Trail,** an easy 1.5-mile path starting just south of the Ash River Visitor Center. The Rainy Lake Visitor Center rents skis and snowshoes.

Camping

Your Voyageurs experience will be excellent during the day, but it isn't complete without a night under the stars. All 126 of the park's campsites are accessible only by boat, and all but a few are equipped with a fire ring, picnic table, privy, tent pads, and bear-proof food locker. The first-come, first-served sites are only intended for use by a single party, and the regular sites accommodate two tents (some larger ones can handle four). A fully accessible campsite on Namakan Lake can be reserved through the Kabetogama Lake Visitor Center. You are also allowed to pitch a tent at undeveloped sites elsewhere in the park as long as you stay 200 yards from any official campsites and a quarter mile from any other developed site. Camping is free, though each party must fill out a self-registration overnight permit. While it should be standard practice anywhere in Minnesota's Northwoods, it is especially important to keep a clean camp at Voyageurs so as not to attract bears—if no food locker is available be sure

to properly hang all food-scented items in a tree (ten feet up and four feet from the trunk).

If you are staying on the mainland many area resorts have RV parking, though the pair of DNR-run campgrounds are your best bet. The beautiful and popular **Woodenfrog Campground,** 218/757-3274, has 61 widely spaced sites on Lake Kabetogama. Also on-site are a swimming beach, two-mile nature trail, interpretive center, and picnic site. The **Ash River Campground,** 218/757-3274, has nine less scenic sites. Both charge $9 per night.

Houseboats

This increasingly popular option for exploring Voyageurs lets you enjoy the wilderness with all the comforts of home. No experience (or license) is needed to drive a houseboat, and the rental company will set you up with everything you need from food and maps to the required fishing boat if you don't have your own. The NPS maintains designated mooring sites with fire rings throughout the park, or you can overnight at one of the resort areas. Currently four companies can set you up with a floating cabin and, according to the National Park Service, all are tightly-run operations. **Voyagaire Houseboats,** 218/993-2266 or 800/882-6287, at Crane Lake is the largest, while **Ebel's Voyageur Houseboats,** 218/374-3571 or 800/253-5475, operates out of Ash River. Both **Northernaire Houseboats,** 218/286-5221 or 800/854-7958, and **Rainy Lake Houseboats,** 218/286-5391 or 800/554-9188, operate on Rainy Lake and are a bit cheaper than the other two. Prices range anywhere from about $225 a day for the basic boat, which sleeps 2–4 people comfortably, to nearly $5,000 a week for the most luxurious model with private bedrooms for a dozen people, hot tubs, entertainment centers, air-conditioning, and other top-notch touches. Spring and fall discounts are as high as 20 percent, and all but Voyagaire have substantial midweek discounts during the summer.

Accommodations

A night in the historic **Kettle Falls Hotel,** 218/374-4404 or 888/534-6835, (see Historic and

Natural Attractions above) is a highlight for many park visitors. The 12 antique-filled rooms in the main lodge share three baths and cost $70 per night, while their modern villas sleep up to eight and cost $140–250 per night and $650–1,250 per week—the villas require a three-day minimum for most of the year. Canoes, kayaks, boats, and everything an angler could need is available, and a shuttle service runs from the Sunset Resort at Ash River. Kettle Falls is only open mid-May through September.

Another 60 lodging options sit on the periphery of the park. Named for its 50-acre home on Rainy Lake **Wind Song Island,** 218/286-5600, offers people with money to burn a chance to get out in the wild without giving up an ounce of luxury. The four rustic but modern cabins are all gorgeously decorated with custom-designed log furniture and hand-woven rugs. Each comes with a canoe, motorboat, and gas grill, and all but one has a private dock. The two- to five-bedroom cabins start at $2,550 per week. Wind Song is only open mid-May through October. The far more casual **Thunderbird Lodge,** 218/286-3151 or 800/351-5133, out near the tip of the peninsula has great Rainy Lake views from most of its quarters. Lakeside lodge rooms start at $74 a night, while the two- to three-bedroom cabins range $150–225 per night and $695–1,099 per week—during the summer cabin rentals require a three-day minimum. Guests get fishing boat rentals and free canoes and paddleboats.

Kabetogama's **Sandy Point Lodge,** 218/875-2615 or 800/777-8595, is a simple, family-friendly fishing resort out at the end of the road. Two-bedroom cabins start at $135/day and $735/week, lodge rooms are $80/day and $475/week, and RV campsites go for $26/day and $160/week. Amenities include a sauna and sandy beach.

Ironically, the largest of the dozen resorts around Crane Lake is also one of the most peaceful. **Nelson's Resort,** 218/993-2295 or 800/433-0743, family-run since 1931, sits along 1.5 miles of private lakeshore over on the quiet end of Crane Lake. Weekly rates for the 27 classic log cabins start at $1,000 for a one-bedroom. Facilities include a wonderful swimming beach, hiking trail, sauna, shuffleboard, and a vegetable garden used to prepare the regular Thursday Swedish Smorgasbord ($18 and open to the public) and other dinners. Nelson's is only open from mid-May through September. The **Pine Ridge Motel,** 218/993-2265 or 888/310-4225, is completely modern inside, but looking at the log exterior you can still imagine it as the trading post-fish shop-bar that it was back in the middle of the 20th century when this was still a truly wild corner of the country. The four comfy rooms cost $69 per night.

There is no single resort association for the park's four gateways, so if you want additional lodging information contact **Crane Lake Visitor & Tourism Bureau,** 800/362-7405, www.visitcranelake.com; **Ash River Trail Commercial Club,** 800/950-2061, www.ashriver.com; **Kabetogama Lake Association,** 800/524-9085, www.kabetogama.com; or **International Falls Convention & Visitors Bureau,** 800/325-5766, www.rainylake.org.

ORR

Far from Voyageurs National Park, Orr is nevertheless the gateway to these famous waters since Highway 53 shuttles just about every park visitor through the surprisingly busy town of 250. The **Orr Travel Information Center,** 4429 U.S. 53, 218/757-3932 or 800/357-9255, is a convenient place to stop and get national park and other regional tourism information. The center is open daily 9 A.M.–6 P.M. during the summer, with hours dropping down to Thursday and Saturday 10 A.M.–4 P.M. and Friday 10 A.M.–5 P.M. the rest of the year. The visitors center is also the site of the **Orr Bog Walk,** a half-mile accessible boardwalk through a variety of wetland habitats, including a tamarack swamp and a black spruce bog. Naturalists sometimes lead guided walks during the summer.

The **Vince Shute Wildlife Sanctuary,** 218/757-0172, one of Minnesota's most remarkable attractions, sits all the way across Pelican Lake. Vince ran a logging camp in these remote woods starting in the 1930s and, like most others living in the wilderness at the time,

THE ARROWHEAD

© TIM BEWER

Vince Shute Wildlife Sanctuary

he routinely shot bears. Eventually though, he figured out that the lumbering giants weren't vicious, just hungry, so he started feeding them in a clearing outside the camp. Soon the "Bear Man," as he became known, had earned a special relationship with the bears, and they no longer feared each other's presence. As Vince's health deteriorated he sought a way to protect his bears' future, and the American Bear Association was formed to not only protect this 360-acre refuge but "to promote the well-being of the black bear through a better understanding of its behavior, biology, and habitat needs." Each day around 30–50 black bears come to eat the food provided for them here and, though it seems somewhat zoolike, these are truly wild bears who only tolerate the presence of humans within the two-acre clearing at the heart of the sanctuary—they remain naturally fearful and elusive everywhere else they wander. From the elevated viewing deck you can watch the young hang out in trees, while the adults roam around eating and resting. Trained naturalists are on hand to answer your questions. Call about their special hiking, photography, and Breakfast with the Bears opportunities. To reach the reserve, head 13 miles west

on County Road 23 and follow the signs. The reserve is open Tuesday–Sunday (plus holiday Mondays) 5 P.M.–dusk during the summer; it does not open during heavy rains. Sundays are the best day to visit since it has by far the smallest crowds. Admission is free, but they really do need your donations.

Most other local tourism activity is focused on 10,945-acre Pelican Lake. About a dozen small, family-run resorts sit on Pelican's wild shore, and the friendly **Deer Lodge,** 218/757-3134, at the lake's quiet back end is as good as any. Rates for the four modern cabins start at $980 a week for a two-bedroom, and they have boats and ice houses for rent. The fanciest lodging in the area is the new lakeside **AmericInn,** 4675 U.S. 53, 218/757-3613 or 800/634-3444, just north of town. Besides the small indoor water park, the hotel features a pool, whirlpool, sauna, and a dock. Standard rooms start at $90, and suites with whirlpools, fireplaces, and balconies are available. If B&Bs are more your style there's the **Hundred Acre Woods,** 5048 Old Hwy. 53, 218/757-0070, a modern home about three miles north of town. The pair of Northwoods-themed guest rooms—there's a sauna in one and a double whirlpool tub in the other—go for $99 and $115 a night. For a meal, most locals will direct you to the **Orr Café,** 4549 U.S. 53, 218/757-3355, where you can get a filling, home-cooked meal for as little as $4. Open daily for breakfast, lunch, and dinner. **Greyhound** buses stop next door at the T. Pattenn Café, 218/757-3908, on their way between International Falls and Duluth. Across the highway you'll find the small **Bois Forte Native Arts & Crafts,** 218/757-3430, which is certainly worth a stop if you have an interest in these things.

SUPERIOR NATIONAL FOREST—LACROIX DISTRICT

The forest's most overlooked district runs along the Canadian border in the the forest's remote north-west corner. For additional details see the Superior National Forest overview earlier in this chapter.

Recreation

Two trails near the Crane Lake resort area, one of the gateways to Voyageurs National Park, lead to wonderful spots on the Vermilion River. The namesake destination of the **Vermilion Gorge Trail,** a three-mile round-trip starting behind Voyagaire Houseboats right in Crane Lake, features sheer granite cliffs with white-water rapids hitting Class V during high water. The fairly easy path is surfaced with gravel most of the way, and interpretive panels discuss the area's human history. Farther up the river is a small picnic area and accessible overlook of **Vermilion Falls** where the river shoots through a ten-foot crack in the rock. From the parking lot a half-mile trail hugs the river past some wild rice beds and "the chute," a stretch of white water—this walk is as scenic, if not more so, than the view of the falls. The six-mile **Astrid Lake Trail** starting at the Lake Jeanette Campground skirts five lakes, crosses a black spruce bog filled with car-nivores pitcher plants, passes some huge boulders dropped here during the last Ice Age, and features half a dozen lakeside campsites. Also see the **Herriman Lake Trail** in the Boundary Waters Canoe Area Wilderness section.

Besides the BWCAW there is fantastic

© TIM BEWER

the Vermilion River in the Superior National Forest

THE ARROWHEAD

paddling on the **Vermilion River,** which flows 39 miles along the western edge of the forest from Lake Vermilion up to Crane Lake. There are many rapids, including some unrunnable waterfalls (well-worn portages take you around) along this wild, cliff-lined waterway, though these lie between long stretches with a barely perceptible current. The campsites and scenery make it a great choice for overnight trips. For some easier paddling, put in to the **Johnson Lake** canoe route, 23 miles northeast of Orr at the end of Forest Road 203. The only access is a half-mile portage, but after that streams connect the trio of narrow, winding lakes with seven campsites on their islands and shorelines. There are two more campsites a few miles down the road on little Franklin Lake, reached by a mile-long portage. You can also portage along the Astrid Lake hiking trail to connect those lakes and the namesake river of the **Hunting Shack** canoe route.

If you prefer seeing nature from behind a windshield, stop by the ranger stations in Cook or Ely and pick up the *Discovery Tour* booklet. It will guide you on a pair of auto tours—one focusing on the Crane Lake area and the other following the Vermilion River and County Road 116 (the Echo Trail) down to Ely—pointing out historic and natural sites along the way.

Camping

The LaCroix District's two campgrounds lie along County Road 116 (the Echo Trail) in the general vicinity of Crane Lake. Both are very good and accept reservations. Because all 12 of its campsites (including the two walk-ins) overlook the lake and most are right next to the shore, **Lake Jeanette** has the highest occupancy rate in the forest. The **Echo Lake** camp has 24 sites plus a beach, dock, and playground and rarely fills up.

Information

The **LaCroix Ranger Station,** 320 N. U.S. 53, 218/666-0020, is located in Cook. It is open daily 6 A.M.–6 P.M. from May through September and weekdays 8 A.M.–4:30 P.M. the rest of the year.

The Iron Range

Though not the only iron range in Minnesota, the Mesabi Range gave up far more ore than the Vermilion and Cuyuna combined and is the only one still worked. A land pocked by massive open pit scars and enormous rusty scrap rock hills, many people dismiss the Iron Range as a tourist destination when, in fact, this is one of Minnesota's most interesting regions. Today the mining industry employs about 4,500 people, a far cry from the 15,000 working here as recently as the 1980s. Mines continue to downsize and close—most recently the LTV Steel Mining Co. shut down their Hoyt Lakes operations in 2001—while former miners talk about how many years they would have had on the job, if they hadn't been laid off. Some parents still give their children the same old advice that they and their grandparents heard in their younger years—get a good education so you can leave—but things are changing. The population's strong work ethic has attracted new industries like manufacturing and call centers to the Range in recent years, and there is talk of developing modern "electric minimills" to produce steel right here at the source. Some people believe this technological revolution could make the Iron Range the center of the steel world. Despite the changes, unemployment remains above the state average and city populations continue to decline.

Although mining will likely continue to fade—and very well could disappear due to cheap foreign steel imports—it remains a vital part of the future. As the region turns to tourism for survival its mining heritage rests at the forefront. The operational and retired mines have become fascinating tourist attractions, and you can watch 37-cubic yard shovels loading 240-ton production trucks at the still operational pits. Environmentalists might cringe, but even the most ardent Luddites are likely to be awed by the scale of it all. Back in the early 20th century, the new mining jobs attracted immigrants from across Europe making the Range nearly as diverse a melting pot as New York City, and that ethnic heritage remains strong here as the various festivals, churches, and menu items will attest. A new travel option, the **Mesabi Trail,** will stretch 132 miles between Grand Rapids and Ely, making it one of the longest paved recreational trails in the world. Eighty miles of trail have been completed so far, and construction through all of the towns featured here, plus the Giants Ridge Resort, should be finished by the end of 2004. A two-day ($3) or annual ($12) Wheel Pass is required for adult users and can be purchased at area businesses or self-service stations at trail access points.

The **Iron Trail Convention & Visitors Bureau,** 403 N. 1st St., 218/749-8161 or 800/777-8497, www.irontrail.org, based in Virginia is one of the best-run tourism organizations in the state, and if you have a particular interest in something—like bird-watching or fishing or shopping—they've probably got a brochure and/or a webpage about it.

HIBBING

Hibbing's a good ol' town.

Bob Dylan, My Life in a Stolen Moment

With just over 17,000 residents Hibbing, "The Iron Ore Capital of the World," is by far the largest Iron Range city. Frank Hibbing founded his town in 1893 on the spot where he discovered iron ore, but with money and people pouring into nearby Virginia, it got off to a very slow start. The roads were poor, drinking water was scarce, and a nationwide financial panic put most people out of work. A couple years later, however, several mines were operating around the village and its existence was secure, but the location was not. By 1915 Hibbing was home to 20,000 people and had a thriving downtown, but the mines were eating their way toward the city from several directions and the Oliver Mining Co. decided that the town had to be moved and so, beginning in 1919, most of the city was transferred to the present site, two miles south. As a payoff the company developed the new downtown; provided low interest loans to families; and built

many civic buildings including a hospital, Village Hall, and high school.

Many famous people have called Hibbing home, including Roger Maris, Kevin McHale, and Vincent Bugliosi, but by far the city's most famous former resident is Robert Allen Zimmerman, known to the rest of the world as Bob Dylan. Bob was born in Duluth in 1941 and his upper-middle-class family moved to Hibbing to run an appliance store when Bob was five years old. After graduating from Hibbing High School in 1959, he moved to Minneapolis and briefly attend the University of Minnesota before ending up in New York City, where he melded folk and rock music, reinventing both in the process. Dylan rarely discusses his Minnesota past and, except for his 10-year high school reunion and the occasional funeral, he has rarely returned—one local theory attributes this to being ashamed of the many lies he told about his boyhood when he first gained fame. Though the city has done little to promote its Dylan history, a slow trickle of fans still make a pilgrimage here. Plans for a Bob Dylan museum have been proposed several times before, and it is certain to happen someday. Ironically his biggest fans are surely hoping that they can't visit it for a long time since Bob has specifically requested that it wait until after his death.

Sights
Hibbing's **Hull Rust Mahoning Mineview** overlooks the world's largest operational open pit iron ore mine and one of the largest mines of any kind, period. Since the first ore was shipped in 1895, more than two billion tons of earth have been removed, creating a cavity over three miles long, 1.5 miles wide, and 600 feet deep. At its World War II peak, around one quarter of all the ore mined in the United States came out of the 30 separate mines that comprised the "Grand Canyon of the North." The Mesabi Range's first strip mine remains one of the few still in operation, and the Hibbing Taconite Company still extracts eight million tons of ore a year. Volunteers, including some retired miners, staff the little visitors center and are glad to answer your questions, plus old mining equipment is on display outside, including a truck that could haul 170 tons;

the trucks in the mine today carry 240. The building is open daily 9 A.M.–6 P.M. from mid-May through September, though the overlook area remains open year-round—if the gate is closed you can walk down. Admission is free. To reach the National Historic Landmark, follow 3rd Avenue East north from downtown for two miles. Two-hour mine tours are available from mid-June through August on Wednesday and Thursday and cost $5. They depart at noon from Iron World Discovery Center in nearby Chisholm, and reservations (218/254-7959 or 800/372-6437) are recommended. Children must be age 10 or older.

The **Hibbing Historical Museum,** 218/263-8522, is small, but definitely worth visiting to see the scale model of North Hibbing as it was in 1913, shortly before the move. The museum is in the lower level of the Hibbing Memorial Building, at the corner of 23rd St. and 5th Ave. E. It is open Monday–Saturday 9 A.M.–4:30 P.M. during the summer, and weekdays 10 A.M.–3 P.M. the rest of the year. Admission is $2. While there pick up the Historical Walks brochure, which details 22 noteworthy buildings around downtown. One of these is **Hibbing High School,** 800 E. 21st St. Education was a priority for the immigrant miners and, as part of the payoff for relocating the city, citizens demanded the best school possible. Construction on the castlelike structure began in 1920; three years and $3,927,325 later the "Palace in the Wilderness" was complete. The remarkable edifice features marble floors, brass railings and doorknobs, murals, statuary, and other ornate interior details, though the coup de grace is the 1,800-seat auditorium—a nearly exact replica of New York City's Capitol Theater, the city's grandest opera house of that age. Its Barton vaudeville organ has 1,949 pipes and is one of just two left in existence, while the crystal chandeliers are valued at $250,000 each. During the summer the building is generally open during the day, and you can just pop in anytime to look around—the auditorium is in the south wing, and the janitors are used to pointing people the right way. You can usually take a look during the school year, too, but stop by the visitors center first to ask.

In 1914 Carl Wickman began shuttling people between Hibbing and the new community of Alice for 15 cents in his Hupmobile car. This simple two-mile route was the beginning of Greyhound Bus Lines, and the whole story is told in the **Greyhound Bus Museum,** 218/263-5814. The collection includes everything from historic baggage tags and belt buckles to one bus from each decade up to the 1980s, including Wickman's original car. The museum is on the way to the Hull-Rust-Mahoning Mineview and is open Monday–Saturday 9 A.M.–5 P.M. and Sunday 1–5 P.M. from mid-May through September. Admission is $3.

There are a handful of **Bob Dylan Sites** that fans will want to seek out. For most of his life in Hibbing, Bob lived in the large square home at 2425 7th Ave. E. (on the corner with 25th St., not 24th St. as obsessed fans would wish). The family is used to people stopping by for a look and will even take your photo in front if they are around, but that doesn't mean it's okay to ring the bell and ask to look inside. You may get that chance down the road though, since the current owners plan to open the house as a B&B someday. The closest thing there is to a museum is the **Bob Dylan Exhibit** in the basement of the Hibbing Public Library, 2020 5th Ave. E., 218/262-1038. Many posters, records, news clippings, and yearbook photos are always on display. The library is open Monday–Thursday 9 A.M.–8 P.M. and Friday–Saturday 9 A.M.–5 P.M., though they do not open on Saturdays during the summer. Another shrine of sorts, and a worthy stop for Dylanphiles, is **Zimmy's,** 531 E. Howard St., a sports bar decorated with Dylan photos and posters (the tattered, autographed L. A. Lakers cap, donated by Bob's mom, is their pride and joy), plus some T-shirts and other items are for sale. Finally, die-hard fans can have a look at the **Moose Lodge,** 421 1/2 E. Howard St., where many of Bob's early bands—The Golden Chords, The Shadow Blasters, Elston Gunn and the Rock Boppers, and The Satin Tones—performed. To see inside, attend the Friday night fish fry.

Recreation

Carey Lake Park, four miles east of town on 25th Street, has 10 miles of trails looping around and along the undeveloped lake. They are open for hiking and biking in the summer, but are used primarily by cross-country skiers; ski rentals are available on winter weekends. The park also has a beach, fishing pier, and some nice picnic spots.

Entertainment and Events

The **Paulucci Space Theatre,** 218/262-6720, presents large-format films and planetarium shows on a 40-foot-diameter domed screen. There are shows daily during the summer and Wednesday–Sunday the rest of the year. The theater is located on the Hibbing Community College campus at 1502 E. 23rd St. The Wednesday night planetarium presentation is free, while all others are $4.

Dylan Days is held the week of May 24th (Bob's birthday) and features Dylan trivia, karaoke, and art works; a poetry contest; and a tour of Dylan haunts. The city's biggest bash is the **Mines and Pines Jubilee** held for nine days over the middle of July. Events include a parade, fireworks, arts and crafts fair, and ice cream social.

Accommodations

The best hotel in town is the **Hibbing Park Hotel,** 1402 E. Howard St., 218/262-3481 or 800/262-3481, where rooms are $73 and guests can use the large pool, whirlpool, sauna, and exercise room. South of town the **Super 8,** 1411 40th St. E., 218/263-8982 or 800/800-8000, charges $61. If money is the only consideration, Hibbing has a many run-down rooming houses. The most presentable and best located is the **Stover House,** 2113 5th Ave. E., 218/263-9819, which mostly does weekly and monthly rentals, but they keep a few rooms available for single nights. The price is $27.

Hibbing's only B&B, the **Adams House,** 201 E. 23rd St., 218/263-9742, is a deceptively large 1927 English Tudor with a screened porch, fitness room, and rec. room with a pool table. The five guestrooms, two with private bath and one kitchenette, are tastefully decorated with antiques and run $80–100.

Food

More than just a Dylan shrine, the **Atrium Restaurant and Zimmy's Grill,** 531 E. Howard St., 218/626-6145, serves the best food in town.

The wide-ranging selection spans burgers to pizza, but Jamaica jerk chicken and tempura shrimp set it apart from the competition. Prices run $6–18 and they are open daily for lunch and dinner.

Another good downtown restaurant is the **Old Howard Saloon and Eatery,** 413 E. Howard St., 218/262-1031. It's a beautiful building with original pressed tin ceilings and even the modern touches maintain the historic feel. The menu includes the usual American entrées, though vegetarians need not fear the "Where Beef is King" motto since they have a few pastas as well. Most items fit into the $5–15 range. Open daily for breakfast, lunch and dinner.

Bach Yen, 2510 1st Ave., 218/263-3647, is one of the best Chinese restaurants outside of the Twin Cities. Dishes range $7–13. Open weekdays for lunch and dinner, and Sat. just for dinner.

It's just a no-nonsense bar, but many locals swear by the hamburgers at **Tuffy's,** 2314 1st Ave., 218/262-1021. They are served daily for lunch and dinner.

Visit the **Sunrise Bakery,** 1813 3rd Ave. E., 218/263-4985, for pasties, potica, porketta, ravioli, and other tastes of the Iron Range. This Hibbing tradition, opened in 1913, also makes deli sandwiches and most of it is surprisingly cheap. Open Mon.–Sat. for breakfast and lunch.

Shopping

A pair of antique stores, **Remember When,** 218/263-8720, and **Antiques on Howard,** 218/362-8449, face each other across Howard Street at 4th Avenue West. **Howard Street Booksellers,** 115 E. Howard St., 218/262-5206, has a little of everything on the shelves.

Information and Services

Hibbing's **Tourist Information Center,** 1202 E. Howard St., 218/262-4166, is staffed by retired women who love to share stories about the town's old days and are your best source of area information. During the summer they are open Monday–Saturday 9 A.M.–5 P.M., and weekdays 10 A.M.–4 P.M. the rest of the year. The staff at the **Hibbing Area Chamber of Commerce,** 211 E. Howard St., 218/262-3895 or 800/444-2246, www.hibbing.org, knows next to nothing about their town, but you can pick up some brochures. They are open weekdays 8–4:30 P.M. The Hull Rust Mahoning Mineview and library also stock area tourism brochures.

Transportation

The **Chisholm-Hibbing Airport,** 218/262-2451, is served by **Northwest Airlink,** 218/262-1391, a couple of times a day. The round-trip fare from the Twin Cities starts at about $200, much less if it's a segment of a longer Northwest flight. Ironically, Greyhound buses no longer come here, but **Lorenz** makes the trip between Minneapolis and Virginia once a day, stopping at the Country Kitchen, 2520 E. Beltline, 218/263-3689. If you need to rent a car you've got **Enterprise,** 218/262-1615, and **Hertz,** 218/262-4528, to choose from. For a cab call **Hibbing Taxi,** 218/263-5065.

AROUND HIBBING

Chisholm

If Walt Disney had been an iron miner instead of a cartoonist Disneyland would have looked a lot

like the **Ironworld Discovery Center,** 218/254-7959 or 800/372-6437. Ironworld, overlooking the massive Glen Mine, is the best place to get the full story on the history and methods of mining in Minnesota—museum displays start at the geological formation of the state and proceed to the present—but Ironworld's exhibits also look at the Range's rich ethnic heritage. Costumed interpreters demonstrate bygone customs and traditions at a fur trappers cabin, American Indian encampment, traditional sod-roofed Sami home, and pioneer homestead. Many weekends see heritage events like Festival Finlandia and Polkafest, plus there are daily music performances and craft demonstrations. The ethnic celebration continues with the dining; order gyros, calzones, fry bread, sarmas, and pasties at the Melting Pot food court, or see what ethnicity is represented at the changing buffet in the dining room. Also at the park you can research your roots in the Iron Range Research Center, one of the Upper Midwest's largest genealogical and local history collections; visit a well-done Civilian Conservation Corps museum; ride a genuine electric trolley; and finish

a traditional Sami home, Ironworld

© TIM BEWER

the day off with a round at Pellet Pete's 19-hole miniature golf course. Ironworld is open daily 9:30 A.M.–5 P.M. (later during some special events) from the end of May through September, and they may open up on weekends further into the fall. The research center stays open year-round. Admission is $8 (though it is reduced to $5 on May weekdays and September weekends). Across from the entrance to Ironworld is the 81-foot **Iron Man Statue,** which is claimed to be the third largest freestanding statue in the nation, behind only the St. Louis Arch and the Statue of Liberty. The miner, holding a pick and shovel, honors those who worked the Mesabi, Vermilion, and Cuyuna Ranges.

Often overlooked by visitors to Ironworld, and understandably so, is the **Minnesota Museum of Mining,** 218/254-5543, which doesn't appear to have changed much since it opened in 1954. The small castlelike building houses most of the mining displays, while outside is a simulated underground mineshaft. The surrounding park is a mining graveyard of sorts, with all kinds of vehicles and implements lying about. There is also a collection of various historical items from old farm tools to old fire engines. Fans of the artist F. Lee Jaques will want to take a look at the model railroad diorama he designed. The museum, along Highway 73, is open daily 10 A.M.–5 P.M. from the beginning of May to early September. Admission is $3.

If you enjoy cars, swing by the **Classic Car Museum,** 305 W. Lake St., 218/254-4201. It's really just a showroom as all of the cars are for sale, but there are always about 40 vehicles that you can admire. Open daily 9 A.M.–5 P.M. during the summer. Admission is $5. As you approach or depart town from the east along Highway 169 look for the **Bruce Mine Headframe,** the last of its kind on the Mesabi Range. The rusting tower lowered and raised the cages that carried miners and ore from the 300-foot-deep mine.

The only hotel in town is the pleasant **Chisholm Inn,** 218/254-2000 or 877/255-3156,

> *Across from the entrance to Ironworld is the 81-foot Iron Man Statue, which some claim is the third largest freestanding statue in the nation, behind only the St. Louis Arch and the Statue of Liberty.*

across from the entrance to Ironworld. Rooms are $89 and amenities include a pool, hot tub, and sauna. Most visitors to town who don't fill up at Ironworld eat at the **Iron Kettle Family Restaurant,** 218/254-3339, which is located along Hwy. 69. The menu, priced between $3–11, offers a little of everything, from pizza to steaks to stir-fry, and breakfast is served all day. Open daily for breakfast, lunch, and dinner. **Lorenz** buses stop at the Chisholm Senior Center, 319 W. Lake St., 218/254-7927, on their roundabout run between Virginia and Minneapolis.

McCarthy Beach State Park

Though McCarthy Beach State Park, 218/254-7979, spreads across 2,311 acres, most facilities and visitors are limited to the narrow isthmus between Side and Sturgeon lakes, with a wide and shallow beach stretching deep into the latter. You can rent a canoe or fishing boat from the park office to further explore the lakes or maybe snare some trout, walleye, or panfish. Elsewhere, 18 miles of decent though unspectacular hiking trails, most open to mountain bikes and horses and groomed for cross-country skiing, follow the park's ridges through red and white pine stands. **Pickerel Lake** is the one noteworthy destination, and the 1.5-mile trail circling it is the only path that sees regular traffic. There are also some nice views of Sturgeon Lake along the **Ridge Trail** that heads north from Pickerel. The main campground has 86 sites in three loops along Side Lake—so get up early for that sunset view. The upper loop is the most secluded and, since all 18 electric sites are in the lower loop, the middle one is also a quiet option. The most peaceful campground is tucked away on Beatrice Lake in the north end of the park. It has 18 horserider and walk-in sites and few facilities.

VIRGINIA

Like the other Iron Range cities, Virginia was a boomtown, built following the discovery of iron

© TIM BEWER

a 240-ton capacity production truck

in the area, but it also became one of northern Minnesota's most important lumber towns. At one point early in its history Virginia had both the world's largest white pine sawmill, the Virginia and Rainy Lake Mill, and the largest iron mine, Missabi Mountain. The dual industry city, platted in the middle of virgin wilderness (hence the name, though it helped that one of the promoters of the new town was originally from the state of Virginia), swelled to 5,000 people in its first year of existence. That same year, 1893, the town was wiped out by a forest fire and, though locals rebuilt, it took a second citywide blaze seven years later to convince Virginians to build with brick, stone, and concrete. Because of its wealth and grandeur Virginia became known as "The Queen City of the North," a moniker it maintains today. Its central location and variety of services make it the best base for visiting the Iron Range.

Sights

The city's main draw is the **Mineview in the Sky** with a panoramic view of the Rouchleau Mine. The massive cavity, cut right along the eastern edge of Virginia, stretches nearly three miles long, a half-mile wide, and 450 feet deep, though the bottom 200 feet are now filled in by water. It produced 300 million tons of ore before closing in 1977. You'll also find a 240-ton capacity production truck and a few other mining vehicles parked at the overlook, and any mining questions can be answered by the staff of the information center. The mineview is located off Highway 53 on the southeast edge of town. The site is open from the middle of May through the end of September from 9 A.M. to 6 P.M. and admission is free. You can get another view of the Rochleau pit at the **Oldtown-Finntown Overlook** in town at the east end of 3rd Street North.

The **Virginia Heritage Museum,** 800 9th Ave. N., 218/741-1136, in Olcott Park is very well presented. Because there are so many mining exhibits in surrounding towns, this museum focuses on logging and also has a good display about the city's twin fires. Relics of the bygone days, such as a foot-operated dentist's drill, are housed in a 1910 Finnish log cabin and 1930s tourist cabin (back then a night cost just $1.50). The museum is open Thursday–Saturday 11 A.M.–4 P.M., and it adds Tuesday and Wednesday from the beginning of May through the end of September. Admission is free. Next to the museum is the **Olcott Park**

Greenhouse. You'll find a **giant loon** (21 feet long) floating in nearby Silver Lake.

Recreation

Mesabi Recreation, 720 9th St. N., 218/749-6719, can set up active travelers with bike, canoe, kayak, snowshoe, and cross-country ski rentals. If you are looking to explore the Range's crystal clear mine pits, you should talk to the people at **Tall Pine Scuba,** 1101-1/2 8th St. S., 218/741-8118 or 800/839-8118. They do sales, service, classes, and air fills.

Entertainment

Chestnut Street, Virginia's main downtown drag, has over a dozen bars (a far cry from the 52 watering holes filling downtown in 1910), and several of these have occasional music or other evening events. The only sure bet, however, is **Razzle's,** 203 Chestnut St., 218/749-0862, which has a range of live rock bands every weekend.

Accommodations

One of the best values around is the **Ski View Motel,** 903 17th St. N., 218/741-8918 or 800/255-7106 (access code 25), on the north side of town. The rooms are old but pass the white-glove test and go for just $44. A sauna is available on a first-come, first-served basis so you don't have to share. Better overall is the **Voyageur North Motel,** 218/741-9235 or 800/235-3524, which has microwaves and refrigerators in the large $55 rooms. It is located at Highway 53 and 13th St. S., which is technically the city of Mountain Iron. Next door at the **AmericInn,** 218/741-7839 or 800/634-3444, $100 gets you not only a modern room but a pool, whirlpool, sauna, and free pass to the Supreme Court Fitness Center downtown. You get the same amenities for just $84 at Virginia's best hotel, the **Park Inn,** 502 Chestnut St., 218/749-1000 or 800/777-4699.

Food

The editors of *Gourmet* magazine won't be making reservations anytime soon, but because of its variety Virginia is the culinary capital of the Iron Range. Most recommended is the historic **Rainy Lake Saloon and Deli,** 209 Chestnut St.,

218/741-6247. The menu, averaging $7, is the most varied in town and includes some Mexican, Italian, and Cajun besides the expected American fare. Open daily for lunch and dinner.

Close on its heals in popularity is **Grandma's Virginia Grill,** 1302 12th Ave. S., 218/749-1960. Wild Cajun chicken with wild rice is typical of their somewhat spiced-up American menu. Entrées average $10. Open daily for lunch and dinner.

The **Whistling Bird,** 101 Broadway St. N., 218/741-7544, five miles southeast of Virginia in Gilbert, draws diners from across the Range for its Caribbean flavorings. Jamaican jerk chicken and shrimp are highlights. Don't worry about the spiciness, the sauce is served on the side, or just order seafood, steak, or one of the international pastas—the Italian sausage and sweet pepper fettuccini is highly recommended. Most dishes are around $10, but some go much higher. Open daily for dinner and reservations are recommended on weekends.

No-frills **Old Mexico,** 302 1st St. S., 218/749-5673, offers a bit of real Mexican *sabor* with platters averaging $6. Open daily for lunch and dinner.

Despite the name, the menu at the **Saigon Café,** 111 2nd Ave. N., 218/741-6465, is mostly Chinese these days since the Vietnamese options just weren't selling. Entrées, including a large number of vegetarian options, average $6. Open daily for lunch and dinner. If you want a Chinese buffet head to **Jue's,** 312 Chestnut St., 218/741-7695, where lunch will cost $6 and dinner $8. Open Mon.–Sat. for lunch and dinner.

There is a coffee shop tucked into the back corner of the **Natural Harvest Food Co-op,** 505 3rd St. N., 218/741-4663, and you can have your caffeine or light meals on the deck overlooking Virginia Lake. Open weekdays for breakfast, lunch, and dinner and weekends for lunch.

The **Italian Bakery,** 205 1st St. S., 218/741-3464, opened for business in 1905 and it is still turning out Iron Range specialties like pasties and potica. It is open Monday–Saturday for breakfast and lunch.

They've lost a lot of the atmosphere by adding a gift shop, but **Canelake's,** 414 Chestnut St., 218/741-1557, still makes handmade candies as they have since 1905.

Shopping

You can get Scandinavian goods at **Irma's Finland House,** 625 9th St. N., 218/741-0204, or a cheap read for the road at the **Paperback Exchange,** 329 Chestnut St., 218/749-1716.

Information and Transportation

Virginia tourism information is available at the Mineview in the Sky. When they are closed, or if you need any additional information, stop by the **Iron Trail Convention and Visitors Bureau,** 218/749-8161 or 800/777-8497, at the corner of 2nd St. N. and 4th Ave. W., open weekdays 8 A.M.–5 P.M. year-round.

Both **Greyhound** and **Lorenz** buses stop at the **Lakshor Motor Inn,** 404 6th Ave. N., 218/741-3360 or 800/569-8131. **C&M Taxi** can be reached at 218/749-4000.

AROUND VIRGINIA

Mountain Iron

The first iron of the Mesabi Range was discovered here in 1890, and two years later the Mountain Iron Mine shipped the first load of ore to Duluth. This town of just under 3,000 residents (2,999 to be exact) has since proudly proclaimed themselves the "Birth Place of the Mesabi Iron Range." Mountain Iron is still home to North America's largest active taconite mining operation, the **Minntac Mine,** which turns out 18 million tons of ore annually. You can get up close and personal with the whole process, every detail of which is overwhelmingly massive, on a free tour led by former Minntac employees. The 90-minute tours begin at an overlook of the East Pit (if you're lucky you'll get to see a blast) and follow the same route as the rocks until the finished pellets are loaded onto the trains. Along the way you will visit the half-mile-long concentrator building where the iron is separated from the rock. Tours depart from the Mountain Iron Senior Center on Main Street on summer Fridays at 10 A.M. and 1 P.M. It is first-come, first-served, and no children under 11 years of age are allowed. Call 218/749-7299 for more information. You can get a quick look at the Minntac Mine, and several smaller abandoned ones, from the **Wacootah Overlook** just east of downtown across from the mine entrance.

In town, directly across from the Senior Center, is a 10-foot-tall statue of Leonidas Merritt, the man who found the "Mountain of Iron," as he called it. You can also admire some taxidermied **albino animals** nearby at Mac's Bar. One block north is an overlook of the **Mountain Iron Mine,** a National Historic Landmark, which crept right up to the edge of downtown before exhausting itself. A 1910 Baldwin steam locomotive and some old mining equipment are parked here, too.

Eveleth

Like Hibbing, iron ore was discovered directly under Eveleth, and in 1900, just eight years after it was founded, the city moved about a mile northeast from its original location. Two mines wrap around the town, and you can get a distant view of the work going on in the pair, now known as the Thunderbird Mine, from the **Leonidas Overlook,** a mile west on town on Fayal Road. Eveleth, like many northern Minnesota towns, has a long hockey history so it makes sense that the **United States Hockey Hall of Fame,** 218/744-5167 or 800/442-7825, is located here. The center isn't huge, but the displays run the gamut from the early history of the game, back when it was played with a ball, to the emergence of women's hockey. You can play games, look at one of the first Zambonis, and watch the 1980 U.S. Olympic team's "miracle" victory over the Soviet Union, which plays continuously. Although the hall is really only for hockey fans, others might at least enjoy the collection of historic ice skates, some as old as 1850. It is open Monday–Saturday 9 A.M.–5 P.M. and Sunday 10 A.M.–3 P.M. and admission is $6. Eveleth is so proud of their hockey history that they have erected the **world's largest hockey stick** downtown in Big Stick Plaza. The Christian Brothers Hockey Stick Company made this 107-foot, 7,000-pound monster using the actual materials and processes for their regular sticks and a 700-pound puck waits for Paul Bunyan's slap shot. The Eveleth Chamber of Commerce across the street sells T-shirts and hands out area tourism brochures. Those who just can't wait for the first snowfall will want to come up for the **Iron Range Snowmobile Grass Drags** held the third Sunday in August.

Simple but spotless rooms at the family-run **Koke's Motel,** 218/744-4500 or 800/892-5107, near downtown cost $44. The biggest and best hotel in town is the **Days Inn,** 218/744-2703 or 888/354-6230, which surrounds a large recreation area with a pool, sauna, mini golf course, and volleyball, among other things. Rooms are $79. Both have ski-wax rooms for guests who need one. The decor doesn't fit the name, but the **Deluxe Café,** 225 Grant Ave., 218/744-4960, is still the most popular restaurant in town. The 12-oz. t-bone steak is $13, while almost everything else on the menu, including half-pound burgers and some salads, is in the $3–7 range. They are open daily for breakfast and lunch and Monday–Saturday for dinner. The low-priced **K&B Drive-Inn,** 218/744-2772, 1.5 miles south of town on Highway 53, still has old-fashioned carhop service, and if you want your sloppy Joe and root beer float clipped to your window in subzero weather you can because they stay open all year long; though most people use the smoke-free indoor dining area in the winter. They are quite proud of both their chicken and pasties. **Greyhound** buses stop downtown at the Range Print Shop, 520 Grant St., 218/744-5673.

Biwabik

Named from the Ojibwe word for valuable, Biwabik was founded in 1892 when iron was discovered in the area. Within a few years the population soared to 3,000 as miners from around the world arrived to work the city's seven mines, the last of which closed in 1956. Today the population is well under 1,000 and falling fast. The number of tourists, however, continues to climb thanks to Giants Ridge, which sits five miles outside of town. Recognizing that tourism was their future, Biwabik began a Bavarian theme back in the 1980s, which now includes the city hall and most downtown buildings. Continuing in the German vein, the annual **Weihnachtsfest** (Christmas Lighting Fest), held the first Saturday in December, is one of the city's biggest events. Following a day of food, crafts,

music, and fireworks, the Christmas lights are turned on in Carl Schuster Park (home to a statue celebrating **Honk the Moose** and the classic children's story he inspired) and the rest of downtown. The lights stay on through March. Preceding the evening fireworks on the 4th of July is the city's century-old **Calithumpian parade** with dozens of clowns and floats judged on humor.

What began as a local ski hill in the 1950s has grown into the multifaceted **Giants Ridge Golf & Ski Resort,** 218/865-3000 or 800/688-7669, which is regularly listed as one of the Midwest's best by both ski and golf magazines. Snowy season visitors have 34 downhill runs, a massive terrain park with a 300-foot half-pipe and bus at its heart, a snowshoe trail climbing to the top of the Laurentian Divide, and 35 miles of world-class cross-country ski trails—initially developed for the U.S. Ski Team—through the adjacent Superior National Forest. As for golf, The Legend is overwhelmingly regarded as the state's best public golf course, and their follow up, The Quarry, is expected to be as good as the original. Other summer diversions include riding the 75 varied miles of mountain bike trails and letting one fly from atop the ski run on the disc golf course. Rentals equipment is available for all of these activities.

Giants Ridge has Play & Stay packages available with hotels as far away as Duluth, though you might as well stay right on-site at the excellent **Lodge at Giants Ridge,** 218/865-7170 or 877/442-6877. Ideal for families, all rooms are two-room suites, many with whirlpool baths and fireplaces, and on-site facilities include a large pool, hot tub, game room, exercise room, and a ski storage/waxing room. Winter high season rates start at $129, though they are almost half that on weekdays during the spring and fall. Just down the road are the fancier **Villas at Giants Ridge,** 218/865-4155 or 800/843-7434, with lakeside condos and cabins ranging from studios to four bedrooms—most come with full kitchens, fireplaces, and whirlpool baths. There's an outdoor pool, private beach, and tennis courts on the grounds. Prices run from $130 to $495 a night and weekly rates are available. The city-owned **Vermillion Trail Park Campground,** 218/742-6331, just west of town on Embarrass Lake, has

40 well-spaced sites ranging from non-electric tent spots for $11 to full hookups for $18.

Alden's Restaurant, 209 Main St., 218/865-6371, has home-cooked meals starting at $5 in a simple, smoke-free dining room. Lunch is mostly sandwiches, while steak and seafood are added for dinner. Open daily for breakfast and lunch and Mon.–Sat. for dinner. **Vi's Pizza,** 215 Main St., 218/865-4164, is just a kitchen attached to a bar, but they do a decent thin-crust 'za for about $10. Open daily for dinner. The somewhat fancy **Timbers Restaurant,** 218/865-7170, at Giants Ridge has a small menu with choices such as honey pecan walleye, porketta sandwiches, penne pasta with venison, and filet mignon, all in the $10–20 range. They've got an outdoor deck and are open daily for breakfast, lunch, and dinner.

Bullwinkle's, 107 Main St., 218/865-6801, one of seven bars in town keeping Giants Ridge guests entertained in the evening, serves up drinks indoors and out and is usually the busiest place in town. They have live music on weekends, while the **R Bar,** 218/865-7000, next door does Karaoke. During the ski season a free shuttle runs between town and Giants Ridge so you can return to your room safely after enjoying the nightlife.

SUPERIOR NATIONAL FOREST—LAURENTIAN DISTRICT

This two-part district running north of the main Iron Range communities and over towards Beaver Bay on the North Shore was named after the north-south continental divide, aka the Laurentian Divide, that runs the length of the forest. In this part of the state, rain falling south of the divide flows into the Atlantic Ocean via the Great Lakes, while to the north it heads north to Hudson Bay. For additional details see the Superior National Forest overview earlier in this chapter.

Recreation

Straddling the Laurentian Divide on Highway 53/169 four miles north of Virginia are the **Lookout Mountain Trails.** The series of loops extends 15 miles back towards a fantastic vista—great for fall color viewing—though unfortu-

nately you have to walk pretty far in to get away from the highway noise. There is a mile-long fitness trail and a brief interpretive trail at the front end, while geological markers in the parking lot discuss the area's unique geology. The 10 groomed miles are some of the area's most challenging cross-country ski trails. Another well-known ski path is the **Sturgeon River Trail,** nine miles north of Chisholm on Hwy. 73, with 20 intermediate-level miles groomed. It's a beautiful (especially the parts that follow the river), though sometimes wet, summer hike. Other worthy and easy hiking opportunities in this portion of the district include the two-mile river-fronting **North Dark River Trail,** on County Road 688 near the Sturgeon River Trail, and the three-mile **Pfeiffer Lake Trail** at its namesake campground. The latter includes a short interpretive trail. The 21 miles of the **Big Aspen Trail** are open to multiple users, including ATV (May 1–Nov. 20 only), horse, and mountain bike riders in the summer and cross-country skiers in the winter. There are some steep hills leading to scenic vistas, but for the most part the trails are pretty easy.

Several more trails lie just off the 59-mile **Superior National Forest Scenic Byway,** which runs through the forest from Aurora to Silver Bay connecting the Iron Range to the North Shore. The main trailhead of the **Bird Lake Trail** lies five miles southeast of Hoyt Lakes and leads to a rolling two-mile loop with a bog boardwalk on the east side of the namesake lake. There is also a nice picnic site here. The majority of the 11-mile trail runs back to town on the south side of the highway, and portions are too wet to hike in the summer but groomed for cross-country skiing in winter. Just south of the Cadotte Lake Campground on Forest Road 416 is the **Otto/Harris Trail** with a path linking loops around each of these quiet fishing lakes. The easy 2.8-mile loop around Otto Lake stays quite close to the shore and is the most scenic part of the eight-mile trail; there are two campsites along it. At the **White Pine Picnic Area** on County Road 2, just north of the byway, a thousand-foot interpretive trail, surfaced with gravel, circles through a stand of white pines where a 150-foot giant is still standing.

Camping

The Laurentian District has three lakeside campgrounds, and all have beaches and take reservations. With 52 sites in four loops **Whiteface Reservoir** is one of the forest's largest camps and one of just two with electric hookups. It is south of Hoyt Lakes in the far corner of the forest. Quieter are the 27 sites nearby at **Cadotte Lake. Pfeiffer Lake**'s 16 sites are located between Tower and Cook.

Information

The **Laurentian Ranger Station,** 218/229-8800, is located in Aurora. It is open weekdays 8 A.M.–4:30 P.M.

Central Lakes

This is Minnesota's backyard. A quick glance at a map shows why the north-central slice of the state is where the average Minnesotan comes to unwind: lakes are abundant (even by Minnesota standards), the forests vast, wildlife is seemingly everywhere, and the Mighty Mississippi River runs right down the middle of it all. Of course, the other factor in its popularity is that you can find all of this just a couple of hours outside the Twin Cities, which is why on summer weekends it seems that just about every other car tooling up and down the major highways is pulling a camper or a boat—or a camper *and* a boat. Although forests cover most of the region, the southern tier is pure farm country; Garrison Keillor's fictional Lake Wobegon tales stem from his time living in a farmhouse near St. Cloud.

Uppgaard Wildlife Management Area

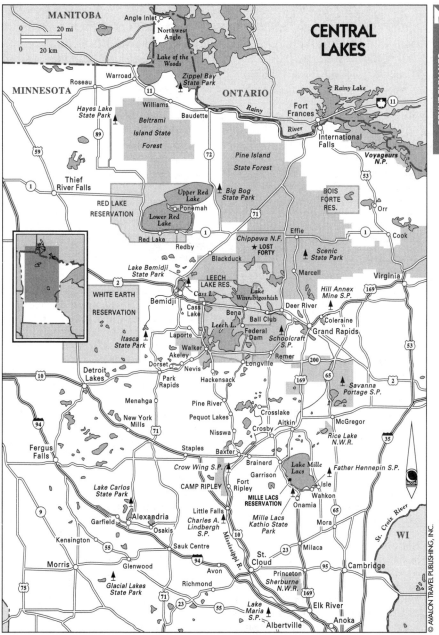

CENTRAL LAKES

CENTRAL LAKES HIGHLIGHTS

Beltrami County History Center, Bemidji

Bog Walk, Lake Bemidji State Park

Charles A. Lindbergh House, Little Falls

Chippewa Discovery Tour, Chippewa National Forest

Chippewa National Forest Headquarters, Cass Lake

Forest History Center, Grand Rapids

Fort St. Charles, Angle Inlet

Itasca State Park

Judy Garland Birthplace and Museum, Grand Rapids

Lost Forty, Chippewa National Forest

Lyle's Logging Camp and Cass Lake Museum, Cass Lake

Mille Lacs Indian Museum

Munsinger and Clemens Gardens, St. Cloud

North Country Museum of Arts, Park Rapids

Oliver H. Kelley Farm, Elk River

Paul Bunyan Statues, Brainerd, Bemidji, Akeley

Savanna Portage State Park

Schoolcraft State Park

St. Cloud

The first city of consequence along the Mississippi River frequently tops quality of life polls and just as often comes in near the bottom on cost of living lists. The St. Cloud area is home to four large colleges and universities, and students make up a big chunk of the city's 59,000 residents. Like any decent college town St. Cloud is a fun place with more than its fair share of good restaurants and nightspots and is growing in popularity as a quick getaway from the Twin Cities. A downtown back on the upswing adds to the city's pleasant character. Because it is located in the heart of the state, St. Cloud rests at the junction of many highways (hence the chamber of commerce's "All roads lead to St. Cloud" slogan), so there is a good chance you'll be passing by. Even if nothing else excites you, be sure to make time for a stroll through the wonderful Munsinger and Clemens Gardens.

History

St. Cloud was born in 1856 when three separate communities, the creatively named Lower Town, Middle Town, and Upper Town—each settled just a few years earlier—merged. A sawmill was the city's first industry and later the city supplied and serviced the new settlements emerging in the wilderness west of the Mississippi River. It was

granite, however, that put St. Cloud on the map. The first quarry opened in 1863, and eventually over 30 more were cut in the area. Quarrying was so important that St. Cloud is still known as Granite City ("Busy Gritty Granite City" or "Nitty Gritty Granite City" to the more poetic). Minnesota granite, noted for its strength, was used to construct the State Capitol and the Cathedral of St. Paul, as well as other buildings around the nation. The solid rock features prominently in downtown St. Cloud as well. Cold Spring Granite is still one of the world's largest granite producers, and you will see many smaller companies around town carving out monuments.

Orientation

Downtown St. Cloud lies west of the Mississippi River along St. Germain (often called Mall Germain, but rarely St. Germain Street), and parking is cheap and easy to find. The St. Cloud State University (SCSU) campus is just to the south. About one quarter of the city lies east of the Mississippi River, though most of the city's recent growth is to the west around the Crossroads Center shopping mall.

St. Cloud began in a three-for-one deal and today history has essentially repeated itself as the city has grown right up against its neighbors Waite

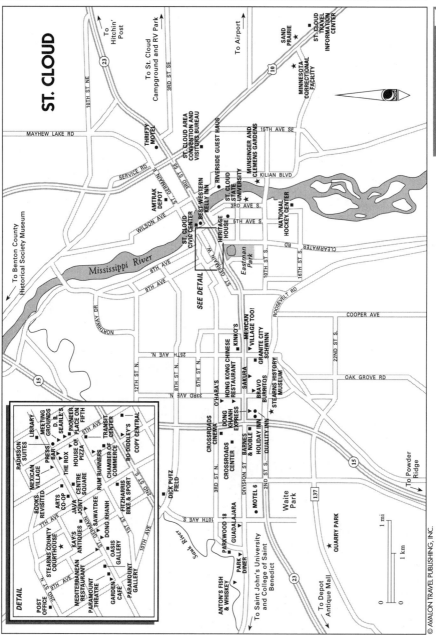

ST. CLOUD

To Hitchin' Post

To St. Cloud Campground and RV Park

To Airport

SAND PRAIRIE

ST. CLOUD TRAVEL INFORMATION CENTER

MINNESOTA CORRECTIONAL FACILITY

10TH ST NE

23

MAYHEW LAKE RD

SERVICE RD

THRIFTY MOTEL

3RD ST SE

ST. CLOUD AREA CONVENTION AND VISITORS BUREAU

RIVERSIDE GUEST HAUS

MUNSINGER AND CLEMENS GARDENS

15TH AVE SE

KILIAN BLVD

10

To Benton County Historical Society Museum

WILSON AVE

AMTRAK DEPOT

3RD ST SE

ST. GERMAIN ST SE

BEST WESTERN KELLY INN

ST. CLOUD STATE UNIVERSITY

3RD AVE S.

5TH AVE S.

NATIONAL HOCKEY CENTER

CLEARWATER RD

Mississippi River

6TH AVE

9TH AVE

ST. CLOUD CIVIC CENTER

ST. GERMAIN ST. W

HERITAGE HOUSE

Eastman Park

10TH ST S.

11TH ST S.

15

NORTHWAY DR.

SEE DETAIL

ST. GERMAIN ST. E

ROOSEVELT RD

COOPER AVE

21ST AVE N.

25TH ST N.

5TH ST N.

KINKO'S

MEXICAN VILLAGE TOO!

GRANITE CITY SCHWINN

22ND ST S.

OAK GROVE RD

12TH ST N.

8TH AVE N.

33RD AVE N.

O'HARA'S

HONG KONG CHINESE RESTAURANT

SAKURA

BRAVO BURRITOS

STEARNS HISTORY MUSEUM

DONG KHANH EXPRESS

15

To Powder Ridge

3RD ST N.

DIVISION ST.

2ND ST S.

CROSSROADS CINEMA

CROSSROADS CENTER

BARNES & NOBLE

HOLIDAY INN

QUALITY INN

10TH AVE S.

DICK PUTZ FIELD

137

MOTEL 6

GUADALAJARA

PARKWOOD 18

Waite Park

QUARRY PARK

Sauk River

PARK DINER

ANTON'S FISH & WHISKEY

To Saint John's University and College of Saint Benedict

23

To Depot Antique Mall

1 mi

1 km

DETAIL

POST OFFICE

2ND ST S.

9TH AVE S.

STEARNS COUNTY COURTHOUSE

MEDITERRANEAN RESTAURANT

PARAMOUNT THEATRE

KAY'S ANTIQUES

ST. GERMAIN ST.

DONG KHANH

SAWATDEE

JAVA JOINT

ARTS CO-OP

BOOKS REVISITED

7TH AVE

RADISSON SUITES

MEXICAN VILLAGE

PRESS BAR

THE ROX

HOUSE OF PIZZA

5TH AVE

LIBRARY

MEETING GROUNDS

D. B. SEARLE'S

PIONEER PLACE ON FIFTH

TRANSIT CENTER

CHAMBER OF COMMERCE

BO-DIDDLEY'S

COPY CENTRAL

RUM RUNNERS

FITZHARRIS BIKE & SPORT

13TH ST.

CENTRE SQUARE

10TH AVE

OASIS GALLERY

GARDEN CAFÉ

PARAMOUNT GALLERY

2ND ST S.

3RD ST N.

© AVALON TRAVEL PUBLISHING, INC.

Park (pop. 6,568) and Sauk Rapids (pop. 10,213). The latter still has its own personality, but you can only tell the former apart by the "Welcome to Waite Park, City with a Smile" sign on Division St. and the confusing change in addresses. St. Cloud is also at the junction of three counties and, while it is the Stearns County seat, parts of the city also lie in Benton and Sherburne.

SIGHTS

Munsinger and Clemens Gardens

The most pleasant way to spend half an hour—or half a day—in St. Cloud is strolling along the east bank of the Mississippi River through these two distinct but complimentary gardens. Clemens Gardens are laid out in the formal European style and the 1,200 rose bushes, the 24-foot Renaissance Fountain (the tallest in any Minnesota public garden), and the English-style White Garden are the highlights of the six geometrically-precise plots. Across Riverside Drive are the wilder Munsinger Gardens, first planted in the 1930s. The flowers, bushes, and lily pond lie at the foot of a mature pine grove, making for a uniquely shady floral experience. You can continue a Mississippi stroll to the north through **Riverside Park** where geese and ducks congregate.

Stearns History Museum

This well-executed county historical museum, one of the state's best, leads you through the history of Stearns County from pre-settlement times to the current day. The two most popular stops are the replica granite quarry and the mint 1919 Pan automobile, which was manufactured in St. Cloud. The museum is open Monday–Saturday 10 A.M.–4 P.M. and Sunday noon–4 P.M. Admission is $4. Call 320/253-8424 for information.

Immediately in front of the museum is the kid-focused Heritage Nature Center, 320/255-7255, where various critters like snakes and rabbits can be observed or handled. It is open daily during the school year and weekends year-round.

Benton County Historical Museum

This diminutive, one-room collection across the river in Sauk Rapids can only dream of reaching

Munsinger Gardens

© TIM BEWER

the level of Stearns County's museum, though kids will surely get a kick out of the horse-drawn school bus fitted with skis. The museum is located at 218 1st Street North, 320/253-9614, and is open Monday, Tuesday, Wednesday, and Saturday 10 A.M.–3 P.M. Admission is free.

Stearns County Courthouse

The solid brick and granite edifice with what looks like a UFO parked on top was completed in 1922, and scenes from the Disney film *The Mighty Ducks* were shot here. You can peek around inside weekdays 8 A.M.–4:30 P.M.

Minnesota Baseball Hall of Fame

This display of old equipment and photos (mostly photos) on the second floor of the St. Cloud Civic Center is for die hard baseball fans only. It is open weekdays 7 A.M.–5 P.M., though if an event is going on at other times the displays are accessible. Admission is free.

St. Cloud State University

With around 15,000 students SCSU is Minnesota's second largest public university after the University of Minnesota-Twin Cities. Other than strolling the pleasant riverside campus, the main diversion here is visiting the pair of tiny art galleries. The **Kiehle Gallery,** 320/255-4717, in the Kiehle Visual Arts Center, brings in several national artists each school year, while the **Atwood Gallery,** 320/255-2205, in the Atwood Memorial Center is open year-round.

Immediately north of the campus, principally along 3rd Avenue South, is the **Southside Neighborhood Historic District,** with dozens of elegant homes from the late 19th and early 20th centuries.

Quarry Park

For a look at the industry that built St. Cloud visit this 653-acre park. Hiking and mountain bike trails lead past 30 abandoned granite quarries last worked in the 1950s. Today the deep pits are filled with water, and swimming is allowed in one (it's a half-mile walk there), many are stocked with trout, and local dive shops offer scuba outings in another of the crystal clear pits. A mining

exhibit and interpretive center is planned, and you might still feel the blasts from other nearby quarries. Call 320/255-6172 for diving or any other information. Admission is $3.50.

Minnesota Correctional Facility

Prisoners chopped and stacked the granite blocks forming the 22-foot-high perimeter of this prison in 1889 and, at just 200 feet shy of one mile, it is claimed as the longest uninterrupted granite wall in the world. The castlelike cellblock at the southwest corner is a lovely site—from the outside, anyway.

Sand Prairie

The Sand Prairie Wildlife Management and Environmental Education Area, 320/255-4279, features 700 acres of prairie, wetland, and forest, most of it under active restoration. Its surroundings are much too urban and habitats much too young to allow a true feeling of wilderness, though it does offer the best birding in the area, and the view from the observation deck at the back end is truly wonderful.

RECREATION

The 2.5-mile paved **Beaver Islands Trail** roughly follows the Mississippi River south of town, though it only has river views along the northern half, and even these are pretty limited. The main trailhead is at 3rd Avenue South and 15th Street. The four miles of groomed cross-country ski trail at **Quarry Park** are lit for night skiing, while downhill skiers have 15 runs (and a tubing hill) to choose from at **Powder Ridge,** 320/398-5295 or 800/348-7734, the highest dropping 290 feet. It is located 16 miles south of town on Highway 15, then turn west on Powder Ridge Road and follow the signs. **Eagle Trace,** 320/558-6066, with 18 holes tucked up against the Mississippi River, is both the most challenging golf course in the vicinity and the most scenic.

ENTERTAINMENT

St. Cloud has embraced the arts and, despite its size, you will never be wanting from a lack of choice. The quality of offerings is high, too, as some groups that normally play much larger towns will make the trip to St. Cloud. The best overall source of what's on is the "Up Next" section of Thursday's *St. Cloud Times.*

The beautifully renovated 1921 **Paramount Theatre,** 913 W. St. Germain, 320/259-5463, is the focal point for the city's arts scene. It hosts touring acts, plus local groups like the **St. Cloud Symphony Orchestra** and the **Central Minnesota Children's Theater.** The **Pioneer Place on Fifth,** 22 5th Ave. S., 320/203-0331, is an intimate historic venue that brings in many of the best Twin Cities' theater companies and also sometimes hosts concerts. Unfortunately, they are dark all summer long. SCSU also has a full range of activities. Call 320/255-4636 to inquire about upcoming events. Not too far west of St. Cloud, the **College of Saint Benedict** and **Saint John's University** jointly run a wonderful fine arts series that brings a eclectic and always interesting mix of music, dance, and theater groups. Call 320/363-5777 for schedule and ticket information.

Nightlife

Around a dozen downtown bars and clubs put bands and/or DJs on stage. Just wander around the corner of St. Germain and 5th Ave. until you find something to your liking, or check the monthly *RiplFX* magazine distributed free around town.

The biggest rock, reggae, and blues bands play the neon-happy **Red Carpet,** 11 5th Ave. S., 320/251-4047. If the music doesn't live up to expectations you've got seven bars over three stories to explore for other diversions. Around the corner the **Press Bar,** 502 W. St. Germain, 320/251-5911, is another St. Cloud music landmark graced mostly by heavy metal and hard rock bands. It also has plenty of other diversions besides the music. **D. B. Searle's,** 18 5th Ave. S., 320/253-0655, has a more varied lineup running from folk to punk.

If rock and roll isn't your style, you can catch an inspired folk singer at **Bo Diddley's,** 216 6th Ave. S., 320/255-9811; don your Stetson and kick up your boots to live country music at the **Hitchin' Post,** 3528 Hwy. 23 E., 320/255-0912, in Sauk Rapids; hear blues on Wednesday nights

at **Legends Bar and Grill** at the Holiday Inn; or chill out to occasional jazz at the downtown **Radisson Suites.**

DJs spin dance music for happy feet Wednesday through Saturday at **The Rox,** 506 W. St. Germain, 320/259-6807; and comedians hitting the national circuit take the stage on Friday and Saturday nights at **Rum Runners,** 102 6th Ave. S., 320/252-4538.

Cinema

Most movies are screened at the **Parkwood 18,** 320/253-4328, in Waite Park with the **Crossroads Cinema,** 320/253-4328, behind the Crossroads Center mall showing six screens of second-run movies for just a buck.

Spectator Sports

The **St. Cloud State Huskies** compete in a full slate of athletics, but it's the Division 1 men's hockey team that gets all the attention. Home ice is the National Hockey Center, which seats 6,000 screaming fans—though getting tickets can be no small feat. Tickets for regular home games are $12 (though the UM-Duluth and North Dakota matchups are $20, and it's $25 for the Minnesota Golden Gophers) and are available by calling 320/255-2137 or 877/727-8849.

The **St. Cloud Riverbats** are a premier team in the Northwoods League, made up of Division I college baseball players who get a minor league experience while keeping their college eligibility. Home games are played at Dick Putz Field, 5001 8th St. N., 320/240-9798, and general admission tickets are just $4.50.

Events

St. Cloud's biggest bash is the **Wheels, Wings, and Water Festival** held over four days in late June. Live music, fireworks, and a powwow are top draws.

ACCOMMODATIONS

Under $50

The **Motel 6,** 815 1st St. S., 320/253-7070 or 800/446-8356, out in Waite Park isn't fancy, but it's a good value at $46. The older but better situated **Thrifty Motel,** 320/253-6320 or 800/898-6320, just off U.S. 10 charges roughly the same.

$50–100

St. Cloud's best hotel is the downtown **Radisson Suites,** 404 W. St. Germain, 320/654-1661 or 800/333-3333. Facilities include a pool, whirlpool, sauna, and fitness center, plus it is connected to the Civic Center by a skywalk. The 103 well-appointed suites go for as little as $79, but expect to pay more. Also joined to the Civic Center is the less flashy **Best Western Kelly Inn,** 100 4th Ave. S., 320/253-0606 or 800/528-1234, with similar amenities but better-valued rooms from just $69.

The large **Holiday Inn,** 75 S. 37th St., 320/253-9000 or 800/465 4329, is a good choice for families. There's a pool, kiddie pool, 30-person whirlpool, sauna, fitness center, volleyball court, and game room. Rooms start at $90. The **Quality Inn,** 70 37th Ave. S., 320/253-4444 or 800/228-5151, across the street has a mini indoor water park with a pool, kiddie pool, hot tub, and two-story waterslide. Rooms start at $80.

B&Bs

The 1903 Queen Anne Victorian **Heritage House,** 402 6th Ave. S., 320/656-5818 or 888/547-4422, near the SCSU campus is fancy but homey. The redbrick building features stained glass windows, hand-carved woodwork, a wraparound porch, and octagon tower, while the four old-looking but completely modern guestrooms have English, German, Swedish, and French themes. Each room has a private bath and rates run $95–135.

Overlooking the Mississippi River not far from Munsinger and Clemens Gardens is the **Riverside Guest Haus,** 912 Riverside Dr., SE, 320/252-2134 or 888/252-2134. The River Room, with a limited Mississippi view, is the favored choice, but the real gem is the Garden Room, with a transparent-roofed and garden-encased balcony. Each has a private bath and is priced at $135.

Campgrounds

The **St. Cloud Campground & RV Park,** 2491 2nd St. SE, 320/251-4463 or 800/690-7045, is a typical family-style RV park and the only camping available right near the city. It has 88 largely shadeless pull-through sites ($27 with full hookups) and a tent area ($22).

FOOD

African

Despite the name the **Mediterranean Restaurant,** 815 W. St. Germain, 320/202-7881, serves Ethiopian and Somali foods like spicy vegetables and fried goat. The half-dozen choices are all priced around $8. Open daily for breakfast, lunch, and dinner.

American

The **Park Diner,** 1531 Division St., 320/252-0080, in Waite Park has got the 1950s atmosphere down inside and out. The massive malts are the best around, as a steady stream of patrons coming through the door for nothing else will attest. Burgers and other menu items average six bucks. Open daily for breakfast, lunch, and dinner.

Anton's Fish & Whiskey, 320/253-3611, just off Division St. at 20th Ave. in Waite Park, opened as a speakeasy during Prohibition. They are still going strong in the same riverside log cabin, and though they have added on considerably to meet demand, the fun Northwoods atmosphere remains intact. Seafood is their specialty, and they fly in the best from both coasts, but they also serve up a flavorful steak and even do a fettuccine primavera. Meals start around $6, but top out much higher.

D. B. Searle's, 18 S. 5th Ave., 320/253-0655, fills four floors of one of the city's most beautiful historic restorations. Half-pound burgers, walleye sandwiches, hoagies, fajitas, pizza, and a couple of pastas for around $7 are representative of the regular menu, while steak and seafood for twice the price are available during dinner. The beer list is 75 strong, and they have a fantastic happy hour. Open Mon.–Sat. for lunch and dinner; bar only on Sunday.

St. Cloud's original brewpub, the fun and casual **O'Hara's,** 3308 3rd St. N., 320/251-9877, has been making its own house brews since 1996. The large menu ranges from a great grilled cheese on sourdough bread for $4 to a 12-oz. New York strip sirloin for $15. Their famous

LAKE WOBEGON

Located about 20 miles north-northwest of St. Cloud and eight miles from Millet, near Holdingford, the "Gateway to Central Minnesota" sits on the western shore of its namesake lake. The Mist County Seat is a one traffic-light town with quiet streets lined by small white frame houses. Time seems to pass slower in Lake Wobegon than in other places and it embodies a stereotypical Americana that only exists in legend, but still rings true to countless people.*

Up until recent years the only outsiders who came to this small (pop. 942) town on the edge of the prairie were those who knew somebody living here or made a wrong turn off the highway and got lost. These days, ever since local boy Garrison Keillor has made it big sharing news and personal observations about his hometown on his *A Prairie Home Companion* radio show ("Where all the women are strong, all the men are good-looking, and all the children are above average"), a great many people want to come and see what it is all about. Those who find it—Lake Wobegon is still not on maps due to a series of surveyors' errors which omitted the fifty-square-mile quadrangle that is Mist County—rarely stay very long, often not even getting out of the car, and almost always find themselves thankful that they don't live here.

History

For a town where so little out of the ordinary happens, Lake Wobegon has a long, interesting history. A few meandering Voyageurs had previously stumbled up the shallow Lake Wobegon River (really just a small stream) from the larger Sauk River to what they called Lac Malheur (Misfortune Lake), though the first recorded history of the area is from 1836 when the Italian Count Carlo Pallavicini camped for a night on the lakeshore. Upon reaching the lake, Pallavicini momentarily believed that he had found the headwaters of the Mississippi River, but he quickly realized that this couldn't possibly be correct. It wasn't until much later that he learned Henry Schoolcraft had identified Lake Itasca as the true source four years earlier. In 1850 a small band of Unitarian missionaries from Boston came in a failed attempt to convert the Ojibwe to Christianity using interpretive dance. The next year Henry Francis Watt, a member of that original party, convinced Benjamin Bayfield, a wealthy New England coffee broker, to return with him to found a city on the lake. New Albion, as the investors named it, though built on a swamp in the middle of nowhere, was promoted as the Boston of the West and attracted many speculators who bet that the St. Paul & Manitoba Railroad would pass through—they even built a train depot and laid out an extra wide Main Street in anticipation. The town almost went bust during the Panic of 1857 and the railroad never arrived because the officials couldn't find it on the map. A spur line was mistakenly built in 1885, but it stopped just short of the town when the error was discovered. Though the original settlers were New Englanders the town grew on the strength of Norwegian Lutherans and German Catholics. The Norwegians had hoped to settle along Lake Agassiz in North Dakota, but found out that it was a prehistoric lake long since vanished. The Germans were initially headed to the Moorhead area, but misread their maps and stopped here—once they discovered the error they stayed put rather than admit their mistake. The Norwegians pushed for changing the name to Lake Wobegon which, in the Ojibwe language, means "we sat all day in the rain waiting for [you]."

Sights

The lovely spring-fed Lake Wobegon covers 678.2 acres and is the town's main attraction. A sandy **beach** with a floating dock to dive off lies just two blocks down from Ralph's Pretty Good Grocery and the best fishing, any local will tell you, is in weedy Sunfish Bay. The **Statue of the Unknown Norwegian** has looked towards the lake from the bend in Main Street since it was carved in 1896. There wasn't enough money to build a pedestal for the granite lad so the plaque honoring the town's early Norwegian settlers that belongs with the statue is on display in the **Mist County Historical Society Museum.** Along with assorted historical artifacts, including a display of old underwear, there are also some old Norwegian crafts. The most unique item on display is the small, black Lake Wobegon Runestone, which, like the more credible and famous Kensington Runestone in Alexandria, purports to prove that Vikings explored the area in 1381. This block, discovered along County Road 2 in 1921 by a Professor Oftedahl or Ostenwald from Chicago, reads "8 of [us] stopped & stayed awhile to visit & have [coffee] & a short nap. Sorry [you] weren't here. Well, that's about [it] for now." The museum is in the musty basement of the town hall and is open normal business hours; get the key from the town clerk. Admission is free. Many fans of the radio show want to get a look at the 1878 **Our Lady of Perpetual Responsibility Catholic Church** which sits on McKinley Street just off Main—you can't miss it. The opulent interior has marble pillars, gold-flecked mosaics in the maroon tile floor, and ornate stained glass windows tucked inside its large stone columns and arches. It's a long, steep climb to the top of **Adams Hill** behind the school, but you will be rewarded with a panoramic view of the town and lake. If you are arriving or departing from the east you could stop at the **Pet-the-Tame-Deer Park,** along U.S. Highway 10.

Practicalities

If for some reason you need to stay in town your only option is **Art's Bait & Night O'Rest Motel,** on the lake outside of town; rooms are cheap but it is not really recommended. The small, aging cabins have uncomfortable furniture, exposed nails on the floor, and the owner is notoriously cranky. Locals crowd the **Chatterbox Café,** on Main Street for home-cooking away from home or a bottomless cup of coffee ($.85 cents for the morning or $1.25 all day). Pot roast and tuna hotdish are the specialties while the hot beef sandwich, liverwurst sandwich, and BLT are other typical menu items. No matter what you order you'll get a heaping platter for just a few dollars. The closest thing to entertainment in town is listening to the pre-Rock 'n Roll classics on the orange and purple jukebox at the **Sidetrack Tap,** a dark, stale beer–scented dive on Main Street where you'll feel right at home if you like to talk about fishing or transmissions. The town's biggest bash is summer's **Toast N' Jelly Days** which has a toast toss, a dunk the pastor booth, and a hotly contested creative Jell-O contest. The winner of the toast cooking contest wins the coveted "Toast of the Town" award. On **Flag Day** (June 14th) Wobegonians famously don red, white, and blue caps and form a living flag.

*In case you didn't already know, Lake Wobegon is not a real town. This all sprang from Keillor's imagination.

half-pound charbroiled burgers (some say the best in St. Cloud) are six bucks. Open daily for lunch and dinner.

Bo Diddley's, 216 6th Ave. S., 320/255-9811, serves up subs and pita pockets—all reasonably priced—plus 30 microbrewed and imported beers in a simple pub-style atmosphere. It's very popular with the college crowd. Open daily for lunch and dinner.

Chinese

Downtown, **Dong Khanh,** 810 W. St. Germain, 320/251-0656, has good food and good service. The menu is fairly limited, but most people choose the buffet ($5 lunch and $7 dinner) anyway. Open Mon.–Sat. for lunch and dinner. Out near the Crossroads Center, **Dong Khanh Express,** 3616 W. Division St., 320/253-2633, does drive-through service.

Another good choice, the fancier **Hong Kong Chinese Restaurant,** 37 33rd Ave. N., 320/251-5907, is hidden away just off Division Street. The menu has all the standard options for around $6, plus fancy tropical drinks. It is open Tuesday–Sunday for lunch and dinner.

Coffeehouses

Meeting Grounds, 14 5th Ave. S., 320/654-9333, has a very peaceful atmosphere. Their organic coffees are the best in St. Cloud, and they are rightly proud of their vegetarian chili, served with homemade bread. Quiet jazz plays in the background as patrons melt into booths and couches by the fireplace. Open daily for breakfast, lunch, and dinner.

Java Joint, 710 W. St. Germain, 320/656-5990, is as far down-market as the Meeting Grounds is up. A youthful crowd makes itself at home in the rummage sale decor, while Black Flag or Fugazi plays on the stereo. Live bands rock the house most weekends. Open Mon.–Sat. for breakfast, lunch, and dinner, and Sun. for lunch and dinner.

Fine Dining

If you want white linens and crystal chandeliers you want **Chanticleer,** 320/654-1661, the house restaurant at the Radisson hotel. Most

of the long-winded dishes—pan-seared beef medallions in a balsamic bordelaise with grilled fillet of black Chilean sea bass ala Nage and maytag blue pomme purées, for example—have a French influence and are priced around $23. Open daily for dinner. Reservations recommended on weekends.

Italian

Despite the name the **House of Pizza,** 19 5th Ave. S., 320/252-9300, offers a broad menu of Italian and American favorites, though its namesake dish is pretty good. Entrées average about $6. Open daily for lunch and dinner.

Japanese

Sakura, 2959 Division St., 320/656-0044, serves St. Cloud's only sushi with nearly two dozen to choose from. On the lighter side of the meat-heavy dinner menu is shrimp and vegetable tempura for $14. For lunch this and all other menu items are about half price. Open Tues.–Fri. for lunch and dinner and just dinner on Saturday.

Mexican

The only authentic Mexican in town is dished up at **Guadalajara,** 1001 Division St., 320/654-9020, out in Waite Park. The recommended House Special is a heaping plate of steak, shrimp, and chicken, but everything on the massive menu is excellent, in part because they make their own chorizo, guacamole, and other staples. Dishes range $4–15, and vegetarians are well catered for. Open daily for lunch and dinner.

Another longtime favorite is **Mexican Village,** 509 W. St. Germain, 320/252-7134. The festive, mock-Mexican courtyard dining area, complete with a fountain, is often full, but service is prompt and platters average $8. The smaller **Mexican Village Too!,** 320/253-8000, is at 20 25th Avenue South. Open daily for lunch and dinner.

Bravo Burritos Mexicantessan & Bar, 68 33rd Ave. S., 320/654-1269, serves a fantastic Southwestern-style burrito stuffed with your choice of eight meats or beans and rice for about $6. Even if you order the mini you're going to be full. Open daily for lunch and dinner.

Thai

Sawatdee, 800 W. St. Germain, 320/240-1135, a branch of the successful Twin Cities Thai empire, has one of the most difficult-to-decide menus in town because it's all so good. The large menu runs $6–13 and you can choose to keep it mild or jack it up to "volcanic." Open daily for lunch and dinner.

Vegetarian

The friendly **Garden Café,** 921 W. St. Germain, 320/252-7125, keeps a small menu of pasta, pizza, tempeh melts, and Belgian waffles—most for around $7—chalked up on the wall by the door. Open Wed.–Sat. for lunch and Mon.–Sat. for dinner.

SHOPPING

St. Cloud is the commercial hub of central Minnesota so you can get just about anything you need here. The main shopping mall is **Crossroads Center,** 4101 Division St., but the commercial build up sprawls along most of Division St. and beyond. Downtown has seen a bit of a revival as of late and now has several interesting shops, as well as the small Centre Square mall anchored by a Herberger's department store. Fine arts in a wide variety of media are available at the **Arts Co-op,** 619 W. St. Germain, 320/252-3242; **Oasis Gallery,** 822 W. St. Germain, 320/258-3700; and the **Paramount Gallery,** 913 W. St. Germain, 320/257-3120. The **Depot Antique Mall,** 320/253-6573, out at I-94 and Highway 23, is jam-packed with merchandise from over 125 dealers. **Kay's Antiques,** 713 W. St. Germain, 320/255-1220, has a smaller selection downtown. Small by their own standards, **Barnes & Noble,** 3940 Division St., 320/251-4537, is still by far the largest bookstore in St. Cloud. **Books Revisited,** 607 W. St. Germain, 320/259-7959, has an outstanding used selection.

INFORMATION AND SERVICES

Tourist Information

The **St. Cloud Area Convention and Visitors Bureau,** 320/251-4170 or 800/264-2940, www

.visitstcloudmn.com, has their offices in a large log building next to the giant waterfall memorializing veterans, police officers, and firefighters who died in service. They are open weekdays 9 A.M.–4 P.M. though the lobby, where the brochure racks are kept, has somewhat longer hours. There is also a small selection of area brochures downtown at the **St. Cloud Area Chamber of Commerce** offices, 110 6th Ave. S. They are open 7:30 A.M.–4:30 P.M. weekdays. Another option is the **St. Cloud Travel Information Center** just to the south on U.S. 10, which stocks statewide travel information. It is open 9 A.M.–5 P.M. daily May through August, and Thursday–Sunday the rest of the year.

Media

The daily *St. Cloud Times* does a good job of local coverage, but for news from around the state and beyond they just can't compete with either of the Twin Cities' papers, both of which are widely available.

KNSR (88.9 FM) is the local public radio news and information station. It's worth checking in occasionally to see what's playing on **KVSC** (88.1 FM), SCSU's student radio station, since it could change from Marvin Gaye to the Meat Puppets at the top of the hour.

Post Office

St. Cloud's main post office is downtown at 915 2nd St. N., 320/251-8220. The counter is open weekdays 8:30 A.M.–5 P.M. and Saturday 8:30 A.M.–11 A.M.

Internet Access

Visitors can get on the Web at **Copy Central,** 211 5th Ave. S., 320/257-2679; and **Kinko's,** 2423 Division St., 320/259-1224.

GETTING THERE AND AWAY

By Air

The **St. Cloud Regional Airport,** 320/255-7292, is four miles east of downtown on Del Tone Road (County Road 7). **Northwest Airlink,** 320/251-8574 or 800/225-2525, makes the short hop to the Twin Cities up to five times a day. As part of a connecting Northwest flight the round-trip fare can be as little as $50.

By Train

Amtrak, 800/872-7245, www.amtrak.com, heads west at 12:40 A.M. and east at 5:11 A.M. from the historic depot at 555 E. St. Germain. Tickets to or from St. Paul cost about $20. The debate seems to never end on the proposed **North Star Line** between St. Cloud and Minneapolis. It's possible it could be running in a few years time, but don't bet on it.

By Bus

Greyhound buses stop at the city's downtown Transit Center, 510 1st St. S., 320/251-5411, five times a day in each direction on the Minneapolis-Fargo run. A one-way walk-up ticket to or from Minneapolis costs $17.

Executive Express, 320/253-2226, runs a shuttle directly to the Minneapolis-St. Paul International Airport from the Holiday Inn, 75 S. 37th Ave., six times a day on weekdays and four on weekends. The trip takes a 1.75 hours and costs $30. Reservations are advisable.

GETTING AROUND
By Bus

St. Cloud's **Metro Transit** buses offer a fairly extensive regional coverage. All routes converge at the downtown Transit Center, 510 1st St. S., except for the three school-year-only Campus Clipper routes, which are used primarily by SCSU students and meet at the Atwood Memorial Center in the heart of campus. The regular fare is $.60 plus $.25 for a transfer (exact change only). Most services run from roughly 6 A.M. to 9:30 P.M. weekdays, and 8 A.M. to 6:30 P.M. on Saturdays. There is a free-fare zone downtown, but it is so small that you might as well just walk. Call 320/251-7433 for more information.

By Taxi

Yellow Cab, 320/251-5050, serves St. Cloud and surrounding communities. You might find them at the taxi stand across from the downtown transit center, but generally you will need to call.

Car Rentals

If you need a car, **Avis,** 2239 Roosevelt Rd., 320/252-4012; **Enterprise,** 3630 W. Division St., 320/240-9000; **Hertz,** 1550 45th Ave. SE, 320/253-9480; and **U-Save,** 2759 Clearwater Rd., 320/656-0666, are there for you.

Bike Rentals

Granite City Schwinn, 2506 1st St. S., 320/251-7540, has mountain bikes and hybrids for $20/day and tandems for $45/day. **Fitzharris Bike & Sport,** 105 7th Ave. S., 251-2844, only rents recumbents and charges $25/day.

AROUND ST. CLOUD
Lake Maria State Park

Lake Maria (ma-RYE-uh) State Park, 763/878-2325, a 1,590-acre remnant of the Big Woods, a maple, oak, and basswood forest that once spread across southeast Minnesota, is one of the nearest wilderness experiences to the Twin Cities. Though best known for its remote trailside campsites and cabins, many of which overlook the 10 small lakes scattered between the rolling wooded hills, Lake Maria is worth a visit even if you just want to take it easy. There is a lakeside picnic site, and the drive to the back end of the park is very beautiful. The park is also a great spot for viewing spring wildflowers and fall colors. The park is known for its population of state-threatened Blanding's turtles—one of four kinds of turtle residing here—easily identifiable by the bright yellow spots on its shell and its bright yellow throat.

The 14 miles of hilly hiking trails (six open to horseback riders) weave a web of interconnected loops across the eastern half of the park. The popular **Big Woods Trail,** a 5.5-mile loop, passes more lakes than any other trail, while the three-mile **Anderson Hill Loop** passes a wonderful hilltop vista and has some prairie for variety. The 1.5-mile **Kettle and Kame Trail** naturally features plenty of classic glacial topography and is the most rugged trail in the park, while the two-mile **Bjorkland Lake Trail** is both the easiest and most popular—excepting the heart-shaped **Zumbrunnen Interpretive Trail,** a short stroll with a marsh boardwalk. Each winter the trails are groomed for cross-country skiing, a three-mile path is packed down for winter hiking, the cabins and campsites are available, and a skating rink is lit in the evening. Snowshoes are available for rent, as are canoes. None of the three log cabins or 17 secluded backpack sites is more than a mile walk from parking area. The simple cabins have bunks for six people, a table, benches, and a wood-fired stove, but no cooking facilities, electricity, or drinking water.

Oliver H. Kelley Farm

Oliver Hudson Kelley, originally from Boston, moved to this Mississippi River homestead in 1850 and taught himself to farm. He quickly became an expert in the emerging field of scientific farming and in 1867 founded the first national farmers' organization, the Order of the Patrons of Husbandry, better known as the Grange, to share new ideas and information among farmers. The Minnesota State Historical Society has revived the farm, now a National Historic Landmark, and hires costumed guides to work the fields using methods from the 1850s to 1870s. The authenticity is impressive in all aspects, right down to the many non-hybridized crops the family planted and unique livestock breeds they raised. The staff can answer just about any questions you have, including how it would be done today, or show you how to do something if you want to give it a try. There's ox-driven plowing in the spring and threshing in the fall, while the kitchen garden always needs weeding and the pigs always need slopping. You can also try your hand at the women's work (remember, this is the mid-19th century) like churning butter, baking bread, canning vegetables, and making soap. Beyond the fields are a pair of nature trails through a restored prairie and along the wooded banks of the Mississippi, while the visitors center has videos and exhibits on the Kelley family, the Grange, and 19th-century farming methods. Many special events take place on the grounds each year, and though most involve farming others include an old-fashioned Independence Day celebration and a re-created Victorian wedding.

The farm is two miles south of Elk River on U.S. 10. It is open Monday–Saturday 10 A.M. to 5 P.M. and Sunday noon–5 P.M. from May through October. The visitors center stays open weekends noon–4 P.M. the rest of the year. Admission to the farm itself is $6, though the visitors center is free. Call 763/441-6896 for more information.

Sherburne National Wildlife Refuge

Though just an hour outside of Minneapolis, the 30,665-acre Sherburne National Wildlife Refuge is a pretty wild place. Established in 1965, much effort has been put into restoring the wetlands, prairies, and oak savanna straddling the St. Francis River. Well over 200 species of bird have been recorded here, and visitors have a good chance of spying common loon, ruffed grouse, wild turkey, osprey, sandhill crane, and many neotropical migrants, like scarlet tanager and Cerulean warbler—plus you are nearly guaranteed to see at least one of the seven pair of nesting bald eagle. Mammals like beaver, otter, fox, and deer are here but harder to find. Your best bet for seeing the varied landscapes and spotting critters is along the 7.3-mile **Prairie's Edge Wildlife Drive.** Along the way you'll pass lakes and ponds filled with waterfowl and shore birds, wildlife observation decks with powerful spotting scopes, a wildflower demonstration area, informational panels, and easy half-mile trails through prairie and woods. Near the refuge headquarters, along County Road 9, are two long hiking trails. Both the five-mile Blue Hills and three-mile Mahnomen trails are a series of interconnected loops winding mostly through oak forest, though the former also passes some prairie and savanna. Neither is especially difficult, though the Blue Hills Trail has more elevation overall. At the front end there is a lookout atop the namesake mound—it's about a one-mile round-trip to the top. Canoes are allowed on limited sections of the St. Francis River and Battle Brook. The refuge trails and waterways are open during daylight hours, though the wildlife drive is generally closed from November through late April. The headquarters, 763/389-3323, is open weekdays 8 A.M.–4:30 P.M. The **Sand Dunes State Forest,** 763/689-7100, immediately south of the refuge has a campground.

Alexandria and Vicinity

ALEXANDRIA

Big Ole, a 28-foot-tall Viking dressed in full battle regalia greets visitors to Alexandria. To some residents, the slogan "Alexandria Birthplace Of America" displayed prominently on his shield is no joke. Despite overwhelming evidence to the contrary, many steadfastly believe that the famous Kensington Runestone (see Gullible's Travels) is authentic and the local chamber of commerce shamelessly promotes this view to keep the curious coming. Even without the stone, Douglas County's 247 lakes and roughly 50 resorts draw thousands of visitors a week during the summer, most of whom pass through "Alex," as the nearly 9,000 locals call their home.

Sights

Alexandria's famous rock is displayed in the **Runestone Museum,** 206 Broadway, 320/763-3160. The Viking section of the museum promotes, rather than examines, the stone's authenticity, even going so far as to show invented maps of the travel route. The museum's other understated historical displays include a good Native American collection. Out back the collection of 19th-century buildings, grandly named **Fort Alexandria,** includes a log home and one-room schoolhouse. The museum is open weekdays 9 A.M.–5 P.M. and Saturday 9 A.M.–3 P.M. From May to September the museum is also open Sunday 11 A.M.–4 P.M. and closes at 4 P.M. on Saturday. Admission is $5.

The two-ton **Big Ole** stands overlooking Broadway just north of the Runestone Museum. He was built of fiberglass in 1964 to accompany the runestone to the World's Fair in New York for the "Minnesota, Birthplace of America" display. An equally huge **replica runestone** sits east of town on Highway 27, though it is scheduled to be moved next to Big Ole.

The Douglas County Historical Society offers half-hour tours of the **Knute Nelson House,** 1219 Nokomis St., 320/762-0382, on weekdays from 9 A.M. to 4 P.M. for $2 per person. Though born in Norway and raised in Wisconsin, Knute

Nelson served Minnesota in Congress, as governor, and most prominently for 28 years as a maverick Republican U.S. Senator. He built his home shortly after arriving in Alexandria in 1871, though he modified it considerably over the years; the bedrooms and living room retain the original furnishings.

You can visit and sample a range of award-winning grape and apple wines at the **Carlos Creek Winery,** 693 County Road 34, 320/846-5443, two miles north of town. Quick tours of the winemaking facility are available upon request, just ask at the counter in the shop, and during the middle of September the winery hosts the popular Grape Stomp and Fall Festival. You can also walk through the stables where Arabian horses are housed and trained. Open Mon.–Sat. 11 A.M.–6 P.M. and Sun. noon–6 P.M.

Thirteen-hundred-acre **Lake Carlos State Park,** 320/852-7200, hugs the north end of its eponymous lake. There is nothing spectacular about the park, but the quiet western half is undeniably beautiful. Thirteen miles of hiking and eight miles of horseback trails lead through the hardwood forests, over the steep glacial hills, and past small hidden lakes. In winter five miles of trail are groomed for cross-country skiing, and snowshoes can be rented at the park office to explore the rest of the park. Most visitors limit themselves to enjoyment in or on the water so the trails offer a great escape. Campers will find 123 sites (81 electric) in two campgrounds; the Upper Campground, especially the northern loop, is far more secluded and also has a couple of walk-in sites. Horseback riders have their own campground. The park is 10 miles north of town on Highway 29.

Recreation

The **Central Lakes Trail,** which stretches 63 miles between Fergus Falls and Avon, is currently being paved. As of 2003 the 18-mile section between Osakis and Garfield, running through Alex, is completed, as is the stretch between Fergus Falls and the Douglas County line. The 17-

mile gap between these two sections is rideable, if you've got a mountain bike. The trail's grand opening is scheduled for 2005.

Arrowwood Stables, 320/762-1124, at the Arrowwood Resort, charges $18 for a 45-minute trail ride. The **Arrowwood Golf Course,** 320/762-8337, also at the resort, and **Geneva Golf Club,** three miles east on Highway 27 and one mile north on Liberty Rd., 320/762-7089, are two good 18-hole public courses near town. PGA pro Tom Lehman, who has a summer home here, golfs at the **Alexandria Golf Club,** 320/763-3604. Though it is a private club, the public is sometimes allowed to play if there are open tee times.

Winter enthusiasts have 15 ski runs, a half-pipe, tubing hill, and 13-miles of cross-country ski trail at **Andes Tower Hills,** 320/965-2455 or 877/542-6337, 15 miles west on Highway 27.

Entertainment and Events

The respected **Theatre L'Homme Dieu,** 320/846-3150, has been performing summer theater near Alexandria since 1961. Performances are held Wednesday to Sunday at 8 P.M. from mid-June to early August at their theatre near Lake L'Homme Dieu. Tickets are $15. The Alexandria Area Arts Association's **AAAA Theater,** 618 Broadway, 320/762-8300, hosts a variety of concerts and plays throughout the year. On the last Sunday in June the **Vikingland Band Festival** attracts a couple dozen marching bands and drum and bugle corps from across the Midwest.

Sports fans who think heart matters more than cash will appreciate the **Alexandria Beetles,** part of the Northwoods League, which puts top college baseball players on the roster while letting them keep their NCAA eligibility. Games take place at Knute Nelson Memorial Stadium, 5th Ave. and Elm St., 320/763-8151, and tickets cost no more than $4.50. The biggest crowds are found Saturday nights at 8 P.M. at the **Viking Speedway,** 320/762-1559, for NASCAR races on the half-mile dirt oval.

Accommodations

The **Skyline Motel,** 605 30th Ave. W., 320/763-3175 or 800/467-4096, look like the set of a 1950s movie, though its 12 rooms have been kept completely up to date inside. A room with a microwave and refrigerator, plus friendly service, is $55. Another older place that has been kept up to date is the **"L" Motel,** 910 Hwy. 27 W., 320/763-5121 or 800/733-1793. The rooms are similar in quality, though priced a little cheaper. Out by the freeway Alexandria's **Holiday Inn,** 5637 Hwy. 29 S., 320/763-6577 or 800/465-4329, has an indoor recreation area with, amongst other things, a pool, fitness center, and volleyball court. The 149 rooms run from $100.

The classiest bed-and-breakfast in town is the **Cedar Rose Inn,** 422 7th Ave. W., 320/762-8430 or 888/203-5333. This antique-filled 1903 Tudor revival with original stained glass and other ornamentation has four lovely guestrooms ranging from $85–140. There is also a sauna in the house and mountain bikes free for guest use. Also in a charming 1903 home is **The Pillars,** 1004 Elm St., 320/762-2700, a more homey option. Five rooms go from $55 with shared bath and $85 with private bath.

Arrowwood, 320/762-1124 or 800/333-3333, run by the Radisson chain is by far the fanciest resort in the area. Its 200 rooms come with all the amenities you'd expect for around $200 and up. The 450-acre grounds have, amongst many other things, a golf course, stables, tennis courts, indoor and outdoor pools, marina, and countless activities for kids. It is located on Lake Darling, four miles northwest of town. In contrast to Arrowwood is the unpretentious, family-run **Woodland Resort,** 218/943-5191, ten miles north of town on Lake Miltona. The eight well-kept lakeshore cabins start at $745/week for a two bedroom.

Food

With service and ambience to match the great food, your best all-around dining option is **Old Broadway,** 319 Broadway, 320/763-3999. Prime rib, their specialty, is served daily, and a 16-oz. cut is $18. Other steak and seafood platters average out to about the same price, while a sampling of Mexican, Chinese, and Italian dishes are all around $9. Open daily for lunch and dinner; reservations recommended.

GULLIBLE'S TRAVELS

8 Goths and 22 Norwegians on exploration journey from Vinland over the West We had camp by 2 skerries one days journey north from this stone We were and fished one day After we came home found 10 men red with blood and dead Ave Maria Save from evil.

On November 8, 1898 Swedish immigrant Olaf Ohman and his 10-year old son Edward were pulling stumps on the family farm about three miles northeast of Kensington. Edward, as the story goes, noticed strange markings on a rock he found under a poplar tree. The 202-pound sandstone slab measured 31 by 16 by six inches and bore the above text on its smooth face while "Have 10 of our party by the sea to look after our ships 14 days journey from this island Year 1362" was carved on an edge. If the runic inscriptions were genuine it would show that Vikings were exploring what is now Minnesota at least as early as 1362, 130 years before Columbus sailed the ocean blue.

After Ohman cleaned it up the stone was displayed in a bank window in Kensington, but when newspapers reported the story the next year it was sent to the University of Minnesota and Chicago's Northwestern University where Scandinavian scholars unanimously declared it a fake. Interest quickly died and Ohman used it as a doorstep. The legend got a second wind in 1907 when Hjalmar Holand, a Norwegian-born historian from Wisconsin with an interest in Scandinavian settlements, bought the stone and became its greatest champion. Holand gave speeches, wrote books and articles, and took the stone to Europe. Constant Larson urged a group of ten Alexandria businessmen to chip in $200 apiece to buy the stone back and then his daughter Lorayne took the stone on tour around the country during much of the 1930s promoting the now legendary Viking exploration. In 1948, after pressure by Minnesota's Congressional delegation, the rock ended up on display at the Smithsonian—which labeled it with ". . . might be one of the most important pieces of evidence for pre-Columbian European exploration of North America."—making it a national phenomenon. The stone continues to travel though it now spends most of its time in Alexandria's Runestone Museum.

Not letting evidence or logic get in the way amateur sleuths have used the stone's 70 words to create a fanciful history. Although exactly which lake is detailed in the carving remains a topic of debate amongst Runestone proponents the generally accepted story has the 30 Vikings, including English astronomer Nicolas of Lynn as navigator, sailing from Vinland (a proven Norse settlement in Newfoundland circa 1000) up to Hudson Bay where Nicolas discovered the magnetic North Pole. They then took the Nelson River to Lake Winnipeg, headed south along the Red River, and followed a now extinct chain of lakes and streams south to Sauk Centre where they performed some religious ceremony at a massive stone altar. For some reason they remained behind and lived out their days with Mandan Indians in the Dakotas.

Not only is the entire legend preposterous on its face, but to believe it you have to ignore a mountain of contrarian evidence. Despite their initial endorsement an embarrassed Smithsonian now considers the rock a fraud and though they do not hold an "official" position the Minnesota Historical Society has spent considerable effort investigating and subsequently denouncing it. In fact, no reputable historian, archaeologist, or linguist backs the stone's validity—those who do are self-taught or work in unrelated fields. Although the reasons are many, the primary factors pointing to a hoax are the lack of any other legitimate archaeological evidence suggesting that Vikings traveled through the continent's interior and the fact that nearly half of the runes didn't exist in the 14th century.

It's highly unlikely that seafaring people who enriched themselves plundering coastlines would end up on the Minnesota prairie, a place where it just so happens that masses of Scandinavians would settle five centuries later. Historians also point out that the idea of Vikings traveling for the sake of exploration is absurd—they would not have headed inland without an economic incentive. Even taking the giant leap that Norsemen would or could have journeyed here the anachronistic message they supposedly left behind gives the prank away. Looking at the runic forms, vocabulary, and grammar nearly half of the text could not have come from the 14th century. As one scholar has stated, the text "is the way my grandfather would write, not my ancestors from the 1300s."

Not that they are needed, but there are plenty of other facts working against the reality of the runestone including: the face is only barely weathered; Ohman was a stone mason; like all other boys his age in Sweden he learned runes in school; Ohman's extensive library contained several books on Swedish history that would have aided him in carving the stone; neighbors remembered Ohman, who had little education but was very smart, expressing a desire to put one over on "them that was educated;" geological surveys show lake levels were not significantly different 500 years ago than they are today; and the Minnesota Historical Society has taped interviews with people who claim their father admitted assisting Ohman to pull off the hoax.

For the most part runestone believers have just one strategy to rely on: claiming the experts are wrong. They contend that the language of the text really was in use back in the 14th century, there are just no surviving examples, and the dozens of 14th century Norse artifacts found in this part of the country and dismissed by archaeologists are in fact real. Supporters also frequently cite the "discovery" of many mooring rocks across this part of Minnesota. The boulders with triangular-shaped holes cut into them—in order to fasten anchor pegs for their boats—are similar to those used by Vikings along the Norwegian coast at that same time, however, these holes have been clearly shown to have been drilled by modern inhabitants for blasting.

More "proof" of the stone's authenticity came in 2001 when a 2,200-pound granite boulder bearing more runes was found on an island a quarter mile from where the Kensington Runestone was unearthed. The AVM stone, so named because it also bears those letters, bears the year 1363 leading to the speculation that the Vikings stuck around the area. Members of the Kensington Runestone Scientific Testing Team presumed the new find genuine; however, instead of being the smoking gun advocates had hoped for, the big breakthrough was revealed as the work of five UofM graduate students in 1985. Their goal at the time was to see if runestone believers would accept their "obviously false" carvings.

Whether the Kensington Runestone was a record of Vikings in Minnesota during the 14th century or a well executed hoax perpetrated by clever immigrant farmers was once a hot topic of discussion in the state—any mention in a newspaper resulted in a flood of letters from both sides—though there is relatively little interest in the topic today. New translations and theories continue to pop up regularly and these still often earn a headline, but most people now accept that it is nothing more than a monument to Scandinavian immigrant humor.

The atmosphere is more relaxed, but the food is also good at **Depot Express,** 104 Broadway, 320/763-7712, in the old Burlington Northern train depot. Steak, seafood, and Italian make up much of the menu, with entrées ranging from under $6 to over $16. Ordering pizza requires choosing from five sauces including "salsa hot sauce" and some creative toppings like wild rice. Dine inside or get in a bit of bird-watching from their patio overlooking Lake Agnes. Open daily for lunch and dinner with live music on weekends.

The city's oldest restaurant, the **Traveler's Inn,** 511 Broadway, 320/763-4000, opened in 1928 and is still going strong. The reasonably priced American fare is complemented by a couple of Italian plates. Open daily for breakfast, lunch, and dinner.

The **Daily Grind,** 518 Broadway, 320/762-7240, serves coffees plus sandwiches and snacks. They are open for breakfast, lunch, and early dinner, but stay open later if a band is playing.

Shopping

Serious shoppers could spend the better part of a day at the half-dozen antique stores downtown on Broadway. **Yesterday's,** 517 Broadway, 320/762-8990; and **Now & Then,** 601 Broadway, 320/763-6467, both have about 30 dealers each, and the latter also has an art gallery and sells Amish furniture. Off Broadway are **The Farmhouse,** 609 N. Nokomis St., 320/762-2243; and **Somewhere in Time,** 514 Nokomis St., 320/762-7275.

Used-book lovers will find the **Vikingland Book Trader,** 605 Broadway, 320/762-8722, worth a browse. The **Scandinavian Gift Shop,** 604 Broadway, 320/763-6363, across the street, sells what it says it does.

Information and Services

The **Alexandria Area Chamber of Commerce,** 206 Broadway, 320/763-3161 or 800/245-2539, www.alexandriamn.org, has offices at the Runestone Museum and they can help you find lodging vacancies.

Transportation

Greyhound buses stop at the B&H gas station, 320/763-7390, along I-94. It is quite far from downtown, so you may want to call **Radio Cab,** 320/763-3333.

Twin Cities Passenger Service, 320/762-1544 or 800/950-2930, runs to and from the Minneapolis-St Paul International Airport twice a day during the week and once on weekends from the parking lot behind the Traveler's Inn, 511 Broadway. A one-way ticket is $36.

AROUND ALEXANDRIA

Sauk Centre

Though you may never have heard of Sauk Centre, in the 1920s it was the most famous small town in America thanks to native son Sinclair Lewis. America's first winner of the Nobel Prize for literature based his 1920 novel *Main Street* on his hometown, and though he called it Gopher Prairie the veil was very thin. The book attacked the simple-mindedness of small town America and, while local residents were outraged, it was both a popular and critical sensation nationally. Ever since then sociologists and journalists have come to Sauk Centre to take the pulse of Middle America. Surprisingly, many residents, especially those who knew the families of the real people behind the characters, still harbor resentment over Lewis' book, though by now most have either forgiven or forgotten—and those who haven't have decided to keep quiet while they capitalize on his fame.

The **Sinclair Lewis Interpretive Center,** 320/352-5201, along I-94 greets visitors arriving from the south. Besides providing an in-depth look at Lewis' life, the center has a brief history of the town and is home to the chamber of commerce. On the same grounds is the restored **Little Red Schoolhouse.** Ask the chamber staff for a look inside. The city wants to sell this land to developers, so the center could be in a new location by the time you visit. It is open weekdays 8:30 A.M.–5 P.M., plus weekends 9 A.M.–5 P.M. during the summer.

In town the **Sinclair Lewis Boyhood Home,** 820 Sinclair Lewis Ave., 320/352-5359, a quaint, 1884 East Lake cottage where Lewis lived from 1889 to 1902, has been restored to the way it

© TIM BEWER

original Main Street

looked when he was growing up. Many of the events in his books actually took place in this house, and you will hear about several during the half-hour guided tours. The house, a National Historic Landmark, is open Monday–Saturday 9:30 A.M.–5 P.M. and Sunday 10:30 A.M.–5 P.M. during the summer. Admission is $3. Lewis was born in the smaller red and white house across the street at number 811, and his ashes are buried in the family plot in Greenwood Cemetery (from the main entrance, it is three rows in and eight monuments to the left) a mile east of downtown on Sinclair Lewis Avenue. Sticking with what works, the city celebrates Sinclair Lewis Days the third weekend of July with a catalog of typical small town Americana including fireworks, a craft show, softball tournament, beauty pageant, and parade. The Sauk Centre Area Historical Society publishes a *Discovery Walking Tour* brochure that points out many other noteworthy buildings in town. The historical society also have a small collection of photos and artifacts in their new **Sauk Centre Area Historical Society Museum** in the

basement of the library, 430 Main St. S., 320/351-8777. It is open Tuesday 2–4:30 P.M. and admission is free.

The city's main attraction not related to Sinclair Lewis, although he did work here for some time (and was fired for reading and sleeping on the job), is the **Palmer House,** 228 Main St., 320/351-9100 or 888/222-3431, a 1901 redbrick hotel and restaurant. Rooms are small but atmospheric and it is far and away the best place to spend the night; rates start at $55. The cheapest beds in town are at the **Hillcrest Motel,** 965 Main St. S., 320/352-2215 or 800/858-6333, where clean and cozy rooms are under $40. You've seen his homes, his museum, and his grave, now, if you're carrying your own shelter, you might as well stay at the **Sinclair Lewis Campground,** just northwest of downtown where 80 sites for $15 each are crammed up against Sauk Lake. As you'd expect, the Palmer House is also *the* place to dine. Pasta primavera ($10) and lemon-baked walleye ($14) are typical entrées from the fairly pricey menu. Cheaper American fare is available at the no-frills **Main Street Café,** 303 Main St., 320/352-5396. **Greyhound** buses stop at Care Free Travel, 620 Sinclair Lewis Ave., 320/352-5781. **Twin City Passenger Service,** 800/950-2930, stops at the Truckers Inn (I-94 and U.S. 71) on its run to the Minneapolis-St Paul International Airport, but the best way to get here is by bike on the paved **Lake Wobegon Regional Trail,** which runs for 28 miles between Sauk Centre and Avon.

Glenwood

The city of Glenwood hugs the northeast edge of 7,110-acre Lake Minnewaska, Minnesota's 13th largest body of water. Splendid views over the lake and town can be had from **Mt. Lookout,** a 90-foot bluff-top overlook on Highway 55 at 14th Ave. NE. Also with worthy views (if only that house wasn't there) is **Indian Mounds Park,** where Princess Minnewaska and Chief White Bear are buried. Take Highway 28/29 to County Road 24 for three miles and look for the sign. Even more Native American lore is on display in town at the excellent **Pope County Historical Museum,** 809 S. Lakeshore Dr., 320/634-3293.

The Helbing Gallery of Indian Arts and Crafts is good enough to have attracted the attention of the Smithsonian Institute, but Cleora Helbing, a Glenwood native who gathered this priceless collection as director of education for the Bureau of Indian Affairs, wanted it displayed in her hometown. The museum also houses displays of old industry and recreation in the 10,000 sq. foot exhibition hall. Out back are a couple of log homes, a one-room schoolhouse, and a building filled with farm machinery and a two-headed cow, amongst other things. It is open weekdays 9 A.M.–4:30 P.M. plus weekends during the summer. Admission is $3. The active Pope County Historical Society also maintains the **Ann Bickle Heritage House & Bremness Gallery,** 214 E. Minnesota Ave. The 1913 Craftsman-style home was Glenwood's fanciest when built and has a lovely English garden in the backyard. The gallery displays the work of local artists. Inquire at the museum about opening times since, at the moment, the historical society doesn't have enough volunteers to keep these open on a regular basis.

You can watch trout swim around in ponds at the **State Fish Hatchery** less than a mile west of town on North Lakeshore Drive. A walleye hatchery also operates from mid-April to mid-May. Open weekdays 8 A.M.–4:30 P.M. Admission is free. Glenwood residents have staged the **Waterama** festival since 1956, making it one of the oldest community festivals in Minnesota. The three days of family fun takes place the last full weekend in July and include a lighted pontoon parade, sailing regattas, water-ski shows, and fireworks.

The only lodging in Glenwood is the 57-room **Scotwood Motel,** 320/634-5105, out at the junction of Highways 55 and 28, where you get a room from $63. It has a pool and a hot tub. The city operates a campground in Barsness Park, but the nearby Glacial Lakes State Park is a better option. The **Franklin Street Diner and Coffeehouse,** 9 N. Franklin St., 320/634-3371, goes beyond the standard cheap family fare with a Monday pizza buffet. Open daily for breakfast, lunch, and dinner.

Glacial Lakes State Park

Although the name celebrates the park's unique geology, Glacial Lakes is actually one of the state's best prairie experiences. Kettle lakes sit nestled in valleys surrounded by rolling fields of big and little bluestem, pasqueflower, and goldenrod. From atop the bare hills, which appear as if they long to be mountain ranges, you can gaze out across a fairly pristine landscape. Both the biology and the geology of the 1,850-acre park are discussed along the half-mile **Prairie-Woodland Interpretive Trail,** which has a beaver lodge along it. The epicenter of park activity is the remarkably pure 56-acre Mountain Lake, the park's largest, where swimming, fishing, and boating (canoes and rowboats are available for rent) are big draws on summer weekends; during the week the park can be nearly deserted. The 39 campsites (14 electric) are nestled in the shade of an oak grove, while six backpack sites are scattered down the 16 miles of hiking trails that cross the warped terrain. Horseback riders have three sites of their own at the head of the 11 miles of trail open to them. In winter follow the six miles of groomed cross-country ski trails or rent snowshoes from the office and explore on your own. Call 320/239-2860 with any questions.

Brainerd Lakes

It's all about a week at the lake. Minnesota's most popular vacation destination spans five counties and five hundred lakes. Brainerd is the unofficial gateway to "Up North" and, for the most part, people spend their time here fishing, golfing, and shopping, but there's also a lot of history to explore, from ancient Native American burial mounds to Charles Lindbergh's boyhood home. Since it all sits just a couple of hours outside of the Twin Cities, the weekend crowds can be a little maddening at times, especially on the roads. Half of all resort revenue for the entire state comes out of this little area, and the lakes suffer more second-home development than anywhere else in Minnesota. For a fun family getaway the Brainerd Lakes area can't be beat—if you're looking for a peaceful wilderness escape then keep on driving.

Lake Country Accommodations

Even with well over 300 choices, finding a room on short notice during summer weekends isn't very easy. If you are having no luck on your own, check with the **Brainerd Lakes Area Chamber of Commerce,** 124 N. 6th St., 218/829-2838 or 800/450-2838, which maintains a vacancy list for their 135 or so members. You can either do the search yourself at www.explorebrainerdlakes.com, or call and let them do it for you. A list is posted outside their office before it closes up for the day.

BRAINERD

Brainerd is an If You Build It They Will Come success story. For over a century Crow Wing, a town built by fur traders, was the northernmost European settlement on the Mississippi River. Naturally Crow Wing's 700 residents expected that the new Northern Pacific Railroad would come through their town, but in 1870 the railroad decided to bridge the river 10 miles north and Brainerd was born. The railroad also chose to build their repair yards here and by 1873 21 stores, 18 hotels, 15 saloons, and five churches had sprung up to serve the new residents, while Crow Wing was already nearly a ghost town.

Though a nationwide financial panic that year hit the town hard it soon recovered. The Northern Pacific was the town's biggest employer and their facilities, still standing east of downtown, were valued at $2 million in 1888. The 1880s were also the peak of the area's logging industry, and some 8,000 lumberjacks would descend on town on payday to drink, gamble, whore, and fight away their salary. Still, town boosters boasted of Brainerd's chivalry and claimed that women were safe on the streets at any hour of the day. The forests were finally cut over by around 1910, but the immense railroad operations, the influx of tourists to area lakes, and the discovery of iron in the nearby Cuyuna Range kept the city moving forward. The massive rail yards are now just a shadow of their former selves and the last paper mill is a pretty small operation, leaving tourism as the lynchpin of the economy.

Brainerd and its western neighbor Baxter have grown right up against each other and are essentially one city; the most noticeable difference between the two is that Brainerd has an actual downtown. Just about all commercial development is stretched out along Highways 210 and

BRAINERD LAKES LINKS

With 33 courses the Brainerd area has grown into Minnesota's premier golfing destination and *Golf Digest* has rated this as the world's 40th best Golf Destination. Acclaimed creators such as Robert Trent Jones Jr., Joel Goldstrand, and Arnold Palmer have carved out many world class holes, that, while not cheap, are veritable bargains when compared with courses of similar quality in better known places.

An informal survey resulted in the following list of central Minnesota's best courses: **Black Brook, Deacon's Lodge, Golden Eagle, The Classic, The Legacy, The Pines** (the state's only five-star public course in *Golf Digest*'s 2002–2003 Places to Play ranking), **The Preserve,** and **Whitefish Golf Club.**

371, which are the roads people drive down to get to the area lakes.

Sights

If you're like me you can't hear the name Brainerd without fond memories of Steve Buscemi uttering the name in the movie *Fargo*. The film also featured a giant statue of Paul Bunyan looming over the highway (you won't find it, though; it was built just for the movie). Brainerd's real Paul Bunyan statue resides at **This Old Farm,** 17469 Highway 18 E., 218/764-2915 or 877/412-4164, seven miles east of town. After the meet and greet with the 26-foot-tall Paul which waves and welcomes children by name, you can enjoy Dick Rademacher's immense private collection of antiques and collectibles. His "hobby gone mad" encompasses over 20,000 items ranging from antique chainsaws to dancing raisin figurines, and much of the collection is housed in historic buildings, including a one-room schoolhouse, log cabin, and the train depot used in the movie *Iron Will*. There is also a Saturday Farmers Market, and each fall you can lose yourself in the 15-acre corn-maze for $6 or shoot it up in the paintball maze for $10—rental equipment is available. During Show Days, the second weekend in August, many artists and enthusiasts descend on the site to show some of the old equipment in operation. The museum is open Thursday–Sunday 10 A.M.–5 P.M. during the summer and admission is $5.

The city's 1917 jailhouse now houses the **Crow Wing County Historical Museum,** 320 Laurel St., 218/829-3268. Naturally, much of the collection is related to the logging era, though railroad, mining, and Native American artifacts are also featured, plus a couple of the old cells were left intact. The highlight is the 1890s all-wood ox-cart. Tours of the sheriff's quarters, restored and furnished as they were in the early 20th century, are given on demand. The museum is open weekdays 9 A.M.–5 P.M. during the summer and 1–5 P.M. the rest of the year, plus Saturday 10 A.M.–2 P.M. Admission is $3.

The ironically-named **Paul Bunyan Nature Learning Center,** 1308 N. County Road 49, 218/829-9620, is just north of town. The kid-focused interpretive center is filled with hands-on plant, animal, and mineral material, naturalists offer various programs, and three miles of hiking trails lead through the 145-acre site. The center is open year-round, though the building's hours vary with the season.

Recreation

The **Paul Bunyan State Trail** starts behind the Paul Bunyan Amusement Center and runs 48 paved miles to Hackensack. You can rent a bike at **Easy Rider,** 415 Washington St., 218/829-5516. They charge $15/half-day, $23/full-day, and also rent in-line skates, canoes, kayaks, cross-country skis, and snowshoes. Over 100 classic bikes are on display. **Paul Bunyan Bike Shuttle & Rental,** 218/839-8093 or 218/568-8422, will deliver bikes right to you and arrange transportation to any location on the trail. If you'd rather ride a horse than a bike, call **Outback Trail Rides,** 218/746-3990. They can take riders of all abilities through the Pillsbury State Forest; a one-hour ride costs $20. They also offer pony rides and a day camp for the kids.

© TIM BEWER

Brainerd's larger-than-life lumberjack

The **Northland Arboretum,** 218/829-8770, covers nearly 500 acres of forest, marsh, and prairie and is best known for its 12 miles of ski trail—three miles are lit at night. The trails are open to hikers the rest of the year. The Nature Conservancy protects a 160-acre jack pine savanna within the preserve, one of just five remaining examples of this rare ecosystem in the state. There is also a garden and reflecting pond based on Monet's garden in Giverny, France, and a native tree trail. The entrance is on NW 7th St. right behind the Westgate Mall. A day pass costs $3 per person or $5 per group. The chamber of commerce distributes a free packet with maps of other ski trails around town.

Downhill skiers and snowboarders have 14 runs on the west shore of Gull Lake at **Ski Gull,** 218/963-4353. They sometimes run a shuttle bus to Brainerd.

Entertainment and Events

Brainerd's history is regaled through song and dance by **Rhythm of the Rails,** which is slated to move out to This Old Farm (see Sights in this section). Performances are held on Thursday, Friday, and Saturday nights at 8 P.M. during the last three weekends of July, and tickets are cheap. **Coco Moon,** 601 Laurel St., 218/825-7955, coffeehouse has occasional music, including a Thursday night bluegrass jam.

The hottest tickets in town are for the races at the **Colonel's Brainerd International Raceway,** 4343 Hwy. 371 N., 218/824-7220, seven miles north of Brainerd. Stock cars, superbikes, and muscle cars race on the three-mile, ten-turn track between May and September. The raceway's weeklong **NHRA Nationals** in mid-August is far and away the town's biggest event.

The **Brainerd Jaycees Ice Fishing Extravaganza** is the world's largest ice fishing tournament with literally thousands of anglers drilling holes on Gull Lake. The $150,000 in prizes are up for grabs the third Saturday in January.

The Brainerd Jaycees Ice Fishing Extravaganza is the world's largest ice fishing tournament with literally thousands of anglers drilling holes on Gull Lake.

Accommodations

A pair of the state's largest and fanciest resorts **Madden's,** 218/829-2811 or 800/642-5363; and **Cragun's,** 218/825-2700 or 800/272-4867, sit next to each other on the south shore of Gull Lake eight miles west of Brainerd and both are very similar—so similar, in fact, that Madden's trap shooting field and USCA sanctioned croquet lawn and Cragun's golf simulator and ban on personal watercraft are some of the few things setting them apart. One other major difference is that Madden's shuts their doors from late October to mid-April and Cragun's operates year-round. Both have beaches, spas, tennis courts, marinas with boat rentals, and a busy scheduled of activities ranging from horseback riding to bonfires, while their golf courses—The Classic and The Legacy—are two of the state's best. Lodging options run the gamut from simple hotel rooms to deluxe lakeside cabins, and summer rates start at $135 and $169 respectively and go way up, though off-season rates can be well less than half these. There is a two-night minimum stay on summer weekends.

The U.S. Army Corps of Engineers' **Gull Lake Recreation Area,** 10867 E. Gull Lake Dr. (on County Road 125 three miles west of Hwy. 371), 218/829-3334 (877/833-6777 for reservations), has 39 shady and well-spaced campsites for $20. The campground stays open year-round, and from mid-September through April the price is $10. Also on-site are a beach, boat launch, and a dozen ancient Native American burial mounds.

Food

Morey's Market & Grille, 1650 Hwy. 371 N., 218/829-8248, is more market than grill, but that hasn't stopped it from becoming one of Lake Country's favorite restaurants. Eight dollars will get you a fantastic sandwich, salad, or seafood selection—you can even choose any fish in the store and they will prepare it according to your wishes. Open daily for lunch and dinner.

If you want to dine with a view, there's no topping the **Knotty Bear,** 218/828-8444, a 65-foot mock-paddlewheeler, cruising Gull Lake on weekends. Their Friday and Saturday sunset dinner buffet costs $42, and the Sunday afternoon brunch spread is $23. The boat departs from Ernie's On Gull Lake, about six miles from Brainerd, from May through September, and reservations are required.

The massive malts at the 1950s-style **371 Diner,** 218/829-3359, north of town along Hwy. 371, are worth going out of your way for, as evidenced by the steady stream of patrons coming through the door for nothing else. Burgers and other menu items average seven bucks. Open daily for breakfast, lunch, and dinner.

The simple **Northwind Grille,** 603 Laurel St., 218/829-1551, downtown serves standard family fare like a roast beef sandwich, taco salad, country fried chicken, and New York strip steak. Breakfast favorites are available all day. The plates are piled high and nothing costs over $10. Open daily for breakfast and lunch, and weekdays for dinner.

The **Eclectic Café,** 717 Laurel St., 218/825-4880, is a youthful, Bohemian coffeehouse, serving exclusively shade-grown coffee and a few cheap sandwiches. Open weekdays for breakfast, lunch, and dinner. Most adults will probably feel more at home at **Coco Moon,** 601 Laurel St., 218/825-7955. Open daily for breakfast and lunch, and Fri.–Sat. for dinner.

Shopping

Brainerd's four antique shops are all located downtown within a block of each other. The largest are **Antiques on Laurel,** 711 Laurel St., 218/828-1584; and **Antiques & Accents,** 214 S. 7th St., 218/828-0724. A few local artists sell their creations at **The Crossing,** 617 Laurel St., 218/833-0416, while **Cat Tale's,** 609 Laurel St., 218/825-8611, carries used books, but has a good Minnesota section stocked with new copies. **Come See What I Saw,** 2469 Hwy. 371, 218/829-3844, is a chainsaw sculpture superstore.

In the winter, over 5,500 fish houses form the temporary city of Frostbite Flats on Mille Lacs.

Information and Services

The **Brainerd Lakes Area Chambers of Commerce,** 124 N. 6th St., 218/829-2838 or 800/450-2838, www.explorebrainerdlakes.com, sits under the city's historic water tower. Their office is open weekdays 8 A.M.–5 P.M. year-round, plus during the summer they are open Saturday 9 A.M.–4 P.M., Sunday 10 A.M.–2 P.M. and stay open until seven on Fridays.

Besides the Brainerd Public Library, 416 S. 5th St., 218/829-5574, you can access the Internet at the Eclectic Café, 717 Laurel St., 218/825-4880, which charges a $1/hour.

Transportation

The **Brainerd-Crow Wing Regional Airport,** 218/825-2166, is northeast of town along Highway 210. **Northwest Airlink,** 218/828-0572 or 800/225-2525, makes the short hop to the Twin Cities up to eight times a day. Round-trip fares start at about $175 (much less if the flight is a segment of a longer Northwest Airlines flight). **Greyhound** buses stop well south of downtown at the Econo Lodge, 2655 Hwy. 371 S., 218/828-0027. **Amtrak** service is half an hour west of Brainerd in the town of Staples.

Budget Rent-a-Car, 218/829-4660; **Enterprise Rent-a-Car,** 218/833-0430; and **National Car Rental,** 218/829-7321, all have branches here, plus **Brainerd Area Taxi,** 218/828-1111, is available 24 hours a day.

MILLE LACS

Two hundred and seven-square-mile Lake Mille Lacs, Minnesota's second largest lake, is an angler magnet. Hundreds of thousands of walleye, a surprising number of them trophy size, are caught yearly making it the top catch, but muskie, smallmouth bass, and northern pike are all enormous and abundant. Marinas, bait shops, and public landings ring the lake, though the easiest way for the occasional angler to land a lunker is to join a launch. These large boats, long a part of Mille Lacs' history, depart from many area resorts. The

MILLE LACS RESERVATION

Total Area - 103 sq. miles
Tribally Owned - 6 percent
Total Population - 4,704
Native Population - 1,171
Tribal Enrollment - 3,292

During the forced migration of Minnesota's Ojibwe to the White Earth Reservation in the mid-19th century, few people remained on their native homelands. One such group, the Non-Removal Mille Lacs Chippewa Band, as they became known to U.S. government officials, resisted and stayed put around Lake Mille Lacs despite the resulting oppression and persecution. Although most of their native lands were cleared for lumber and then made into dairy farms, eventually the reservation—albeit a diminished one—was restored thanks to the few hundred resilient members left behind. Most tribal lands lie on the south side of the lake though other parcels are scattered

widely across Pine and Aitkin Counties. Tribal headquarters are in Onamia.

Thanks to its location on a large lake and its proximity to the Twin Cities the tribe has been very successful and uses much of its tourism and gaming revenue to buy more land. In the process their gaming enterprises (they run casinos in Onamia and Hinckley) has reduced the tribe's unemployment rate to an unusually low three percent. Tourism, however, is a double-edged sword as the influx of visitors drives up property values, making the purchase of land expensive for the tribe.

The area's native singing and drumming once caught the ear of Grateful Dead member Mickey Hart, who featured two songs by the tribe's own Little Otter Singers on the *Honor The Earth Powwow: Songs of the Great Lakes Indians* album recorded for Hart's "The World" music series. The well-known song and drum group has other releases available too.

action doesn't let down even a little in the winter when over 5,500 fish houses, linked by plowed roads and regular shuttle service, form the temporary city of Frostbite Flats. You can rent one of these fish houses, decked out with propane heaters and electrical generators for lights and television, from area resorts by the day or overnight.

Though it often seems like it, fishing isn't the only diversion here. Nature lovers will love Mille Lacs Kathio State Park, and there is plenty of room on the lake for sailing and windsurfing. If you just want a scenic country drive, the less developed north and east shores deliver.

Sights

The Ojibwe tell their own story at the **Mille Lacs Indian Museum,** 320/532-3632, a cooperative venture between the Mille Lacs Band and the Minnesota Historical Society. The museum traces their history and displays let you learn about their fantastic beadwork, the significance of what you'll see at a powwow, and modern sovereignty issues. The heart of the center is the Four Seasons Room, where life-sized dioramas show what life was like here 200 years ago.

Cooking and craft demonstrations are held frequently, and native-made products are for sale in the restored 1930s trading post, one of many that operated along the shore in those days. The museum is located along U.S. 169 eight miles south of Garrison. May through August it is open Monday–Saturday 10 A.M.–6 P.M. and Sunday noon–6 P.M., plus Thursday–Saturday 10 A.M.–5 P.M. and Sunday noon–5 P.M. the rest of the year. Admission is $6.

The **Mille Lacs Lake Museum,** 405 W. Main St., 320/676-3945, in Isle has a small local history hodgepodge in a pair of old one-room schoolhouses. The highlight is the Model T modified to run as a snowmobile. It is open Friday 1–7 P.M., Saturday 10 A.M.–4 P.M., and Sunday 1–3 P.M. during the summer. Admission is free.

Of interest to serious bird-watchers are Hennepin and Spirit Islands, two rocky islets in the south end of the lake, that together comprise the **Mille Lacs National Wildlife Refuge.** Though they cover just over half an acre (the nation's smallest NWR), the islands are nevertheless a vital nesting habitat for the Caspian and common terns and are used by many other migrating species

CENTRAL LAKES

© TIM BEWER

bandolier bag at Mille Lacs Indian Museum

unusual to the area, such as arctic loons and Baird's sandpipers. Bring a good pair of binoculars since the islands are closed to the public and visitors are requested to approach no closer than 100 feet. You don't need to boat out to the islands for good bird-watching though, some 230 species of birds have been recorded around the lake, and bald eagles are frequently spotted soaring overhead.

Don't forget to get your picture taken with the **giant walleye sculptures** in Garrison and Isle.

State Parks

Two state parks grace the lake's southern shore. At just 318 acres **Father Hennepin State Park,** 320/676-8763, over by Isle, is used primarily for its two large campgrounds (103 sites, 41 electric) and for access to the lake at its beach, fishing piers, and boat launches. It's also worth spending some time trying to spot the albino deer along the four miles of rolling hiking trails, half of which are groomed for cross-country skiing in the winter. Hennepin Island is visible from the beach.

Mille Lacs Kathio State Park, 320/532-3523, is 10,585 beautiful acres of steep forested hills and deep lakes. While a quick look at a map explains why the French dubbed the region Thousand Lakes (only later was it applied to Spirit Lake, as the Dakota called it), Kathio, as this specific spot on the southwest shore is known, is a name without meaning. The Dakota called it Izatys and so did French explorer Daniel Greysolon, Sieur du Lhut in 1679 after he became the first European to travel here. Someone mistranscribed the "Iz" in his journal to a "K" and later mispronunciations resulted in Kathio. Izatys was an important civic and religious site for the Dakota before they were driven out by the Ojibwe in the Battle of Kathio, a legendary three-day battle that not all historians are convinced really occurred. The archaeological record here actually extends back 9,000 years to the earliest nomadic Paleo-Indians, and more than 20 significant archaeological sites have been uncovered so far, leading to designation of the park as a National Historic Landmark. The whole human history, as well as natural topics, are presented at the park's informative **Kathio Interpretive Center.**

The park's most popular walk is the **Touch the Earth Trail,** a self-guiding loop behind the Interpretive Center. It passes through a variety of forest types, including a tamarack bog via a boardwalk. The wonderful 3.2-mile **Landmark Trail** combines history and scenery. Just a short distance from the parking area the trail passes ancient burial mounds and the site of a former Dakota village with signs explaining how life was once lived here. The trail continues past lovely lake views over the interior hills. The rest of the park's 31 miles of hiking trail (25 of which are shared with horseback riders) are seldom used during the summer because they can be very muddy and buggy; however, since maples are abundant they are absolutely wonderful for fall color. You'll find the steepest hills along the northernmost loops, while the seldom-used trails south of the river are less hilly overall, though far from flat. In winter 20 miles of trail are groomed for beginner and expert skiers and are often mentioned as Minnesota's best. Both skis and snowshoes are available for rent, and there is a popular sledding hill. Mille Lacs Kathio also has a vertigo-inspiring 100-foot **fire tower** to climb, a swimming pond, and canoes and rowboats are available for rent if you want to paddle the Rum River or the lakes along it.

Just about every site in the two campgrounds is shaded and secluded. The Petaga Campground has 48 regular campsites (22 electric) plus five camper cabins with heat, electricity, and screened porches and three secluded walk-in sites. Much more peaceful are the 26 sites in the primitive Ogechie Campground. Horse riders have a separate camp.

Other Recreation

The **Rum River** spills out of Mille Lacs' southwest end and can be paddled all the way to Anoka where it feeds the Mississippi, a trip of 148 miles. The first eight miles to Onamia cuts across Mille Lacs Kathio State Park and flows through three lakes. It's an easy day trip. Downstream from Onamia all the way to Princeton the Rum is shallow and rocky with a few small rapids and may need to be waded at times; ask locally about water levels. Another recommended day trip (though a campsite allows this to be an overnighter, too) is the 15 miles from U.S. 169 to Milaca. The wildest and most scenic part of the river is the winding stretch between Princeton and Cambridge. If you want to be guided down the river, call or stop by **Lundeen's Tackle Castle,** 320/532-3416, at the junction of Highways 169 and 27.

Eleven miles of the **Soo Line Trail** between Onamia and Isle are paved for bike riders. You can rent bikes in Isle at **Hardware Hank,** 150 W. Main St., 320/676-8670. **White Bear Ranch,** 320/532-5706, near Onamia, offers horseback riding trips.

Entertainment and Events

Besides gambling, the **Grand Casino Mille Lacs,** 320/532-7777 or 800/626-5825, operated by the Mille Lacs Band Ojibwe, also hosts big-name musical acts a couple times a month. It's mostly country and western performers, but there is sometimes a little variety. The Mille Lacs Band also hosts two powwows: the **Memorial Pow-**

wow is held on Memorial Day, and the **Mille Lacs Annual Powwow** takes place the third weekend of August.

Accommodations

There are over three-dozen resorts on the lake, but that large number doesn't represent the limited choices you have since most are aging family-run fishing establishments. On the other end of the spectrum is **Izaty's Golf and Yacht Club,** 320/532-3101 or 800/533-1728, a popular getaway for Twin Citians on the lake's south shore, with a 120-slip marina. Other amenities on the 650 acres include a pair of 18-hole golf courses (two of the state's best), tennis courts, indoor and outdoor pools, a beach, and boat rental. The Kids' Klub lets parents do their own thing during the day. The rooms, as fancy as the surroundings, include four-bedroom lakeshore townhouses with kitchens and fireplaces costing $495 and hotel rooms from $129. Much simpler and more fishing focused is **Eddy's Lake Mille Lacs Resort,** 320/532-3657 or 800/657-4704, between Garrison and Onamia. Besides the 80 motel rooms ($90) with a pool, whirlpool, and sauna, Eddy's has a large marina, launch and guide service, and a free shuttle to the casino.

The **Grand Casino Mille Lacs Hotel,** 320/532-7777 or 800/468-3517, has 284-rooms, yet they're often full on weekends. Standard quarters cost $95, while two-room suites with fireplaces and whirlpools are almost twice that. Guest amenities include a pool, whirlpool, sauna, and exercise room. The **Garrison Inn & Suites,** 320/692-4050 or 800/456-4000, has a pool, whirlpool, and good rooms from $95. The **Northern Inn,** 125 N. Main St., 320/495-3332, in Wahkon has basic but spanking-new rooms from $69 and is a good value for this area.

Food

The home-cooking at **Svoboda's Spotlite,** 111 Madison St., 320/692-4692, in Garrison is a family tradition for many locals. The food is scrumptious, portions large, and prices low. They are open daily for breakfast and lunch with dinner served weekends.

Another casual place is **Eddy's Waterfront,**

320/532-3657, at Eddy's Lake Mille Lacs Resort along U.S. 169 about five miles north of Onamia. For a real Minnesota feast there is all-you-can-eat walleye on Friday and Saturday nights, and you can even give them your day's catch and let them cook it up for you. The mostly American menu ($5–15) even has several vegetarian options. Open daily for breakfast, lunch, and dinner.

For variety, nothing comes close to the Grand Casino. The inevitable **Grand Buffet** isn't quite up to Las Vegas standards, but it features over 100 items for $7 lunch and $9–16 dinner. The **Grand Northern Grill,** open 24 hours, serves a standard American menu averaging $10. Their **Woodlands Steakhouse,** with steak and seafood averaging $20, tries to be elegant.

The fanciest dining of all is at **Izatys.** The menu is surprisingly creative, with items such as Bayou pasta, Southwest salmon, and nuevo Latino pork chops. Try fried walleye cheeks ("the calamari of Lake Mille Lacs") as an appetizer. Lunch entrées run $8–20 and dinner is considerably more expensive. Open daily for lunch and dinner.

Fans of useless trivia will want to know that Garrison, with just 213 residents, is the smallest town in the world with a McDonald's.

Shopping

Scattered antique stores and generic gift shops pop up all around the lake, but Isle has the most varied and interesting selection. Tops on the list is **Someday Isle . . .,** 250 W. Main St., 320/676-1962, operated by a dedicated bunch whose enthusiasm is infectious. Local artists sell a variety of work including hand-woven rugs, many of which are made on-site—visitors can often take a seat at a loom and give it a try. There is also workspace for artists, many of whom tutor local children. Though the Grand Casino has a gift shop with a few Native American crafts, anyone interested in these items should do their shopping at the Mille Lacs Indian Museum.

Information

You can pick up brochures or ask questions at the **Mille Lacs Lake Tourism Office,** 320/532-5626 or 888/350-2692, www.millelacs.com, located

in Onamia's renovated depot. The depot also houses a small art gallery. It is open weekdays 9 A.M.–4 P.M. In Garrison, a little hut along U.S. 169 is staffed Thursday–Monday 9 A.M.–5 P.M. from May through September.

Transportation

Lorenz buses stop at the Gateway gas station, 320/532-3787, just south of Onamia, Grand Casino Mille Lacs, and the Super America gas station, 320/692-4999, in Garrison on their run between Minneapolis and Virginia.

SOUTH OF BRAINERD
Crow Wing State Park

Considering its location—nine miles south of Brainerd along Highway 371—you'd expect Crow Wing State Park, 218/829-8022, to be overflowing with visitors, but in their rush to get up to the lake most people drive right on by, leaving the park nice and peaceful. Allan Morrison established a trading post here at the junction of the Mississippi and Crow Wing Rivers in 1823. The town, also named Crow Wing, that grew up around it was for half a century the northernmost European settlement on the Mississippi, and many of the state's most influential early citizens settled here. Clement Beaulieu came in 1847 to run the American Fur Company's operations, and he built what was in its day a stately mansion. It was about this time that the economy was transitioning from fur to timber, and several mission churches were established. Crow Wing's population reached 700, but when the Northern Pacific Railroad chose to cross the Mississippi ten miles to the north, where the city of Brainerd now stands, Crow Wing quickly died. Today a boardwalk leads through the old village site with signs discussing life in that era, though all that remains is the Greek Revival **Beaulieu House** and a couple of cemeteries—the church only dates to 1958. A section of the Woods Trail, traveled by oxcart caravans between St. Paul and Winnipeg from the 1840s to 1860s, also remains.

After visiting the modest historic site, be sure to explore some of the rest of the 2,077-acre park. The park lies at a spot where the state's

© TIM BEWER

the Mississippi River at Crow Wing State Park

three primary biomes—deciduous forest, coniferous forest, and prairie—merge, and the varied habitats make for good wildlife viewing. The 14 miles of hiking trail (six miles are groomed for cross-country skiing) are at their best where they hug the Mississippi, especially at the Chippewa Lookout, just a short climb from the boat launch. There are some rolling hills, but the trails are generally very easy. The paddling is excellent here and with calm waters it's ideal for families. Most people just canoe around the park, though longer trips on either river are excellent, especially the 10 undeveloped miles of the Mississippi downstream to the Nokasippi River. The park office has canoes and rowboats for rent, and there is a canoe-in campsite on the Mississippi. The shady campground features 60 wooded sites (12 electric) and a camper cabin.

Camp Ripley

Camp Ripley is one of the largest National Guard facilities in the United States and around 60,000

troops train here annually, many in winter skills. Visitors can pick up a self-guided tour brochure, which leads you around the base, but the main reason to stop is the **Minnesota Military Museum,** 320/632-7374. It houses several absorbing displays about all aspects of conflict from weapons to war bonds. Artillery, tanks, helicopters, and the like are displayed outside. The displays are so well done that even the most ardent pacifist will find them interesting. During the summer the museum is open Wednesday–Sunday 10 A.M.– 5 P.M., and Thursday–Friday 9 A.M.–4 P.M. the rest of the year. Admission is free. The best time to visit the base is mid-September of odd-numbered years for **Camp Ripley Community Appreciation Day** when the public are offered tours, demonstrations, and vehicle rides.

LITTLE FALLS

Charles A. Lindbergh Jr., who grew up in Little Falls, put this Mississippi River town on the map. When Lucky Lindy landed his single engine Spirit of St. Louis in Paris in 1927, he immediately became one of the most famous people in the world but he never forgot his hometown. He made several return visits over the rest of his life and wrote longingly of his life there in several books. Little Falls, likewise, continues to celebrate its most famous son.

French traders named these rapids Painted Rocks and Lt. Zebulon Pike, who wintered in a small fort here in 1804, called the falls "a remarkable rapid in the river, opposite a high piney island." Sadly, visitors today can only imagine what a wonderful scene it must have been since the falls now lay buried behind a hydroelectric dam. The rapid drop in the river was a natural spot to develop early industry, and the first dam and sawmill were built in 1849. Many more mills followed, making Little Falls a very prosperous city in its day, as evidenced by the solid downtown business district and many fine homes around it.

Sights

Lindbergh spent all of his boyhood summers in a modest 1.5-story house south of town, and lived here permanently from 1917 to 1920 to run the family farm. Now a National Historic Landmark, the **Charles A. Lindbergh House** remains almost exactly as he left it when he departed to study engineering at the University of Wisconsin. Not only are the furnishings original, but during your tour you'll see bullet holes from a gun mishap and some of the secret hiding places Lindbergh pointed out to contractors while restoration work was done. Next to the home is the **Lindbergh History Center,** 320/632-3154, dedicated in 1973 by Charles himself, commemorating the whole Lindbergh family. Exhibits about Charles Jr.'s inventions, conservation efforts, and writings clearly show that he lived a remarkable life beyond the single flight he is remembered for. There is also a 23-minute movie about Lucky Lindy's life, warts and all, and a replica of the Sprit of St. Louis' cockpit. Both are open May through Labor Day, Monday–Saturday 10 A.M.–5 P.M. and Sunday noon–5 P.M., and Saturday–Sunday through October. Closed October–May. Admission is $5.

The Lindbergh home sits at the entrance to the 436-acre **Charles A. Lindbergh State Park,** 320/616-2525, named for the more famous Lindbergh's father, whose family donated the land in his honor. The elder Lindbergh was a progressive Republican congressman (his anti-war stance cost him later elections for U.S. Senate and Minnesota governor) and pioneering conservationist. Although the park is small, walking the six miles of hiking trails or dipping a paddle in Pike Creek will satisfy nature lovers. The excellent campground has 38 (15 electric) wooded and well-spaced sites. For even more seclusion there is a backpack site that can be reached by foot or canoe. Canoes are available for rent in the summer, as are snowshoes in the winter. Cold-season visitors will also find 5.5 miles of groomed cross-country ski trails, and **Pap's Sport Shop,** 64 E. Broadway, 320/632-5171, has ski rentals.

The Morrison County Historical Society's **Charles A. Weyerhaeuser Memorial Museum,** 320/632-4007, is named for, but not specifically about, the great lumber baron. It is a small but well-presented collection with some interesting items from the logging era and an actual beaver top hat, the fashionable item that spawned the

North American fur trade. The museum is just south of the Lindbergh House, and a wooded trail along the Mississippi leads between them. It is open year-round Tuesday–Saturday 10 A.M.–5 P.M., plus Sunday 1–5 P.M. during the summer. Admission is free.

The neighboring **Weyerhaeuser and Musser Historic Homes,** both built in 1898, were erected by Charles A. Weyerhaeuser and Richard Drew Musser, the sons of lumber magnates Frederick Weyerhaeuser and Peter Musser. The twin mansions behind the Convention and Visitors Bureau (CVB) now comprise the city-owned Linden Hill Conference and Retreat Center, 320/616-5580 or 800/794-0809, but are open to visitors with advanced notice 9 A.M.–3 P.M. when not in use for gatherings. Inside you will find the lavish interiors filled with a mix of original and period furnishings, plus a large doll collection and *Wizard of Oz* memorabilia. Even if you find the houses closed or don't want to shell out the $10 per person for a tour, a visit here is still worthwhile for a look at the exteriors and a walk through the nine-acre riverside grounds.

Pack thousands of rods, reels, lures, motors, and similar objects into a large room and you've got the **Minnesota Fishing Museum,** 304 W. Broadway, 320/616-2011. Highlights of the impressive collection include artistic spearing decoys, flys, and old boat engines dating back 1902—and you don't have to fish to find the history interesting. The museum is open Tuesday–Saturday 9 A.M.–5 P.M. year-round, plus Sunday noon–4 P.M. during the summer. Admission is $3, except on Tuesdays when entry is free.

The best part of **Pine Grove Park & Zoo,** 1200 W. Broadway, 320/632-3263, is the stand of old-growth white pines hovering over the picnic area. The modest zoo houses mostly Minnesota animals like timber wolf, black bear, elk, bison, and cougar, plus a few exotics including tiger and emu. The zoo is open daily 8 A.M.–8 P.M. during the summer, and 8 A.M.–4 P.M. the rest of the year. Admission is free.

Entertainment and Events

Maple Island Park hosts free outdoor concerts on summer Sundays, while the **Hole-in-the-**

Day Players perform musicals and dinner theater during the summer. Call the Great River Arts Association, 320/632-0960, for details about these and other special events. The weekend after Labor Day is the **Little Falls Arts & Crafts Fair** which, with over 1,000 exhibitors, is one of the largest in the Midwest.

Accommodations

The friendly **Clifwood Motel,** 1201 Haven Road, 320/632-5488, is nothing special, but clean rooms with refrigerator and microwave are just $38. The national chains are east of town at the junctions of Highways 10 and 27. Cheapest is the **Super 8,** 320/632-2351 or 800/800-8000, with rooms from $52, while the **Country Inn,** 320/632-1000 or 800/456-4000, has a pool and whirlpool and rooms starting at $89.

Little Falls has a pair of B&Bs that are open on a limited basis. The 1890 French Second Empire **Randall House,** 200 4th St., SE, 320/616-5815, accepts guests Friday to Sunday evenings year-round and the rest of the week during the summer or around special events. A night in one of the four simply decorated rooms, which share three bathrooms with claw-foot tubs, is like a visit to grandma's house. Rates are $75–85 a night. One block over is **Lottie Lee's,** 206 3rd St. SE, 320/632-8641, a cozy 1907 Tudor home. A night in one of the three guestrooms, each with a private bath, begins at $85. Lottie's is open from May to September.

Charles A. Lindbergh State Park has a very pleasant campground.

Food

For a meal, most locals will direct you to the **Black & White Hamburger Shop,** 116 SE 1st St., 320/632-5374, a local landmark and a very fun place to dine. The menu features nearly 30 sandwiches, such as a Jamaican jerk hamburger, Italian sausage, and a black bean burger, for about $5 and steak and chicken dinners for about twice that; plus you won't be bored since the walls are full of antiques and uniques. Open daily for breakfast, lunch, and dinner.

For a snack you can't do any better than **Pete & Joy's Bakery,** 121 E. Broadway, 320/632-6388, where the doughnuts, muffins, pies, and bread are all fantastic and unbelievably cheap. Open Mon.–Sat. for breakfast and lunch.

No matter where you decide to dine, consider getting your order to go and eating it in Maple Island Park, just south of downtown, where you can enjoy the flowers and fresh air and watch the Mississippi River race by.

Information and Transportation

The **Little Falls Convention and Visitors Bureau,** 606 SE 1st St., 320/616-4959 or 800/325-5916, www.littlefallsmn.com, is housed in the ornate Burton-Rosenmeier House. It is open weekdays 9 A.M.–5 P.M., plus Saturday 10 A.M.–3 P.M. during the summer. **Bookin' It,** 113 1st St. SE, 320/632-1848, is a small locally-owned bookstore with a decent regional section.

Greyhound buses stop twice a day at McDonald's, east of town along U.S. 10, on their way between Minneapolis and Grand Forks, North Dakota.

EAST OF BRAINERD

Crosby

Crosby sits on the edge of the narrow Cuyuna Iron Range, named for homesteader Cuyler Adams, who first found iron here in 1904, and his St. Bernard Una. Though much smaller than the Mesabi and Vermilion Ranges, over 100 million tons of ore were extracted between 1908 and 1984. The Range's heyday is remembered at the **Croft Mine Historical Park,** 218/546-5466, on the north side of town. On your hour-long guided tour you'll get to see and touch old mining equipment—the Croft was worked from 1916 to 1934—and learn a lot about the history of mining from knowledgeable guides. The highlight is a re-created mineshaft, while the rest of the park has a ho-hum museum filled mostly with old photos, a few historic buildings, and some rusting mining equipment. The park is open daily in the summer 10 A.M.–6 P.M., and tours depart on the half-hour until 4:30 P.M. The underground experience costs $4.50, though the other exhibits are free. There's more mining memorabilia plus other historical artifacts at the

Cuyuna Range Historical Museum, 101 1st St. NE, 218/546-6178, housed in a 1910 Soo Line Depot. It is open weekdays 10 A.M.–4 P.M. during the summer and admission is $1.

A big part of the range's future is the **Cuyuna Country State Recreation Area,** which is taking shape around Crosby. Still in the acquisition and development stage, Cuyuna will eventually cover 5,000 acres and encompass over 20 lakes—15 of which are deep mine pits now filled with water—and 25 miles of undeveloped shoreline. Although there are no trails, with just short portages between them paddlers can easily reach isolated lakes, and the office staff can recommend a loop route that avoids private property concerns. Another interesting feature are the up-to-200-foot-high piles of excess rock, now covered with trees that, like the man-made lakes, look completely natural. At present the only developed facilities are boat accesses, though a campground is likely in the near future, and as more land is acquired trails will be marked and maintained. Currently anglers come for the 50,000 trout stocked annually, and scuba divers have discovered the clear water of the pits. Divers can rent gear, get a tank filled, or join a group dive at Brainerd's **Minnesota School of Diving,** 712 Washington St., 218/829-5953 or 800/657-2822. If you want to know more about the area, contact the park office in Ironton at 307 3rd St., 218/546-5926.

While most closely associated with mining, Crosby now bills itself as "The Official Antique Capital of the Lakes Area," and there were eight antique stores on Main Street at last count. For recreation of another sort, call **Blackhoof Ranch,** 218/546-8101, to do some horseback riding. If you are here the second Saturday in June make a quick detour north to the village of Cuyuna for their annual **Wood Tick Races.**

One of the state's most unusual lodging options calls Crosby home. The over-the-top **Nordic Inn,** 210 1st Ave. NW, 218/546-8299, nordic@vikinginn.com, isn't just another bed-and-breakfast; it's a Medieval Brew and Bed. Owner Richard Schmidthuber (he's adopted the nickname The Crazy Viking, but you'd probably call him that anyway) is a self-taught scholar of Viking history and one of the fully-decked-out marauders you'll

see in the stands at Minnesota Vikings home games. To live out his Norse dream he converted an old church into a Viking realm, complete with five Viking-themed guestrooms (one is dedicated not to the Norse but the NFL variety and comes complete with Astroturf carpeting, lockers, and a urinal) running $65–125. At night, for an added fee, you can dress in Viking attire and join in interactive dinner theater or just relax in the Valhalla room with its unique hot tub and grill. He offers tours of his kingdom daily at 4 P.M. and has many Viking weapons and wares for sale. For even more Norse amusement visit the **Viking Games and Trade Fair** held annually during Father's Day Weekend. Competitors throw axes and stones, shoot bows and arrows, and row alongside a Viking encampment.

The **Hallett House,** 22418 Hwy. 6, 218/546-5433 or 877/546-5433, is a grand 1920s home set on 13 wooded acres half a mile east of Crosby. The five guestrooms, ranging from large to huge, all have private baths and are tastefully decorated. Though there is ample common space in the house, guests tend to congregate in the screened-in gazebo out back. Owners Scott and Bob serve a scrumptious breakfast and make all guests feel welcome. Prices run from $85–135. Seven miles south of town on Highway 6 is **Ruttger's,** 218/678-2885 or 800/450-4545, one of the first resorts in the state. With a pair of links, Ruttger's is known as a golfers' destination, but they have all the other amenities that you would expect from a top-of-the-line facility like this. Zig's is an excellent dining room and many area residents come here to eat. Prices run $163–291, depending on room type and other factors. The resort is open from late April to the end of October. You can also camp in town at the purely functional, RV-only **Crosby Memorial Park,** 218/546-5021, for $16.

For a family-style meal you can't do any better than the **Heartland Kitchen,** 131 W. Main St., 218/546-5746. The standard American menu, spiced up just a little by such items as teriyaki glazed chicken breast, averages $6. Open daily for breakfast and lunch. For ribs, many locals head four miles north on Highway 6 to **TJ's Riverside,** 218/546-6878, a no-frills joint on the banks of the Mississippi River. The menu spans $2 veggie burgers to $14 steaks, and they are open Wednesday–Sunday for breakfast, lunch, and dinner.

Aitkin

William Aitkin, for whom the city and county are named, was a prominent fur trader who opened a school for the local Ojibwe here in 1832. An actual town wasn't established, however, until 1871 when the arrival of the railroad facilitated logging. Steamboat service ran up and down the Mississippi River between Aitkin and Grand Rapids until the 1920s, and when river levels are low the ribs of sunken steamers still rise to the surface. The city became not only a major supply center for the logging camps, but a major release valve for the lumberjacks of the surrounding camps who arrived with pockets full of cash to drink, whore, gamble, and fight before heading back to work. The money, from both the legitimate and illegitimate businesses, soon made the town prosperous, and it remains healthy today despite the dwindling fortunes of most of the surrounding Cuyuna Range towns.

Aitkin's main claim to fame is the Fish House Parade. The day after Thanksgiving, dolled-up ice fishing shanties and similarly unique and humorous floats make their way down Minnesota Avenue.

Aitkin's main claim to fame is the **Fish House Parade.** The day after Thanksgiving, residents pull their dolled-up ice fishing shanties and similarly unique and humorous floats down Minnesota Avenue. The rest of the year your best bet for entertainment is the **Jacques Art Center,** 121 2nd St. NW, 218/927-2363. The center is named for Francis Lee Jacques, former Aitkin resident and one of America's premier wildlife artists, best known for his work at the American Museum of Natural History in New York City. It contains many of the prolific artist's paintings and a pair of his three-dimensional "duoramas," an art form he invented. The center also hosts bimonthly exhibits from local artists. It is open Tuesday–Saturday 11 A.M.–4 P.M. and admission is free. The **Depot Museum,** 20 Pacific St., 218/927-3348, on the south side of downtown has railroad, logging, riverboat, and other historical memorabilia. It is open Wednesday,

Friday, and Saturday 10 A.M.–4 P.M., plus the same hours on Tuesdays during the summer. You might also want to catch a flick in the **Rialto Theatre,** 220 Minnesota Ave. N., 218/927-2824, a 1937 moviehouse with a funky marquee and a psychedelic art deco interior. In its day this was as fancy as they came.

Best bet for spending the night is the spic-and-span **40 Club Inn,** 950 2nd St. NW, 218/927-2903 or 800/682-8152, where $70 gets you use of a pool, hot tub, and sauna. The county also maintains seven **campsites** on the Mississippi River at the end of 4th Ave. NW for $9 a night. The **Birchwood Café,** 120 Minnesota Ave. N., 218/927-6400, open daily for lunch and dinner, has tasty family fare averaging $5. **Lorenz** buses stop at the Roadside Restaurant, 100 2nd St NE, 218/927-2113, on their run between Minneapolis and Virginia.

Rice Lake National Wildlife Refuge

One of Minnesota's oldest national wildlife refuges covers over 18,000 acres around its namesake lake. Surrounding the refuge area like a giant horseshoe are a series of glacial hills that trap much of the water that accumulates here, and as the low-lying areas fill with sediment and vegetation they become floating peat bogs. This build-up of decaying vegetation creates a nutrient-rich growing environment which, in part, accounts for the vast beds of wild rice in the lake that are still harvested by Native American each fall. The lake's plentiful food sources also attract waterfowl in staggering numbers during the fall migration—the refuge is most famous for attracting upwards of 100,000 ring-necked ducks. Two pair of bald eagles nest on the refuge, and songbirds like LeConte's sparrow, Connecticut warbler, and yellow rail are common in the uplands. In total around 230 species of bird have been recorded here. Lucky visitors might spot a black bear or timber wolf, though white-tailed deer and beaver are more common.

Almost everything of interest to visitors is

found along the 9.5-mile auto tour (generally open to vehicles May though November), which cuts through the heart of the refuge. A brochure discusses the history of this area and points out ancient Native American burial mounds. A seven-mile chain of hiking trails crosses forest and field, and the .75-mile **Twin Lakes Trail** that skirts Twin Lakes, a bog, and a flower-filled field is arguably the most scenic. In winter, half of the trails are groomed for cross-country skiing. The observation tower near the end of the drive lets you truly appreciate how large and shallow the lake is, while North Bog Road, branching off the auto tour, offers close-up views of a peat bog in various stages of succession. The visitors center, 218/768-2402, which has a few nature displays, is open weekdays 8 A.M.–4 P.M. throughout the year, plus in summer the Friday closing time is extended until seven and it opens on Saturday 8 A.M.–4 P.M.

NORTH OF BRAINERD

Highway 371, once an ancient Native American footpath and later a lumber wagon route known as the Leech Lake Trail, funnels thousands of people to area lakes every day during the summer, and the action doesn't let up much in the winter. Nisswa, Pequot Lakes, and Crosslake are busy shopping and supply centers for those recreating at the abundant resorts and second homes.

The **Paul Bunyan State Trail,** a former railroad bed now paved between Brainerd and Hackensack, parallels Highway 371 for most of its 48-mile route—when completed the trail will stretch 100 miles to Bemidji. Thankfully, it sidesteps the nonstop sprawl along the highway south of Nisswa. Development tails off to the north, making for a fairly scenic ride, even though it is right along the highway. Bike rental is available in several trailside towns, plus **Paul Bunyan Bike Shuttle & Rental,** 218/839-8093 or 218/568-8422, will deliver your cycles right to you; they charge $15/half-day and $25/full-day.

If you're a bird-watcher pick up the ***Birds of the Byway*** brochure at any area tourism office. It points out 15 top spots on the Paul Bunyan Scenic Byway, a 48-mile signed drive along area

roads and, with the variety of habitats it passes, 100 species days are not unheard of.

Nisswa

Early settlers chose the name Hill's Crossing for their growing village in 1898, but since there was already another town with that name the Post Office chose the name of the man who submitted the denomination petition and dubbed it Smiley. Ten years later citizens chose the Ojibwe word for Three in reference to the main lakes around town, known today as Roy, Nisswa, and Clark. This reasonably attractive town is pretty much all about shopping—well over half the businesses in town are gift shops of some sort—and this makes it the busiest destination in the Brainerd Lakes area. If you can, visit Nisswa on a summer Wednesday to watch the weekly **turtle races.** The sluggish sprints are held rain or shine in the parking lot behind the Nisswa Trailside Information Center, and around 500 kids participate each week. The first heat of the day is at 2 P.M. and the event lasts for an hour. There is no entry fee, though turtle rental costs $2.

Nine historic buildings moved to the edge of downtown make up the **Nisswa Pioneer Village,** 218/963-0801. The fully furnished buildings include a one-room schoolhouse, bank, and several log homes, while railroad relics are kept across the street in the old caboose and train depot. Many forgotten skills are demonstrated here during **Nisswa Pioneer Day** at the end of August, and there are two days of Scandinavian folk music and dance during early June's **Nisswa Stämman Festival.** The museum is open Wednesday–Saturday 10 A.M.–3 P.M. from mid-June through August, plus the same hours on the few Saturdays preceding the main season. Admission is $1 for the Pioneer Village, while the train displays are free.

If you are here for the **Paul Bunyan State Trail** you can rent a ride at **Trailblazer Bikes,** 218/963-0699, in the Nisswa Square mall and **Martin's Sport Shop,** 218/963-2127, downtown on Main Street—the former has tandems available and the latter also leases in-line skates, cross-country skis, and snowshoes. Both charge $15 for a half-day and $25 for a full day. For

© TIM BEWER

Nisswa Pioneer Village

some less strenuous recreation there's the **Nisswa Family Fun Center,** 218/963-3545, two miles south of town. Ten dollars gets you unlimited access to a waterslide, in-line skating track, video games, and a walk-through maze.

The downtown **Nisswa Motel,** 218/963-7611 or 800/254-7612, has simple but spotless rooms from $68. Two-night minimums apply on summer weekends, and bicyclists get a ten percent discount during the week. **Grand View Lodge,** 218/963-2234 or 800/432-3788, just to the west of town on Gull Lake, opened in 1919. The original log lodge—surrounded by some 24,000 flowers—is still at the center of things, but they've since expanded over 550 acres. Most of that is taken up by their four golf courses. The Pines is Minnesota's only five-star course on *Golf Digest's* 2002–2003 Places to Play ranking, while Deacon's Lodge and The Preserve both scored four and a half. Their seven Laykold tennis courts are world-class, too: *Tennis* magazine rated Grand View as a top 50 resort. Other top-notch facilities include an indoor pool area with a waterslide, 1,500-foot sandy beach, boat rentals, and five

restaurants. There's a multitude of special kids programs available day and night, while scheduled activities for adults run the gamut from water-skiing to ice carving demonstrations to massage lessons. With all the various facilities, special packages, and seasonal discounts they offer it's tough to pin down a price, but in general you're looking at about $330 a night per bedroom in the summer and there are often multinight minimum stay requirements. These prices include breakfast, dinner, and use of most facilities. Rates at some of their nearby satellite properties are cheaper.

Though there is an espresso bar and bakery open in the morning, deli sandwiches served for lunch, and a popular brunch buffet on Sunday, it is the dinner menu that has made downtown's Nisswa Grille, 218/963-4717, one of the most popular restaurants in the lakes area. Selections like walleye, wild mushroom risotto, and barbecue duck average $15, and many choices come as family platters intended to be shared. There's also a good wine and beer selection and sometimes live music. They are open daily. Weekend dinner reservations are a good idea in the summer, though seating in the upstairs oyster bar is first-come, first-served. Locals are quick to recommend the **Bar Harbor Supper Club,** 8164 Interlachen Rd. (County Road 77), 218/963-2568, west of town on the north shore of Gull Lake. Back in its heyday this was such a renowned club that it attracted the likes of Duke Ellington and Tommy Dorsey to play for the Chicagoland gangsters and others who came out for the night. After the grand original burned down in 1968 they moved across the street to more modest digs. The something-for-everyone menu runs from a $3 grilled cheese to a $79 lobster, and it's hard to beat a table on the lakeside deck. Open daily for lunch and dinner year-round, and you can come by car, boat, or snowmobile. Lounge singers and jazz acts still perform on weekends.

Besides the plethora of downtown shops, retail addicts will also want to browse the **Nisswa Flea Market,** 218/829-8667, a gathering of arts, crafts, and antique vendors held summer Saturdays south of town on Highway 371. The **Rainy Days Bookstore,** 218/963-4891, downtown on Main Street has a really good Minnesota section. **Greyhound** buses stop downtown at the chamber of commerce's **Nisswa Trailside Information Center,** 218/963-2620 or 800/950-9610, www.nisswa.com, which is staffed weekdays 9 A.M.–5 P.M. and weekends 10 A.M.–2 P.M. during the summer, while in the winter they close on Sundays and an hour earlier during the week.

Pequot Lakes

Founded as Sibley Siding in 1894, postal officials eventually insisted that the name be changed because there was already another Sibley in the state. It became Pequot six years later—Lakes was added in 1940. One legend of the name says that O-Pequot was a daughter of a White Earth Ojibwe Chief who let the first settlers gather for Sunday services in her home, while another says that it just happened to be the first Indian-sounding word (the Pequot were a small tribe from Connecticut) that popped into the mind of the postal official charged with making the choice. Pequot was an important rail center and the massive park

dividing the downtown was once filled with warehouses and train yards—the **Paul Bunyan State Trail** runs down the middle of it. The chamber of commerce's **Trailside Information and Hospitality Center,** 218/568-8911 or 800/950-0291, www.pequotlakes.com, is housed in a renovated depot; it's open daily 9 A.M.–5 P.M. in the summer, and Monday–Saturday 10 A.M.–5 P.M. the rest of the year. Elsewhere in town is the inevitable concentration of gift shops, though Pequot is much less of a tourist trap than Nisswa.

Little Pequot's two claims to fame are true one-of-a-kinds. Most obvious is the fishing bobber water tower. Legend has it that Paul Bunyan got it caught in the scaffolding and he just let them keep it. Pequotians also celebrate the area's logging heritage with **Bean Hole Day.** On the first Tuesday after the 4th of July (unless it falls on a Monday), 150 gallons of baked beans are buried in a rock-lined pit and then dug up the next day at noon to feed the assembled masses. The old logging camp tradition was revived in 1935 and today 2,500 people take a bite. An arts and crafts fair and other events are held concurrently.

The **Pequot Lakes Area Museum,** 218/568-5324, below the bobber has a small collection of just about anything they can get their hands on. It is open Friday and Saturday 11 A.M.–4 P.M. and admission is $1. Anyone with a fear of heights won't even want to look up at the **Pequot Lakes Fire Tower,** but everyone else can scramble to the top of the 100-foot steel spire for some superb forest views. It is located half a mile east of town on County Road 11, and it's a steep climb uphill from the parking lot. The **Laughing Loon,** 218/568/4127, mock-paddlewheeler tours the Whitefish Chain of Lakes from June through September. Though the exact night tends to change, they run a weekly dinner cruise; reservations are required. **Whispering Pines Riding Stable,** 218/562-4377 or 866/546-9383, out by the Breezy Point Resort offers one-hour trail rides between May and October.

The combination of big rooms and little touches makes the **AmericInn,** 218/568-8400 or 888/568-8400, one of the best small hotels in all of Minnesota—and they've got the awards to prove it. There is a pool, whirlpool, and sauna indoors, plus volleyball, croquet, and a patio ringed by birdfeeders in the large backyard. Standard Northwoods-themed rooms cost $120, and there is a two-night minimum stay on summer weekends. The same owners run a 49-site RV campground next door. It is located about a mile north of town along Highway 371. Two prominent resorts rest on area lakes. Straddling Upper Whitefish and Lower Hay lakes since 1902 is the family-focused **Driftwood Resort,** 218/568-4221 or 800/950-3540, with golf, tennis, volleyball, swimming pools, a beach, free boats, and pony and fire engine rides among the many amenities, plus waiters dress in Old-world costumes for the Friday night Smorgasbord. They have 24 one–four bedroom cabins and charge $468 per adult per week during the summer peak. Driftwood is only open May through September. Five miles east of Pequot on Pelican Lake is the posh and enormous **Breezy Point Resort,** 218/562-7811 or 800/432-3777, with a pair of 18-hole golf course and an ice arena amongst the top-flight amenities. Their 250 varied rooms and cabins start at $109 but go much higher.

The **Timberjack Smokehouse,** 218/568-6070, two miles south of the bobber on Hwy. 371, is Pequot's most frequently recommended restaurant. Best known for ribs, the steak and seafood menu runs $6–23 and they have a Friday night fish fry. Open Tues.–Sun. for lunch and dinner.

By far the most varied menu is downtown at **Sibley Station,** 218/568-4177, another local favorite. Salads, subs, gyros, pastas, pizza, sandwiches, steak, and seafood—and their famous soups, good enough to be a meal unto themselves—run $6–19. Open Mon.–Sat. for lunch and dinner.

The **Plaid Duck,** 218/568-7440, is a Main Street coffee shop that also serves wine and beer. Open daily for breakfast and lunch.

Greyhound buses stop at the Northern Food King, 218/568-5995, grocery store right at the corner of Hwy. 371 and Main St.

Crosslake

The Crosslake Logging Company opened a camp here in the 1870s and 1,400 men lived at the "Old Headquarters" during its peak. The company moved on in 1912, but around this same time many tourist camps chose to open on the back end of the Whitefish Chain of Lakes for the sunset views and so the little village on the eastern shore of Cross Lake survived. Today this tourism-dependent city straddles County Road 66 for about four miles and has just about everything a vacationer could want, from birch bark lampshades to boat rentals. There's also a waterslide and a pair of miniature golf courses.

Down by the junction of County Roads 66 and 3, the closest things there is to a downtown, is the **Historic Log Village,** 218/692-5400, with half-a-dozen old log buildings and a replica general store filled with historical artifacts. The buildings are open on weekends 11 A.M.–4 P.M. during the summer. Admission is free. About three miles west of town along County Road 16 is the unique **Uppgaard Wildlife Management Area,** 218/828-2228. The scenic, 110-acre tract surrounds two lakes and is the state's first and only "landscaping for wildlife demonstration area."

Historic Log Village, Crosslake

© TIM BEWER

Even if you have no interest in this subject, it's a scenic walk and there's a good chance of spotting wildlife along the easy 1.5-mile trail. Paddlers will enjoy the 19-mile trip to the Mississippi along the **Pine River,** a little known but very scenic paddling stream. It's a very easy run with just a few small rapids.

The **Pine Terrace Resort,** 35101 Pine Terrace Rd., 218/543-4606 or 800/950-1986, is exactly what a family resort should be: small and peaceful with a great view right out your cabin. There are no other resorts and only a few other houses on the scenic, wooded Star Lake and no personal watercraft or large boats are allowed. The twelve spic-and-span cabins, ten on the lake and two perched up on the hill, each come with a boat (motors extra), dock, and grill. The standard two-bedroom cabins go for $755 a week, and there are other cheaper and pricier options. Although it looks and feels thoroughly modern today, the **Manhattan Beach Lodge,** 39051 County Road 66, 218/692-3381 or 800/399-4360, was actually built in the 1920s and hosted many Chicagoland gangsters in the 1930s. Each of the 18 rooms has a sunset view over Big Trout Lake and facilities include a small beach, whirlpool, sauna, and exercise room. Prices start at $109, and there is a two-night minimum on peak weekends. The U.S. Army Corps of Engineers' **Crosslake Recreation Area,** 218/692-2025 or 877/444-6777, at the junction of County Roads 3 and 66 is about as good as a 125-site RV campground can be. The $25 sites are all shaded, and

there is also a beach and boat launch here. **Loveland's Resort,** 13710 County Road 16, 218/692-2511, 888/692-2511, has a 35-foot, four-person houseboat available for $150 per night.

Famous Dave's Barbeque, 33816 County Road 3, 218/692-7427, is a barn-shaped roadhouse on the south side of town. The award-winning, St. Louis-style ribs are the specialty of the house, but they splash the sauce on chicken, beef brisket, burgers—even catfish—and serve it up with Southern sides like corn on the cob and baked beans. Most items are in the $7–12 range. Open daily for lunch and dinner. **Pine Peaks Restaurant,** 218/692-4100, just north of the junction of County Roads 3 and 66, has simple and cheap family fare. Breakfast is served all day, and they feature a Friday night fish fry. Open daily for breakfast, lunch, and dinner. For fine dining try the **Manhattan Beach Lodge,** whose eclectic menu includes lasagna, pad thai, Cajun burgers, and honey-pecan battered walleye. Vegetarians will find more choices than at most Northwoods restaurants. Lunch runs $6–18 and dinner $10–26. Open daily for lunch and dinner during the summer and Tues.–Sun. for dinner during the winter—spring and summer hours vary.

The **Brainerd Lakes Area Chambers of Commerce** staffs an Information Center at the junction of County Roads 3 and 66. It is open Monday–Saturday 10 A.M.–4 P.M. during the summer and the same times on Saturday during May and September.

Headwaters

When Henry Rowe Schoolcraft stepped onto the shore of Lake Itasca in 1832, he not only identified the source of the Mississippi River but also ensured that generations of visitors would follow in his footsteps. Over half a million people are drawn to the region annually, and not just to amble across the mighty river's meager headwaters at Itasca State Park, but also to visit family-friendly Park Rapids, the surprisingly artsy college-town Bemidji, and a collection of quirky tourist-trap villages. They're all set in a legendary forest, big enough to give birth to Paul Bunyan.

PARK RAPIDS

The "Gateway to Itasca State Park" centers around a bustling, old-fashioned downtown and its unique center-of-street parking, a legacy of logging days when streets were built extra-wide to accommodate oxcarts making U-turns. Logging was the early mainstay of the local economy with several mills operating on the Fishhook River, but tourism, fueled by the establishment of Itasca State Park in 1891 and aided by the arrival of the railroad that same year, gained its foothold early. The hordes of visitors drawn by a wealth of outdoor recreation—not just in the state park, but also on the Heartland State Trail and dozens of nearby lakes—have not drained this city of its down-to-earth personality.

Sights and Recreation

Two museums, the **Hubbard County Historical Society** and the **North Country Museum of Arts,** 301 Court Ave., 218/732-5237, share a home in the original Hubbard County Courthouse. On the bottom floor, local history is showcased in typical fashion: rooms stuffed with artifacts including old typewriters, farm tools, and women's clothing dating back to the 1880s. There's also a replica classroom from a circa-1905 school and a cabin interior showing the quality of local life when residents were pioneers on a challenging frontier. The art museum upstairs houses a permanent collection of 15th through 19th-century European paintings, attributed not to the Old Masters, but to their lesser-known followers, plus some African and Native American art. Rotating exhibits in adjoining galleries highlight contemporary work by regional artists. The museums are open Tuesday–Sunday 11 A.M.–5 P.M. May through September, except closed Sundays in May and September. Admission to both is just $1.

The **Heartland State Trail** starts in downtown Park Rapids and continues 49 paved miles north on an abandoned railroad grade to Cass Lake, passing many lakes along the way.

Entertainment and Events

The **Northern Light Opera Company** stages summertime productions at Riverside Methodist Church, 1005 Park Ave. N. Call 218/732-7096 for information on schedules and tickets. You can take in plays on summer weekends at **Long Lake Theater,** 218/732-0099, seven miles south of town in Hubbard. **Silver Star Festival Park,** 218/237-STAR, near town on Highway 34, stages several music festivals throughout the summer, ranging from polka to blues, while the **Black Moose Coffee House,** 311 S. Main St., 218/237-1313, has live music on Friday nights. Park Rapids has many events; one of the largest is the

Summertime Art & Craft Celebration, a craft fair held the last weekend in July.

Accommodations

The **Gateway Guest House,** 203 Park Ave. N., 218/732-1933 or 877/558-8614, is an arts-and-crafts-style 1920s B&B, lovingly restored by the friendly owners. The four guestrooms have shared baths and one has a private balcony; guests also have access to a sauna, hot tub, TV room, parlor with fireplace, and an inviting front porch bedecked with flowers. The Gateway's location is great, too—very close to downtown, and right across the street from the Heartland Trail. Rates are $60 per night.

Carolyn's Hideaway, 11203 County Road 32, 218/732-1101 or 800/484-1058 (code 6088) offers a more woodsy experience north of town on Sloan Lake. It's a cedar-log B&B with three units, including a tower with great views and a private deck. Canoes and bikes are free for guest use, and there are a sauna, pool table, and hiking trails on the property. Wine and cheese are served each evening and dinner is available. Rates are $59–99.

The **Lady Slipper Inn,** 51722 270th St., 218/573-3353 or 800/531-2787, between Park Rapids and the Tamarack National Wildlife Refuge sits on 160 acres with two spring-fed ponds and a cedar bog. There are trails on the property, and guests have free use of snowshoes, as well as canoes and paddleboats. The five guestrooms each have a private bath, whirlpool tub, fireplace, and deck. Rates include breakfast, and dinner can also be arranged. Rooms run $100–115.

Lee's Riverside Resort Motel, 700 North Park Ave., 218/732-9711 or 800/733-9711, offers a quiet setting on the Fishhook River, yet is just a short walk to downtown. The six log cabins each have two bedrooms and a full kitchen, while the three motel rooms come with a microwave and refrigerator. Most units have carports and guests have access to the swimming area, free canoes and paddleboats, and a picnic area. A night in a cabin starts at $72, while the motel rooms are about $55. Next door the **Terrace View Motor Lodge,** 716 Park Ave. N., 218/732-1213, is old and a bit odd, but clean and priced right at $45 per night. The newer

C'mon Inn, 1471 Highway 34, 218/732-1471 or 800/258-6891, charges from $65, and has a pool, hot tub, and game room.

Food

The **Rapid River Logging Camp,** 218/732-3444, north of town (take U.S. 71 to County Road 18 and follow the signs), offers a unique dining experience in the bygone spirit of logging camp mess halls. An all-you-can-eat set menu is served on tin plates and cups at wooden tables and benches. There are several log structures and antique logging machinery on the grounds. They serve breakfast, lunch, and dinner all summer long.

The **Minnesoda Fountain,** 205 Main St. S., 218/732-3240, has a huge selection of ice cream goodies, as well as sandwiches and subs in the $7 range. The checkerboard floor and counter stools lend nostalgic ambience. It's open daily for lunch and dinner.

The **Great Northern Café,** 218 1st St. E., 218/732-9565, offers inexpensive diner fare, including five kinds of French fries, stuffed potatoes, and homemade pie. It's open daily for breakfast and lunch and Monday–Saturday for dinner.

Gilbert's, 309 3rd St. E., 218/237-6190, offers imaginative cuisine in a setting decorated like an outdoor patio on the Mediterranean. The lunch menu features creative sandwiches like pepper jack roast beef on black bean bread for $7. Dinner includes many of the same sandwiches plus steaks. During the summer Gilbert's serves lunch and dinner daily and hours are somewhat reduced in the winter.

The **Schwarzwalk Inn,** 122 Main St. S., 218/732-8828, specializes in German cuisine: the wiener and bratwurst plate is $7 and the schnitzel dinner is $10. There's a good wine list, and, of course, beer. Breakfasts are huge and American-style. Schwarzwalk is open daily for breakfast and lunch and Monday–Saturday for dinner.

The **Black Moose Coffee House,** 311 S. Main St., 218/237-1313, is a large, cozy space downtown with log furniture and a fireplace. They have a full espresso bar, sandwiches, wraps, and pastries. Open daily for breakfast, lunch, and dinner.

Shopping

Candles!, 218/732-9368, has a huge selection of candles from around the world, as well as an on-site candle factory that you can tour for free weekdays at noon in the summertime. It's located three miles north of town on U.S. 71. **Rich's Antiques,** 409 Park Ave. S., 218/732-3949, is a large antique store, and **Beagle Books,** 112 W. 3rd St., 218/237-2665, is an independent bookstore with a small Minnesota section.

Summerhill Farms, 218/732-3865, about six miles north of town on U.S. 71, is a seven-shop complex on a former dairy farm selling everything from women's clothing to gourmet chocolate. The blue-painted farm buildings are only open during the summer.

Information and Services

The **Park Rapids Area Chamber of Commerce,** 1204 Park Ave. S., 218/732-4111 or 800/247-0054, www.parkrapids.com, offers information on Park Rapids proper, as well as surrounding communities, and can find a room or cabin for visitors arriving last minute. In summer the office is open Monday–Thursday 8 A.M.–5 P.M., Friday 8 A.M.–7 P.M., Saturday 9 A.M.–5 P.M., and Sunday 11 A.M.–3 P.M. The rest of the year they open weekdays 8 A.M.–5 P.M.

WEST OF PARK RAPIDS

Three unique little towns, each boasting a world-class tourist trap, lie between Park Rapids and Walker, and the **Heartland State Trail** links them all.

Dorset

Tiny Dorset's claim to be "The Restaurant Capital of the World" seems preposterous at first glance, but the numbers don't lie. With a population of 22 and four restaurants, there probably isn't any other town in the world that can beat the per-capita average. With five gift shops, plus an old-time photo studio, it could probably compete for a world gift shop title, too. Downtown Dorset is really just a single block, surrounded by quiet fields, where shops and restaurants line up along an Old West-style boardwalk and the community ethos has distinctly more to do with play than work.

None of Dorset's four restaurants will be gracing the pages of *Gourmet* Magazine, but they are friendly enough—and Dorset itself is picturesque enough—to attract diners from miles around. The **Dorset Café,** 218/732-4072, features family fare like broasted chicken, baked lemon pepper cod, and steak. It's the only place in town open year-round, serving dinner daily and opening for lunch on weekends. **Compañeros,** 218/732-7624, offers Mexican fare, mostly in the $6–8 range. They serve lunch and dinner daily. The **Dorset General Store & LaPasta Italian Eatery,** 218/732-0275, serves American breakfasts, burgers and pastas for lunch, and a full Italian menu ($8–12) at dinner. It's open for three meals daily. The **Dorset House Restaurant & Soda Fountain,** 218/732-5556, specializes in homemade pizzas and also offers imaginative soups and sandwiches, burgers, and chicken entrées, plus an all-you-can-eat dinner buffet and a large selection of dairy treats. It's open for lunch and dinner daily. Besides a good Minnesota section, **Sister Wolf Books,** 218/732-7565, has an espresso bar.

Of course, a town of such culinary fame must have a food festival, and the annual **Taste of Dorset** is held the first Sunday in August. You can sample foods on the boardwalk or enter the minnow races, though the day's highlight is the election of the Mayor of Dorset; to be a candidate you just have to plunk down $1. If you're interested in staying in town there's the **Heartland Trail B&B,** 218/732-3252. The town's 1920 schoolhouse has been converted to a homey inn without losing its spacious schoolhouse feeling. The six guestrooms (in the old classrooms) each have 12-foot ceilings and a private bath, plus guests can also make themselves at home on two outdoor decks, or in the library or the TV area. The B&B is located right next to the namesake trail, and guests can rent bikes on-site. Rates range $70–90, and the B&B closes up for the winter. For more information about Dorset, pick up the annual **Dorset Daily Bugle,** a tongue-in-cheek local rag, or check out www.dorsetmn.com.

Nevis

No one seems to know where the name Nevis came from, but since there is an island named Nevis in the West Indies and a Ben Nevis mountain in Scotland, it is assumed one of these landmasses was the inspiration. What is known is that this compact town on the east end of Lake Belle Taine is home to the **world's largest tiger muskie.** The big fish was constructed in 1950 from cedar and redwood and lives under a roof in a small park a block north of Highway 34. Real animals are the area's secondary attraction. The **Northland Bison Ranch,** 22376 Glacial Ridge Trail, 218/652-3582 or 877/453-9499, a mile northwest of town is a working buffalo ranch raising animals for meat and for various parts used in Native American art. You can tour the ranch (for $5) Tuesday–Sunday at 10:30 A.M., 1:30 P.M., and 3:30 P.M. during the summer, or stop by the gift shop year-round. The **Minnesota Emu Ranch,** 218/652-2303, on the lakeshore raises 500 of the massive flightless birds. Call for details about public tours.

Akeley

As the Heartland State Trail enters Akeley from the west it passes over a trestle above the Crow Wing River, which flows out of the eleventh lake in the Crow Wing Chain, a system of lakes popular with canoeists and a central factor in the town's history. Akeley was once an important logging town that boomed when the Red River Lumber Company, the popularizer of the legend of Paul Bunyan (see The Larger Than Life Lumberjack), opened a sawmill here in 1898. Over the next 19 years they cut up eight million trees before packing up and moving their operations to California. The town continued to grow for another decade, peaking with a population of 4,512 people in 1930. Since then the town has slowly declined, and today there are exactly 4,100 less residents.

There is no shortage of **Paul Bunyan statues** in Minnesota, but since Akeley claims to be Paul's birthplace it's appropriate that the tallest Paul resides here. Located right on Main Street, Akeley's Paul bends down on one knee allowing visitors to take a seat on his outstretched palm. The statue is only 25 feet tall, but he'd be twice this if

THE LARGER-THAN-LIFE LUMBERJACK

Paul Bunyan is the pinnacle of American tall tales. His early years are lost to time, but it is assumed that the first stories of the extraordinary lumberjack circulated through the logging camps of Minnesota, Wisconsin, and Michigan in the late 1800s, though apparently they were not very widespread. The immigrant lumberjacks, whose sense of humor was as vast as the new land they conquered, created a colleague so large that his meals were cooked on a griddle greased by men using hams as skates, so strong that he could fell 20 trees in a single stroke, so fast that he could blow out his lantern and jump into bed before the room became dark, and so smart that he trained beavers to build dams for him. The flamboyant lumberjack has since starred in a Disney movie, had an acclaimed opera written about him, and been featured on a U.S. postage stamp.

Paul's over-the-top stories may have originated in lumber camps, but they didn't gain a popular audience until after most of the forests of his birthplace had been cleared. James MacGillivray, a *Detroit News* reporter, first put the legendary lumberjack in print in 1910 with a brief mention in the story "The Round River Drive." Four years later Minneapolis ad man and former Minnesota lumberjack William Laughead put the myth in the national spotlight with a series of illustrated pamphlets sharing the exploits of Paul as well as extolling the virtues of the Red River Lumber Company for whom they both worked. In 1922 Laughead expanded the tales in *The Marvelous Exploits of Paul Bunyan as told in the camps of the white pine lumberman for generations, during which time the loggers have pioneered the way through the north woods from Maine to California, collected from various sources and embellished for publication.* The book became so popular that Red River began publishing annual editions and gave away over 100,000 of them over the next two decades. The popularity of these tales led to serious analysis by University professors and an endless stream of children's books.

In Minnesota Paul Bunyan lives on in more than just legend. His name graces everything from bowling alleys to bike trails to Internet service providers—ironically, there is even a Paul Bunyan Nature Center—and many old logging towns like Bemidji honor him and his contemporaries with giant fiberglass statues. The most widespread reminder of Paul are Minnesota's many lakes which, according to legend, are the footprints of his partner Babe the Blue Ox, who "weighed more than the combined weight of all the fish that ever got away."

he stood up. Right behind him the **Akeley Paul Bunyan Historical Museum,** 218/652-2369, has a hodgepodge of local historical items, including logging tools and photographs spanning the town's history. It's open daily noon–4 P.M. during the summer and admission is free. The family-owned **Red River Museum,** 218/652-4371, on the east side of town displays items specifically related to the Red River Lumber Company: model trains, logging artifacts, and Paul Bunyan memorabilia. There's also a collection of carved birds. It's open Tuesday–Saturday 10 A.M.–6 P.M., and Sunday noon–5 P.M. during the summer. Admission is $4. Akeley is also home to the **Woodtick Musical Theater,** 218/652-4200 or 800/644-6892, which presents a two-hour Grand Ole Opry-like stage show with a satirical Minnesotan touch. Catch the summer-only shows at 8 P.M. Wednesday–Saturday or at 3 P.M. Wednesday–Thursday for $12.50.

One of the area's best-known restaurants lies west of town. **Brauhaus,** 28234 Hwy. 34, 218/652-2478, features German specialties like plum glazed duck and *rinderbraten* (roast beef), as well as American favorites like steak and seafood, most in the $10–20 range. There's a large selection of imported wine and beer, and the staff is garbed in traditional German costumes. During the summer it's open daily for dinner and Sundays for lunch, while in the spring and fall the hours reduce to Thursday–Sunday for dinner.

ITASCA STATE PARK

Established in 1891, Itasca was Minnesota's first state park and it remains one of the best loved. At nearly 33,000 acres, harboring the humble headwaters of the Mississippi River and a wealth of history, Itasca is a state park with national significance; in fact, it's a National Natural Landmark. One could easily spend a week here getting to know the shores of Lake Itasca, learning about the history of exploration and conservation in the park, spotting wildlife in a landscape covered by towering pine forests and over 100 deep glacial lakes, and staring in awe at the diminutive inauguration of North America's greatest river.

History

Though he wasn't the first white man to pass through, explorer Henry Rowe Schoolcraft did identify this as the source of the Mississippi River in 1832. He was accompanied here by the Ojibwe guide Ozawindib and created the name Itasca for the lake from which the river flows by combining the middle syllables of the Latin phrase *Veritas caput,* meaning "true head." Subsequent decades saw various challenges to Schoolcraft's claim, but in the late 1800's Jacob V. Brower—a historian, anthropologist, and land surveyor—largely put the matter to rest. Though Lake Itasca is fed by five tributaries, Brower determined that its outflow is the first point where the volume of water is great enough to truly be called a river. It was Brower who spearheaded efforts to establish Itasca State Park and thus protect the virgin pine stands from Minnesota's burgeoning logging industry. On April 20, 1891, the proposal squeaked through the Minnesota state legislature. An era of wilderness tourism had begun, and today Itasca preserves the majority of Minnesota's 15,000 remaining acres of virgin pine forest.

Jacob V. Brower Visitor Center

Itasca's 14,000-square-foot visitor center is designed to be environmentally friendly: it's made of recycled, nontoxic materials, uses low-flow faucets in the restrooms, and is efficiently heated. Exhibits in the main hall include explanations of why Lake Itasca is considered the Mississippi's true source, wildlife displays, and varied interactive historical artifacts, though the best place to start is the short orientation film. The excellent gift shop is stocked full of nature and history related books. It is open in summer 8 A.M.–8 P.M. Saturday–Thursday and 8 A.M.–9 P.M. on Friday. Winter hours are daily 8 A.M.–4:30 P.M. Other places to pick up information are the campground office, the North Entrance station, and Douglas Lodge. The park's phone number is 218/266-2100.

Mississippi Headwaters

Though it leaves Minnesota as a mile-wide behemoth, here in Itasca the Mississippi River is just a small stream tumbling over a pile of rocks. And, though small, the Mississippi here flows with purpose, running fast right from the start. A raindrop falling into Lake Itasca will reach the Gulf of Mexico 2,552 miles and 90 days later dropping 1,475 feet along the way. Given that the Father of Waters drains two-thirds of the United States and holds a cherished place in the American imagination, it's no surprise that almost everyone who comes to Itasca wants stroll over it. A 600-foot accessible trail leads to the small, man-made rock dam marking the clear outflow from the lake—if you don't want to get your feet wet there's also a bridge to take you across. A small museum near the parking area details the expeditions of Henry Rowe Schoolcraft and other explorers. It's open daily 9 A.M.–5 P.M. from May through mid-October.

Sights from Douglas Lodge to the Headwaters

Across the main park drive from the visitors center **Douglas Lodge** anchors a small village of historic buildings on the south end of Lake Itasca. Completed in 1906, the log and stone structure's large lobby has a stone fireplace and wicker furniture, and it's worth a peek inside even if you aren't staying in one of the rooms or eating in its dining room. Nearby, the 1940 **Forest Inn** is the most significant contribution of the CCC workers who labored in Itasca during the Great Depression. It features a large, cathedral-ceilinged meeting room and houses a summer-only gift shop. Many other historic log structures—including the **Dormitory, Clubhouse,** and **Fireplace Rooms**—were renovated during the 1980s and '90s. Pick up the *Historic Buildings Tour*

crossing the headwaters of the not-yet-mighty Mississippi, Itasca State Park

© TIM BEWER

brochure for more information on the construction and renovation of these buildings. A quarter-mile down the Dr. Robert's Trail, which leaves from the pier below Douglas Lodge, the **Old Timer's Cabin** is worth a look for its almost comical construction: it's a small cabin built of logs so enormous that it only took four to complete each wall.

Heading north from Douglas Lodge (which you can do by car, bike, or foot) there are two prime lookout spots on the east shore of Lake Itasca. **Preacher's Grove** is a parklike stand of 250-year-old pines, named for preachers' conventions once held there, and the **Peacepipe Vista** is a wooden platform a mile or so farther north. The small, summer-only **Itasca Museum** focuses on the park's homesteading history. The **Wegmann Store Ruins** in this vicinity mark the spot where Theodore Wegmann, the park's first game warden, and his wife Johanna ran a small store and post office in the park's early days. Alongside the ruins of their cabins a reconstructed version of their homestead gives a sense of what the original was like. The Wegmanns and 12 others are buried in the nearby **Pioneer Cemetery,** with graves dating to 1898. The **Indian Cemetery,** also in the area, is a series of Native American burial mounds.

Sights along Wilderness Drive

The rest of Itasca's sights—at least those within easy walking distance—are strung along the **Wilderness Drive,** a 10-mile one-way route shared by cars and bicycles that traces the outline of the 2,000-acre **Itasca Wilderness Sanctuary.** The **Forestry Demonstration Area** is a CCC plantation with interpretive markers detailing the basics of forest management. **Minnesota's largest red and white pines** are each a short distance from the Wilderness Drive. Nearby, the **Bison Kill Site** is a historic spot where Native Americans historically hunted buffalo; interpretive signs explain the history. **Nicollet Cabin,** a restored 1917 cabin, is less than a mile down the Nicollet Trail, and a good place for a picnic. The Wilderness Drive passes **Elk Lake,** sometime contender for the headwaters title, before ending up back at the Douglas Lodge area. The **Aiton Heights Fire Tower** near the end of the drive is reached by hiking about three-quarters of a mile from the parking area on Wilderness Drive or via the 1.5-mile Deer Park Trail, which starts at

Douglas Lodge. The 110-foot tower can be climbed (except during the winter) and interpretive signs detail forest canopy wildlife and the history of fire towers.

Trails

The 33 miles of hiking trails in Itasca range from short bog boardwalks to isolated paths near remote lakes. The shortest, easiest hikes are the **Headwaters Trail,** which is 600 feet long and wheelchair-accessible, and the 800-foot **Big Pine Trail** that leads to Minnesota's largest white pine tree.

The **Dr. Roberts Trail** is an accessible two-mile walk near Douglas Lodge that starts out as a bog boardwalk—great for orchid viewing—before reaching the Old Timer's Cabin and continuing along Lyendecker Lake. The 0.8-mile **Aiton Heights Trail** leads from a parking area off Wilderness Drive, through maple-basswood stands, to the Aiton Heights Fire Tower. The **Deer Park Trail** is 3.1 miles long, wide and grassy, and leads past many small lakes and several hike-in campsites—beaver and otter are often spotted here. Large stands of mature red pine lend their name to **Red Pine Trail,** a 1.2-mile connector between Deer Park and the Ozawindib Trail. The **DeSoto Trail** is another wide, grassy lane passing through stands of aspen on the way to Hernando DeSoto Lake; it's 2.7 miles long.

The Ozawindib Trail and Eagle Scout Trail are both really parts of the **North Country National Scenic Trail,** (see North Country National Scenic Trail) stretching from North Dakota to New York State. Itasca's 13 miles of this 4,200-mile route pass through the southwest quadrant, the park's most undisturbed corner.

The **Brower Trail** is an excellent way to travel between Bear Paw Campground and the Douglas Lodge area; it's two miles long and hugs the shore of Lake Itasca, passing the Peacepipe Vista and Preachers' Grove along the way, and frequently serving up bald eagle and loon sightings. The 1.5-mile **LaSalle Trail** leaves the Pine Ridge Campground and passes through a pine regeneration area where you might see woodcock "peenting" in the spring.

On the west side of Wilderness Drive the **Landmark Interpretation Trail** affords access to a deer exclosure, while the **Blowdown Trail** is known as a birding loop and also gives a close-up look at wind-damaged trees. The **Bohall Trail** leads out to Bohall Lake and is the only trail that goes into the Itasca Wilderness Sanctuary. All three paths are a half-mile in length. The 2.5-mile **Two Spot Trail** and 3.8-mile **Nicollet Trail** are both great places to spot wildlife in Itasca's wild interior.

A 5.8-mile paved **bike trail** runs along the east shore of Lake Itasca, connecting the Mississippi Headwaters with Douglas Lodge. It is gently rolling along most of its length and cross-country skiers use it in wintertime. Bikers can continue around the Wilderness Drive for another 10 miles. Other trails used by cross-country skiers include Aiton Heights, Deer Park, DeSoto, Eagle Scout, Nicollet, North Country Trail, and Red Pine—31 miles are groomed in total.

Other Recreation

Canoeists favor Itasca's four "main" lakes: Itasca, Elk, Mary, and Ozawindib. In spring, some canoeists take on the Mississippi River, but this becomes impossible later in the year when the water level drops. Motorboats are also permitted on the four main lakes and, though there are no size restrictions, there is a 10-mph speed limit.

The ***Chester Charles*** excursion boat makes a 90-minute journey around Lake Itasca, following the same route taken by Schoolcraft. Naturalists narrate the $10 tours, giving information about the history of the park as well as pointing out wildlife—loon and bald eagle sightings are common. The boat runs from late May through early October. Call 218/732-5318 for reservations and information.

Itasca Sports Rental, 218/266-2150, rents a wide selection of outdoor including bikes, canoes, motorboats, paddleboats, surfbikes, and camping equipment. They also offer fishing licenses, bait, fish freezing, and battery charging. It's located at the boat launch on Lake Itasca and is open daily May through mid-October. Snowshoes can be rented at the visitors center.

There's a **swimming beach** just south of the Brower Inn.

Camping

Two drive-in campgrounds with full facilities are located along Lake Itasca's eastern shore. Both cost $12 or $15 with electric hookup. With 158 sites (65 electric) the **Pine Ridge Campground** is the larger of the two and stays open year-round. The northern loops—Poplar and Pine—have more widely spaced sites and lack electricity so they are most peaceful in the park. The **Bear Paw Campground,** right on the lakeshore, has 79 campsites (34 electric) and 11 of these are cart-in sites. Itasca also has 11 **backpack sites** for $7 on or very near the park's smaller lakes.

Accommodations

Itasca lodging facilities are open Memorial Day to mid-October and reservations, which are essential (though you might find openings on short notice during the week), can be made at 866/857-2757 or www.stayatmnparks.com.

The 1905 **Douglas Lodge** is a lovely, historic log building with leafy views of Lake Itasca from its deck and dining room. Most guestrooms have double beds and shared baths and cost $55. There are also several two-bedroom suites with private baths for $84. The **Nicollet Court Motel** next door offers rooms with private baths for $52 and, though it lacks the historic pedigree of the lodge, it's still a beautiful log building with a fireplace in the lounge.

There are also a variety of **cabins** available for rent in Itasca. Near Douglas Lodge, 15 cabins ranging from one to three bedrooms are scattered along the lakeshore. All have living rooms and some have fireplaces and screened porches. Prices range $84–148 depending on size and number of guests. Housekeeping cabins near the Bear Paw Campground sleep four people and have full kitchens, but no private showers (guests can use the campground showers). They cost $85. Four **fireplace rooms**—essentially motel units in a CCC-era building—have fireplaces and screened porches and sleep two people. These cost $73. A single housekeeping cabin on Lake Ozawindib has a large living/dining area with a fireplace and primitive toilet facilities. The cabin comes with the use of a boat and is the most remote lodging available within the park. It costs $120 and sleeps up to eight.

Another lodging option—equally appealing, and much less expensive—is the **Mississippi Headwaters Hostel,** 218/266-3415, housed in another historic log building that once served as park headquarters. The Hostelling International-affiliated facility offers 31 beds with shared bath, a full kitchen and dining area, coin laundry, living area with fireplace, and an outside fire ring. The basic, cozy amenities are used more often by families than the expected twenty-something backpackers, though all are welcome. Prices are $15–17 a night for HI members and $3 more if you're not a member. They are closed for much of the spring and fall.

Bert's Cabins, 218/266-3312, a private resort just a mile from the Headwaters on Wilderness Drive, also run on the May–October schedule but reopens during January and February for winter enthusiasts. There's a pool and playground on-site.

Dining

Douglas Lodge has a full-service restaurant serving three meals a day from Memorial Day through early October. Diners have lovely views from the restaurant's picture windows or from the outside deck in back. Prices are reasonable with most options, such as wild rice hotdish and a buffalo burger platter, under $10. Breakfast features wild rice pancakes. The snack bar at the North Picnic Area's **Brower Inn** offers inexpensive sandwiches, salads, desserts and beverages during the summer.

BEMIDJI

Stretched along the shore of 6,765-acre Lake Bemidji and energized by an infusion of thousands of college students, the "First City on the Mississippi" (population 11,917) has a sophisticated feel that belies its size. Bemidji is an art-friendly place with an excellent history museum and enough good restaurants to distract you from outdoor activities for a day or so.

History

The city takes its name from the Ojibwe phrase Bemiji-gau-maug (Cutting sideways through),

RED LAKE RESERVATION

Total Area - 1,260 sq. miles
Tribally Owned - 100 percent
Total Population - 5,162
Native Population - 5,071
Tribal Enrollment - 9,264

More than just about any tribe in the United States, the Red Lake Ojibwe have done things their own way. The band lives collectively on land that has never been subdivided: Oregon's Warm Springs tribe is the only other in the United States that also successfully resisted allotment. In the late 19th century, as they struggled against outside pressure to subdivide their Rhode Island-sized home, they chased off surveyors, missionaries, and other outsiders who might pose a threat. With no land in private hands none can be sold to outsiders without the approval of all and thus, unlike the checkerboard reservations of all other Minnesota tribes, the Red Lake band still owns all of the land (excepting a few small chunks sold to a railroad) within its borders. Red Lake is also one of the nation's few "closed" reservations meaning that outside a few federal matters the reservation retains total control over all criminal and civil affairs. Consistent with their fierce independence, Red Lake is also the only Ojibwe band that does not belong to the Minnesota Chippewa Tribe Federation.

The Red Lake Reservation encompasses all of Lower Red Lake, the largest lake within Minnesota, as well as much of Upper Red Lake and this land, much of it wetland, is one of the most pristine environments in the state. The reservation also includes the majority of the Northwest Angle and scattered parcels across nine counties. Tribal headquarters are located in Red Lake, an important Dakota village during the French fur trade era, while the little villages of Redby, Little Rock, and Ponemah are the reservations' three other communities. The latter is one of the most traditional Native towns in the Lower 48 and English remains a second language for many adult residents across the reservation.

Though Red Lake suffers economically because of its isolation, it has managed to succeed in several natural resource industries including logging and gravel mining. The Red Lake Fisheries Association, the oldest Native-controlled marketing co-operative in North America, began in 1929 and had 300 members until lax regulation of the walleye harvest forced its closure. They are currently trying to revive the population. Cranberries and wild rice are still small industries but with tens of thousands of acres suitable for cultivation they have great potential. The tribe's Seven Clans Casinos operate in Red Lake, Warroad, and Thief River Falls.

which describes the diagonal path the Mississippi River cuts through the lake. A trading post and sawmill opened in the late 1800s and settlers, mostly Scandinavians, soon followed. As the town grew throughout the 1890s, logging established itself as the area's primary industry, and it remains important today. The coming of the railroad in the next decade was also instrumental in the town's growth. Bemidji has been the seat of Beltrami County since 1897, and Bemidji State University (BSU) opened in 1919. Tourists arriving en masse during visits to the Chippewa National Forest and Itasca State Park have given the city an economic mix that ensures its vitality.

Sights and Recreation

You can't miss Bemidji's most famous attraction:

the giant statues of **Paul Bunyan and Babe the Blue Ox.** The Northwoods folk heroes stand on the downtown waterfront greeting visitors as they arrive in town. Built in 1937 for a winter carnival, Paul and Babe graced the pages of *Life* magazine that same year and soon inspired the whole trend of oversized sculptures in Minnesota. Right next to the statues, the CVB has a hokey display of Paul's personal effects, including a giant toothbrush and boxer shorts. There's also a fireplace built with stones from 48 states and the Canadian provinces.

Bemidji is something of an artist's haven and its credentials include a **sculpture walk** around the downtown. Twenty public sculptures are on display, and a brochure available at the visitors center points you to their locations. Sculptures

© TIM BEWER

the original Paul and Babe statues

change annually and are available for sale. The **Bemidji Community Art Center,** 426 Bemidji Ave. N., 218/444-7570, is a gallery space located in a historic Carnegie Library. It showcases changing exhibits by regional artists, and the work of many locals is for sale in the gift shop. It's open Tuesday–Friday 10 A.M.–4 P.M.

The **Beltrami County History Center,** 130 Minnesota Ave. SW, 218/444-3376, is housed in the 1912 Great Northern Depot, beautifully restored—keeping the original woodwork and terrazzo floor—and reopened as a state-of-the-art museum in 2001. Unlike many local history museums Beltrami is professionally curated, using photographs, maps, and artifacts to tell coherent stories about the area's past; the result is one of the state's best history facilities. A telegrapher's station and a collection of Native American artifacts are on permanent display, while other exhibits change every 18 months. The museum is open weekdays 9 A.M.–4 P.M. and Saturday 10 A.M.–4 P.M. and costs $3.

The **Headwaters Science Center,** 413 Beltrami Ave., 218/444-4472, is a kid-oriented museum featuring many hands-on exhibits. Visitors can study a living stream, climb into a bear den, and shoot their friends with an air cannon, plus the staff conducts demonstrations on various topics ranging from stone tools to hydroponic gardening. The Science Center also has a very cool gift shop stocking toys and supplies for budding scientists. The museum is open Monday–Saturday 9:30 A.M.–5:30 P.M. and Sunday 1–5 P.M.; admission is $3.

Concordia Language Villages, 218/586-2214 or 800/450-2214, north of town on Turtle River Lake, is a unique facility housing four culturally authentic "villages," replicating the architecture and atmosphere of France, Germany, Finland, and Norway, plus Spain is on the way. Casual visitors can call ahead for a free guided tour, though if you've got the time take part in one of their 12 language immersion programs. These range from three days to four weeks and are geared for all age groups and abilities. A stay at Concordia includes international cuisine and other emulations of daily life abroad.

For something on the opposite end of the entertainment spectrum drop a few bucks at one of the town's small amusement parks. **Paul Bunyan Amusement Park** next door to the visitors center includes miniature golf, a few carnival rides, and a rideable miniature railroad. It's open daily 11 A.M.–9 P.M. The **Putt'n'Go Amusement Park,** 218/751-7333, west of town along U.S. 71 has a waterslide, go-karts, miniature golf, and batting cages. It's open daily 11 A.M.–10 P.M. Both are only in operation for the summer season.

The **Buena Vista Ski Village,** 218/243-2231, has 16 runs for downhill skiing and snowboarding, plus a half-pipe and tubing park. You can also take a sleigh ride when it's snowy or a covered wagon ride during the fall color season. Buena Vista is located 15 miles north of town on County Road 15.

Lake Bemidji State Park

Only five miles north of town, Lake Bemidji State Park, 218/755-3843, is a popular place. Most come to enjoy the lakefront—public boat access and boat rentals make the park a good place for fishing, and there is a sandy swimming beach below the visitors center—though nature lovers are well served, too. With its various habitats, including upland red and white pine forests, jack pine barrens, and scattered wetlands, the 1,688-acre park is home to diverse flora and fauna. The park's premier hike is the **Bog Walk,** a 1,200-foot boardwalk leading through a spruce-tamarack bog before winding up at isolated Big Bog Lake. Interpretive signs along the way discuss the formation of bogs and the life forms visible from the trail, including the insectivorous sundews and pitcher plants, plus myriad orchids—most bog flowers bloom in late spring and early summer. The wheelchair-accessible boardwalk is reached via a one-mile gravel path. The Bog Walk connects to a 15-mile network of longer trails across the park including the 3.6-mile **Old Logging Trail** and 2.5-mile Pinewood Trail, which wind through mixed pine and aspen forests. Flowers are also abundant along the **Sundew Pond Boardwalk,** an easy mile-long walk down the **Fish Hawk Trail.** The mile-long **Rocky Point Trail** near the visitors center climbs a bluff overlooking the lake. Off-road bikes are allowed on five miles of trail, while the northern trailhead of the **Paul Bunyan State Trail** is also located at the park—currently the northern end is only paved for the first five miles, though when completed (probably many, many years from now) it will run 100 miles south to Brainerd. Winter brings eleven miles of groomed trail for cross-country skiing and snowshoe rentals. The 95-site (43 electric) campground includes is quiet and shady, though not especially secluded.

Entertainment and Events

Bemidji State University hosts a full spectrum of theater and music, including a two-day jazz festival in February; call 218/755-3863 for scheduling and ticket information. The **Paul Bunyan Playhouse,** 314 Beltrami Ave., 218/751-7270, one of the oldest professional summer theaters in the nation, stages drama, comedy, and musicals, while the **Northern Inn-Prov Comedy Club** at the Northern Inn Hotel brings in touring stand-up acts on Friday and Saturday nights from September through May.

The **Uptown Caffe,** 523 Minnesota Ave., 218/444-5282, hosts live music or poetry readings on many Friday nights throughout the year.

Bemidji has a busy schedule of events, starting with January's **Brrrmidji Polar Daze,** a week-long celebration of winter with snow sculpture and sled dog races. In February, Buena Vista Ski Area hosts **Logging Days,** where participants relive the historic logging era with demonstrations, logging-camp-style meals, and sleigh rides. July sees the **First City Celebration of the Arts,** a 10-day event offering art exhibitions and live music. Concordia Language Villages hosts several **International Days** during July and August, and the public is invited to experience languages, food, and music from around the world.

Accommodations

The **Edgewater Inn,** 1015 Paul Bunyan Dr. NE, 218/751-3600 or 800/776-3343, sits on 650 feet of private beach. Standard rooms start at $67 while suites cost up to $265—all guests have access to the hot tub, sauna, and steam room. The large **Northern Inn,** 3600 Moberg Dr., 218/751-9500 or 800/667-8485, is a full-service hotel with a pool, sauna, game room, fitness center, and even a beauty salon. Rooms come with first-class touches like free cocktails, and rates start at $99. The most basic rooms in town are at the **Midway Motel,** 1000 Paul Bunyan Dr. NE, 218/751-1180, and they go for $45.

Ruttger's Birchmont Lodge, 218/444-3463 or 888/788-8437, on the lake's north shore is Bemidji's premier entry in the large resort category, and they offer a variety of lodging options. The Main Lodge offers some great bargains with basic rooms for as little as $41, while rooms in the Cedar Lodge have extra amenities like fireplaces, decks, and balconies and prices starting at about three times as much. Some lakeview cottages have screened porches, fireplaces, and kitchenettes; rates range $87–169 per night. The completely modern lakefront townhomes have complete kitchens and maid service with weekly rates running $475–645. All of these are early and late summer prices—during the peak season, prices more than double. Ruttger's has an appropriately fancy restaurant on-site, a marina that rents boats, indoor and outdoor pools, tennis courts, and a private sandy lakeshore.

Taber's Historic Log Cabins, 2404 Bemidji Ave. N., 218/751-5781, offers a more rustic experience in 1930s log cabins. The site is convenient to downtown but near the lakeshore and feels secluded. Most cabins have full kitchens and special features include antique, handcrafted log furniture, and antique cookstoves. Right next door is the landmark Taber's Bait and Tackle, Bemidji's oldest bait shop. Taber's is open May through October and prices range from $50–95 per night or $250–475 weekly.

Beltrami Shores, 218/586-2518 or 888/746-7373, is a resort and a B&B in one. The lovingly decorated and relatively pristine spot sits on Beltrami Lake 10 miles north of town. The resort has seven restored one- and two-bedroom cabins hugging the lakeshore, with peak rates ranging $500–995 for a week, and they are available from mid-May through early October. The B&B portion of Beltrami Shores is brand-new, and just as beautifully decorated as the cabins. Three rooms with Northwoods decors sleep from one–five guests and all rooms have private baths. There's a lounge with fireplace, a cozy library, three-season porch, and two decks. The B&B price is $85 and there is a two-night minimum stay. There's a swimming area, firepit, playground, and cedar swings, and guests have free use of beach toys and kayaks. Fishing boats, motors, hydrobikes, and canoes are available for rent.

Food

Union Station/First City Brewery & Grill, 128 1st St., 218/751-9261, is a fine restaurant in a historic railroad depot where diners can choose from the casual brewery room, more formal dining room, or outdoor patio. The lunch menu includes pizzas, portabella sandwiches, and pastas for around $7–10, while steaks and seafood from $15–27 and glorious desserts are added for dinner. Handcrafted ales and a big wine list round out the experience. It's open weekdays for lunch, daily for dinner, and they do a big Sunday brunch.

Another upscale choice is **Tutto Bene,** 300 Beltrami Ave., 218/751-1100. The lunch menu features Italian soups and grilled panini sandwiches for around $6, while dinner features classic Italian dishes with handmade pastas for around twice that. There's a stylish, modern dining room but the beautiful outdoor patio is the place to be. Open for lunch and dinner Mon.–Sat.

Keith's Pizza, 110 Paul Bunyan Dr. SE, 218/751-7940, does brick oven-baked pizza and features a garlic white sauce, as well as more traditional pies. Open daily for lunch and dinner during the summer then dropping the Sunday lunch in the off-season.

Local favorite **Raphael's Bakery & Café,** 319 Minnesota Ave. NW, 218/444-2867, has homemade breads, pastries, and cakes, plus very inexpensive soups and sandwiches in an old-fashioned atmosphere. If you only sample one thing here make it the wild rice bread. Open Mon.–Sat. for breakfast, plus weekdays for lunch.

The **Uptown Caffe,** 523 Minnesota Ave., 218/444-5282, is a coffee shop with a full espresso bar, pastries and desserts, and inexpensive lunches including homemade soups, salads, and sandwiches on focaccia and bagels. Rotating art exhibits add to the atmosphere. It's open for breakfast and lunch daily and stays open late on weekends.

Shopping

The **Bemidji Woolen Mills Factory Store,** 301 Irvine Ave. NW, 218/751-5166, offers all kinds of wool items—shirts, jackets, sweaters, gloves, and blankets—and is quite a popular destination. **Gallery North,** 503 3rd St. NW, 218/759-9813, sells affordable works by local artists in just about any media and artist demonstrations occur daily. **Grandma's Attic,** 218/759-8931, in the same building is a large and well-organized antique mall.

Information and Services

The **Bemidji Visitors & Convention Bureau,** 218/444-3541 or 800/458-2223, www.visitbemidji.com, right next to the Paul and Babe statues on the waterfront, offers a wealth of information, including hotel and resort vacancy listings. It is open weekdays 8 A.M.–6:30 P.M., Saturday 9 A.M.–6 P.M., and Sunday noon–5 P.M. in the summer season, and weekdays 8 A.M.–5 P.M. and Saturday 10 A.M.–2 P.M. the rest of the year.

Cyber Bugs Paradise Café, 311 3rd St. NW, 218/444-2927, is a Hawaiian-themed coffee shop with high-speed Internet connections, as well as other hi-tech services: digital camera, printers, fax machines, scanning, and networked games.

Transportation

The **Bemidji/Beltrami County Airport,** 218/751-1880, is located west of town on U.S. 2.

Northwest Airlink, 800/225-2525, makes the hour-long flight to the Minneapolis-St. Paul airport up to four times a day, and round-trip fares start around $175—much less if it is a segment of a longer Northwest flight. **National,** 218/751-1880, and **Enterprise,** 218/759-9960, both located at the airport, rent cars.

Greyhound buses stop at 909 Midway Dr. S., 218/751-7600, on their way to and from Minneapolis.

Chippewa National Forest

Encompassing three of the state's largest lakes, plus the infant Mississippi River and thousands of acres of forest and wetland, the Chippewa National Forest is absolutely packed with recreational opportunities. Established in 1902 the 1.6 million-acre preserve (over 660,000 acres are managed by the Forest Service) was the first National Forest in the eastern United States. Fully half of the forest's acreage is made of lakes, streams, and wetlands, including Leech Lake and Lake Winnibigoshish, the third and fourth largest lakes in Minnesota respectively. In total there are 1,300 lakes within the forest boundaries. Most campgrounds sit lakeside and, though most resorts are warm-season fishing lodges, there is accommodation for all tastes.

The Chippewa is home to a greater percentage of breeding bald eagles that anywhere else in the Lower 48—most years there are about 170 pair—and spotting them is a highlight for most forest visitors. Most build their sofa-sized nests in stands of towering red and white pine, but the best viewing is from large lakes and major rivers where the birds circle overhead in search of food or perch in trees along the shoreline. Federal Dam on Leech Lake, Winnie Dam on Lake Winnibigoshish, and Knutson Dam on Cass Lake are all productive fishing grounds for eagles and thus good places to spot them, especially during the winter since the churning water doesn't freeze. The birds also frequently soar over the Mississippi, so a canoe trip or a drive along U.S. 2 often yields sightings. More eagle-watching information is available at forest offices. Just about all other Northwoods

wildlife resides in the forest, too, including osprey, great gray owl, common loon, ruffed and spruce grouse, northern goshawk, black-backed woodpecker, deer, pine marten, wolverine, fisher, porcupine, black bear, moose, bobcat, cougar, lynx, and the rarely seen but sometimes heard timber wolf. In total, nearly 250 species of bird have been recorded here.

Towns within the forest—Walker is the biggest—got their start as lumbering centers; the timber industry no longer runs the show around here quite as completely as it once did, but about one percent of the forest is still cleared each year. The Leech Lake Ojibwe Reservation sits within the forest, as does the north-south continental divide, also called the Laurentian Divide: rain falling to the south of the line flows to the Gulf of Mexico via the Mississippi River, while water to the north enters the ocean via Hudson Bay. Historical sites include many CCC-era camps and several stands of old-growth pine, preserved by fortunate error and forward thinking conservationists.

Recreation

The Chippewa has over 160 miles of nonmotorized trails for hikers with routes ranging in length from the one-mile walk through the old-growth red and white pine at the Lost Forty to a 68-mile portion of the **North Country National Scenic Trail** (see the North Country National Scenic Trail description elsewhere in this chapter) stretching from New York to North Dakota. Most of the hiking trails in the forest (the North

NORTH COUNTRY NATIONAL SCENIC TRAIL

When completed the North Country Scenic Trail will stretch 4,200 miles across seven states from Lake Sakakawea in central North Dakota to Lake Champlain in eastern New York. It will be the longest hiking trail in the nation. Currently over 1,700 miles have been certified by the National Park Service since the trail's inception in 1980 and another 800 miles are now hikable.

Minnesota's 850-mile slice enters from the east near Jay Cooke State Park and then turns north and merges with the **Superior Hiking Trail** (SHT). The next 400 or so phenomenal miles follow the SHT, noted for ridgetop views of Lake Superior and an abundance of waterfalls, turning inwards towards the Canadian border and crossing through the remote and rugged Boundary Waters Canoe Area Wilderness along the Border Route and Kekekabic trails. From Ely the trail heads west along an as yet to be determined route to the Chippewa Na-

tional Forest which holds the next completed segment—a beautiful and wild 68-mile stretch across the southern border. Work is progressing rapidly on a new trail across the Paul Bunyan State Forest which will link the Chippewa with another excellent section through the remotest corner of Itasca State Park. After 13 miles through the park the trail continues to the west for another eight miles. There is currently no completed trail beyond this, though the route will almost certainly cross both the Tamarac National Wildlife Refuge and Maplewood State Park. Beyond Maplewood the trail will lead out of the forests of the east and into the Great Plains, eventually crossing the Red River into North Dakota.

For more information contact the North Country Trail Association, 229 E. Main St., Lowell, MI 49331, 888/454-6282. Their website, www.northcountrytrail.org, is an especially helpful resource and includes trail condition reports.

Country and Shingobee trails are notable exceptions) are also open to off-road bikes, plus the Forest Service has designated a number of road routes. Most are easy or moderate, though those looking for a challenging ride will find it—Suomi Hills is considered the most difficult mountain bike route in the forest. There are also hundreds of miles of unpaved forest roads, most fairly rough, that bikers looking to get off the beaten path can explore at will; bring a compass and map. Snowmobilers can take advantage of 330 miles of groomed trails and many forest roads, including nearly half of the 112-mile **Soo Line Trail,** the longest motorized recreation trail in Minnesota, which connects Cass Lake to Moose Lake along an abandoned rail bed.

There is good fishing right across the state, but the Chippewa National Forest encompasses some of the best of the best. These nationally recognized fishing waters provide ideal habitat for a wide variety of species. Deep basins like Benjamin Lake, Bee Cee Lake, and Diamond Lake harbor rainbow and lake trout, while more shallow, nutrient-rich lakes, including Blackduck, Winnibigoshish, Cass, and Leech, are home to walleye, muskie, northern pike, bass,

and panfish. Walleye are the area's most sought-after species, though Leech Lake is a widely known muskie factory. Facilities and services for anglers abound throughout the forest, and there are seemingly as many bait shops as there are lakes. If you haven't got a boat and don't want to hire a guide, sign up with launch services on Leech Lake, Cass Lake, and Lake Winnibigoshish. Remember that on the largest lakes, windy conditions preclude the use of small boats.

Canoeists and kayakers have loads of water to choose from, too. Nine designated routes ranging in length and difficulty cover the forest's largest lakes and most secluded streams. There's a two-mile route on the slow-moving Shingobee River, highly recommended for families, while the Turtle and Mississippi are other easy paddles with good eagle-viewing opportunities. More difficult routes follow the Big Fork River, which has some white water, and the 120-mile Chippewa Headwaters Loop connecting Lake Winnibigoshish, Leech Lake, and Cass Lake via the Mississippi and other waterways. Canoeing on the large lakes is dangerous in high winds, so use caution and get weather information from the Forest Service before setting out. Many of the forest's rivers have primitive campsites, facilitating multi-day excursions.

Fall colors normally reach their peak around the third week in September; call the Forest Service's National Color Hotline (800/354-4595) during September and October to get the up-to-the-minute scoop. The **Edge of the Wilderness National Scenic Byway,** stretching 47 miles between Grand Rapids and Bigfork, is a favorite leaf peeping route.

Camping

Chippewa has 23 campgrounds. Almost all are on or near the forest's major lakes and the majority lie in the Blackduck and Deer River districts. Most are officially open mid-May to mid-September, though camping is allowed at any time; however, there will be no water or facilities available. Each campsite has a picnic table, fire grate, tent pad, and parking spot. Beyond that facilities vary, though only Norway Beach and Stony Point have electric hookups, flush toilets, and showers. A few of the larger, more developed campgrounds—Norway Beach, Deer Lake, O-Ne-Gum-E, Clubhouse Lake, and Stony Point—take reservations (for a $9 non-refundable fee) at 877/444-6777 or www.reserveusa.com. Camping rates in summer range $12–16, depending on how developed the campground is, while most camping in the winter is free.

Over 400 "dispersed" backpacking sites are sprinkled throughout the forest. For more information on these free and typically very primitive options, as well as more developed hike- and canoe-in sites, inquire at one of the district offices or call 218/335-8600. Forest Service rules also permit you to camp anywhere on public land, as long as you're 150 feet from any water source or trail and observe Leave No Trace (www.lnt.org) outdoor ethics. Though registration isn't required for backcountry camping, checking in at a ranger station is always a good idea, especially to find out about any current fire restrictions.

Information

There are four ranger districts in the Chippewa: Blackduck, Deer River, Walker, and Marcell—you may see outdated information referring to the Cass Lake District, but this no longer exists. The **Forest Headquarters,** 200 Ash Ave., 218/335-8600 (218/335-8632 TTY), r9_chippewa_public@fs.fed.us, www.fs.fed.us/r9/chippewa, in Cass Lake can give general information and is open weekdays 7:30 A.M.–5 P.M. during the summer, and 8 A.M.–4:30 P.M. the rest of the year. District stations are usually the best place to get specific advice about sites and activities in each area. The Forest Service publishes a slew of free maps and information sheets about activities and facilities, and there's also a very handy foldout map available for $6 if you want a more detailed view.

Cass Lake

Though not actually within the forest, Cass Lake is a regular stop for visitors because it lies right along U.S. 2 near many of the most popular forest destinations. The body of water for which this sleepy town was named was originally dubbed Red Cedar Lake, a translation of the Ojibwe name. During his 1832 expedition to find the source of the Mississippi River, Henry Rowe Schoolcraft renamed it in honor his friend, Lewis Cass, who as Territorial Governor led an expedition here twelve years earlier and errantly declared this the great river's source. The area's logging industry was centered here in the late 1800s and was so large that the city's population exceeded 7,000 at the turn of the 20th century. These days, Cass Lake has about 850 inhabitants and a strong Ojibwe heritage.

Lyle's Logging Camp and Cass Lake Museum, 218/335-6723 or 800/356-8615, right in town at the junction of Highways 2 and 371, features an evocative reconstruction of a logging camp as it would have appeared during the timber industry's early 20th-century heyday. Lyle Chisholm, who had worked as a logger since he was 11, built the authentic bunkhouse, mess hall, tool shop, and other buildings, and these are enhanced by recorded narratives. The museum, in a former railroad depot, houses wildlife and local history exhibits. They are both open Monday–Saturday 9 A.M.–5 P.M. during the summer and admission is $4. Known as the Log Palace, the remarkable **Chippewa National**

LEECH LAKE RESERVATION

Total Area - 1,310 sq. miles
Tribally Owned - 3 percent
Total Population - 10,205
Native Population - 4,561
Tribal Enrollment - 8,219

The Mississippi and Pillager Ojibwe bands first arrived in the wooded and swampy areas of north central Minnesota around the mid-18th century, originally making their homes on the small islands of Leech Lake. The reservation was created in a series of treaties and executive orders between 1855 and 1874 and an 1864 resettlement plan developed by the U.S. Government called for moving all of Minnesota's Ojibwe here, though the relocation effort was redirected to the White Earth Reservation three years later. It was at Sugar Point—now known as Battle Point—on the northeast shore of Leech Lake that the Ojibwe Chief Bug-Oh-Nay-Geshig and his followers successfully fought off the army who

had been sent to arrest him on trumped up charges. Their goal was to intimidate the Ojibwe into giving up their land and timber rights. The Battle of Sugar Point, fought in 1898, is sometimes described as "the last deadly battle in the United States between the American military and the American Indian."

Today, the reservation expands over parts of Beltrami, Cass, Hubbard, and Itasca counties and 75 percent of the Chippewa National Forest was land that had once been part of the reservation. Itasca State Park, surrounding the headwaters of the Mississippi River, was another portion taken out of Ojibwe control. Tribal headquarters are located in Cass Lake, with other key native settlements at Onigum, Ball Club, and Bena. Leech Lake-run casinos operate at Cass Lake, Deer River, and Walker. While tourists bring much income to the tribal community locals also harvest wild rice on some 40 lakes to sell locally as well as on the international market.

Forest Headquarters, 218/335-8600, is presumed to be the largest log structure in Minnesota. Constructed in 1935 from giant red pine the three-story structure surrounds a 50-foot-high fireplace built from glacial boulders. The Finnish log construction style uses only grooves and notches to fit the logs together, while hand-crafted interior features include gnarled stair railings, split log steps, and hand-hammered ironwork. Also inside are Forest Service and natural history exhibits. You can look around during business hours weekdays 7:30 A.M.–5 P.M. in summer, and 8 A.M.–4:30 P.M. the rest of the year.

The **Heartland State Trail** is paved all the way to Park Rapids, 49 miles to the southwest. It's used mostly by bikers, but horseback riders and hikers are welcome, too. There's no bike rental in town at the time of this writing, but since the paving was just completed that is sure to change soon. **Sailstar Marina,** 218/335-2316, rents fishing and pontoon boats, while canoe rental, shuttle service, and guided tours are available at **Adventure Tours and Rental,** 218/335-8858 or 800/635-8858, at the Shangri La Resort west of town.

Cass Lake **powwows** are regionally known. Three take place every summer—Memorial Day, the Fourth of July, and Labor Day—at the Veterans Memorial Grounds near the Palace Casino. Other events include the **Mi-Gi-Zi Festival** on the second weekend in June, featuring a Northwoods triathlon (run/canoe/bike), plus all the usual music, food, and crafts and the winter-themed **Chain Reaction** on the second weekend in January.

About three dozen family- and fishing-focused resorts sit on the surrounding lakes with about half of those on Cass Lake itself. **Sah-Kah-Tay Resort,** 218/335-2424 or 800/232-3224, north of town on Cass Lake's west shore is typical. There are nine housekeeping cabins near the shady lakefront, and guests have access to games, paddleboats, an outdoor fireplace, and boat rentals. Cabins have two–five bedrooms and cost $105–205 daily or $515–1025 weekly. The large **Palace Casino Hotel,** 218/335-8935 or 800/442-3910, at the Leech Lake Band Ojibwe's tropically-themed Palace Casino has a pool, hot tub, and a game room. Regular rooms are $60 and the whirlpool suites go for $70, plus they have a few RV campsites. **Sportsmen's Pizzeria,** 115 2nd St. NW, 218/335-6771, has specialty pies under $15, plus sandwiches on Native American frybread and fried chicken. They're open weekdays for lunch and Monday–Saturday for dinner. There are also plenty of food choices at the casino. The **Cass Lake Information Center,** 218/335-2250 or 800/356-8615, www.casslake.com, is on the frontage road north of U.S. 2. They're open weekdays 8 A.M.–4:30 P.M. and they add Saturdays during the summer. In addition to providing information on the national forest and the community, they can help you find hotel and resort vacancies on short notice.

BLACKDUCK DISTRICT

Blackduck

Just north of the forest Blackduck is a tidy community of 696 named after the lake just west of town. In the Ojibwe's days the 2,700-acre Blackduck Lake was a favorite feeding place for ducks and so many descended that they obscured the water surface and inspired the name. The town honors its namesake birds with two giant **black duck statues.** One is in a small park at along U.S. 71 and the other sits near the fire station on Main Street. Over 60 whittlers come to show off their decoys and other carvings during the **Woodcarvers Festival** the last Saturday in July.

All rooms at the **AmericInn,** 218/835-4500 or 800/634-3444, at the intersection of Highways 71 and 30 have a refrigerator and microwave and start at $65. There's also a pool, whirlpool, sauna, and exercise room. The **Drake Motel,** 172 Pine Ave., 218/835-4567 or 888/253-8501, is a smaller and more economical option with 11 basic rooms (two with kitchenettes) going for as little as $40. The **Countryside Restaurant,** 218/835-3333, next to the AmericInn has inexpensive home-cooking: omelets, steaks, country fried chicken, and a salad bar. It's open for breakfast, lunch, and dinner daily. The **Hillcrest Supper Club,** 20250 Tepee Hill Ln. NE, 218/835-4250, boasts a beautiful setting on Blackduck Lake and a menu of steak, seafood, and other entrées like Polynesian ham, most in the $10–15 range. Hillcrest is open for dinner Tuesday–Sunday.

Recreation

The Blackduck district contains many of the Chippewa National Forest's most popular historic and natural areas. Many of these fall within the **Ten Section Area,** a stand of old-growth pines east of Cass Lake that was the first area protected by law in 1902 and is thus the historical heart of the forest. The **Norway Beach Recreation Area,** on the east shore of Cass Lake, is one of the forest's most heavily visited spots. People are drawn by the developed campground and the beach, as well as the **Norway Beach Visitor Information Center,** 218/335-2283. The CCC-era building houses interpretive displays and, during the summer, an on-site naturalist conducts programs. It's open Wednesday–Saturday noon–5 P.M. from May to September. Four of the 18 paved miles of the **Mi-Ge-Zi Trail,** used by hikers and bikers, passes along the shore through Norway Beach and continues on to Cass Lake where it connects to the Heartland State Trail, while a two-mile **nature trail** gives a close-up look at the huge red pines. Out on Cass Lake itself **Star Island** contains a very unusual feature: 195-acre Lake Windigo, featured in *Ripley's Believe It Or Not* as the "lake in the island in the lake." Hiking the six-mile **Star Island Trail** is a good way to see most of the 1,000-acre island, named for its four-point shape. Many local resorts offer Star Island tours in the summer.

Pennington Bog, a 107-acre cedar swamp 14 miles northeast of Cass Lake on County Road 39, is a great place to see rare orchids—early to mid-summer is the best time to visit. Another bog walk, this one part of the six-mile **Webster Lake** trail system, has interpretive panels discussing the bog's carnivorous pitcher plants. The trailhead is at the Webster Lake Campground, seven miles south of Blackduck on County Road 39, and then three miles southeast on Forest Roads 2207 and 2236.

The **Blackduck Lookout Tower,** three miles south of Blackduck on County Road 39, then a short drive west down County Road 300, was in use from the mid-1930s until 1970. You are free to climb the tower for a smashing view of the forest. Farther north, the famous **Lost Forty** is a 144-acre section of virgin pine, spared from

CENTRAL LAKES

logging by a surveyor's error in 1882. There's a one-mile trail through the enormous trees, many of which are up to 350 years old and harbor bald eagles and other wildlife—the largest pines are on the area's east end. To reach the Lost Forty from Blackduck take County Roads 30, 13, and 29 about 25 miles east to Dora Lake and head north on County Road 26 for two miles to Forest Road 2240, then follow that for about 1.5 miles. Nearby, Island Lake contains **Elmwood Island,** an undeveloped island with a half-mile trail through a stand of upland cedar. Occupied by CCC workers from 1935 to 1941, **Camp Rabideau** is six miles south of Blackduck on County Road 39. A one-mile interpretive trail highlights the 17 original buildings remaining here from which CCC workers—the "Tree Army"—conducted forest management and construction projects during the Depression. Considered a historical site of national importance because of the enormous legacy of the CCC, the camp is under restoration to preserve what were originally meant to be temporary structures.

The Chippewa Discovery Tour runs 50 miles between Cass Lake and Blackduck taking in many of the sights listed above and is a great way to get acquainted with the layout of this part of the forest and to learn about the natural and human history. Most of the route follows Highways 10 and 39 and part of it also comprises the state designated Scenic Highway Scenic Byway.

Popular road bike routes in the district, mostly unpaved, include a moderate 27-mile loop through the **Lost Forty,** an easy twelve-mile loop near **Webster Lake,** and a moderate 26-mile route through **Norway Beach** and the rest of the Ten Section.

The **Turtle River, Mississippi River** and **Pike Bay Connection** are designated canoe routes; Pike Bay is considered a historic route and is fairly difficult, with six portages in eight miles. The three-mile **Carter Lake Trail** and the 10-mile **Meadow Lake Trail** are designated for cross-country skiing, though not groomed.

Camping

The **Norway Beach Recreation Area,** the Chippewa's largest and most popular campground, has four separate loops: Chippewa, Cass Lake, Norway Beach, and Wanaki, with a total of 170 sites. All have flush toilets and showers, and the Chippewa Loop is one of only two campgrounds in the forest with electric hookups. A boat ramp gives access to Cass Lake and there's a swimming beach and picnic area. Reservations are accepted. The other large campground by Blackduck is named **Winnie,** since it sits on the west shore of enormous Lake Winnibigoshish. It has a swimming beach, boat ramp, and 35 sites in a stand of large red and white pines.

Knutson Dam has 14 sites on the north side of Cass Lake and is known both for good fishing and its Mississippi River canoe access. **Noma Lake,** also noted for fishing, has 14 sites in a stand of birch and a boat launch. **Webster Lake** has 14 sites among large red pines, plus a boat ramp and direct access to some of the district's best hiking. The tiny **Star Island** campground, with three free sites, provides a spectacular location, though there is no drinking water.

Information

The **Blackduck Ranger Station,** 218/835-4291, is located on the south side of Blackduck along U.S. 71. It is open Monday–Thursday 7:30 A.M.– 5 P.M. and Friday 7:30 A.M.–4 P.M. There is also the handy **Norway Beach Visitor Information Center** detailed above.

MARCELL DISTRICT

Marcell

The only town of consequence in this chunk of the forest, Marcell is an outpost of about 30 souls. Settled in 1901 on the shores of Turtle Lake to support the logging industry, the town's buildings were moved south to the railroad tracks in 1911 when the industry had finally cut over the whole area. Marcell remains a logging town and makes a good supply stop, with gas, groceries, and sporting goods. The **Timberwolf Inn,** 218/332-3990, two miles north of town on Highway 38, has 12 rooms for about $50 in a modern log building. The on-site restaurant serves breakfast on the weekends and dinner daily during the summer. Sandwiches run about $6, though their specialties—ribs, chicken, and seafood—range $10–25. The **Buckhorn Resort,** 218/832-3723 or 800/450-6628, south of town has an exceptional setting on Caribou Lake, one of Minnesota's deepest and clearest. There are five older red chalet-style cabins along the shore and two beautiful modern four-bedroom log lodges—all of which come with a fishing boat. Guests have access to a game room, a dock, and a Finnish-style wood-fired sauna. Prices range $90–225 per night (there is usually a three-night minimum) and $540–1,500 per week.

Scenic State Park

The name says it all. This 3,360-acre park right on the edge of the national forest protects virgin pine shorelines of half a dozen lakes. Along with the huge trees other park highlights include fishing, swimming, paddling (canoe rentals are available), a bog walk, and a hike along **Chase Point,** a long esker dividing Coon and Sedgwick Lakes. In total there are 14 miles of hiking trail and three of those are groomed for cross-country skiing each winter, while bird-watchers come here just to add spruce grouse to their life lists. The history of the CCC is told in the historic log pavilion with its grand stone fireplace and original log-and-branch furniture, and the park naturalist leads fire tower tours on summer Saturdays. There are a variety of lodging opportunities—95 drive-in campsites (20 electric) are divided between Chase Point Campground, on a hill above Coon Lake, and Lodge Campground near the beach and fishing pier—the latter is a bit more convenient, though the former is generally more scenic and secluded. There are also two backpack sites about a mile in from the parking area and five lakeside canoe sites—four of which can be reached on foot as well. Finally, a four-bedroom guesthouse comes with a boat. Call 218/743-3362 with any park inquiries.

Recreation

The Marcell District is characterized by many smaller lakes and dispersed camping, making it one of the more secluded corners of the forest. Several areas have been set aside for nonmotorized use and contain beautiful opportunities for hiking, biking, and backpacking.

The **Trout Lake Recreation Area,** 16 miles south of Marcell off Highway 38, contains 11 lakes in its 6,000 nonmotorized acres. There are five miles of hiking and biking trails, groomed for skiing in the winter, within the Trout Lake area, and Spider Lake has over two-dozen primitive campsites on its shore. The **Joyce Estate,** reached by a short hike, is a 1924 hunting camp built by a wealthy logging family with 40 buildings, including a main lodge, servant's cabins, and outdoor facilities like a golf course and greenhouse. Many of the buildings are constructed in the Adirondack style, with log architecture and stickwork. You can wander the grounds and admire the plushness of the Joyces' version of roughing it.

Suomi Hills Recreation Area, also nonmotorized, covers an area of rolling hills on the west side of Highway 38. Twenty-one miles of trail accommodate hikers, bikers, and skiers and are accessible from two marked trailheads along the Highway. Mountain bikers consider this the choicest ride in the whole forest. This area is ideal for overnight camping, with enough miles of trails and few enough visitors to ensure solitude among the numerous small lakes. A CCC camp on the north end of Suomi Hills was used to house prisoners of war during World War II. Suomi is known as a fall color destination, and hikers will also find morel mushrooms and blueberries in season. Within Suomi Hills the **Miller Lake Geologic Area** is reached by a short hike from a fire road off Highway 38. Miller Lake, a "disappearing lake," broke through an earthen levy at its south end in 1982; beavers subsequently built a dam at the breach, but that too washed away in 1993 once again sending the lake into oblivion. More beaver activity is visible today.

A short interpretive loop called the **East Lake Pines Trail** is located on the north shore of East Lake (accessible by boat only) and explains how glaciers created kettle lakes as it leads through old-growth red pines. Near **Thydean Lake** on Forest Road 2180, not too far north of Marcell, is a meadow noted for its bounty of butterflies. There are three designated road bike routes, mostly unpaved: **Clubhouse Lake** (moderate, five miles); **Little Ruby** (easy/moderate, ten miles); and **Wirt/Talmoon Loop** (moderate/difficult, 35 miles).

Three driving tours feature highlights of the Marcell District. The **Edge of the Wilderness National Scenic Byway** covers 47 miles of Highway 38 between Grand Rapids and Effie. Its 14 stops include Trout Lake, a tamarack bog, and the Laurentian continental divide. Marcell marks the byway's approximate midpoint. The **Chippewa Adventure Tour** is 17.5 miles and focuses on wildlife-viewing opportunities (bald eagles, wetland birds, beaver, and ruffed grouse in particular) and various kinds of forest and marsh habitats. A 39-mile **Fall Color Tour** includes the Chippewa Tour, plus adds a long stretch of Highway 38.

Camping

The two developed campgrounds in the Marcell District have swimming beaches and are named for the noted fishing lakes they sit on. **Clubhouse Lake** has 47 sites, a boat ramp, and accepts reservations. The **North Star** camp has 38 generally quieter sites.

Information

The **Marcell Ranger Station,** 218/832-3161, is located on the north edge of Marcell along Hwy. 38. It is open weekdays 8 A.M.–4:30 P.M.

DEER RIVER DISTRICT

Deer River

Most people stop at Deer River (pop. 903) right on the edge of the forest for supplies or to gaze at the car-sized **northern pike statue** by the Deer River Welcome House. Other than gas, food, lodging, and the photo-ready fish, the nonprofit **White Oak Society,** 33155 Hwy. 6, 218/246-9393, is the principal reason to come to town. Members, most of whom are volunteers, reenact the Great Lakes voyageur days of the early 1800s at their reconstructed fur post. There's an Ojibwe village, clerk's and bourgeois quarters, blacksmith shop, smokehouse, and canoe building shed. The society hosts the **White Oak Rendezvous and Festival** the first weekend of August during which you can

watch historical demonstrations (atlatl tossing and clay oven cooking, for example) and take part in workshops on activities like canoe building and quill calligraphy. There's also lots of period food and beer. Father's Day weekend sees **Camping with Historical Attitude,** during which society members camp in the manner of the voyageurs and invite the public to camp alongside them. They run a small campground with 25 RV sites; there are no hookups and they cost $10. The gift shop is a historically-accurate company trading post with such items as fabrics, tomahawks, and copper kettles. **Bahr's Motel,** 109 Division St., 218/246-8271, has 22 very basic but clean rooms starting at $35, plus some kitchenette units that can sleep seven for $83. The **Rivertown Diner,** 315 Main Ave., 218/246-9690, has all-American food at rock-bottom prices; most sandwiches and breakfasts are under $5. It's open for three meals daily. The Leech Lake Ojibwe's **White Oak Casino,** 45830 U.S. 2 W., 218/246-9600 or 800/653-2412, is just west of town.

Lake Winnibigoshish

Not quite the tongue twister it appears to be, Winnibigoshish is pronounced basically like it is spelled using a hard "O." If that's too intimidating just call it "Big Winnie" like everyone else does. Big it certainly is—with 116 miles of shoreline (less than 5 percent developed) and 70,000 acres, Minnesota's fourth largest lake dominates this part of the forest. The long name the Ojibwe bestowed upon it means Miserable-Wretched-Dirty-Water, because storm winds can churn up the muddy bottom, but the scores of anglers and boaters who flock to its shores are enough proof that Winnibigoshish is a misnomer.

A third of the National Forest campgrounds are bunched around the northeast end of the lake and just over a dozen resorts sit on its shore. A good family-friendly choice is the **Eagle Nest Lodge,** 218/246-8701 or 800/356-3775, at the lake's northeast end (on a large bay known as Cut Foot Sioux Lake). With 14 housekeeping cabins, some with fireplaces, and a beautiful stretch of sandy beach, the resort is a tidy, peaceful escape. Naturalist programs, a game room, sailboats, and canoes are some of the many on-site activities and facilities, plus visitors can rent fishing boats. Rates range $128–600 nightly and $640–3,000 weekly during the summer peak—they also offer "mini-weeks" (Sat.–Tues. or Tues.–Sat.). The **Gosh Dam Place,** 38589 Hwy. 46, 218/246-8202, has 20 basic motel rooms popular with anglers. Half have private baths and cost $29 per person, and the rest have shared baths and cost $22 per person. The on-site restaurant serves breakfast, lunch, and dinner daily, most meals are under $10.

Schoolcraft State Park

One of the least-visited state parks in Minnesota, Schoolcraft preserves both natural and human history along a meandering stretch of the Mississippi River. It is named for Henry Rowe Schoolcraft, who is believed to have camped here during his expedition to identify the river's source. Virgin pine covers much of its 295 lovely acres, and the marshy area around the Vermilion River in the park's southern half contains an oxbow lake. Besides stands of red and white pine (including one 300-year-old specimen), spruce, jack pine, and fir, the two miles of looping hiking trails pass wild rice fields and beds of yellow and white water lilies. Near the lake are the remnants of the Dobson homestead, believed to be the first in the township. The rustic campground has 28 sites and there are two canoe sites on the Mississippi. Call Hill Annex Mine State Park, 218/247-7215, for information.

Bena

Sitting smack-dab in the middle of the forest is the **Big Fish Supper Club,** 218/665-2333, with a classic meat and potatoes menu, but that's not why you should stop. It's the 65-foot-long, 14-foot-tall tiger muskie sitting next to it that the restaurant took its name from. Built as a drive-in in 1958, it now just serves as storage space, but that doesn't take away the magic for curious road trippers. It's also a popular find for postcard collectors and even made it into the classic tourist trap montage at the beginning of *National Lampoon's Vacation.* The Big Fish is open for three meals daily in the summer; the rest of the year they serve breakfast and lunch Thursday–Sunday and dinner daily.

Longville

Longville, a little town at the end of Girl Lake, is known as the Turtle Race Capital of the World

© ERIKA HOWSARE

Bena's big fish

CENTRAL LAKES

based on their popular reptilian racing on summer Wednesdays. Though the turtles start sprinting at 2 P.M., race day begins an hour earlier with a street full of other kiddie activities like mini-golf and Chicken Dance contests. You can rent a turtle if you don't have your own.

Recreation

The **Cut Foot Sioux Trail** is a 22-mile loop that follows the Laurentian Continental Divide and passes numerous small lakes and the north end of Cut Foot Sioux Lake where there are several campgrounds. The trail passes a fire tower (climbing it is not allowed) and leads through the Cut Foot Experimental Forest, a forest management laboratory. Starting at the same place is the **Simpson Creek Trail.** Thirteen miles of nonmotorized path give access to a cedar swamp, red and white pine stands, glacial eskers, and eagle-watching spots on the shore of Cut Foot Sioux Lake. Both trails are used by hikers, bikers, and skiers. The **Cut Foot Sioux Visitor Center,** 218/246-8233, houses a local and natural history museum and is open weekdays 9 A.M.–4:30 P.M., staying open until 9 P.M. on Wednesday. It sits about 16 miles northwest of Deer River on Highway 46 at its intersection with Highway 35. Nearby, the original **Cut Foot Sioux Ranger Station** is one of the oldest surviving structures in the U.S. Forest Service's eastern region. Built in 1908, it was used as a ranger station, honeymoon cabin, and tool shed over the years until it was restored in the 1990s. It's decorated the way it was in 1911, when a ranger and his wife called it home. You can sign out keys from the visitors center to see the inside.

North of Lake Winnibigoshish, the 22-mile **Pigeon Lakes Loop** is a moderately challenging unpaved mountain bike route. The U.S. 2 bridge over the Mississippi River, eight miles east of Deer River, is a noted spot for viewing bald eagles. Lake Winnibigoshish, including the two Cut Foot Sioux lakes and Little Ball Club Lake, are top fishing spots known for walleye, northern, muskie, bass, and panfish.

Camping

The Deer River District contains the forest's only horse campground, the **Cut Foot Sioux Horse Camp.** It has 23 campsites and is surrounded by 120 miles of rideable road and trail. The district's drive-in campgrounds are clustered on Cutfoot Sioux Lake, an isolated offshoot of Lake Winnibigoshish, and most have boat ramps. Both **O-Ne-Gum-E** and **Deer Lake** have 48 sites and accept reservations; the latter also has a swimming beach. Smaller and generally quieter are **Mosomo Point,** an angler favorite; **West Seelye Bay; East Seelye Bay;** and **Williams Narrows** with good bald eagle viewing—none have more than 23 sites and the first and the last two have swimming beaches. **Tamarack Point** has 32 sites on Lake Winnie's south shore.

There is also the U.S. Army Corps of Engineers' **Lake Winnibigoshish Recreation Area,** 218/326-6128, with 22 shady campsites, eight of them electric, right next to the dam. They cost $15 and can be reserved through the same company that handles the National Forest camps.

Information

The **Deer River Ranger Station,** 1037 Division St., 218/246-2123, is located on Highway 46 north of Deer River. It is open weekdays 8 A.M.–4:30 P.M. You can also get information at the **Cut Foot Sioux Visitor Center.**

WALKER DISTRICT
Walker

By far the biggest and busiest town in the forest, Walker (pop. 1,069) bustles with visitors tramping between the restaurants and gift shops. It sits on the western arm of busy Leech Lake—Minnesota's third largest with 122,610 acres of water and 154 miles of shoreline. Though this part of the forest is more heavily developed than the rest, the activity isn't overwhelming. Walker is best known for celebrating a big-headed, spotted fish that's so ugly it's cute. The **International Eelpout Festival,** one of Minnesota's best known community celebrations, is held the second weekend of February and features fishing tournaments, a fish house parade, and lots of cold-defying outdoor revelry to close out the ice fishing season. The eelpout, a flatheaded freshwater cod, is also known as a burbot or lawyer.

Normally reviled by anglers, it's actually a tasty catch and the 10,000 or so people who descend on the town for the festivities can sample it boiled, barbecued, or battered and fried.

The **Cass County Museum,** 201 Minnesota Ave. W., 218/547-7251, covers local history with a historic schoolhouse, Ojibwe and Dakota art and artifacts, animal mounts, and much more. It's open weekdays 10 A.M.–5 P.M. during the summer and costs $3. With Leech Lake considered one of the world's best walleye factories, the **Minnesota Fishing Hall of Fame,** 218/547-2000, has broad appeal in this neck of the woods. The collection features videos, plaques, photos, and other memorabilia of legendary anglers, plus there are games and a fishing pond with bait and tackle provided. It sits just north of Walker on Highway 371 in the Walker Outlet Center and is open daily 10 A.M.–5 P.M. during the summer. The whole experience is free. Five miles south of town at the junction of Highways 371 and 200 is **Moondance Ranch and Adventure Park,** 218/547-1055, which offers 20 acres of activities, including "formula K" go-karts, miniature golf, a water slide, arcade, wagon rides, and a zoo with black bears, a Siberian tiger, and 100 other animals. They also offer horseback riding through the forest and host dozens of county fair-quality rock bands during mid-July's **Moondance Jam** music festival. Various passes for different areas of the park range $6–23. Open daily 9 A.M.–9 P.M. in the summer and Wed.–Sun. 10 A.M.–9 P.M. during the spring and fall. Also out at this junction the Leech Lake Ojibwe provide nonstop gaming action at their **Northern Lights Casino,** 218/547-2744 or 800/252-7529. Fifteen miles to the northwest is the **Forestedge Winery,** 35295 Hwy. 64, 218/224-3535, which crafts wines out of rhubarb, blueberries, cranberries, plums, and other fruits that can easily withstand harsh northern winters. You can sample and buy the wine and tour the farm Tuesday–Saturday 10 A.M.–5:30 P.M. and Sunday noon–5 P.M. from mid-May through December.

Walker lies very near the mid-point of the 49-mile **Heartland State Trail,** a wide paved path running from Park Rapids to Cass Lake. The **Back Street Bike & Ski Shop,** 201 5th St. N., 218/547-2500, a block from the trail, has bike rentals for $10 for two hours or $20 for the whole day, plus in-line skate and cross-country-ski rentals. While there is a lot to do on land in and around Walker, most people come here to get out on the lake and the easiest way to do that is with **Coborn's Leech Lake Cruises,** 218/547-4150, which runs three times a day during the summer: noon, 3 P.M., and 9 P.M., though only the 3 P.M. cruise runs on Sundays. They run a more limited spring and fall schedule. The cost is $14. The **City Dock Launch Service,** 218/547-1662, runs daily trips for anglers seeking walleye and muskie, and they'll fillet and freeze your catch if you get lucky. Trips run in summer only and cost $45 for a half-day or $65 for a full day and you can rent equipment if you need it. Leech Lake is one of the state's top sailing waters, and you can rent a boat or take a lesson at **Fleet Sails,** 201 5th St., 218/547-1188 or 888/276-5539. If you want horsepower instead of wind power, try **Walker Rental,** 8045 SautBine Rd. NW, 218/547-3656 or 888/831-1465, which has pontoons and ski boats, plus water skis, tubes, and canoes.

Over fifty resorts sit on the shore of Leech Lake. **Adventure North,** 218/547-1532 or 800/294-1532, with a prime location on Pine Point, is one of the fanciest. Five cabins—some quite large—and a suite in the historic lodge range $115–480 nightly and $795–2,410 weekly. Gourmet meals are also available, as are numerous fishing, hunting and snowmobiling packages. There's a nice stretch of beach, a heated outdoor pool, and a harbor on-site. Cheaper and more sprawling, **Huddle's Resort,** 218/836-2420 or 800/358-5516, has no less than 52 cottages, plus townhouse units. The resort has two swimming beaches, docks on Leech Lake and smaller Rat Lake across the road, and a slew of organized activities like bingo, movies, scavenger hunts, and dances. Rates range $99–275 daily and $575–1,675 weekly. West of town on Kabekona Lake, **Cry of the Loon Lodge,** 218/224-2651 or 800/524-1979, is an immaculate, erudite resort with three cabins and a lodge suite, each with its own fireplace and deck or patio, and lovely lake views. There's a library, game room, and waterfront area for guests' use, with free fishing boats, canoes, kayaks and paddleboats. Rates range $90–140 nightly and $425–725 weekly. The **Country Inn,** 218/547-1400 or 800/456-4000, south of town on Hwy. 200, has 46 rooms, four whirlpool suites, and four two-room suites. All have refrigerators and microwaves and there is a pool and whirlpool. Rates range $89–117.

The variety of dining options in Walker far exceeds all other forest towns. The casual **Pepper's Beach Bar & Grill,** 218/547-1662, has indoor and outdoor dining right at the city dock. The menu includes burgers, fish baskets, salads, bar munchies, steak, and seafood with most options in the $7–15 range. They're open daily for lunch and dinner during the summer, dropping down to weekends only in the spring and fall, and closing up completely in the winter. The **Outdoorsman Café,** 511 Minnesota Ave. W., 218/547-3310, has a similar menu plus breakfasts and most of their dinner platters are only about $6. It's open for breakfast daily, and lunch and early dinner Monday–Saturday. **Walker Bay Coffee Company,** 603 Minnesota Ave., 218/547-1183, has a big-city coffee shop ambience and the best vegetarian selection around. Besides the obvious they have breakfast pastries, soups, salads, ice cream, and grilled sandwiches for about $5. It's open for three meals on Monday–Saturday, plus summer Sundays. **Café Zona Rosa,** 101 5th St., 218/547-3558, serves lunch and dinner daily in summer and Thursday–Saturday in winter. In addition to Mexican standards, there are wraps, pastas, and seafood entrées; most are priced in the $7–11 range. The cantina specializes in margaritas. **Wok-Er,** 617 Michigan Ave., 218/547-3955, has basic takeout or dine-in Chinese food, including huge Mongolian-style entrées. Most menu items, as well as the buffet, are priced around $7. It's open for lunch and dinner daily with a midnight buffet on Saturdays. The **Ranch House Supper Club,** 9420 Hwy. 371 NW, 218/547-1540, in a secluded setting four miles north of town has daily all-you-can-eat specials served in covered wagon booths. The regular menu includes ribs, steaks, seafood,

sandwiches, and a salad bar and you shouldn't pass up the chance to try their house specialty: honey-buttered popovers. It's open for daily for dinner plus lunch on Sunday.

The **Leech Lake Area Chamber of Commerce,** 205 Minnesota Ave., 218/547-1313 or 800/833-1118, www.leech-lake.com, has information on Walker and the rest of the region. They're open weekdays 9 A.M.–5 P.M. and Saturday 10 A.M.–2 P.M., and if you are arriving last minute they can you find a vacant room, not always an easy thing to do around here. For those who don't have their own wheels, **Greyhound** buses stop at Hardees, 201 Minnesota Ave., 218/547-2664.

Recreation

Leech Lake itself takes up much of the Walker district; other recreational areas are scattered around the area south of the lake. **Shingobee Recreation Area** is five miles southwest of Walker off Highway 34 and was developed as a downhill ski area during the CCC era in the early 1930s. Today it's a favorite of cross-country skiers, hikers, and canoeists. The six-mile **Shingobee National Recreational Trail** winds through the area's cedar, spruce, and balsam woods. Rolling topography provides scenic vistas and a couple of places for sledding. The **North Country National Scenic Trail** (see North Country National Scenic Trail elsewhere in this chapter) also passes through Shingobee and the slow-moving **Shingobee River** provides a beautiful, easy canoe route. The eight-mile **Gadbolt Lake** road bike route is nearby to the southeast, and the 15-mile **Hanson Lake** route is a slightly harder bike loop around several small lakes. Both are unpaved.

Lake Erin is another family favorite with a half-mile interpretive trail around the lake and wetland areas that provide good wildlife spotting opportunities. Other hikes in Walker district are eight-mile **County Road 50** through aspen and red pine, and 12-mile **Goose Lake Trail** (through wetlands) that is groomed for skiing in winter.

The **Boy River** between Leech and Iguadona lakes is favored by canoeists for its excellent bird-watching. The eight-mile **Pike Bay Connection** is a more difficult canoe route with a number of portages.

Federal Dam, where Leech Lake empties into the Leech Lake River, is a well-known eagle-watching site.

Camping

Stony Point, a 44-site campground that juts into Leech Lake northeast of Walker, is very popular due to its scenic location, electric hookups, and modern facilities (showers and flush toilets). There's also a boat ramp and swimming beach, and the grassy sites are surrounded by old-growth forest with some trees over 200 years old. Reservations are accepted.

Mabel Lake with 22 sites near the Boy River and **South Pike Bay** with 24 sites and access to the Pike Bay Connection canoe route are more secluded and primitive. Both have beaches and boat ramps.

Information

The **Walker Ranger Station,** 201 Minnesota Ave. E., 218/547-1044, is located on the south edge of town and is open weekdays 7:30 A.M.–4:30 P.M.

Grand Rapids and Vicinity

GRAND RAPIDS

Founded on the riches of the forest, this lumber town (pop. 7,764) got its start in 1870; however, it took 20 years and the arrival of the railroad before it blossomed into a real village. The initial transport was via steamboats that ran upstream from Aitkin to the namesake rapids, a wild five-foot drop stretching nearly half a mile long that is now buried behind the Blandin Dam. Despite its unpredictability, steamer service didn't completely die out until the 1920s. The journey took about a day if conditions were good, but when water levels dropped passengers often had to help push the boat over shoals. The remains of wrecked boats still poke out of the river when water levels are low.

Though Grand Rapids sits on the edge of the Mesabi Iron Range it never became a mining center. Lumbering and paper-making became the city's economic foundation, and they are still the lynchpins today, though tourism is growing in importance. Highways 2 and 169, two busy cross-state routes that converge here, are the principal reasons people pass through Grand Rapids, though the proud hometown of Judy Garland has several worthwhile at-tractions and its small-town friendliness makes them all the more appealing.

Sights

The Minnesota Historical Society's **Forest History Center,** 218/327-4482, is a well-executed living history museum re-creating Camp #1 of the Northwoods Logging Company. After learning about the history of logging in Minnesota in the museum (don't miss the short film of Minnesota's last log drive), you'll be led back to the year 1900 in the logging camp. Camp employees will explain their duties, answer question, and share stories—such as the cook's efforts to sneak prunes into the lumberjacks' meals to keep them regular. Visits to the bunkhouse, horse barns, and blacksmith's shop offer a good taste of what a lumberjack's life was like. Down on the Mississippi River you'll visit the wanigan, a floating cook shack that fed the men who traveled downstream with the logs. Reforestation is discussed in the 1934 Forest Service patrolman's cabin and you'll learn about fire spotting at the top of the 100-foot-tall lookout tower. The camp reenactors are in action Monday–Saturday 10 A.M.–5 P.M. and Sunday noon–5 P.M. from June through mid-October.

> *Grand Rapids is more than a little proud to be the birthplace of Judy Garland. The Judy Garland Festival takes over town on the fourth weekend in June and usually attracts several of the original Munchkins.*

The museum and trails are open weekdays the rest of the year; call for times. Admission is $6 and worth every penny.

For a look at a modern component of the lumber industry take a tour of the **Blandin Paper Company,** 116 3rd St. NW, 218/327-6682. The massive complex dominates the downtown business district and turns out magazine papers for publications such as *Time* magazine and the Lands' End catalog. Free tours through the mill are offered Wednesday–Friday 10 A.M.–4 P.M. during the summer; no open-toed shoes or children under 12 are allowed.

The **Judy Garland Birthplace and Museum,** 2727 U.S. 169 S., 218/327-9276 or 800/664-5839, is a loving shrine to the star of *The Wizard of Oz,* who lived here until she was four. Born in 1922, she was Frances Ethel Gumm when she crashed her older sisters' performance at their parents' Grand Rapids theater, making it through *Jingle Bells* before being carried off the stage. The museum preserves the Gumms' little white house with its cast-iron stove and other reminders of life in the mid-1920s. Other than the piped-in *Oz* soundtrack, the house feels like a lived-in home. There's also a straightforward presentation of Garland's career and the sad demises of seemingly all the Gumm family members. The memorial gardens feature the Judy Garland Rose and—of course—a field of poppies. The museum is open daily 10 A.M.–5 P.M., though appointments are required from mid-October to mid-May. Next door the **Children's Discovery Museum,** 19 NE 4th St., 218/326-1900 or 866/236-5437, is full of hands-on exhibits including *The Wizard of Oz* materials. It is open Monday–Saturday 10 A.M.–5 P.M. and Sunday noon–5 P.M. Admission is $3 for either or $5.50 for both.

There is more Judy Garland memorabilia at the **Itasca Heritage Center,** 10 NW 5th St., 218/326-6431, housed in the Old Central School, an imposing 1895 Romanesque stone structure with a yellow brick road leading to the front door. Other exhibits found at the top of the beautiful wooden central staircase cover Ojibwe culture, the trapper era, logging, and papermaking. The museum and its interesting gift shop are open weekdays 9:30 A.M.–5 P.M. and Saturday 9:30 A.M.–4 P.M., plus summer Sundays 11 A.M.–4 P.M. Admission is $4.

Across the street the **MacRostie Art Center,** 405 1st Ave. NW, 218/326-2697, is a nonprofit art gallery with an eclectic mix of local artworks. There's a worthwhile gift shop, too, with pottery, jewelry, and handmade cards. It's open Monday–Saturday 10 A.M.–5 P.M.

Recreation

The **Mesabi Trail** is still a work in progress, but when finished this ribbon will run 132 miles to Ely, making it one of the longest paved recreational trails in the country. Most paving between Grand Rapids and Embarrass should be completed by the end of 2004, though the final stretch to Ely is still being planned. The trailhead is located at the fairgrounds, 1336 NE 3rd Ave., and a $3 two-day or $12 annual Wheel Pass is required; you can buy one at the trailhead or Itasca Bike, Ski & Fitness Centre, 316 NE 4th St., 218/326-1716. The **Taconite State Trail** is another long-distance trail stretching to Ely, though it is not surfaced and is used primarily by snowmobilers.

Mount Itasca, 218/245-3487, a few miles north of town near the village of Coleraine, is a year-round recreational park, though it is busiest in the winter for downhill skiing and snowboarding. There are also some challenging cross-country ski trails, a biathlon course, and a year-round ski jump, plus hiking and mountain biking in the warmer months. Downhill lift tickets are $12, though use of the trails in the summer is free. The CVB can direct you to many other skinny ski trails in the area.

Dan Bergerson of **Great Outdoors Equipment, Inc.,** 218/326-9775, runs guided dogsled trips ranging from a three-hour introduction (including dinner at a local restaurant) to overnight adventures. Prices range $55–300 and you can even drive the team. If you want to travel by horse **K&K Stables,** 218/245-3814, offers trail rides of varying lengths, from just an hour ($20) to overnight trips in the Chippewa National Forest ($175). Their 400-acre ranch is about 20 miles northeast of Grand Rapids on County Road 59.

Grand Rapids has four 18-hole golf courses just 15 minutes from downtown. Best of the bunch is **Wendigo,** 218/327-2211 or 888/554-6539. Rounding out Grand Rapids' "Grand Slam of Golf" are **Pokegama,** 218/326-3444 or 888/307-3444; **Sugarbrooke,** 218/327-1462 or 800/450-4555; and **Eagle Ridge,** 218/245-2217 or 888/307-3245.

Entertainment and Events

Grand Rapids is more than a little proud to be the birthplace of Judy Garland. The **Judy Garland Festival** takes over town on the fourth weekend in June and usually attracts several of the original Munchkins. The festival also includes a candlelight vigil celebrating Judy's birthday, *Wizard of Oz* screenings, and a collector's exchange with Judy and Oz memorabilia booths. The city's biggest summer bash is the **Tall Timber Days Festival,** the first weekend in August, featuring lumberjacking events, chainsaw carving, turtle and canoe races, and a craft show.

The **Mississippi Melodie Showboat,** 218/259-0814 or 866/336-3426, is a yearly summer recreation of the days when entertainment traveled up the Mississippi River by steamboat. During the last three weekends in July a small paddle-wheel steamboat arrives and docks at an outdoor stage on the riverbank, then disgorges costumed performers who sing and dance with a live band. Performances are held Thursday–Saturday at 9 P.M. with a 5 P.M. matinee on Saturday. Tickets are $9.

The **Myles Reif Performing Arts Center,** 720 Conifer Dr., 218/327-5780, is a large space in a beautiful modern building on the forested edge of Grand Rapids. Offerings include everything from jazz combos to comedians to children's theater.

Accommodations

With 122 rooms the **Sawmill Inn,** 2301 Pokegama Ave., 218/326-8501 or 800/235-6455, is not only the city's best hotel, but also the largest. Rooms, starting at $86, have rustic logging-themed decor, and the pool, whirlpool, and sauna are in a skylit courtyard. **The Country Inn,** 2601 U.S. 169 S., 218/327-4960 or 800/456-4000, also has a pool and hot tub, plus an exercise room.

Prices range $73–117. The lakeside **Forest Lake Motel,** 1215 NW 4th St., 218/326-6609 or 800/622-8590, and the **Itascan Motel,** 610 S. Pokegama Ave., 218/326-3489 or 800/842-7733, both have basic but clean rooms starting at $42, plus kitchenettes are available.

South of town on the north shore of Sugar Lake is the upscale **Ruttger's Sugar Lake Lodge,** 218/327-0454 or 800/450-4555, a well-known golf resort. For non-golfers, or those who need a diversion between tee times, there are also bikes, sailboats, canoes, and paddleboats available for guest use. Lodging options range from studio lodge rooms to three-bedroom town homes and are priced from $105 to $489; various golf and meal packages are also available, and there is a two-night minimum stay on summer weekends. Some units have kitchens, fireplaces and whirlpools.

On the north edge of town is the **Judge Thwing House,** 1604 County Road A, 218/326-5618, an antique-filled 1910 arts-and-crafts-style house that's been converted to a four-room B&B. Guests can relax on the porch or in the country-style living room. Rooms with private baths are $65–70, and those with shared bath are $60.

Food

Forest Lake Restaurant, 1201 NW 4th St., 218/326-3423, features a pair of dining rooms. The expensive steakhouse has entrées like roasted prime rib au jus starting at $15, while the more casual upstairs has plenty of sandwiches and pastas in the $7–10 range. It's open daily for breakfast, lunch, and dinner.

The **Hometown Café,** 18 NW 4th St., 218/326-8646, opens at 5 A.M. for greasy spoon breakfasts and burgers, plus pie. They pack the locals in Monday–Saturday for breakfast and lunch.

South of town on Pokegama Lake is the **Harbor,** 20184 U.S. 169, 218/326-1756, a steak-and-seafood joint with a bar and a view. Steak runs $21 and there are salads in the $9 range. Open daily for dinner.

Connected to the MacRostie Art Center is the **Brewed Awakenings,** 105 NW 4th St., 218/327-1088, coffeehouse. They have pastries, soups, espresso, and a big-city artsy atmosphere with live entertainment on weekends.

Shopping

The Old Central School, home of the Itasca Heritage Center, also houses several worthwhile craft shops, including **Stained Glass with Class,** 218/327-7964, and **ABC's of Quilting,** 218/326-9661. **Second to None,** 214 NW 1st Ave., 218/327-0789, is an antique shop with lots of dishes and furniture, plus some books and toys. **The Village Bookstore** at 201 NW 4th St., 218/326-9458, in the Central Square Mall has a good Minnesota and Native American selection, plus lots of outdoors guides.

Information and Services

The **Grand Rapids Area Convention and Visitors Center,** 1 3rd St. NW, 218/326-9607 or 800/335-9740, www.visitgrandrapids.com, is open weekdays 8:30 A.M.–5 P.M. They track lodging vacancies, which can be useful during the summer.

Transportation

Northwest Airlink, 218/326-6657, flies between the **Grand Rapids/Itasca County Airport,** 218/326-0893, and the Twin Cities up to three times a day. Prices for the round-trip flight start around $175—much less if it is a segment of a longer Northwest flight.

Car rental is available downtown from **Hertz,** 815 NW 4th St., 218/326-9421, and at the airport through **ACAR,** 218/326-9421.

Lorenz buses stop in Grand Rapids at Vanity Dry Cleaners, 401 NE 1st Ave., 218/326-3726, on their roundabout run between Minneapolis and Virginia.

HILL ANNEX MINE STATE PARK

One mile long, three quarters of a mile wide, and 500 feet deep, the Hill Annex open pit mine gave up 63 million tons of iron ore during its 65 years of operation. The massive cavity was turned in to a tourist attraction shortly after the mine shut down in 1978, and the 90-minute tours take you past many original mining facilities—some tours include a pontoon ride on the lake that now fills the bottom of the pit. Along the way you'll learn about the mine operation, which began with horsepower and eventually

became the range's first all electric mine. Tours of a different sort are also available, and they are an even bigger hit with children. Guides will lead you on fossil hunts in the exposed rock, and the marine relics such as snails, clams, and shark's teeth you'll dig up prove that this area was under water during the Cretaceous period (some 144 to 66 million years ago). The mine's old Clubhouse has been converted into the park office and a museum with exhibits about the mine and fossil displays (including a crocodile jaw found here). You can also get a quick look at the mine from the overlook outside the clubhouse. The mine tours costs $6 and depart daily on the hour between 10 A.M. and 4 P.M. during the summer—the fossil tours are only available twice a week, at 12:45 P.M. on Wednesday and Saturday. The free Clubhouse museum is open daily 8 A.M.–6 P.M. during the summer, and weekdays with reduced hours the rest of the year. For more information, call 218/247-7215.

SAVANNA PORTAGE STATE PARK

This remote 16,000-acre park is a lovely tract of near-wilderness centered on a historic portage between the Mississippi River watershed and Lake Superior-bound St. Louis River. The six-mile Savanna Portage connecting the East Savanna River with the West Savanna River was used for centuries by Dakota and Ojibwe and then by fur traders who arrived in the region in 1763. After poling or dragging their canoes through miles of narrow, sharp turns the Voyageurs had to trudge through at least 1.5 miles of knee-deep muck while shouldering 150-pound packs. Even with a canal dug to shorten the walk this was one of the most dreaded portages in the entire Northwest. The entire transit process used to take the fur-laden men as long as five days. The savanna of the name doesn't refer to an actual grassland, but rather the marsh along the eastern portion of the trail.

In total there are 22 miles of hiking trail within the park, and mountain bikes are allowed on nearly half of them. Sixteen miles are groomed for cross-country skiers of all abilities. You can retrace part of the Voyageurs' route along the remote **Savanna Portage Trail,** an often wet and somewhat challenging 11-mile round-trip—the summer mosquito hordes add a bit of historic authenticity to the hike. Another popular path is the hilly, two-mile **Continental Divide Trail,** suitable for hikers as well as bikers, which follows the divide and offers a great vista of the forest along the way. It connects to the flatter **Wolf Lake Trail** with an observation deck overlooking Wolf Lake and the surrounding tamarack lowlands at the end. As the easy **Lake Shumway Trail** encircles its namesake lake it traverses a beaver dam and provides a good opportunity to see other wildlife along its 1.5-mile path—a short **bog boardwalk,** lined by orchids and carnivorous pitcher plants, branches off the trail. The 1.6-mile **Esker Trail** attests to the park's glacial past and takes you past a spruce-tamarack bog. Explore more spruce forest and spot the warblers that inhabit them along the mile-long **Black Spruce Trail.** There's a historic homestead and excellent wildflower viewing along the one-mile **Anderson Road Trail.** The **Remote Lake Trail** on the west side of the park connects to the trail system in the Remote Lake Solitude Area of the adjacent Savanna State Forest.

Besides hiking, people come to Savanna Portage to swim in Loon Lake and to fish for panfish, trout, and bass on this and other waterways—only electric motors are allowed on the four main lakes. Canoeists may prefer the island-studded and aptly named Remote Lake. Canoes and fishing boats are available for rent. In the south end of the park, at the confluence of the Prairie and West Savanna Rivers, there's a wild rice field and more fishing.

Those spending the night have many options. The park has 64 campsites, some on the lakefront. Both loops are woodsy and pleasant, but the northern one is quieter since the 18 electric sites are all in the southern loop. The best places to pitch a tent are the seven backpacking sites scattered around the park; the one on Wolf Lake can also be reached by canoe, and there's a very remote one down the Savanna Portage Trail. Non-campers can enjoy the surroundings in either the rustic camper cabin (available April through October) or the Garni Cottage with heat, water, and electricity in the north end of the park on Savanna Lake. The Garni, which sleeps six, is open year-round. For general park information call 218/426-3271.

Waters of the Dancing Sky

Although it's just a puddle compared to Lake Superior, **Lake of the Woods** is a pretty remarkable body of water. The nation's largest lake after the five Great Lakes and the Great Salt Lake sprawls out over 1,486 square miles and has 65,000 miles of shoreline and an oceanlike feel, especially when strong winds toss up six-foot waves. A remnant of Glacial Lake Agassiz, Lake of the Woods is relatively shallow, averaging just 26 feet in depth. It encompasses an astonishing 14,582 islands and despite the area's brief summers and frigid winters (40 below zero nights are not uncommon), some of them harbor prickly pear cactus.

Needless to say, if you are here to fish you will find everything you need; area towns seemingly have as many bait shops and fishing guides as the lake has fish. The lake competes with Lake

Mille Lacs as the state's top walleye factory (some proud locals call this the Walleye Capital of the World), though muskie, northern pike, smallmouth bass, and crappie are also abundant, and lake sturgeon are recovering. The recreational fishing scene here churns on year-round with ice fishing becoming more popular each year. Heated fish house rental is big business, and you can even spend the night out on the lake in a sleeper fish house stocked with full kitchens and beds. Dozens of resorts ring the lake and, unlike elsewhere in Minnesota, most rent by the day rather than the week. Just about all of them are geared exclusively for hunters and anglers, but that doesn't mean those who don't fish (or just don't want to spend all their time doing it) won't enjoy themselves up here—each of the small town has a golf course and historical museum, there are some beautiful state parks in the area, and wildlife viewing is spectacular in the **Beltrami Island State Forest.**

Several designated scenic touring routes through Lake of the Woods County highlight natural and historical points of interest. The **Waters of the Dancing Sky Scenic Byway** (so named because the chance of seeing the Northern Lights is good up here) stretches 191 miles across the top of Minnesota, following Highway 11 from Karlstad to International Falls. The 75 miles of this route between Roseau and Greenbush, known as the **Borderland Trail,** once sported upwards of two million orchids every summer, principally Minnesota's state flower the showy Lady's-Slipper. The widening of the highway has reduced their numbers, but it is still an impressive show in some places. The peak blooming season depends on the weather, but is generally from mid-June to early July. Drives through the Beltrami Island State Forest include a Fall Color Drive, Bog Drive, Blueberry Pickers' Drive (the berries ripen in midsummer and are free for the picking), and Homestead Drive passing pioneer cemeteries and remnants of homesteads.

The small communities around the lake live for fishing and hockey—even much more so than most other Minnesota towns-and, though they aren't exactly tourist meccas, they can meet most of your needs.

BAUDETTE

The border town of Baudette (pop. 1,104) is 12 miles up the Rainy River from Lake of the Woods; nevertheless, with most of the resorts nearby, it is the primary hub for those visiting the lake, and it is a laid-back place where much of the activity centers around fishing. The **Lake of the Woods County Museum,** 119 8th Ave. SE, 218/634-1200, covers local history, both human and natural. There are exhibits on Native American cultures, early settlers, and the industries that have driven the area's economy over the years: logging, commercial fishing, agriculture, and pharmaceuticals. You can view the museum, including the re-created schoolroom and general store, Tuesday–Saturday 10 A.M.–4 P.M. dur-

ing the summer. Admission is free. **Lake of the Woods Nature Tours,** 218/634-1059, offers guided trips focusing on both nature and history, including bird-watching, wildflowers, and Native American culture. Tours are available year-round and cost $100 for a single person and $200 for a group. Any doubts about the locals' love of fishing will be put to rest when you see **Willie the Walleye.** The region's two-ton, 40-foot-long mascot "leaps" out of the Rainy River along Highway 11. Baudette celebrates its fishy mascot on **Willie Walleye Day,** the first Saturday in June, with a craft fair, street dance, beer garden, and walleye lunches.

Practicalities

West of town on Highway 11, the **AmericInn,** 218/634-3200 or 800/634-3444, has a pleasant fireplace in the lobby, plus a pool, hot tub, and heated fish-cleaning house. Rates start at $69. The nearby **Walleye Inn Motel,** 218/634-1550 or 888/634-5944, is a much cheaper option with rooms as low as $32. The **Wildwood Inn B&B,** 218/634-1356 or 888/212-7031, is in a choice spot on wooded Wheeler's Point at the mouth of the Rainy River. The inn has five bedrooms, each with a private bath and unique decoration. Some have fireplaces and all guests start the day with full gourmet breakfast; other meals are available by request. Common spaces include a porch and a great room with fireplace, TV, and a forest view. Rates start at $110. Typical of the many fishing resorts in the area is the friendly and modest **Schuster's,** 3140 Hwy. 172 NW, 218/634-2412 or 800/243-2412, also in a great location by the river's mouth. The 15 fully equipped one- to three-bedroom cabins range $80–250 daily. There are boats for rent, a launch service, and anglers appreciate the calm waters here.

The **Ranch House,** 203 W. Main St., 218/634-2420, "Home of the Monster Pancakes," has some huge breakfasts—two steaks and three eggs for $10, for example. There are also more modest breakfasts and burgers for around $6, and dinners like pan-fried walleye for $14. The atmosphere is homey and locals gather here to catch up on town gossip. Open daily for breakfast, lunch, and dinner. **Rosalie's,** 1229 W. Main

St., 218/634-9422, next to the AmericInn is a more upscale option with dinners like pesto fettuccine alfredo, stuffed walleye, and their signature prime rib for $10–15. It's open weekdays for lunch and daily for dinner.

Lake of the Woods Tourism, 930 W. Main St., 218/634-1174 or 800/382-3474, www.lakeofthewoodsmn.com, offers information and vacancy searches for the entire region. In summer, they're open weekdays 9 A.M.–6 P.M., Saturday 10 A.M.–6 P.M., and Sunday 10 A.M.–4 P.M.; hours are reduced to weekdays 9 A.M.–4:30 P.M. in the off-season.

ZIPPEL BAY STATE PARK

Zippel Bay State Park, 218/783-6252, protects nearly 3,000 acres of forest, though it is defined by water. Besides the protected cove that lent the park its name, there's a two-mile sand beach along Lake of the Woods just waiting to be strolled. Not surprisingly, swimming, fishing, boating, and beachcombing bring in most visitors. Though you would be lucky to see one, the adorable piping plover nests on the beach. Just 50

breeding individuals reside on the entire lake, and yet this is the largest remaining population of this endangered bird on all of the Great Lakes. The six miles of hiking trail through the forest—the system is expanded to eleven miles for cross-country skiing—afford a chance to spot wildlife and wildflowers. In Zippel Bay itself, a fishing pier, boat ramp, and marina service anglers in search of walleye, sauger, and northern pike. Four campgrounds with a total of 57 sites are nestled in the woods; none have electric hookups but showers are available.

WARROAD

Warroad, the only American port on Lake of the Woods, lies along what was once a well-traveled route, a figurative war road followed by the Dakota and Ojibwe who frequently attacked each other in an effort to control this fertile area. Today Warroad is a well-kept town with tree-lined streets and thousands of petunias lining the main route in the summertime. Most of Warroad's 1,722 residents eat, sleep, and breathe hockey (they've dubbed themselves Hockeytown

© ERIKA HOWSARE

Father Aulneau Memorial Church

USA) so it's only appropriate that one of the world's leading hockey stick manufactures was founded here by native sons and Olympic gold medalists (1960) Bill and Roger Christian. Bill's son David got a second-generation gold during 1980's Miracle on Ice run. You can tour the **Christian Brothers Hockey Stick Factory,** 1001 State Ave. NE, 218/386-1111, weekdays at 10:30 P.M. and 3 P.M. to get a glimpse of the manufacturing process. It's located on Highway 11 on the west side of town. Tours are free. **Marvin Windows,** 802 State Ave. N., 218/386-1430, the city's other major employer and the second largest window manufacturer in the United States, also offers free factory tours. They are available weekdays at 9:30 A.M. and 1:30 P.M., and you must call ahead.

Regional history is laid out at the **Warroad Heritage Center,** 202 Main St., 218/386-2500. On display are artifacts relating to Native Americans, the fur trade, European settlement, the fishing industry, and the current economic mainstays of hockey sticks and windows. The museum is open Monday–Saturday 1–5 P.M. and Sunday 1–4 P.M. Admission is free. The **Ka-Back-A-Nung Trail** is a 2.5-mile walk through town highlighting various historical sites; pick up a brochure with directions at the Heritage Center. The highlight of the walk is the 1904 **Father Aulneau Memorial Church,** 202 Roberts Ave. NE, said to be the largest all-weather log church in the world. Bird-watchers shouldn't be in too much of a rush to get out of town since the marshes and sandbars near the Warroad Marina are very productive for waterbirds, and two observation towers in Warroad City Park offer wide views.

Though only a small patch of their reservation lands lie here, the Red Lake Band Ojibwe operate the **Seven Clans Casino,** 218/386-3381 or 800/815-8293, right on the Warroad River near the marina. The casino hosts the **Warroad Traditional Pow-wow** the first weekend in June in the city park.

Practicalities

The **Super 8,** 909 N. State St., 218/386-3723 or 800/800-8000, is owned by the Lake of the Woods casino and offers weekday casino packages. Rates start at $50. With 70 rooms the **Patch Motel,** 801 State Ave. NW, 218/386-2723 or 800/288-2753, is the city's largest, and it has a hot tub and game room. The **Can-Am Motel,** 406 Main Ave. NE, 218/386-3807 or 800/280-2626, offers a hot tub and sauna; rooms start at about $60 at both. The **Hospital Bay B&B,** 620 Lake St. NE, 218/386-2627 or 800/568-6028, is a newly restored 1905 Victorian that once served as Warroad's first hospital. It's located right on Hospital Bay on the Warroad River and has four guestrooms with private baths and antique furnishings ranging from $60–120. They have dock space with access to Lake of the Woods and can arrange fishing trips. The **Warroad City Campground,** 218/386-1004, is huge—165 sites including 68 electric—and crowded, but it has a good location near the marina and city park. There are showers, a fishing pier, and an outdoor swimming pool. One night costs $14–20.

The **Lakeview Restaurant,** 1205 E. Lake St., 218/386-1225, has beautiful Lake of the Woods vistas and a fireplace in the dining room and classic American fare from $5. It serves breakfast, lunch, and dinner daily. Breakfast at the **Patch Restaurant,** 701 State Ave. NE, 218/386-2082, includes pigs in a blanket and Belgian waffles with fruit (both around $5) and is available all day. Lunch features hamburgers and buffalo burgers for around $6, while more upscale options such as steak, chicken, and pork chops averaging $10 and lobster tail topping out at $24 are added to the dinner menu. Open daily for breakfast, lunch, and dinner. **Time Out Pizza,** 603 Cedar Ave., 218/386-3764, has pasta, burgers, fried chicken, and a salad bar. A large Hawaiian pie costs $16, while an eight-piece box of chicken goes for $10. They're open daily for lunch and dinner.

Local and regional information is available at the **Warroad Area Chamber of Commerce,** 311 State Ave N., 218/386-3543 or 800/328-4455, www.warroad.org. They are open weekdays 8 A.M.–5 P.M.

NORTHWEST ANGLE

One of the strangest quirks of geography in the United States, the Northwest Angle is a large,

DRIVING TO THE ANGLE

Heading between Warroad or Roseau and Angle Inlet you will first pass through a manned Canadian Customs station. Have your vehicle registration and a photo ID with you. Americans and Canadians can cross with any state issued ID though they should bring a birth certificate just in case—everyone else needs a passport. The Warroad station never closes in either direction while the Roseau station is open daily 8 A.M.–midnight.

After a remote drive through Manitoba (remember that posted speed limits are in kilometers/hour) you'll reenter the United States and travel eight more miles to Jim's Corner, a four-way intersection. Stop at the videophone and press the American flag button to report to U.S. Customs. Stop here again when leaving to call Canadian Customs. They will give you a number to prove that you cleared customs, just in case you're stopped. If the videophone isn't working use the regular payphone to call either country's customs office. The number for U.S. Customs is 218/386-1676 and Canadian Customs can be reached at 807/274-3655, ext. 240.

Back at the Warroad and Roseau ports of entry you'll be questioned again by U.S. officials, and though border crossings get more scrutiny than they did pre-9/11 reentry to the United States is still generally a breeze.

Astronomer I. L. Tiarks located the northwesternmost point of the lake and dropped a line south from there to the 49th parallel, creating the "chimney" shape that rises from the top of Minnesota today. It is the northernmost point in the continental United States, making little Angle Inlet the Lower 48's northernmost town.

Today, the Angle is still defined by its separateness. The vast majority of the land is uninhabited and officially a part of the Red Lake Ojibwe Reservation, and telephone service didn't reach the Angle until the 1990s. Angle Inlet residents—there are around 100—are a tight-knit group. Children, from kindergarten through sixth grade, attend the only state-funded one-room schoolhouse in Minnesota, before being bused to Warroad to continue their education. Though tourism is the main industry, dirt roads and a harsh climate ensure that the visitors don't overwhelm the place. When visitors do come, they usually do so to fish, though bird-watching is becoming another major draw. The "town" of Angle Inlet isn't much more than a large fishing camp, and everything is quite basic and very laid-back. Life seems to happen out on the lake, fishing and exploring islands, more than it does on land. The Northwest Angle also encompasses a few inhabited islands, including Oak and Flag.

The drive from Warroad or Roseau to Angle Inlet is about 60 miles, with the first 40 miles paved. A floatplane from Baudette or Warroad makes the trip in about 20 minutes.

Sights and Recreation

The only actual tourist attraction on the Angle is **Fort St. Charles,** a reconstruction of the longest occupied French fort on Minnesota soil. St. Charles was established in 1732 by Pierre Gaultier de Varennes, sieur de La Vèrendrye and a band of French-Canadian voyageurs. The fort served as a center of exploration and fur trading, and La Vèrendrye spent his years venturing west desperately searching for the Northwest Passage. The fort was abandoned in 1763 when Great Britain gained control of the territory. When built it sat on the mainland, but now, due to a rise in the lake level, the re-created log cabins and stockade (on the exact locations of

wooded peninsula completely cut off from the rest of the nation by a corner of Manitoba, Canada. Due to crude maps and a surveyor's error, early government officials believed the Mississippi River headwaters lay west of Lake of the Woods. This caused a long period of confusion, starting with the 1783 treaty that gave the United States independence from Great Britain. The treaty mandated that the international boundary should follow the Rainy River to the Lake of the Woods, cut through the lake, then head due west from the northwest corner of the lake to the Mississippi River. When the British realized that the Mississippi is actually 140 miles to the south, the question of the boundary was reopened—the issue wasn't completely resolved until 1925.

the original structures) sit a short ways off it on Magnuson's Island. The free site is maintained by Angle Outpost Resort, 218/223-8101 or 800/441-5014, and it never closes. At Northwest Point, near Angle Inlet are the ruins of Nor'West Angle, a 19th-century Canadian village that had 800 inhabitants at its peak. It's in an advanced state of decay but still worth poking around, especially in the cemetery. Golfers should note that the Angle has the northernmost golf course in the Lower 48. The nine-hole **Northwest Angle Country Club,** 218/223-8001, course has the additional distinction of sand greens. You don't even have to haul your clubs all the way up here since rentals are available.

Out in the center of the lake, 15 miles from Angle Inlet, is the 762-acre **Garden Island State Recreation Area,** 218/783-6252. Named after the corn, squash, pumpkin, and potato gardens tended here by Native Americans as early as the 18th century, Garden Island is today primarily used by anglers wanting to stretch their legs or fry up the day's catch at the picnic area. There are sandy beaches for swimming or strolling, and the island is a productive bird-watching locale—several bald eagles nest here. In the winter timber wolves cross the frozen lake to hunt, and snowmobilers stop for a rest in the park shelter. Camping is prohibited. While out boating, many visitors also take in the views from the top of **Massacre Island** or Falcon Island's **Eagle Rock.** Both are easy to moderate hikes.

Island Passenger Service, 218/223-8261, offers water-taxi service to Oak and Flag Islands; Fort St. Charles; Kenora, Ontario; and other points around the lakes. You can also take a two-hour sightseeing cruise, which includes a stop at the resort of your choice, for $60 per person or $25 per person with four or more passengers.

Practicalities

There are 14 resorts up here—half on the mainland and half out on Oak and Flag islands—and most offer all-inclusive fishing packages. **Jake's Northwest Angle Resort,** 218/223-8181 or 800/729-0864, is a mainland mainstay. They've got six cabins with full kitchens and decks that sleep four–eight people and cost $35 per person

with a $95 minimum per cabin. Jake's also has a campground with 35 electric sites—five of which are available for daily and weekly rentals. Though they're geared mainly toward RVers, who pay $20, tent campers are welcome for $15. All guests have access to Jake's marina and can hire fishing guides. In winter, Jake's provides fish houses for ice fishing and transportation to the best fishing spots via bombardier. Out on Oak Island, **Bonnie Brae Resort,** 218/223-8411 or 800/772-8411, offers more upscale lodging in two- and three-bedroom condos, each with private decks and access to a shared hot tub. A lounge, snack bar, docks, and rental boats are available. Three-day packages, including boat rental, start at $255 per person, while daily rates for visitors with their own boats start at $50. The resort also arranges transportation.

Places to eat include **Pine Creek Pub,** 218/223-9731, across from Jake's, with a full bar and pool table. The house specialty is prime rib, served on Saturday nights, for $15. **Grumpy's,** 218/223-8511, at the Northwest Angle Resort has a similar menu with lots of fried appetizers, and most dinners cost $10–13. Both are open daily for all three meals.

Basic supplies are available at Jake's and at **Northwest Angle Services,** 218/223-4251; however, it's worth stocking up on most of what you'll need in Warroad or Roseau before making the trip. Also, don't count on buying gas up here, as the only fuel available is meant for boats and quite expensive. Local information is available from the **Northwest Angle and Islands Chamber of Commerce,** 866/692-6453, www.lake-ofthewoodsresorts.com.

ROSEAU

Roseau (pop. 2,750 people) is the largest and fastest growing city in this part of the state. It was established as a fur trade post on Roseau Lake by the Hudson's Bay Company way back in 1822. The lake, really more of a wetland area, was later drained for agriculture. Like Warroad, its principal on-ice rival, this town is hockey mad. The Rams have made more appearances at the state high school hockey tournament than any other team in Minnesota and have sent seven alumni to the NHL, including the Broten brothers Neal, Aaron, and Paul. In the summer of 2002 a flood devastated Roseau. Though many downtown shops and restaurants were being renovated at the time of this writing, some business owners were facing the prospect of moving or closing down. Listed below are attractions and businesses not wiped out by the flood; check Main Street for additional survivors.

Roseau bills itself as the "Snowmobile Capital of the World," and though many people and publications call it the birthplace of the snowmobile, that just isn't true. It was, however, a player in snowmobiling's infancy. **Polaris Industries** opened here in 1945 as a manufacturer of farm equipment, but a decade later they began producing snowmobiles and became the first company to mass-produce a snowmobile for individual use. Today Polaris is a billion-dollar corporation and one of the world's leading manufacturers of recreational vehicles. You can see snowmobiles and ATVs being assembled during a tour of their 500,000 sq. foot facility. The free tours depart Monday–Saturday at 4 P.M. Just north of the plant at 205 5th Ave. SW is the free Polaris museum and gift shop, the **Polaris Experience Center;** it's open Monday–Saturday noon–8 P.M. and Sunday noon–6 P.M. Call 218/463-4999 for further information.

Two miles west of town on Highway 11, the **Pioneer Farm and Village,** 218/463-1820, tells the story of the early settlers in reconstructed buildings, including a cabin, general store, church, and cigar factory. It's open weekdays noon–5 P.M. from May through September and admission is free. Less ambitious is the **Roseau County Historical Museum,** 108 2nd Ave. NE, 218/463-1918, with many Native American relics. It was damaged during the flood, so call to check on hours.

Practicalities

The most upscale lodging in town is the **AmericInn,** 1090 3rd St. NW, 218/463-1045 or 800/634-3444, with a pool, sauna and whirlpool. Regular rooms start at $69, while two-room suites with a fireplace and whirlpool

are $150. The very basic **Evergreen Motel,** 304 5th Ave NW, 218/434-7685, has nine simple rooms and 13 efficiency apartments with refrigerators and microwaves. Rates range $32–$44. **Roseau City Park,** 218/463-1792, has 10 electric RV sites and 10 tent sites for $12 and $7 per night respectively.

Branigan's, 205 5th Ave SW, 218/463-0993, is located in a renovated creamery and is decorated with historic photos. It has a huge menu featuring steaks, seafood, pastas, salads, and the like. Open daily for lunch and dinner. **Pam's Pantry,** 218/463-3979, in the same plaza has an espresso bar, ice cream, and gourmet groceries. **Earl's Drive-In,** 1001 3rd St NE, 218/463-1912, along Highway 11 has very inexpensive burgers, chili, ribs, and fried chicken. It's open daily for lunch and dinner during its April–September season. Other downtown restaurants, including a pizzeria and a Chinese restaurant, were closed due to flooding but may reopen.

The **Roseau Tourism Bureau,** 100 2nd Ave. NE, 218/463-1542 or 800/815-1824, http://city.roseau.mn.us/tourism, in city hall provides information for visitors. They are open weekdays 8 A.M.–4:30 P.M. Various brochures for the area are also available at the Cenex convenience store and the Polaris Experience.

HAYES LAKE STATE PARK

Swimming and fishing in the 200-acre manmade lake is the park's top draw, but thanks to its remote location this 2,950-acre park is also an excellent destination for wildlife lovers. Wildlife is abundant and rare wetland plants, like orchids and gentians, grow in the park's large bogs. One of the highlights of the 13 miles of level hiking trails hugging the lake and river is the short **bog boardwalk** near the campground. The half-mile **Pine Ridge Nature Trail** is an easy, interpretive trail at the end of the lake offering the chance to see a beaver lodge and maybe some of its residents. Along the **Homestead Interpretive Trail** you'll pass an early 1900s homestead and gravesite, as well as scenic views of the Roseau River. For longer hikes the **Moose Ridge Trail** on the lake's south shore is the least used and thus the

© TIM BEWER

preferred option for spotting wildlife. Seven miles of path are open to horseback riders, five for mountain bike riders, and six are groomed for cross-country skiing. The 35 sites (nine electric) in the modern campground and two nearby walk-in sites overlooking the lake are all very private. For those less inclined to rough it, there are two rustic camper cabins, one with electricity. For more information about the park, call 218/425-7504.

Red River Valley

Few would rank the stretch of Minnesota tucked up against North Dakota as the state's most beautiful or exciting region—in fact, most would rank it dead last in both categories. Nevertheless, it is anything but boring. This commonly held stereotype stems from the endless farm fields checkering the improbably flat terrain covering most of the area. However, sandwiched between the farms are the lakes and hills around Fergus Falls and Detroit Lakes, some excellent parks and wildlife refuges, and a touch of big city energy in Fargo-Moorhead.

Still, there is no denying that agriculture is the heart and soul of the region. This is, in fact, the east end of the Great Plains: where the West begins. The Red River Valley proper (more properly the Valley of the Red River of the North to distinguish it from the other Red River Valley in Texas and Oklahoma), a remnant from the last Ice Age, spreads an average of 50 miles wide along the Red River of the North. This mucky, meandering groove flows north to Canada and forms the upper half of Minnesota's western border along the way. A sea of tallgrass and wet prairie, broken only by the occasional riverbottom forest, once covered this land. Today, all but a few scattered fragments of the prairie have been plowed under and most of the wetlands drained to access some of the most fertile farmland in the world. Though the growing season is short the rich soil, coupled with abundant rain and snow, makes this excellent farming territory. Wheat, sugar beets, potatoes, corn, and sunflowers are some of the top crops. The latter are a beautiful sight in the fall when fields of the golden giants stretch to the horizon.

Phelps Mill

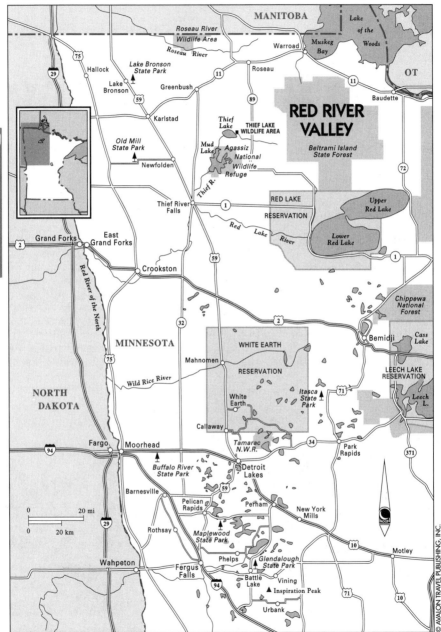

RED RIVER VALLEY HIGHLIGHTS

Agassiz National Wildlife Refuge
Anishinaabe Cultural Center and Gallery,
  Detroit Lakes
Buffalo River State Park
Hjemkomst Center, Moorhead

Maplewood State Park
Otter Trail Scenic Byway
Phelps Mill, Phelps
Rourke Art Museum & Gallery, Moorhead
Tamarac National Wildlife Refuge

Moorhead and Vicinity

Minnesota's western outpost, along with its bosom buddy Fargo, North Dakota, forms the largest metropolitan area (175,000 people) between Minneapolis and Spokane. Still, it remains off the beaten path for tourists. Fargo-Moorhead (some proud locals choose to call it Moorhead-Fargo) is rightly considered one place and, unlike the bickering siblings of Minneapolis and St. Paul, it is a cordial and cooperative partnership—most of the time. In fact, the "Other Twin Cities" were jointly awarded the National Civic League's All American City prize in 2000.

In most regards Moorhead plays second fiddle to Fargo, but even with just a third the population of its western neighbor, Moorhead (pop. 32,177) has a much more interesting and diverse menu of attractions for visitors. Fargo may have earned considerable national attention when the Coen Brothers named their movie after it, but don't come looking for movie locations—almost none of the story or filming took place here.

History

Transportation made Moorhead what it is today. By the 1820s caravans of huge wheeled oxcarts, made entirely of wood, screeched across the prairie (grease would have mixed with dirt and quickly worn away the axles; as it was they still had to be changed up to four or five times per trip), to service the pioneer outposts. These trains, up to 200 carts long by the 1840s, carried tons of pelts south through the Red River Valley along the Pembina Trail, then cut east across the Minnesota River Valley to the offices of the American Fur Company at Fort Snelling. The first steamboat, hauled overland in pieces from Little Falls, ran up the Red River in 1859, and soon the oxcart caravans came here to transfer their loads on the boats and barges for the five-day journey north toward Winnipeg. Settlers poured in, and a proper town developed in 1871 when the Northern Pacific Railroad chose this site to cross the Red River. The "Gateway to the West" opened a year later, and by the end of the decade Moorhead had grown into one of Minnesota's largest and most important cities.

As settlers moved into the western frontier, Fargo would grow to be the dominant city, but at the end of the 19th century Fargo seemed to exist largely to fuel Moorhead's growth. By 1885 Fargo became known as the Divorce Capital of the World, since North Dakota residents could get a "ten-minute divorce." Those seeking to end their nuptials came to Fargo and lived it up across the river in Moorhead at the city's symphony, opera, and bars for 90 days until they could get their business over with and go home. In 1889 North Dakota went dry and Moorhead's bars thrived, at least until Clay County followed suit.

SIGHTS

Hjemkomst Center

The focal point of the Hjemkomst (YEM-komst) Center, 202 1st Ave. N., 218/299-5511, is the 76-foot Viking ship built in a potato warehouse by local guidance counselor Robert Asp, who had long dreamt of sailing to Norway. Although Asp died shortly after finishing

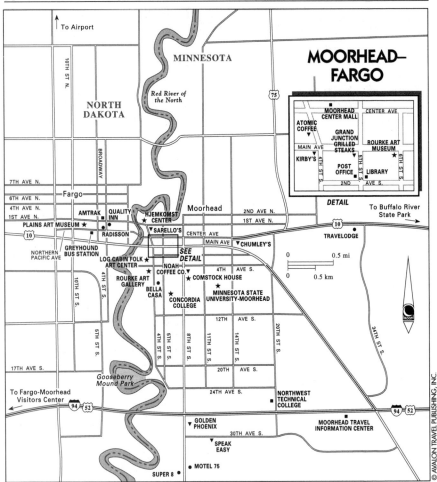

construction, the *Hjemkomst* completed the 6,000-mile voyage from Duluth, Minnesota, to Bergen, Norway, in 1982. The center, literally built around the ship, also houses a handful of displays about the ship's construction, the voyage, and Vikings. Be sure to watch the documentary film about the voyage. Just as interesting and historically accurate is the **Hopperstad Stave Church,** another labor of love by a local resident. The rocketlike chapel with steep, wood shingled roofs topped by carved dragons, is a full-sized replica of a 12th-cen-

tury church in Vik, Norway. Built entirely of wood, except where modern building codes demanded otherwise, it is an impressive sight. A guide takes visitors inside on the hour between April and October. The rest of the year it is open by reservation only. Downstairs are the often-overlooked local historical displays of the **Clay County Museum** (most interesting is the Scandinavian cultural exhibit in the hallway) and the **Red River Valley Exhibit.** The center is open Monday–Saturday 9 A.M.–5 P.M. and Sunday noon–5 P.M. Admission is $6.

© TIM BEWER

Hopperstad Stave Church, Hjemkomst Center

Comstock House

Moorhead wouldn't be what it is today if it weren't for the Comstock family. Solomon, the patriarch, earned a fortune in banking and railroads and used his wealth and influence to create the college that would grow to become Minnesota State University Moorhead (MSUM). He also served as a state senator and along with his wife, Sarah, helped establish Moorhead's first public library. Their daughter Ada continued the family's interest in promoting education; she was named the first dean of women at the University of Minnesota and later rose to president of Radcliffe College. Their 1882, 11-room Victorian mansion, 506 8th St. S., 218/291-4211, was the largest and fanciest house in Moorhead and showed Comstock's optimism for the young community in those early days. What sets apart a tour of this house is that the family left their furniture, clothing, books, dishes, and lovely tapestries behind so visitors can really see how they lived. The house is open for guided tours Satur-

day and Sunday 1–4:15 P.M. from late May through September. Admission is $4.

Art Museums

The small but grand 1913 Federal Post Office Building makes a fitting home for the **Rourke Art Museum,** 521 Main St., 218/236-8861. The permanent collection spans ancient to modern and includes a large selection of African and Native American works, and an outdoor sculpture courtyard is to be completed soon. Admission is $3. The smaller **Rourke Gallery** is housed in an 1875 mansion at 523 4th Street South, and though you probably wouldn't expect to find a Picasso in Moorhead, you will here. Admission to the gallery is $2. Both are open Friday–Sunday 1–5 P.M.

Though it is in Fargo, the **Plains Art Museum,** 704 1st Ave. N., 701/232-3821, got its start in Moorhead and spent over three decades there before moving to this wonderfully adapted 1904 warehouse. Only a fraction of the 2,500-piece permanent collection, which includes such artists as Warhol and Chihuly, is on display at any one time, but the three floors host a continuous stream of exhibitions. The gallery is open Tuesday and Thursday 10 A.M.–8 P.M., Wednesday, Friday, and Saturday 10 A.M.–6 P.M., and Sunday noon–6 P.M. Admission is $3, except on the second and fourth Tuesday of each month when it is free.

The **Log Cabin Folk Art Center,** 315 4th St. S., 218/299-5252, has a busy summer schedule of adult and children's workshops in such crafts as wood carving, candle making, and painting, plus weekly art exhibits and concerts. A more limited calendar of adult classes and special events continue in other seasons. The center is open Monday and Wednesday 1–5 P.M. and Tuesday and Thursday 6:30–8:30 P.M., plus other times for special events.

Both MSUM and Concordia have art galleries on campus. The gallery at MSUM's **Rolland Dille Center for the Arts,** 218/236-2151, is the larger of the two and has changing exhibitions throughout the year. Concordia's small **Cyrus M. Running Gallery,** 218/299-3310, is on the second floor of the Frances Frazier Comstock Theatre, right in the center of campus, and they only show work during the school year. Admission to both is free.

S. S. Ruby

For the full scoop on the Red River's history and ecology, take a ride on this 20-passenger pontoon boat. The 45-minute cruises depart from under the First Avenue Bridge in Moorhead and offer a surprisingly scenic experience. The service runs weekends from May–October, weather and river condition permitting. The service runs weekends mid-May–mid-September, weather and river conditions permitting. Boats depart on the hour Tuesday and Friday 5–8 P.M. and weekends 1–8 P.M., and the price is $6. Call 701/306-7829 for reservations.

RECREATION

The Red River is an almost a forgotten asset amongst locals, but it makes for a great day of lazy canoeing. Even right in the city you get a near-wilderness experience along its wooded banks, while extended journeys north pass a mix of farms, forest, and prairie and can also be scenic. River Keepers, 218/235-2895, can give you all the information you need to make a trip. In town, paved bike trails run up and down both sides of the Red River and are connected by three bridges.

A full range of outdoor equipment, from canoes to snowshoes, is available at **MSUM's Recreation and Outing Center,** 218/236-2265, based in the Comstock Memorial Union.

ENTERTAINMENT

Nightlife

Moorhead's live music leader is **Kirby's,** 315 Main Ave., 218/233-2617, with mostly rock acts on the calendar, but they get a little of everything. They promote themselves as "The Corner That Rocks," but a better slogan would be "The Best Dive in the Fargo-Moorhead Area," as one friendly bar jockey put it. **Ralph's Corner Bar,** 218/233-3351, across the street, and the **All-Star Bowl,** 309 17th St. N., 218/233-2020, also have live rock bands, while you might find a

country band on stage at **Chumley's,** 1608 Main Ave., 218/236-7813. If you want to dance, then join the college crowd at the **I-Beam,** 1021 Center Ave., 218/233-7700.

Campus Events

MSUM offers everything from musicians to mentalists and the public is usually invited. Call 218/236-2260 for a schedule of events. The MSUM Planetarium, 218/236-3982, presents five different shows throughout the year in Bridges Hall. The mini-universe is turned on Sunday at 2 P.M. and Monday at 7 P.M. during the school year, and Thursdays at 7 P.M. during the summer. Admission is $3. To find out what's happening at Concordia College, which has a more limited, but equally varied calendar, call 218/299-4366. Both the **MSUM Theatre,** 218/236-2271, and the **Concordia College Theatre,** 218/299-3314, produce four shows during the school year, and MSUM's Straw Hat Players put on an additional five performances during the summer.

Classical Music

The **Fargo-Moorhead Symphony Orchestra,** 218/233-8397, performs in various locations on both sides of the river. Their most popular performances are theme nights (such as Science Fiction-related songs), which try to take symphonic music to new audiences. They often perform in conjunction with the **Fargo-Moorhead Civic Opera,** 701/239-4558.

Cinema

Moorhead's only movie theater is the **Safari 7 Discount,** 218/236-5240, which shows second-run movies; however, there is an exciting alternative during the summer. **MSUM's Summer Cinema** presents silver screen classics each June and July at Weld Hall's Glasrud Auditorium. Pipe organ music is played during silent films and before every show. All seats are just $2.

Events

The **Scandinavian Hjemkomst Festival** is one of the nation's largest celebrations of Nordic heritage. You can discover the ethnic music, dance, crafts, food and more over five days around the second to last weekend in June. Moorhead's newest bash is **Hullaballoo,** which aims to have something for everybody over Labor Day weekend.

Barnesville, 20 miles southeast of Moorhead, hosts one of Minnesota's finest festivals, **Potato Days.** Events include potato sculpture, a potato sack fashion show, potato golf and billiards, mashed potato wrestling, and a hotly contested potato picking competition. The excessive silliness draws upwards of 13,000 people (six times the population) to this quiet town every year on the weekend before Labor Day.

ACCOMMODATIONS

Hotels

From late May to early August **MSUM** rents out some of their student housing in Snarr Hall, 218/236-2145. The price per night is $12 for a dorm bed in a shared room or $16 for a guaranteed private room. There are discounts for longer stays.

The city's cheapest hotels are out at the junction of I-94 and U.S. 75 where both the **Motel 75,** 218/233-7501 or 800/628-4171, and **Super 8,** 218/233-8880 or 800/800-8000, have rates under $50. Moorhead's best hotel is the **Travelodge,** 3027 S. Frontage Rd., 218/233-5333 or 800/578-7878, along U.S. 10. Immaculate rooms start at $80, and there is a pool and whirlpool.

The hotels nearest to downtown Moorhead are actually in downtown Fargo. The best rooms in either city are at the towering **Radisson,** 201 N. 5th St., 701/232-7363 or 800/333-3333, which is a bit of a bargain if you can get their $75 rate, though the normal price is $99. Amenities include a pool, sauna, whirlpool, and exercise room. The nearby **Quality Inn,** 301 3rd. Ave., 701/232-8850 or 888/232-8850, is also good and only charges $69, though it doesn't have the sauna and exercise facilities.

B&B

Just behind Concordia College, in a simple 1912 home filled with lovely woodwork, is **Bella Casa,** 721 5th St. S., 218/287-3741. The tasteful furnishings include a mix of antiques and European-themed art. Bella Casa attracts many artists

and other visitors from the nearby colleges and, not surprisingly, gets a large number of return guests. The four guestrooms share three baths and cost $70 a night.

Campgrounds

The best camping around is at **Buffalo River State Park,** but the RV-focused **KOA Kampground,** 218/282-2200, along I-94 is much closer.

FOOD

Arguably Fargo-Moorhead's best restaurant, **Sarello's,** 28 Center Mall Ave., 218/287-0238, is superb from start to finish. Ignore the strip mall location because you'll walk into a contemporary interior more in line with Manhattan or London than Moorhead. Chef Christian D'Agostino trained at the Culinary Institute of America, and owners Anthony and Sarah Nasello have put together a world-class wine list. The food and service are both excellent, but the best thing is how affordable it is for what you get. While some seafood and meat dishes such as roasted rack of lamb top out in the $20 range, several pastas dishes (try the *Penne all'Arrabiata*) go for $9. For lunch you can get grilled portabello mushroom, fillet of salmon, or a dozen other entrées for around $8. Open weekdays for lunch and Mon.–Sat. for dinner. Reservations strongly recommended.

A popular Moorhead original is **Speak Easy,** 1001 30th Ave S., 218/233-1326, where the decor is 1930s gangster chic. The dinner menu has pastas around $10 and steaks for twice that, while lunch is more casual with meatball sandwiches and lasagna from $3–7. Open Mon.–Sat. for lunch and daily for dinner.

For a home-cooked meal you can't do better than **TnT's Center Mall Café,** 510 Center Ave., 218/287-6090. Sandwiches and salads run $3–6, and there are many daily specials including pie and coffee for two bucks. Open daily for lunch and dinner and weekdays for breakfast.

The city's best Chinese is served at the **Golden Phoenix,** 816 30th Ave. S., 218/236-7089. Items such as scallops in black bean sauce and orange-flavored chicken offer variety from the standard Chinese options. The average entrée price is $8, as is the dinner buffet. Open Tues.–Sun. for lunch and dinner.

Better than the chains, **Grand Junction Grilled Steaks,** 109 5th St. S., 218/287-5651, serves hot subs for around $4, and their french fries are quite good, too. Open daily for lunch and dinner.

Moorhead has a pair of relaxing java outlets. The **Noah Coffee Co.,** 420 8th St. S., 218/233-2193, took over an old house near the MSUM campus and has several cozy nooks and crannies to melt in to. **Atomic Coffee,** 15 4th St. S., 218/299-6161, takes a minimalist approach with nothing but changing art displays gracing its brick walls. Both are open late nightly.

SHOPPING

The **Moorhead Antique Mall,** 218/287-1313, out along I-94 has 60-odd dealers under one roof. Much smaller, but still worth a browse, is **Old Market Antiques,** 312 7th Ave. S., 218/287-1767, near downtown. For general shopping there is the **Moorhead Center Mall** downtown and plenty of other shops along I-94 and Hwy. 10.

INFORMATION AND SERVICES

Tourist Information

The **Fargo-Moorhead Visitors Center,** 2001 44th St. SW, 701/282-3653 or 800/235-7654, www.fargomoorhead.org, is located in a mock grain elevator along I-94 in Fargo. During the summer they are open weekdays 7:30 A.M.–7 P.M., Saturday 9 A.M.–6 P.M., and Sunday 10 A.M.–5 P.M. The hours are weekdays 8 A.M.–5 P.M. and weekends 10 A.M.–4 P.M. the rest of the year. While there, check out the **Celebrity Walk of Fame** where over 100 notables have left handprints and scrawled their names. Stars who have dipped their mitts run the gamut from Richard Simmons to Gene Simmons and Dr. Ruth to John Updike. The **Moorhead Travel Information Center** on I-94 has information on the rest of Minnesota.

Media

The best source for local information is *The Forum,* Fargo-Moorhead's daily newspaper, or talk radio **KFGO** (790 AM). **KMSC** (1500 AM), MSUM's student radio station, plays everything from Michael Hedges to Marilyn Manson.

The best cultural calendar is in the free weekly *High Plains Reader.*

Post Office

Moorhead's main post office is at 119 Fifth St. S., 218/236-6001, and is open weekdays 8 A.M.–5:30 P.M. and 9–11 A.M. on Saturday.

TRANSPORTATION

Getting There and Away

Hector International Airport, 702/241-8168, on the north side of Fargo is served by **Northwest,** 800/225-2525, with eight flights a day to Minneapolis; and **United Air,** 800/241-6522, with three a day to both Denver and Chicago O'Hare. Expect to pay about $200 for the Twin Cities flight, much less if you add it as a leg of a connecting Northwest flight.

The **Amtrak,** 701/232-2197, Empire Builder stops in Fargo at the small depot at 420 4th St. N., at 2:10 A.M. on its way to Chicago and 3:49 A.M. on its way to Seattle/Portland.

The **Greyhound** Bus Station is at 402 Northern Pacific Ave., 701/293-1222 or 800/231-2222, in Fargo. Buses depart for Minneapolis/St. Paul ($32 one-way) four to six times a day, and they run west to Bismarck ($43 one-way) and beyond three to four times throughout the day. Also departing from the Greyhound Station, **Jefferson Lines,** 701/293-1222 or 800/451-5333, has a daily run in each direction between Sioux Falls, SD, and Winnipeg, Manitoba. The Sioux Falls run departs at 4:30 P.M. and the one-way fare is $43. The Winnipeg service leaves at 3 P.M. and costs $46.

Getting Around

Metropolitan Area Transit, 701/232-7500, has six Moorhead routes that offer comprehensive coverage of the city, though there are no buses on Sunday or after 7 P.M. The fare is $1 for adults and $.50 for students and seniors. Call **Doyle's Yellow Checker Cab,** 218/233-1354, for taxi service.

The only national car rental agency in Moorhead is **U-Save,** 1036 1st Ave. N., 218/271-8994, though many of the other large agencies have branches at Fargo's airport, including **Avis,** 701/241-1580; **Budget,** 701/241-1575; **Hertz,** 701/241-1533; and **National,** 701/241-1576.

BUFFALO RIVER STATE PARK

Straddling the Buffalo River is one of Minnesota's largest and healthiest prairies. Restoration of this vanishing ecosystem began back in 1979 with the cooperation of The Nature Conservancy, who owns the adjoining 2,855-acre Bluestem Prairie Scientific and Natural Area. The **Wide Sky Trail** north of the river offers the easiest views of the annual floral explosion, plus good opportunities for spotting the copious birds, while other stretches of the 12-mile trail system (five miles groomed for cross-country skiing) wind through the native hardwood forest along the riverbottom. The best way to learn about the park's four distinct habitats (river, forest, oak savanna, and prairie) is to follow the half-mile **Savanna Cutoff Trail,** which passes through each of them. Keep your eyes peeled along the steep riverbanks for bison skulls and bones, which are occasionally uncovered. If you want to see prairie chickens doing their courtship dance in April, reserve a **viewing blind** as early as possible from The Nature Conservancy (218/498-2679). A picnic area, swimming pond, and 44 (35 electric) campsites sit in the woods along the river and it is these, not the prairie, that draw most visitors so, even on a busy summer weekend, the trails are likely to offer a peaceful escape once you get beyond earshot of the beach. Call 218/498-2124 with any park questions.

Tucked up against the northeast edge of the park is the **Minnesota State University–Moorhead's Regional Science Center,** 218/236-2904, which offers nature programs for school groups and the general public, plus hiking/cross-country ski trails through their 300 acres of prairie and forest. Also located here is the Paul Feder Observatory with a 16-inch reflecting telescope. The nature center is open May–October on Sunday 1–5 P.M., and there are guided trail walks on Sundays at 2 P.M. The trails are open throughout the year and admission is free.

Lakeland

Although its waters drain to the Red River, the area southeast of Moorhead has little else in common with the rest of the region. Glaciers carved out 1,277 lakes in what are now Otter Tail and Becker counties, making this the surprising site of one of Minnesota's greatest concentration of lakes. The lakes themselves have made this a popular travel destination with Minnesotans and North Dakotans. Geologically the 20-mile-wide swath of hills and valleys is known as the Leaf Hills, and it extends all the way south to Willmar. The Otter Tail River, which crosses the county, is the principal source of the Red River of the North.

FERGUS FALLS

Unlike its neighbors Detroit Lakes and Alexandria, the Otter Tail County Seat doesn't rely on tourism for its economic health. This makes it a less exciting, but much more pleasant, place to visit. Fergus Falls straddles the Otter Tail River, and it grew up and thrived as a milling town; when the railroad arrived its future was guaranteed. Today Fergus Falls is a rapidly growing town of nearly 13,500 people with a lovely main street—Lincoln Avenue in this case—where cobblestone sidewalks and trees front the 19th-century brick facades. Joseph Whitford, who in 1857 staked out the town site, named it after James Fergus, the man who financed his expedition. Neither witnessed the town's growth. Fergus never set foot in the area, and Whitford died soon after he came, years before the first settlers arrived.

Sights and Recreation

Locals are rightly proud of their excellent **Otter Tail County Historical Museum,** 1110 W. Lincoln Ave., 218/736-6038. The lifelike displays on a wide variety of topics make this one of the state's best local history museums. Most impressive are the 1916 Main Street and the agricultural displays. Old varieties of food and flowers are grown out front in the heirloom garden, and the seeds are then sold in the museum's gift shop. The museum is open Monday–Friday 9 A.M.–5 P.M. and Saturday 1–4 P.M., plus Sunday 1–4 P.M. during the summer. Admission is $2.

The **Prairie Wetlands Learning Center,** 218/736-0938, located just south of town on Hwy. 210, is a 3,225-acre environmental education center run in partnership between the U.S. Fish & Wildlife Service and the city of Fergus Falls. Inside is a small hands-on exhibit area that will eventually be expanded, but the main reason to visit is to admire the prairie and wetlands along the 4.5 miles of trails. The exhibits are open Monday–Friday 8 A.M.–4 P.M., plus Saturday 10 A.M.–6 P.M. June–August. The grounds are open daily from dawn to dusk.

The **Fergus Falls River Trail** follows the Otter Trail River downtown between Veteran's Park and Union Ave. It is a pleasant half-mile walk with a steady stream of historical markers reliving the city's early days. Fergus Falls is the western terminus of the **Central Lakes Trail,** which stretches 63 miles to Avon along an abandoned rail line. As of 2003 the first 25 miles have been paved from Fergus to the Douglas County line, and the entire trail should be surfaced by 2005 so expect a steady stream of bikers to descend on the town in the near future.

Don't leave town without taking a look at the **world's largest otter** in Adams Park just southeast of downtown along County Road 82. Rothsay, 16 miles up the freeway, has its own entry in the Minnesota big-statue contest: a 13-foot-tall, 18-foot-long **prairie chicken** in full mating display—it, too, is the world's largest.

Entertainment and Events

A Center for the Arts, 124 W. Lincoln Ave., 218/736-5453, a restored 1920s Vaudeville theater, is the pride and joy of Fergus Falls. It hosts movies, music, plays, and more throughout the year. If you get a chance, attend one of the silent movies to hear the accompaniment of the Mighty Wurlitzer pipe organ. The lobby also serves as an art gallery for local artists.

The area's biggest event is the **Lake Region Pioneer Threshing Show,** which draws fans of bygone farming machinery and practices. The massive show takes place in the nearby town of Dalton the weekend after Labor Day. In town, celebrate the seasons with **SummerFest** in early June and the **Frostbite Festival** the first weekend in February.

Accommodations

Most of Fergus Falls' hotels are clumped together around I-94 and Hwy. 210. The barnlike **Motel 7,** 218/736-2554, surrounds decent, larger-than-average rooms from $47. Best in town is the **Best Western The Falls Inn,** 218/739-2211 or 800/293-2216, which is connected to the city's convention center. Rooms run $85–130, and it has a pool, whirlpool, and fitness center.

There are no B&Bs in town, but 11 miles north on Jewett Lake is the friendly **Forest Lodge Farms,** 218/736-0306 or 800/950-0306. The 1880s farmhouse, greatly modified over the years, has five rooms with and without private baths from $60–120 a night. There is good bird-watching down by the lake, and the owner, Kate Sasseville, knows all about the surrounding area.

The area's state parks have excellent camping so there should be no need to stay at the city's **De-Lagoon Park,** which hasn't a lick of shade for its 22 sites. On the plus side, a night costs just $5.

Food

Ask anyone in town which of Fergus Falls' restaurants is the best and **Mabel Murphy's,** 3401 Hwy. 210 W., 218/739-4406, is the only answer you will get. The menu has steaks, salads, seafood, and pastas, many under $10, and the Old World atmosphere is warm and inviting. The dining room is open weekdays for lunch and daily for dinner.

While Mabel's is the city's best, the **Viking Café,** 23 W. Lincoln Ave., 218/736-6660, is its runaway favorite. The Viking opened in 1946 and about the only thing that has changed since then are the prices. Still, none of the home-cooked standards on the menu cost more than $6. They are open daily for breakfast and lunch plus early dinners except Sunday.

Hunan Spring, 220 W. Cavour St., 218/739-

5889, in the City Center Mall comes recommended for Chinese. Their lunch buffet is $5.50 for lunch and $7 for dinner. **Tomacelli's Pizza & Pasta,** 218/739-6373, in the same mall has an all-you-can-eat lunch buffet with pizza, soup, and salad for $6. Both are open daily for lunch and dinner.

Barringer's Coffee House, 127 E. Lincoln Ave, 218/736-2090, also has soup, sandwiches, and snacks. Open Mon.–Sat. for breakfast and lunch.

Shopping

Fergus Falls' largest antique store is **Classic Antiques and Collectibles,** 119 W. Lincoln Ave., 218/739-5464, while **Periwinkle Place,** 222 E. Washington Ave., 218/739-2800, also has a good selection. The more modest **Collector's Corner,** 218/736-2210, is down in the basement at 221 W. Lincoln Ave. In the same building, the **Nordic Galleri,** 218/739-9665, has a bounty of Scandinavian fare.

Information and Transportation

The **Fergus Falls Convention & Visitors Bureau,** 218/739-0125 or 800/726-8959, www.visitfergusfalls.com, is located downtown at 202 South Court Street and distributes information for all of Otter Tail County. There is also a good selection of brochures available at the Otter Tail County Historical Museum.

Greyhound buses stop twice a day on their run between Minneapolis ($36 one-way) and Fargo ($14) at the Spur gas station, 1425 W. Lincoln Ave., 218/736-2786.

THE REST OF OTTER TAIL COUNTY

Although the land around Fergus Falls is pretty dry, Otter Tail County has an amazing 784 lakes. Fishing is excellent here, and there are more than enough resorts and bait shops to take care of you if a day or a week communing with a rod and reel is what you desire. Fish are certainly not the only attraction, though. There are plenty of small towns, historic sites, and natural areas worth a visit and some excellent places to spend the night whether you want to pitch a tent or be pampered. Even

more appealing than the sites themselves is driving between them. This is rural Americana at its best. All of the following, except for artsy New York Mills, lie along the **Otter Trail Scenic Byway,** a circular, 150-mile marked route along country roads. Get an early start and you could cover it all in a day, but that would be seriously rushing things. Better to take your time and enjoy the ride.

Phelps Mill

There is no point in saving the best for last. The first stop along the byway, if traveling clockwise from Fergus Falls, is the impressive Phelps Mill. Not only is it a beautiful site when viewed from outside, but the original equipment is still in place, and you can walk through all four levels to learn how the process, advanced for its day, worked. The Maine Roller Mills, as it was known, began producing flour in 1889. It continued grinding wheat and rye until 1939 when it was abandoned and the town that grew up alongside it slowly vanished. The **Phelps Mill Festival,**

© TIM BEWER

abandoned one-room school house in Otter Tail County

an arts and crafts fair with music and a children's activity area, takes over the grounds the second weekend in July. The mill doesn't keep regular hours, but it is open early (whenever the caretaker comes around) to dusk from roughly May to October, but the weather, not the calendar, makes the determination. Admission is free.

Maplewood State Park

Soaring, tree-covered hills and deep, lake-filled valleys define Minnesota's sixth largest state park. The aspen, maple, and oak that dominate the forest put on a fantastic display of fall color, while the park's prairie has its own brilliant show during the summer. Hikers have 25 miles of trail, ranging from gentle to wild, to choose from across the 9,250-acres, and come winter 13 miles of these are groomed for cross-country skiing. The easiest routes are the **Grass Lake Interpretive Trail** and the **Woodland Nature Trail,** both of which have signs discussing park ecology. For longer romps, head to the south end of the park. Boats and canoes can be rented from the park office to explore the various lakes. Also consider an early morning or evening visit to the wildlife observation blind near the Lake Lida Campground. Seventy-one campsites (32 electric) and a fully-accessible camper cabin are spread over four campgrounds; the shaded and secluded Knoll and Hollow camps are the best. For even more privacy get one of the three backpacking sites in the south end of the park. Horseback riders touring the 20 miles of trails open to them have their own camp. Call 218/863-8383 for more information.

> *Maplewood State Park's aspen, maple, and oak put on a fantastic display of fall color, while the park's prairie has its own brilliant show during the summer.*

Pelican Rapids

Surprisingly, little Pelican Rapids (pop. 2,400) is one of the most ethnically diverse cities in the state, with residents originating from all corners of the globe. Mexicans and Vietnamese came some time ago for jobs, and more recently Bosnians, Croatians, Kurds, and Sudanese have left their war-torn lands and found a safe haven in this town. This cultural diversity is celebrated, pri-marily in its edible form, in mid-June during the **International Friendship Festival.** The main reason to stop the rest of the year is for a look at the **world's largest pelican.** The 18-foot-tall steel bird sits below Mill Pond Dam in E. L. Peterson Park. Many people also enjoy a stroll across the 250-foot suspension bridge here. If you arrive on a Tuesday morning between mid-June and mid-August, you can watch children race minnows next to Pelican Drug. The starting time is 10:30.

Set amidst 800 acres of rolling prairie and forest a mile north of town is the **Prairie View Estate B&B,** 43581 County Road 9, 218/863-4321 or 800/298-8058. The cozy 1927 home was built by the proprietor's grandparents on land home-steaded two generations before that. The three rooms, each with a private bath and many original fur-nishings, start at $65. About 10 miles east of town on Spirit Lake is another historic B&B, **The Log House & Homestead,** 218/342-2318 or 800/342-2318. Five rooms are split between the 1889 log house and the 1902 home-stead, which sit on 115 wild acres. Rates range $110–195. Just north of town the **Pelican Motel,** 900 N. Broadway, 218/863-3281 or 800/423-1172, has 16 basic rooms from $40. **Sherin Memorial Park,** a few blocks east of downtown on Hwy. 108, has a small and shady campground. Tent sites are $5 and RV hookups are $10; however, the camping is much better at Maplewood State Park. For a meal you could do much worse than the cheap home-cook-ing at **The Rapids,** 40 N. Broadway, 218/863-1726. Open daily for breakfast and lunch.

Perham

Perham's claim to fame are the faster-than-you'd-expect **Perham International Turtle Races.** The 10-foot sprints take place downtown in City Hall Park every Wednesday at 10:30 A.M. throughout the summer. Between heats kids can take a ride on the **Perham Express,** a mock train that runs up and down the city's streets. Next to the reptilian speedway is the **Doll Museum,** 135 E. Main St., 218/346-7710 or 800/634-6112, the collection of

Pelican Rapids

local octogenarian Verona Larson. Around 500 dolls, new and old, including Native American dolls, Japanese dolls, and Cabbage Patch Kids, are now on public display. The building also houses the chamber of commerce. It is open Monday–Saturday 9 A.M.–5 P.M., plus Sunday 1–4 P.M. in the summer. Admission is $2. Perham's other small museum is **The History Museum of East Otter Tail County,** 230 1st Ave. N., 218/346-7676. The collection is modest, but it is well presented. Open Mon–Sat. 10 A.M.–5 P.M. and Sun. 1–4 P.M. Admission is free.

If you want to spend the night there is a **Super 8,** 218/346-7888 or 800/800-8000, with rooms from $50. The city's best restaurant is the **Station House,** 103 E. Main St., 218/346-7181, where the menu ranges from a taco salad to a vegetarian garden burger to a T-bone steak. Few items are over $10, and they are open daily for breakfast, lunch, and dinner. **Greyhound** buses stop twice a day on their run between Minneapolis and Fargo at the Perham Oasis gas station, 218/346-7810, along U.S. 10.

New York Mills

Though the Otter Trail Scenic Byway turns south

at Perham, a detour on U.S. 10 to this unique community is definitely in order. The **New York Mills Regional Cultural Center,** 24 N. Main Ave., 218/385-3339 or 888/877-1969, is a true anomaly—a town this small (pop. 1,158) shouldn't have an arts center this good. Housed in a lovingly restored 1885 red brick mercantile, the center hosts an impressive calendar of music, theater, storytelling, film, comedy, and much more. Their low-priced workshops are even more diverse and have included painting, bookbinding, mime, and playing the jaw harp. Work from regional artists is displayed in the gallery and sold in the gift shop. It is open Tuesday–Saturday 10 A.M.–5 P.M. plus Sunday 11 A.M.–3 P.M. in the summer. Admission is free. The center also oversees the **New York Mills Sculpture Park** along U.S. 10, which has some really interesting work in a truly horrible setting. Arguably the center's greatest contribution is the **Great American Think-Off;** an annual philosophy competition held each June. A 750-or-less-word essay on a topic such "is honesty always the best policy?" and "which is more dangerous—science or religion?" narrows the hundreds of hopefuls down to four finalists who battle it out head to head in a live debate. Entries are received from around the globe and the event is usually broadcast live on C-SPAN. Five miles outside of town is the **Finn Creek Museum,** 218/385-2233, an 18-acre Finnish farm site with the original 1900 house and sauna as well as many other relocated buildings from that era. To get there head east on Centennial 84 Dr. and follow the signs. It is open daily 1–5 P.M. during the summer and admission is free. The best time to visit is the last weekend during the **Finn Creek Summer Folk Festival** with Finnish music and dance and historical exhibitions such as blacksmithing.

Decisions, decisions. At the **Whistle Stop Inn B&B,** 107 Nowell E., 218/385-2223 or 800/328-6315, guests must choose between three fully decked out, turn-of-the-century railroad cars including an 1893 caboose, and two plush rooms in the lovely 1903 Victorian home. Rooms in the house are $70 or $80, the caboose is $95, and the huge rail cars are $140. The **Mills Motel,** 102 Miller St., 218/385-3600, is a modern, well-run hotel with rooms running $32–64. The **Eagles Café,** 31 N. Main Ave., 218/385-2469, has cheap and tasty home-cooking. They are open

Monday–Saturday for breakfast, lunch, and dinner and just breakfast and lunch on Sunday. **Greyhound** buses stop at the County Road 67 exit of U.S. 10 twice a day on the run between Minneapolis and Fargo.

Glendalough State Park

Though Glendalough is one of Minnesota's newest state parks, it is also one of its oldest protected natural areas. Since 1903 this spot served as a private resort and game farm and entertained such dignitaries as Presidents Eisenhower and Nixon. The various owners had limited impact on their land, and much of the park's 1,931 acres of marsh, hardwood forest, remnant prairie, and more than nine miles of undeveloped shoreline on six lakes, is remarkably pristine. Clearly the most unusual aspect of the park is Annie Battle Lake, a designated **Heritage Fishery.** Because fishing was limited on the 335-acre lake over the last century, largemouth bass, panfish, and walleye are large and plentiful. To preserve the status quo for future generations of anglers, strict regulations, including no motors (even electric), no fish-finding devices, and catch-and-release only

© TIM BEWER

Whistle Stop Inn B&B

on some species, are in effect. Fish aren't the only species found in abundance. Waterfowl, including loons, are common on Glendalough's lakes, bald eagles nest on the shores, and you are almost certain to spot deer in the prairie along the entrance road in the early evening. Lake Emma is the park's prime wildlife viewing spot. The **Beaver Pond Interpretive Trail** is another good spot, and Sunset Lake is excellent for bird-watching. In total there are eight miles of trails with six of these groomed for cross-country skiing in the winter. The park office rents canoes, rowboats, and snowshoes. When you are not communing with nature there is a picnic area and sandy beach, and Glendalough's campground is one of the state's best. All 22 cart-in sites are wooded and well spaced. There are also four camper cabins and, during the summer, three sites on Annie Battle Lake are reached by boat, bike, or foot. Call 218/864-0110 with any park questions.

Battle Lake

The nearest town to Glendalough is Battle Lake, home of **Chief Wenonga,** a towering fiberglass sculpture overlooking the lake on the north end of town. In 1795 the real chief, leading a band of Ojibwe warriors, suffered a massive defeat by the Dakota on this spot in a battle for control of these productive hunting and fishing grounds. Tucked in amongst the many gift shops along Lake Avenue is the nonprofit **Art of the Lakes Gallery,** 108 S. Lake Ave., 218/864-8606, with works for sale in all media by some 75 member artists. They also sponsor various workshops throughout the year and the Battle Lake Art and Craft Fair the second weekend in August. It is open daily during the summer, but just weekends the rest of the year. If shopping isn't your thing—though that is really what Battle Lake is all about—two area stables, **Silver Sage Guest Ranch,** 218/864-8007; and **Shady Oaks Riding Stable,** 218/367-2699, offer horseback riding. On summer Thursdays at 11 A.M. they shut down a block of Main Street (which they can do because Main Street is not the main street) and let kids race turtles, though it is a smaller affair than in nearby Perham.

One of the region's best places to spend the night is the **Xanadu Island Bed & Breakfast,** 218/864-8096 or 800/396-9043, five miles out of town. In the 1920s and 1930s this five-acre island on the north end of Elbow Lake was a luxurious summer retreat for the rich and famous. A one-lane road, enshrouded by a lovely tunnel of trees, now connects the island to the mainland. The rustic main lodge, with an enclosed porch and open deck, has five bed-and-breakfast rooms running $95–155 per night; rooms at the upper end of the price scale have fireplaces and/or hot tubs. Behind the main house the old servants quarters and boathouse have been converted into spacious and fully equipped cottages from $625 per week, though they lack the charm of the rooms in the house. The workaday **Battle Lake Motel,** 218/864-5208, is just a stone's throw north of Chief Wenonga on Hwy. 78. Its rooms run $47 and are usually filled with anglers. Far and away the best restaurant in town is **Stub's Dining Hall,** 631 Lake Ave. N., 281/864-9929, which specializes in steak and seafood and has a whole section of the menu dedicated to combinations of the two such as "steak and walleye" ($16) and "ribs and lobster chunks" ($18). The piano bar is an unexpected bonus. Open Mon.–Sat. for lunch and dinner. Many locals swear by the hamburgers at **Shoreline Lanes,** 505 Lake Ave. N., 218/864-5265. In fact, one area nurse tells me that she has had patients on their deathbeds whose last wish was to have just one more.

Vining

If it weren't for local construction worker Ken Nyberg, the only reason to stop in Vining would be to fill up your gas tank. Nyberg's hobby is making larger-than-life steel sculptures, and he has made Highway 210 his gallery. Spread out along the length of the tiny village you'll find, among others, a square knot, foot, and pliers about to squash a giant roach.

Inspiration Peak

The views from the second-highest point in Minnesota make this hill worthy of its name, though when autumn color arrives you might think its original name, Leaf Hill, is most appropriate. A steep quarter-mile walk on a paved path from the picnic area takes you to an overlook at the summit of the 1,750-foot hill for panoramic views. Nobel Prize-winning author Sinclair Lewis, who promoted protecting the area as a park, describes the scene best: "a glorious 20 mile circle of some 50 lakes scattered among fields and pastures, like sequins fallen on an old Paisley shawl." The peak is 4.5 miles west of Urbank on County Road 38.

DETROIT LAKES

The village of Detroit was founded in 1871 as a service center along the newly built Northern Pacific rail line. "Lakes" was added in 1926 because of continued postal mix-ups between it and some other city way off in Michigan. The town of over 7,000 sits at the north end of the glacially formed lakes and hills known as the Leaf Hills, and it is these bodies of water that serve as its livelihood today. The economy is heavily dependent on the thousands of families who flock here each summer to pass a week at one of the 50-plus resorts in the vicinity and drop dollars at the small amusement parks, waterslides, and miniature golf courses in and around town. Some people come just to land a lunker with legendary marathoner Dick Beardsley, who lives nearby and runs a fish-

ing guide service (218/846-9230, www.dick-beardsley.com) in town.

Sights and Recreation

The **Anishinaabe Cultural Center and Gallery,** 921 8th St. SE, 218/847-3651 or 800/890-3933, is hidden away in an industrial park on the east side of town. Opened in 1995 the center has been active in politics and social work, as well working to preserve and promote Ojibwe culture. Throughout the year musicians, dancers, and storytellers come to perform or teach classes in the traditional round room. Regular drumming and dancing sessions are held on Thursday afternoons during the summer, and special exhibits are often on display in the gallery. The gallery also sells the work of dozens of artists, from traditional drums to contemporary paintings. If you want to learn about Ojibwe history or contemporary issues you can't do much better than this; the enthusiastic staff loves to sit down and share their history, and guests are welcome to stay for dinner to meet other members of the community. The center is open weekdays 9 A.M.–7:30 P.M., Saturday 9 A.M.–3 P.M., and Sunday noon–3 P.M. during the summer, and weekdays 9 A.M.–5 P.M. the rest of the year.

WHITE EARTH RESERVATION

Total Area - 1,167 sq. miles
Tribally Owned - 10 percent
Total Population - 9,192
Native Population - 3,378
Tribal Enrollment - 21,083

The White Earth Reservation was never the historic homeland of any Ojibwe people. The U.S. Government created it with the intent of moving all of the Ojibwe people in Minnesota, Wisconsin, and Michigan here. Due to pressure and payoffs from the government many did settle in scattered communities across the reservation, but most refused or returned home after arriving. The village of White Earth, named for the white clay found in abundance here, is the largest native community on the reservation and home to the tribal headquarters. The other notable native communities are Nay-

tahwaush, Pine Point, Rice Lake and Elbow Lake. Fifty-three wild rice beds are spread out across the reservation and hundreds of thousands of pounds of the sacred grain are harvested each year by the tribal-owned Manitok Wild Rice Company. The tribe also owns a garment manufacturing plant and the Shooting Star Casino in Mahnomen, the area's largest employer.

The White Earth band's most famous member is the environmentalist Winona LaDuke who was Ralph Nader's Vice Presidential running mate for the Green Party in 1996 and 2000. LaDuke's White Earth Land Recovery Project is part of a larger effort by the tribe to regain land that it has lost over the years; much of it due to unscrupulous land sales authorized by the 1889 Nelson Allotment Act and other similar laws, as well as tax delinquency.

Almost everyone will find something of interest at the somewhat disheveled **Becker County Museum,** 714 Summit Ave., 218/847-2938, whether it be the 1910 Maxwell car, the two-headed cow, the collection of classic hats, or the pair of polar bears. The museum is open weekdays 8 A.M.–5 P.M. and Saturday 1–5 P.M. and admission is free.

The narrow, mile-long **City Beach** is a huge summertime draw and boats and bikes can be rented at several spots along the beachfront. There is a three-story-tall waterslide across from the beach at the end of Washington Ave., while most of the other summertime mini-amusement parks are just south of town along Highway 59.

Two companies sitting side by side on Hwy. 34 seven miles west of town, **K&K River Tubing,** 218/847-2808; and **Charlie's Ottertail Tubing,** 218/847-3258, run trips on the Otter Tail River. Both run two-hour trips for about $6. **Timberline Ranch,** 218/847-3886, offers trail rides on horseback during the summer. An hour-long ride is $18 and must be reserved a day in advance. Longer rides are also available. There are seven golf courses within 10 miles of town. **Wildflower,** 888/752-9945, at the Fair Hills Resort, and the **Detroit Country Club,** 218/847-5790, are the most challenging.

Winter sports enthusiasts have **Detroit Mountain,** 218/847-1661, with 15 runs for skiers and snowboarders, plus a half-pipe and tubing hill. The Mountain is located three miles east of town on Hwy. 34 and also has a three-mile cross-country ski trail, though the best place to ski is **Maplelag** (see Accommodations).

Entertainment and Events

Although several area bars feature entertainment occasionally, the city's primary spot for nightlife is **Islands,** 1375 West Lake Dr., 218/847-8731, which has a regular schedule of DJs and live bands.

The **Northwest Water Carnival** has grown from humble beginnings in 1935 to 10 days of family events. Highlights are a chili cook-off, carnival, night golf, and a massive parade. It begins the first Saturday after the 4th of July. Each August 50,000 people pack the Soo Pass Ranch south of town for **WE Fest,** one of the largest country music festivals in the world. For ticket or other information call 800/493-3378.

Thirty-five miles north of Detroit Lakes in the small city of Mahnomen is the White Earth Ojibwe's popular **Shooting Star Casino,** 218/935-2701 or 800/453-7827. Attached to the casino are a 392-room hotel, RV park, a couple of restaurants, a fitness center, and the Cabaret Ballroom, which brings in big-name entertainment. The band also sponsors the **White Earth Powwow** on the weekend closest to June 14th in the village of White Earth north of Detroit Lakes.

Accommodations

Across from the beach the simple **Holiday Haven Motel,** 220 West Lake Drive, 218/847-5605, has rooms from $40. Also on the lake are the storybook, red and white **Fairyland Cottages,** 410 West Lake Drive, 218/847-9991, which have changed little since the 1940s. They are so classic that they were featured in the postcard montage at the beginning of the movie *National Lampoon's Vacation.* One-bedroom cabins go for $60/night and $350/week, and there are also two- and three-bedroom cabins available. Heading east out of town you'll find the **Best Western Holland House,** 615 U.S. 10 E., 218/847-4483 or 800/338-8547, whose primary attraction is a 133-foot indoor waterslide. Other amenities included in the $109 room price are a pool, whirlpool, and sauna.

The only bed-and-breakfast in the area is five miles southeast of town along U.S. 10. The **Acorn Lake B&B,** 30680 Acorn Lake Rd., 218/334-5545 or 888/571-9904, has five rooms from $55 with shared bath, to a two-room whirlpool suite with private entrance for $99. Weather permitting, breakfast is served on the deck. There is a beach, and guests who want to poke around the lake can use one of their boats.

Maplelag, 218/375-4466 or 800/654-7711, has all the best aspects of the summer camp of your childhood with everything you now expect as an adult, and guests come from around the world to experience one of Minnesota's best winter resorts. Cross-country skiing is the main focus, and 33 miles of groomed trails for all abilities cross their 660 acres. Lessons are available in traditional, skating, and telemarking styles, and top-quality equipment is available for rent. Other than hitting the slopes, guests can also try just about every winter activity there is including snowshoeing, dogsledding, skijoring, kicksledding, and ice-skating. After a long day on the trails unwind in the hot tub and sauna (both open 24 hours), make an appointment with one of the licensed massage therapists, or dip into the bottomless cookie jars before heading back to relax in your TV- and telephone-less rooms. A three-day winter weekend package including meals runs $202–258, and they are closed most of the summer. Maplelag is located 20 miles north of Detroit Lakes (near Callaway) on Little Sugarbush Lake. A more typical family-style resort with a good reputation is **Lakecrest Resort,** 24013 U.S. 10 W., 218/847-5459 or 800/435-5459. It has 17 fully equipped cabins two miles west of town on Long Lake. Mid-summer rates for a two-person cabin start at $761 a week, but are as low as $170 October–May.

Food
The casual and ever popular **Lakeside 1891,** 200 West Lake Dr., 218/847-7887, set in a historic hotel, has a menu ranging from BLTs to fajitas to steaks and prices ranging $5–17. Open daily for lunch and dinner. **Main Street Restaurant,** 900 Washington Ave., 218/847-3344, is a typical small town café with burger baskets for $5. They are open daily for breakfast, lunch, and dinner. The **Chinese Dragon,** 808 Washington Ave., 218/847-2177, has an impressively large menu with over two-dozen vegetarian options and an average price of $8 per plate. Open daily for lunch and dinner. In the same mall is the **Sunflower Hill Coffee Co.,** 218/847-8870, which has light meals and snacks.

Information and Transportation
The **Detroit Lakes Regional Chamber of Commerce,** 700 Washington Ave., 218/847-9202 or 800/542-3992, www.visitdetroitlakes.com, has information about the city and surrounding lakes area. They are open weekdays 8 A.M.–5 P.M. In the summer they're also open Saturday 8:30 A.M.–5 P.M. and Sunday 10 A.M.–1 P.M. and don't close until 6 P.M. on weekends.

Amtrak trains stop at around 3 A.M. on their east and westbound runs. The depot is downtown at 116 Pioneer St. **Greyhound** buses stop twice a day next to the Budget Host Inn, 895 U.S. 10 E., 218/847-5878, on the run between Minneapolis ($36 one-way) and Fargo ($12).

TAMARAC NATIONAL WILDLIFE REFUGE
The beautiful Tamarac National Wildlife Refuge is spread out over 43,000 acres at the convergence of Minnesota's three primary ecosystems—prairie, northern hardwood forest, and northern pine forest—creating an impressive variety of flora and fauna. Nearly half the area is wetlands, which increases the biological diversity even more. Bird-watchers have got a shot at seeing over 250 species. Common loon, bald eagle, ruffed grouse, and ruby-throated hummingbird are prevalent, and trumpeter swans were reintroduced starting back in 1987 and are not too difficult to find. The more than 40 mammalian species include black bear, beaver, river otter, fisher, moose, and timber wolf. Just about everything of interest to visitors is in the southern third of the refuge (below County Road 26), which is open year-round; the northern section is generally off-limits March–September. The best place to begin a visit is the centrally located **visitors center,** 218/847-2641, which has interpretive displays, a gift shop, and knowledgeable staff on hand to answer your queries. They lead free guided tours at 11 A.M. on Thursdays during the summer. The **Blackbird Auto Tour,** a five-mile, one-way route starting near the visitors center, is both scenic and excellent for wildlife observation. It is open to cars, weather permitting, which is generally May through early November. The best bet for hiking is the **Old Indian Trail,** which leads for 1.5 miles through a maple forest.

The Far Northwest

Relatively few tourists to Minnesota make it out this far, and with all there is to see and do in the rest of the state that's understandable. That doesn't mean, however, that there is no reason to visit this forgotten corner. For someone who has never been to the Great Plains just driving through here will be a worthy new experience. As you approach the widely scattered towns, grain elevators loom in the distance looking larger than the Sears Tower. Up close though, you can almost see the small towns dying right before your eyes. On the other hand, a few mid-sized cities have diversified their economies and are thriving. But towns are the exception—here farms are the rule. Being surrounded for so long by so little you can quickly come to feel lonely, sometimes it even seems a little eerie, and when a rumbling thunderstorm is rolling toward you it can be downright scary. Just imagine how the pioneers felt as they stared out across the endless sea of prairie, unlike anything they had ever seen before, that was to become

their new homes. Their legacy is to be found in both the rusting farm equipment and crumbling shells of old houses sprinkled along the roads and in the shiny new silos and tractors in the fields.

THIEF RIVER FALLS

Thief River Falls is the largest and fastest growing city in northwest Minnesota. The town sits where the Thief River joins the larger Red Lake River, and the abundant waterpower was first exploited for sawmills in the 1880s. Norwegians were amongst the earliest settlers, and today half of the city's 8,410 residents claim at least some Norse ancestry, making this the most Norwegian city in the nation. The Dakota and later the Ojibwe made it their home long before this, and an Ojibwe village remained at the river junction until 1904—a statue of Chief Red-Robe overlooks the site. The city really began to grow when the Great Northern and Soo Line Railroads made this a center for shipping wheat. The city is the best base for visiting the nearby Agassiz National Wildlife Refuge, a bird-watcher's paradise.

Sights and Recreation

The city's most interesting attraction is the **Arctic Cat factory,** 218/681-8558, where you can watch snowmobiles and ATVs being born. Your tour guide will lead you right through the factory floor along the assembly lines and under conveyor belts to show you the whole operation from start to finish. Many things have changed since 1962 when the plant opened but, while you'll see robotic welding and computerized diagnostics, most of the work is still done by hand by the plant's 1,300 employees. Snowmobiles are only produced March through Thanksgiving, though ATVs roll off the lines year-round. The free, hour-long tours depart weekdays at 1 P.M. throughout the year. There are times, however, especially at the beginning of the year, when the lines are down, so it would be wise to call ahead.

Seventeen historic buildings have been moved from across the county to the **Peder Engelstad**

© TIM BEWER

Abandoned homes dot the Red River Valley.

Pioneer Village, 218/681-5767. All of them, including the one-room schoolhouse, barbershop, general store, and candy shop are stocked with appropriate furnishings and provisions. The museum also has a collection of old vehicles (including a 1926 Model T) and farm equipment, though their pride and joy are interesting Native American and Norwegian exhibits. They host several special events each year to reenact pioneer days. The village, located just off Hwy. 32, is open daily during the summer 1–5 P.M. Admission is $3.

The city's 7.3-mile **Riverwalk** trail system roughly follows the Red Lake River through town and has 15 historical markers along its path. Most of the route follows city streets, but some of the sections through parks are pleasant. The trails along the Northland Community and Technical College at the north end and the Greenwood Trails at the south are your best bets for quiet riverside strolls. If you want to bike the route, stop by the **Pathfinder Bike & Bait Shop,** 206 N. Knight Ave., 218/681-3116, where rentals are just $5/day.

For a more active outing you could paddle the **Red Lake River** all the way to East Grand Forks, a 127-mile trip. The Red Lake River is one of the few canoeable rivers in the region and is generally a quiet paddle, though there are some easily navigable boulder fields between St. Hilare and Crookston, which can create up to Class II rapids. The wooded banks are steep to around Red Lake Falls before giving way to low farmland.

Entertainment and Events

Thief River Falls doesn't have any interesting festivals, but the **All Nation's Cultural Festival** held the second weekend of July in nearby St. Hilare makes up for it. Dancers and musicians representing cultures from around the globe perform on stage, while a fur trade encampment and children's events take place concurrently. Admission is $8 per day or $14 for both. There are also many historical goings-on at Peder Engelstad Pioneer Village.

Eight miles south of town on U.S. 59 is the **Seven Clans Casino,** 218/681-4062 or 800/881-0712. Besides gaming, the Red Lake Ojibwe-owned facility has a 151-room hotel and 40,000 square-foot indoor water park with four waterslides.

Accommodations

Both the **T-59 Motel,** 1510 U.S. 59 SE, 218/681-2720; and the **Hartwood Motel,** 1010 Main

the Red River Valley, right in the middle of it all

Ave. N., 218/681-2640, have basic rooms from $35. The best rooms in town are at the spanking new **C'Mon Inn,** 1586 Hwy. 29 SE, 218/681-3000 or 800/950-8111. Standard rooms start at $59, and there is a pool and whirlpool. Crammed between the river and Highway 32 is the city-owned **Thief River Falls Tourist Park,** 218/681-2519, with 64 electric campsites from $11 and unlimited space for tents for just $7.

Food

A short way north of downtown is **Dee's Kitchen,** 811 Atlantic Ave. N., 218/681-9907, a local favorite that does everything right. A quarter-pound burger is $3 and a hearty shrimp basket is $7, and they are open daily for breakfast and lunch plus weekdays for dinner. The friendly **Evergreen Eating Emporium,** 700 Hwy. 32 S., 218/681-3138, has an English Tudor decor, but serves up a solid American menu ranging from a veggie burger for $6 to a steak and crab platter for $22. Open daily for lunch and dinner. **China King,** 304 3rd St. E., 218/681-3858, gets the nod from most locals as the best Chinese in town. Dinner averages $6 and they are open daily for lunch and dinner.

Information and Services

The **Thief River Falls Visitors and Convention Bureau,** 2017 U.S. 59, 218/681-3720 or 800/827-1629, www.ci.thief-river-falls.mn.us, is at the southeast entrance to town. They are open weekdays 8:30 A.M.–5 P.M.

Transportation

Thief River Falls Regional Airport, 218/681-7680, is two miles south of town on Hwy. 17. **Northwest Airlink,** 218/681-6688 or 800/225-2525, makes the two-hour flight to the Twin Cities twice a day and round-trip fares are around $200, much less if it is a segment of a longer Northwest flight.

CROOKSTON

Crookston's main claim to fame is the massive channel catfish that gather below the dam on Red Lake River. Anglers commonly land channel cats in excess of 10 pounds and some tip the scale

© TIM BEWER

Minnesota has some unique road hazards.

at over 20. While Crookston is home to the **Polk County Historical Museum,** 719 E. Robert St., 218/281-1038, with an assortment of relocated historic buildings and just about anything old they can get their hands on (open daily noon–5 P.M. late May–mid-September; admission is free), the city's living history is more interesting. **Widman's Candy Shop,** 116 S. Broadway, 218/281-1487, opened in 1911 and hasn't changed much since then. Now run by a fourth generation Widman, the store still sells homemade candy, their famous hand-dipped potato chips, and old-fashioned fountain drinks. Even the prices hark back to the bygone days with malts for just $1.65. A few blocks over, the **Grand Theatre,** 124 E. 2nd St., 218/281-1820, opened in 1910 as a Vaudeville stage and is now one of the oldest continually-running movie theaters in the United States. The **giant oxcart statue** (the world's second largest, as best as I can determine) north of downtown along U.S. 75 is certainly worthy of a road trip photo. The **Red Lake River,** one of the few canoeing rivers in northwest Minnesota, offers 50 miles of gentle paddling to East Grand Forks where it joins the Red River.

Practicalities

Both the **Golf Terrace Motel,** 1731 University

Ave., 218/281-2626; and the **Motel Country Club,** 719 Groveland Ave., 218/281-1607 or 888/314-0105, have decent rooms for $35, though neither has a golf course. The latter does have a pleasant riverside location on three acres. A big step up in quality is the **Northland Inn,** 2200 University Ave., 218/281-5200 or 800/423-7541, where a $60 room gets you a pool and hot tub. The city's **Central Park,** 218/281-1242, has an almost shadeless campground. Tent sites are $6, while trailers and RVs cost $10.

All of the city's restaurants have voluntarily gone smokefree. The best of them is the **University Station,** 218/281-5210, at the Northland Inn, which has salads, steaks, and stir-fry ranging from $6–20. Open daily for breakfast, lunch, and dinner. For a drink or a snack try **The Novel Cup,** 101 W. Robert St., 218/281-4830, a tiny coffee shop/bookstore at the corner of Broadway and Robert Street. It is open Monday–Saturday for breakfast and lunch.

The small **University of Minnesota–Crookston** campus is the town's cultural anchor, and the public is invited to most events. Call 800/862-6466 to see what is on. **Greyhound** buses stop at the Amoco gas station at 1749 University, 218/281-3908, on their once-a-day run between Grand Forks ($10 one-way) and Minneapolis ($58).

AGASSIZ NATIONAL WILDLIFE REFUGE

Twenty-three miles northeast of Thief River Falls is Minnesota's largest National Wildlife Refuge and one of its oldest. Named for Glacial Lake Agassiz, which shaped this land some 10,000 years ago, Agassiz has 61,500 acres, most of it wetlands, in the ecological transition zone between the pine forests to the east and tallgrass prairies to the west, and nearly 23,000 additional acres of state-managed wildlife lands border the refuge. Wetlands like these once covered a much larger area of the Red River Valley, but a massive network of drainage ditches opened up the land to farming. They also increased the severity of spring floods along the Red River. You can never expect to spot a moose in the wild, but

wood lilies, Old Mill State Park

your chances at Agassiz, which normally has a population of around 250, are as good as anywhere in the state. Concentrate on willow thickets during the rut in September and October. Two wolf packs also roam the refuge, and bear, fisher, otter, and bobcat are among the other 47 species of mammal found here. Elk even wander in on rare occasions. One hundred and thirty-three bird species nest here and more than twice that can be observed during the year. Rare species, such as boreal chickadee and Mississippi kite, have earned Agassiz recognition as one of the best bird-watching sites in the United States.

Despite its size, public access is very limited. Other than County Road 7, which crosses the southern half of the refuge, casual visitors are restricted to the four-mile **Lost Bay Habitat Drive,** which leads you right through some prime wildlife viewing territory, and two concise, wooded **hiking trails;** all are open May–October. Birding is also good on roads along the edge of the refuge. For an impressive panorama climb the 100-foot-tall **observation tower** during snow-free months. It is right near the refuge office, 218/449-4115, on County Road 7. Several free, primitive campsites are available on the adjacent state managed wildlife lands.

OLD MILL STATE PARK

This peaceful, 407-acre wooded preserve circles a small collection of historic structures. The Old Mill in question is actually two small restored flour mills, one steam-powered and one water-powered, which were both built along the Middle River in 1889 and 1896, respectively. A furnished log cabin sits next to the mill, adding to the experience. The mill is powered up each year on the last Sunday in August during **Grinding Days.** Despite its small size the park hosts a decent sampling of wildlife, which might be spotted on the seven-mile web of **trails** that crosses the mostly forested park. In winter the trails are groomed for cross-country skiing and skis and snowshoes can be rented from the park office. Twenty-six (10 electric) campsites and a swimming pond round out the experience. For further information call 218/437-8174.

LAKE BRONSON STATE PARK

You know that if such an off-the-beaten-path park attracts over 125,000 visitors a year it must be pretty good. Following a major drought in the 1930s that dried up wells in Bronson and Hallock, the South Branch Two River was dammed as a hedge against future disasters. As one of the few lakes in the area, 330-acre Lake Bronson became a magnet for locals looking to swim, fish, and canoe. While the lake draws the vast majority of visitors, this is a well-rounded park with 14 miles of trails, abundant wildlife, and several minor historic sites. The 3,720-acre park encompasses a mix of prairie and aspen forest, and if you'd like to see a moose in the wild this is an excellent place to look. The **Aspen Parklands Interpretive Trail** is a good place to learn about the park's ecology, but if you really want to get away from it all head through the forest and oak savanna in the far east end of the park. The eastern half of the five-mile trail around the lake is also scenic, while the western portion is paved for biking. In winter seven miles of trails are groomed for skiing, and snowshoes can be rented from the office. Campers are well covered with 194 sites (35 electric) in three campgrounds. The mostly wooded **Two Rivers Campground** is quieter and has more secluded sites, but if you can get a lakeside site in the **Lakeside Campground,** take it for the views. Additionally, four backpacking sites are set along the river, and there are a couple of canoe-in sites on Moose Island. These sites can't be reserved, but they are almost always available. Call 218/754-2200 with any park questions.

RED RIVER VALLEY

Prairieland

Minnesota's southwest corner is relentless farm country speckled with historic sites, most related to the region's original cultures. Though it is still romantically linked with its prairie, all but tiny fragments of the original landscape have been plowed under. In its place are some of the nation's highest-yielding corn and soybean fields, and most of the harvest is sold by some of the most innovative and profitable farmer-owned cooperatives in the world. Prairie restorations, some quite extensive, are under way in many places, and at Blue Mounds State Park bison roam free once again, albeit behind three miles of fence.

Despite having several of the state's most unusual attractions most people, including Minnesotans, dismiss southwest Minnesota. One-of-a-kind must-sees include the world's largest ball of twine rolled by just one man and an actual two-story outhouse, as well as the Pipestone National Monument and Jeffers Petroglyphs, two of the most important Native American spiritual sites in the state. For some, a pilgrimage to Walnut Grove, former home of Laura Ingalls Wilder, is just as spiritual. This may not be what you came to Minnesota for, but to ignore this part of the state is to miss the variety that makes it so special.

© TIM BEWER

Sod House on the Prairie bed-and-breakfast

PRAIRIELAND HIGHLIGHTS

Blue Mounds State Park
Harkin Store, near New Ulm
Jeffers Petroglyphs
Lac Qui Parle State Park
Laura Ingalls Wilder Museum, Walnut Grove
Nobles County Pioneer Village, Worthington

Pipestone National Monument, Pipestone
Sod House on the Prairie, Sanborn
Twine Ball, Darwin
Two-Story Outhouse, Belle Plaine
Wind Farms, around Lake Benton

Minnesota River Valley

The Minnesota River cuts 330 miles across the bottom of the state before joining the Mississippi River at the Twin Cities. The first major tributary of the Mississippi flows through a deep, miles-wide valley cut during the last Ice Age by the draining of Glacial Lake Agassiz (see Red River Geology in the Red River Valley chapter). The state took its name from the river, adapting the Dakotas' Minnay Sotar (Sky-tinted Water). The best way to visit the towns and parks along it is to follow the various highways and back roads of the Minnesota River Valley Scenic Byway, a 300-mile route from Belle Plaine to Browns Valley. Unlike the monotonous driving through the rest of southwest Minnesota, the journey is often beautiful. Distinctive pink signs with a bald eagle in flight mark the route, but with so many twists and turns it can be difficult to keep your bearings, so a map (available free by calling 800/473-3404 or from any tourist office along the way) is recommended.

TWIN CITIES TO MANKATO

Minnesota Valley State Recreation Area

Most of the low-lying valley between Belle Plain and the Mississippi River is protected by a series of parklands, most notably the Minnesota Valley National Wildlife Refuge, and this multiunit park that covers most of the ground upstream of Shakopee. The landscape is principally wet meadow and floodplain forest, though the valley walls and bluff tops are lined by oak forest and oak savanna remnants. The principal feature of the 5,500-acre park, besides the river, is the **Minnesota Valley Trail,** a 35-mile riverside route open to hikers, mountain bikers, horseback riders, and snowmobilers. Overall it's not a very challenging ride, though there are some sandy areas and heavy rains can make mud pits out of long stretches. Trail access in the north is available along Highway 41 at Nysen's Lake, in the middle along County Road 9, and in the south along County Road 57. Severe erosion has forced the closure of five miles of trail between County Road 9 and the trail center in the Lawrence Unit; call the park office at 952/492-6400 to check on the status of this section. If you want to follow the river by canoe or kayak, you can put in along Highway 25 north of Belle Plaine. It's an easy, rapids-free route with numerous canoe-in campsites. Boat ramps are found at every road crossing downstream to Shakopee and most of the rest on toward the Mississippi River.

The park headquarters, campgrounds, and the restored 1857 Samuel B. Strait House (you can go inside to read historical panels about how the former settlement here grew up with the steamboat and died with the railroad; open summer weekends 9 A.M.–3 P.M.) are found along County Road 57 in the Lawrence Unit. The rustic Quarry Campground has 33 shady and well-spaced campsites, including eight walk-ins. There is also a horse-rider campground here and five miles of level hiking trail are groomed for cross-country skiing in the winter.

PRAIRIELAND

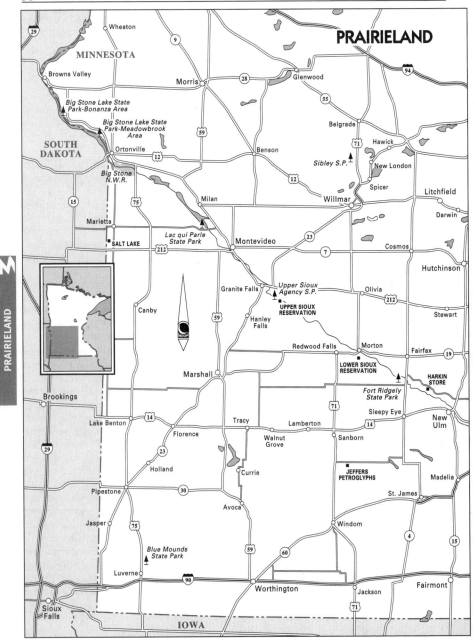

PRAIRIELAND

PRAIRIELAND

MINNESOTA

SOUTH
DAKOTA

Wheaton

Browns Valley

Morris

Glenwood

Big Stone Lake State
Park-Bonanza Area

Big Stone Lake State
Park-Meadowbrook
Area

Ortonville

Benson

Belgrade

Hawick

Sibley S.P.

New London

Spicer

Litchfield

Big Stone
N.W.R.

Milan

Willmar

Darwin

Marietta

SALT LAKE

Lac qui Parle
State Park

Montevideo

Cosmos

Hutchinson

Canby

Granite Falls

Upper Sioux
Agency S.P.

UPPER SIOUX
RESERVATION

Olivia

Stewart

Hanley
Falls

Redwood Falls

Morton

Fairfax

LOWER SIOUX
RESERVATION

HARKIN
STORE

Marshall

Fort Ridgely
State Park

Brookings

Lake Benton

Tracy

Lamberton

Sleepy Eye

New
Ulm

Florence

Walnut
Grove

Sanborn

Holland

Currie

JEFFERS
PETROGLYPHS

Madelia

Pipestone

St. James

Jasper

Avoca

Windom

Blue Mounds
State Park

Luverne

Sioux
Falls

Worthington

Jackson

Fairmont

IOWA

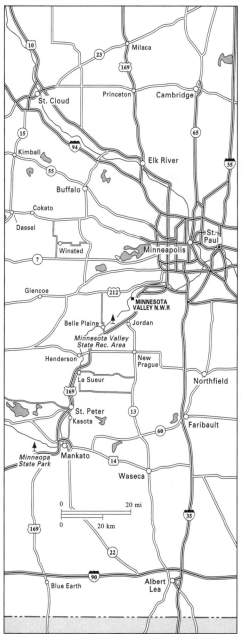

© AVALON TRAVEL PUBLISHING, INC.

Belle Plaine

The "Beautiful Prairie" is home to one of the most unusual tourist attractions in the nation—a real **two-story outhouse.** The five-holer is connected by a skywalk to the **Hooper-Bowler-Hillstrom House,** 410 N. Cedar St., 952/873-6109, as the Belle Plaine Historical Society calls it. Samuel Bowler, the home's second owner, added the skycrapper to accommodate his large number of children. It's actually not as ominous as it seems; the upper chamber is set back a few feet so all materials drop behind a wall. The rest of the rooms in the 1871 home are furnished from three periods: the 1850s, the 1890s, and the early 1900s. If you don't want to take the hour-long tour of the rest of the house, they will let you just grab a look at the single feature that prompted you stop in the first place. The house is open Sunday 1–4 P.M. during the summer. Admission is $2.

Emma Krumbee's, a mini tourism empire along Highway 169, takes care of most travel needs. They manage the **AmericInn,** 952/873-6017 or 800/634-3444, with sparkling new rooms from $83, plus a small pool, whirlpool, and game room, as well as **Emma Krumbee's Restaurant and Bakery,** 952/873-4334, (open daily for breakfast, lunch and dinner), with delicious home-cooking averaging $7. Behind them is a you-pick apple orchard, site of the annual **Great Scarecrow Festival,** where over 100 scarecrows are on display along with a petting zoo and pony rides for the kids. Held from mid-September to late October, it is one of Minnesota's most attended annual events. **Greyhound** buses stop at the Amoco/Oasis Market, 952/873-6762, north of town along Highway 169.

Le Sueur

This former steamboat stop, founded as a city in 1853, was named after Pierre Le Sueur, a French explorer credited as the first European to travel up the Minnesota River. He was sent here in the late 17th century by the King of France to help keep the peace between the Dakota and the Ojibwe.

One small house in the center of this unassuming town gave birth to two of America's most

© TIM BEWER

the humble birthplace of the Mayo Clinic and Green Giant

well-known and successful enterprises: the Mayo Clinic and Green Giant. English born Dr. William Mayo built this boxy home himself in 1859 and set up his first medical practice on the second floor. Five years later, after an appointment to the Civil War draft enrollment board, he relocated to Rochester, where his practice grew into the Mayo Clinic. A decade later the Cosgrove family moved into the house, and in 1903 Carson Nesbit Cosgrove founded the Minnesota Valley Canning Company, later renamed Green Giant because of the overwhelming popularity of their mascot. Hour-long tours of the **W. W. Mayo House,** 118 N. Main St., 507/665-3250, as it is now known, offer a glimpse of life in the 1860s, the time period reflected in the house's furnishings, a few of which were used by the Mayo family. Costumed guides recount the family's histories (Louise Mayo's story is as interesting as her husband's) and daily lives. During the summer the home is open Tuesday–Saturday 10 A.M.–4:30 P.M. and Sunday 1–4:30 P.M., plus Saturday–Sunday 1–4:30 P.M. beginning in mid-May and ending in mid-October. The house is decorated for 1860s- and 1920s-style Christmases the first weekend in December. Admis-

sion is $2. Tours start next door in the **Mayoview History Center,** which has a short video introduction and a gift shop.

Green Giant headquarters left Le Sueur in 1979 when Pillsbury purchased the company; now all that remains is a small research center and a large Green Giant history room at the **Le Sueur City Museum,** 709 N. 2nd St., 507/665-2050, filled with everything from old cans of corn to Green Giant dolls. Except for an impressive display of antique radios, the rest of the collection is the usual small town miscellany. The museum is open weekdays 9 A.M.–noon and daily 1–4:30 P.M. during the summer, and Tuesday–Thursday 9 A.M.–4:30 P.M. the rest of the year. Admission is free.

Few visitors stick around very long, but if you are so inclined it won't cost you much. The **Le Sueur Downtown Motel,** 510 N. Main St. 507/665-6246, has spotless rooms for $36, while the **Le Sueur Diner,** 507/665-2080, in the Valleygreen Square Mall at the end of North Main Street serves cheap American fare. It is open daily for breakfast and lunch and Monday–Saturday for dinner. **Greyhound** buses stop at the Downtown Motel.

St. Peter

St. Peter is just your average small city (pop. 9,747), but things could have been much different. In February 1857, shortly before Minnesota would become the 32nd state, a bill moving the capital from St. Paul to this young city passed the Territorial Legislature. But, before the bill could reach the desk of Governor Willis A. Gorman, who happened to be from St. Peter, Representative Joe Rolette of Pembina, the committee chair, took the bill and hid out in a St. Paul hotel room playing poker until the session adjourned. The governor did sign a copy of the bill, but the courts overturned the law because it was not the actual bill passed by the legislature. As a reminder of the shenanigans, Highway 169 runs down an especially wide main street laid out in anticipation of the move.

Just north of town is a natural ford in the Minnesota River (then named the St. Peter River, hence the city's name) known as the Traverse des Sioux (Sioux Crossing). Over several weeks in the summer of 1851 the Sisseton and Wahpeton bands of Dakota met with American negotiators at a busy trading post here and eventually signed the Traverse des Sioux Treaty giving up over 24 million acres of land in southern Minnesota, as well as Iowa and South Dakota. The unkept promises made in this treaty (and the Mendota Treaty signed by the Mdewakanton and Wahpekute Dakota two weeks later) played a large part in the Dakota Conflict a decade later. The **Treaty Site History Center,** 507/934-2160, details the events leading up to the signing and the tragedies following it. The museum also covers other events in Nicollet County history. The restored prairie surrounding the museum is a state historic site, and a mile-long trail with interpretive signs along it leads down to the river. The best guess at where the actual signing ceremony took place is just up and across the highway, but there is nothing to see except a big rock with a plaque embedded in it. The museum, located a mile north of town on Highway 169, is open Tuesday–Saturday 10 A.M.–4 P.M. and Sunday 1–4 P.M. Admission is $3.

The city's other significant attraction is the **E. St. Julien Cox House,** 500 N. Washington Ave., 507/934-4309, an excellent example of Gothic/Italianate architecture. The striking red and gold house is fully restored and furnished with 1880s Victorian period pieces, and they've done such a good job that it looks lived in. A costumed guide will tell you about upper-class life from this time during an hour-long tour. Outside are a flower and herb garden and a carriage house with old wagons and sleighs. The house is open 1–4 P.M. the first and third weekends of the month between mid-May and early September. The popular Christmas at Cox House is held the first two weekends in December and admission is $3, or $5 for a combination ticket with the Treaty Site History Center.

If you call ahead you can arrange a visit to the museum of the **St. Peter Regional Treatment Center,** the first psychiatric hospital in the state, which opened in 1866. The museum is in the Center Building; the original hospital structure contains just about anything old they could find, from the fancy employee china to straitjackets. You can visit anytime between 7:30 A.M. and 3:30 P.M. and admission is free. Call 507/931-7250 to make an appointment. The small **Arts Center of St. Peter,** 315 S. Minnesota Ave., 507/931-3630, has a new exhibition from local and regional artists about once a month. The gallery is open Thursday 1–8 P.M., Saturday–Sunday 1–5 P.M.

The top hotel in town is the **AmericInn,** 700 N. Minnesota Ave., 507/931-6554 or 800/634-3444, with a pool, whirlpool, sauna, and rooms from $73. For the budget-minded there is the **Viking Jr. Motel,** 507/931-3081, south of town on Highway 169. Simple but clean rooms, stocked with a refrigerator and microwave, are $40. **Riverside Park,** 507/931-0665, near downtown has a dozen first-come, first-served campsites and a tent area along the Minnesota River for $7 or $12 with electric hookup. **Ooodles Café,** 402 S. 3rd St., 507/931-4455, is a deservedly popular stop for home-cooked American fare. They have a long list of sandwiches, heaping breakfasts (served all day), and all-you-can eat dinner specials. Entrées average $5. Open daily for breakfast and lunch and weekdays for dinner. The **St. Peter Food Co-op,** 119 W. Broadway, 507/934-4880, has a small deli/bakery where you can also get a good meal for about $5. Open daily for breakfast, lunch, and dinner. For some fine dining head 1.5 miles south of town on Highway 22 to **The Country Pub,** 507/931-5888 or 888/395-5888, which combines a quiet country setting with a big city menu. Dishes like grilled asparagus salad, lamb T-bone, Florentine stuffed chicken breast, and Louisiana shrimp gumbo average about $17. In the summer their screened porch is the place to be. Open weekdays for lunch and dinner and just dinner on Saturday. Reservations are recommended.

Greyhound buses stop at the Freedom Valu Center, 625 S. Minnesota Ave., 507/931-6841, once a day on the run from the Twin Cities to the south. **Land to Air Express,** 507/625-3977 or 888/736-9190, vans make the trip to the airport four times a day during the week and three on weekends for $21 one-way. They stop at Hometown Travel, 400 South 3rd Street.

MANKATO

Settled in February of 1852, before the terms of the Traverse des Sioux Treaty were even formalized, Mankato sits right where the Minnesota River takes a sharp left turn toward the Mississippi. The origin of the city's name is something of a mystery. Mahkato means Blue Earth in Dakota and refers to the greenish-blue clay found along the Blue Earth River, which empties into the Minnesota on the west side of town. Legend has it that this was the name chosen by the founders, and a later printing error was never corrected. The story has been repeated so often and for so long that it is now accepted as fact by most people, but more likely than not that actual origin lies with a survey map published in 1843 by Joseph Nicollet. The name Mahkato reminded the famous explorer and cartographer of a German folktale about a "water-spirit" named Mankato (he was in fact mistaken; according to the Blue Earth County Historical Society there is no such character) so he used that name on his map.

There is absolutely nothing special about this Mahkato clay, but in the late 17th century Pierre Charles Le Sueur, a French lieutenant who explored the area, sent a sample back to France where it was declared copper-bearing. Le Sueur returned several years later and reportedly shipped

THE DAKOTA CONFLICT

"Taoyateduta is not a coward and he is not a fool . . . Kill one-two-10, and 10 times that many will come to kill you . . . Braves, you are little children—you are fools. You will die like the rabbits when the hungry wolves hunt them in the Hard Moon. Taoyateduta is not a coward. He will die with you."

Chief Little Crow

Prompted by a decade of broken promises and underhanded dealings by the U.S. government the Dakota in Minnesota, led by Chief Little Crow (Taoyateduta), began attacking white towns and farmsteads in August of 1862 in order to take back the land they had ceded a decade earlier. With the army occupied by the Civil War many Dakota believed that they could defeat the Americans, and initially it looked like they might succeed. The attacks resulted in widespread panic and abandonment of just about every settlement in southwestern Minnesota. Before the army, led by former governor Sibley, rounded up hundreds of combatants and chased most of the other warriors west, nearly 500 civilians and soldiers had been killed. An estimated 71 Dakota, including 38 hung in unison in Mankato, the largest mass execution in the country's history, died in the uprising. Almost all remaining Dakota, including many who had risked their own lives to protect settlers, were evicted from the state, though this action served both as punishment and protection since vigilantes would have almost certainly killed anyone who remained. The tragic episode essentially spelled the end of Native American resistance in Minnesota though subsequent battles between the Dakota and the United States, such as Little Big Horn and Wounded Knee, flared out west through the rest of the century.

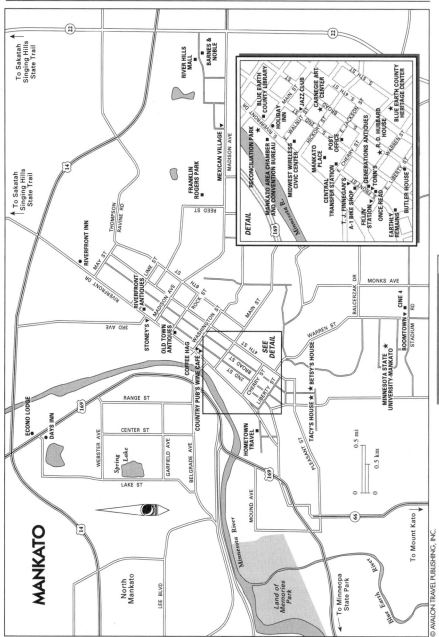

MANKATO

To Sakatah
Singing Hills
State Trail

To Sakatah
Singing Hills
State Trail

RIVER HILLS
MALL

BARNES &
NOBLE

RIVERFRONT INN

FRANKLIN
ROGERS PARK

MEXICAN VILLAGE

MADISON AVE

REED ST

THOMPSON

RAVINE RD

MAY ST

RIVERFRONT DR

LIME ST

RIVERFRONT
ANTIQUES

MADISON AVE

6TH

ROCK ST

WASHINGTON ST

MAIN ST

MONKS AVE

BALCERZAK DR

STADIUM RD

CINE 4

BOOMTOWN

STONEY'S

OLD TOWN
ANTIQUES

3RD AVE

COFFEE HAG

COUNTRY PUB'S WINE CAFE

2ND ST

BROAD ST

4TH ST

SEE
DETAIL

CHERRY ST

LIBERTY ST

WARREN ST

BETSY'S HOUSE

TACY'S HOUSE

MINNESOTA STATE
UNIVERSITY-MANKATO

ECONO LODGE

DAYS INN

RANGE ST

CENTER ST

WEBSTER AVE

GARFIELD AVE

BELGRADE AVE

Spring
Lake

LAKE ST

HOMETOWN
TRAVEL

PLEASANT ST

MOUND AVE

North
Mankato

LEE BLVD

Minnesota River

Land of
Memories
Park

To Minneopa
State Park

Blue Earth River

To Mount Kato

0.5 mi

0.5 km

PRAIRIELAND

© AVALON TRAVEL PUBLISHING, INC.

DETAIL

RECONCILIATION PARK

S. RIVERFRONT DR

BLUE EARTH
COUNTY LIBRARY

HOLIDAY
INN

MANKATO AREA CHAMBER
AND CONVENTION BUREAU

MIDWEST WIRELESS
CIVIC CENTER

MAIN ST

WALNUT ST

HICKORY ST

CENTRAL
TRANSFER STATION

T. J. FINNEGAN'S

A-1 BIKE SHOP

FILLIN'
STATION

ONCE READ

EARTHLY
REMAINS

MANKATO
PLACE

POST
OFFICE

E. CHERRY ST

N. BROAD ST

TONN'S

CARNEGIE ART
CENTER

JAZZ CLUB

S. 2ND ST

E. JACKSON ST

GENERATIONS ANTIQUES

R. D. HUBBARD
HOUSE

WARREN ST

E. LIBERTY ST

BUTLER HOUSE

BLUE EARTH COUNTY
HERITAGE CENTER

Minnesota R.

169

two tons of the blue earth down the Mississippi River toward France in 1701, though somehow it never made it. The clay, in fact, did not contain copper. Le Sueur was almost certainly aware of this fact from the start and simply used the sample as a ruse to procure a license to trade furs in the area, an endeavor that proved very lucrative.

The city grew rapidly as a transportation and supply center for the prairie frontier. Steamboats led the way, but were unreliable due to the shallow river, and stagecoaches soon came along a military road connecting Mankato with St. Paul. The railroad arrived in 1868, and Mankato became a hub for four different lines. By 1880 it was the fourth largest city in the state and the success of surrounding farms made it very prosperous. Today Mankato is the largest (along with North Mankato, which lies across the river but is otherwise indistinguishable) and most cultured city in the southwest, though farming remains important to the economy.

The most infamous chapter in the city's history came very early. The 303 prisoners convicted and sentenced to death following the Dakota Conflict were brought to Mankato. President Lincoln, after hearing an urgent plea from Bishop Henry Whipple, spared the lives of all but the convicted murderers and rapists and 38 men were hung simultaneously from a single gallows on December 26, 1862. A crowd of 3,000 (watched over by 2,000 soldiers there to keep the peace if needed) waited hours in the bitter cold to witness what remains the largest mass execution in U.S. history. A nine-foot buffalo sculpted from local Kasota limestone stands in Reconciliation Park, near the sight of the execution, as a memorial to that time.

Sights

Mankato's principal attraction is the **R. D. Hubbard House,** 606 Broad St. S., a three-story, white-brick French Second Empire mansion full of fancy woodwork, marble fireplaces, stained glass windows, and Tiffany lamps. Built in 1871, the Blue Earth County Historical Society has restored and refurnished it to its 1905 appearance. The carriage house next door, fronted by a small flower garden, has a collection of antique vehicles. Tours

begin on the hour between 1 and 4 P.M. every weekend from May through September. Admission is $2. The historical society also runs the nearby **Blue Earth County Heritage Center,** 415 E. Cherry St., 507/345-5566, a small local history museum with various historical artifacts, including some really nice Dakota pieces. It is open Tuesday–Saturday 10 A.M.–noon and 1–4 P.M. Admission is $2. The museum also has a petite display about hometown hero Maud Hart Lovelace, author of the classic Betsy and Tacy books. The Deep Valley setting for her stories was really Mankato, and if you are a fan of the series you'll want to get a copy of the ***Betsy-Tacy Places in Mankato*** self-guided tour brochure; it's available at the Heritage Center and the Blue Earth County Library, 100 Main St. E., 507/387-1856. The tour, created in part by Lovelace herself, leads you past 55 sites featured in the 13 books including Betsy and Tacy's houses (333 Center St. and 332 Center St. respectively) both now owned by **The Betsy-Tacy Society,** 507/345-8103. They hope to open them as museums someday, but for now you can only visit if you call in advance.

The Carnegie Library, mentioned frequently in Lovelace's books, is now the **Carnegie Art Center,** 120 Broad St. S., 507/625-2730. It hosts monthly exhibits by local and regional artists and occasionally sponsors workshops and lectures. It is open Wednesday, Friday, and Saturday 1–4 P.M. and Thursday 1–7 P.M. from September to July. Admission is free.

There is more to see on the campus of the **Minnesota State University-Mankato** (MSU). The small **Conkling Art Gallery,** 507/389-6412, in Nelson Hall, right in the center of campus, hosts many traveling exhibitions during the school year. When there is a noteworthy astronomical event, such as a lunar eclipse or passing comet, the Astronomy Department opens up their Standeford and Andreas Observatories for public viewing. Call 507/389-6208 to find out if anything is scheduled. Die-hard fans of the purple and gold flock to Blakeslee Field from late July to mid-August for **Minnesota Viking training camp.** Practices are free and open to the public, while intra-squad scrimmages and games against other NFL teams cost $7. Tickets are available from the Mankato Area Chamber and Convention Bureau and the MSU athletic office, 507/389-3000.

Minneopa State Park

Southern Minnesota's largest waterfall sits five miles west of Mankato on Highway 169 in Minneopa State Park, 507/389-5464. The 45-foot twin falls dropping into a rocky gorge on Minneopa Creek (Minneopa means water falling twice in the Dakota language) is far and away the most popular feature of the park and has been attracting sightseers since the mid-19th century. A short-lived summer resort was built here in 1858, and a village grew up around the nearby train station. Both went bust following the grasshopper plagues of the 1870s, though the train continued to bring thousands of tourists each summer. Recognizing the beauty and popularity of the area, the legislature made this Minnesota's third state park. Another popular feature is the German-style Seppman windmill, one of the state's earliest gristmills. Completed in 1864 it could grind 150 bushels of wheat per day in the right conditions. The arms were blown off by a tornado in 1890 and never replaced, but the medieval-looking tower is still a beautiful sight. The mill is perched above the valley and from here you get the best views of the boulder-strewn (these glacial erratics were carried over a hundred miles south by the last glacier) prairies of the river valley terrace. You'll see the wide plain up close as you approach the mill, either by road or along the 4.5 miles of hiking trail that loop through it. These trails are groomed for cross-country skiing in the winter. Birders will be rewarded with both grassland and woodland species like bluebirds, bobolinks, shrikes, belted kingfishers, and both eastern and western meadowlarks. Take one of the spurs that lead down to the river and you might see beaver, pelican, or northern green heron.

Recreation

The paved **Sakatah Singing Hills State Trail** follows 39 miles of former railroad bed through farms, forest, and small towns between Mankato and Faribault. The **A-1 Bike Shop,** 526 S. Front St., 507/625-2453, has bike rentals for $15 a day or $30 for the whole weekend.

In its peak season **Mount Kato,** 20461 Hwy. 66, 507/625-3363 or 800/668-5286, just a mile south of town, has 19 downhill ski and snowboard runs, the largest dropping 240 feet, and a tubing run. From May through October mountain bikers ride the seven miles of trail, most of it wooded single track. They have bikes for rent.

Entertainment and Events

The biggest events in town, from professional wrestling to Broadway musicals, take place at the **Midwest Wireless Civic Center,** 507/389-3001. Overall the best source of entertainment in town is **Minnesota State University-Mankato.** Call 507/389-1866 or 800/722-0544 to find out what's happening on campus. The city is also home to the **Mankato Symphony Orchestra,** 507/625-8880; **Minnesota Valley Chorale,** 507/625-8278; and the **Merely Players Community Theatre,** 507/388-5483.

MSU's 13,000 students keep the nightlight active. **Boomtown,** 1610 Warren St., 507/625-9264, is a busy campus bar, but South Front Street downtown is the best bet for barhopping. The most varied choice here is **T. J. Finnegan's,** 520 S. Front St., 507/388-3664, a self-styled "sports rock café," with dancing most nights, a Sunday night comedy show, and award-winning wood-fired pizza.

The **Jazz Club,** 200 Walnut, 507/387-5100, puts bands on stage Wednesday–Saturday nights; shows often start early and cover charges are low, if there is one at all. **Country Pub's Wine Café,** 301 N. Riverfront Dr. 507/345-1516, also has some weekend jazz. The **Coffee Hag,** 329 N. Riverfront Dr., 507/387-5533, has folk performances on weekends, and the **Fillin' Station,** 634 S. Front St., 507/344-0345, hopes to do the same in the near future.

Mankato's three movie theaters, each showing first run films, are the **Mall 4,** 12 Civic Center Plaza, 507/625-2385, downtown in the Mankato Place Mall; the **Cine 4,** 220 Stadium Rd., 507/625-1763, next to MSU; and the **Movies 8,** 1850 Adams St., 507/625-3553, at the River Hills Mall.

Some of the hottest tickets in town are for the

MSU Mavericks men's hockey team, who take on their WCHA (a premier Division I conference, all other MSU sports are Division II) rivals at the Midwest Wireless Civic Center. Tickets cost $13 and are available by calling MSU Athletics at 507/389-3000. Another noteworthy sports team is the **Mankato Moondogs,** 507/625-7047, a member of the Northwoods League, which allows top Division I college baseball players to get a minor league experience while keeping their college eligibility. Home games are played at "The Frank" (Franklin Rogers Park) from June to the middle of August. All tickets cost $5.

The annual **Mankato Pow-wow** is held in Land of Memories Park the third weekend of September.

Accommodations

The cheapest motel in town is the small **Riverfront Inn,** 1727 N. Riverfront Dr., 507/388-1638, with basic but decent rooms from $45; all come with a microwave and refrigerator. Don't expect to watch the sunset over the river—the inn is named for the street, not the body of water. Ten dollars more gets you a whirlpool and sauna at the **Econo Lodge,** 111 W. Lind Ct., 507/345-8800 or 800/553-2666, on the north side of town along Highway 169. The **Days Inn,** 1285 Range St., 507/387-3332 or 800/329-7466, across the street is a bit newer and charges $75 with a pool and whirlpool. The city's biggest and best hotel is the **Holiday Inn,** 101 E. Main St., 507/345-1234 or 800/465-4329. Besides the good location, $97 gets you a pool, whirlpool, sauna, fitness center, and game room.

The **Butler House,** 704 S. Broad St., 507/387-5055, the city's first and only B&B, is a lovely and cozy 1905 English-style home with frescoes of local scenes painted on the walls and a screened porch with a swing in the back. The five guestrooms, two with double whirlpools and one with a fireplace, run $89–139.

Minneopa State Park, detailed above, has 67 (six electric) decent campsites and one camper cabin. Most sites are shady and screened from the adjacent sites.

Food

The hip **Country Pub's Wine Café,** 301 N. River-front Dr., 507/345-1516, could probably make a go of it in Minneapolis's Warehouse District. The casual, vine-covered space serves over 100 wines by the glass, and though the menu is limited to panini sandwiches, pizza, and cheese plates—all averaging $7—it is still one of the most recommended restaurants in town. There is usually live jazz on weekends. Open Tues.–Fri. for lunch and Mon.–Sat. for dinner.

Stoney's, 900 N. Riverfront Dr., 507/387-4813, is a popular casual family restaurant with a touch of class. The something-for-everyone menu includes beef stroganoff, turkey walnut salad, barbecue pork ribs, beer-battered walleye, lasagna, and steak. Prices, averaging out to about $10, are quite reasonable. Open daily for lunch and dinner.

The **Mexican Village,** 1630 E. Madison Ave., 507/387-4455, with its festive mock-Mexican decor is the favorite of Mankatoans for south-of-the-border flavor. All the usual choices average $8. Open daily for lunch and dinner.

Tonn's, 617 S. Front St., 507/388-5710, has a standard Chinese menu, but since the owners are Cambodian they've thrown in some dishes from home like lemon grass chicken. Few items are over $6 in this no-frills joint, but the food is above average. Open Mon.–Sat. for lunch and dinner.

There's a pair of choices for top quality java: **Coffee Hag,** 329 N. Riverfront Dr., 507/387-5533, (open Tues.–Sun.) in Old Town; and the **Fillin' Station,** 634 S. Front St., 507/344-0345, (open Mon.–Sat.) downtown. The former offers more on the artistic end, while the latter has shady seating outside. Both are open early to late.

Shopping

Most day-to-day shopping is east of town along Madison Avenue and around the large **River Hills Mall,** 1850 Adams St., an area known as Hilltop. The downtown **Mankato Place** mall has few stores left. The most interesting shopping is along North Riverfront Drive in historic **Old Town,** where you'll find several gift shops plus two large antique stores: **Old Town Antiques,** 523 N. Riverfront Dr., 507/386-0600; and **Riverfront Antiques,** 1027 N. Riverfront Dr., 507/388-5152. There are even more antiques downtown along South Front Street, including **Generations Antiques,** 615 S. Front St., 507/345-7551; and **Earthly Remains,** 731 S. Front St., 507/388-5063, the city's largest. Local artists sell their wares at the small gift shop in the **Carnegie Art Center,** 120 Broad St. S., 507/625-2730. Best bet for books is the **Barnes & Noble,** 1859 Adams St., 507/386-0110, right across from the River Hills Mall, while **Once Read,** 629 S. Front St., 507/388-8144, downtown has a varied used inventory.

Information

Though tourists are a low priority, your best source of information is the **Mankato Area Chamber & Convention Bureau,** 112 Riverfront Dr., 507/345-4519 or 800/657-4733, www.mankato.com/cvb. Their office in the restored Union Depot is open Monday–Friday 8 A.M.–5 P.M. They also maintain a booth in the center of the River Hills Mall.

Transportation

Greyhound buses stop at the Econo Lodge on the north side of town once a day on their way to and from Minneapolis. It might be more convenient to travel with **Land to Air Express,** 434 Patterson Ave., 507/625-3977 or 888/736-9190, who do the trip to the airport four times a day during the week and thrice on weekends. A one-way fare is $24, and it is best to make reservations.

The city of Mankato's **Heartland Express,** 507/625-7433, is a limited local bus service available Monday through Saturday during the day. All routes, except for a campus circulator, stop at the Central Transfer Station (maps and schedules are posted here) on Cherry Street in front of the Mankato Place mall. The fare is $1.25.

For a taxi call **Kato Cab,** 507/388-7433.

NEW ULM

New Ulm revels in its Teutonic heritage. Sixty-six percent of the city's 13,594 residents claimed German ancestry in the last census, which gives New Ulm the nation's largest percentage of any single ethnicity amongst cities with 5,000 or more residents. The Brown County seat was settled in 1854 by two groups of German colonists

who established a "planned socialist utopian German community on the American prairie." Germans continued to emigrate to the growing city, and within 15 years the town had five breweries. The mother tongue could still be heard on city streets well into the 1960s, and even today a large percentage of locals can get by in this second language. A completely unrelated claim to fame is that most of the world's Velveeta is made here.

During the Dakota Conflict, nearly 1,000 settlers from across southwestern Minnesota sought shelter in New Ulm. The center of town was fortified and the volunteer soldiers sent to protect it managed to repel a pair of fierce attacks, though the second victory was a spectacularly hollow one as the Dakota warriors still managed to torch 190 of the town's 225 homes. So terrified were the settlers that children were kept in basements with gun powder kegs to be detonated if the Dakota should break through the island of defense. Recognizing the inevitable, Colonel Charles Flandrau retreated and led the terrified people to Mankato where they waited out the end of the war.

Sights

The better-than-average **Brown County Historical Museum,** 2 N. Broadway St., 507/233-2616, is most noteworthy for its layered German Renaissance design; the 1910 building originally served as the post office. The principal exhibits are the Dakota room, with a wonderful collection of exquisite artwork and displays about the Dakota Conflict, and Made in Brown County (aka the "beer, brats, and bricks exhibit") about the industries that the town grew up on. The museum is open weekdays 10 A.M.–5 P.M. and Saturday 1–5 P.M. year-round, plus Sunday 1–5 P.M. during the summer. Admission is $2.

The **Minnesota Music Hall of Fame,** 27 N. Broadway St., 507/354-7305, a block down from the museum pretty much contains just photos and concertinas. Though the inductees include such heavyweights as Bob Dylan, Bobby Vee, and Eddie Cochran, to enjoy yourself you need to be fan of Syl Liebl, "Whoopee John" Wilfahrt, and other polka kings. It is open Thursday–Saturday 10 A.M.–4 P.M. during the summer and admission is $3.

© TIM BEWER

the Brown County Historical Museum

The **Wanda Gág House,** 226 N. Washington St., 507/359-2632, is the childhood home of the famous children's book author and illustrator (*Millions of Cats, ABC Bunny, Tales From Grimm,* etc.), whose prints now hang in galleries around the world. The rooms of the restored house have family photos and some of her art hanging on the walls. While mostly of interest to fans of the artist, it also has a few unique architectural features worth a look. The home is open on summer weekends 1–5 P.M. Admission is free.

Another historic home open to tours is the 1887 Queen Anne Victorian **John Lind House,** 622 Center St., 507/354-8802, formerly the residence of the state's 14th governor and now a combination events center, office building, and museum. For a dollar you can take a quick tour of the house Friday–Sunday 1–4 P.M. between April and December; during the summer it is open the same hours all week long.

New Ulm's 45-foot-tall **Glockenspiel,** one of the few freestanding carillon clock towers in the world, stands at the north end of downtown at Minnesota Street and 4th Street North. The bells—all two tons worth—chime and the three-

foot-tall polka figures spin around daily at noon, 3 P.M., and 5 P.M., plus 10:30 A.M. and 1 P.M. during festivals.

The towering **Hermann Monument** (officially it's the National German-American Monument) was erected in 1897 to honor Hermann of Cherusci, who united the German tribes and drove out the Romans in 9 A.D. The 32-foot statue of the sword-bearing warrior stands at the top of a 102-foot tower, itself perched atop one of the city's highest points. The views across the town and the Minnesota River Valley from the top are fantastic, but the climb itself, a spiraling staircase to the top and then a wriggle through the trap door, is fun on its own. It is open daily 10 A.M.–4 P.M. during the summer, plus during Oktoberfest weekends. To get there follow Center St. west out of downtown to Hermann Heights Park.

Other Teutonic monuments include the **German-Bohemian Immigrant Monument** along German Street and 2nd Street North. The small statue (dwarfed by its massive pedestal) has a dual perspective: from the front the family is walking forward to a new life, but when viewed from behind they appear to be dancing. If you've ever traveled across central Europe, you'll recognize many of the design elements in the Baroque **Cathedral of the Holy Trinity,** 605 N. State St. Construction was completed in 1893, though interior work continued for another eight years. You can take a look underneath the twin spires daily 7 A.M.–5 P.M. A free **Walking Tour of Historic New Ulm** brochure available at the museum and the Visitor Information Center leads you past dozens of other historic structures in the downtown area.

The most noteworthy bit of German heritage in the city is the **August Schell Brewing Company,** 507/354-5528 or 800/770-5020. The popular local brewery has remained at the same lovely riverside setting and under the same family of owners since its founding in 1860. Though you only see a dash of the brewery's operations the one-hour tours are entertaining nonetheless, thanks to the knowledgeable beer fanatics leading them. During the summer, tours depart at 3 and 4 P.M. weekdays and on the hour between 1 and 4 P.M. on weekends; the rest of the year tours are only offered on Saturday at 1 P.M. and 2:30 P.M. Your $2 ticket includes a post-tour tasting session. Tours start in the Museum of Brewing (open daily noon–5 P.M. during the summer; free), which features old brewery and family items. Sitting behind the main brewhouse is the grand mansion Mr. Schell built for his retirement. Though the building is closed to the public, everyone is welcome to roam amongst the flowers, butterflies, and peacocks in the garden fronting the house. A deeryard sits in back. The grounds are open daily 8 A.M. to dusk. The brewery is located on the south side of town; take Broadway to 18th Street South and follow the signs.

Libations of the grape variety are made at **Morgan Creek Vineyards,** 507/947-3547, eight miles south of town; take Highway 15 to County Road 24. The gift shop and tasting room are open May through December, Friday and Saturday, 11 A.M.–9 P.M., and Sundays noon–5 P.M. Tours of the underground facility are available on the hour weekends 1–4 P.M. through October.

Flandrau State Park

Tucked into the Cottonwood River Valley on the west edge of the city is 805-acre Flandrau State Park, 507/233-9800. The most popular features are the campground (see Accommodations) and the large sand-bottomed swimming pool, but the eight miles of hiking trails aren't bad. The least used, though arguably the best, trails in the park are the forested **Old Island Loop** and **River Loop** in the south end. A steep set of steps climbs up the oak covered bluff and then gradually drops down into the valley again where the rest of the two-mile figure eight is generally level. This part of the park is your best bet for spotting wildlife. Probably the most popular trail is the half-mile round-trip, also eased by steps, up to the overlooks across the valley at the end of the **Indian Point Trail.** To enjoy the grasslands in the northern end of the park follow the **Bluebird Trail,** an easy half-mile loop inside of it, or the **Grassland Trail,** a one-mile loop around the outside of it that climbs to an overlook. The trails are groomed for cross-country skiing in the winter, and both skis and snowshoes are available for rent.

Events

The city's biggest shindig is **Heritagefest,** celebrating all things German during the second and third weekends in July. The massive event features entertainment on five stages (including bands from the homeland), a 100-unit parade, and the hundreds-strong "tuba mania" concert. Photogenic masked Narren stroll the festival grounds. Performing a cannon firing drill nightly is the **New Ulm Battery,** a most unusual relic. The 42-man, horse-drawn artillery unit was formed following the Dakota Conflict and is the only known Civil War outfit of its kind still in existence.

Of course, the city celebrates **Oktoberfest** with dancing, music, food, and free-flowing Schell's beer the first two weekends in October. New Ulm also celebrates **Fasching,** the "German Mardi Gras," designed to chase winter away, on the Saturday before Ash Wednesday, while Schell's Brewery hosts a **Bock Fest** on the same afternoon.

Accommodations

The **Holiday Inn,** 2101 S. Broadway St., 507/359-2941 or 800/465-4329, is nothing special, but it's easily the city's best hotel. Amenities include a pool, whirlpool, sauna, fitness center, and game room. Rates start at $79. The best of the city's cheapies is the **Colonial Inn,** 1315 N. Broadway St., 507/354-3128 or 888/215-2143, where older rooms are a good value at $35. The **Super 8,** 1901 S. Broadway St., 507/359-2400 or 800/800-8000, has more modern rooms from $53.

The city's pair of B&Bs are both in lovely homes. **The Bohemian,** 304 S. German St., 507/354-2268 or 866/499-6870, is the more flashy of the two. The 1899 East Lake Victorian is bedecked with stained glass and even has an Asian-inspired parlor. Each of the seven main house and carriage house guestrooms have private baths, and four have their own whirlpools. Prices run from $70–140. The homey **Deutsche Strasse,** 404 S. German St., 507/354-2005 or 866/225-9856, has five guestrooms, two with shared bath, priced at $79 and $89 in an 1894 home.

Flandrau State Park has a pair of campgrounds with 90 (35 electric) rather crowded and moderately shaded sites. The three walk-in sites here offer a semblance of solitude.

Food
German food is easy to come by in New Ulm. **Veigel's Kaiserhoff,** 221 N. Minnesota St., 507/359-2071, opened its doors in 1938 and is the city's oldest and most beloved restaurant. The meat-laden menu (a 1/3 pound hamburger leads the special weight watchers category, and vegetarians are completely out of luck) has both German and American favorites averaging $10 per platter. Open daily for lunch and dinner.

The more casual **20th Street Grill,** 1927 S. Broadway St., 507/359-1255, also features steak, seafood, and schnitzel, but selections like pasta, gyros, and a salad bar give the menu variety. Entrées average about $9, and they also have a Friday fish fry. Open daily for lunch and Mon.–Sat. for dinner.

You can get a filling meal for around $5 at the no-nonsense **Ulmer Café,** 115 N. Minnesota St., 507/354-8122. It's a good choice for breakfast. Open daily for breakfast and lunch.

The city's two Chinese restaurants, **Main Jiang House,** 206 N. Minnesota St., 507/354-1228;

and **King Buffet,** 400 N. Minnesota St., 507/354-6668, serve ordinary small town Chinese. Both have the same owners and recipes and almost exactly the same menu; the main difference is that the former charges a little bit less and the latter has a larger buffet. Both are very cheap and open daily for lunch and dinner.

The Backerei, 27 S. Minnesota St., 507/354-6011, has really good and really cheap confections, while the small **Cornerstone Coffee,** 213 S. Minnesota St., 507/354-5552, has the best java in town. Both are open Monday–Saturday for breakfast and lunch.

Shopping
Downtown remains the city's principal shopping district, though many stores are stretched out along Broadway Ave. to the south. Shop to a serenade of polka music and cuckoo clocks at **Domeiers,** 1020 S. Minnesota St., 507/354-4231, an old-world store bursting with imported German goods. The **GutenTag Haus,** 127 N. Minnesota St., 507/233-4287, and **Christmas Haus,** 203 N. Minnesota St., 507/233-4350, also sell German gifts. Old World heritage of a different sort is available at **The Sausage Shop,** 301 N. Broadway St., 507/354-3300. Dozens of varieties, from kielbasa to blood sausage to wild rice brats, are made in-house.

The tiny **Council for the Arts in New Ulm (CANU),** 220 N. Minnesota St., 507/233-2268, sells and displays work from local artists. **Antiques Plus,** 117 N. Broadway St., 507/359-1090, is the city's largest antique shop. **Bookshelves & Coffeecups,** 123 N. Minnesota St., 507/359-4600, has a decent selection of used books and good espresso, while **Rieke's Books,** 13 N. Minnesota St., 507/354-7833, has both new and used titles, including a good local interest section.

Information and Services
The New Ulm Chamber of Commerce's **Visitor Information Center,** 1 N. Minnesota St., 507/233-4300 or 888/463-9856, www.newulm .com, is helpful, knowledgeable, and friendly. They are open Monday 8 A.M.–6 P.M., Tuesday–Friday 8 A.M.–5 P.M., Saturday 10 A.M.–

4 P.M. year-round, plus Sunday noon–4 P.M. during the summer.

The **Larkspur Market,** 16 N. Minnesota St., 507/359-2500, a combination gift shop and coffeehouse, has public Internet access.

NEW ULM TO THE SOURCE

Harkin Store

This wonderful little state historic site really transports you back to a bygone era. The village of West Newton, a steamboat stop halfway between New Ulm and Fort Ridgely, was a bustling place in 1870 with mills, hotels, saloons, a school, and, of course, a general store. When the railroad came through in 1873 it bypassed West Newton and the town, which was also suffering from a grasshopper plague, quickly faded away. The store didn't close until 1901, but it did little business in the ensuing years, serving almost exclusively as the local post office. The store shut its doors with much of the original stock—cigars, fabric, boxes of soap, nails, and patent medicines—still on the shelves and costumed staff, reliving the heydays of the 1870s, can give you prices and explain what some of the unusual gadgets are for. The store is eight miles northwest of New Ulm on County Road 21. Throughout the summer it is open Tuesday–Sunday; during May, September, and the first half of October it is open on weekends only; closed the rest of the year. The hours are 10 A.M.–5 P.M. Admission is just $1. Call 507/354-8666 for information.

Fort Ridgely State Park

Fort Ridgely was built in 1853 at the edge of the newly created Dakota reservation lands to keep the peace as settlers poured into southwest Minnesota. Nine years later the fort was attacked twice during the Dakota Conflict, but neither offensive was successful. The Fort had no stockade, just six cannons, and with ravines on three sides was in a poor defensive position, so had the 1,000 or so Dakota been better organized or more aggressive they surely could have overtaken the 180 soldiers bunkered down here. The fort became obsolete after the war since the Dakota had been exiled, and it was abandoned

just a decade later. The commissary, the only remaining building, has been restored by the Minnesota Historical Society and now houses displays about life in the fort. The center is only open during the summer Tuesday–Saturday 10 A.M. to 5 P.M. and Sunday noon–5 P.M., though the grounds are accessible year-round. The **Fort Ridgely Historical Festival,** a Civil War-era reenactment with music, demonstrations, and an 1860s baseball game, is held every fourth weekend in June.

Much of the rest of the 584-acre park is taken up by a nine-hole golf course with artificial greens. Eleven miles of hiking trail cross the park and those on the east side are hilly and forested, while those through the prairie to the west are generally level. All but a mile are open to horses, and four miles are groomed for cross-country skiing, though the sledding hill (inner tubes can be rented for $2) is the more popular. The campground has two sections. The modern camp has 22 sites (eight electric) jam-packed against the road, though on the plus side some are alongside Fort Ridgely Creek. The quieter rustic camp has 17 shady and widely spaced sites. Horseback riders also have their own camp. Call 507/426-7840 for more information.

Morton

A pair of historic sites and a large casino lure tourists to this small town. It developed alongside the granite quarries first dug here in 1886, and the Cold Spring Granite Company still works several of them on a limited basis.

Just north of town is the **Birch Coulee Battlefield,** 507/697-6321, scene of one of the bloodiest battles of the Dakota Conflict. Though the site amounts to little more than an empty field with a few sticks staked into it, this is by far the most interesting site relating to war because the design lets you imagine yourself as an observer at the real event. Captain Joseph Anderson and his men from Fort Ridgely were out on a mission to bury the civilians killed over the previous two weeks. Wrongly assuming that the Dakota had left the area, they set up camp on a hill near Birch Coulee Creek on the evening of September 1, 1862. During the night, 200

LOWER AND UPPER SIOUX RESERVATIONS

Lower Sioux
Total Area - 2.7 sq. miles
Tribally Owned - 100 percent
Total Population - 335
Native Population - 294
Tribal Enrollment - 930

Upper Sioux
Total Area - 2 sq. miles
Tribally Owned - 100 percent
Total Population - 57
Native Population - 47
Tribal Enrollment - 369

The original Dakota reservations in Minnesota, as established by the Traverse des Sioux and Mendota treaties, stretched along the Minnesota River, ten miles wide on each side. The Lower Sioux Reservation extended from Little Rock Creek (just west of the Harkin Store) to the Yellow Medicine River while the Upper Sioux lands continued from Yellow Medicine up to Big Stone Lake. After the Dakota were expelled from Minnesota following the 1862 Dakota Conflict (see The Dakota Conflict earlier in the chapter) some 7,000 people fled to South Dakota or were resettled in Nebraska. In the 1880s a few Dakota families defied the government and returned to their homeland in the Minnesota River Valley. By the end of the decade the federal government recognized these settlements, though the reservations weren't formalized until the 1930s, at which time they were granted some additional lands.

The Lower Sioux Community, across the river from Morton, got its start in 1884 when Chief Good Thunder returned from South Dakota and purchased 80 acres near where Bishop Henry Whipple had run his mission, a spot traditionally known to the Dakota as Cansa'yapi (Where They Marked the Trees Red). Whipple was a faithful friend of the Dakota and the man who had convinced President Lincoln to spare the lives of most of those condemned for their roles in the uprising. Good Thunder and other returning Dakota were soon joined by a few families who had managed to remain in the state under the protection of influential fur trader Alexander Faribault. The tribe's major industry, besides their Jackpot Junction casino, is traditional hand-thrown, hand-painted pottery.

The families of the Upper Sioux community returned to Pejuhutazizi Kapi (The Place Where They Dig for Yellow Medicine) near the far southeast end of their former reservations lands, just south of Granite Falls. Though not as profitable as most others in the state their Firefly Creek Casino has been a vital economic stimulant for the band.

Dakota warriors, led by Wamditanka (Big Eagle), surrounded them and attacked just before dawn. The Dakota kept the U.S. soldiers under siege for 36 hours, killing 20 men and 90 horses in the process. They only fled when reinforcements arrived the next afternoon. Quotes from Captain Anderson and Chief Wamditanka, along with sketches done by a soldier, provide a full accounting of the battle. Admission is free. A **Gathering of Kinship Pow-wow** is held at Birch Coulee in early September. The field is three miles north of Morton; take Highway 71 and follow the signs.

To learn more about the causes of the war and the history of the Dakota, cross the river to the **Lower Sioux Agency,** 507/697-6321. The post, established in 1853, served as the distribution center for food and funds called for by the Traverse des Sioux Treaty. It was also an educational center for the few Dakota who wanted to learn the European way of life. In their first organized attack of the war, the Dakota looted and then destroyed the post on August 18, 1862. Just one building, a restored 1861 warehouse built of stone, remains standing, though interpretive signs along the trails point out the locations and functions of others, while life at the agency and other aspects of the Dakota culture and resistance are discussed in the visitors center. Many special events reliving Dakota, fur trade, and pioneer culture are held during the year. The agency is located on County Road 2, about a mile east of the casino. It is open Monday–Saturday 10 A.M.–5 P.M. and Sunday noon–5 P.M. from May through Labor Day, daily 1–5 P.M. in September and October, and Saturday and Sunday 1–5 P.M. December–February. Admission is $4.

The Lower Sioux Community's **Jackpot Junction,** 507/644-3000 or 800/946-2274, was Minnesota's first casino. Besides gaming this busy complex has three restaurants, hosts live music every weekend, and includes the nearby **Dacotah Ridge Golf Course,** 507/644-5050, one of the state's best. The **Lower Sioux Lodge** hotel has standard rooms for $75 and suites for $200, plus 40 RV sites in the summer. The **Lower Sioux Community Wacipi** (powwow) is held the second full weekend in June. Just west of town at the junction of Hwys. 71 and 19 is the **Morton Inn,** 507/697-6498 or 800/245-9800. The modern rooms aren't fancy but a bargain at $40, and they have a free 24-hour shuttle to the casino.

In town you'll find a couple of gift shops and the **Renville County Museum,** 441 N. Park Dr., 507/697-6147, with the usual assortment of historic artifacts. On the grounds are a farm machinery shed, a blacksmith shop, and a pair of one-room schoolhouses, one furnished as it was in the day and the other housing a large collection of Red Wing pottery and Depression-era dishes and glassware. The main building is open Tuesday–Friday 10 A.M.–4 P.M., plus Saturday 10 A.M.–4 P.M. and Sunday 1–4 P.M. during the summer. Admission is $1. On a hill near the museum are two fifty-foot granite columns commemorating those who died at the Birch Coulee battlefield and six Dakota who risked their own lives to save many others during the uprising.

Redwood Falls

The waterfalls that this city took its name from are found in **Alexander Ramsey Park.** Larger than the city itself "The Park" has six miles of trail, two of them paved for bikes, winding past Ramsey Falls, a beautiful dual waterfall, and the smaller Redwood Falls. Also in the park are some quiet picnic areas, a fitness course, 18-hole golf course, and a sad little zoo. Ramsey Creek is stocked with brown trout each spring.

A half-mile west of town on Highway 19 is the **Redwood County Museum,** 507/637-3329, with 27 rooms full of historical artifacts and dis-

plays in the former Redwood County Poor Farm. Highlights of the diverse collection, quite large for such a small town, include a foot-and-a-half-long meteorite, frightening old medical instruments, and dozens of mounted birds. There is also a small display about Richard W. Sears. The founder of the Sears, Roebuck Co. was the depot agent for the Minneapolis and St. Louis Railroad in North Redwood when he sold his first shipment of watches in 1886 and realized that there was money to be made in the mail-order business. Out back is a one-room schoolhouse and building full of antique cars and farm machinery. The museum is open Thursday–Sunday 1–5 P.M. May through September. Admission is $2. Downtown at East 2nd Street and South Jefferson is the 1860s **Redwood County Jail,** currently being restored by the Redwood County Historical Society. The historical society's other project is the **Gilfillan Estate,** 507/249-3451, eight miles southeast of town on Highway 67. In 1882 St. Paul lawyer and businessman Charles Duncan Gilfillan left the big city and purchased 13,000 acres here to raise cattle. Remarkably, the home he built in 1882 was turned over to the historical society with all of its possessions, much of it dating back to the 1920s. It's like a visit to your grandparents' house, if they happened to be wealthy farmers out on the prairie and had a large collection of antique farm equipment in the outbuildings. The grounds also host FarmFest, an annual farmers' convention, in early August. It is open summer weekends 1–4:30 P.M. and admission is $3.

Mad-scientist types arrive in town the second weekend in June to show off their latest creations at the **Minnesota Inventors Congress,** 507/637-2344 or 800/468-3681, the nation's oldest invention convention. While none of the products displayed here have changed the world, many will end up on store shelves after being examined by manufacturers who arrive incognito.

The cheapest lodging in town is the simple but spotless **Motel 71,** 1020 E. Bridge St. (U.S. 71), 507/637-2981 or 800/437-4789, where rooms are just $35. A step up is the nearby **Dakota Inn,** 410 W. Park Rd., 507/637-5444 or 800/287-5443, run by the Lower Sioux Community of Dakota, with rooms from $54 plus a pool, whirlpool, and a free shuttle to the Jackpot Junction Casino. **Alexander Ramsey Park** has a 28-site (15 electric) first-come, first-served campground; the price is $10. The **Calf Fiend Café,** 220 E. 2nd St., 507/637-3728, a bright-yellow coffeehouse, is a popular place for lunch. Besides the usual long list of drinks they serve soups, sandwiches, and pasta salads. They are open Monday–Saturday from very early to very late.

Upper Sioux Agency State Park

Perched on the riverside bluffs where the Yellow Medicine River joins the Minnesota, this 1,280-acre park affords some quality views of the Minnesota River Valley, but was actually established for its historical significance. This was the site of the Yellow Medicine (aka Upper Sioux) Agency, established in 1853 to administer the terms of the Traverse des Sioux Treaty. Food and cash, as provided by the treaty, were doled out here, and some Dakota families came to learn modern farming methods, though most rejected attempts to "civilize" them. By 1862 the site had grown into a small village, but the warring Dakota torched it during their failed uprising that summer. The local Dakota opposed the conflict and helped lead residents to safety. While the story is interesting, the remains are not. Only one brick employee duplex still stands; historical signs mark the foundations of others. For an actually interesting bit of history come the first weekend in August for the **Upper Sioux Wacipi** (powwow).

Though small, the park has a lot of natural diversity, ranging from restored prairies to forest to wetlands, and 18 miles of hiking and horseback riding trail leads through it all. In winter most of the trails are claimed by snowmobilers, though cross-country skiers have two miles of groomed track and the office also rents snowshoes. The long, steep sledding hill is one of the park's most popular features. The Yellow Medicine River Campground, on the edge of the prairie, has 34 widely spaced sites (14 electric), including three walk-ins, in a mix of shade and sun. A pair of authentic tepees are available between Memorial Day weekend and the end of October for $20—they are very popular, so reserve well in advance. The Riverside Campground is an open

grassy area along the Minnesota River with all sites available first-come, first-served. There is also a horse-rider campground. Call 320/564-4777 for additional park information.

Granite Falls

The founders of this city of just over 3,000 came to run mills along the fast-dropping Minnesota River, and even today a hydroelectric plant still generates the town's power. **Andrew J. Volstead,** former mayor of Granite Falls and long-serving Minnesota congressman, is best remembered as the author of the Volstead Act, which established enforcement provisions for Prohibition. He wrote the bill not as a crusader, but only because as chair of the House Judiciary Committee the job fell in his lap. Volstead was most proud of his work to establish farmer cooperatives in the United States. His home at 163 9th Avenue has been restored and is a National Historic Landmark. While it now houses a pair of social service organizations, some informational panels about Volstead and the history of cooperatives are crammed into the front parlor. You can view them if the offices are open. The rest of the city's history, from its ancient geology to pioneer life, is laid out at the **Yellow Medicine County Historical Museum,** 320/564-4479, on the south edge of town at the junction of Hwys. 23 and 67. There are many Native American displays inside, and an old log cabin and log church sit behind the main building. The museum is open Tuesday–Friday 11 A.M.–3 P.M. and Saturday–Sunday noon–4 P.M. from mid-May to mid-October. Admission is $1. Five miles southeast of town on Highway 67 is the small **Firefly Creek Casino,** 320/564-2121, operated by the Upper Sioux Dakota.

The **Super 8,** 845 U.S. 212 W., 320/564-4075 or 800/800-8000, isn't fancy, but it's the best hotel in town. Rooms are $59. The campground at **Memorial Park,** 320/564-3011, about a mile southeast of town along Highway 67, is sub-par, but on the plus side tent sites cost just $3, while electric sites are $7. **DeToy's,** 845 U.S. 212 W., 320/564-2280, is your basic American family restaurant with broasted chicken the specialty and most items under $6. Breakfast is served all day. Open daily for breakfast, lunch, and dinner. **Greyhound** buses stop at the Tri County Co-op, 1297 Granite St., 320/564-2525.

Swensson Farm Museum

Olof Swensson, a Norwegian immigrant, settled here in 1873. Visiting his 22-room brick home, built in 1901, is like stepping back in time; his family lived here until the 1960s, and many of the original furnishings remain. Also on the site are his ingeniously constructed timber-framed barn and the family burial plot. During your visit you will also learn a little about Olof's dabbling as a writer, preacher, and political activist. The museum is located halfway between Granite Falls and Montevideo on County Road 15, three miles southeast of the hamlet of Wegdahl. It is open Sundays 1–5 P.M. during the summer and admission is $3. Call 320/269-7636 for information.

Montevideo

Montevideo's founders were so impressed by the views of the Minnesota and Chippewa River Valleys that they borrowed the name of the Uruguayan capital, which in Latin means From the Mount I See. They now maintain a sister-city relationship with their southern counterpart, and the downtown plaza is named in honor of José Artigas, the father of Uruguayan independence. The 11-foot bronze statue of Artigas was a gift of the Uruguayan people in 1949.

The city's primary attraction is **Historic Chippewa City,** 320/269-7636, an interesting collection of relocated and restored historic buildings. The two dozen structures include a general store, blacksmith shop, one-room schoolhouse, firehouse, newspaper office, and bank. Each is filled with tools of the trade creating what approximates a late-19th-century village. The museum, southwest of downtown at the junction of Hwys. 59 and 7, is open Monday–Friday 9 A.M.–5 P.M. and Saturday and Sunday 1–5 P.M. from May through September (though no weekend hours after Labor Day). Admission is $3. Just south of downtown along 1st Street is the **Milwaukee Road Heritage Center.** It is still a work in progress (thus it has no set hours yet), but the restored 1901 Chicago, Milwaukee & St. Paul Railroad Depot houses a small collection of rail-road-related artifacts, and across the street are a few old railroad cars and a still-functional turntable. A mile to the east on Hwy. 212 is a 51-foot granite obelisk and historical marker commemorating the release of 269 Dakota-held captives and the surrender of some 1,200 warriors at the end of the Dakota Conflict. The small park, now known as **Camp Release,** was the site of Col. Henry Sibley's military camp.

If you will be staying here you've got several good options. The **Country Inn,** 1805 Hwy. 7 E., 320/269-8000 or 888/201-1746, is the best hotel for many miles around. Rooms go from $90, and amenities include a pool and whirlpool. Just across the street the **Viking Motel,** 1428 Hwy. 7 E., 320/269-6545 or 800/670-0777, is the cheapest in town. Rooms are small and simple, but clean and cost just $33. The **Lagoon Park Campground,** 320/269-7572, along the Chippewa River just northwest of downtown, is a shady, better-than-average municipal campground. The 10 campsites with electric and water hookups are just $10. Four miles northwest of town the **Broodio at Moonstone Farm,** 9060 40th St. SW, 320/269-8971, offers a unique and relaxing getaway. Richard and Audrey Arner run an antibiotic- and hormone-free beef farm and have converted their old henhouse into a simple cottage heated by a wood-burning stove. Many writers and artists come here for the peace and quiet. Guests can use the bathroom facilities in the main house or the nearby outhouse and get a simple continental breakfast in the morning.

The locals' runaway favorite for dining out is the fantastic **Valentino's,** 110 S. 1st St., 320/269-5106, probably the classiest small town café you'll ever find, yet none of their homemade sandwiches and salads are over $6. They are open Monday–Saturday for breakfast and lunch, plus Sunday lunch outside the summer months. An even bigger surprise is **Java River,** 210 S. 1st St., 320/269-7106, a coffeehouse and bakery that would make it in the Twin Cities. Besides the roster of coffees, they serve low-priced soups and sandwiches, including some veggie options, and ice cream. They also offer Internet access and sometimes host live music. Open Mon.–Sat for breakfast, lunch, and dinner.

Lac qui Parle Mission

Joseph Renville, an independent fur trader with a French father and Dakota mother, established his trading post here in 1826. A decade later Renville invited missionaries to educate and Christianize the Dakota, though few accepted the religious or cultural overtures. The mission was shut down in 1854, but during their time at Lac qui Parle, Renville helped the missionaries write the first translation of the Bible into the Dakota language and complete the first Dakota dictionary. Inside the small wooden church, a reconstruction of the 1841 original, are a few displays about the Dakota, their language, and the missionaries' work. The first church bell to ring in Minnesota hung in the steeple of this church and what is believed to be that bell is on display. Almost a mile up County Road 32 is an overlook of the site of **Fort Renville,** his original fur trading post, which operated until the 1830s. It's most interesting for the lake view, especially when migrating geese congregate here in the fall. The mission is open daily 8 A.M.–8 P.M. from late April through Labor Day and admission is free. Call 320/269-7636 for additional information.

Lac qui Parle State Park

Lac qui Parle State Park, just down the road from the mission, sits at the foot of the Lake That Talks, as the Dakota called it. But it wasn't spirits they were listening to, it was migrating geese. Flocks of up to 200,000 gather on this natural widening of the Minnesota River during the late October peak, more than any other spot in the state, and their collective honking is an astonishingly loud experience. Though the park is only just over 1,000 acres in size, the adjacent **Lac qui Parle Wildlife Management Area** protects some 35,000 acres along a 25-mile-long stretch of the river. This huge and well-managed preserve accounts for the remarkable abundance of not just geese, but all wildlife. Other notable species nesting here include white pelican, prairie chicken, and bald eagle. The latter congregate here in the winter and can be seen feeding on the Minnesota River below the Lac qui Parle (aka Churchill) dam. They also feast on geese that overwinter on the lake.

The park has six miles of trails for hiking, horseback riding, and cross-country skiing; all are flat and easy, though they are often a bit wet. The 2.5 miles of loops through the bottomland forest behind the campground are beautiful and some of the best wildlife-watching trails anywhere in Minnesota. Canoeing down the Lac qui Parle and Minnesota Rivers or along the shore of the lake itself is another good way to see animals. Canoes can be rented and shuttle service arranged down by the dam. If you are just looking to relax, there is a small, sandy beach. The campground has 42 (21 electric) widely spaced, though largely shadeless, sites; better are the 11 walk-in sites nearby. Horseback riders have a separate camp all to themselves. For any questions call 320/752-4736.

Milan

Exactly why this tiny village, founded by Norwegians, was named after the Italian city is unknown. Some of its Scandinavian past is on display at the **Arv Hus Museum,** 236 Main St., 320/734-4868, an eclectic little collection of local history and Norwegian art in an old harness shop. It is open "by chance or appointment" and admission is free. Around the corner from the museum is Karen Jenson's **Trestuen Gallery & Studio,** 104 Lincoln, 320/734-4715. She sells her own rosemaling, as well as wood carvings and other Scandinavian crafts from several local artists. The town is also home to the surprising **Milan Village Arts School,** 320/734-4952, which offers classes in various folk arts from lefse making to Australian dot painting.

Big Stone National Wildlife Refuge

Named by the Dakota for the tall granite outcroppings rising along the river, Big Stone's 11,521 acres are a vital haven for migrating birds and a magnet for bird-watchers. The bottomland forests and grasslands (including 1,700 acres of prairie) fronting 11.5 miles of the Minnesota River host 240 bird species over the course of a year, most notably waterfowl and warblers. The easiest way to see the refuge and its inhabitants is along the five-mile **Prairie Drive Auto Tour.** The easy .75-mile **Rock Outcrop Hiking Trail** is also worthwhile. Along both you'll learn about local history and ecology, see the prairie, and get a chance to climb the beautiful, lichen encrusted granite mounds. For the best views of the huge autumnal waterfowl concentrations, drive along the **East Pool Wildlife Observation Drive** off Highway 75 at the refuge's eastern border. All other refuge roads not posted as restricted are also open to hiking. A canoe is a great way to explore the refuge, though paddling is only allowed from mid-April through the end of September. A worthwhile trip down the Minnesota River begins at the main entrance (along Highway 75, two miles south of Ortonville) and continues down to the Highway 75 bridge. The NWR abuts the Lac qui Parle WMA so you can continue the scenic river trip much farther down river.

Ortonville

Ortonville, which grew up on granite quarrying and corn canning, sits at the foot of Big Stone Lake. The narrow 30-mile lake is the source of the Minnesota River and also forms the Minnesota-South Dakota border. The main building of the **Big Stone County Museum,** 320/839-3359, houses a hodge-podge collection of antique items for home and work, plus a few locally discovered fossils and a handful of Native American artifacts. The outdoor displays include a furnished 19th-century log cabin and blacksmith shop. The highlight is old Artichoke Lake General Store building, which is now filled with over 500 stuffed birds, most from the area, and thousands of Native American arrow and axe heads. The museum is located southeast of town at the junction of Hwys. 12 and 75. It is open Monday–Saturday 10 A.M.–5 P.M. and Sunday 1–4 P.M. Admission is free.

The **Econo Lodge,** 320/839-2414 or 800/553-2666, out on Highway 75, is Ortonville's best hotel. Large rooms are $55. Most locals eat at the no-frills **Too Mad Café,** 204 2nd St. NW, 320/839-2470, and you should, too, since the food is good, the portions are large, and the prices are low. Open Mon.–Sat. for breakfast and lunch and Thurs.–Sat. for dinner.

Big Stone Lake State Park

Big Stone Lake State Park, created in 1961 to preserve some land on the lakeshore before it was all developed, is a three-for-one deal. The first unit you come to, the **Meadowbrook Area,** contains most of the park's 990 acres and has the most facilities, including the basic 37-site (10 electric) campground. Right next to the campground is a beach and you can also rent canoes. The half-mile Bluebird Trail, noted for its spring and summer wildflowers, has two easy loops through a prairie restoration. Eleven miles farther up the road is the smaller **Bonanza Area.** Much of this unit is covered by a rare undisturbed glacial till hill prairie and oak savanna and has been designated a Scientific and Natural Area. The Hiking Club Trail is a wooded half-mile loop with a few small hills. It passes tiny Benkowski Falls along the way. Between the two, a mile from the Bonanza unit, the **Overlook Area** is just that, an overlook perched high above Big Stone Lake. Both the Meadowbrook and Bonanza units have lakeside picnic areas and boat launches. The majority of visitors are here to fish—Big Stone Lake is noted for walleye, but also yields bluegill, perch, northern, and channel catfish. Call 320/839-3663 for more park information.

Browns Valley

Continue to the end of Big Stone Lake and you'll pass several apple orchards before ending up in this small village stuck out at the end of Minnesota's hump. Browns Valley was founded in 1866 by Joseph R. Brown, a leader in the formation of the Minnesota Territory, cowriter of its constitution, and prominent lobbyist of the federal government on behalf of the local Dakota. His son Sam made a famous "Paul Revere Ride" that year to warn settlers of threatened attacks by the Dakota. **Sam Brown Memorial Park,** 320/695-2110,contains a restored log cabin that served as his home, a trading post, stagecoach stop, tavern, and inn. It now houses a tiny Sam Brown and local history museum. The park also has a furnished one-room schoolhouse. The buildings are open during the summer Friday–Sunday 1–6 P.M. and admission is free. Famous amongst archaeologists, **Browns Valley Man** was discovered in 1933 by amateur archaeologist William H. Jensen in the gravel ridge just south of town. The skeleton has been dated to 8,000 B.C., making it one of the oldest found in the Americas.

South of the River

LAURA INGALLS WILDER HISTORIC HIGHWAY

Walnut Grove, twice the home of the famous children's author and the setting of the popular TV show *Little House on the Prairie,* is one of the most popular destinations in southwest Minnesota. A few other towns along Highway 14 also have Laura Ingalls Wilder connections. Whatever you do, don't miss Jeffers Petroglyphs.

Sleepy Eye

Although the real Ingalls family likely passed through here on their way to Walnut Grove, they had next to no connection to the town. The TV family, however, visited often and Laura even married Almonzo Wilder there—in real life the marriage took place in De Smet, South Dakota. The village took its name from Sleepy Eye Lake on the northwest edge of town, which honors the Sisseton Dakota chief Ish-Tak-Ha-Ba (Sleepy Eyes) who lived here near the end of his life. Remembered fondly by explorers and settlers as "a friend of the Whites" he died in South Dakota in 1860, but in 1902 his remains were returned to his homeland, and he now rests below a 50-foot-tall granite obelisk in front of the **Sleepy Eye Depot Museum,** 100 Oak St., 507/794-5053. The museum itself has a small collection of random artifacts from the town's past and present, including plenty of Sleepy Eye Milling Co. memorabilia, now hot collectors' items. It is open Tuesday–Saturday 2–5 P.M. from May through mid-December and admission is free. A bronze larger-than-life statue of the chief stands across the street next to the post office. **Del Monte Foods,** 507/794-2151, have been in Sleepy Eye since 1930, and they offer tours of their pea and corn canning facility on the west edge of town during the production season, generally June through October. You must call ahead, though you can often visit on short notice. Tours generally take an hour, though what you see depends on what's going on in the plant on the day you visit.

The best hotel in town is the **Best Western Inn of Seven Gables,** 1100 Main St. E., 507/794-5390 or 800/852-9451, where $79 will get you a large room plus use of the pool and whirlpool. The 20 rooms at the **Orchid Inn,** 500 Burnside St. SE, 507/794-3211 or 800/245-493, go for as little as $20 and, while you get what you pay for, you could do a lot worse. The **W. W. Smith Inn,** 101 Linden St. SW, 507/794-5661 or 800/799-5661, is a friendly B&B with four guestrooms (some private bath, some shared) and a carriage house with hot tub priced from $85. The 1901 Queen Anne Victorian is filled with stained glass, carved woodwork, and period furnishings. Camping is free at the eight shady sites in **Sportsmen's Park** off Highway 4 on the north side of the lake. The handful of no-frills cafés on Main Street are your best bet for breakfast or lunch, while for dinner, other than fast food and bar food, your only choice is the old-fashioned supper club at the Orchid Inn with walleye, beef stroganoff, and filet mignon for around $10 and lighter fare like burgers and spaghetti for half that.

Sod House on the Prairie

Two authentically constructed soddies sit in the middle of a restored tallgrass prairie, and it's the closest you'll come to seeing how the pioneer families of Laura Ingalls' day lived. The main house is furnished with period pieces, and interpretive signs on the grounds explain what Laura Ingalls' real life was like. To get the full pioneer experience don't just visit, spend the night. You cook on a wood-burning stove, read by oil burning lamps, carry in your own water and, yes, use a sod outhouse. If you want, there is even period clothing to wear. Though obviously not for everyone, the house is much nicer than you would expect and has a wood floor (the Ingalls' was earthen) and plaster walls. The homes are open daily 10 A.M.–5 P.M. from April through October, though B&B checkout is noon so you might not get to look in the main house until after then. Admission $3. Spending the night costs $100 for a couple, plus $10 for each additional person,

© TIM BEWER

Jeffers Petroglyphs

and children of all ages are welcome. The Sod House is just east of Sanborn; take Magnolia Ave. south of Highway 14. For information, reservations, or to arrange a guided tour contact the ultra-friendly McCone family at 507/723-5138.

Jeffers Petroglyphs

Over 2,000 ancient petroglyphs carved by Native Americans on an exposed shelf of bedrock lie exposed on this 80-acre state historic site. Many of the buffalo, deer, elk, turtles, thunderbirds, humans, weapons, and other similar subjects were cut 5,000 years ago, while it appears others are as recent as the 1750s. The glyphs likely served a ceremonial purpose, and this remains sacred ground for many tribes—religious ceremonies are still held here on occasion. While signs point out many of the shapes, scan the rock patiently as you walk amongst them and others will just appear to you. They are most dramatic during the long shadows of early morning and late evening. Even if there weren't a single carving this would be a worthwhile trip, as the small islands of pink quartzite surrounded by the sea of prairie makes this is one of the most beautiful spots in Minnesota. It is also a great place to see the subtleties of prairie ecology since each of the three main types of prairie—wet, mesic, and dry—are represented, and together they contain well over 100 species of flower and forb. Amongst the many plants are prickly pear cactus and the federally-threatened prairie bush clover. The 33-acres surrounding the rocks are native, while the rest is a very healthy restoration.

After appreciating the glyphs most people just return to the parking lot, but if you continue around the site on the mile-long trail you'll pass a shiny and smooth "buffalo rub" (bison would brush/rub themselves up against rocks to help shed their thick winter coats). The visitors center has a few displays about life on the prairie and an artistic, but not very informative, multimedia presentation. Outside the center you can take aim at a Styrofoam buffalo with an atlatl—a weapon that predates the bow and arrow.

Jeffers is located 12 miles south of Sanborn. Take Highway 71 to County Road 10 and follow the signs. During May and September it is open Friday and Saturday 10 A.M.–5 P.M. and Sunday noon–5 P.M. Summer hours are Monday–Friday

10 A.M.–5 P.M., Saturday 10 A.M.–8 P.M., and Sunday noon–8 P.M. Admission is $4. Call 507/628-5591 for information.

Walnut Grove

Walnut Grove was settled and grew like just about every other small prairie town in southwestern Minnesota and would be as unremarkable as the rest of them if it wasn't for one former resident.

LITTLE HOUSE *OF* THE PRAIRIE

E arly settlers on the prairie built sod houses for one logical reason—there weren't very many trees. But, out on the frontier a dirt dwelling had many other practical advantages. They were strong, dirt-cheap (pardon the pun), and could be quickly taken down and reassembled elsewhere should the need arise. The sod bricks, cut three to four inches thick, were held together by the dense network of prairie roots and formed remarkably durable walls and ceilings. The two-foot thick walls not only made a sturdy home, but a climate controlled one: the effective insulation kept them warm in the winter and cool in the summer. Soddies did have a downside, of course. They could suffer smoke drafts (especially irritating considering that buffalo chips were the primary fuel source) and they would get damp if the roof wasn't up to snuff. Practical matters aside, living in a well built soddy was not the unpleasant experience one would expect. Interior walls would be smoothed down with an ax and covered with lime whitewash, clay, canvas, or newspaper. Most pioneers also built a window or two into their homes. Although most settlers were very poor over time they could enhance their soddy with all the comforts of a city home.

Eventually railroads brought cheap lumber to the prairie and sod walls were slowly replaced with traditional wood frame construction, though some farming families didn't give up their soddies until the middle of the 20th century. The art of sod construction hasn't died out completely: the Sod House on the Prairie bed-and-breakfast not far from Walnut Grove lets you live like the resourceful pioneers for a night.

Laura Ingalls Wilder, author of the "Little House" series of books that inspired the TV show *Little House on the Prairie,* arrived as a seven-year-old girl and lived here for five years (1874-76 and 1877-79). The Ingalls family and other homesteaders who made their way west to this spot along the banks of Plum Creek found rich soil and plentiful game, which made the difficulty of living in the prairie frontier worthwhile. The family lived alternately out on the farm and in town where Charles Ingalls worked various jobs. The settlement quickly grew into a proper village, and Walnut Grove was incorporated in 1879. Charles was elected the first justice of the peace, but later that year his insatiable wanderlust and lack of farming success prompted a move to De Smet in the Dakota Territory. Laura described life here in her book *On the Banks of Plum Creek.* Although her books, written while she was in her 60s and 70s, are fictional and were never meant to be historical records, many of the episodes she describes really did happen or are based loosely on real events. The TV show, however, just borrowed a few names and general events and is nearly 100 percent fiction.

The real story of Laura and her family, both in Walnut Grove and elsewhere, is told at the **Laura Ingalls Wilder Museum,** 507/859-2358 or 800/528-7280. The collection includes many family photos and mementos, like Laura's sewing basket and quilt, plus displays about several of the real people she mentioned in the Plum Creek book, such as Johnny Johnson and the Olesons, who in real life were the Owens. Displays about the TV show include the home's fireplace mantle and even replicas of various buildings constructed of toothpicks. A real fan could spend many hours taking it all in, though even those who've never heard of *Little House on the Prairie* will find it interesting. There are also displays about the town's past, and in back are several old buildings, including a one-room schoolhouse. It is open daily 10 A.M.–6 P.M. during the summer, Monday–Saturday 10 A.M.–5 P.M. and Sunday noon–5 P.M. during May and September, and it closes an hour earlier each day in April and October. Call ahead about times from November through March. Admission is $3. You can also roam the original **Ingalls homestead,** now a spic-and-span farm that

Charles would be proud of. The sod home alongside Plum Creek, which Laura described as "small, but clean and pleasant," that they lived in before building a proper cabin is long gone, of course, and just a small depression remains. It is located 1.5 miles north of town on County Road 5. You can visit daily from May through October, and the gate is kept open until dusk. Admission is $3. Fanatical Little Housers will not want to miss **"Pa's Bell,"** which hangs in the steeple of the English Lutheran Church at the corner of 5th and Wiggins streets. Charles donated his last $3 toward its purchase, and Laura tells the story in her Plum Creek book. People at the museum can direct you to other Wilder sites, such as where Laura worked and went to school. To get an idea of what the land looked like when the Ingalls' lived here, take a look at The Nature Conservancy's 80-acre **Wahpeton Prairie** tucked up against the Cottonwood River. It is located six miles north of town on County Road 5, a mile east on 170th St., and then half a mile north on Duncan Ave. The best time for Little House fans to visit are any of the last three weekends in July for the **Wilder Pageant,** a theatrical reenactment of Laura's life. The pageant is a mighty big production and is held in an outdoor amphitheater on the banks of the Plum Creek just west of town. Besides the play, a craft show, Laura and Nellie look-alike contest, and historical reenactments take place during some or all of these weekends. Pageant tickets cost around $7 and can be ordered at 888/859-1670.

Surprisingly, with all the tourists who come here, Walnut Grove has no lodging, just a 40-site campground at Upper Plum Creek Park two miles southwest of the museum. The well-spaced sites start at $10 and the park also has a beach. No doubt someone will open a B&B soon, but until then the nearest place with a bed is seven miles down the road in Tracy. There is also the **Lamberton Motel,** 507/752-7242, ten miles east on Highway 14, with basic but clean rooms for $35. The no-frills **Nellie's Café,** 507/859-2384, on Highway 14 has sandwiches (but no cinnamon chicken) for around $2.50. It is open daily for breakfast and lunch and weekdays for dinner.

Tracy

Laura Ingalls' first train ride was the eight-mile hop from Walnut Grove to Tracy, fancifully described in her book *By The Shores of Silver Lake,* so it's fitting that the highlight of the **Wheels Across the Prairie Museum,** 507/629-3661, is the railroad display. The original depot no longer exists; however, the bench inside the one here now is one of the six that was in the original, and some people come just to sit in it hoping that they are sitting where Laura once did. You can raise your odds of roosting in history by visiting the **End-O-Line Railroad Park and Museum,** 507/763-3708, 13 miles south in Currie, which has a pair of the original benches. The rest of the museum's collection includes just about anything old they can get their hands on and, as the name suggests, a large number of old vehicles. It is located along Highway 14 on the west side of town and is open daily 1–5 P.M. during the summer. The **Valentine Inn,** 385 Emory St., 507/629-3827, a 1902 Victorian home that once served as a hospital, was saved from the wrecking ball by the Beierman family, who have lovingly restored and furnished it. The five guestrooms, each with a private bath, start at $85. In the summer guests tend to congregate on the wraparound porch. Quiet **Swift Lake Park,** just north of town, has a handful of campsites for $5 or $8 with electric hookup. The **Cozy Grove Motel,** 507/629-3350, along Highway 14 on the west side of town isn't a complete fleabag, but it is in desperate need of an overhaul and even at just $28 it is overpriced—it gets a mention only because of the lack of lodging in Walnut Grove. The **Red Rooster Restaurant,** 507/629-9959, is a truck stop and the most popular restaurant in town. They serve all the standard American meals from corn dogs to rib eye steaks, plus a few extras like gyros and pizza, with nothing over $9. It is open daily for breakfast, lunch, and dinner.

PIPESTONE

Pipestone's first settler didn't put down roots until 1873, and the village wasn't incorporated until almost a decade later. The city developed later than many other towns in southwest Minnesota because people feared living so close to the sacred quarries still worked by the Dakota. Once the settlers did finally come though, it grew fast. By the end of the 19th century four railroads passed through town, and promoters took to calling it Little Chicago. It never grew into a metropolis, but the city's former prosperity is evident in the ornate buildings gracing the downtown. Constructed with distinctive red Sioux Quartzite (the dark red was quarried in Pipestone and the pink comes from nearby Jasper), the downtown looks like no other. It is a much older history, though, that brings most visitors to Pipestone. Native American culture remains strong here, and the quarries that once kept people away now make Pipestone one of the most visited cities in southwest Minnesota.

Pipestone National Monument

For many Native Americans the Pipestone National Monument, 507/825-5464, is one of the most sacred places in North America. Quarrying of pipestone, so named because it is carved primarily into traditional Native American ceremonial pipe bowls (the commonly used name peace pipe is a misnomer), is believed to have begun here in the late 16th century. Though there are other sources of pipestone, the Catlinite found here exists nowhere else in the world. The finished pipes from these quarries were so highly revered that tribes across most of North America traded for them, and this land was a neutral ground between all tribes at various points in history. It became a unit of the national park service in 1937 after the Yankton Dakota, who had been guaranteed unrestricted access through an 1858 treaty, sold their rights to the federal government, though Native Americans are still the only ones allowed to quarry here. The process nearly died out in the first half of the 20th century, but today interest has been revived and quarriers from across the United States and Canada still dig through some 10 feet of solid quartzite by hand to reach the 1–3 inch-thick layer of pipestone. During late summer and fall you will probably see people working one of the many pits. The visitors center not only explains the entire

process of making a pipe, but from April to October you can watch local Dakota artists carving them. The finished products, along with other Native crafts, are for sale in the gift shop.

Although the stone is the main focus, there is much more to see in this 282-acre park. The .75-mile **Circle Trail** leads along a beautiful ridge of quartzite with a waterfall and many interesting rock formations. Much of the site is covered by virgin tallgrass prairie and signs along the trail point out many of the plants, as well as some of the uses the Dakota had for them. On your way in or out of the park take a look at the Three Maidens, six large granite boulders named in honor of two legendary women (who said names have to be logical?) who live inside them. The Dakota leave offerings of food and tobacco here for the guardian spirits of the quarry. The park is open Monday–Thursday 8 A.M.–6 P.M. and weekends 8 A.M.–8 P.M. during the summer, and daily 8 A.M.–5 P.M. the rest of the year. Admission is $2.

Other Sights

For more information on the history and art of pipemaking or Dakota culture visit the **Little Feather Center,** 317 4th St. NE, 507/825-3579. Don't be fooled when you enter; for some odd reason the front of the building contains a display of dolls, but you'll find a good museum of Dakota cultural art and artifacts in back. Of course, pipes and other crafts are for sale, too. Hours vary and admission is free.

The **Pipestone County Museum,** 113 Hiawatha Ave. S., 507/825-2563, has an interesting collection of items related to the city's history and a good Native American collection, plus they host many special events. It is open daily 10 A.M.–5 P.M. and admission is $3. At the museum you can pick up the *Pipestone: Past and Present* walking tour booklet, which details three dozen buildings in one of Minnesota's largest historic districts. One of the most interesting is the **Moore Block,** 102 E. Main St., next to the museum, which is adorned with over a dozen whimsical gargoyle-like sculptures. Legend has it that the vacant niche held a nude Eve statue, removed after an outcry by modest citizens.

Across from the entrance to the national monument is **Fort Pipestone,** 507/825-4474, really just a gift shop with a selection of generic gifts to go along with its high-quality Native American goods, but you should visit to see the replica 19th-century fort surrounding it. Open daily during the summer 9 A.M.–8 P.M. and 10 A.M.–6 P.M. during May and September. Admission is free.

Entertainment and Events

In Longfellow's poem *The Song of Hiawatha* Gitche Manito, the Great Spirit, calls all the nations to Pipestone (*On the Mountains of the Prairie, On the great Red Pipe-stone Quarry*) to end all war. During the **Song of Hiawatha Pageant** the story is acted out on land and water by a cast of 200 in a high-tech, 3,500-seat outdoor amphitheater. Performances take place at sundown the last two weekends in July and the first weekend in August. Tickets cost $10.

For real Native American culture attend either the **Pipestone Original Indian Community Pow-wow,** the last weekend in July, or the **Honoring the Elders Pow-wow,** the last weekend in August. Another Native event held here is the **Gathering of the Sacred Pipes Sundance,** hosted in early August by the American Indian Movement. This deeply spiritual gathering draws Native Americans from across the United States and Canada, and while non-Native visitors are allowed at this event it is not meant for them. If you have a deep interest in Native issues and culture and are interested in attending, contact the CVB for more information.

Civil War Days, held the third weekend of August in even numbered years, attracts around 400 living history re-enactors and over ten times as many onlookers. Admission is $5.

The **Pipestone Center for Performing Arts,** 104 E. Main Street, 507/825-2020 or 877/722-2787, offers a busy year-round schedule of music, theater, dance, and other special events. A block down the street the **Quarry Twin Theatre,** 204 E. Main St., 507/825-3522, shows first-run films.

Accommodations

The **Historic Calumet Inn,** 104 W. Main St., 507/825-5871 or 800/535-7610, is so good that spending a night here is reason enough to visit Pipestone. The 1888 hotel has been completely modernized, but the historic character is omnipresent, from the grand staircase to the claw-foot tubs. You should request one of the rooms furnished with antiques, though the "modern" rooms are also very nicely appointed. Rates start at just $79, a veritable bargain considering what you'd pay in larger towns for something similar.

The large, basic rooms at the **Arrow Motel,** 600 8th Ave. NE, 507/825-3331, are the cheapest in town at $35. Better is the **Super 8,** 605 8th Ave SE, 507/825-4217 or 800/800-8000, which charges $63.

Across from the entrance to the national monument is the **Pipestone RV Campground,** 507/825-2455, a standard RV park, except that they rent a pair of tepees. These cost $28 per night and can fit six campers.

Food

The **Calumet Inn** is tops in the dining department, too. Filet mignon, apple-smoked pork chop, and Cajun chicken fettuccine are typical of the meat-heavy menu, though they are most proud of their wild rice soup. Prices range $5–17. Open daily for breakfast and lunch, and Mon.–Sat. for dinner.

Lange's Café, 110 8th Ave. SE, 507/825-4488, a Pipestone institution, is open 24/7. The mostly American menu also includes a selection of pastas and few items are over $8. Try the chicken with almond-raisin sauce followed by their homemade ice cream for desert.

Dar's Pizza, 607 8th Ave. SW, 507/825-4261, serves a top quality thin-crust. A large one-topping is $12. They are open daily for dinner and will deliver.

For excellent bakery follow your nose to **Brummel's Bread Basket,** 214 E. Main St., 507/825-5911. Open Mon.–Sat. for breakfast and lunch.

Shopping

Ceremonial pipes and other Native American crafts are for sale all over town. After the Pipestone National Monument, the best place to look is at the **Keepers of the Sacred Tradition of Pipemakers,** 400 N. Hiawatha Ave., 507/825-3734 or

PRAIRIELAND

888/550-8675, in the restored 1880 Rock Island Railroad Depot—look for the 28-foot pipe sculpture. They also have a small coffee shop.

By far the largest antiques center is **The Antique Attic,** 504 8th Ave. SE, 507/825-5719. Other places with small selections of past goods include the **Gallery on Main,** 110B W. Main St., 507/562-1267; **Liberty Pawn, Coins, and Antiques,** 224 W. Main, 507/825-4404; and the Historical Calumet Inn.

Information and Transportation

The friendly and efficient **Pipestone Convention and Visitors Bureau,** 117 8th Ave SE, 507/825-3316 or 800/336-6125, www.pipestoneminnesota.com, is open weekdays 8 A.M.– 5 P.M. The Pipestone County Museum also has tourism information available.

Greyhound buses arrive and depart once a day at **Lange's Café.**

NORTH OF PIPESTONE

Lake Benton

This quiet town of 700 hugs the southern end of its 2,875-acre namesake lake, a popular boating destination. The city is best known for sitting right at the center of the world's largest wind power project: a nearly 100-mile chain of over 450 modern **wind turbines** stretching along the Buffalo Ridge. This new generation of generators soars well over 200 feet high; they are so efficient that on a windy day just one creates enough energy for all 250 of the town's homes. The towers have quickly become southwestern Minnesota's newest cash crop, bringing much needed money into one of the poorest parts of the state, and there is still no end in sight as the wind farms continue to expand. Studies show that southwest Minnesota has more wind power potential than all of California and could conceivably produce enough electricity for the entire state. Local officials are so enamored with the future of wind energy that they have declared themselves the "Original Wind Power Capital of the American Midwest" and even worked a three-blade design into the downtown streets. Not only are the turbines producing cheap, clean energy for tens of thousands of people and providing new jobs, they have become a tourist attraction. For an up-close view, head two miles west on Highway 14 and then take the unnamed road north to the towers.

Minnesota's newest cash crop

You can learn more about wind energy, as well as local history, at the **Heritage and Wind Power Learning Center,** 110 Center St., 507/368-9577. It is open weekdays 10 A.M.–5 P.M. year-round, plus the same hours on Saturday and noon–5 P.M. on Sunday during the summer. Admission is free.

On the way to the aforementioned wind turbine viewing spot is **Hole-in-the-Mountain County Park** with an 1860 pioneer cabin, hiking trails, and a small ski hill with towrope. A fur trade reenactment takes place in the park the second weekend of August. Two miles south of town along Highway 75, The Nature Conservancy's 775-acre **Hole-in-the-Mountain Prairie** preserve crosses a line of steep hills and valleys. The best views of the wildflowers and other flora are available along the dirt road just south of the sign. The lovely **Lake Benton Opera House,** 507/368-4620, an 1896 downtown edifice that looks like the offspring of a church and a fire station, hosts several dramatic and musical productions each year. Finally, if you love to shop you are in luck because Lake Benton has an unexpected proliferation of gift and antique shops.

The Burk family restored an 1888 Italianate home following a destructive fire, filled it with lovely decorations, and opened the **Benton House B&B,** 211 W. Benton St., 507/368-9484. The three guestrooms, all with private bath, start at $65. Outside of town on the shore of Lake Benton is the quiet and friendly **Wooden Diamond B&B,** 504 Shady Shore Dr., 507/368-4305. The oversized guestroom comes with a private entrance, deck, refrigerator, microwave, and use of a pontoon boat. It costs $70 per night. Head three miles east on Highway 14 and follow the signs. Both establishments offer "no frills" discounts if you skip breakfast and snacks. If price is the only consideration, head for the **Highway 75 Motel,** 507/368-9354, which has tiny and old rooms just north of town for $28. **Hole-in-the-Mountain County Park** has 50 wide-open campsites for $5/tents and $12/RVs. For reservations call 507/368-9350. The **Country House,** 507/368-4223, just east of town on Highway 14, is the city's top restaurant. Steak and seafood dominate the menu and their specialty, prime rib, is served on Friday and Saturday. Entrées average $12 in the main

dining room, or you can get sandwiches and the like for about half that in the more casual lower dining room. Open daily for dinner. A pair of cheap, small town cafés will fill you up during breakfast and lunch.

Prairie Coteau Scientific and Natural Area

Ten miles northeast of Pipestone on Highway 23, just past the village of Holland, is one of the region's few large remnants of original prairie. The healthy, 329-acre grassland blankets a steep hill allowing for a progression from dry prairie species along the ridge to wet prairie vegetation at the bottom. Over 40 species of butterfly flutter between the more than 200 species of wildflower. There are no trails, but you are welcome to explore on your own. The field is most colorful along the ridge top, so don't be put off by the steep climb. The line of wind generators following the Buffalo Ridge (see Lake Benton above) lies just north of the preserve.

I-90
Luverne

The Rock County Seat was founded as a mail stop along the military road between Blue Earth, Minnesota, and Yankton in the Dakota Territory. The original plan called for the city to sit below the cliffs of Blue Mounds State Park, but town founder Philo Hawes, who upon first seeing the hills called this area a Garden of Eden, found a better supply of lumber a short ways to the south. Internationally renowned photographer Jim Brandenburg feels a similar connection to the park's prairie. Though he lives in Ely, Brandenburg was born in Luverne and recently opened the **Brandenburg Gallery,** 211 E. Main St., 507/283-1884, here. Many of the prints for sale are of his better-known northern subjects, but much of the work comes from the park and other prairies. Consider a visit to the gallery before going up to the park; Brandenburg is such an amazing photographer that seeing his photos will give you a greater appreciation of it.

The city's other worthy attraction is the **Hinkly House Museum,** 217 N. Freeman Ave.,

507/283-2115, a 12-room Victorian mansion filled with many original furnishings. The costumed guides—one is the granddaughter of original owner R. B. Hinkly—are assisted during tours by members of the local 4-H club who play the roles of house servants. Hinkly ran a quarry and the basement has vaults for storing dynamite and a display of quarrying tools. Just down the street is the **Rock County Historical Museum,** though its collection is primarily of interest to local residents. Both are open Tuesday, Thursday, and Saturday 2–4 P.M. during the summer. Admission is $2 for either building or $3 for both. Conveniently located between the two museums is the **Carnegie Cultural Center,** 205 N. Freeman Ave., 507/283-8294. The former library now hosts monthly art and historical exhibitions and special events such as music and storytelling. Work from local artists is sold in the gift shop. They are open weekdays 1–5 P.M., Saturday 10 A.M.–4 P.M., and Sunday 1–4 P.M., plus during the summer they stay open until 7 P.M. on Thursdays. For a blast from the past watch a flick at the **Verne Drive-In Theatre,** south of the freeway on Hwy. 75, 507/283-0007; or the **Palace Theatre,** 104 E. Main St., 507/283-8526, a former Vaudeville house. Although there is a lot going on during **Buffalo Days,** held the first weekend in June, the most notable event is the **buffalo chip throwing contest.** For those who don't know what a buffalo chip is, here's a clue—contestants take aim at a toilet.

North of town along Highway 75 is the **Hillcrest Motel,** 507/283-2363 or 800/588-3763, where cozy and spotless rooms cost just $38. By far the best hotel in town is the **Comfort Inn,** 801 S. Kniss Ave. (U.S. 75), 507/283-9488 or 800/228-5150, where $85 gets you use of a small pool and whirlpool. Luverne's only B&B is **Our House,** 611 N. Kniss Ave., 888/283-9340, with three guestrooms for $65. All have private baths and there is a grill in the backyard. For a simple but delicious meal head to **J J's Tasty Drive-In,** 804 S. Kniss Ave., 507/283-8317, where $4 will get you a burger, fries, and a malt. Motorcycle fans can admire the 1949 Harley Davidson displayed inside. They are open daily for breakfast and lunch as long the weather permits. For some-

thing a little fancier there's the **Magnolia Steak House,** 507/283-9161, a longtime favorite down at the Interstate. They have their own meat market attached so you know the beef is top quality. Dinner prices range $7–20, and they are only open Monday–Saturday for dinner. **Greyhound** buses stop at the Cenex gas station, 507/283-3942, along I-90.

Blue Mounds State Park

Although it receives far fewer visitors than most of Minnesota's state parks and can't offer the deep wilderness of the state's largest, in many ways Blue Mounds is one of the best. The namesake mound at the heart of the park, which appeared blue to the earliest settlers passing by in the distance, is a massive outcrop of Sioux quartzite bedrock rising gradually from the west and ending in a spectacular 1.5-mile-long cliff. This ridge, nearly 100 feet tall in many places, is one of the best rock-climbing sites in the state; all climbers must get a free permit from the park office. The mound and most of the 1,800-acre park is topped by original tallgrass prairie that, though it has been degraded by livestock grazing, was never plowed, thanks to the shallow, rocky soil. Remarkably, bison graze on the prairie once again, almost as they did through the early 19th century. The only difference is that this herd of around 45 remains behind three miles of fence. Though the bison are enclosed, they do remain wild, so never walk right up to the fence if they are nearby since they can break through it as if it were a paper bag—and they sometimes do.

The hiking here is arguably the best in southwest Minnesota, and all 13 miles of trail crossing the prairie are beautiful. The easiest is the **Mound Creek Trail** leading around the lakes and campgrounds. The distant vistas from the **Upper Cliffline Trail** are spectacular, and when combined with the scenic views of the cliff itself from the **Lower Cliffline Trail** form an ideal though somewhat difficult hike; several cutoffs let you take in the best of both without hiking the full five-mile loop. The **Western Loop Trail** and the **Upper and Lower Mound Trails** in the south end of the park lead right through the heart of Blue Mounds' prairie and also have some hills

© TIM BEWER

Buffalo roam in Blue Mounds State Park.

along the way. Bird-watchers seeking western species could have a field day along these trails. It's about a mile round-trip from the interpretive center to the park's highest point via the Upper Mound Trail. Along the way up to the peak stop to investigate the 1,250-foot line of rocks perfectly aligned to east and west. No one knows who built them or when.

The large campground overlooking Upper Mound Lake has 73 sites (40 electric), though for a more peaceful and secluded night there is a separate 14-site cart-in campground. The park is just four miles north of Luverne on Highway 75; call 507/283-1307 for information.

Worthington

Some of the first settlers to arrive on the shore of Lake Okabena were members of the National Colony Company, a temperance group whose influence on local laws lasted well into the 20th century. Those seeking out the 785-acre lake today include a large number of windsurfers who find steady and strong winds—many contests have been held here, including the 2003 U.S. Nationals. The town's biggest claim to fame is the **Great Gobbler Gallop.** Worthington annually pits a turkey in a main street race against a contender from Cuero, Texas, which also claims to be the Turkey Capital of the World. They've been squaring off since 1973 and Worthington's bird, always named Paycheck ("Nothing goes faster than a paycheck"), leads the overall series. Other events during **King Turkey Days** (the second Saturday after Labor Day) include a parade and pancake feed. The **Prairie Expo,** with modern exhibits about the past and present of southwest Minnesota, was supposed to be a major destination for travelers but it failed almost immediately after opening. By all accounts the displays were excellent and so someday it might reopen, but don't bet on it. For now, it is the biggest white elephant in the state.

Its sheer size makes the **Pioneer Village,** 507/376-3125, out at the fairgrounds one of the best local history museums in the state. Over three dozen historic buildings, including a print shop, one-room school house, farm house, and general store, have been moved from around the county. Most are filled with appropriate furnishings and fixtures creating mini museums. Other interesting displays are a sod house, large assortment of old vehicles, and the barbed wire collection. It is open Monday–Saturday 10 A.M.–5 P.M. and Sunday 1–5 P.M. during the summer. Admission is $3. The **Nobles County Historical Society Museum,** 507/376-4431, has a small collection of artifacts in the basement of the Nobles County Library, 407 12th St. It is open Monday–Friday 1–5 P.M. Also in the library's basement is the small **Nobles County Art Center,** 507/372-8245, with monthly exhibits by regional artists. Open Mon.–Sat. 2–4:30 P.M. Admission to both is free. If something cultural is happening in town it's probably at the large, art deco **Memorial Auditorium Performing Arts Center,** 714 13th St., 507/376-9101.

The cheapest beds in town, with good reason, are at the **Oxford Motel,** 1801 Oxford St., 507/376-6126. One night will set you back $29. Not fancy, but still a big step up, are the **Sunset Inn,** 507/376-9492, at the junction of Hwys. 59 and 60; and the **Budget Inn,** 1231 Oxford St., 507/376-6136. Both have small rooms for around

M

PRAIRIELAND

$45. Worthington's largest hotel, the **Travelodge,** 507/372-2991 or 800/578-7878, across from Prairie Expo, has rooms with microwave and refrigerator for $55, plus a small pool, whirlpool, and sauna. Best in town is the **Holiday Inn Express,** 1250 Ryan's Rd., 507/372-2333 or 800/ 225-8828, just south of the freeway. Eighty-six dollars gets you a spanking new room plus use of the pool, whirlpool, and exercise room.

Dining in Worthington is a pleasant surprise. Because of the large number of immigrants living here, there are several quality ethnic restaurants. The menu at **Bangkok Cuisine,** 1719 East Ave. 507/376-9009, is evenly split between Chinese and Thai, but because of local tastes the Thai chef fries up Chinese meals 90 percent of the time. They are located south of town along Highway 59 and are open Tuesday–Saturday for lunch and dinner. Expect to spend about $5 for lunch and $8 for dinner. No compromises are made at **El Taco,** 418 10th St., 507/372-5039, where a killer Mexican platter costs about $5. Open Wed.–Sun. for breakfast, lunch, and dinner. By all accounts the best American fare is at **Michael's,** 507/376-3187, which specializes in steak and seafood in the $8–15 range. It is located on the east side of town where Highway 59 joins Highway 60. They are open Monday–Saturday for dinner only.

You can get statewide information four miles south of town at the **Worthington Travel Information Center** along Highway 59. While there you can admire the large herd of **llamas** and **alpacas. Greyhound** buses stop at the Cenex gas station, 507/376-6080, at I-90 and Highway 59.

Fairmont

Fairmont, the Martin County Seat, hugs a long, north-south chain of lakes. It was founded in 1857 by E. Banks Hall and William Budd, whose names still grace the lakes on which they built their cabins. A decade and a half later a group of Oxford and Cambridge educated English settlers arrived and the new methods of growing beans they developed helped save the town during the grasshopper plague of the 1870s. The English, riding in full crimson regalia, also introduced fox hunting to Minnesota and soon became known statewide as the Fairmont Sportsmen.

Some of the more unusual artifacts in the large, though otherwise ordinary, collection of the Martin County Historical Society's **Pioneer Museum,** 304 E. Blue Earth Ave., 507/235-5178, are a motorcycle from 1912, a radio from 1924, and a pair of wooden roller skates. It is open Monday–Thursday 8:30 A.M.–4:30 P.M. and Friday–Saturday 1–4:30 P.M. Admission is free. **Heritage Acres,** 827 Lake Ave., 507/235-9625, is a private agricultural history museum overlooking Sisseton Lake on the west side of town. The 40-acre grounds have several historic structures including a home, church, train depot, and one-room schoolhouse. You can walk the grounds anytime, though the buildings can only be visited during festivals or by appointment. You can while away a long time watching the enclosed **prairie dog colony** at the Heritage Acres entrance. The **Texas Longhorn cattle** grazing behind the McDonalds just south of the freeway on Highway 15 are another animal attraction.

If you are staying in town be sure to see what's on stage at the **Fairmont Opera House,** 45 Downtown Plaza, 507/238-4900, built in 1901 and added to the National Register of Historic Places 80 years later after almost being demolished for a parking lot. The yearly calendar regularly gets many bigger names than you would expect for a town this small; recent bookings have included The Glenn Miller Orchestra, Junior Brown, and Harmonious Wail.

The top hotel in town is the **Holiday Inn,** 507/238-4771 or 800/785-4066, right off the freeway on Highway 15. Large rooms start at $99, and their many amenities include a pool, hot tub, sauna, game room, exercise room, and even an indoor putting green. The **Budget Inn,** 1122 N. State St., 507/235-3373, is showing its age, but the rooms are clean and just $42 with refrigerator and microwave. There is also a pool, hot tub, and sauna. Two of the city's most popular restaurants are right across the street from each other on Highway 15. **The Ranch,** 1330 N. State St., 507/235-3044, has steak, seafood, and sandwiches, plus a handful of extras like spaghetti and stir-fry. Very little is over $10. Open daily for breakfast, lunch, and dinner. **China Restaurant,** 1400 N. State St., 507/235-8148, has a huge menu with many items, like spicy orange chicken, that you wouldn't expect to find in a small town. Expect to spend about $5 for lunch and $8 for dinner. They are open daily for lunch and dinner and will deliver to area hotels. **Greyhound** buses stop at the Holiday Inn.

Blue Earth

What's green, 47 feet tall, weighs 8,000 pounds, and greets visitors with a hearty "Ho, Ho, Ho?" No, not Godzilla doing his Santa Claus impression; it's the **Jolly Green Giant,** of course. Arms akimbo and a smile on his face, he surveys the pea and corn fields around town that are harvested by General Mills, the latest owner of this merry mascot. He wears a red scarf in the winter and a leather vest and bandana at times in July and August as a gesture to motorcycle riders heading to rallies in South Dakota and Iowa. The jolly one isn't Blue Earth's only claim to fame. In 1917 Walter Schwen devised a process for coating ice cream in chocolate and the Eskimo Pie was born, though back then it was called a Chocolate Dream.

Although the giant is the primary reason to stop in Blue Earth, if you are here you might as well visit the city's two small museums. The **James B. Wakefield House,** 405 E. 6th St., 507/526-5421, built in 1868 by one of the city's founders, is laid out as though a family from about a century ago were still living there and happened to label all their possessions with index cards. Across the street in the city's old library is the **Etta C. Ross Museum,** 324 E. 6th St., a hodge-podge collection of anything old they can

get their hands on. Both are open weekdays 9 A.M.–2 P.M. and admission is free. The Faribault County Historical Society also maintains a one-room schoolhouse, log cabin, blacksmith shop, and post office (all appropriately equipped) at the fairgrounds and opens them up during the County Fair at the end of July. **Minnesota's first stained glass window,** initially installed in Christ Church in St. Paul, now shines in the 1871 Church of the Good Shepherd a few blocks from the museums at the corner of East 8th and South Moore Streets. If you want to get inside to see it, ask at the museum and, if someone is available, they will take over.

Both of the town's hotels are out at I-90 and Highway 169. Rates at the **Super 8,** 507/526-7376 or 800/800-8000, start at $55. For $21 more you'll get a similar quality room with a refrigerator and microwave, plus a swimming pool and hot tub for guest use at the **AmericInn,** 507/526-4215 or 800/634-3444. Camping is free for two nights along the Blue Earth River at the fairgrounds north of town; there are electric hookups. **Hamilton's,** 209 S. Main St., 507/526-3287, is a longtime local favorite for family fare with prices running $5–16. Open daily for breakfast and lunch, and Mon.–Sat. for dinner. Carhops still take your order at the **Cedar Inn,** 326 N. Grove St., 507/526-5612. The prices are equally old-fashioned; hamburgers, corn dogs, and ice cream are all under a buck. It is open daily for lunch and dinner, but only from the end of March to the end of September. **Greyhound** buses stop at the Texaco gas station, 507/526-5225, in front of the statue.

M

PRAIRIELAND

Little Crow Lakes

Though Kandiyohi and Meeker Counties have a high concentration of lakes this is still, like the rest of southwest Minnesota, thoroughly farm country. Except for drivers racing along Highway 12 from the Twin Cities to South Dakota and anglers shacking up for a week at a resort for some fishing in the summer, this part of Minnesota sees few visitors. Darwin, however, is worth going out of your way for.

WILLMAR AND VICINITY

The Kandiyohi County Seat is a growing, though not very exciting, city of over 18,000 that serves as the regional commercial center. Though the first settlers built log cabins around Foot Lake over a decade earlier, the city of Willmar was founded as a railroad town in 1869. It soon became a hub of James J. Hill's Great Northern empire and remains an important railroad town with the Burlington Northern & Santa Fe Railway's busy switching yard one of Willmar's major employers.

Sights

Area history is on display at the **Kandiyohi County Historical Museum,** 610 U.S. 71 NE, 320/235-1881. The Native American display is small but interesting and the Horseless Carriage, circa 1900, is another highlight. Other objects from the museum's collections are kept next door in the Sperry House, built on this site in 1893 and restored to its appearance at that time. It can be toured during the summer and around Christmas. Other displays on the grounds that can be visited during the summer include a one-room schoolhouse, agricultural equipment collection, and log cabin. The museum is open Monday–Friday 9 A.M.–5 P.M., plus Saturday–Sunday 1–5 P.M. in the summer. Admission is free.

A pair of privately owned museums will appeal to fans of internal combustion. The **Mikkelson Collection,** 418 Benson Ave. SE, 320/231-0384, is packed with vintage boats, including over a dozen rare Falls Flyers ("The Jaguar of Boats") and outboard motors, various other boating ar-

tifacts, and hundreds of toy boats and motors. The set hours are Saturdays 9 A.M.–4 P.M., but it is often open during the week, too. Admission is $6. On the other side of town is the **Schwanke Museum,** 3310 U.S. 71 S., 320/235-4341, which covers most of the rest of the motorized spectrum. The private collection has over 100 classic cars, trucks, and tractors, plus another 200 related items. It is open Monday–Saturday 1–4 P.M. between April and November; call for winter hours. Admission is $5.

Recreation

The **Glacial Lakes State Trail** is an 18-mile path connecting Willmar with Spicer, New London, and Hawick. The 12 miles from Willmar to New London is paved, while the last section is crushed granite. The trail continues to Richmond, but it is still being developed and some bridges are out.

Robbins Island Park, covering the peninsula dividing Foot Lake from Willmar Lake, has a beach, plenty of shady space for picnics, and a short nature trail.

Entertainment and Events

Touring music and theatrical acts take the stage at the **Willmar Education and Arts Center,** 611 5th St. SW, 320/231-8560, while locals produce six shows a year at the **Barn Theatre, 321 4th St. SW, 320/235-9500. The Kandi 6,** 1605 1st St., 320/235-2131, is a six-screen movie theater in the Kandi Mall.

Willmar's biggest bash is late June's **Willmar Fests.** A sand sculpture contest, bed races, international banquet, and a performance by the award-winning Little Crow Water Ski Team are highlights.

Accommodations

The two best hotels, the **Holiday Inn,** 320/235-6060 or 877/405-4466; and the newer **Comfort Inn,** 320/231-2601 or 877/241-5215, are attached to the Willmar Conference Center on the east edge of town along Highway 12. Both have a pool, whirlpool, fitness center, and rooms from about

$80. The primary difference between the two is that the former has a sauna and game room. Not quite as nice, but a better value is the older **Colonial Inn,** 1102 S. 1st Ave., 320/235-4444 or 800/396-4445. The rooms, which are better than the outside appearance would suggest, start at $40.

The deceptively large **Corner Garden Inn,** 615 Becker Ave. SW, 320/214-3552 or 800/387-6379 ext. 4549, is a very entertaining B&B. The expanded 1914 Prairie Style home has a billiard room, heated outdoor pool, and three public rooms to unwind in. The four antique-filled guestrooms, each with a private bath, are priced from $95–135, and some have whirlpools and fireplaces.

Food

If Lake Wobegon's Chatterbox Café had a real-life counterpart, the classic **Town Talk Café,** 210 5th St. SW, 320/235-0567, could be it. It's got cheap, home-cooked, American fare served in a truly classic setting. Breakfast is served all day. Open Mon.–Sat. for breakfast and lunch.

Besides caffeinated beverages the **Daily Grind,** 400 Litchfield Ave. SW, 320/235-3835, serves soup and sandwiches; order a combo of the two for $4. There is live music on Thursday nights. Open weekdays for breakfast, lunch, and dinner, and Sat. for breakfast and lunch.

El Tequila, 1111 1st St. S., 320/235-2415, serves some really good Mexican fare with a large menu ranging from $3–11. Open daily for lunch and dinner.

Shopping

Willmar's main shopping drag is 1st Street, centered around the Kandi Mall, but the handful of interesting stores are all downtown. **The House of Jacobs,** 421 Litchfield Ave. SW, 320/235-2191, is one of the state's largest Scandinavian stores. Besides selling clothes, crafts, books, food, and other items from the old country, they also make their own lefse.

Mr. B's Chocolatier, 540 Benson Ave. W., 320/235-1313, makes and sells exquisite Belgian-style chocolates. Choose from assorted gift boxes or chocolate corncobs and other country-style molds. They're expensive but extraordinary.

A pair of antique shops, **Olson's,** 320/235-0423, and **L&Js,** 320/231-3748, share the same building at 614 Benson Ave. SW.

Information and Transportation

The **Willmar Lakes Area Convention and Visitors Bureau,** 2104 U.S. 12 E., 320/235-3552 or 800/845-8747, www.seeyouinwillmar.com, has a rack of brochures for all of Kandiyohi County. They are open Monday–Friday 9 A.M.–5 P.M.

Greyhound buses stop at the Central Lakes Co-op, 2550 E. U.S. 12, 320/214-7813.

NORTH OF WILLMAR

Spicer

Spicer is a mini resort town on Green Lake, the largest body of water in the area. While it hops during the summer it is very quiet the rest of the year. Besides swimming, fishing, boating, or sailing on the lake you can get your kicks on the go-kart track or bumper boats at **Big Kahuna Park,** 320/796-2049, or **Wally's Waterslide,** 320/796-4040; both have miniature golf courses. **Spicer Bike and Sports,** 320/796-6334, along the **Glacial Lakes State Trail** (see Willmar above) rents bikes and in-line skates. All are on the south side of town along Highway 23. The **Green Lake Bible Camp Chapel,** 320/796-2181, is 1.5 miles east of town on Lake Avenue. Built in the Norwegian stave style it is certainly worth a quick look.

A dozen small, summer-only resorts dot the many lakes surrounding the town, but by far the best lodging is the charming **Spicer Castle,** 11600 Indian Beach Rd., 320/796-5870 or 800/821-6675, spicercastle@spicercastle.com, on Green Lake. This English country-style mansion, built in 1895 by town founder John Spicer, is now an exquisite eight-room inn with an additional two renovated cottages on the grounds. With little obvious modernization and much of the family's original furnishings intact, the house has not just the look of a century past, but the feel as well. Rooms run from $80–145; all have private baths and a few have whirlpools. You don't need to be a guest at the Castle to join one of their five-course **Murder Mystery dinners** (Fridays year-round plus Saturdays from September

PRAIRIELAND

to June; $46) or **Dinner Cruises** (Thurs.–Sat. nights plus Wed. lunch during the summer; $30). If you just want a regular hotel the **Northern Inn,** 154 Lake Ave. S., 320/796-2091, right in town across from big and busy Saulsbury Beach, has modern rooms from $80, plus a pool, whirlpool, and sauna. The **Westwood Café,** 142 Lake Ave. N., 320/796-5355, is your typical small town restaurant with burgers, salads, steaks, and the like averaging $6. Open daily for breakfast and lunch, and Mon.–Sat. for dinner.

Sibley State Park

Sibley State Park, 320/354-2055, sits near the southern end of the Alexandria Moraine, a band of glacially formed hills and lakes stretching north to the city Detroit Lakes. **Mount Tom,** the tallest of these hills, was once a lookout for the local Dakota and, like most high places, it held spiritual significance for them, too. From the observation tower you can take in a broad vista of the surrounding lakes, forest, and farms. Historically, oak savanna and prairie were the main landscapes, but today forest covers most of the 3,016-acre park. Shortgrass prairie remnants remain on some of the hills, and many old farm fields are being restored to the native prairie and oak savanna. With a mix of grasslands, woodlands, and lakes, bird-watching can be pretty good here.

Eighteen miles of hilly hiking trails, half open to horseback riders, wind through the park's forest and field. The **Mt. Tom Trail,** a three-mile loop climbing from Lake Andrew to Mt. Tom, is the most popular. Several shorter loops branch off the south end, and the **Oak Hills Trail** lets you cut off the not-so-scenic southern tip. Arguably more scenic, and definitely more peaceful overall, is the horse path along the north end of the park. The three-mile western loop is easier and passes through less forest. For a short, easy hike try the **Pondview Interpretive Trail,** a paved loop around a pond with signs discussing park ecology. More interpretive signs are found on the **Woodland Wildlife Trail,** which follows the beginning of the five-mile paved bike trail. Both are a mile long and start by the interpretive center. Lake Andrew bustles with swimmers, boaters,

and anglers all summer long, while smaller Henschien and Swan Lakes, connected by a portage and a small stream, offer some scenic canoeing. Canoes and rowboats can be rented during the summer. In winter a ten-mile web of challenging, groomed cross-country ski trails covers the main part of the park. The western half of the park has no trails, but would be a good place to explore by snowshoe.

Campers have 134 sites (53 electric) in two campgrounds. A little over half of them, including all the electric ones, are crammed together next to the beach and main picnic area. They are shady and convenient if you have kids, but the Oak Ridge Campground, a mix of open and wooded sites, all widely spaced, is much more peaceful and scenic. Horseback riders have their own 50-person camp.

HIGHWAY 12 EAST OF WILLMAR

Litchfield

The Meeker County seat is a quiet city of 6,542 whose main claim to fame is the 1885 **Grand Army of the Republic Hall,** 308 Marshall Ave., 320/693-8911, one of the few remaining in the nation and the last in Minnesota. The Ladies of the G. A. R., descendents of Union veterans, still hold their annual meeting here. It houses a small but interesting collection of Civil War artifacts, but the building itself is the most interesting feature, as it was designed to resemble a military fort, giving the diminutive structure a degree of stature. An addition in back houses the **Meeker County Historical Society Museum,** two floors of the usual historical artifacts highlighted by an 1868 log cabin. They are both open Tuesday–Sunday noon–4 P.M. and admission is free. A Civil War living history encampment takes place across the street in Central Park Labor Day weekend (most of the action is on Saturday) in even-numbered years. In odd-numbered years the town hosts a period artillery competition with muskets, cannons, and the like. Another historical relic, the **Starlite Drive-In Theatre,** 320/693-6990, still screens double and triple features. On the other side of town is Lake Ripley, very popular for boating and fishing. Surrounding its shore you'll find a small floral garden, a beach, municipal campground (320/693-7201), and the 18-hole Litchfield Golf Club (320/693-6425).

The modern **Scotwood Motel,** 1017 E. Frontage Rd., 320/693-2496 or 800/225-5489, has a pool, whirlpool, and rooms from $65. **Greyhound** buses stop here on their way to and from Minneapolis. Six miles southwest of town on 300 acres fronting Star Lake is the luxurious **Birdwing Spa,** 21398 575th Ave., 320/693-6064. A few of the many rejuvenation options include massages, pedicures, yoga, herbal wraps, TAErobics, gourmet meals, and canoe trips. You will be pampered into submission, but the bill will shock you back to reality: a weekend overnight starts at $395. Best bet for a bite to eat is the busy **Main Street Café,** 226 N. Sibley Ave., 320/693-9067, where you can get a solid home-cooked meal for around $4. Be sure to take time to look at the historic photos hanging on the wall. Open daily for lunch and dinner.

Darwin

Everyone should make the trip to tiny Darwin (pop. 276), just over an hour from Minneapolis, to experience the extraordinary, one-of-a-kind genius of Francis A. Johnson. Johnson, son of U.S. Senator Magnus Johnson, gave the tiny village its one claim to fame: the **world's largest ball of twine made by just one man.** This "magnificent sphere" is 11 feet tall, 12 feet-nine inches wide, and weighs nearly nine tons—it used to weight 11 tons, but all the water has finally evaporated out. He rolled his first strand of baler twine in March of 1950 and didn't stop until 1979, using railroad jacks to move the ball around when it got large. There are other giant twine balls out there, some even a bit bigger, but they are just pitiful imposters—all were collective efforts and were inspired by Johnson's creation. When Johnson died in 1989 the city spurned a generous offer from the Ripley's Believe It Or Not folks and moved it into town, where a Plexiglas enclosed shelter protects it from souvenir hunters. The ball has since been made vaguely famous by the epic Weird Al Yankovic song *The Biggest Ball of Twine in Minnesota.* Weird Al had

befriended Johnson and, according to the folks in Darwin, still visits town when he gets a chance.

Though he will always be known as the man who rolled the twine ball, Johnson was also an obsessive whittler and collector—he died with nearly 500 hammers and 7,000 pencils. A few of the tens of thousands of functional wooden pliers he carved—one cut from a matchstick and another stretching 6.5 feet with 19 progressively smaller pliers cascading from the handles—are now on display in the **Darwin Depot Museum,** 320/693-7544, along with a handful of historical Darwin photos and artifacts. Though you can see the twine ball and museum in just a few minutes, you could easily spend hours listening to the local volunteers tell stories about Johnson. It is open daily 9 A.M.–4 P.M. during the summer, and is also open in the spring and fall, though you need to call ahead to find out when. Admission is free. A full range of twine ball memorabilia—T-shirts, hats, magnets, coffee mugs, key chains, Christmas ornaments, twine ball starter kits, and more—are for sale in the museum. When it is closed you can still get some mementos next door at the Twine Ball Inn restaurant, named after a line from Weird Al's song, or the Darwin Municipal Liquor Store up on the highway.

Dassel

Any railroad enthusiasts passing by will want to stop at **The Old Depot Museum,** 651 U.S. 12 W., 320/275-3876. The 1913 Great Northern Depot, moved here from Cokato, is now filled with one of the state's top collections of railroad art and artifacts. The museum is open daily 10 A.M.–4:30 P.M. from Memorial Day weekend through September. Admission is $2.50. Work is under way to renovate the large **Universal Laboratories Building** to house a museum about ergot, a fungus that grows on wheat, used in blood clotting medicines that were processed here during World War II.

Cokato

The city's name, roughly derived from the Dakota language (In the Midst of), is an appropriate enough title today since it lies halfway between

Minneapolis and Willmar. The well-presented **Cokato Museum,** 175 W. 4th St., 320/286-2427, focuses on the town's Swedish and Finnish roots. Displays include a reconstructed log home, a Finnish sauna, and an early dentist's office that will make you cringe. Ask the attendant to take you up the street to the **Akerlund Photo Studio,** which was opened in 1902 and looks just as it did when operations ceased in the 1950s. His apartment tucked away in back is equally remarkable since it has been left nearly exactly as it was when

furnished in 1927. The museum is open weekdays 9 A.M.–4:30 P.M. (closed Mon. Nov.–April), Saturday 10 A.M.–4 P.M., and Sunday noon–4 P.M. Admission is free.

The **Third Street Inn,** 370 3rd St. W., 320/286-7099, has three guestrooms in a lovely 1880 brick home that is entirely for guest use, though the proprietors do live nearby. The rooms, one with a sauna, one a steam bath, and the other a separate living room, each cost $55. A continental breakfast is served in the morning.

Bluff Country

When the last five to ten glaciers bulldozed their way across North America they spared most of southeast Minnesota. Though their icy lobes slid around this area, the torrential meltwaters rushed right through it, carving away hundreds of feet of sandstone and limestone. The gorgeous result is a rugged region of steep valleys capped by limestone bluffs and lined by wildly meandering streams that continue to slowly carve the valleys. This unique region is often errantly called the Driftless Area. The true Driftless Area is a 10,000-square-mile wedge across parts of Wisconsin, Illinois, and Minnesota that wasn't gouged by any glaciers over the last million years—in Minnesota it only encompasses a thin strip along the Mississippi River in Winona and Houston counties. The rest of the region beyond this, which some geologists call the Pseudo Driftless Area, was buried by earlier glaciations, though it is visually identical to the real thing, hence the confusion. Even geologists can only differentiate it by locating the scattered pockets of thin, highly eroded glacial till that remain.

There is a lot of variety in this little corner of the state. Moving inland from the spectacular 500-foot bluffs and historic river towns hugging the Mississippi you'll find blue-ribbon trout streams, the state's most popular bike trails, Minnesota's largest Amish settlements, and cosmopolitan Rochester. The land levels out as it moves west, slowly fading into the Great Plains.

© TIM BEWER

Lake Pepin

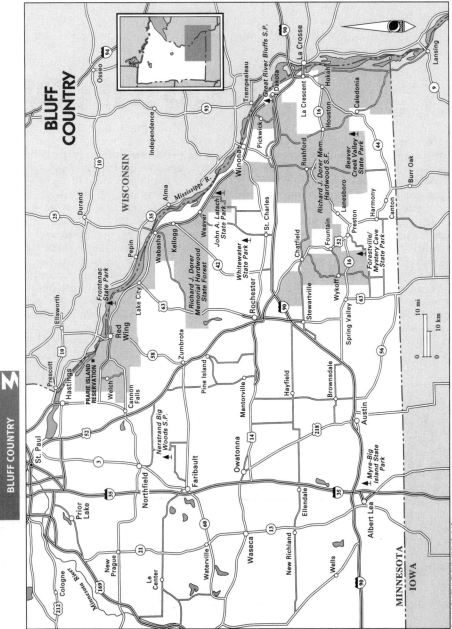

BLUFF COUNTRY

© AVALON TRAVEL PUBLISHING, INC.

BLUFF COUNTRY HIGHLIGHTS

Amish Tours, Harmony and Lanesboro

Blufflands State Trail

Driving the Great River Road

Eagle Watching, Winona, Red Wing

Ed's Museum, Wykoff

Forestville/Mystery Cave State Park

Great River Bluffs State Park

LARK Toys, Kellogg

Mayo Clinic, Rochester

Prairie School Banks, Owatonna and Winona

SPAM Museum, Austin

Great River Road

We move up the river—always through enchanting scenery, there being no other kind on the Upper Mississippi.

Mark Twain, Life on the Mississippi, *1883*

Life on the Mississippi has changed considerably since Twain penned these words, but the statement remains as true as ever. Below its confluence with the St. Croix River the "Father of Waters" quickly expands, spanning two to three miles (up to five by La Crescent) while towering, half-dome bluffs hedge it in along the rest of its Minnesota journey. Highway 61 hits the bluffs as it approaches Red Wing and meets the river at Lake City, and from this point on you'll have unrivaled scenery. There is ample opportunity to turn inland and climb the mountainlike terrain for glorious valley views that stretch on toward infinity. Though you are never far from one of the historic river towns, the floodplain and impossibly steep hills thwart development allowing moments where you can imagine yourself deep in a lost wilderness. Wildlife, best enjoyed from a canoe in the river's backwaters, but quite often seen from behind the wheel, abounds all year long. Each fall waterfowl, shorebirds, and raptors follow the valley south to warmer wintering grounds. For bald eagles the river *is* their winter residence, and well over a thousand fish in the open waters along Minnesota.

Though the age of paddlewheel steamboats peaked even before Mark Twain did, for many they remain synonymous with the Mississippi and a few paddlewheelers still ply these waters, though today you are much more likely to view one of the river's many barges.

HASTINGS AND VICINITY

Hastings' first European settler, Henry Bailly, came to this strategic spot, where the St. Croix River meets the Mississippi, in 1850 under the guise of running a trading post, but he really was in wait to claim the site for development the moment the ink dried on the Dakota treaties. That, as anticipated, happened the next year and a city was soon plotted and named for Henry Hastings Sibley, the future first governor of Minnesota. It was a city poised for greatness. Steamboat travel was difficult upriver of this point so many warehouses, mills, banks, and other businesses associated with the river trade arose here and the city prospered. Navigational improvements organized by shippers allowed the commercial emergence of Minneapolis and St. Paul and spelled the end of Hastings' prominence.

Just 20 minutes from St. Paul, this city of 18,000 is a popular day trip from the Twin Cities. Most come to shop the galleries, gift shops, and antique stores along historic Second Street, whose two busiest blocks remain largely intact from the beginning of the 20th century. The **Hastings Area Chamber of Commerce and Tourism Bureau,** 111 3rd St. E., 651/437-6775 or 888/612-6122, www.hastingsmn.org, gives out a free map with a detailed walking/driving tour. It highlights most of the 64 buildings listed on the National Register of Historic Places, including the

BLUFF COUNTRY

Le Duc-Simmons Mansion, 1629 Vermillion St., an impressive 1865 Gothic Revival home slated to become a local history museum someday, and the modest **Fasbender Clinic** (now Edward Jones Investments), a Frank Lloyd Wright design at the corner of Hwy. 55 and Pine Street.

An elevated observation platform at **Lock and Dam #2,** just northwest of town, lets you watch boats and barges get a 12-foot lift. It is open daily 8 A.M.–dusk from April through November. The **Mississippi River Interpretive Center** could open nearby as soon as 2004. Another worthy diversion is **Vermillion Falls Park,** located on the west side of town just off U.S. 61. The small falls lies behind the Gardner Flour Mill, the oldest continuously operating flourmill in the state, and drops into a narrow gorge that runs around the city. A bike trail, part of a 15-mile loop of both roads and paved trail circling the city, follows the river; downstream it leads past the almost haunting **Ramsey Mill** ruins, built by the state's first Territorial Governor in 1857.

Outside of town the **Alexis Bailly Vineyard,** 18200 Kirby Ave., 651/437-1413, the state's first winemaker using all locally-grown grapes, opens their doors for tastings ($2) and sales on Friday, Saturday, and Sunday, 11 A.M.–5 P.M., from June to mid-November. To get there head south on U.S. 61 to 170th Street East, and then west for two miles. Although it is only open to the public the last full weekend in July during the **Antique Power Show,** you may want to drive past the **Little Log House Pioneer Village,** 651/437-2693, a large and impressive collection of old buildings and vehicles spread out over 40 acres. To get there head south on U.S. 61 for six miles to 220th Street East.

All of Hastings' hotels are on the south side of town on or near U.S. 61. The cheapest is the locally owned **Hastings Inn,** 1520 Vermillion St., 651/437-3155. Large, basic rooms are $59, and they have some kitchenettes. Amenities include a pool, whirlpool, game room, and sauna. Much newer and nicer is the **Country Inn & Suites,** 300 33rd St., 651/437-8870 or 800/456-4000, also with a pool and whirlpool. Standard rooms start at $89, while two-room suites with whirlpools and fireplaces are $139. For some-

thing really special try the **Thorwood Inn,** 315 Pine St.; and **Rosewood Inn,** 620 Ramsey St., 651/437-3297 or 800/846-7966. Two of the city's most beautiful historic homes, both built in 1880, have been renovated for all-out luxury and are now jointly managed with an eye for detail, making them two of the most elegant and romantic inns in the state. Most rooms have whirlpools and fireplaces and, while prices start at $97, most cost much more. A private dinner can also be arranged if ordered ahead of time, and occasionally they plan special dinner evenings with chamber music and limousine service.

The well-regarded Italian meals at the **Mississippi Belle,** E. 101 2nd St., 651/437-4814, Hastings' fanciest dining, will only set you back about $10 per plate. They are open Tuesday–Sunday for lunch and dinner. More casual is the popular **Levee Café,** 100 Sibley St., 651/437-7577. Sandwiches dominate the menu, but a few seafood and pasta dishes are available; all average $6. Open daily for lunch and dinner, plus weekends for breakfast. **Professor Java's,** 202 E. 2nd St., 651/438-9962, is a quality coffeehouse with a good sandwich menu. They are open daily for breakfast, lunch, and dinner.

Visiting boaters can dock up and stock up at **King's Cove,** 651/437-6186; or **Hastings Marine,** 651/437-9621. **Airport Passenger Service,** 800/869-5796, vans make five runs a day between La Crosse, Wisconsin, and the Minneapolis-St. Paul International Airport stopping in town at the AmericInn, 2400 Vermillion St., 651/437-8877. The fare is $34 round-trip and reservations are required.

Prairie Island

The 2,400 slot machines and 64 blackjack tables at the Prairie Island Dakota's **Treasure Island Resort and Casino,** 651/388-1171 or 800/222-7077, are surrounded by a Caribbean decor, and they claim to have the largest nonsmoking gaming space in the Midwest. If you are here in July you can join the **Prairie Island Dakota Wacipi** (powwow). The 150-passenger *Spirit of the Water* cruise boat runs on the Mississippi River Wednesday through Sunday from May through October. Afternoon sightseeing trips

PRAIRIE ISLAND RESERVATION

Total Area - 1.9 sq. miles
Tribally Owned - 100 percent
Total Population - 199
Native Population - 166
Tribal Enrollment - 582

The small island home of the Prairie Island Mde-wakanton Dakota sits on the Mississippi River 30 miles downriver from St. Paul. Like the rest of the state's Dakota the Prairie Island band was expelled from Minnesota following the bloody Dakota Conflict. The Secretary of the Interior established the present reservation in 1889 for the Dakota who returned to their homes instead of staying in exile in South Dakota and they continued to purchase land for the tribe through 1934, expanding their home to its present size. The reservation was officially recognized in 1936. Soon after this the U.S. Army Corp of Engineers built Lock and Dam

#3, burying about half of the tribe's low-laying island under the river and adding about half of the rest to the floodplain.

Their Treasure Island Casino, opened in 1984, is one of the state's most profitable but the biggest issue for the tribe today is "The Nuke." In 1973 Northern States Power (now Xcel Energy) built the Prairie Island Nuclear Generating Plant less than half a mile from the community, an act the tribe calls the second invasion. Despite not having an adequate evacuation plan for this busy island—with casino guests there can be as many as 11,000 people on the island at a time and the only road out is both vulnerable to floods and crossed by 20 to 25 trains a day—NSP was granted permission to store spent nuclear fuel on the island. Though the tribe has resisted the plant and its expansion from the start they have had only minor victories in the courts and the legislature.

cost $11, while lunch, brunch, and dinner cruises are anywhere from $18 to $30. The attached 250-room hotel features a swimming pool with a waterfall, a pair of hot tubs, fitness center, arcade, and rooms from $99. If you are driving your bedroom it can be parked in the large RV park for as little as $10. You can also come by boat since they have a full-service marina. There are several restaurants on-site including the Las Vegas-worthy **Tradewinds Buffet;** prices vary but it's generally $8 for lunch and $11 for dinner.

Turn down the road just before the casino and you'll pass the Prairie Island Nuclear Generating Plant (whose bright idea was it to build a nuclear power plant on the Mississippi River?) before coming to **Lock and Dam #3,** the busiest lock on the Upper Mississippi River. Approximately 20,000 recreational boats get an eight-foot lift each year, and you can watch them from the elevated viewing platform. It is open daily 8 A.M.–dusk from April through November.

Welch

Well away from the Mississippi River but just 2.5 miles south of Highway 61, quaint and quiet

Welch is worth a detour even if you just drive down into the valley for a quick peek. The tiny bluff-ringed town on the Cannon River so resembles a New England village that is stood in as one in the film *Here On Earth.* Welch is at the midpoint of the **Cannon Valley Trail,** a 19-mile paved bike and cross-country ski path between Red Wing and Cannon Falls. Just as popular as a ride on the trail is a trip on the river. **Welch Mill Canoeing & Tubing,** 651/388-7716 or 800/657-6760, will set you up for easy five- or 12-mile trips down the Cannon. Canoe rentals are $20 for the short ride and $25 for the full trip, while tubing trips are just $6. Added to the recreation mix in winter is **Welch Village,** 651/222-7079, with 40 downhill ski and snowboard runs, the largest dropping 350 feet, plus a half-pipe and terrain park. If you want to stay overnight, your only option is the basic, 150-site **Hidden Valley Campground,** 651/258-4550, just outside town along the Cannon Valley Trail. They charge $22, plus $2 more for electricity, and also rent inner tubes. The **Trout Scream Café,** 651/388-7494, downtown will fill you up with cheap sandwiches and ice cream. They are open daily for breakfast and lunch.

BLUFF COUNTRY

RED WING

The answers are yes. Both Red Wing Pottery and Red Wing Shoes hail from this flower-filled river town, one of the prettiest on the Upper Mississippi. Just an hour from St. Paul and Rochester, this vibrant city of 16,000 has a largely intact 19th-century downtown, a gift to all from previous city leaders who were ahead of their time in historic preservation. You can enjoy the results by just strolling downtown and the residential neighborhood next to it or pick up the *Footsteps Through Historic Red Wing* brochure at the historical museum or visitors center and follow the trio of walking tours.

History

A Dakota summer village had stood at the base of Barn Bluff since at least 1805, the year Lieutenant Zebulon Pike came through to explore the new lands acquired by the United States in the Louisiana Purchase. Half a century later the city was named for the chief that Pike met, Whoo-pa-doo-to (Wing of Scarlet), whose descendents resided in town through the middle of the 20th century. The first European settlers were Swiss Protestant missionaries who established an outpost here in 1837. Though they left eight years later, Rev. John Aiton revived the mission in 1848, and an official post office was opened two years later. The town didn't really take off, however, until the U.S. Land Office opened here in 1855. Waves of settlers claiming land on the western prairies filtered through, and a busy trade center emerged to serve them. By the end of the decade the population exceeded 1,250.

Even with the Civil War raging to the south the city thrived through the 1860s (the population more than tripled) with wheat leading the way, and soon Red Wing was the world's largest wheat port. As farmers shifted to other crops and the steamboats lost most of their business to the railroads its importance as a wheat market soon declined, but Red Wing never experienced the predictable economic bust because so many diverse industries had sprung up here. By the end of the century Red Wing had swapped superiority by becoming one of the nation's largest flour milling

centers. The innovative La Grange Mill, one of dozens in and around Red Wing, ground its first flour in 1877, and their Gilt Edge and Old Glory brands earned such acclaim that the company exported half of their output to Europe. Pottery also rose to prominence in the 1870s. The area's first potter was German immigrant Joseph Pohl, who sold some of his creations to neighbors in 1861, though he only remained in the area for a couple of years. A few potters followed in his footsteps, but with very limited success. In 1878 the Red Wing Stoneware Company finally got the business model right, and five years later they were joined in the clay trade by the Minnesota Stoneware Company. Eventually the companies merged and operated under the Red Wing United Stoneware and Red Wing Potteries names until the company folded in 1967. Their early crocks, water coolers, and butter jars are the most famous and desirable products with collectors, but as populations shifted to the cities the company diversified into flower pots, dinnerware, and even sewer pipe—if you live in the Midwest there's a good chance that some still runs under your town. Today two small companies keep the Red Wing Pottery tradition alive.

The city's first shoe factory opened in 1861, and eventually a tannery opened to supply them. Red Wing Shoes, just "The Shoe" to locals, sewed its first pair of boots in 1905 and within a decade production reached 200,000 pairs a year. Though they now annually manufacture millions of shoes in over 150 styles in their four plants (a pair here plus another two in Missouri and Kentucky), it remains a family-owned enterprise.

Sights

The **Goodhue County Historical Museum,** 1166 Oak St., 651/388-6024, perched high above the town, has a better-than-average local history collection on display. Highlights are the fossils and agates in the geology room, the ancient pottery and modern crafts in the Native American exhibit, and the Red Wing Pottery. Kids can climb in a Dakota tepee and try on clothes from centuries past. The museum is open Tuesday–Friday 10 A.M.–5 P.M. and Saturday–Sunday 1–5 P.M. Admission is $5.

© TIM BEWER

Red Wing's boat house village

There's an even larger pottery display at the **Red Wing Pottery Museum,** 2000 Old West Main St., 651/385-7716 or 800/977-7927, at historic **Pottery Place,** a former pottery factory that has been transformed into one of the most beautiful shopping malls you'll ever visit. The extensive collection, organized by the Red Wing Collectors Society, spans the earliest salt-glazed crocks to the expensive dinnerware made at the end of the company's history. From June through October the mall and museum are open Monday–Friday 9 A.M.–7 P.M., Saturday 9 A.M.–6 P.M., and Sunday 11 A.M.–5 P.M., while the hours the rest of the year are Monday–Saturday 10 A.M.–6 P.M. and Sunday 11 A.M.–5 P.M. Admission is free.

The story of the city's other famous industry is told at the little **Red Wing Shoe Museum,** 314 Main St. The company, whose headquarters is just upstairs, doesn't offer factory tours, but you can see the whole process here, from cutting the hide to final inspection. You won't wear out a pair of boots purchasing the finished product since the Red Wing Shoe Store is right next door.

Barn Bluff (343 feet tall)looming over downtown has always been a dominant landmark on the river, and its magnetic appeal has lured countless visitors to the top. Most famous was Henry David Thoreau, who climbed it during his 1861 journey to Minnesota. A set of steps leading up the backside makes the climb easier these days, though the steep route means you still have to earn the wonderful city and river views. The extensively bolted bluff faces are an increasingly popular rock-climbing destination. You can follow Scenic Skyline Drive to the top of **Sorin Bluff** for another scenic overlook of the city. The view isn't quite as good, but it comes with a lot less effort. Each winter about 100 bald eagles winter in the Red Wing area, and they can be seen up-close and personal at **Colville Park,** where dozens perch in the cottonwood trees when not fishing in the Mississippi. **Red Wing River Boat Rides,** 651/455-7983, depart from Levee Park daily at noon and 3 P.M. for an hour-long ride up to Lock and Dam #3 or down to Lake Pepin, poking into the backwaters where possible. A ride on the 20-passenger *Maggie,* a transport boat used during the Vietnam War, costs $10.

Botanist Alexander Anderson, inventor of the process behind "Puffed" wheat and rice, built his country estate and laboratory five miles west of

BLUFF COUNTRY

downtown. After he died his family donated the land and home to promote the arts, and today the **Anderson Center,** 651/388-2009, provides classes and hosts resident artists and short-term fellows. While they don't have an actual gallery, art is hung in the halls of the main building; you can see it weekdays 9 A.M.–5 P.M. There is also plenty of outdoor sculpture on the grounds, and guests are welcome to climb the water tower.

Recreation

The paved **Cannon Valley Trail** follows the bluffs above the Cannon River for 20 miles from Red Wing to Cannon Falls along a former railroad bed. A $3 Wheel Pass, available from local merchants or at trailhead pay stations, is required for adults. **Four Seasons Bike,** 2301 Old West Main St., 651/385-8614; and the **Outdoor Store,** 1811 Old West Main St., 651/388-5358, rent bikes for $25/day, both offer tandems and recumbents.

Hikers should head inland to the Hay Creek unit of the **Richard J. Dorer Memorial Hardwood State Forest,** 612/345-3216, where 17 miles of rugged trail climb the steep valleys and follow the ridge tops. In winter about a third are groomed for cross-country skiing. The principal trailhead, which also has a quiet picnic area and good trout fishing nearby, is four miles south of town on Hwy. 58, and then 1.5 miles north on the gravel road by Dressen's.

Paddlers can run the lovely 25 miles of the Cannon River from the city of Cannon Falls to the Mississippi. With just a few Class I rapids, it's an easy run suitable for families. There are no rentals available in Red Wing, though you can arrange this and shuttle service from **Cannon Falls Canoe & Kayak Rental,** 615 N. 5th St., 507/263-4657 or 877/882-2663, at the start of the run or in the village of Welch (see above). Exploring the labyrinth of Mississippi River backwaters surrounding town can also be great fun.

The **Mississippi National Golf Links,** 651/388-1874, on the south edge of town has a pair of courses often ranked among the state's best.

Entertainment and Events

The immaculately restored 1904 **Sheldon Theatre,** 443 W. 3rd St., 651/385-3667, has a busy, year-round schedule of theatrical and musical performances.

Nightlife spans Friday night jazz at **Jimmy's Pub** in the St. James Hotel, to weekend acoustic acts at the **Blue Moon Bagel Co.,** 427 W. 3rd St., 651/385-5799, to karaoke, DJs, and live bands at little **Guppies,** 325 Bush St., 651/385-8994. There isn't much else.

The city's biggest blowout is the **River City Days Festival,** the first full weekend in August, with a parade, talent show, ice cream social, arts and crafts fair, and dragon boat races. People take the latter event very seriously, and in the weeks leading up to the big event you'll sometimes see racers practicing. Hundreds of artists take over the downtown the second weekend in October for the **Fall Festival of the Arts.**

Accommodations

Red Wing has several top-notch bed-and-breakfasts, each in antique-filled, historic homes. The most distinctive building is the 1857 **Lawther Octagon House,** 927 W. 3rd St., 651/388-1778, which not only has some quirky twists and turns inside, but also a strong historic feel. Irish immigrant James Lawther came to this country at age 19 and took a gamble by purchasing the bulk of land around town. When the railroad came through he cleaned up—by some accounts he was briefly the wealthiest man in Minnesota—and built his dream home at age 25. Each of the five guestrooms, priced $115–200, has a private bath and some have whirlpool tubs.

Even bigger than it looks from the outside the **Candlelight Inn,** 818 W. 3rd St., 651/388-8034 or 800/254-9194, is an elegant 1877 Victorian mansion built by a former manager of the Red Wing Stoneware Company. Most of the home's original features, including copious woodwork and some stained glass windows, remain intact while a screened front porch is a pleasant addition. The friendly hosts have plenty of advice about Red Wing to share and they'll even give you a penny for your thoughts. Each of the five guestrooms, priced $139–199, has both a private bath and a fireplace: three have whirlpools.

The colorful **Moondance Inn,** 1105 W. 4th St., 651/388-8145, is an 1874 Italianate with a large front porch and museum-quality living room. Two of the five large guestrooms have views of Barn Bluff, where the stone for the house was quarried, and each has its own double whirlpool. Prices are $165 or $189.

Modern in comparison to the others the **Golden Lantern Inn,** 721 East Ave., 651/388-3315 or 888/288-3315, is no less distinguished. The 1932 Tudor Revival built by the president of Red Wing Shoes has abundant public space, though in the evening guests tend to gather for s'mores in the garden fireplace. Breakfast is available in the formal dining room, the screened porch, or your own room—the latter option is especially popular in Helen's Suite, which has a private balcony. Each of the five guestrooms has a private bath, a double whirlpool tub and/or fireplace, and is priced $149–215.

The only lodging right downtown is the venerable **St. James Hotel,** 406 Main St., 651/388-2846 or 800/252-1875, which was so highly regarded when it opened in 1875 that trains adjusted their schedules so passengers could stop for a meal. The Red Wing Shoe Company gave it a multi-million dollar restoration in 1977, reestablishing it as one of the top hotels on the river. Though thoroughly modernized it maintains its Victorian feel; there's even a pipe organ in the lobby. All 61 rooms are uniquely decorated with Amish quilts and antiques and most have river or bluff views. Rates start at $89.

As for ordinary hotels, the **Rodeway Inn,** 235 Withers Harbor Dr., 651/388-1502 or 800/228-2000, offers a pool and whirlpool for $73, and the **AmericInn,** 1819 Old West Main St., 651/385-9060 or 800/634-3444, adds a sauna and $16 to the bill. The only cheap lodging in Red Wing is the **Parkway Motel,** 3425 U.S. 61, 651/388-8231 or 800/762-0934, with basic but clean rooms with microwave and refrigerator for just $39.

Food

The **Port** restaurant at the St. James Hotel is the cream of the crop of Red Wing restaurants. The seasonal menu features such choices as macadamia-encrusted walleye, gnocchi, and roast rack of lamb. The decor is suitably elegant for the prices, which generally run $20 and up. It is open daily for dinner and reservations are recommended. The **Veranda,** also in the St. James, overlooks the river and has an outdoor patio. Much more casual than Port, it's still the second most formal restaurant in town. Typical lunch choices are walleye and chips, wild mushroom and asparagus linguini, and grilled salmon, while steak and eggs or pecan pancakes make it the top option for breakfast. Prices run $8–16. Open daily for breakfast and lunch, plus Fri.–Sun. for dinner. Sunday brunch at the St. James is served in the fifth floor **Summit Room**—$18 gets you a mighty big spread.

The only Red Wing restaurant that gets mentioned in the same breath as the Port is the **Staghead,** 219 Bush St., 651/388-6581. The principally Italian menu (about $8 for lunch and $9–19 for dinner) is served in an unpretentious but beautifully restored 1884 setting. They also have an excellent beer and wine list. Music fans who wondered whatever became of Greg Norton after the breakup of Hüsker Dü may be surprised to find that he prepared their dinner; he's been the Staghead's head chef for many years. Open Mon.–Sat. for lunch and Tues.–Sun. for dinner.

The most varied menu is at **Liberty's,** 303 W. 3rd St., 651/388-8877, a Red Wing institution since 1975. It's a casual family restaurant with burgers, steak, seafood, Italian, Mexican, a Friday fish fry, and breakfast served anytime. Prices run $4–18. Open daily for breakfast, lunch, and dinner, and they'll even pick you up at your boat or hotel.

Many Red Wingites are thankful for the opening of **Fiesta Mexicana,** 2555 W. Main St., 651/385-8939. All of the authentic south-of-the-border flavors are under $10. Open daily for lunch and dinner.

Braschler's, 410 W. 3rd St., 651/388-1589, has a truly spectacular bakery and a small soup, salad, and sandwich menu. Open Mon.–Sat. for lunch and dinner. The most popular spot for caffeine is **Lily's,** 419 W. 3rd St., 651/388-8797, which also serves $6 deli sandwiches and salads. Open Tues.–Sat. for breakfast, lunch, and dinner, plus Sun. for breakfast and lunch.

BLUFF COUNTRY

Shopping

Shopping is a key component of the Red Wing experience. Although many people make special trips for the pottery and antiques, there's quite a bit more available, most of it found in two main areas. Up along Old West Main Street, in what is known as the Historic Pottery District, you'll find a growing conglomeration of outlet stores, while specialty shops downtown lean toward the refined. Two companies continue the city's pottery heritage, and you can watch the products being made by hand at both of them. The revival began in 1987 at the **Red Wing Stoneware Company,** 651/388-4610 or 800/352-4877, which throws the classic crocks and jugs plus other customary and contemporary products. You can watch the potters work any time on weekdays through a shop window or take a factory tour at 1 P.M.; an additional 10 A.M. tour is added during the summer. They are located 4.5 miles west of town along U.S. 61. **Red Wing Pottery Sales,** 1995 Old West Main St., 651/388-3562 or 800/228-0174, has produced salt-glazed wares since 1996.

You can buy footwear direct from the source at the **Red Wing Shoe Store,** 314 Main St., 651/388-6233. For factory seconds scan the shelves at **Hughes Shoes,** 405 W. 3rd St., 651/388-6132; and **Walt's Shoe Service,** 312 4th St., 651/388-5510.

Antique lovers could easily spend half a day or more browsing the many shops. The best place to start is at the **Pottery Place** mall, 2000 Old West Main St. Here you'll find **Pottery Place Antiques,** 651/388-7765, and **Old Main Street Antiques,** 651/388-1371, two superb multi-dealer showrooms with plenty of Red Wing Pottery merchandise. Other equally large and worthy Red Wing stores are **Al's Antique Mall,** 1314 Old West Main St., 651/388-0572; **Antiques Of Red Wing,** 307 Main St., 651/385-5963; and **Memory Maker Antiques,** 419 Main St., 651/385-5914. Three small stores rounding on the scene are **Hill Street Antiques,** 212 Hill St., 651/388-0736; **Rocky's Lil' Emporium,** 213 Bush St., 651/388-9840; and **Teahouse Antiques,** 703 W. 4th St., 651/388-3669.

The **Canyon Trail Gallery,** 321 Main St., 651/388-5972, has sculpture and paintings from Minnesota and the West, much of it with a Native American theme. Regional artists get a shot at the small **Red Wing Arts Association Gallery,** 315 W. 4th St., 651/388-7569, in City Hall.

For an ethnic treat there's **Irish Macushlas,** 314 Main St., 651/385-0667; **Ruth's German Haus,** 1518 Old West Main St., 651/388-0516; the **Uffda Shop, 202 Bush St., 651/388-8436 (Scandinavian); and Whitehawk Gifts,** 1504 Old West Main St., 651/388-0354 (Native American).

Hobgoblin Music, 920 Hwy. 19, 651/388-8400, sell dulcimers, guitars, mandolins, banjos, bagpipes, drums, flutes, and similar folk instruments in their restored barn north of town. Stoney End Harps are manufactured in the lower level, and you can watch them come to life through a viewing window.

The **Red Wing Book Company,** 406 Main St., 651/388-7274, in the St. James Hotel, has a good local interest section with many Mississippi River titles.

Information and Services

You can get just about any question answered at the **Red Wing Visitors' Center,** 418 Levee St., 651/385-5934 or 800/498-3444, www.redwing.org, in the city's historic train depot. The lobby is open daily 8 A.M.–8 P.M. to pick up brochures, and it is staffed weekdays 8 A.M.–5 P.M.

Transportation

The **Amtrak,** 651/385-5934, Empire Builder service arrives at the city's historic depot from St. Paul at 9:04 A.M., while the western service comes through at 8:46 P.M. A walk-up day return ticket from St. Paul costs $28, half that with an advanced purchase. **Airport Passenger Service,** 800/869-5796, vans run five times a day between La Crosse, Wisconsin, and the Twin Cities stopping in Red Wing at the AmericInn. A round-trip ticket costs $44. Reservations are highly recommended.

If you are arriving by boat there is short-term dockage at Levee Park alongside downtown. For additional boating services **Bill's Bay Marina,** 651/388-0481; **Ole Miss Marina,** 651/388-8643; and **Red Wing Marina,** 651/388-8995, can meet your needs.

The Red Wing RIDE, 651/388-0332, minibuses run between downtown and Old West Main Street for $1. You can tour the town in a 1931 Studebaker or similar classic car with **Riders Express,** 651/380-9652, or from the air with **River Valley Sightseeing Flights,** 715/594-3999. Prices depend on where you want to go and what you want to see, but each has set itineraries from $100 and $65 respectively.

RED WING TO WABASHA

Frontenac State Park

This 2,773-acre state park stretches along four miles of Lake Pepin, a 28-mile-long widening of the Mississippi River. Most facilities, including a picnic ground with great Mississippi views on Point-No-Point, are perched atop a forested 450-foot bluff. Moving inland down the back of the bluff you'll find a diverse ecosystem of prairie, oak savanna, floodplain forest, and a small lake, and the varied habitats make for great bird-watching: some 260 species have been recorded here. Most noteworthy are the many species of migrating warblers that pass through in early May, while the prothonotary and Cerulean warblers, rare in Minnesota, nest in the bottomland forests.

Frontenac has nearly 15 miles of hiking trail. The most popular is the short and easy **Bluffview Trail,** an interpretive path that offers both forest and grassland scenery. Heading for 1.5 miles atop the 450-foot ridge in the opposite direction and returning down along the river is the more rewarding **Bluffside Trail.** The local advice is to return up hill on the east end, which is a more gradual climb. At the far end of the trail, behind the campground, is **In-Yan-Teopa,** a giant rock with a hole carved through its heart by glacial meltwaters. There is an overlook with a historical marker above the stone, but to see the hole you must walk down the trail. Beginning at the parking area along Highway 61 the .75-mile **Sand Point Trail** cuts through wetlands on a long boardwalk and leads out to Lake Pepin, where you can stroll the beach. This is the most noteworthy spot in the park for bird-watchers, and interpretive signs along the way discuss the history and ecology of the area. The other trail starting

here is a short and easy unnamed walk that loops past some small Native American burial mounds. In the winter the park maintains a steep sledding hill and grooms 5.5 miles of ski trail which, unfortunately, intersect with snowmobile trails at several points. The web of trails through the center of the park twists through a mix of field and forest and past the remnants of a 19th-century quarry that supplied limestone for the Cathedral of St. John the Divine in New York City.

The 58 shady sites in the campground are spaced close together, but all have trees between them. The 19 electric sites are in the first two loops, so if you are tenting reserve a site in the back two. Better yet, take one of the four cart-in campsites, which are less than half a mile down a trail. Call 651/345-3401 with any park questions.

Mount Frontenac

Across the highway from the park is **Mount Frontenac,** 651/388-5826 or 800/488-5826, a ski resort and golf course nestled in the bluffs. These links are considered some of the most scenic in the state, while the biggest of the 11 ski runs drops 420 feet. The facility is owned by the Prairie Island Dakota, who offer discounted stay and play packages at their nearby Treasure Island Resort and Casino.

Lake City

On June 28, 1922, 18-year-old Ralph Samuelson strapped two eight-foot pine boards to his feet, grabbed hold of an old clothesline, and let an airplane pull him across the Mississippi River just offshore of Lake City; on that day water-skiing was born. Replicas of his original skis (he broke the originals while skiing) are on display at the Lake City Area Chamber of Commerce, 212 S. Washington St., 651/345-4123 or 877/525-2348, www.lakecity.org. Lake City, as this 28-mile widening of the Mississippi River is known, is the Upper Mississippi's top spot for sailing, water-skiing, and boating. With 625 slips, the city-owned **Lake City Marina,** 651/345-4211, is the largest marina on the Upper Mississippi. If you don't have your own boat **Sail Away of Lake City,** 651/345-5225, rents a variety of craft including sailboats and pontoons. Currently there are two golf courses in the area, the 18-hole **Lake City Country Club,** 651/345-3221; and the nine-hole **Lake Pepin Golf Course,** 651/345-5768, though people across the state are anxiously awaiting the opening of the Hale Irwin-designed **Mississippi Jewel,** 651/345-5999 or 800/747-8676, which should begin life in July 2004.

Great River Vineyard, 35680 U.S. 61, 877/345-3531, three miles north of town, has seven acres of trellises, but instead of fermenting their grapes they produce juice, jelly, and jam. You can also pick your own grapes. They are open to the public Monday–Saturday 9 A.M.–5 P.M. and Sunday noon–5 P.M. from mid-Aug. through mid-Oct. There are also a couple of apple orchards selling directly to the public (Aug.–Nov.) along the highway near town.

Most of the city's hotels, including several really old and cheap properties, sit north of town along Highway 61. A step up from those at the bottom is the family-friendly **Sunset Motel,** 1515 N. Lakeshore Dr., 651/345-5331 or 800/945-0192. It's got an outdoor heated pool, beach, game room, and fish-cleaning house, and they'll even pick you up at the marina. They charge $68. Much newer is the **AmericInn,** 1615 N. Lakeshore Dr., 651/345-5611 or 800/800/634-3444, with a pool, whirlpool, sauna, and rates from $85.

The local choice for home-cooking away from home is **The Galley,** 100 E. Lyon Ave., 651/345-9991, with a typical all-American roster of steak, seafood, and sandwiches—most of it for around $5 and none of it over $10. They also serve a Friday fish fry and a Sunday breakfast buffet. Open daily for breakfast, lunch, and dinner. The relaxing **Rhythm & Brew Coffeehouse,** 220 E. Chestnut St., 651/345-5335, has a small menu of soups and sandwiches. They host live acoustic performers on weekends. Open daily for breakfast and lunch (except closed Sun. in winter), plus Fri. and Sat. for dinner. **Chickadee Cottage,** 317 N. Lakeshore Dr., 651/345-5155, a combination gift shop and restaurant, serves made-from-scratch meals like omelets and Swedish meatballs, plus afternoon tea is available—all prices are between $4–8. Open Tues.–Sun. for breakfast and lunch between April and November.

Airport Passenger Service, 800/869-5796, vans make five runs a day between La Crosse, Wisconsin, and the Twin Cities, stopping in town at the AmericInn. It costs $50 round-trip and reservations are required.

WABASHA

Wabasha is Minnesota's most timeless river town; replace the cars on Main Street with horse and buggies and you'd have a scene almost straight out of the last act of the 19th century. Only 15 buildings in the seven-block historic district were erected after 1900, and the Wabasha Bridge hanging behind it adds a scenic flourish. In 1826 fur trader Augustine Rocque, whose father was French and mother Dakota, built a trading post here, and since the site has been continuously occupied since that day Wabasha claims to be Minnesota's oldest city. It acquired the name Cratte's Landing in 1838 after Oliver Cratte built a home and blacksmith shop here, but five years later the growing settlement was renamed in honor of the respected Dakota chief Wa-pa-shaw who held sway over the area at that time. The town thrived as a lumbering, milling, and boat-building center between 1850 and 1880 and at that time was one of the largest wheat markets along the river. As the railroads usurped its importance as a shipping center the town stagnated, and for most of the 20th century the beautiful downtown was pretty much left alone.

The town's current claim to fame comes as the home of Jack Lemmon and Walter Matthau in the *Grumpy Old Men* movies, though they were filmed almost entirely elsewhere in the state: Faribault for the downtown and St. Paul for the neighborhood. The only Wabasha location is the St. Felix Church shown for few seconds during the opening credits in the original. Screenwriter Mark Steven Johnson grew up nearby in Hastings, and his grandfather—Old Man Gilbert—lived in Wabasha. Though the movies are fictional, many of the characters and incidents are based on real people and events.

Sights and Recreation

Each winter the Mississippi River around Wabasha

UPPER MISSISSIPPI RIVER
NATIONAL WILDLIFE AND FISH REFUGE

Established in 1924 to protect smallmouth bass spawning grounds, the Upper Mississippi River National Wildlife and Fish Refuge follows the river for 261 miles from just above Wabasha south to Rock Island, Illinois. It is the longest wildlife refuge in the Lower 48. Along the way it encompasses over 233,000 acres of river, islands, forest, marshes, sloughs, backwater lakes, sandbars, and scattered prairie remnants, almost all of it in the floodplain.

The refuge headquarters is in Winona at 51 East 4th Street, 507/454-7351 or 800/657-3775. They have maps and brochures and can answer just about any question you might have.

Wildlife

The refuge is home to 57 species of mammals including white-tailed deer, coyote, fox, otter, and beaver; the endangered Blanding's and wood turtles and 51 other reptile and amphibian species; and 118 kinds of fish ranging from the minnows to sturgeon.

Birds have been the biggest winners in the United States Fish and Wildlife Service's conservation efforts. Over 300 species have been recorded here and the river is one of the continent's principal migration corridors. Geese and ducks are especially abundant. Each fall up to 75 percent of the North American population of canvasback ducks may be seen on river Pools 7 and 8 around La Crosse, Wisconsin. Up to 12,000 tundra swans can be seen in late October and early November around Weaver Bottoms as they pass through during the fall migration. Bald eagles are year-round residents—nearly 100 pair nest in the refuge—though they are most impressive in winter when they congregate below dams and at the mouths of tributaries—where the water doesn't freeze over. The Wabasha and Red Wing areas are the top winter viewing spot on the Minnesota side. Heron and egret rookeries, often hundreds of nests strong, are found in the more remote areas. Other birds commonly found in the refuge are sandhill crane, turkey vulture, pheasant, wild turkey, Eastern bluebird, yellow warbler, and an increasing number of American white pelicans. Endangered and threatened species residing here include osprey, peregrine falcon, red-shouldered hawk, great egret, and yellow-crowned night heron.

Paddling

Lazy canoeing is fantastic in the quiet backwaters where countless side channels and sloughs wind through hundreds of wooded islands. In the summer, acres of water lilies and other flowering water plants are in bloom. In addition to the up close and personal look at the river's rich flora and fauna the backwaters offer adventure and solitude; you can explore at will, enjoy getting lost, and for the most part motorboats can't make it back there. The braided backwater labyrinths are most abundant in the upper sections of each pool where the construction of the locks and dams have had less effect on the river. Because of heavy boat and barge traffic the main river channel is not a good place to canoe; even just crossing it can be difficult. The largest barges need a mile to stop and they can not steer out of your way!

Boaters of all kinds can camp on refuge islands for up to 14 days at a single site. During waterfowl hunting season (generally late September to mid-November in Minnesota) camping is only allowed outside closed areas and on sites visible from the main channel. Downed wood may be used for campfires, though cutting of any tree is, of course, prohibited.

is home to one of the largest concentrations of bald eagles in the Lower 48. They come south to Wabasha because the rapid current keeps the river open year-round, allowing them to fish. The early birds show up around the beginning of November, though the best viewing, when over 200 can be seen on most days, doesn't begin until December. Most stick around through March. Just before they leave, a sharp peak occurs (the record daily count was 697) as other eagles that went farther south stop here on their trip back home. Although sightings are all but guaranteed during this time, they aren't exactly rare the rest of the year since 30 pair nest in the area. The **National Eagle Center,** 152 Main St., 651/565-4989, with educational displays, knowledgeable staff, and a pair of the real thing, is a must-see. Angel and Harriet cannot be released back into the wild because of permanent disabilities, so they eye up visitors face-to-face on the back deck. The center also provides spotting scopes and knowledgeable volunteers 1–3 P.M. on weekends during the winter at the **Eagle Observation Deck** in back. You can also get some up-close looks at several pullouts along the highway just to the north of Wabasha between Reads Landing and Camp Lacupolis. The best viewing times are mornings and early evenings when they dive into the river for fish; during the middle of the day they can be seen perched in trees. The Center is open year-round Tuesday–Sunday 10 A.M.–4 P.M. and admission is free. The current facility is just a temporary home. A much larger and more involved center is planned for the riverfront with a hoped-for 2004 opening.

Two museums sit about two miles outside of town. To the north in the hamlet of Reads Landing is the **Wabasha County Historical Museum,** 651/345-3987, which occupies a musty 1870 schoolhouse, only the second brick school built in Minnesota. The most interesting of the historical hodgepodge is the pearl button display; this was once a very lucrative industry all along the river. There is farm machinery in the back annex and a few exhibits have been moved down to the old Post Office, including copies of some letters sent by Pa and Laura Ingalls to family across the river in Pepin, Wisconsin, the town where Laura was born. It is open Friday

and Saturday noon–4 P.M. during the summer. Admission is free. To the south along Hwy. 60 is the far more interesting **Arrowhead Bluffs Museum,** 651/565-3829, an eclectic private collection of old farming and logging tools, arrowheads and similar Native American artifacts, old bottles, and one of every Winchester gun model (including commemoratives) from 1866 to 1982. Mounted wildlife from across North America include moose, polar bear, javalina, rattlesnake, and scorpions. It is open daily 10 A.M.–6 P.M. May through December. Admission is $4.

If you want to take a short spin around the river, rent a fishing boat or pontoon from **Great River Houseboats,** 1009 E. Main St., 651/565-3376.

The **Coffee Mill Bluff,** 651/565-2777, ski area right on the edge of town has 11 runs, the longest dropping 425 feet, making it the tallest in southern Minnesota.

Entertainment and Events

Wabasha's biggest bash is the **Riverboat Days Festival** held in late July. Highlights include lumberjack shows, dog Frisbee, and craft and antique fairs. Come February it's time for the **Grumpy Old Men Festival** with ice golf, softball in the snow, dead fish relay races, and a fish house parade. Indoors there's cribbage, bingo, music, Raghetti's Spaghetti Feed, and a look-alike contest.

Accommodations

Unquestionably *the* place to stay in town, or along this whole stretch of river for that matter, is the **Anderson House,** 333 W. Main St., 651/565-4524. In operation since 1856 this is the oldest continuously operating hotel west of the Mississippi, and some things haven't changed since then. If you've got a chill they'll bring you a hot brick in a quilted envelope, and if you've got a cold they'll prepare you a mustard plaster. Plus, as if the hotel wasn't unique enough, they have a dozen cats waiting to share your room, should you desire. The felines are free, but in high demand, so reserve them early. Many of the rooms still have original furnishings; the buckling hallways only add to the hotel's charm. Rates start at $94; some of the largest suites run $200.

There's also some history at the **Bridgewa-**

ters **Bed and Breakfast,** 136 Bridge Ave., 651/565-4208, cmoore@clear.lakes.com, a large 1903 Queen Anne Victorian with a wraparound porch and six antique-filled guestrooms. Rates run $79 with a shared bath to $145 for spacious quarters with double whirlpools.

The cheapest rooms—just $45—are at the small **Wabasha Motel,** 1110 Hiawatha Dr. E., 651/565-9932, just south of town.

For the ultimate river experience, reserve a floating home from **Great River Houseboats,** 1009 E. Main St., 651/565-3376. A four-passenger craft is $400 for a two-night rental, while a luxury boat sleeping ten goes for over a thousand dollars for a weekend.

The **Kruger Campground,** five miles west of town along Hwy. 60, in the Richard J. Dorer Memorial Hardwood State Forest, 651/345-3216, is a peaceful primitive campground with 19 shady and widely spaced sites for $9. Nine miles of hiking trails, including a .75-mile wheelchair-accessible path, lead through the forested bluffs.

Food

Though not the actual bar from the *Grumpy Old Men* movies, **Slippery's,** 10 Church Ave., 651/565-4748, did lend them its name. The casual riverside, boat-in restaurant has an outside deck, while interior decoration includes several set pieces from the movies—both films play continuously in the dining room. Putz burgers, Catfish Hunter sandwiches, and Mexican dishes run about $5, while pasta and steak are available for dinner. They also do a popular Friday-night fish fry. Open daily for lunch and dinner.

The **River Town Café,** 119 Pembroke Ave. S., 651/565-2202, is a no-frills family joint right downtown with burgers and other sandwiches for about $4. Open daily for breakfast, lunch, and dinner.

The best location for coffee and a snack is the **Flour Mill Bakery,** 146 W. Main St., 651/565-4070, which has a patio overlooking the river and some really good baked goods. Open Tues.–Sun. for breakfast and lunch.

Information and Services

The **Wabasha Area Chamber of Commerce,**
160 W. Main St., 651/565-4158 or 800/565-4158, www.wabashamn.org, is open Monday–Friday 9 A.M.–5 P.M. On weekends someone at the eagle center next door should be able to answer your questions.

Transportation

Airport Passenger Service, 800/869-5796, vans make five runs a day between La Crosse, Wisconsin, and the Twin Cities, stopping in town at the Mobil gas station, 825 Pembroke Ave. S., 651/565-2324, just west of downtown. The round-trip fare is $54 and reservations are required. If you are arriving via the Mississippi there is a courtesy dock right behind downtown, while the full-service **Wabasha Marina Boatyard,** 1009 E. Main St., 651/565-4747; and **Parkside Marina,** 829 W. 3rd St., 651/565-3809, can take care of any other boating needs.

WABASHA TO WINONA
LARK Toys

The last thing you would expect to find in little Kellogg, population 439, is one of the world's greatest toy stores, but there it is. LARK stands for Lost Arts Revival by Kreofsky and the family-run enterprise, which now attracts hundreds of thousands of visitors annually, began in 1983 when Donn and Sarah Kreofsky began making wooden toys in their garage. Word spread and soon they were stocking FAO Schwatz and 2,500 other retailers. Burned-out by the big-business side of things they decided to open their own toy store. It has grown into a 31,500-square-foot complex, and now the largest independent toy store in North America sells everything from board games to chemistry sets to Russian nesting dolls to wind-up toys plus, of course, the handmade wooden toys that started it all.

The one-of-a-kind **LARK Carousel** ($1) takes riders for a spin on 18 whimsical, hand-carved creatures like a goldfish, otter, and loon. The thousands of antique toys from the 1900s through the 1960s on display throughout the store will no doubt bring back memories. Also on-site are a small café and miniature golf course. LARK, 507/767-3387 or 888/747-5275, is open weekdays 9 A.M.–5 P.M., and weekends 10 A.M.–5 P.M. for most of the year, but only Friday–Sunday during January and February.

Weaver Bottoms

One of Minnesota's most impressive migrations begins in mid-October when tundra swans swoop down from above the Arctic Circle and take a monthlong break on the Mississippi before continuing to their East Coast wintering grounds. In good years this shallow backwater area, stretching four miles between the hamlets of Weaver and Minneiska, has seen as many as 12,000 swans in a single day; the peak comes within a few days of Nov. 10. The best viewing spot is at the top of the hill next to St. Mary's Cemetery, 1.75 miles south of Weaver—look for the bald eagle's nest here. Another good spot is the observation deck at Weaver Landing. Occasionally you might also spot them from downtown Minneiska. Because of the heavy traffic, stopping along U.S. 61 to take a look is not a good idea. The best swan watching is actually across the river in Alma, Wisconsin, where volunteers are available daily 9 A.M. to dusk to answer questions.

Drive along County Road 84 (which joins U.S. 61 about 1.5 miles north of Weaver) and you'll pass 1000 acres of rolling sand dunes, some as high as 30 feet. Most are protected as the **Kellogg-Weaver Dunes Scientific and Natural Area,** on land owned and managed by The Nature Conservancy.

John A. Latsch State Park

Twelve miles before Winona a trio of 500-foot-tall bluffs—Faith, Hope, and Charity—are perched high above the Mississippi in this seldom-visited state park. The aptly named **Riverview Trail,** a lung-chugging half-mile set of steps, climbs 450 feet through the forest and past a prairie remnant to the top of Charity Bluff, the tallest of the three. The views, of course, are superb. The only camping is at seven rustic walk-in sites. If you have any questions, call 507/932-3007.

The park is named in honor of a Winona businessman and avid Mississippi River angler who, around the turn of the 20th century, was chased off a farmer's land when he attempted to take shelter from a storm. In order to prevent similar affronts from occurring to anyone else ever again, he spent two million dollars to purchase over 18,000 riverside acres and then gave it away for use as parks and wildlife habitat. His campaign later inspired the creation of the Izaak Walton League, whose first act was to promote the creation of the Upper Mississippi River Wildlife and Fish Refuge.

Directly across from the park is **Lock and Dam #5** where you can watch boats get a nine-foot lift. The observation area is open daily 8 A.M.–dusk from April through November.

WHITEWATER STATE PARK

The large Whitewater River Valley, filled with spring-fed streams and tall limestone bluffs, cuts through the heart of southeast Minnesota before merging with the Mississippi near Weaver. The name, bestowed by the Dakota, speaks not of frothy rapids but rather its milky springtime color caused by clay deposits accumulating during high water. When European settlers moved into the valley to farm, they cleared the steep hills and, by the turn of the 20th century, as a direct result of their actions, severe flooding began. By the 1930s the floods had become epidemic—the village of Beaver flooded 28 times in 1938 alone—and frustrated people abandoned their homes. The DNR purchased the most erosion-prone lands and taught farmers to change their land use practices. Today, the 28,000-acre Whitewater Wildlife Management Area comprises nearly half of the valley, and the restoration efforts have made this something of a natural paradise. The popular 2,800-acre park lies adjacent to the WMA but was established for its beauty decades before the state stepped in to stop the floods.

The valley is a great bird-watching destina-

> *The name Whitewater State Park, bestowed by the Dakota, speaks not of frothy rapids but rather its milky springtime color caused by clay deposits accumulating during high water.*

tion, and the 237 recorded species include Cerulean warbler, Louisiana waterthrush, Acadian flycatcher, and other species at the far northwest extent of their ranges. Whitewater is also one of the best places in the state to enjoy spring wild-flowers. For more information about the natural and human history of the valley, stop by the Whitewater Valley Visitor Center at the park office. The most popular of the many naturalist programs held here discusses the facts and myths of rattlesnakes and includes a chance to see a live one. Call 507/932-3007 for information about the programs or anything else related to the park.

Recreation

There are two kinds of hiking trails at Whitewater, steep and flat. The best representative of the latter is the mile-long **Trout Run Trail,** a self-guided interpretive path that cuts back and forth across its namesake creek. The 2.7-mile **Coyote Point Trail** and 4.2-mile **Dakota Trail** climb the 250-foot bluffs on the west side of the park leading to some wonderful vistas, particularly Eagle Point and Signal Point along the latter trail. The .75-mile **Chimney Rock Trail** is the easiest, and thus most popular, bluff-top climb. Steps on the steepest parts of all three trails make the climbs a bit easier. In the winter the level trails are groomed for cross-country skiing, while snowshoe rentals let you explore the rest of the park.

The Whitewater River and some of its tributaries are some of the state's top trout runs with ample brown, brook, and rainbows. Currently the DNR is trying out a winter catch-and-release season on a portion of this river.

The Whitewater River can be canoed down to the Mississippi River, though low water levels and frequent snags make it a tough journey. If you want to go anyway, start the 17-mile trip in the village of Elba, the last town in the valley. Despite the name the river has no natural rapids, though there are some small ones around bridges.

The most popular spot in the park on hot summer days is the wide, sandy beach.

Camping

Whitewater has a pair of campgrounds and, in an exception to the general rule, the larger one is

the better of the two. The 75 sites (47 electric) in the Cedar Hill Campground are mostly shady and widely spaced, while most of the 31 sites across the river at Gooseberry Glen are crowded closely together. There are four walk-in sites, plus a camper cabin is available April–October.

Elsewhere in the Valley

Several unique natural and historic attractions are found near the park. A map available at the park office details these and many others, and park naturalists often lead tours to these satellite sites. The **Elba Fire Tower** is perched atop a bluff three miles northeast of the park. Some 600 steps lead up to the tower, which you can climb (during daylight hours between April and October) for spectacular views of the valley's farms and forests. You can hunt for (and almost certainly find!) **fossils** to the west of the park along County Road 9 about seven miles from Hwy. 74; the site is between the river and the church. Scan the sedimentary rock, cut away for the road, and you'll find the calcified remains of ancient plants and animals that lived here hundreds of millions of years ago, back when this land was buried under the ocean. Most common are clamlike brachiopods, snails, moss animals (bryozoans), and sea lilies. The park office has a handy identification guide available. The **Crystal Springs Trout Hatchery** rears over 400,000 brook, rainbow, lake, and splake trout annually. You can visit the facility weekdays 8 A.M.–4:30 P.M.

WINONA

The largest of Minnesota's river towns below St. Paul was founded as Montezuma in 1851 by Orren Smith, captain of the steamboat Nominee, who needed a location between Galena and St. Paul to load fuel wood. Within two years it had grown into a town of 300 and was renamed Winona (Firstborn Daughter in the Dakota language). Not only did steamboats resupply themselves here but, when the local land office opened, settlers heading west poured in to secure farms and purchase provisions needed for a new life on the prairie. By the end of the decade nearly a

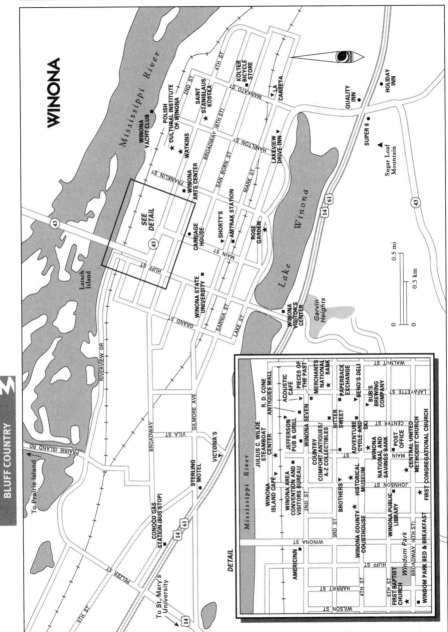

WINONA

Mississippi River

Lake Winona

WINONA YACHT CLUB
POLISH CULTURAL INSTITUTE OF WINONA
SAINT STANISLAUS KOSTKA
WATKINS
KOLTER BICYCLE STORE
LA CARRETA
QUALITY INN
HOLIDAY INN
SUPER 8
Sugar Loaf Mountain
WINONA ARTS CENTER
LAKEVIEW DRIVE-INN
SEE DETAIL
CARRIAGE HOUSE
SHORTY'S
AMTRAK STATION
ROSE GARDEN
WINONA STATE UNIVERSITY
WINONA VISITOR'S CENTER
Garvin Heights

2ND ST
4TH ST
MANKATO ST
HAMILTON ST
BROADWAY (6TH ST)
SAN BORN ST
MARK ST
FRANKLIN ST
MAIN ST
HUFF ST
SARNIA ST
LAKE ST
GRAND ST
RIVERVIEW DR

Latsch Island

43

14 61

43

0.5 mi
0.5 km
0

To Prairie Island
PRAIRIE ISLAND RD
GILMORE AVE
BROADWAY
VILA ST
STERLING MOTEL
VICTORIA'S
CONOCO GAS STATION (BUS STOP)
61 14
PELZER ST
5TH ST
To St. Mary's University
14

BLUFF COUNTRY

DETAIL

Mississippi River

WALNUT ST
LAFAYETTE ST
CENTER ST
MAIN ST
JOHNSON ST
2ND ST
3RD ST
WINONA ST
HUFF ST
HARRIET ST
WILSON ST
BROADWAY (6TH ST)
5TH ST
4TH ST

R. D. CONE ANTIQUES MALL
PIECES OF THE PAST
MERCHANTS NATIONAL BANK
ACOUSTIC CAFE
PAPERBACK EXCHANGE
BENO'S DELI
BUB'S BREWING COMPANY
JULIUS C. WILKIE STEAMBOAT CENTER
JEFFERSON PUB & GRILL
WINONA SEVEN
BITTER SWEET
ADVENTURE CYCLE AND SKI
WINONA ISLAND CAFE
COUNTRY COMFORT ANTIQUES/A-Z COLLECTIBLES
WINONA NATIONAL AND SAVINGS BANK
POST OFFICE
CENTRAL UNITED METHODIST CHURCH
WINONA AREA CONVENTION AND VISITORS BUREAU
BROTHERS
HISTORICAL MUSEUM
FIRST CONGREGATIONAL CHURCH
WINONA COUNTY COURTHOUSE
WINONA PUBLIC LIBRARY
Windom Park
AMERICINN
FIRST BAPTIST CHURCH
WINDOM PARK BED & BREAKFAST

© AVALON TRAVEL PUBLISHING, INC.

dozen sawmills were turning and the town thrived. Flour mills also went up in the 1850s, and the settlers who had previously passed through town continued to enrich it by shipping their harvest back from as far west as South Dakota, first by oxcart and then in 1862 along the Winona and St. Peter Railroad. Ironically, by the 1880s this treeless, barren plain had become one of Minnesota's greatest lumber towns and the fourth largest grain market in the country, reportedly producing more millionaires than any other similarly sized city in the nation.

By the late 19th century, cities farther west had appropriated much of the flour business, and around the turn of the 20th century the surrounding forests had largely been cleared. As the old industries died out new ones, like brick making, dairying, meatpacking, sauerkraut (at one time Winona produced more than any place west of Chicago), and quarrying arose to keep the city prosperous. **Sugar Loaf Mountain,** visible from across the city and well beyond, is a 500-foot-tall monument to the latter industry. The 85-foot pinnacle at the top appears natural, but is, in fact, the remains of an 1880s quarry. If you want to climb it, a well-worn trail leads up the south side of the peak from the redbrick building serving the city's water reservoirs on West Burns Valley Rd. Today, despite a population of over 27,000, it is a fairly sleepy town.

Sights

Paying homage to the city's past is the **Julius C. Wilkie Steamboat Center,** 507/454-1254, a full-sized paddlewheeler replica in Levee Park. The lower level is a small museum with photos and memorabilia from the steamboat era, while a splendid Grand Salon fills the upper deck. An actual steamer was once on display in this park, but when it burned down the Winona County Historical Society built the Wilkie in its place using the engine and paddlewheel salvaged from the original. The Wilkie is open Wednesday–Sunday 10 A.M.–4 P.M. from mid-May through mid-September. Admission is $3. For a bit of the real thing, board the *Julia Belle Swain,* 608/784-4882 or 800/815-1005, one of just five steam-powered paddlewheelers left prowling the river.

The boat itself was crafted in 1971, but the reciprocating engines were salvaged from a 1915 ferryboat—the whole elegant setup offers a pretty remarkable time warp. Though this gorgeous vessel is based in La Crosse, Wisconsin, they make Winona a home away from home so there is ample opportunity to take a ride during their June to October season. Two-hour evening sightseeing cruises cost $20, while lunch and dinner options are $45–49.

The **Winona County Historical Museum,** 160 Johnson St., 507/454-2723, is one of the state's most interesting local history museums. Most impressive are the lumber mill diorama and the balcony-level timeline beginning during the Ice Age and ending in the 1960s. Children can explore replicas of a cave, tepee, and steamboat pilothouse. The museum is open Monday–Friday 9 A.M.–5 P.M. and Saturday–Sunday noon–4 P.M. (weekdays only during Jan. and Feb.). Admission is $3. The Historical Society also maintains the **Bunnell House,** three miles south of town in the hamlet of Homer. Willard Bunnell, a trader who supplied lumber to passing steamboats, was Winona County's first permanent white settler. He built this Rural Gothic wood frame house in the early 1850s, making it one of the oldest surviving houses in the state. From the outside it looks like a movie-set haunted house, and inside it is furnished as it might have been in the mid-1800s. It is open Wednesday–Saturday 10 A.M.–5 P.M. and Sunday 1–5 P.M. during the summer. Admission is $3.

During the last half of the 19th century several thousand Polish immigrants settled in Winona's east end, and today the city has the nation's largest concentration of Poles from the Kashubian region. The still growing **Polish Cultural Institute of Winona,** 102 Liberty St., 507/454-3431, makes an effort to both tell and preserve their history. An interesting selection of Polish crafts and books are for sale in the brightly painted gift shop. The center is open Monday–Friday 10 A.M.–3 P.M., Saturday 10 A.M.–noon, and Sunday 1–3 P.M. from May to November. Admission is free. One block over on East 3rd Street is the **Watkins Heritage Museum,** 507/457-6095. Displays cover the entire history of the

© TIM BEWER

the Julius C. Wilkie Steamboat Center

company, from the days of peddling Dr. Ward's Vegetable Anodyne Liniment, "good for man or beast," via horse-drawn wagon in 1868 to its current line of nearly 400 products sold door-to-door by 80,000 North American salespeople. Though primarily just a collection of old bottles, boxes, and tins, it is far more interesting than you would expect. It is open Monday–Friday 10 A.M.–4 P.M. and Saturday 10 A.M.–2 P.M. Admission is free.

Though many historic buildings have been lost over the years, downtown Winona is still the most architecturally interesting city between St. Paul and Galena, and over 100 structures are listed on the National Register of Historic Places. The *Historic Downtown Walking Tour* brochure, available at visitors center, CVB, and Historical Museum, details about two dozen of them, most dating from the last half of the 19th century. They also offer a taped driving tour. The banks designed by prominent Prairie School architects are the most noteworthy edifices. The 1912 **Merchants National Bank,** 102 E. 3rd St., designed by William Purcell and George Elmslie, has an intricate terra cotta arch over the front door and amazing stained glass windows that are even beautiful

from the outside. It is open Monday–Thursday 9 A.M.–4 P.M. and Friday 9 A.M.–5 P.M. The 1914 George Maher-designed **Winona National and Savings Bank,** 204 Main St., creatively combines Egyptian Revival with the classic Prairie School style. An odd, little museum on the second floor has a couple of placards on the bank's history, a wall full of antique guns, and dozens of trophies from African safaris, including various hippo, baboon, wildebeest, and elephant body parts. Open weekdays 8:30 A.M.–5 P.M. and Sat. 9 A.M.–noon. Many of the city's fanciest Victorian homes surround **Windom Park.** The bronze statue in the center of the fountain is of the city's namesake, a Sioux maiden who, according to legend, threw herself off a Mississippi bluff rather than marry a man she did not love. Though not on the brochure don't miss the impressive **Church of Saint Stanislaus Kostka** at 625 East 4th Street. Topped by a towering, silver dome the 1894 church combines a Greek cross plan with Romanesque and Baroque elements.

The greatest reminders of Winona's past wealth are its stained glass windows, many made by Tiffany and other famous studios. These fabulous works of art adorn churches and other buildings all over town. The aforementioned banks and Church of Saint Stanislaus Kostka are three of the most spectacular examples. If you can stop by during normal business hours the **Watkins Company** headquarters, 150 Liberty St., and the **Winona County Courthouse,** 171 W. 3rd St., are also worth a look. The Historical Museum has displays about stained glass, as well as a large window of its own. Though less easy to visit, the **First Baptist Church,** 368 W. Broadway St.; **Central United Methodist Church,** 114 W. Broadway St.; and **First Congregational Church,** 161 W. Broadway St. are also impressive. It's not just the number of stained glass windows that lead some to call Winona the "Stained Glass Capital" of the USA. Winona is also home to seven studios that make, restore, and repair windows worldwide. A couple of them give tours, but only to large groups.

Winona has several good parks. **Lake Park,** the city's most popular, surrounds Lake Winona. Of most interest to tourists is the modest rose garden on the north side. It also has fishing piers, a disc golf course, and band shell. Most of Winona sits on a giant sandbar that was once, a very long time ago, an island in the Mississippi, and at that time Lake Winona was a channel of the Mississippi River. Though securely locked to the shore these days, Winona retains the moniker "The Island City on the Mississippi." You can get an impressive overview of Winona, the Mississippi River valley, and up to 30 miles beyond from the overlook at **Garvin Heights City Park** perched 575 feet above the city. Down in the valley itself **Prairie Island Park** has a mile-long trail through the bottomland forest and a large deer yard with white-tails and wild turkey.

Recreation

There are a lot of options in and around Winona to keep the active set busy—what follows just scratches the surface. If you'll be spending any amount of time here, get copies of the excellent maps and brochures published by the CVB for detailed biking, hiking, paddling, cross-country skiing, and bird-watching advice.

The most challenging, but also most remote and rewarding off-road biking is the 6.5-mile Plowline Trail west of Winona in the Bronk Unit of the **Richard J. Dorer Memorial Hardwood**

State Forest, 507/523-2183. To reach the trailhead go northwest of town on U.S. 61 to County Road 23 and follow it south for three miles. For a leisurely family ride, follow the 5.5-mile path that circles Lake Winona. Road riders will find the country roads through the narrow valleys surrounding Winona to be peaceful, beautiful, and quite challenging territory. The most popular cross-country skiing right in the city is on the nine miles of groomed trail through the forested hills behind **St. Mary's University. Adventure Cycle and Ski,** 178 Center St., 507/452-4228, rents bikes, in-line skates, and cross-country skis, while the **Kolter Bicycle Store,** 400 Mankato Ave., 507/452-5665, just has bikes.

Winona, home of We-no-nah Canoes, one of the world's leading canoe and kayak manufacturers, is a great spot to begin an exploration of the maze of Mississippi River backwater channels. There are canoe rentals at Prairie Island Park. The Winona District office of the **Upper Mississippi River National Wildlife and Fish Refuge,** 51 E. 4th St., 507/454-7351 or 800/657-3775, can offer maps and information.

Entertainment and Events

Both **Winona State University,** 507/457-2456, and the smaller **Saint Mary's University,** 507/457-1600, have varied schedules of music, theater, speakers, films, and similar cultural events. The general public is welcome at most of them. The **Winona Arts Center,** 228 E. 5th St., 507/453-9959, is a small, volunteer-run venue occasionally hosting films, music, and art displays.

Having played their first gig in 1915 the **Winona Municipal Concert Band** is reportedly the oldest continuously performing musical group west of the Mississippi. They take the stage at the Lake Park Band Shell Wednesday nights at 8 P.M. all summer long.

Winona State University's 7,200 students generate a small nightlife. The busiest bars in town are **Bub's Brewing Company,** 65 E. 4th St, 507/457-3121; and **Brothers,** 129 W. 3rd St., 507/452-7673; both occasionally have live music. The **Acoustic Café,** 77 Lafayette St, 507/453-0394, also has live music, usually on the lighter side, every weekend.

BLUFF COUNTRY

For a movie, head downtown to the **Winona Seven,** 70 W. 2nd St., 507/452-4172, Winona's only movie theater.

Winona has a diverse calendar of events highlighted by **Steamboat Days,** a busy five-day festival at the end of June with all the usual events like fireworks and a carnival, plus a kiddie parade, fishing contests, craft show, and bed races. Winona celebrates its Polish past with **Polish Heritage Days** in early May and **Polish Apple Day** (*Smaczne Jablka*) in mid-October.

Accommodations

Rooms in Winona can be very hard to come by on summer weekends, so plan ahead as far as possible. Winona has several budget, family-run hotels, but they are all decades past their prime and only of interest to penny-pinchers. Best of the lot is the **Sterling Motel,** 1450 Gilmore Ave., 507/454-1120, where next to nothing has changed since it opened in the 1950s. Basic but clean rooms with refrigerators are $42. A far better facility and a the best value in the area is the **Midwestern Motel,** 507/452-9136 or 800/213-9136, a few miles north of town on U.S. 61 near Minnesota City. Spotless, new rooms run from $29.

The **Super 8,** 1025 Sugar Loaf Rd., 507/454-6066 or 800/800-8000, sits right below Sugar Loaf Mountain and charges $62. The **Quality Inn,** 956 Mankato Ave., 507/454-4390 or 800/562-4544, is starting to show its age, but still, with a pool, whirlpool, game room, and a 24-hour restaurant attached, it's a good deal at $79. The best located hotel is the **AmericInn,** 60 Riverview Dr., 507/457-0249, which sits by the river. Regular rooms start at $89, plus they have a two-story lighthouse room with Mississippi views for $132. Facilities include a pool, whirlpool, and sauna. TVs in the bathroom are just one of the touches that makes the **Holiday Inn,** 1025 U.S. 61 E., 507/453-0303 or 888/292-0303, Winona's fanciest hotel. The $99 room price includes use of a sauna, exercise room, whirlpool, and separate children's and adult pools.

The **Windom Park Bed & Breakfast,** 369 W. Broadway St., 507/457-9515, has four charmingly decorated guestrooms, all with private bath, in a beautiful 1900 Colonial Revival home. Two luxury suites with whirlpools and fireplaces sit out back in the renovated carriage house. There is a surplus of public space, and all guests are treated to a five-course breakfast in the morning and wine and cheese in the evening. Rooms in the house start at $99, while the carriage house rooms are $175. The **Carriage House Bed & Breakfast,** 420 Main St., 507/452-8256, one of the longest operating B&Bs in the state, has its four guestrooms in a renovated 1870 carriage house that still maintains some unique original features. Each of the rooms, ranging $80–150, has a private bath and a pair of them have whirlpool tubs and fireplaces. Guests can borrow bikes, including a tandem, to explore the city after eating the continental breakfast.

The 198-site **Prairie Island Campground,** 507/452-4501, north of town is your typical large municipal campground, though the riverside location, complete with a beach, is a bonus. The nightly rate is $17 electric and $14.50 nonelectric. Campers looking to enjoy natural surroundings should consider the nearby state parks or, better yet, take a boat or canoe out to one of the myriad islands around the city.

Food

Ask anyone in town where to eat and after telling you about the great restaurants across the river in Wisconsin they will almost certainly suggest the casual **Jefferson Pub & Grill,** 58 Center St., 507/452-2718. The menu spans spicy black bean burgers, walleye filet sandwiches, fettuccini, and T-bone steaks with prices in the $6–16 range. The attached Sidetrack Tap bar has an impressive roster of beers. Open daily for lunch and dinner.

For Italian the top choice is **Victoria's,** 1213 Gilmore Ave., 507/452-9150, a branch of the longtime Rochester favorite, in the Winona Mall. Most dishes are priced around $6. Open daily for lunch and dinner.

Shorty's, 528 Center St, 507/452-2622, a classic neighborhood diner, is a throwback to the 1950s, and if you want to listen in on town gossip this is the place. The menu includes burgers for $2, heaping breakfast platters (served all day) for $4, and steaks for under $10. Open Mon.–Sat. for breakfast, lunch, and dinner, and Sunday for breakfast and lunch.

Carhops still take your order at the **Lakeview Drive-Inn,** 610 E. Sarnia St, 507/454-3723. They serve reasonably priced sandwiches, ice cream, and homemade root beer and classic car collectors gather here to show off their wheels. They are open daily 11 A.M.–11 P.M. during their short spring to fall season.

The authentic Mexican at **La Carreta,** 550 Mankato Ave, 507/454-3700, is very tasty, and the usual entrées, plus a few less common ones, average $7. They are open daily for lunch and dinner.

Beno's Deli, 78 E. 4th St., 507/452-2761, is a basic but beloved sandwich bar downtown in the old city hall. They are open Monday–Saturday for breakfast and lunch. Another place with good, cheap sandwiches is the **Acoustic Café,** 77 Lafayette St, 507/453-0394, a busy but still cozy coffeehouse. They are open daily early to late.

If you want a snack with a side order of Mississippi River-watching there's the **Winona Island Café,** 507/454-1133, next to the Wilkie. It is open daily for lunch and dinner during the summer and fall.

Shopping

As you'd expect, most of the city's shopping is out along Highway 61, though a number of gift shops have claimed homes in historic buildings downtown. One of the largest is **Pieces of the Past,** 79 E. 2nd St., 507/452-3722, which sells things that look old, including handcrafted furniture. On the same block is **Bitter Sweet,** 50 E. 2nd St., 507/452-0000, with homemade candies a highlight.

By far the largest antique store in town is the **R. D. Cone Antiques Mall,** 66 E. 2nd St., 507/453-0445. **Country Comfort Antiques,** 79 W. 3rd St., 507/452-7044, and **A-Z Collectibles,** 507/454-0366, in the basement of the same building, are also worth a browse.

Used books are sold at each of the antique stores listed above, the Winona County Historical Museum, and **Paperback Exchange,** 79 E. 3rd St, 507/452-5580. The latter has the largest selection, but romance novels take up half the shelf space.

Information and Services

The **Winona Visitor's Center,** 507/452-2278, just off the Highway on Lake Winona, is staffed weekdays 9 A.M.–5 P.M. and weekends 10 A.M.–4 P.M. from April to November. You can also get information at the **Winona Area Convention and Visitors Bureau,** 67 Main St., 507/452-2272 or 800/657-4972, www.visitwinona.com; it is open weekdays 8 A.M.–5 P.M. all year long.

The endlessly varied **KQAL, (FM 89.5),** Winona State University's student radio station, is a welcome break from the usual vanilla of commercial music stations.

Transportation

The **Amtrak,** 65 E. Mark St., 507/452-8612, Empire Builder service arrives from St. Paul at 10:09 A.M. and the western service comes through at 7:44 P.M. A same-day purchase return ticket from St. Paul costs $50; it's just $33 with an advanced purchase. **Jefferson Lines** and **Greyhound** buses stop at the Conoco gas station, 507/452-3718, out along U.S. 61. Both connect to the Twin Cities via Rochester. **Airport Passenger Service,** 800/869-5796, vans make five runs a day between La Crosse, Wisconsin, and the Twin Cities stopping at the Quality Inn. The fare is $64 round-trip and reservations are highly recommended.

Locally, **Winona Transit,** 507/454-6666, has a limited citywide bus service available weekdays until around 6 P.M. The city also has two cab companies: **Economy Cab,** 507/454-7433; and **Yellow Cab,** 507/452-3331. **Hertz,** 275 W. 2nd St., 507/454-2888; and **Enterprise,** 1111 W. Service Rd., 507/454-4462, are the national car rental agencies in town.

There is public dockage for short-term visitors arriving by boat right by the Wilkie Steamboat Center. For overnighters there is the **Winona Yacht Club,** 24 Laird St., 507/454-5590, and **Winona Municipal Harbor (Dick's Marine),** 507/452-3809, over on Latsch Island—both are full service facilities.

SOUTH OF WINONA

Pickwick Mill

Two miles off Highway 61 on County Road 7 is the restored Pickwick Mill, 507/452-9658, which operated from 1856 to 1980. Today the building

THE MODERN MISSISSIPPI

Before the 1840s steamboats had a hard time navigating the Upper Mississippi River because of the abundance of sandbars, low water, and snags. In 1845 wheat interests formed the Mississippi River Improvement Company to better navigation by removing wrecks and snags. The U.S. Army Corps of Engineers dredged a four-and-a-half foot deep shipping channel in 1878 and over time it was expanded, but despite these efforts cargo continued to shift to the more reliable railroads. By 1918 river transport was virtually dead. Business leaders, concerned about a lack of competition, pushed Congress for action to restore commerce on the river and they authorized a nine-foot channel maintained by a series of locks and dams. Construction on what was then one of the world's largest public works projects began in 1931. Today 29 locks and dams, the last completed in 1964, move 90 million tons of cargo, principally wheat, logs, oil, and fertilizer, up the river between St. Louis and Minneapolis. A typical 15-barge tow stretches a quarter mile and carries the equivalent of 990 semi-trucks or 225 train cars.

The 670-mile aquatic stairway brought commerce back, but it also changed the river forever. Originally the Mississippi had several winding channels with many rapids and shifting sand bars, but the series of pools created by the dams made it more like a lake habitat than that of a river. The current was slowed by both the main dams and the smaller wing dams (underwater rock piles) that help maintain the channel. The excessive sedimentation that has resulted has become a serious threat to the river and many fish populations are in serious decline. Critics also claim that the barges' wake erodes the shoreline.

Although it's unlikely to happen in our lifetimes many would like to remove the dams and let the real river return. This would spell the end of commercial river transport, but shipping by rail would be cheaper anyway since maintaining commerce on the river costs hundreds of millions of federal dollars annually. The Corps, which is addicted to enormous projects and hates to take no for an answer, has other plans: they are pushing a one billion dollar lock expansion plan. When their own lead economist determined that the benefits couldn't even come close to justifying the costs Corps leaders removed him from the study. A resulting investigation showed that top brass at the Corps—who have met behind closed doors with barge interests including ConAgra, Cargill, and American Commercial Barge Lines—cooked the books to justify the program. Some of the evidence included internal emails and memos with such phrases as "He directs that we develop evidence or data to support a defensible set of capacity enhancement projects" and "The push to grow the program is coming from the top down." Independent analysis has backed up the original conclusions and while the brouhaha is in the courts the Corps continues to "study" the project. This is just one of many controversial projects that makes the Corps one of the most reviled federal agencies by both environmentalists and taxpayer advocates.

has been extensively fixed up inside, but most of the original machinery and some assorted supplies remain, much of it just lying around where the last owners left it. The mill no longer grinds grains, but the 20-foot waterwheel still turns the complex series of wooden gears. While the inside is interesting, the solid, six-story limestone building is most impressive from the outside. The mill is open Tuesday–Sunday 10 A.M.–5 P.M. June through September and weekends in May and October. Admission is $3. You can dine with a mill view across Big Trout Creek at the popular **Pickwick Inn,** 507/454-7750.

Great River Bluffs State Park

This 3,000-acre bluff-top park is managed as a "natural" park so development is limited to a small picnic area, campground, and six miles of wide, level hiking trails linking eight overlooks. The north-facing vistas offer some of the best Mississippi River views anywhere, but don't overlook the valley views to the south, which are also impressive. If you don't want to walk to the overlooks, there is a good one of the river along the road to the campground. As you walk the trails you'll also see several small goat prairies (on slopes so steep that only goats could graze them) riding some of the bluff tops. Ironically, they get more sunlight than any other natural community in Minnesota, but because they freeze easily woody plants that would otherwise establish themselves are killed off. The **King's Bluff Nature Trail,** a 2.5-mile round-trip, has interpretive signs along it discussing these and other ecological topics. In winter the trails, plus a few miles of additional loops, are groomed for cross-country skiing, snowshoes can be rented at the park office, and there is a steep sledding hill. The primitive campground with 31 shady and widely spaced sites is one of the best spots along the river to pitch a tent. Additionally, a five-site bicycle campground down along U.S. 61 is available for those pedaling the Great River Road. Call 507/643-6849 with any park questions.

La Crescent

Gritty little La Crescent is all about apples. The first orchard in the state was planted here in 1857 and today, with seven growers working 550 acres, La Crescent has justifiably declared itself the "Apple Capital of Minnesota." Half a dozen orchards, most selling direct to the public, ring the town with many located along the **Apple Blossom Scenic Drive.** The 19-mile marked route climbs the bluffs above La Crescent and then returns along the river; many people just follow the most scenic half of the route, which turns back at Dakota. The trees are in their glorious white bloom around mid-May, and apples are available from late July until mid-November, though the valley views are superb all year long. Three miles above town is **Lock and Dam #7** where an elevated platform lets you watch boats get an eight-foot lift. In the winter you'll likely see bald eagles fishing here. The State of Minnesota has a **Travel Information Center** here, too. The city's **Apple Festival,** held over four days around the third weekend in September, has orchard and packing plant tours, a soap box derby, big wheel races, arts and crafts fair, and the King Apple Grand Parade. It's a mighty big event for such a small town.

The only hotel in town is the **Ranch Motel,** 200 Chestnut St. S., 507/895-4422. It's a well-worn property but the rooms are large, clean,

and priced at only $34 weekdays and $49 weekends. There's not much choice in dining either. **Corky's Pizza and Ice Cream,** 25 S. Walnut St., 507/895-6996, downtown, which has expanded the menu to include sandwiches, salads, and burgers, has the most variety and consistently low prices. Open daily for lunch and dinner. In both cases (dining and lodging) you are better off looking across the river in La Crosse, Wisconsin.

Beaver Creek Valley State Park

A long but recommended detour inland from La Crescent brings nature lovers to this fine example of Minnesota's driftless topography. Spring-fed Beaver Creek cuts a deep, narrow valley through the bluffs, and this cool and quiet 1,200-acre park straddles nearly six miles of it. Because the park protects the majority of land in the upper part of the watershed, the little creek and surrounding landscape are remarkably pristine. The valley is filled with virgin hardwood forests and native patches of prairie cling to

© TIM BEWER

Beaver Creek Valley State Park

some south and west facing slopes. Fly fishers will appreciate the challenge of the naturally reproducing, trophy-sized brown and brook trout—so healthy is the aquatic population that a special winter catch-and-release season has been added. The park is a top bird-watching spot, and several species like Cerulean warbler, Louisiana waterthrush, and the rare Acadian flycatcher that are at the far northwestern ends of their range nest in the park.

Eight miles of hiking trail follow the valley. For a complete Beaver Creek experience climb 250 feet up the bluffs to the nearest overlook along the **Switchback Trail** for a long view down the valley, and then walk through what you've just been admiring along the **Beaver Creek Val-** ley Trail, a level and easy two-mile round-trip along the creek heading out to a prairie. If you are lucky, you might spy a five-lined skink with its bright blue tail along the adjoining **Plateau Rock Trail** and **Quarry Trail** that climb the east side of the valley and are worthwhile trails even without a chance of lizards. The campground has 42 sites right along the road—the valley is just too narrow for any setback. The farther in you go the more peaceful the sites become, and not just from less traffic. All 16 electric sites are at the head of the campground, and they are more widely spaced as you move towards the back; a half dozen walk-in sites sit way at the end. There is also a single camper cabin. Call 507/724-2107 with any park questions.

Rochester

The average Minnesotan knows just two things about Rochester: it is home to the Mayo Clinic and it is an exceedingly dull city. "I don't need to go to Rochester, I'm not sick" is a common attitude. The "boring" label is so strongly ingrained, in fact, that the CVB gives locals familiarization tours just so that if someone asks them what there is to do in town they don't answer "Nothing." While the prevailing wisdom is not completely wrong—frankly Rochester does rank fairly low on the excitement scale—the odd combination of big city and small town surprises most first-time visitors, of whom, between "The Clinic" and conventions, there are hundreds of thousands annually. It really is worth a visit.

Though the city is synonymous with modern technology (besides the Mayo Clinic Rochester has IBM's largest single building), the giant corncob water tower on the south side of town is a reminder of Rochester's agricultural roots. Olmsted County's first settlers were New England farmers. In 1854 one of them, George Head from Rochester, New York, built a log cabin home/hotel/saloon at a waterfall on the South Branch Zumbro River. A proper town, fueled by flourmills, soon sprang up here, and when a name was needed Head suggested Rochester because the rapids here reminded him of the Genesee River in his former hometown.

After an 1883 tornado devastated the city, Dr. William Mayo opened a hospital that would later grow into the world-renowned Mayo Clinic. Today the Mayo name and legacy permeate the city. The clinic has brought gleaming skyscrapers and some cosmopolitan flair to this city of 86,000. This sophistication, along with a deep civic pride, makes Rochester a regular contender (and frequent winner) on "Most Livable" city rankings. Rochester was doing all right before the hospital opened and might have even become southern Minnesota's leading city without it, but Dr. Mayo single-handedly put Rochester on the map, and it certainly would not be the economic axis that it is today without him. Originally nicknamed the "Queen City," it prefers the "Med City" label these days.

Orientation

Though many of the city's top attractions sit in the southeast end of the city, you can find just about anything you want or need in the bustling downtown. Beyond the center most businesses stretch out along Hwys. 52 and 63, Civic Center Drive, and 2nd Street to the west of downtown. There is very little of interest to tourists (or most

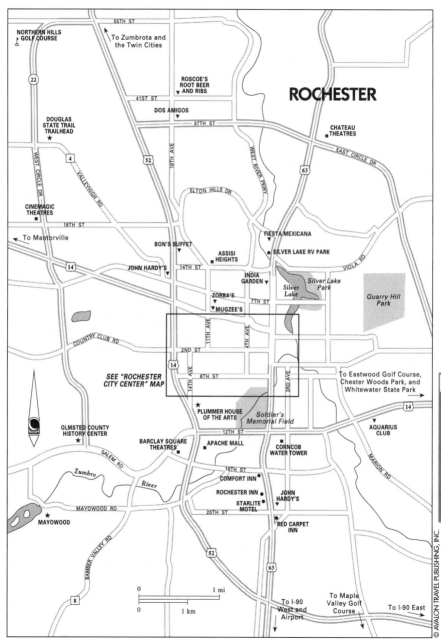

NORTHERN HILLS
GOLF COURSE

To Zumbrota and
the Twin Cities

55TH ST

ROSCOE'S
ROOT BEER
AND RIBS

DOS AMIGOS

ROCHESTER

22

41ST ST

37TH ST

CHATEAU
THEATRES

DOUGLAS
STATE TRAIL
TRAILHEAD

4

WEST CIRCLE DR

VALLEYHIGH RD

18TH AVE

52

WEST RIVER PKWY

EAST CIRCLE DR

63

ELTON HILLS DR

CINEMAGIC
THEATRES

19TH ST

To Mantorville

BON'S BUFFET

FIESTA MEXICANA

SILVER LAKE RV PARK

14

JOHN HARDY'S

14TH ST

ASSISI
HEIGHTS

INDIA
GARDEN

Silver
Lake

Silver Lake
Park

VIOLA RD

Quarry Hill
Park

ZORBA'S

MUGZEE'S

7TH ST

Silver
Lake

COUNTRY CLUB RD

11TH AVE

4TH AVE

2ND ST

14

14TH AVE

6TH ST

3RD AVE

To Eastwood Golf Course,
Chester Woods Park, and
Whitewater State Park

SEE "ROCHESTER
CITY CENTER" MAP

14

PLUMMER HOUSE
OF THE ARTS

Soldier's
Memorial Field

AQUARIUS
CLUB

Moon

OLMSTED COUNTY
HISTORY CENTER

BARCLAY SQUARE
THEATRES

APACHE MALL

12TH ST

CORNCOB
WATER TOWER

MARION RD

SALEM RD

Zumbro

River

16TH ST

COMFORT INN

ROCHESTER INN

STARLITE
MOTEL

JOHN HARDY'S

MAYOWOOD RD

20TH ST

MAYOWOOD

RED CARPET
INN

BAMBER VALLEY RD

52

63

8

0   1 mi

0   1 km

To I-90
West and
Airport

To Maple
Valley Golf
Course

To I-90 East

BLUFF COUNTRY

© AVALON TRAVEL PUBLISHING, INC.

locals for that matter) in the eastern half of the city. Rochester is divided into quadrants, and all addresses have a NE, NW, SE, or SW suffix. The dividing intersection is Center Street and Broadway (U.S. 63). An extensive downtown pedestrian subway and skyway system connect the main Mayo Clinic buildings, Civic Center, Centerplace Galleria mall, parking ramps, and most of the large downtown hotels.

SIGHTS
Olmsted County History Center
The county historical society's modest collection includes a classic soda fountain, an early IBM display, and, of course, quite a bit on the Mayo Clinic. Kids can get up-close and personal with the hands-on log cabin, tepee, and rag-rug loom. Far and away the most interesting display is the chunk of wood impaled by blades of grass during the 1883 tornado. The furnished 1862 log cabin and 1885 one-room schoolhouse in back are open during the summer only. The museum is on the far southwest side of town at 1195 W. Circle Dr. (County Road 22) SW. Call 507/282-9447 with any questions. It is open Tuesday–Saturday 9 A.M.–5 P.M. and admission is $4.

Mayowood Mansion
Mayowood, the country estate of clinic cofounder Dr. Charles Mayo, once covered 3,000 acres and included eight farms; a man-made lake with landscaped islands; a greenhouse made of old X-ray plates; and extensive Japanese, English, and Italian gardens. The elegant 48-room mansion at the center of it all was built as a summer home in 1911, and sometime in the 1920s he added a hydroelectric dam and moved out here permanently. Another two generations of Mayos resided here until 1965 when the family left the "Big House," as Dr. Charlie called it, and most of its furnishings to the Olmsted County Historical Society. Though financing still stands in the way, they hope to begin resurrecting the extensive formal gardens, which currently stand in ruin. The home is located at 3720 Mayowood Rd. SW. Call the museum with any questions. The schedule varies annually so it is best to call ahead, though typically

the one-hour home tours are offered weekends from mid-May through mid-October, plus a couple of weekdays during the summer. Special Christmas tours are held in November, and the grounds are one stop on a citywide gardens tour held each June. Admission is $10.

Plummer House of the Arts
Henry Plummer, another doctor made obscenely wealthy during his time at the Mayo Clinic, built this 49-room, five-story, English Tudor mansion in 1917. Plummer (designer of the clinic's Plummer Building) was also a noted engineer, and he worked such innovative features as a central vacuum system, power garage door opener, intercom, and gas furnace into his Quarry Hill home. All of the furniture was left behind with the house, though it still feels somewhat empty. Despite the name, there are no art displays. The arts label stems from his wife Daisy, a tireless promoter of the arts. Today the home is used primarily for weddings and other special events, though you can

the Mayo Clinic's Plummer Building

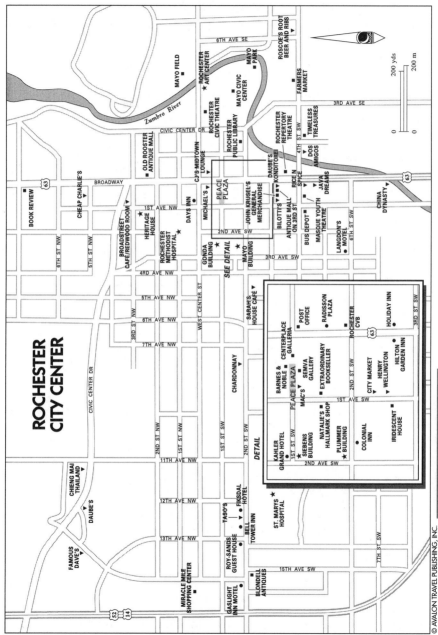

ROCHESTER CITY CENTER

© AVALON TRAVEL PUBLISHING, INC.

BLUFF COUNTRY

THE CLINIC IN THE CORNFIELD

The Mayo Clinic began with a tragedy. In August 1883 a tornado leveled half of Rochester killing 31 and injuring hundreds more. Rochester had no medical facility so hotels, offices, and dance halls transformed into emergency rooms. Desperate doctors, including William Worrall Mayo and his sons, enlisted nuns from the Sisters of St. Francis as nurses. The crisis inspired Mother Alfred Moes to propose building a hospital and she enlisted the support of Dr. Mayo. The order raised $40,000 and opened Saint Marys Hospital in 1889. The "Clinic in the Cornfield" as it was known was southern Minnesota's first hospital and it served the needs of rural residents for hundreds of miles.

While W. W. Mayo created the clinic his sons, William J. and Charles H., both expert surgeons, were the pioneers that made it the world-renown center it is today. Back then doctors washed their hands after surgery, but not before. Dr. Charlie and Dr. Will were among first doctors in the nation to sterilize equipment before surgery and they made the new antiseptic and aseptic techniques standard procedure in their hospital. They also pioneered the concept of medicine as a cooperative science with specialists consulting amongst themselves in a teamwork approach to patient care. This revolutionary concept made the Mayo Clinic the world's first integrated group practice: today it is the largest. By the 20th century the Mayo name was known far and wide and the actual clinic was growing as fast as its reputation. Patients weren't the only ones flocking to Rochester to take advantage of the Mayo doctors' skill and ingenuity; other physicians came to learn from the best and in 1915 the clinic organized the world's first formal graduate training program for physicians.

In 1919 the Mayo brothers transferred all of the clinic's assets and the bulk of their life savings to a charitable, nonprofit group now called the Mayo Foundation; from that point on all profits have gone towards medical education and research. These have always been core components of the clinic's mission and many breakthroughs have come out of Rochester including the first test of surgical samples that was quick enough to allow diagnosis and repair in a single operation, the cure for tuberculosis, the first hip replacement surgery, and, most recently, a rapid anthrax test. Dr. Charlie, noticing that milk was the source of illness in a large percentage of his patients, even went as far as establishing his own dairy herd at his Mayowood estate to prove to area farmers that pasteurizing milk was cost effective.

Today the Mayo Clinic continues to rank amongst the best health care facilities in the world. The country hospital that began with 27 beds now has its own zip code and has treated over six million people from over 100 countries including presidents and royalty. Branches have since opened in Florida and Arizona and the Rochester facility alone occupies 13 million square feet, has 26,000 employees, and treats well over 300,000 patients a year.

visit the house Wednesday and the first and third Sunday of the month 1–5 P.M. during the summer. The 11-acre grounds with forested trails and a small floral garden are free and open to the public year-round from sunrise to sunset. Admission is $3. Call 507/281-6160 with questions.

Heritage House

For a look at a more modest, though still upper-class, home visit Heritage House, 225 1st Ave. NW, 507/286-9208. When the wrecking ball threatened it in 1972 citizens raised some money, moved it to Central Park (the city's original town square), and restored it. The 1875 home was one of the few downtown buildings to survive the 1883 tornado, and many of the original features and furnishings remain. Except for the fancy dresses on display in the various rooms, it looks like you've dropped in on the Whiting family back in their day. The guides know the story behind just about every chair, lamp, and doorknob and will tell you as little or as much as you want to know about family life in the late 19th century. The house is open for tours on Tuesday, Thursday, and Sunday 1–3:30 P.M. during the summer.

The Rochester Carillon

Inside the pinnacle atop the Mayo Clinic's grand

Clinic Visits

Guided tours begin at 10 A.M. though come early because it is preceded by an interesting 15-minute film on the history of the Mayo family and the early years of the clinic. You don't see anything beyond the main public areas during the 90-minute tours—they can't exactly walk you into the operating rooms—but you'll get the full scoop on the history and daily operations plus some of the artistic highlights will be pointed out. A more detailed hour-long art and architecture tour begins in the afternoon at 1 o'clock. The collection, mostly donated by patients and benefactors, includes such heavyweights of the art world as Warhol, Rodin, and Chihuly, as well as work by renowned local sculptor Charles Gagnon. Both tours are free, offered weekdays only, and start in the Judd Auditorium on the subway level of the Mayo Building. Call 507/284-9258 for information.

If you don't mind missing the stories or having someone around to answer questions you can see everything and more on your own—maps are available at any of the information desks. Currently there is no self-guided art tour brochure, but supposedly one is in the works.

The Gonda Building, referred to as the "Front Door" of the Mayo Clinic, is the newest of the clinic's 70 buildings. It has some of the largest works of art (including a much talked about Dave Chihuly blown-glass chandelier) and an interesting modern design: a self-guided tour brochure is available.

In contrast to the sleek, modern Gonda Building is the gargoyled Plummer Building. The city's showpiece edifice cost three million dollars to build in 1928 and even Bill Gates probably couldn't finance it today. Henry Plummer joined the Mayo brothers in 1901 and became the clinic's jack of all trades. Not only was he an accomplished physician, but he introduced the now ubiquitous dossier medical records system where a single file is kept for a patient, designed the first large scale intercom system, and was even such a skillful architect that he designed the building named after him. The Mayo Historical Suite, a mini-museum on the third floor (open weekdays 8 A.M.–5 P.M.) has lots of old photos, the Mayo brothers' original office furniture, and some frightening surgical instruments from the past. Also worth a look are the lobby, the massive front doors, and the Medical Library Reading Room on the 14th floor.

Unique X-rays of a snake that swallowed a pair of light bulbs and similar subjects are displayed in the Patient Education Center and on the subway level of the Siebens Building, and more historical displays are found in the adjacent hallway.

Saint Mary's Hospital also has a self-guided tour brochure, though pretty much the only thing worth seeing is the small historical display right by the main entrance of the Francis Building. It has some of W. W. Mayo's original surgical tools and the hospital's first operating table.

Plummer Building is one of the most complete carillons in North America. The 56 bronze bells cover four-and-a-half octaves; the largest stands six feet tall and weighs in at four tons, while the smallest is just 19 pounds. Live concerts, encompassing everything from show tunes to hymns, are performed Monday nights at 7 P.M. and Wednesday, Thursday, and Friday at noon, plus on various holidays. The best place to hear them is about 500 feet downwind, but since that is unpredictable it is probably best to take a seat around the "Boy With a Dolphin" statue in front of the Mayo Building. Call 507/284-8294 to arrange a tour.

Rochester Art Center

The often overlooked Rochester Art Center, 320 Center St. E., 507/282-8629, has two floors of changing exhibits, primarily by local and Midwestern artists, plus frequent classes, lectures, films, and other special events. It is open Tuesday–Saturday 10 A.M.–5 P.M. (closing at nine on Thurs.) and Sunday noon–5 P.M. Admission is free. If you arrive and find the building is gone, look on the other side of the Civic Center since that means a much-delayed expansion has finally happened.

Silver Lake Park

If you've been wondering why the goose theme is

so prevalent in Rochester, visit this large park just north of downtown where upwards of 35,000 Canadian honkers congregate over the winter, a result of the local power plant keeping the lake ice-free. They are here the rest of the year, too, though in much smaller numbers. If you don't have your own bread you can buy goose feed at the parking lot north of 7th St. on the west side of the lake. Paddleboats and canoes are available here for a trip around the lake.

RECREATION

Quarry Hill Park, 701 Silver Creek Rd. NE, 507/281-6114, a 300-acre oasis, is no lost wilderness, but for an urban park it's not too shabby. Five miles of hiking trail wind through the forest and grassland, though wherever you decide to hike includes a pass though the 20-acre hilltop savanna at the center of the park. In the winter cross-country skis and snowshoes can be rented. The kid-focused Nature Center (open Mon–Sat. 9 A.M.–5 P.M. and Sun. noon–5 P.M.) has interactive displays, touch tables, an indoor bee hive, a 1,700-gallon Minnesota fish aquarium, a life-size T-Rex skull model, and over 100 animal mounts. Admission is free. The main entrance is located off County Road 22 on the east side of the city.

The paved **Douglas State Trail** follows a former railroad bed through 13 miles of farmland between the northwest edge of Rochester and Pine Island. Bikers also have another 29 miles of paved trail crisscrossing the city. The most popular routes follow the Zumbro River and the smaller creeks that empty into it, though the trails branch off to many other locations and the system is expanding continuously. You can access these trails across from the Douglas Trail trailhead.

The paved of the city's seven public golf courses are the **Northern Hills Golf Course**, 4800 West Circle Dr. NW, 507/281-6170; and **Eastwood Golf Course**, Eastwood Rd. SE 507/281-6173. Though it's not a very challenging course, the limestone bluffs at the **Maple Valley Golf Course**, 507/285-9100, 15 minutes southeast of Rochester, make it the area's most scenic by far.

ENTERTAINMENT

A quick glimpse at the tapestry of flyers covering record store windows might lead one to believe that the city is a hotbed of cultural activity, but closer inspection shows that they are almost all promoting clubs and events in Minneapolis and La Crosse, Wisconsin. This pretty much tells you all you need to know about Rochester's paltry entertainment roster. The noticeably slim Entertainment section in the Thursday edition of the **Rochester Post-Bulletin** is the best source of what's going on in town. You can also call the Arts Event Hotline at 507/288-ARTS.

Nightlife

CJ's Midtown Lounge, 8 S. Broadway, 507/289-7478; and **Mugzee's**, 524 11th Ave. NW, 507/281-8055, are a pair of beer and shot joints with live bands. The former has rock acts nightly, while the latter does weekend blues. The classy **Redwood Room**, 300 1st Ave. NW, 507/281-2451, has live music on the lighter side nightly, usually jazz. Tops for dancing is the **Aquarius Club**, 1201 Eastgate Dr. SE, 507/281-5229, out by the University Center.

Classical Music

The **Rochester Orchestra and Chorale**, 507/286-8742, founded in 1919 serves up eight shows a season at the Mayo Civic Center. Tickets start at $10. Also popular is the **Choral Arts Ensemble**, 507/252-8427, a 40-voice choir performing classical and jazz pieces several times a year at the beautiful Assisi Heights convent, 1001 14th Street North. Ticket prices begin at $6.

Theater

Both the **Rochester Civic Theatre**, 220 E. Center St., 507/282-8481; and the **Rochester Repertory Theatre**, 314 1/2 S. Broadway, 507/289-1737, offer comedies, dramas, and musicals at their respective homes. Tickets are $15 at each. Children take the stage between October and June at the **Masque Youth Theatre**, 14 4th St. SW, 507/287-0704, performing anything from fairy tales to Shakespeare, and tickets are as low as $5.

Freebies

Free **Down By the Riverside Concerts** are held on Sunday nights in July and August in Mayo Park behind the Civic Center. Despite the name the Thursday night **Riverside Galleria Series** concerts are held in Peace Plaza, which is not on the river. The schedule for both varies from rock to jazz to classical to folk, and they start as 7 P.M. and 6:30 P.M. respectively.

Cinema

Rochester has three movie theaters, all on the outskirts of town. The 15-screen **CineMagic Theatres,** 507/280-0333, on the west side and the 14-screen **Chateau Theatres,** 507/536-7469, not too far north of downtown, are both ultra-modern facilities. **Barclay Square Theatres,** 1300 Salem Rd. SW 507/281-0366, is an older six-screen cinema near the Apache Mall. There is no longer a movie theater downtown, but the Chateau Theatres run a free shuttle from the Radisson hotel at 2:30 and 6 P.M.

Spectator Sports

The **Rochester Honkers** play in the Northwoods Baseball League, made up of top Division I college players who get minor league experience while keeping their college eligibility. Home games are played at Mayo Field, 403 E. Center St., 507/289-1170, and tickets are $3–6. The **Minnesota Chill,** one of four teams in the women's U.S. Professional Volleyball league, play a 21-game spring season at the Mayo Civic Center. They were the league's inaugural season champions in 2002, though the league's future is in doubt.

Events

The city's biggest blowout is **Rochesterfest,** an eight-day affair with a sandcastle contest, kite festival, hot air balloon race, bike races, and an 1860s baseball game—not to mention the usual food, parade, music, and carnival rides. It begins the third weekend in June. The ever-popular **Midwestern Lumberjack Championships** are always held concurrently with Rochesterfest in Silver Lake Park. A much smaller, but equally fun shindig is the **Greek Festival** held each August at the Civic Center.

ACCOMMODATIONS

One of the most remarkable things about Rochester is how good a value the hotels are. At last count Rochester claimed around 70 hotels and motels, mostly a result of the large number of people coming here for treatment at the Mayo Clinic, though the city does a brisk convention business, too. Just about every hotel has shuttle service available to the hospitals, and most have kitchenettes available for long-term visitors. The **Rochester Lodging & Hospitality Association** has a fairly complete list of choices at www.rochesterlodging.com/dir.htm, and the CVB offers a handy search feature at www.rochestercvb.org/accommodations.asp.

Hotels and Motels Under $50

Downtown: Literally held together by duct tape in a few places **Langdon's Motel,** 526 3rd Ave. SW, 507/282-7425, charging just $27, is the cheapest hotel in town. You get what you pay for, but the rooms are large, clean, and the owners are very eager to please. The **Colonial Inn,** 114 2nd St. SW, 507/289-3363 or 800/533-2226, opened its doors in 1906 and today a night in the very small $34 rooms is like stepping back to that time. A couple of rooms with shared bath are even cheaper.

St. Marys: A whole row of older, no-frills hotels catering almost exclusively to patients and their families front St. Marys Hospital. Rooms at each of them are creaky, but absolutely spotless. The **Bell Tower Inn,** 1235 2nd St. SW, 507/289-2233 or 800/448-7583; **Gaslight Inn Motel,** 1601 2nd St. SW, 507/289-1824 or 800/658-7016; and **Roy-Sands Guest House,** 1307 2nd St. SW, 507/285-0554; with rooms from around $45 are typical.

South Broadway: There is no shortage of cheap hotels on the south side of town either. Both the **Rochester Inn,** 1837 S. Broadway, 507/288-2031 or 800/890-3871; and the **Starlite Motel,** 1921 S. Broadway, 507/289-3908 or 800/981-2622, are very basic but fine and charge from $35. Rooms are eight dollars more and about that much better at the **Red Carpet Inn,** 2214 S. Broadway, 507/282-7448 or 800/658-7048, which also has a small pool.

All three have microwaves and refrigerators in most rooms.

Hotels and Motels $50–100

Downtown: The leader of the pack in Rochester's crowded hotel scene is the **Radisson Plaza,** 150 S. Broadway, 507/281-8000 or 800/333-3333, the city's only four-diamond facility. Guest facilities include a pool, whirlpool, sauna, and fairly large exercise room. You'll probably end up paying more, but weekend specials as low as $69 (a fantastic bargain) are available for their large, well-appointed rooms.

The **Hilton Garden Inn,** 225 S. Broadway, 507/285-1234 or 800/445-8667, the most recently constructed downtown hotel, has well-appointed rooms plus a pool, whirlpool, and exercise room. Rates start at $79.

The historic **Kahler Grand Hotel,** 20 2nd Ave. SW, 507/280-6200 or 800/533-1655, opened its doors in 1921. It has a grand lobby; over 700 rooms; and a domed, skylit recreation area with pool, whirlpool, sauna, and exercise room. The small standard rooms start at $69, though larger facilities are also available.

A less fancy option, but one also full of character, is the **Days Inn,** 6 1st Ave. NW, 507/282-3801 or 800/329-7466, a renovation of a 1917 building. Rates for the smallish standard rooms are $53, though full sized rooms don't cost all that much more.

St. Marys: The **Fiksdal Hotel,** 1215 2nd St. SW, 507/288-2671 or 800/366-3451, is a bit nicer than most of the other hotels along this stretch and has microwaves and refrigerators in all the rooms, plus a second floor patio.

South Broadway: The **Comfort Inn,** 1625 S. Broadway, 507/281-2211 or 800/228-5150, with a pool, whirlpool, and mini indoor water playground, makes a good choice for families. Rates start at $80.

Campgrounds

The miserably crowded **Silver Lake RV Park,** 1409 N. Broadway, 507/289-6412, is the closest to downtown and the Mayo Clinic. They have 55 sites and charge $29 for a full hookup including cable TV. There is a far better camp-ground (52 sites, 35 electric) seven miles east of the city at **Chester Woods Park,** 8378 U.S. 14 E., 507/285-7050. Rates are $12 with electricity and $10 without.

FOOD

Rochester goes to sleep early, and during the week many restaurants have the chairs on the tables by nine o'clock. Refreshingly the city has a strict smoking ban in public places and this includes all restaurants.

American

Mac's, 20 1st St. SW, 507/289-4219, is a simple café on Peace Plaza where they will serve you a heaping platter in no time flat, though you are welcome to linger like many of the coffee-sipping regulars do. Steak, seafood, salads, and a few Greek standards average $8, and breakfast is served all day. Open daily for breakfast, lunch, and dinner.

The casual **McCormick's,** 507/281-8000, on the skyway level of the Radisson, has sandwiches, salads, and pastas for around $8, but it is the downright incredible Sunday brunch buffet (all-you-can-eat for $11) that sets it apart. Open daily for breakfast, lunch, and dinner.

The restaurant below the pig statue is **Cheap Charlie's,** 11 5th St NW, 507/289-7693, an aptly named local favorite since it opened in 1955. Although the low prices attract many to this small lunch counter, the family recipes (passed on to the new owners) are top-notch. They've got burgers and other sandwiches for $2.50 and chicken, steak, and fish dinners for just twice that. Open Mon.–Fri. for breakfast, lunch, and dinner, plus Sat. for breakfast and lunch. They now have an outlet in the Center-place Galleria mall.

Another all-American place that has been going since the middle of the 20th century is **Taso's,** 1223 2nd St. SW, 507/289-2690. Next to nothing is over $6, and they still drop a sprig of parsley on each plate. Since it sits directly across from St. Marys Hospital many of the patrons are patients, which leads to some interesting eavesdropping. Open daily for breakfast, lunch, and dinner.

There are several very cheap (and healthy, of course) cafeterias in the main **Mayo Clinic** buildings.

Asian

There's nothing fancy about **China Dynasty,** 701 S. Broadway, 507/289-2333, though it is the only restaurant in town that doesn't do Chinese by the numbers. Heaping entrées from the small menu average $5 for lunch and $8 for dinner, and it deserves the many "best of" awards it has won over the years. Open daily for lunch and dinner.

What sets **Bon's Buffet,** 1652 U.S. 52 N., 507/281-9699, apart from the rest of the pack isn't that it has one of, if not the largest, buffets in town, but the Mongolian grill where you choose your ingredients and sauces and let their cooks stir-fry it. The buffet costs $6 for lunch and $10 for dinner. Open daily for lunch and dinner.

The no-frills **Chieng Mai Thailand,** 1123 Civic Center Dr. NW (in the Barlow Plaza strip mall), 507/287-9897, Rochester's only Thai kitchen, has a huge menu evenly split between Siamese and Chinese, with some choices from Cambodia and Vietnam, too. The daily lunch buffet costs $7, as do most of the 200-plus menu items. Open daily for lunch and dinner.

India Garden, 1107 N. Broadway, 507/288-6280, has an extensive menu covering the whole of the subcontinent, though their tandoori dishes are the specialty of the house. Most entrées average $10, or you can sample at will from the all-you-can-eat buffet. Open daily for lunch and dinner.

Rice N' Spice, 401 S. Broadway, 507/529 0974, a friendly little Indian grocer downtown, serves cheap sandwiches and *samosas.* Open daily for breakfast, lunch, and dinner.

Bakery

The people behind the city's beloved German restaurant **Daube's** also run the best bakery in Rochester. Their main location is on the city's north side at 1310 5th Pl. NW, 507/289-3095, though their scrumptious cookies, rolls, tortes, pretzels, and breads are also available downtown at their Pastry Pavilion, 155 1st Ave. SW (subway level of the U.S. Bank Building), 507/252-8878; and Konditorei, 14 3rd St. SW, 507/280-6446.

Barbecue

Aficionados of barbecue are in for a treat with three award-winning choices. Both **John Hardy's,** 929 W. Frontage Rd. N., 507/288-3936, and 1940 Broadway S., 507/281-1727, (open daily for lunch and dinner); and **Roscoe's Root Beer and Ribs,** 4180 18th Ave. NW, 507/281-4622, and 603 4th St. SE, 507/285-0501 (open Tues.–Sun for lunch and dinner, though the latter location, with outdoor seating only, is seasonal) are locally owned roadhouses. The statewide favorite **Famous Dave's,** 431 16th Ave. NW, 507/282-4200, (open daily for lunch and dinner), is more upscale. You can get a meal for under $10 at each of them.

Deli

City Market, 212 1st Ave. SW, 507/536-4748, is a small gourmet grocer with deli sandwiches and salads for about $5. The lunch-hour lines may look long, but they zip right along. Open weekdays for lunch and an early dinner.

Eclectic

You should be able to please everyone in your group at **Henry Wellington,** 216 1st Ave. SW, 507/289-1949, where the large, fun menu spans Italian, Mexican, seafood, steaks, barbecue ribs, salads, and more. The street is fairly quiet, so outdoor dining is pleasant here. Prices range $7–20. Open weekdays for lunch and daily for dinner.

In a move that should be celebrated the **Centerplace Galleria** forbids chains from its food court so not only do you get more variety (there is Indian, Lebanese, and sushi) than most malls, you can enjoy some really good food. It is open daily for lunch and weekdays for dinner.

Fine Dining

The **Broadstreet Café,** 300 1st Ave. NW, 507/281-2451, housed in a delightful warehouse renovation, gets many votes among locals as the best restaurant in town. Pesto-crusted salmon, garlic ostrich with mango, and grilled duck breast, all for about $25, typify the creative, yet unpretentious menu. Open daily for dinner and weekdays for lunch.

Before you walk through the wall of wine into the candle-lit dining room, check out the photos of celebrities who have dined at the venerable **Michael's,** 15 Broadway S., 507/288-2020. Greek dishes are the specialty of the house, but make up only a small part of the meat and seafood menu. Prices run $8–29, with most right in the middle of the span. Open Mon.–Sat. for lunch and dinner.

French

Chardonnay, 723 2nd St. SW, 507/252-1310, the city's only French restaurant, calls a Victorian home, home. Steak and seafood, all for about $30 a plate, form the backbone of the changing menu. With hundreds of bottles to choose from, theirs is the best wine list in town and has earned *Wine Spectator* magazine's Award of Excellence. Open Mon.–Sat. for dinner.

German

By day **Daube's,** 14 3rd St. SW, 507/280-6446, is a wonderful bakery and sandwich shop, but at night they break out the sausages, schnitzels, and sauerbraten. Begin your meal with the pickled herring and wash it down with imported beer or wine. Entrées average $16. Open Mon.–Sat. for breakfast, lunch, and dinner.

Greek

Although both Mac's and Michael's (listed under American and Fine Dining) are well known for their Greek fare, only the casual **Zorba's,** 924 7th St. NW, 507/281-1540, has an extensive Greek menu. Entrées average $10 and the large combination platters are a good deal at $20 for two people. Open daily for lunch and dinner.

Italian

With a shockingly large menu (the chicken section alone is longer than many restaurants' complete rosters) ordering a meal at **Victoria's,** 20 2nd Ave. SW, 507/280-6232, in the Kahler Grand Hotel, can be a real dilemma. The choices run from mix and match pastas to pork tenderloin Sorrento, and there's even walleye with alfredo sauce. The prices, running $8–26 for dinner (everything is a couple dollars less during lunch), are reasonable and the portions are large. Open daily for lunch and dinner.

A much different choice for Italian is the **Red-**

wood Room, 300 1st Ave. NW, 507/281-2978, where the changing menu features just a dozen intricate choices like smoked turkey pasta and lobster ravioli. Not to detract from the food, but the intimate, candle-lit, jazz-infused basement space is itself enough reason to dine here. Open weekdays for lunch and daily for dinner.

Mexican

Once the only Mexican restaurant in Rochester, there is still none better than **Fiesta Mexicana,** 1645 N Broadway NE (in the Northbrook Shopping Center), 507/288-1116. This ultra-friendly family-run place has a large menu with all the usual, plus some creative additions like potato chimichangas. None of their platters exceed $10. Open daily for lunch and dinner.

The similarly priced **Dos Amigos,** 20 4th St. SE, 507/282-3300, and 1726 37th St. NW, 507/536-4527, is also good. The large menu goes beyond the usual and they serve an interesting *salsa blanca* with the complimentary chips. Open daily for lunch and dinner.

Middle Eastern

Sarah's House Café, 420 2nd St. SW, 507/281-5888, is a simple little joint serving falafel, humus, gyros, lentil soup, and other Near East dishes for about $5. Traditional water pipes are available on the front patio for smokers. Open daily for lunch and dinner.

Pizza

The dumpy, red-vinyl **Bilotti's,** 304 1st Ave SW, 507/282-8668, has a full Italian and American menu, but it is their piled-high, thin-crust pizzas that keep them popular. A large cheese is just $9. Open daily for dinner and weekdays for lunch.

SHOPPING

Rochester is the regional shopping center for a large chunk of southeast Minnesota, so there is little you can't find here. The **Apache Mall** with around 80 stores is the largest outlet, though the smaller **Centerplace Galleria** right in the heart of downtown has a far more interesting selection of shops.

Rochester is a good place to shop for antiques. The largest stores, each with about 20 dealers, are the **Old Rooster Antique Mall,** 106 N. Broadway, 507/287-6228; and the **Antique Mall on Third Street,** 118 3rd St. SW, 507/287-0684. **Mayowood Galleries,** 20 2nd Ave. SW, 507/288-2695, in the Kahler Grand Hotel is small, but everything is top shelf. Other shops worth a browse are **Blondell Antiques,** 1408 SW 2nd St. SW, 507/282-1872; **Iridescent House,** 227 1st Ave. SW, 507/288-0302; **John Krusel's General Merchandise,** 22 3rd Ave. SW, 507/289-8049; and **Timeless Treasures,** 40 4th St. SE, 507/288-3398.

The large **SE Minnesota Visual Artists (SEMVA) Gallery,** 16 1st St. SW, 507/281-4920, fronting Peace Plaza downtown has work for sale in just about all possible media. For a truly unique remembrance of Rochester or a gift for someone who already has everything, get yourself some **Goose Poop Art.** Gary Blum's unique creations are available at **Natalie's Hallmark Shop,** 101 1st Ave. SW (in the Marriott subway), 507/288-4715. For an ethnic gift there is the **Dream Lady Gallery,** 507/288/2892, in Kahler Grand Hotel; and **The Nordic Shop,** 507/285-9143, in the Centerplace Galleria mall, selling Native American arts and crafts and Scandinavian imports respectively.

The **Barnes & Noble,** 15 1st St. SW, 507/288-3848, downtown on Peace Plaza isn't just the city's best bookstore, it's also one of the most beautiful anywhere. Their conversion of the 1927 Chateau Theatre kept the castle facade, night sky ceiling, and sunburst marquee. Even bibliophobes should take a look inside. Barnes & Noble, 507/281-7950, has a second location in the Apache Mall. Just around the corner from Peace Plaza is the **Extraordinary Bookseller,** 112 1st Ave. SW, 507/289-2407, one of the best used bookstores outside the Twin Cities. The **Friends' Bookstore** at the Rochester Public Library, 101 2nd St. SE, 507/287-2612, is small, but quite good. **Book Review,** 611 N. Broadway, 507/285-1600, has comics and lots of cheap paperbacks. **Pied Piper,** 8 17th Ave. NW (in the Miracle Mile Shopping Center), 507/281-1890, is a really good children's bookshop.

The **Rochester Downtown Farmers Market** is held at 4th St. and 4th Ave. SE on Saturday mornings from May through October.

INFORMATION AND SERVICES

Tourist Information

The very knowledgeable staff of the **Rochester Convention & Visitors Bureau,** 150 S. Broadway, 507/288-4331 or 800/634-8277, www.rochester-cvb.org, are available to answer your questions weekdays 8 A.M.–5 P.M.

The weekly *Rochester Area Visitor* brochure and the monthly *Rochester Magazine* are available along the skyway and in most hotels.

Media

The city's daily newspaper is the *Rochester Post-Bulletin,* though the *Star Tribune* and *Pioneer Press* from the Twin Cities are also widely available.

Post Office

The downtown post office, 102 S. Broadway, 507/287-1240, is open weekdays 8:30 A.M.–5 P.M.

Internet Access

Besides the library, the only public Web access is at the girlish **Java Dreams** coffee shop, 415 S. Broadway, 507/282-4477, which has a free computer for customer use.

GETTING THERE AND AWAY

By Air

Rochester International Airport, 507/282-2328, Minnesota's second busiest, is eight miles south of the city along Highway 63. **Northwest Airlink,** 800/225-2525, makes the short hop to the Twin Cities up to 11 times a day, and you can add this flight on to a longer Northwest flight for as little as $50. **American Airlines,** 800/433-7300, has four flights a day to Chicago O'Hare Airport for as little as $150.

Rochester Airport Shuttle, 507/282-2222, runs between the airport and major hotels for $9 per person. A taxi will cost about $22 to downtown.

By Bus

Jefferson Lines and **Greyhound** charge $23 one-way for the Minneapolis to Rochester route. The bus depot is at 405 1st Ave. SW, 507/289-4037.

Both **Rochester Direct,** 507/280-9270 or 800/280-9270, and **Rochester Express,** 507/282-8673 or 800/479-7824, run vans to the Minneapolis-St. Paul International Airport with drop off and pick up at most of the city's major hotels. It is about a 90-minute trip, and both charge $23 one-way. Reservations are required for the trip north and recommended heading south. The frequent service can also be used to reach towns along the way or the Mall of America. Rochester Express also has two vans a day to Winona (scheduled to coincide with Amtrak trains) and service to Decorah, Iowa (twice daily); La Crosse, Wisconsin (twice a week); and Cannistota, South Dakota (twice monthly).

GETTING AROUND

By Bus

Rochester City Lines, 507/288-4353, is a comprehensive bus system. All routes begin and end downtown on 2nd Street SW between 1st and 2nd Avenues. A Transit Information Center with route maps, schedules, and free phones for live assistance is located on each side of the street. Eight routes run along 2nd Street SW, and two go down South Broadway, the two places tourists are mostly likely to go. The fare is $1.

By Taxi

Taxis aren't rare on the streets of Rochester but flagging one down isn't routine, so if you need one call **Yellow Cab,** 507/282-2222.

Car Rentals

Avis, 507/288-5655; **Budget,** 507/252-5055; **Hertz,** 507/288-2244; **National,** 507/288-1155; and **Thrifty,** 507/252-5045, all have airport branches. Downtown you will find **Avis,** 507/288-5222, at the Kahler Grand Hotel and **National,** 507/288-1331, at the Holiday Inn.

Organized Tours

Rochester Express, 507/282-8673 or 800/479-7824, offers a variety of one-day tours in and around the city, including down to the Amish region around Lanesboro and out to the Mississippi River. They charge a minimum of $25 per person.

AROUND ROCHESTER

Mantorville

This petite community (it's actually home to over 1,000 people, but you'd never know by looking at it) survives on tourism—half of all businesses in town are antique and gift shops—but it grew up on limestone. The Mantor Brothers, Peter, Riley, and Frank, came here from out east in 1853 and built a sawmill and gristmill on the Zumbro River, though they chose this particular spot with eyes on opening a quarry. Mantorville limestone has built buildings across the state and beyond. Naturally it was the material of choice for local architects, a factor that led to the entire downtown's inclusion on the National Register of Historic Places.

Up on the hill and across from the 1871 Dodge County Courthouse (the oldest working courthouse in the state, unfortunately destroyed aesthetically by the incompatible modern annex) is the **Dodge County Historical Society Museum,** 507/635-5508. The main building, the former St. John's Episcopal Church, built in 1869, now contains a small but eclectic collection of historical curios, plus there's an 1856 house and 1883 one-room schoolhouse on the grounds. All of the museum buildings are open Tuesday–Saturday noon–4 P.M. from May through mid-October, plus the church is open Thursday–Saturday 10 A.M.–4 P.M. the rest of the year, except for a one-month closure beginning in mid-December. Admission is $2. Just down the street is the **Restoration House,** 507/635-5140, a fully restored and furnished 1856 home. It once served as a county office building and what was then the county's only prison cell still sits in the basement. In back is the even more interesting **Old Log Cabin,** built at roughly the same time. It was home to the cooper for the nearby Mantorville Brewery (now in ruins) and many barrel-making tools are on display in the basement. Both buildings are open for tours 1–5 P.M. daily except Monday from May through October.

© TIM BEWER

Zumbrota Covered Bridge

The city's top historic site isn't a museum but a restaurant. The **Hubbell House,** 502 N. Main St., 507/635-2331, has been in continuous operation since 1854 when it opened as a stagecoach stop. The current building, filled with antiques and Civil War memorabilia, went up in 1856, replacing the original log hotel. The varied menu includes such choices as seafood crepes, vegetable lasagna, raspberry chicken, and filet mignon. Everything on the smaller lunch menu is under $10, while dinner runs $7–40. Open daily except Mon. for lunch and dinner. The **Mantorville Theatre Company,** 507/635-5420, is best known for their booable summer melodramas, though they do a few other productions during the rest of the year, too. Tickets for the weekend shows start at $6. Their home base is the Mantorville Opera

House, 5 5th St. NE, a 1918 Vaudeville theater. The purely functional **Stussy Memorial RV Park,** 507/635-5170, has ten shadeless sites along the river for $20 with full hookups.

Zumbrota

On your way to or from Rochester be sure to stop for a look at Minnesota's only remaining original covered bridge. The 116-foot **Zumbrota Covered Bridge** was built in 1869 to serve the stagecoach route between St. Paul and Dubuque, Iowa. When a modern steel span replaced the barnlike structure in 1932 sensible locals insisted on preservation not demolition, though it didn't actually make it back over the riffling Zumbro River again until 1997. It now sits just one block from where it originally stood.

BLUFF COUNTRY

Amish Country

Take some of the best scenery southeast Minnesota can throw at you; add bucolic bike trails, trophy trout streams, and the old order way of life; mix with a dash of luxurious indulgence; and you get Fillmore County, southern Minnesota's most popular destination. The state's largest Amish community rings Harmony, and a chance to brush up against their way of life is a big draw, but the bike trails snaking through the deep valleys bring in most of the masses and have given Lanesboro hegemony in the county's tourist trade. While this is primarily a summer and fall destination—the Root River Valley is a remarkable fall color canvas—more and more people are heading here in the winter to ski.

Most of what is detailed in this section lies along or near Highway 16, the federally designated **Historic Bluff Country Scenic Byway,** a winding 88-mile ribbon coming up the bluff-lined Root River Valley from Hokah near the Mississippi River. West of Lanesboro the road leaves the valley to wind through the rolling farm fields trimmed with patches of forest and streams.

If you are here to cast a fly, the South Branch Root River above Preston and the streams that feed it are considered by many to be the best trout waters in the state, while Duschee Creek outside Lanesboro and Trout Run Creek east of Chatfield also come highly recommended.

LANESBORO

Little Lanesboro is one of the loveliest towns in Minnesota. The entire downtown business district is listed on the National Register of Historic Places, and the plumb limestone bluff rising 320 feet behind it couldn't be any more perfect a backdrop.

The Southeastern Minnesota Railroad reached the valley in 1868, and Lanesboro was founded as a summer resort by and for East Coast bigwigs that same year. The financiers dammed the Root River to create a lake for sailing and summer homes and built the three-story Phoenix Hotel,

a luxurious dwelling filled with hand-carved oak woodwork, imported crystal chandeliers, and marble topped dressers. The Phoenix did decent business until burning down in 1885 (despite what you expect from the name, it was not rebuilt), though Lanesboro never became the great resort area its promoters had hoped; it turns out they were just ahead of their time. The city did thrive during the 19th century and well into the 20th, though it was milling, not tourism, that created the initial boom. Lanesboro hit the skids in the 1960s and during two decades of decline saw most businesses go belly up leaving a downtown filled with vacant storefronts.

The rail line that created the town almost single-handedly re-created it in 1985 when the first five miles were converted into the Root River State Trail. Lanesboro is now one of the most popular travel destinations in the state and, though fewer than 800 people reside here, many times this converge on the city every weekend during the summer and fall—you'll probably tour half the town while searching out a parking space. Dozens of businesses now cater to the mostly affluent visitors, who pedal the trails and shop by day and pamper themselves with the fine dining and historic lodging at night. Just about everything of note is found along Parkway Avenue, the city's main drag, though many shops have popped up on Coffee Street, too.

Sights

The **Lanesboro Historical Museum,** 105 Parkway Ave. S., 507/467-2177, began with the donation of wood carvings of local barber Hans Olson and, though these are still the highlight of the collection, it has now expanded to include various other historical artifacts from the town's early days. The museum is open 11 A.M.–3 P.M. (quite often earlier and later too, if someone is around), daily from May–October and weekends the rest of the year.

Avian Acres, 507/467-2996 or 800/967-2473, 1.5 miles southwest of town, is first and foremost

© TIM BEWER

a wild bird supply superstore, but tourists are more likely to make the trip for the 100-critter petting zoo. To get there, take County Road 8 west and follow the signs down the mountain-like road. The store and menagerie are open daily (even holidays) 9 A.M.–7 P.M. Admission to the petting zoo is $2.50—or free if you spend enough in the store.

The **Eagle Bluff Environmental Learning Center,** 507/467-2437 or 888/800-9558, is a primarily a residential group conference center with educational and team-building programs, though the small nature center with displays on karst geology (open 8 A.M.–4:30 P.M. weekdays and 10 A.M.–4 P.M. weekends) and some of the hiking trails are also open to the public. The monumental overlook of the Root River Valley, an easy quarter-mile stroll from the nature center, is alone is worth the trip up here. Take County Road 8 two miles west of town, turn right on County Road 21, and follow the signs.

The DNR's **Lanesboro Fish Hatchery,** 507/467-3771, produces over 750,000 brown and 400,000 rainbow trout annually and, while most are let loose in this area, they end up in streams all across Minnesota. A video shown in the office (located across the bridge) presents the beginnings of the rearing process, and then you can see the rest of it in person. You'll see the most fish in the ponds and raceways during June and July, though there is something to see all the time. The fish farm is located along Duschee Creek (appropriately one of the state's best trout streams) a mile south of town on Highway 16 and is open Monday–Friday 7 A.M.–4:30 P.M.

To see something you just don't see every day, drop by the **Lanesboro Sales Barn** on the east end of town. This is one of the largest livestock markets in the Upper Midwest, and an average of 1,000 head of cattle, often twice that, are auctioned off during the Wednesday slaughter auction beginning at 8:30 A.M. The regular livestock auction on Friday at 11 A.M. is mostly cattle, but also pigs, sheep, and goats.

Both **Flaby's Amish Tours,** 507/467-2577 or 800/944-0099, and **R & M Amish Touring,** 507/467-2128, will take you out to Amish farms in their vans. Both charge $20 per person, though R&M will offer a small discount if the guide rides in your car. You can book a space at the Cottage House Inn and Stone Mill Suites respectively.

BLUFF COUNTRY

BLUFFLANDS STATE TRAIL

A pair of immensely popular trails, collectively known as the **Blufflands State Trail,** are the ideal way to experience the beauty of southeast Minnesota. The 60 miles of paved path lead through the wooded valleys and past the towering limestone bluffs and rolling farm fields that define this corner of the state. As a bonus deer, pheasant, and wild turkey encounters are fairly common. The bikers and in-line skaters who flock here to use these trails are largely responsible for the area's economic resurrection. Heaviest use comes during the summer, but cross-country skiers make them year-round attractions.

The shade covered **Root River State Trail** winds along its eponymous waterway for most of the 42 miles between Fountain and Houston. It crosses 47 bridges along the way. The trail largely follows an abandoned railroad grade and is almost completely level except for a steep half-mile climb about five miles from the Houston end. Riders doing one-way trips should note that there is an appreciable downhill from west to east.

The just as beautiful **Harmony-Preston Valley State Trail,** an offshoot of the Root River Trail, leads 18 miles south to Harmony and has two distinct segments. The northern half crisscrosses Camp Creek, Watson Creek, and the South Branch Root River—like the Root River Trail, it is generally flat and pleasantly shady. Beginning at County Road 16, about five miles south of Preston, the trail leaves the old railroad grade and climbs steeply out of the valley over leg-burning hills. For many, it is a welcome break from the usual flat and straight miles of Rail-to-Trail conversions. Eventually you are rewarded for the effort with a sweeping view of the path you just traced. Beyond this there are just rolling hills on into Harmony. Another nine miles of trail, tentatively dubbed the **Forestville State Trail,** between Preston and Forestville/Mystery Cave State Park could be completed by 2005.

Lanesboro, located along the western half of the Root River Trail and just five miles from the Harmony-Preston Valley Trail, is the main base for most riders, though each of the quaint rural communities along the trail has lodging and/or camping.

Recreation

The **Root River State Trail** cuts straight through the heart of town, while the **Harmony-Preston Valley State Trail** begins about five miles away. Canoeists, kayakers, and inner tubers can follow the **Root River** more directly. Both the north and south branches cut past towering bluffs and sheer limestone cliffs and are easy routes with generally nothing more than the occasional Class I rapid. The North Branch is widely considered the most scenic trip and is thus the most popular. The 30 miles between Chatfield and the confluence of the two branches near Whalen can be done in about 12 hours, though several campsites make it a great overnight trip, and a landing at Moen's Bridge right in the middle allows for more manageable day trips, too. Below Whalen the valley widens and continues to expand for all of the 55 miles to the Mississippi River. Highway 16 hugs the river most of the way down, and though this makes for an incredible drive it diminishes the quality of the paddling. For just a short jaunt consider the winding five-mile, 90-minute trip between Lanesboro and Whalen. A pair of outfitters in town can set you up with just about everything you need for some time on the trail or the river. The **Little River General Store,** 105 Coffee St., 507/467-2943 or 800/994-2943, has a most impressive array of bikes including tandems, recumbents, tandem recumbents, and even side-by-side two- and six-seater surreys. Shuttle service is available along the entire trail system with advanced notice. Canoes, kayaks, inner tubes, cross-country skis, and snowshoes are also available for hire. The smaller, though generally cheaper, **Root River Outfitters,** 102 Parkway Ave. S., 507/467-3400, has bikes, canoes, inner tubes, and fly-fishing equipment. Both companies provide shuttle service with all watercraft rentals.

Entertainment and Events

The well-respected **Commonweal Theatre Company,** (based in the St. Mane Theatre building),

206 Parkway Ave. N., 507/467-2525 or 800/657-7025, produces six shows throughout the year. Tickets are $15. During the summer the theater hosts the live radio broadcast of the *Over the Back Fence* musical variety show; a seat in the audience costs $3 or you can listen in on KFIL (103.1 FM/1060 AM).

Also during the summer live bands, blues and rock more often than not, play the patio at the **Riverside on the Root** restaurant on Wednesday nights. The public is always welcome at the monthly **barn dances** at the Sons of Norway Hall, 200 Parkway S., 507/498-5452.

Buffalo Bill Cody, a friend of David Powell, a famous Dakota doctor who lived in town, spent a great deal of time in Lanesboro in the years before and after forming his Wild West Show, and the town celebrates the connection by naming its biggest festival **Buffalo Bill Days.** The community blast has music, arts and crafts, a parade, and lots of food the first weekend in August. **Art in the Park,** every third Sunday in June, attracts nearly 100 vendors and thousands of buyers. There's a **standstill parade** the third Saturday in May in Whalen, four miles east of Lanesboro.

Accommodations

With eight in and around town, little Lanesboro is the bed-and-breakfast capital of Minnesota. Yet, even with another 16 hotels, historic inns, and cottages, it is very difficult to find a room on summer weekends without booking months in advance. Thankfully for last-minute visitors the Lanesboro Visitor Center keeps a list of vacancies in and around town, and when the city is full up don't fret, there are plenty of quality options in the nearby towns.

The colorful **Historic Scanlan House,** 507/467-2158 or 800/944-2158, one of Lanesboro's first B&Bs, looks like a people-sized gingerbread house. The 1889 Queen Anne Victorian on the south end of town is jam-packed with antiques and knickknacks, and each of the seven guestrooms has a private bath and most also have whirlpool tubs. A couple of rooms go for as little as $105, while the largest suite tops out at $225.

Local legend has it that Michael Scanlan built his grand home to prove he was the town's "most successful Irishman." His main competition for the honor was Cady Hayes, who started construction of this equally grand Queen Anne mansion, now the **Cady Hayes House,** 500 Calhoun

© TIM BEWER

side-by-side on the Root River State Trail

Ave. S., 507/467-2621, the next year. The three guestrooms, one decked out with Amish furniture, another with a large rosemaled Norwegian bed, and the third, a two-room suite, furnished with antiques, each have a private bath and are priced $80–115.

The venerable **Mrs. B's Historic Lanesboro Inn,** 101 Parkway Ave. N., 507/467-2154 or 800/657-4710, is right along the river and trail—this is one of the few businesses that predates it—in the heart of town. Each of the 10 cozy rooms in the impressive 1870 limestone building have a unique character, whether it is the rosemaled and hand-carved Norwegian beds, Amish quilts, or fireplaces. The front parlor has a baby grand piano, fireplace, and library. Rooms cost $99 to $109. They also manage a pair of large one-bedroom apartments that can sleep six.

Another classic 19th-century limestone structure on the north end of town has been converted into the **Stone Mill Suites,** 100 Beacon St. E., 507/467-8663 100, 866/897-8663. Many original features, like the thick interior walls and wooden beams, have been left exposed and some of the larger rooms have lofts and fireplaces. The 10 themed rooms run $110–140.

For a real treat, book a room at the **Berwood Hill Inn,** 507/765-2391 or 800/803-6748, a museum-quality Victorian mansion surrounded by an incredible garden. Room rates begin at $155, but if you want to be pampered you can't do much better than this. Each of the four luxurious guestrooms in the house has a private bath and two have whirlpool tubs, while a simple cottage (the bathroom is inside the main house) is available for $90. A gourmet breakfast is included in the price, and lunch and dinner options are available with advance notice. It is located four miles west of town.

The friendly **Brewster's Red Hotel,** 106 Parkway Ave. S., 507/467-2999, has eight individually decorated rooms in an 1870 home that climbs a steep hill. The simple quarters starting at $55 are a good value, plus there are three one-bedroom apartments for $125. The patio and deck are a nice place to unwind.

The 14 rooms at the **Cottage House Inn,** 209 Parkway Ave. N., 507/467-2577 or 800/944-0099,

are thoroughly modern, but most are decorated with antiques and at $70 they are a good value.

The city runs a pair first-come, first-served campgrounds: 43 RV sites with water and electric hookups are jammed together at Sylvan Park, though the pond-side tent sites are decent. The 16 RV sites between the river and the high school football field at the nearby **Riverview Campground** are a bit more spread out, but you need to come over to the park for showers. Both charge $17 for RVs and $10 for tents.

Food

The most talked about restaurant in town is the **Victorian House,** 709 Parkway Ave. S., 507/467-3457, a posh French restaurant (with a French chef) where a four-course meal will run about $30. They are open Tuesday–Saturday for dinner and reservations are required.

Mrs. B's Historic Lanesboro Inn, 101 Parkway Ave. N., 507/467-2154 or 800/657-4710, the city's original gourmet kitchen, serves a $30 four-course prix fix dinner with a single sitting Wednesday–Sunday evenings at 7. The menu changes daily, but expect creative dishes such as roast pork tenderloin with Thai red pepper peanut sauce, pesto mashed potatoes, or herb asparagus bisque.

The menu is more varied, the atmosphere more casual, but the food just as clever and commendable at the **Old Village Hall,** 111 Coffee St. 507/467-2962. Entrées such as garden angel-hair pasta, pecan-crusted quail, and pork tenderloin with an apple and date glaze run $15–22. The trailside deck is a popular place to dine. They are open daily for dinner and weekends for lunch between May and November with reduced hours, generally weekends only, the rest of the year.

Naturally, most of the tables at the laid-back, blues-infused **Riverside on the Root,** 109 Parkway Ave. S., 507/467-3663, overlook the river. Pizza is their specialty, and you can get a large from $13, while the sandwiches and pastas rounding out the menu run $6–11. Nightly specials include Mexican and prime rib. The kitchen is open mid-April through November with dinner daily, lunch daily during the summer and weekends the rest of the year, and breakfast on summer weekends.

The menu at the **Trail Inn Café,** 111 Parkway Ave. N., 507/467-2200, a simple family restaurant, covers mostly the basics like a hamburger, turkey club, and broasted chicken with a few extras like elk burgers and pizza. Most everything is under $8. Open daily for lunch and dinner except closed Mon. during the winter.

Last, but certainly not least, is **Das Wurst Haus,** 117 Parkway Ave. N., 507/467-2902. The meat, bread, sauerkraut, and mustard for their brats, Ruebens, and other German-style sandwiches are all made from family recipes passed down to the new owners. The Haus also brews its own root beer, serves an extraordinary number of ice cream cones, and at any time you could hear a random act of polka. Barry Levenson, curator of the Mount Horeb Mustard Museum (www.mustardmuseum.com) and the world's foremost authority on all things mustardy, has declared the Fabian family recipes to be "perhaps the most authentic German-style mustards made in America." Open daily for lunch between March and November.

Lanesboro

© TIM BEWER

Shopping

Just about every other business downtown is selling antiques or Amish crafts. You can buy the latter, plus produce and baked goods, directly from the source on Saturday mornings when a small farmers market convenes in Sylvan Park. The **Cornucopia Art Center,** 103 Parkway Ave., 507/467-2446, is small, but carries top quality and often reasonably priced work by dozens of regional artists. **Frank Wright,** woodworker extraordinaire, primarily carves spoons and chopsticks. You can pick up his hand-carved wares at the Cornucopia Art Center or in his workshop/store at 106 Coffee St., 507/467-3376. The **Scenic Valley Winery,** 101 Coffee St., 507/467-2958 or 888/965-0250, primarily produces fruit vintages like rhubarb, raspberry, and wild plum, plus green pepper and onion cooking wines. Free samples are always available. Next door is **Candy Lane,** 201 Parkway N., 507/467-3731, with Amish and other homemade candies. You can help yourself (though donations

are appreciated, of course) to the books and magazines in the lobby of the Lanesboro Library, 202 Parkway Ave. S., 507/467-2649.

Information and Services

The helpful **Lanesboro Visitor Center,** 507/467-2696 or 800/944-2670, www.lanesboro.com, is located one block east of Parkway Ave. along the Root River Trail. It is generally open Sunday–Thursday 10 A.M.–4 P.M. and Friday–Saturday 9 A.M.–5 P.M.

WEST OF LANESBORO

Preston

The Fillmore County Seat is quite a bit larger than Lanesboro, but a whole lot quieter due to the scarcity of tourists. "America's Trout Capital," as they have declared themselves, is tucked into a deep bend of the **South Branch Root River** and the fishing is superb from here all the way up to Forestville/Mystery Cave State Park. For most,

BLUFF COUNTRY

the main reason to come to Preston is to leave it, either along the river or via the **Harmony-Preston Valley State Trail.** The 14-mile trip by water to Lanesboro has just a few small riffles along the way and is a much less traveled route than that below Lanesboro, though this is in part because it is a difficult run when water levels are low.

The simple **Trailhead Inn,** 112 Center St., 507/765-2460, sitting right where it says it does, has 10 fairly large rooms from $70, plus a whirlpool room for $105. The **Country Hearth Inn,** 809 U.S. 52 N., 507/765-2533 or 888/378-2896, charges $86 for similar rooms, but also has a pool and whirlpool for guest use. The fanciest rooms in town are at the **JailHouse Inn,** 109 Houston St., NW, 507/765-2181. The 1869 brick building did serve as the courthouse and jail, but it has been completely gutted and gussied up, and now the only evidence of its former use are the room names and the original bars left behind in the "Cell Block." Each of the 12 cozy rooms has a unique touch, whether it be Amish furnishings, antique decorations, or claw-foot tubs. Rates start at $75, though the largest whirlpool suites are more than double that. A few miles outside of town off County Road 17, right between the river and the trail, is **The Old Barn Resort,** 507/467-2512 or 800/552-2512. The massive campground (130 RV and 40 tent sites) is as crowded as you'd expect it to be, but the location makes it a good choice anyway. The barn itself houses the offices; a busy restaurant; game room; and a four-room, 44-bed hostel in the basement, while a swimming pool and 18-hole golf course ring it. Rates are $17, $18, and $25 for a tent site, hostel bed, and RV site with full hookups respectively.

Locals looking for a nice night out come from across the county to dine at the **Branding Iron,** 507/765-3388, a casual supper club perched above town along U.S. 52. Steak and seafood average $15 and sandwiches and salads are about half that. Open daily for lunch and dinner. For something simpler there's **The Brick House On Main,** 104 E. Main St., 507/765-9820, a small coffeehouse with panini sandwiches, ice cream, and a full slate of caffeinated beverages. It's an ideal post-ride rest stop. Open daily (closed Sun. Nov.–April) for breakfast and lunch.

The Brick House, Trailhead Inn, and Old Barn all rent bikes; the latter two also have inner tubes and the Old Barn has canoes.

Fountain

Other than accessing the **Root River State Trail,** which has its western terminus here, the main reason to stop in Fountain is the **Fillmore County History Center,** 202 County Road 8, 507/268-4449, the largest museum in the area by far. The historical medley contains thousands of objects from the distant and not-so-distant past, like fossils, old toys, housewares, clothes, classic cars, and farm equipment. Their 36 restored Oliver tractors date back to the 1920s. Outside are a furnished one-room schoolhouse and a spruced-up log cabin from the late 1860s. The museum is open year-round Monday–Friday 9 A.M.–4 P.M., plus Saturday and Sunday 1–4:30 P.M. from mid-June to mid-October. Admission is free.

Fountain is named for the abundant natural springs in the area, and the results of those springs has lent the town its motto, "Sink Hole Capital of the U.S.A." There are about 100 of these small, usually shallow pits right around town; look for round clumps of trees. One is fenced off directly across from the museum. You can see many more along County Road 8 west of town and from a viewing platform just down the Root River Trail.

Wykoff

Until 1989, when Ed Krueger died, there was no reason for visitors to come to this sleepy village. Unlike anything you've ever seen **Ed's Museum,** 100 S. Gold St., is a meticulously organized monument to messiness. The town's most colorful character ran the Jack Sprat grocery store on the lower level of this simple building and resided upstairs. When his wife died in 1940, Ed pretty much stopped throwing things away and he left the store, and everything in it, to the town on the condition that it be turned into a museum. The local historical society fixed up the building, tossed out tons—literally—of what they decided was rubbish, and ordered the rest of his hoard to a degree of orderliness that would pass boot camp muster—and probably make Ed turn in his grave. Still, the collection is amazing, and careful scanning of the boxes and shelves will reveal some surprising finds, like his mummified cat Sammy and a jar with 25 gallstones. Other things laying about the store include junk mail, every magazine he ever subscribed to, and unsold store merchandise from the 1940s. Thankfully some things, like his desk, were left in their original state, and there are photos of the store before its unfortunate rearranging. Most of the furnishings in his second floor home were purchased at the time of his marriage in 1923, and next to nothing has changed since then; you really feel as though the pre-1940 Ed might come home any minute. The extraordinary Ed's life is on display Saturday and Sunday 1–4 P.M. during the summer, though you can make appointments to visit other times. Admission is free. If the museum is closed, inquire across the street at **The Bank Gift Haus,** 105 S. Gold St., 507/352-4205.

The Historic Wykoff Jail Haus, 219 N. Main St., 507/352-4205, is an original 1913 jailhouse that the town has renovated into a B&B. For $63 you can sleep on bunks in the two original cell blocks or use the fold-out bed in the sitting room. It's not fancy, but hey . . . you're in jail! The price includes breakfast at the nearby **Gateway Inn,** 118 Gold St. N., 507/352-4221, a classic small town café open daily for breakfast and lunch, plus Friday night for a fish fry.

Spring Valley

Spring Valley has just over 2,500 inhabitants, enough to make it the largest town in the county. Laura Ingalls Wilder and her husband Almanzo, whose parents moved here from New York when he was 13, attended the Methodist-Episcopal Church in Spring Valley during 1890 and 1891. Today the simple church with its lovely stained glass windows houses part of the **Spring Valley Historical Museum,** 221 Courtland St. W., 507/346-7659. Although it's the primary draw, there is only a handful of Wilder photos and memorabilia. The rest of the historical hodgepodge includes an antique camera collection; 1874 horse-drawn fire wagon; funeral wreaths woven from human hair; and an exhibit on Richard Sears, founder of Sears, Roebuck & Co., who was born in nearby Stewartville. Across the

street is the 1865 Washburn-Zittleman House, furnished as it would have been at the turn of the 20th century. Another building has school, military, and agricultural displays. The museum is open 10 A.M.–4 P.M. daily during the summer, and weekends in September and October. Admission is $3 for any one building or $5 for all. The Wilder's home is gone, but if you want to see their barn ask the staff for directions.

The William Strong House, 508 N. Huron Ave., 507/346-2850 or 888/350/6452, is a gorgeous 1879 Second Empire mansion with five comfy, antique-filled guestrooms and an inviting front porch. Rooms start at $95. The **Shady Rest Motel,** 710 N. Broadway (U.S. 52), 507/346-2625, has eight very simple rooms for $39. **Elaine's Café,** 125 S. Broadway, 507/346-7492, is a no-nonsense joint where locals linger over coffee and catch up on town news. The menu's got burgers for $2 or a roast beef dinner for $5. Open daily for breakfast and lunch and weekdays for dinner.

FORESTVILLE/MYSTERY CAVE STATE PARK

You can do more in one afternoon at this diverse park than most vacationers do all weekend. Explore Minnesota's longest cave, step back to the 19th century in the village of Forestville, hike the wooded hills and valleys, and dip a line in three of Minnesota's best trout streams. For general park questions call 507/352-5111.

Historic Forestville

Founded in 1853 Forestville, like many other fledgling communities in the south of the state, became a rural trade center for area farmers. One hundred and ten people lived here at its peak, but when the newly formed Southern Minnesota Railroad bypassed the town in 1868 it faltered, and by 1890 Thomas Meighen had acquired the entire town and all the surrounding land. Each of the fifty remaining residents worked for Meighen on his farm, in his general store, or at his saw and feed mills. Today part of the village is brought to life, as it would have been in the summer of 1899, by costumed interpreters portraying actual town residents. During the 90-minute living history tours you'll get to compare prices in the General Store (with much of the original stock left on the shelves when it closed in 1910), sample something fresh from the oven in the Meighen's kitchen, and help the farm laborers in the garden. The site is open Tuesday–Fri 10 A.M.–5 P.M., Saturday 11 A.M.–6 P.M., and Sunday noon–5 P.M., plus the same hours on weekends in September and October. Admission is free. Call 507/765-2785 for more information.

Mystery Cave

The entrance to Minnesota's longest cavern is five miles west of the main park. Thirteen miles of winding passage were carved into the limestone bedrock over many thousands of years, and the South Branch Root River still feeds this living cave before flowing through the park proper. Park naturalists lead visitors past the stalactites, stalagmites, and underground ponds. The standard one-hour tour follows a lit, wheelchair-accessible concrete path. During the summer, tours are offered daily 10 A.M.–5 P.M., plus weekends 10 A.M.–4 P.M. from mid-April through the end of October. At least a couple of times a day during summer weekends a two-hour tour using handheld lanterns leads along a gravel path through a different level of the cave; there are fewer formations along the way but you will see larger passages. Both tours cost $7, and you might want to bring something warm to wear since the cave remains a constant 48 degrees. Call 507/937-3251 with any cave questions.

Trails

Most of the 15 or so miles of trail in the 3,100-acre park have some climbs, though they are generally very scenic so your effort is rewarded. One of the more popular routes is the mile-long climb up the **Sandbank Trail** to the overlook. Follow the **Ravine** and **Maple Ridge** trails, both of which lead out from Historic Forestville, to enjoy the profusion of spring wildflowers. The **Big Spring Trail** is the only easy path, though it can be very wet, and there is no bridge over Canfield Creek near the end. If you hike the whole two miles to the Big Spring at the head of the valley, you'll experience a microclimate 10 degrees cooler than the

rest of the park. Look carefully in the winter and spring when there is no vegetation in the way and you'll find hidden caves and springs near many of the trails. Most of the trails are open to and popular with horseback riders, and about half are groomed for cross-country skiing in the winter. A paved bike path along the river will lead here from Preston by as early as 2005.

Camping

The quiet campground has 73 sites in three loops. Those in loop A are the best, all shaded and widely spaced, while B and C are mostly shady; all 23 electric sites are in loop C.

HARMONY

This friendly town lies right between the area's two largest Amish communities. The Amish drop into town quite frequently, and you are much more likely to pass their horse-drawn buggies around here than anywhere else. The region's biggest tourist draw, after Lanesboro, got its name rather spontaneously. When a discussion of what to call the newly formed town became overly heated one exasperated member of the group stood up and exclaimed, "Let's have harmony here!" The opposing sides pondered the statement briefly, and they have had Harmony ever since.

Sights and Recreation

Michel's Amish Tours, 45 Main Ave. N., 507/886-5392 or 800/752-6474, offers ride-along tours Monday–Saturday 9 A.M.–3 P.M. year-round for $25 per car. **Amish Country Tours,** 507/886-2303, in the Village Depot, has both van and ride-along tours between mid-April and early November. The van tours ($11 per person) depart at 11 A.M., 1:30 P.M., and 3:30 P.M. with added times on Saturday as needed, while ride-alongs ($25 per car) are available 9 A.M.–4 P.M.

In 1924 a farmer followed the squeals of his missing pigs and found they had fallen into a deep cavern and **Niagara Cave,** 507/886-6606 or 800/837-6606, opened to the paying public ten years later. Stalactites, stalagmites, flowstone, and fossils are found in many of the large caverns, though the highlight of this living, growing cave is the 60-foot underground waterfall. You follow a paved and wooden path the whole way so you won't get very muddy, but bring a jacket since the temperature remains a constant 48 degrees. The one-hour tours depart at least every half-hour daily 9:30 A.M.–5:30 P.M. from May through September, and weekends 10 A.M.–4:30 P.M. in April and October. Admission is $8. The cave is four miles outside Harmony: take Hwy. 139 south and follow the signs. If you arrived in town by bike but don't wish to ride out to the cave, Amish Country Tours, 507/886-2303, in the Depot will drive you out and back for a buck.

Ada Austin of **Austin's Mohair,** 507/886-6731, has created one of the most impressive enterprises in the state. The Old Goat Woman, as she calls herself, keeps over 200 furry goats on her purple-trimmed farm and gift shop, and together with a dozen stay-at-home moms turns out a most impressive variety of goat-made gifts. The wool is woven into socks, sweaters, blankets, Christmas stockings, and yarn; the horns are cut into buttons; and cheese, fudge, and soap are brewed from the milk. Goat sausage is quickly becoming a top seller. While you shop your kids can feed and pet her kids. Most Amish tours make a stop here, but you are welcome to visit on your own—just head east for about a mile on U.S. 52 and take the first gravel road to the north. The farm is open daily April though December and Monday–Saturday the rest of the year, and the hours are roughly 8 A.M. until 5 P.M.

The **Harmony Toy Museum,** 30 Main Ave. S., 507/867-3380, displays over 4,000 playthings plus, in a recent move toward diversification, old tools, crafts, and paintings. Everybody, no matter how old or young, will find something from his/her childhood. Like a garage sale gone mad, Wesley Idso's personal collection of handmade and store-bought toys has unwittingly grown into one of the state's best folk art displays. And, no matter how hard you plead, none of it is for sale. The doors are usually open Monday–Saturday 10 A.M.–5 P.M. and Sunday noon–5 P.M. from May through September. Admission is $1.

When Slim Maroushek was diagnosed with Multiple Sclerosis he decided he needed a new career—he chose wood carving. **Slim's Woodshed,** 160 1st St., NW, 507/886-3114, is a combination classroom, store, and museum, and the collection of carvings from around the globe is absolutely worth the $1 admission. Slim opens his doors Monday–Saturday 9 A.M.–5 P.M. plus Sunday noon–4 P.M. from April to December.

Harmony is the southern terminus of the **Harmony-Preston Valley State Trail. Kingsley Mercantile,** 2 Main Ave. N., 507/886-2323 (closed Sundays), rents bikes or you can let the Country Lodge hotel arrange one for you. There is no regular shuttle service here, but if you are staying in town the proprietors of your hotel or B&B will probably be able to make arrangements.

The **Harmony Interpretive Center,** a small local history museum, should be open in the visitors center by the time you read this.

Entertainment

The **Jem Theatre,** 14 Main Ave. N., 507/886-7469, is a small renovated 1940s movie house, showing first-run films on weekends for $3. It's the only movie theater in Fillmore County. **Hats Off,** 35 1st Ave. NW, 507/886-6311, in the old American Legion building hosts Sunday night polkas and square dances.

Accommodations

The **Country Lodge,** 525 Main Ave. N., 507/886-2515 or 800/870-1710, is a very friendly and homey hotel in a renovated creamery. Regular rooms are just $55, and those with whirlpools cost $85. **Slim's Bunkhouse,** 160 1st St. NW, 507/886-3114, at Slim's Woodshed has three simple rooms with a shared bath for $35.

The **Selvig House Bed & Breakfast,** 140 Center St. E., 507/886-2200 or 888/887-2922, is a beautiful 1910 home with an enclosed porch and country decorations. Each of the three guestrooms has a private bath and are priced at $90; one has its own second floor porch with a swing. Carol and Ralph know a lot about their town and love to share history and advice. A newer B&B, the **Gourmets' Garden,** 507/886-2971, is in a completely modernized 19th-century farmhouse on a 10-acre hobby farm a couple of miles out of town. The chef owners not only prepare a fanciful breakfast but, upon request, serve up

A PEOPLE APART, A PEOPLE TOGETHER

And be not conformed to this world: but be ye transformed by the renewing of your mind, that ye may prove what is that good, and acceptable, and perfect, will of God.

Romans 12:2

The country roads around Harmony are lined with Amish farmsteads. Spend even a little time here and you'll pass bearded men (sans mustaches since they associate these with the military) and bonneted women in their plain, home-sewn clothes clopping along in horse-drawn buggies or out working the fields.

Scattered pockets of Amish dot Minnesota farm country, about 3,000 in total, but Fillmore County's community is the largest. Driven west by rising land prices the first Amish relocated here from Ohio in 1974. Southeast Minnesota appealed to the transplants because of the abundance of wood, natural springs, and creameries. From just an initial few the tight-knit community has grown to about 100 families (700 people) in five church districts. A second and entirely separate group numbering about 35 families came up from Iowa in the mid-1990s and now resides to the southwest of Harmony. Both are strict Old Order sects. A less austere community, also relocated from Iowa, resides not too far away to the north near St. Charles.

The Ordnung

Ironically, though the Amish were born of the Radical Reformation today they constitute the most conservative faction of American society. While some Amish sects are less strict the Old Order of Fillmore County have retained much of their 17th-century culture. They travel by horse and buggy, light their homes with kerosene lamps, and cook on wood-burning stoves. Children study English in school though their mother tongue remains the German dialect known as Pennsylvania Dutch (Deutsch), and Sunday worship is conducted in High German. Among the modern developments that they reject are indoor plumbing, musical instruments (emotions might be stirred), daylight savings time, zippers, rubber tires, and insurance.

Amish doctrines, while varying slightly from community to community (there is no central Amish organization), all stem from the core belief that the Bible is the literal word of God and are maintained in the *Ordnung* (Order), a strict, unwritten moral code. The twin tenets remain separation and obedience, the latter referred to *Gelassenheit* (literally "submission to authority," though often translated as humility), which promotes exclusive and tightly knit communities. The simplicity and self-denial that defines the Amish lifestyle wards off temptation and promotes self-sufficiency.

Church elders are willing to strike a balance between change and tradition and though they always aim towards the latter the Amish are not quite as stuck in the past as they appear. While they do not use electricity in their homes (if you see an Amish household with power lines it is because most deeds require the electrical system to remain in working order until the property is paid off), diesel engines are one technology that the Amish have widely embraced. Motors are used in woodworking shops, to pump water, and in many aspects of farming. Commercial dairying in particular requires adherence to strict storage and sanitation rules which simply can not be met without a touch of technology. Automobiles too are an accepted part of Amish life; owning and driving them, however, are not since this would result in inequality and make travel too easy. Just about every Amish family in Fillmore County has a close relationship with someone who owns a car that they can pay for rides. They also ride Greyhound and Amtrak when visiting relatives back east.

Modern Conflicts

From the start the Amish have been at conflict with the society around them, or more accurately society has been in conflict with the Amish around them. Today's Amish are almost completely free to practice their beliefs as they desire though problems occur when their strict biblical interpretations run counter to the law. One of the most important examples is in education. Amish children attend private one-room schools through the 8th grade—the Old Order prohibits formal education beyond this—a belief that by the 1950s had created quite an uproar in many places. The issue was, for the most part, settled in 1972 by a unanimous Supreme Court decision (Wisconsin v. Yoder) exempting the Amish and similar groups from compulsory school attendance laws.

A more recent and enduring example is the use of slow-moving vehicle signs. In the interest of public safety many Amish affix the familiar orange triangles to the rear of their buggies, but others, mostly elders, refuse because to do so means putting their faith in "worldly symbols" rather than God. An outline of silver reflective tape was a solution accepted reluctantly by most states, but not Minnesota. Back in the 1980s the Highway Patrol argued that this method was insufficient because it only let drivers know that something is ahead but does not communicate that it is moving at a slow speed. A 1986 compromise permitting black triangles with a white outline pleased neither side completely and lasted just a year. The state and other proponents of mandatory signage, including most Harmony area residents, argued that safety concerns outweighed a religious view that was not even held by all church members. Additionally they pointed out that the Amish opposition to the orange safety signs was inconsistent with their use of orange hunting attire. As many Fillmore County Amish ended up in jail over repeat violations the Minnesota Supreme Court, citing Wisconsin v. Yoder amongst other things, overturned the convictions. Today very few use the orange triangles and thus deadly car-buggy accidents continue to occur.

Meet the Amish

Signs like "Quilts" or "Eggs and Honey" fronting Amish farms don't just advertise what the farm produces, they invite you to stop and buy. In some cases you will meet the family though many rely on the honor system. On Saturdays during the summer and fall many drive their buggies into Harmony and Lanesboro or park along U.S. 52 to sell their wares: bread, produce, jellies and jams, honey, candy, baskets, furniture, and one-of-a-kind Amish quilts are all common.

Though you are welcome to ask, they tend not to like discussing their culture or religion with the English, as all outsiders are called; the fact is they don't let you on to their property to be sociable, they just want your money. To learn about their lives and customs or just get an explanation of what you are seeing join a tour or hire a ride-along guide in Harmony or Lanesboro. A typical tour lasts about 2.5 hours and visits a woodworking shop and around five farms with different items for sale. While the van tours are becoming the method of choice the ride-along guides have the advantage of letting you set the route; decide what sort of things you wish to see or buy and they will lead you to a farm that has it. Reservations are recommended for all companies.

Whether touring with a guide or on your own do not take photos of people, a practice they believe is forbidden by the Second Commandment. Also, never stop at an Amish house on a Sunday or a religious holiday.

three- or five-course dinners. Most ingredients are picked from their organic gardens. They also offer cooking classes and have bikes available. The pair of guestrooms with bubbler massage tubs and private entrances cost $130.

The purely functional **Harmony Municipal Campground,** on the north side of town on 4th Street, has six sites with electric hookups for $8, or you can just throw your tent up anywhere else for half that. **Austin's Mohair** (see above) has four campsites ($10) along a road traveled frequently by their Amish neighbors, and children from neighboring farms will come by to sell you firewood. There is room for RVs, but the primitive sites have just a picnic table, fire ring, and a porta-potty.

Food
The no-frills **Harmony House,** 57 Main Ave. N., 507/886-4612, serves up burgers and sandwiches for about $3 and fried chicken, steak, and beer-battered fish dinner platters for $9. Open daily for breakfast, lunch, and dinner.

While the Harmony House tends to be the locals' top choice, tourists take up most of the tables at the **Intrepid Traveler,** 121 Main Ave. N., 507/886-2891, a classy but casual café with a daily menu of pasta and meat, with such choices such as penne with vegetables, herb roasted game hen, and blackened catfish all for about $15. Vegetarians are sometimes out of luck.

Shopping
Many shops downtown sell Amish goods and/or antiques, and an informal **Amish farmers and craft market** sets up by the grain elevator on Saturday mornings during the summer and fall. For something completely different stop by **Nordsving Welding,** 507/886-6201, on 2nd Street NW behind the visitors center, and pick up a "lawn bird." The **Clover Art Gallery,** 35 Center St. E., 507/886-3313, sells the work of regional artists; the quality is very high, though so are the prices. In the same building is **Skandinavien Blomma,** 25 Center St. E., 507/886-2201, with Scandinavian imports from candy to clothing.

Information
Get all the local information you need at the **Harmony Visitor Center,** 15 2nd St. NW, 507/886-2469 or 800/247-6466, www.harmony.mn.us. They are open daily 9 A.M.–5 P.M. from June through September, and daily 10 A.M.–4 P.M. during May and October. The **Historic Bluff Country Regional Convention and Visitors Bureau,** 507/886-2230 or 800/428-2030, hbc@means.net, covering the entire region, has their offices in the same building. They are open Monday–Friday 9 A.M.–5 P.M. year-round and keep a list of accommodations vacancies.

I-35 Corridor

The west side of southeast Minnesota lies just beyond the hills and valleys that define this corner of the state. This is the start of the flat farm country of the Great Plains, and agriculture is the principal industry. Excepting Northfield, a vibrant college town, these Interstate-hugging cities, all county seats with populations roughly around 20,000, are exceptionally ordinary, but herein lies their charm. Blocks of unblemished 19th-century storefronts line the streets as a testament to their former prosperity; architecture and history fans can get walking tour brochures for each town at the local history museums or chambers of commerce. Yet, unlike some other cities chock-full of classic architecture—Stillwater for instance—with businesses aimed primarily at the throngs of tourists, Faribault, Owatonna, Albert Lea, and Austin remain genuine Main Street shopping districts with family-owned shoe stores, pharmacies, lunch counters, and the like still thriving. So stop, have a look around, and take the pulse of Middle America.

NORTHFIELD

This charming city straddling the Cannon River exudes a European charm. John North, a progressive-thinking lawyer from New York, founded

The City of Cows, Colleges and Contentment in 1855. He constructed the Ames Mill (today the home of Malt-O-Meal) the next year and the flour it produced, using a new and improved milling process, won an award at the 1876 Centennial Exposition World's Fair in Philadelphia. While milling declined toward the end of the 19th century, many locals turned to dairy cows—area farmers were amongst the first in the nation to raise Holsteins for their livelihood—and by the early 1900s Northfield was one of America's leading dairy centers. Agriculture remains the area's top industry, though Northfield's fortunes rest squarely on its two high-ranking colleges. Tops is Carleton College, known as the "Harvard of the Midwest" for attracting more National Merit Scholars than any other liberal arts college in the county. St. Olaf College, well known for its music program, holds tightly to its Norwegian roots and is the home of the national archives of the Norwegian-American Historical Society. Together the pair, founded in 1866 and 1874 respectively, have nearly 5,000 students, and while it's impossible to know what would have come of Northfield had the schools not thrived, it certainly wouldn't be the vibrant place it is today.

Ironically, this beautiful and cultured town is most famous for a violent bank robbery. On September 7, 1876, the James-Younger gang, led by the infamous Jesse and Frank James, rode into town and raided the First National Bank, but the robbery was foiled by the courageous townsfolk. Joseph Heywood, the acting cashier, refused to assist, even though the safe was unlocked (none of the outlaws tried to open it on their own and they only got away with $26.60, all in coins), a brave act of resistance for which he was fatally shot. Alerted men took up the fight on the streets, killing two of the eight outlaws. The remaining six, including the James brothers, were pursued across the state by a posse that grew as large as 1,000 and eventually each was captured or killed. Hollywood has rehashed the affair many times, but never once bothered to do so accurately. Though the robbers later told conflicting stories about the heist, Cole Younger asserted that they ventured all the way up to Minnesota

from Missouri because the bank held funds of two carpetbaggers they despised (Adelbert Ames, who ran the mill, had been a Northern general and was later appointed governor of Mississippi by President Grant, and General Benjamin Butler of Massachusetts); thus some observers consider it the last battle of the Civil War.

Sights
The First National Bank is now part of the **Northfield Historical Society Museum,** 408 Division St., 507/645-9268. Though the counter is a replica, the safe, clock (permanently set to 1:50), and other items are original, and it looks exactly as it did on that fateful day. One room has displays about the robbery, including some of the outlaws' guns and a saddle, plus a small back room hosts rotating exhibits on other aspects of city history. If you can't be here for the annual reenactment of the shoot-out you can watch it on video. The museum is open Tuesday–Saturday (plus Mon. during the summer) 10 A.M.–4 P.M. and Sunday 1–4 P.M. Admission is $3. The Museum Store has a fine selection of local and Minnesota-related books and gifts, including seemingly every Jesse James book in print. The *Outlaw Trail* brochure available at the museum and chamber details sites in Northfield and beyond where they ate, slept, rendezvoused, and hid out. The *Northfield Historic Points of Interest* brochure leads you on an architectural tour of the town; one of the stops is the modest home of Norwegian born author O. E. Rölvaag. Just down the street from the museum the small **Northfield Arts Guild Gallery,** 304 Division St., 507/645-8877, displays and sells the work of artists from across southeast Minnesota. Open Mon.–Sat. 10 A.M.–5 P.M., except closing at 8 P.M. on Thurs. For most visitors, a wander through downtown and a stroll along the river followed by a rest in lovely **Bridge Square** is the highlight of a visit to Northfield. The downtown park hosts special events, like concerts and pie baking contests, every Thursday night during the summer, plus special events at other times.

The scenic St. Olaf and Carleton campuses possess several minor attractions. The **Carleton College Art Gallery,** 507/646-4469, is in the

BLUFF COUNTRY

lower level of the school's Concert Hall, though plans are under way for a new and much larger gallery. It hosts exhibitions of the college's permanent collection, plus traveling exhibits, and is open Monday–Wednesday noon–6 P.M., Thursday and Friday noon–10 P.M., and weekends noon–4 P.M. during the school year. Student work is always on display in the art department's **Boliou Hall.** The **Goodsell Observatory,** 507/646-4000, is a beautiful 1887 Richardsonian Romanesque building. If the skies are clear on the first Friday of the month, you can gaze at the planets through its original 16.2-inch refractor during the first two hours after dark. All three are centered on the Bald Spot (where you'll probably have to dodge flying disks—this school is mad about ultimate Frisbee) in the center of campus. Nearby, behind the Cowling Recreation Center, is a petite **Japanese Garden.** St. Olaf's main art gallery, the **Flaten Art Museum,** 507/646-3248, features work by regional, national, and international artists, while student work is exhibited across the hall in the **Virginia and Jennifer C. Groot Gallery.** They are located in the Dittmann Center right in the center of campus.

Recreation

Four hundred acres of forest and field along the east bank of the Cannon River north of town comprise the lower half of Carleton College's **Cowling Arboretum.** There is no sign marking the entrance, but a parking lot at the main trailhead sits along Hwy. 19, just before the bridge. If you'd rather paddle down the Cannon, a state designated Wild and Scenic River, it's 11 easy miles through a mix of forest and farm to Lake Byllesby Regional Park, just before the city of Cannon Falls. The best scenery is found along the final 25 miles of the river between Cannon Falls and the Mississippi River (see Red Wing). Above Northfield it's a generally peaceful 16-mile, six–eight-hour paddle down the mostly wooded valley from Faribault, and there are several campsites along the way.

Entertainment

The very active **Northfield Arts Guild,** 507/645-8877, produces six musical, comedic, and dramatic plays a year, including some for children. Their offices are at 304 Division Street, though the NAG Theater is across the river at 411 West 3rd Street. Tickets are either $11 or $12, depending on the performance. There is usually something interesting going on at **Carleton College,** 507/646-4000, and the public is usually welcome. To see what's on at **St. Olaf** call 507/646-3002.

Two wonderful basement pubs face each other across the river. While both the **Contented Cow,** 302 Division St., 507/663-1351; and **Froggy Bottoms,** 305 Water St. S., 507/664-0260, each has its own personal faunal theme, they have much in common including riverside patios, live music on weekends, and smoke-free air. The evening-only Cow has a British theme so there is beer and a wee bit of food from the Isles, plus a stack of board games waiting to be played. The Frog's small patio is tucked right up against the river and can be enjoyed during lunch most days.

Events

The **Defeat of Jesse James Days,** one of the biggest festivals in Minnesota, spans five days, but the highlight takes just seven minutes. The infamous raid and shoot-out between the brave citizens of Northfield and the James-Younger gang is reenacted in front on the First National Bank six times on Saturday and Sunday. The festival begins on Wednesday with a graveside service for Joseph Lee Heywood and Nicolaus Gustavson, the two innocent men killed during the robbery attempt, and is followed by an antique tractor pull, rodeo, arts and crafts show, parade, and old-time patent medicine show, among other things. It all takes place the weekend after Labor Day. The city of Madelia, 65 miles to the east, reenacts the capture of the Younger Brothers the following weekend.

The **St. Olaf Christmas Festival,** begun in 1912, draws thousands to Northfield in early December and reaches a much larger audience with a national broadcast on PBS. Hymns, carols, and other choral works are performed by the acclaimed St. Olaf Choir and other vocal groups with accompaniment from the St. Olaf Orchestra: over 500 student musicians in total. Another musical event is the **Bridge Chamber Music Festival** the first weekend in June.

Accommodations

The undisputed top lodging option is the **Archer House,** 212 Division St., 507/645-5661 or 800/247-2235, a grand French Second Empire inn right downtown. Erected in 1877, the hotel has been completely modernized without sacrificing its historic character. The 36 individually decorated rooms have various little extras like claw-foot tubs and four-poster beds, and just over half have whirlpool tubs. Ranging $75–140 they are a good value. If the Archer House is full, consider the completely modern **Country Inn,** 300 Hwy. 3 S., 507/645-2286, 800/456-4000, across the river from downtown with rooms from $72. At $49 the **College City Motel,** 875 Hwy. 3 N., 507/645-4426 or 800/775-0455, has the cheapest beds in town. The rooms (each with a refrigerator and microwave) are simple, but nicer than the dreary exterior would lead you to believe.

The friendly **Magic Door Bed and Breakfast,** 818 Division St. S., 507/664-9096, info@ magicdoorbb.com, is a large 1899 home tastefully decorated with antiques. The three guestrooms, each with a private bath and whirlpool tub, start at $135, while the largest suite is $185.

Food

Refreshingly, most of the city's restaurants are smoke-free. Northfield's most beloved restaurant is the **Ole Store and Café,** 1011 St. Olaf Ave., 507/645-5558, just below St. Olaf college. The menu includes diverse home-cooked choices, such as pan fried walleye, cashew chicken stir fry, and a grilled veggie sandwich, all for about $7, though what most people talk about are the Ole Rolls—sinfully rich and delicious cinnamon caramel buns. Open Tues.–Sat. for breakfast, lunch, and dinner, and Sun. for breakfast and lunch. The cozy **Tavern of Northfield,** 212 Division St., 507/663-0342, below the Archer House Inn, has something for everyone. The menu spans lamb pitas, steak sandwiches, jambalaya, roast duck, fettuccine marinara, and bean burritos, while the prices range $3–18. Open

daily for breakfast, lunch, and dinner. You can get soup, a hoagie, and a beer for under $5 at **Hogan Brothers' Acoustic Café,** 415 Division St. S., 507/645-6653—they've got ice cream and bakery, too. This casual and inviting space hosts live music on weekends during the school year.

Few towns this small have the variety of ethnic options that Northfield does, including the Afghani delights of **Byzantine,** 201 Water St. S., 507/645-2400. The menu actually reaches across the Near East to Greece, and even includes fish and chips, fried chicken, and steak for the less adventurous in your party. Dishes average $9 and they are open Monday–Saturday for lunch and dinner. **Chapati,** 214 Division St. S., 507/645-2462, serves some wonderful tandooris, biryanis, and curries for around $11. Mild is the standard, but if you request it hot they will deliver. The menu is large, though if they are busy you are limited to the $7 buffet during weekday lunches. Open daily for lunch and dinner. **Las Delicias,** 317 Division St. S., 507/664-0200, is a superb counter-service café with a small menu of wonderful Guatemalan and Mexican dishes for about $5. Open Mon.–Sat. for lunch and dinner. Also highly recommended for south of the border flavor is **El Tequila,** 1010 Hwy. 3 S., 507/664-9139. It has a much larger selection and prices running $3–11. Open daily for lunch and dinner.

With everything delicious and cheap, the **Quality Bakery,** 410 Division St., 507/645-8392, lives up to its name. Open Tues.–Sat. for breakfast and lunch. The **Goodbye Blue Monday,** 319 Division St. S., 507/663-6188, coffeehouse is a popular student hangout with good coffees, homemade bakery, and free Internet access. Open daily early until late.

Information and Services

The **Northfield Chamber of Commerce,** 205 3rd St. W., 507/645-5604 or 800/658-2548, www.northfieldchamber.com, next to the Country Inn along Hwy. 3 is open Monday–Friday 8 A.M.–5 P.M.

As Time Goes By, 425 Division St. S., 507/ 645-6700, is an excellent used book shop, while **River City Books,** 306 Division St., 507/ 507/646-7754, carries new titles.

BLUFF COUNTRY

Transportation

If you aren't driving, the easiest way to get here from the Twin Cities is with **Care Tenders,** 507/664-3859, who will pick you up at the airport and deliver you right to your destination in town. A round-trip is $40 per person and 48 hours advance notice is required. **Jefferson Lines** buses stop at the Big Steer Travel Center, 507/645-6082, located west of town at the junction of I-35 and Highway 19. With 24-hour advanced notice **Northfield Transit,** 507/645-7250, will pick you up or drop you off at Big Steer for $4. They also run a very limited in-town bus service.

NERSTRAND BIG WOODS STATE PARK

Midway between Northfield and Faribault is a nearly 3,000-acre remnant of the Big Woods, once a vast island of forest in the surrounding prairie and oak savanna, that stretched from Mankato almost to St. Cloud. The primary destination is the mile-long **Hidden Falls Trail.** The wide waterfall at its back end is very impressive in high water, almost looking man-made, though the path is worthwhile even when the flow of Prairie Creek is reduced to just a trickle. Relatively few visitors wander the peaceful rolling hills and valleys crossed by the rest of the 14-mile web of trails. The best time to visit is in the spring when some 50 species of wildflower bloom in the park. Look for sharp-lobed hepatica, wood anemone, nodding trillium, March marigold, bloodroot, Dutchman's breeches, and the endemic Minnesota trout lily, the only federally-endangered plant in Minnesota. You'll pass one of the greatest blossom concentrations on the way down the steep hill to the falls. Most of these bloom in April, though the vivid show continues well into May. The seven miles of trail in the north half of the park are groomed for cross-country skiing, and snowshoes for rent from the park office let you explore the rest of the park. The campground has 51 sites. For the most part the 24 without electricity are fully shaded, while the others are generally open. Call 507/334-8848 with any park questions.

FARIBAULT

While you may have never heard of Faribault (FAIR-ih-bo) you likely are familiar with its products: Tilt-A-Whirl carnival rides, Faribault Woolens, and Butter Kernel canned vegetables. You might also have seen the city before since its historic downtown stood in as Wabasha in the *Grumpy Old Men* movies. Fur trader Alexander Faribault established his first post in the area in 1826 before moving to the present town site, where the Straight River joins the Cannon, a decade later. He established the town in 1852 immediately following ratification of the Traverse des Sioux Treaty, and within a few years it was a prosperous city. Today this quiet town has more buildings on the National Register of Historic Places than any other community of its size in Minnesota. The many schools established during the 1860s, including the Minnesota State Academy for the Blind and the Minnesota State Academy for the Deaf, both still in operation, led to the moniker "Athens of the West." (The Faribault Regional Center—variously known as the School for Idiots and Imbeciles, the Minnesota Institute for Defectives, and the School for Feeble-Minded and Colony for Epileptics—closed in 1998.)

Today the quiet town of Faribault has more buildings on the National Register of Historic Places than any other community of its size in Minnesota.

A good time to visit town is the second weekend in September for the **Faribault Area Airfest & Balloon Rally,** which features a variety of airships; the **Tree Frog Music Festival** runs concurrently.

Sights

The oldest building in the city, the **Alexander Faribault House,** 12 1st Ave. NE, 507/334-7913, was built in 1853 by the city founding father. It was one of the first (possibly *the* first) wood-frame homes constructed in southern Minnesota and is one of the state's oldest surviving buildings. It has been restored and filled with period furnishings. It is usually open Monday–Friday 1–4 P.M. during the summer, and admission is $1. More history is on display at the small **Rice County Historical Society Museum,** 1814 2nd Ave. NW, 507/332-2121, where much of the space is taken up by a well-executed mock Main Street display. The Native American artifacts are also interesting. The museum is open Monday–Friday 9 A.M.–4 P.M., plus 1–4 P.M. during summer weekends. Admission is $3. The log cabin, church, one-room schoolhouse, and shed filled with farm machinery out back are only open by appointment.

The **Faribault Woolen Mill,** one of just three sheep to sweater mills left in the nation, diverts the largest number of visitors off the freeway and into town (just follow the signs). The fifth generation family enterprise has been weaving top quality wool fabrics, most famously Faribo blankets, since 1865, and free tours of the entire operations are available weekdays at 10 A.M. and 2 P.M. Their large outlet store at 1819 2nd Ave. NW, 507/334-1644 or 800/448-9665, is open Monday–Saturday 9 A.M.–5:30 P.M. and Sunday noon–5 P.M., and the mill tours begin here.

Stop by to shop, sign up for a class, or just watch some carving at the **Ivan Whillock Woodcarving Studio,** 122 1st Ave. NE, 507/334-8306. Other locals artists vend their wares at the small **Faribault Art Center,** 210 Central Ave. N., 507/332-7372.

Recreation

Faribault is the eastern terminus of the **Sakatah Singing Hills State Trail,** a 39-mile paved path leading to Mankato along an old railroad bed. The trailhead is along Hwy. 21, just north of the **Faribault Area Chamber of Commerce,** 507/334-4381 or 800/658-2354, www.faribaultmn.org. You could also depart town along the **Cannon River,** a state designated Wild and Scenic River. It's a generally peaceful 16-mile, six–eight hour paddle down the mostly wooded valley to Northfield, and there are several campsites along the way. For a quiet hike follow the 10 miles of trails at the **River Bend Nature Center,** 507/332-7151, particularly those along the Straight River. The 750 acres of forest and prairie

is a good bird-watching area, and the Interpretive Center is filled with animal mounts. It is located on the southeast edge of town: take Hwy. 60 and follow the signs.

Practicalities

If you are going to stay in town it should be at the family-run **Lyndale Motel,** 904 Lyndale Ave N., 507/334-4386 or 800/559-4386, which sits right on the Cannon River—you can watch herons wade in the river right from your window. Rates start at $38. The Lyndale is the stop for **Jefferson Lines** buses. Farther north at the junction of Lyndale Ave. (Hwy. 21) and I-35 is the newly constructed **Days Inn,** 507/334-6835 or 800/329-7466, a good value at $50. It has a pool and whirlpool.

Don't let the name fool you, you can get a rock solid meal at **Wimpy's,** 520 Central Ave. N., a truly classic lunch counter and a local favorite since 1936. Nothing on the menu, including a seven-ounce sirloin steak, is over $8. Open daily for breakfast, lunch, and dinner. Locals also love **The Depot Bar & Grill,** 311 Heritage Place, 507/332-2825, in a renovated train depot downtown by the river. The menu, ranging $5–20, covers sandwiches, salads, steak, seafood, and Southwestern. Open daily for lunch and dinner. South of town near the junction of Hwy. 21 and I-35 is the wonderful **El Tequila,** 951 Faribault Rd., 507/332-7490, with real-deal Mexican platters for around $7. They are open daily for lunch and dinner. The old-fashioned **Dusek's Bakery,** 223 Central Ave. N., open Tues.–Sat. for breakfast and lunch, is a great spot for a snack, and the prices are unbelievably low.

OWATONNA

Legend has it that Chief Wadena once relocated his entire village south to this spot so that his daughter Owatonna, deathly ill following the famine of the harshest winter they had ever seen, could drink the healing waters of the area's mineral springs. Though there is likely no truth to the tale, generations of Native Americans did travel here to quaff the curing waters of the springs feeding the "Ouitunya"

National Farmer's Bank

River. Mapmakers ironically translated this crooked river's name to Straight, though a better translation would be "morally strong" or "honest." The city's founding fathers, the earliest of whom built their cabins here in 1854, kept the original for the town. Like most cities around here it prospered early, first with milling and soon after with the railroad.

Sights

Though the claim seems dubious, according to the Minnesota Office of Tourism **Cabela's,** 507/451-4545, the hunting and fishing superstore along the freeway north of town, is the second most visited tourist attraction in the state. Regardless of exactly where it ranks, this 150,000 sq.-foot center is a big deal. It has become a mandatory tour bus stop, and they even offer a shuttle service to local hotels and Owatonna's small airport for people who fly in just to shop—though it's not all about shopping. Literally hundreds of animal mounts—at least 100 white-tailed deer alone—are on display throughout the store. A 35-foot-tall mountain features North American species like polar bear, elk, beaver, and wild turkey,

while creatures from the African plains like elephant, rhino, hartebeest, and baboon are spread out along the north wall. Minnesota fish swim in the 60,000 gallons of freshwater aquarium. It's not exactly the American Museum of Natural History, but it's a very impressive collection. The store is open Monday–Saturday 8 A.M.–9 P.M. and Sunday 10 A.M.–6 P.M.

Even if you are in a hurry to get elsewhere, exit the freeway and take a moment to admire the Louis Sullivan-designed **National Farmer's Bank,** 101 N. Cedar Ave., a Prairie School masterpiece inside and out. Now Wells Fargo, the world-renowned 1908 bank is a National Historic Landmark and was even featured on a postage stamp. You can admire the stained glass arches (even beautiful from the outside), murals, and 2.25-ton chandeliers weekdays 8 A.M.–5:30 P.M. and Saturday 8 A.M.–noon. It sits across from Central Park, one of the few town squares in the state. Another fine Prairie School design, the **Federated Insurance Companies** building, 148 E. Broadway, is just a block east.

The Steele County Historical Society's **Village of Yesteryear,** 1448 Austin Rd. (on the south side of town at the fairgrounds), 507/451-1420, has fifteen 19th-century structures like log cabins, a blacksmith shop, general store, one-room schoolhouse, and a print shop. Each is appropriately equipped, and the furnishings of the 1876 St. Wenceslaus of Moravia Church are largely original. The "Please Touch" stickers on many items are a nice feature. You can see the buildings from the outside anytime, but indoor visits are only possible with guided tours at 1:30 P.M. and 3:30 P.M. daily except Monday. The season runs from May though September. Admission is $5.

The Minnesota State Public School for Dependent and Neglected Children opened in 1886 and served nearly 13,000 children during its 60 years of operation. During its peak in the 1920s it housed 500 children, making it the largest in the nation. Owatonna was chosen, in part, because it was believed that area farmers in need of workers would adopt kids. The **State School Orphanage Museum,** 540 W. Hills Circle, 507/451-2149, is really just a small collection of photos, plus a few artifacts in a City Hall hallway, but the accompanying stories are both frightening and heartwarming. It's hard to believe that in its day this was a very progressive institution. It is open weekdays 8 A.M.–5 P.M. and weekends 1–5 P.M. Admission is free. The **Owatonna Arts Center,** 507/451-0533, in the same building has monthly exhibits by area artists. It is open Tuesday–Sunday 1–5 P.M. and admission is usually free.

Practicalities

The **Holiday Inn,** 2365 43rd St. NW, 507/446-8900 or 800/465-4328, next to Cabela's features an indoor water park with waterslides, lazy river, waterfall whirlpool, and more. There is also a game room and fitness center. You might get a room for under $100. The aging but clean **Oakdale Motel,** 1418 S. Oak Ave., 507/451-5480, on the south side of town charges as little as $40 for a room with a microwave and refrigerator. **Jefferson Lines** buses stop here. Quality wise the **Super 8,** 1818 U.S. 14 W. (at I-35), 507/451-0380 or 800/800-8000, lies between them and charges $51.

The most unusual menu in the region is at the **Northwoods Cache** on the second floor of Cabela's. Wild game ingredients include ostrich, elk, and caribou sandwiches and bison and venison bratwurst, each for about $6. Open Mon.–Sat. for breakfast, lunch, and dinner, plus Sun. for lunch. The fanciest restaurant in town is **Jerry's Supper Club,** 203 N. Cedar Ave., 507/451-6894, with mostly steak and seafood on the menu. Lunch averages $8, while the dinner menu starts here and goes up—way up. Open daily for lunch and dinner. Simpler is **Costas' Candies & Restaurant,** 112 N. Cedar Ave., 507/451-9050. It has an all-American menu with a few Greek favorites and you can fill up for $6. The homemade sweets in the candy counter are awfully tough to resist. Open weekdays for breakfast, lunch, and dinner and Sat. for breakfast and lunch. The festive **El Tequila,** 1830 S. Cedar Ave., 507/444-9490, is rightly popular for south-of-the-border flavors. Entrées average $7, and they are open daily, except Monday, for lunch and dinner.

The **Owatonna Area Chamber of Commerce and Tourism,** 320 Hoffman Dr., 507/451-7970 or 800/423-6466, www.owatonna.org, on the west side of downtown has office hours weekdays 8 A.M.–5 P.M., though you can pick up brochures and maps in the lobby anytime.

ALBERT LEA

The Freeborn County Seat is centered on a low hill between Fountain and Albert Lea Lakes. Lieutenant Albert Lea, who led a surveying expedition across the region in 1835, initially named the larger of the two Fox Lake after spying a white fox run by it. Several years later, the famous French explorer Joseph Nicollet came through the area and renamed it in Lea's honor. Even though Interstates 35 and 90 intersect here, making it "The Crossroads of the Upper Midwest," the town sees few tourists. The city's museums, however, are worth a stop.

Sights

The **Freeborn County Historical Museum,** 1031 Bridge Ave., 507/373-8003, north of downtown at the fairgrounds, is the area's best local history collection. The main hall houses the usual artifacts, plus gold records and quite a bit of memorabilia from native son Eddie Cochran. The old toys are interesting, too. During the summer you can visit the one-room schoolhouse, cobbler shop, 1853 log cabin, and other historic structures out back. The main museum building is open Tuesday–Friday, 10 A.M.–5 P.M. year-round, plus Saturday 1–5 P.M. during the summer. Admission is $5. Ask at the museum if you would like to see the **Itasca Rock Garden,** a unique outdoor folk sculpture; it is on private property, but visits are allowed.

Just about everyone will find something of interest at the **Story Lady Doll & Toy Museum,** 131 N. Broadway Ave., 507/377-1820, whether it be the Raggedy Ann, Princess Diana, Cat in the Hat, or 19th-century china dolls, or handmade Navajo dolls. There are over 1,500 dolls (and despite the name hardly any toys) in total. Open Tues.–Sat. noon–4 P.M. Admission is $2.

It's easy to dismiss small town art centers, but you'll probably be surprised by the creative offerings at the **Albert Lea Art Center,** 224 S. Broadway Ave., 507/373-5665. New displays by serious Midwest artists are hung monthly, and work by local artists is on consignment at the center's shop. It is open Tuesday–Friday noon–4 P.M. and Saturday 10 A.M.–2 P.M. Admission is usually free, sometimes a buck.

The **Blazing Star Bike Trail,** when completed, will connect Albert Lea with Myre-Big Island State Park, a six-mile trip. Currently two miles of the paved trail lead along the north end of Albert Lea Lake from Frank Hall Park. During the summer you can float around Albert Lea Lake on the **Pelican Breeze Cruise Boat,** 507/383-2630, a double-decker pontoon that also departs from the park. A 90-minute narrated tour ($8) departs every Saturday and Sunday at 2 P.M., and there is a Friday evening pizza cruise ($12) at six. Fountain Lake's Bancroft Bay Park on the far north end of town hosts the annual **Big Island Rendezvous,** Minnesota's largest fur trade era reenactment. Over 1,000 costumed traders camp out and demonstrate the crafts, games, and music of the early 1800s. Admission is $8 per day.

Myre-Big Island State Park

Across Albert Lea Lake from the city is Big Island, as all locals call it. Oak savanna and prairie, including expansive prairie wetlands, dominate most of the park, though the 116-acre island itself, protected from the fires that perpetuated the prairies, is covered by a dense northern hardwood forest. The 1,600-acre park protects eight of the lake's 20 miles of shoreline, and hundreds of migrating waterfowl converge on the wetlands. Some 16 miles of hiking trail loop through the whole of the park. The best destination for birders is the 1.5-mile **Great Marsh Trail,** which follows the rolling hills around a large pond; there is a viewing blind along the south end. The freeway hum is pretty loud, but the birds don't mind. The **Bur Oak Esker Trail** crosses four miles of similar terrain, plus the lakeshore and minus the wetlands. The glacial moraine of the last Ice Age not only formed the lake, but also an esker, and the north end of this trail follows it. Four lakeside backpack sites, reached by foot, mountain bike, or canoe, are stretched out along this trail. The easiest path, the mile-long **Big Island Trail,** is also the most popular. Five miles of trail, including those on the Big Island, are groomed for cross-country skiing. With 34 thickly wooded sites (half of them electric) and a camper cabin, Big Island is the better of the park's two campgrounds. All 63 sites (15 electric) in the White Fox Campground are out in the open. The lake is too shallow for a beach, but there is a picnic area and boat launch and rental canoes are available. Call 507/379-3403 for more information.

Practicalities

Not far off I-35, the **Country Inn & Suites,** 2214 E. Main St., 507/373-5513 or 800/456-4000, also has a pool and fitness center, plus a whirlpool, and rooms with the chain's usual cozy touches from $79. Just down the street the simpler **Super 8,** 2019 E. Main St., 507/377-0591 or 800/800-8000, charges just $51. If B&Bs are your thing, you have a pair to choose from. The fanciest is the **Victorian Rose Inn,** 507/373-7602 or 800/252-6558, inn@victorianrose.net, a storybook 1898 mansion with four guestrooms ($85–95), each with a private bath. The nearby

Fountain View Inn, 310 N. Washington Ave., 507/373-2899, an antique-filled home (the owner Bonita *loves* to tell stories about her turn-of-the-20th-century house) sitting right on Fountain Lake. Three of the four rooms (priced from $95–150) overlook the lake, and you have the option of a pontoon breakfast.

One of the biggest surprises in all of Minnesota is **Crescendo,** 118 S. Broadway Ave., 507/377-2425, a trendy gourmet bistro with a Mediterranean menu and a decor right out of Greenwich Village. The menu changes with the seasons, but pan-seared halibut with capers and chive salsa and spaghetti with basil pesto—all ranging between $9–22—are typical. Locally grown ingredients feature prominently, and they fly the seafood in fresh from the coasts. Open Thurs.–Sat. for dinner. At the other end of the spectrum is the cheap home-cookin' of the humble **Abrego's Café,** 120 S. Washington Ave., 507/373-5469. Paintings of hunters in snowshoes hang next to sombreros and maracas on the wall, and a roast beef dinner sits next to chicken enchiladas on the menu. It's so popular that some people who work downtown have lunch here just about every day. Open Mon.–Sat. for breakfast and lunch and Fri. for dinner.

The ultra-friendly staff of the **Albert Lea Convention & Visitors Bureau,** 143 W. Clark St., 507/373-3938 or 800/345-8414, www.albertlea.org, will be happy to help you with any questions you may have. Office hours are weekdays 8 A.M.–5 P.M. **Jefferson Lines** buses stop at the Texaco gas station, 2302 E. Main St., 507/373-6814.

AUSTIN

The area's first European settler, a trapper named Austin Nichols, built his cabin along the Cedar River in what would become the city of Austin in 1853. The city became an important regional rail center in 1867, though it could be said that the modern town was born in 1887 when George Hormel opened his butcher shop. This trivial operation grew into the Hormel Foods Corporation, maker of SPAM and much more. Hormel, now a Fortune 500 company (the only one in

Minnesota outside the Twin Cities metro), is still headquartered here and also keeps its research and development arm in town. Spend even a moment here and it will become evident just how proud the 23,000 residents of the Mower County seat are to live in the land of SPAM: the Hormel name pops up all over town, the high school athletes are Packers, **SPAMtown USA** banners line the main thoroughfares, and you'll even find the mystery meat on many restaurant menus.

Sights

Learn everything you always wanted to know about Spam (but were afraid to ask) at Hormel Foods' humorous **SPAM Museum,** 1937 Spam Blvd. (just north of downtown along Main St.), 507/437-5100 or 800/LUV-SPAM. Believe it or not, this celebration of America's luncheon meat is one of the best executed museums in the state. Following the 15-minute film *SPAM, A Love Story,* the endless conveyor belt of navy and yellow cans will lead you past interactive multimedia displays on George Hormel's first butcher shop, SPAM at war, historic ads, including those by George Burns and Gracie Allen, and much more. One of Monty Python's greatest achievements airs continuously, and you can also show off your SPAM knowledge by playing the SPAM Exam game show with host Al Franken. At the end you can purchase a SPAM-emblazoned doll, necktie, basketball, or wine glass in the gift shop. The extravaganza is open Monday–Saturday 10 A.M.–5 P.M. and Sunday noon–4 P.M. Admission is free.

The rest of the town's history—plus more about George Hormel—is told at the **Mower County Historical Center,** 1303 SW 6th Ave., 507/437-6082, a collection of about 20 historic buildings including a log cabin, blacksmith shop, and one-room schoolhouse plus an M-4 Sherman tank and steam locomotive. None of the buildings are left open, so if you want to visit them you'll need to be led around by a volunteer. If you have an interest in this sort of thing, the best bet is to see it in Albert Lea. Open Mon.–Fri. 10 A.M.–4 P.M. Admission is $5. The **SPAMtown Belle,** 507/433-1881, a toylike miniature paddlewheeler built in 1956, chugs around East Side Lake. The half-hour trips cost $2 and are available every

Friday, Saturday, and Sunday 5–8 P.M. during the summer. Although it is now a YMCA events center, not a museum, if you stop by the **Hormel Historic Home,** 208 4th Ave. NW, 507/433-1213, you can get a quick tour of the luxurious former residence of the meat plant's founder. Though built in 1871, it has been restored to the glory of the 1920s, when the family moved out. It is open weekdays 10 A.M.–5 P.M., except closing at 4 P.M. during the summer. Cycling fanatics will enjoy a look at the nearly 60 bicycles dating back to 1868 on display at the **Rydjor Bike Shop,** 219 Main St. N., 507/433-9093. Open daily except Sunday.

Hormel hosts **SPAM Jam,** the town's biggest bash, the second weekend of June. There is music (including the harmonies of the SPAMETTES female quartet), celebrity appearances, a classic car show, SPAM cooking contests, and much more. Another noteworthy event is **Stories From the Heartland,** the last weekend in February. Nationally known storytellers from across the United States come to spin yarns and lead workshops. There are opportunities for audience participation. Most events take place at the historic **Paramount Theatre,** 125 4th Ave. NE, a 1929 Spanish Colonial gem.

Practicalities

Most of the city's hotels line I-90 on the north side of town, including the **Holiday Inn,** 1701 4th St NW, 507/433-1000 or 800/985-8850, easily the city's best. There's a pool, whirlpool, sauna, fitness center, game room, and putting green under the dome, and the rooms start at $100. Next door the **Days Inn,** 700 16th Ave NW, 507/433-8600 or 800/329-7466, charges $60 for decent rooms. The rooms at the **Austin Downtown Motel,** 209 1st Ave. SE, 507/433-

At the SPAM Museum, following the 15-minute film SPAM, A Love Story, an endless conveyor belt of navy and yellow cans leads you past interactive multimedia displays on Hormel's first butcher shop, SPAM at war, historic ads, and much more.

2375, are small and *way* past their prime, but at just $30 the price is right.

Jerry's Other Place, 1207 N. Main St., 507/433-2331, a family restaurant fronting the SPAM Museum, seems to always be packed. A large meal of steak, seafood, sandwiches, pasta, and the like will run you $5–20. Open daily for breakfast, lunch, and dinner. For a table with a view there is **The Old Mill,** 54446 244th St., 507/437-2076. Known far and wide, as much for being in an 1873 flour mill—the dining room overlooks the waterfall cascading down Ramsey Dam—as the food, the Old Mill has been a restaurant since 1949. The supper club menu is mostly steak and seafood, and you can eat for under $10, but expect to pay a lot more. To get there take 6th Street north of town, veer right and then left at the intersections, and follow the road for about two miles until you see the sign. Open weekdays for lunch and Mon.–Sat. for dinner. At the other end of the spectrum is **White's Tendermaid,** 217 4th Ave. NE, 507/437-7907, a closet-sized lunch counter with low-priced malts and burgers. Get an espresso or panini sandwich at the **Brick House,** 412 3rd Ave NE, 507/434-2417, a small coffee shop on the east side of downtown. Open daily for breakfast and lunch. Eight dollars is the average price of the impressively large selection of entrées at **El Mariachi,** 227 Main St. N., 507/434-5975. Open daily for lunch and dinner.

The friendly and helpful **Austin Convention and Visitors Bureau,** 329 Main St. N., 507/437-4563 or 800/444-5713, www.austincvb.com, is across the street from the SPAM Museum. They are open weekdays 8 A.M.–5 P.M. **Jefferson Lines** buses pick up and drop off at the Mower County Transit Center, 202 4th Ave. NE, 507/433-5767.

Resources

Suggested Reading

Just about every bookstore, new and used, has an extensive Minnesota section, but none can compare to the exhaustive inventory at the Minnesota History Center, 345 Kellogg Blvd. W., 651/296-6126, in St. Paul.

Required Reading

Mohr, Howard. *How To Talk Minnesotan.* New York: Penguin, 1987. A thoroughly hilarious primer on not only how to talk like, but how to be, a Minnesotan. Although Mohr claims that his book is only "a good deal," it is absolutely a heckuva deal.

History

Carley, Kenneth. *The Dakota War of 1862.* St. Paul, MN: Minnesota Historical Society Press, 2001. A balanced and accessible account of Minnesota's other Civil War.

Folwell, William Watts: *A History of Minnesota.* St. Paul, MN: Minnesota Historical Society Press, 1969. This encyclopedic, four-volume set is unquestionably the best historical resource available, at least up to the 1920s when it terminates.

Lass, William E. *Minnesota: A History.* New York: W. W. Norton & Co., 2000. The most readable account of the state's past, and one of the few to continue up to the present day.

Meier, Peg. *Bring Warm Clothes.* Minneapolis, MN: Minneapolis Star & Tribune Co., 1981. Meier's compilation of letters, diary entries, photographs, and paintings offer a truly fascinating look at the past—from the early explorers through World War II—as told by ordinary Minnesotans.

People

Berg, A. Scott. *Lindbergh.* New York: Penguin Putnam, 1998. The definitive biography of the only Minnesotan more famous than Jesse "The Body" Ventura. This Pulitzer-prize winning work shows just how complex Lindbergh really was.

Cary, Bob. *Root Beer Lady: The Story of Dorothy Molter.* Duluth, MN: Pfeifer-Hamilton Publishers, 1993. One of the most remarkable legends of Minnesota's Northwoods, city girl Dorothy Molter left Chicago to live off the land on remote Isle of the Pines in what is now the Boundary Waters Canoe Area Wilderness.

Holmquist, June D. (editor). *They Chose Minnesota: A Survey of the State's Ethnic Groups.* St. Paul, MN: Minnesota Historical Society Press, 1988. An in-depth but not too scholarly look at the people who made Minnesota. It tells where the people came from and where they went, but most importantly it explains why and shares plenty of interesting anecdotes along the way. Many updated and expanded individual chapters of *They Chose Minnesota* are also available as part of *The People of Minnesota* series of books.

Ventura, Jesse. *I Ain't Got Time to Bleed.* New York: Penguin, 2000. The whole story, from getting drunk down by the river in high school to the Navy SEALs to a biker gang to the wrestling ring to Hollywood to the Capitol—right from the mouth of "The Body" himself. Whether you love him or hate him, few people have lived a life like this.

Zochert, Donald. *Laura: The Life of Laura Ingalls Wilder.* New York: Avon, 1994. The true story of the author whose books inspired the *Little House on the Prairie* TV series.

Literature

Ervin, Jean (editor). *The North Country Reader.* St. Paul, MN: Minnesota Historical Society Press, 2000. This diverse anthology of Minnesota writers spans the state from the prairie to the North Shore and from the pioneer days of the mid-19th century to the turn of the 21st. The 37 featured authors include F. Scott Fitzgerald, Sinclair Lewis, O. E. Rölvaag, Garrison Keillor, Gordon Parks, Carol Bly, and Henry Rowe Schoolcraft.

Keillor, Garrison. *Lake Wobegon Days.* New York: Viking Penguin, 1985. Keillor's classic novel shares the complete story of the fictional small Minnesota town he made famous on his *A Prairie Home Companion* radio show. A truly delightful read whether you've ever heard the show or not.

Keillor, Garrison. *W.L.T: A Radio Romance.* New York: Viking Penguin, 1992. My favorite work of Keillor's is this humorous look at the early days of radio in Minnesota and the colorful characters working on and off the air.

Lewis, Sinclair. *Main Street.* New York: Signet Classics, 1998. This full frontal attack on the small-mindedness of small town America is one of Lewis' most acclaimed works. Though he named the town Gopher Prairie it was a very thinly veiled portrayal of Sauk Centre, his hometown. *Main Street* was selected for the 1921 Pulitzer Prize, but, since it failed to depict a positive view of American life, the trustees of Columbia University overturned the vote.

Wilder, Laura Ingalls. *On the Banks of Plum Creek.* New York: Harper & Row, 1973. The only one of the nine Little House books that deals extensively with Wilder's time in Minnesota. The Ingalls family faced many hardships while living in a sod home near Walnut Grove. While the series is fiction, much of it is based on real events and it gives a good account of pioneer life in the 1870s.

Nature

Douglas, Paul. *Prairie Skies: The Minnesota Weather Book.* Stillwater, MN: Voyageur Press, 1990. An entertaining read about every Minnesotan's favorite topic of conversation. It is filled with lovely photos, interesting facts, and clear explanations.

Eckert, Kim. *A Birder's Guide to Minnesota.* Plymouth, MN: Williams Publications, 1994. Minnesota's bible of birding covers 800 sites with detailed maps to help you spot specific species. It also provides superb background information on Minnesota species and seasons. Anyone with even a casual interest in bird-watching should travel with a copy.

Henderson, Carrol and Lambrecht, Andrea, et al. *Traveler's Guide to Wildlife in Minnesota.* St. Paul, MN: Minnesota's Bookstore, 1997. A bulky but otherwise excellent guide to 120 of the top wildlife viewing spots in Minnesota with maps and detailed information about what species you can expect to see as well and when and where to look. It is written by experts at the DNR.

Madson, John. *Where the Sky Began: Land of the Tallgrass Prairie.* Ames, IA: Iowa State Press, 1996. A beautifully written yet intricately detailed look at the complex ecology and long history of the tallgrass prairie. Sure to add to your appreciation of the prairie.

Moyle, John B. and Evelyn W. *Northland Wildflowers: The Comprehensive Guide to the Minnesota Region.* Minneapolis, MN: University of Minnesota Press, 2001. The standard reference to Minnesota's wildflowers. It details over 300 species and is filled with photos for easy identification.

Ojakangas, Richard W. and Charles L. Matsch. *Minnesota's Geology.* Minneapolis, MN: University of Minnesota Press, 1982. As close to the complete story of the state's formation as one could hope for. It is filled with maps, charts, and photos which make following the detailed descriptions fairly easy, even for those without a geology background.

Olson, Sigurd. *Songs of the North.* New York: Penguin, 1987. Olson was such a powerful force for conservation in the Boundary Waters, where he spent most of his years, that reading his works is the next best thing to being there. This collection of 20 essays comes from such classic books as *The Singing Wilderness* and *Listening Point.*

Sansome, Constance Jefferson. *Minnesota Underfoot: A Field Guide to Minnesota's Geology.* Stillwater, MN: Voyageur Press, 1983. Detailed descriptions for 56 of Minnesota's most unique geological features. The writing is clear enough for the layperson and detailed enough for geologists. The many maps and photos help you pinpoint the features discussed in the text.

Tekiela, Stan. *Birds of Minnesota.* Cambridge, MN: Adventure Publications, 1998. This field guide only details about a quarter of Minnesota's birds, but has excellent photos. A good choice for beginning bird-watchers.

Tester, John R. *Minnesota's Natural Heritage: An Ecological Perspective.* Minneapolis, MN: University of Minnesota Press, 1995. This excellent book, beautifully illustrated and filled with helpful charts and graphs, offers a detailed and comprehensive overview of Minnesota ecology. It's required reading in many college courses, but so well written that those with no science background can easily take it all in.

Outdoor Recreation

Beymer, Robert. *Boundary Waters Canoe Area.* Berkeley, CA: Wilderness Press, 2000. This two-volume guide (Western Region and Eastern Region) is the ultimate resource for planning a trip in the BWCAW. Multiple routes are recommended from every entry point.

Breining, Greg. *Paddling Minnesota.* Helena, MT: Falcon Publishing, 1999. The bible of Minnesota paddling describes and maps over 100 lake and river trips.

Farris, Mike. *Rock Climbing Minnesota and Wisconsin.* Helena, MT: Falcon Publishing, 2000. A very useful guide covering 10 locales in Minnesota. Photos and maps help you identify the hundreds of routes.

Johnson, Mickey. *Flyfisher's Guide to Minnesota.* Belgrade, MT: Wilderness Adventures Press, 2001. A very comprehensive listing of where, when, and how.

Johnson, Steve. *Mountain Biking Minnesota.* Guilford, CT: Globe Pequot Press, 2002. Sixty-three off-road rides for all abilities.

Pukite, John. *Hiking Minnesota.* Helena, MT: Falcon Publishing, 1998. The 87 featured hikes, each of them mapped, offer a good selection of what the whole state has to offer.

Slade, Andrew (editor). *Guide to the Superior Hiking Trail.* Two Harbors, MN: Ridgeline Press, 2001. This great, map-filled guide can lead you along the entire trail or help you choose a good day hike. Detailed background information will help you appreciate everything you see along your hike.

Weinberger, Mark. *Short Bike Rides in Minnesota.* Guilford, CT: Globe Pequot Press, 1998. A handy little guide that describes and maps 40 scenic rides across the state, most of them loops.

Description and Travel

Federal Writers' Project of the Works Progress Administration. *The WPA Guide to Minnesota.* St. Paul, MN: Minnesota Historical Society Press, 2002. Originally published in 1938 as *Minnesota: A State Guide,* this wonderful document is far too outdated to be of any help as a travel guide, but it offers a fascinating look at the state's folklore and remains an invaluable historical resource.

Gebhard, David and Martinson, Tom. *A Guide to the Architecture of Minnesota.* Minneapolis, MN: University of Minnesota Press, 1991. Even if you have just a casual interest in architecture, this book will be a welcome resident in your glove box. It contains quick profiles of thousands of buildings in nearly 300 towns across the state.

Olsenius, Richard. *Minnesota Travel Companion.* Minneapolis, MN: University of Minnesota Press, 2001. Brief historical background on Minnesota's towns and natural features. Not nearly as detailed as *The WPA Guide to Minnesota* mentioned above, but it's a lot easier to find and has wonderful early photos from the Minnesota Historical Society collections.

Perich, Shawn. *The North Shore: A Four-Season Guide.* Duluth, MN: Pheifer-Hamilton Publishers, 1992. The detailed history and interesting stories make this mile-by-mile guide a wonderful companion to a Lake Superior visit.

Pohlen, Jerome. *Oddball Minnesota.* Chicago, IL: Chicago Review Press, 2003. Although you'll find similar content in the book you are currently holding, this tome offers a proper look at eccentric Minnesota from the place Tiny Tim suffered his fatal heart attack to the Willie the Worm Man statue.

Simonowicz, Nina. *Nina's North Shore Guide.* Minneapolis, MN: University of Minnesota Press, 1999. The most complete scoop on the North Shore available.

Photography

Minnesota is so singularly beautiful that I've seen very few photo collections that aren't spectacular. These are a few personal favorites.

Brandenburg, Jim. *Chased By The Light.* Minnetonka, MN: NorthWord Press, 2001. These Boundary Waters and North Shore photos would be special no matter what circumstances they were taken under, but for this collection Brandenburg limited himself to just one photo a day for 90 autumn and winter days. Truly amazing.

Keillor, Garrison and Richard Olsenius. *In Search of Lake Wobegon.* New York: Viking Studio, 2001. A look, through the words of Keillor and black and white photos of National Geographic photographer Olsenius, at the small towns of Stearns County that the fictional Lake Wobegon is based on.

Ryan, Greg and Sally Beyer. *Minnesota: Simply Beautiful.* Helena, MT: Farcountry Press, 2001. Stunning photos of city and country, though mostly the latter.

Ryan, Greg and Douglas Wood. *Minnesota: The Spirit of the Land.* Stillwater, MN: Voyageur Press, 1995. A celebration of Minnesota wilderness from the tallgrass prairie to the boreal forest.

Cuisine

Hauser, Susan Carol. *Wild Rice Cooking.* New York: The Lyons Press, 2000. Wild rice is more than just a food to Native Americans and this beautiful little book tells the complete story of the official state grain. It also has 80 recipes.

Legwold, Gary. *The Last Word on Lutefisk.* Minneapolis, MN: Conrad Henry Press, 1996. Everything you always wanted to know about reconstituted cod soaked in lye (but were afraid to ask). Includes a lutefisk dinner directory.

McKey, Gwen and Barbara Moseley (Editors). *Best of the Best from Minnesota.* Brandon, MS: Quail Ridge Press, 1997. Over 400 of just what the name says, from uniquely

Minnesotan dishes such as Norwegian flat bread and wild rice soup to the just plain delicious like meatless lasagna and frozen mint dream dessert.

Millang, Theresa. *The Great Minnesota Hot Dish.* Cambridge, MN: Adventure Publications, 1999. Easily the most Minnesotan cookbook out there. It contains classics hot dishes (local vernacular for casserole) like tater tot and tuna noodle as well as breakfast burrito and other modern takes on the historic art form.

Children

Bowen, Betsy. *Antler, Bear, Canoe: A Northwoods Alphabet Year.* Boston: Houghton Mifflin Co., 2002. An alphabet book that takes children through typical sights and activities during a year in the Northwoods. Even adults will love Bowen's woodblock prints in this or any other of her other children's books.

Butler, Dori Hillestrand. *M is for Minnesota.* Minneapolis, MN: University of Minnesota Press, 1998. A fun, fact-filled picture book.

McCarthy, Ann E. *Critters of Minnesota Pocket Guide.* Cambridge, MN: Adventure Publications, 2000. This little book has facts and photos of 50 Minnesota mammals and birds.

Shaw, Janet. *Kirsten's Story Collection.* Middleton, WI: Pleasant Company Publications, 1990. Kirsten, of the popular American Girl series, is a nine-year-old Swedish girl whose family immigrates to Minnesota in 1854. During the six-story series, combined into one book, she encounters a bear, goes to school, and has her house burn down.

Stong, Phil. Honk: *The Moose.* Duluth, MN: Trellis Publishing, 2001. A classic, Newbery Medal-winning tale from 1935 of a moose who comes to live in town. It is based on a true story from Biwabik.

Internet Resources

Access for All
www.accessminnesota.org
Travel information about Minnesota aimed at persons with disabilities.

Adelsman's Cross-Country Ski Page
www.skinnyski.com
The state's best source for cross-country skiing information.

Fishing Minnesota
www.fishingminnesota.com
More than anyone could ever want to know about landing a lunker in Minnesota, including regularly updated fishing reports from across the state.

Minnesota Department of Natural Resources
www.dnr.state.mn.us
A wealth of information about state parks, bike trails, canoe routes, fishing, cross-country skiing, snowmobiling, and just about all other outdoor recreation, as well as the natural history of Minnesota.

Minnesota Gaming Directory
www.minnesotagaming.com
A listing of Minnesota's 18 casinos.

Minnesota Golfer
www.mngolfer.com
A searchable database with detailed information about all of the state's courses.

Minnesota Grown Directory
www.minnesotagrown.com
A searchable directory of agricultural products, from blueberries to buffalo, available for purchase straight from the producer.

Minnesota Historical Society Visual Resources Database
http://collections.mnhs.org/visualresources
This fascinating, searchable collection of historical photos and drawings has nearly 200,000 images with more being added.

Minnesota Newspaper Directory
www.mnnews.com
Get the latest news and gossip from Minnesota towns. If a paper has a website, you'll find the link here.

Minnesota Office of Tourism
www.exploreminnesota.com

Minnesota Ornithologists' Union
http://biosci.umn.edu/~mou/index.html
A wealth of information for bird-watchers.

Minnesota Snow
www.mnsno.com
Covers downhill skiing and snowboarding in Minnesota.

North Star-Minnesota State Government Online
www.state.mn.us
The official web portal for the state government, with links to a wide variety of information.

Index

M

Index

M
Index

Acknowledgments

This book would not have been possible without the assistance of countless people at chambers of commerce, CVBs, historical societies, parks, DNR offices, and other organizations who sent me information, answered my questions, and assisted me during my visits across the state. The following were especially helpful: Brad Toll, Thomas Getzke, Penny Petersen, Ed Robb, Pat Christopherson, Melissa Quirk, Marie Koski, Darla Moore, Ethel Orr, Betty Wanhala, Joyce Barott, Barb Oswell, Doug Schmitz, Linda Fryer, Judy Sellman, Shawn Mason, Ed Oerichbauer, Judy Okerstrom, Joni Hagstrom, Kathy Moore, Becky Peterson, Ione Miller, Christine Steussy, Jeannine Windels, Dorothy Russell, Betty Sayers, Trent Redfield, Marlene Karnatz, Amy Ankrum, Denise Solma, Mick Myers, Chris Roelfsema-Hummel, Janet Timmerman, Betty McCabe, Jessica Pots, Emily Peck, Terry Sveine, Scott Larson, Rosella Peterson, Kristina Falck, James Lundgren, Bob Musil, Vern Jackels, Mark Peterson, Anneliese Detwiler, Mary Tulp, Herman Transburg, Kathy Hartl, Joyce Jacobson, Holly LaVallie, Curt Johnson, Chuck Lennon, Cheryl Offerman, Joan Michel, Nancy Overby, John Ryan, Liz Torgerson, Robert Dana, Joan Galli, Kevin Johnson, Steve Mueller, Gerda Norquist, Scott Pengelly, Al Stevens, Steve Piragis, Terry Eggum, Norma Malinowski, Judy Ness, Steve Robertsen, Yvonne Schmidt, Barb Soderberg, Renee Uhan, Catherine Crawford, Mary Graves, Lee Grim, Kathleen Przybylski, Gayle Coyne, John Leinen, Bruce Adelsman, Anthony X. Hertzel, Jim Benton, Marnie Werner, Pete Boulay, and David Berg. My apologies to anyone I forgot.

Extra special thanks to: Erika Howsare who wrote most of the Headwaters, Chippewa National Forest, Grand Rapids and Vicinity, and Waters of the Dancing Sky sections of the Central Lakes chapter; Bill Wroblewski who helped me write the Native American reservation and sod house sidebars; Tom Huhti for loaning me most of the European Contact portion of the introduction; Scott Anfinson for taking the time to help me with the state's prehistory and archaeology; Howard Hobbs for setting me straight on the driftless area; David Nohrenberg for the Ode to St. Urho translation; and all the wonderful people I worked with at Avalon including Naomi Adler Dancis, Grace Fujimoto, Kevin McLain, Amber Pirker, Julie Leigh, and Amy Scott.

Others that I owe a debt of gratitude to for one reason or another are Damien Andrajack, Karen Bewer, Tim Boock, Anna Dunklee, Kirsten Frickle, Marcia Howard, Dan Mirocha, Temmy Solarin, Beth Stanciu, Eve Stein, and Kim Wroblewski.

Winter Sports

U.S.~Metric Conversion

1 inch = 2.54 centimeters (cm)
1 foot = .304 meters (m)
1 yard = 0.914 meters
1 mile = 1.6093 kilometers (km)
1 km = .6214 miles
1 fathom = 1.8288 m
1 chain = 20.1168 m
1 furlong = 201.168 m
1 acre = .4047 hectares
1 sq km = 100 hectares
1 sq mile = 2.59 square km
1 ounce = 28.35 grams
1 pound = .4536 kilograms
1 short ton = .90718 metric ton
1 short ton = 2000 pounds
1 long ton = 1.016 metric tons
1 long ton = 2240 pounds
1 metric ton = 1000 kilograms
1 quart = .94635 liters
1 US gallon = 3.7854 liters
1 Imperial gallon = 4.5459 liters
1 nautical mile = 1.852 km

To compute Celsius temperatures, subtract 32 from Fahrenheit and divide by 1.8. To go the other way, multiply Celsius by 1.8 and add 32.

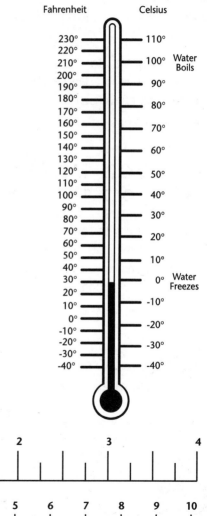

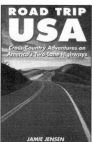

Keeping Current

Although we strive to produce the most up-to-date guidebook humanly possible, change is unavoidable. Between the time this book goes to print and the moment you read it, a handful of the businesses noted in these pages will undoubtedly change prices, move, or even close their doors forever. Other worthy attractions will open for the first time. If you have a favorite gem you'd like to see included in the next edition, or see anything that needs updating, clarification, or correction, please drop us a line. Send your comments via email to atpfeedback@avalonpub.com, or use the address below.

Moon Handbooks Minnesota
Avalon Travel Publishing
1400 65th Street, Suite 250
Emeryville, CA 94608, USA
www.moon.com

Editor: Amy Scott
Series Manager: Kevin McLain
Copy Editor: Julie Leigh
Graphics Coordinator:Amber Pirker
Production Coordinator:Amber Pirker
Cover Designer: Kari Gim
Interior Designers: Amber Pirker, Alvaro
    Villanueva, Kelly Pendragon
Map Editor: Naomi Adler Dancis
Cartographer: Kat Kalamaras
Proofreader: Erika Howsare
Indexer: Judy Hunt

ISBN: 1-56691-482-5
ISSN: 1545-2158

Printing History
1st Edition—January 2004
5 4 3 2 1

Some photos and illustrations are used by permission and are the property of the original copyright owners.

Front cover photo: © Mary Liz Austin
Table of contents photos: © Tim Bewer

Printed in the United States by Malloy

Winter Sports

Acknowledgments

This book would not have been possible without the assistance of countless people at chambers of commerce, CVBs, historical societies, parks, DNR offices, and other organizations who sent me information, answered my questions, and assisted me during my visits across the state. The following were especially helpful: Brad Toll, Thomas Getzke, Penny Petersen, Ed Robb, Pat Christopherson, Melissa Quirk, Marie Koski, Darla Moore, Ethel Orr, Betty Wanhala, Joyce Barott, Barb Oswell, Doug Schmitz, Linda Fryer, Judy Sellman, Shawn Mason, Ed Oerichbauer, Judy Okerstrom, Joni Hagstrom, Kathy Moore, Becky Peterson, Ione Miller, Christine Steussy, Jeannine Windels, Dorothy Russell, Betty Sayers, Trent Redfield, Marlene Karnatz, Amy Ankrum, Denise Solma, Mick Myers, Chris Roelfsema-Hummel, Janet Timmerman, Betty McCabe, Jessica Pots, Emily Peck, Terry Sveine, Scott Larson, Rosella Peterson, Kristina Falck, James Lundgren, Bob Musil, Vern Jackels, Mark Peterson, Anneliese Detwiler, Mary Tulp, Herman Transburg, Kathy Hartl, Joyce Jacobson, Holly LaVallie, Curt Johnson, Chuck Lennon, Cheryl Offerman, Joan Michel, Nancy Overby, John Ryan, Liz Torgerson, Robert Dana, Joan Galli, Kevin Johnson, Steve Mueller, Gerda Norquist, Scott Pengelly, Al Stevens, Steve Piragis, Terry Eggum, Norma Malinowski, Judy Ness, Steve Robertsen, Yvonne Schmidt, Barb Soderberg, Renee Uhan, Catherine Crawford, Mary Graves, Lee Grim, Kathleen Przybylski, Gayle Coyne, John Leinen, Bruce Adelsman, Anthony X. Hertzel, Jim Benton, Marnie Werner, Pete Boulay, and David Berg. My apologies to anyone I forgot.

Extra special thanks to: Erika Howsare who wrote most of the Headwaters, Chippewa National Forest, Grand Rapids and Vicinity, and Waters of the Dancing Sky sections of the Central Lakes chapter; Bill Wroblewski who helped me write the Native American reservation and sod house sidebars; Tom Huhti for loaning me most of the European Contact portion of the introduction; Scott Anfinson for taking the time to help me with the state's prehistory and archaeology; Howard Hobbs for setting me straight on the driftless area; David Nohrenberg for the Ode to St. Urho translation; and all the wonderful people I worked with at Avalon including Naomi Adler Dancis, Grace Fujimoto, Kevin McLain, Amber Pirker, Julie Leigh, and Amy Scott.

Others that I owe a debt of gratitude to for one reason or another are Damien Andrajack, Karen Bewer, Tim Boock, Anna Dunklee, Kirsten Frickle, Marcia Howard, Dan Mirocha, Temmy Solarin, Beth Stanciu, Eve Stein, and Kim Wroblewski.

U.S. ~ Metric Conversion

1 inch = 2.54 centimeters (cm)
1 foot = .304 meters (m)
1 yard = 0.914 meters
1 mile = 1.6093 kilometers (km)
1 km = .6214 miles
1 fathom = 1.8288 m
1 chain = 20.1168 m
1 furlong = 201.168 m
1 acre = .4047 hectares
1 sq km = 100 hectares
1 sq mile = 2.59 square km
1 ounce = 28.35 grams
1 pound = .4536 kilograms
1 short ton = .90718 metric ton
1 short ton = 2000 pounds
1 long ton = 1.016 metric tons
1 long ton = 2240 pounds
1 metric ton = 1000 kilograms
1 quart = .94635 liters
1 US gallon = 3.7854 liters
1 Imperial gallon = 4.5459 liters
1 nautical mile = 1.852 km

To compute Celsius temperatures, subtract 32 from Fahrenheit and divide by 1.8. To go the other way, multiply Celsius by 1.8 and add 32.

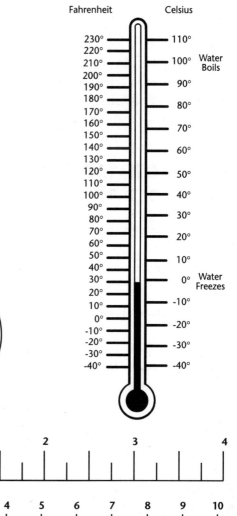

Fahrenheit   Celsius

230° — 110°
220°
210° — 100°   Water Boils
200°
190° — 90°
180°
170° — 80°
160°
150° — 70°
140° — 60°
130°
120° — 50°
110°
100° — 40°
90°
80° — 30°
70°
60° — 20°
50°
40° — 10°
30°
20° — 0°   Water Freezes
10°
0° — -10°
-10°
-20° — -20°
-30° — -30°
-40° — -40°

inch 0   1   2   3   4

cm 0 1 2 3 4 5 6 7 8 9 10

Keeping Current

Although we strive to produce the most up-to-date guidebook humanly possible, change is unavoidable. Between the time this book goes to print and the moment you read it, a handful of the businesses noted in these pages will undoubtedly change prices, move, or even close their doors forever. Other worthy attractions will open for the first time. If you have a favorite gem you'd like to see included in the next edition, or see anything that needs updating, clarification, or correction, please drop us a line. Send your comments via email to atpfeedback@avalonpub.com, or use the address below.

Moon Handbooks Minnesota
Avalon Travel Publishing
1400 65th Street, Suite 250
Emeryville, CA 94608, USA
www.moon.com

Editor: Amy Scott
Series Manager: Kevin McLain
Copy Editor: Julie Leigh
Graphics Coordinator: Amber Pirker
Production Coordinator: Amber Pirker
Cover Designer: Kari Gim
Interior Designers: Amber Pirker, Alvaro Villanueva, Kelly Pendragon
Map Editor: Naomi Adler Dancis
Cartographer: Kat Kalamaras
Proofreader: Erika Howsare
Indexer: Judy Hunt

ISBN: 1-56691-482-5
ISSN: 1545-2158

Printing History
1st Edition—January 2004
5 4 3 2 1

Text © 2004 by Tim Bewer.
Maps © 2004 by Avalon Travel Publishing, Inc.
All rights reserved.

Avalon Travel Publishing is a division of Avalon Publishing Group, Inc.

Some photos and illustrations are used by permission and are the property of the original copyright owners.

Front cover photo: © Mary Liz Austin
Table of contents photos: © Tim Bewer

Printed in the United States by Malloy